THE PACIFIC C

WASHINGTON
504.8 miles

Pasayten Wilderness
North Cascades National Park
Glacier Peak Wilderness
Alpine Lakes Wilderness
Mt. Rainier
Goat Rocks
Mt. Adams
Columbia River

OREGON
455.8 miles

Eagle Creek
Mt. Hood
Mt. Jefferson
Three Fingered Jack
Mt. Washington
Three Sisters Wilderness
Diamond Peak Wilderness
Mt. Thielsen Wilderness
Crater Lake National Park
Sky Lakes Wilderness
Mt. McLoughlin

CALIFORNIA
1691.7 miles

Marble Mountain Wilderness
Russian Wilderness
Trinity Alps Wilderness
Castle Crags Wilderness
Mt. Shasta
Burney Falls State Park
Hat Creek Rim
Lassen Volcanic National Park

Sierra Buttes
Donner Pass
Granite Chief Wilderness
Desolation Wilderness
Yosemite National Park
Ansel Adams Wilderness
John Muir Wilderness
Mt. Whitney
John Muir Trail
Sequoia-Kings Canyon Nat'l Parks
The High Sierra
Kennedy Meadows

The Sierra Nevada
Tehachapi Mountains
Mojave Desert
Mt. Baden-Powell
San Gabriel Mountains
San Bernardino Mountains
San Gorgonio Wilderness
Mt. San Jacinto
San Jacinto Mountains
San Felipe Hills
Anza-Borrego Desert
Laguna Mountains

YOGI'S PCT HANDBOOK

Jackie McDonnell

Published by: Yogi's Books LLC
                98837 Kennedy Meadows Road
                Inyokern, CA 93527

To order additional copies of *YOGI'S PACIFIC CREST TRAIL HANDBOOK* and to obtain updates, go to [www.yogisbooks.com].

If you have any questions, or if you have current trail information to add, please email us: [yogisbooks@gmail.com].

Unless another author is identified, all information in this book is from Jackie McDonnell's personal observations.

FANTASTIC PEOPLE

Thanks to David Miller "Awol" for allowing us to use his town map symbols.
Thanks to all hikers who contributed their experiences.

READ THIS DISCLAIMER

A thru-hike of the Pacific Crest Trail involves a myriad of scenarios which could be life-threatening or dangerous. Hitchhiking, icy passes, lightning, fords, glissading, postholing, extreme heat, extreme cold, lack of water, bears, mountain lions, and more all pose threats to people on the trail. Bad things could happen. I am not an expert on any of the topics discussed in this Handbook. None of the people who comment in this book are experts. I'm simply presenting how we dealt with the situations we had at any given point on the trail. What worked for us won't necessarily work for you.

When you walk the trail, you assume the risks associated with all aspects of a Pacific Crest Trail hike. You alone are responsible for your safety. Reading this book will not prevent bad things from happening.

YOGI'S STORY

I can't place a finger on exactly WHEN I discovered long distance hiking. I do remember one sleepless night in the mid-90's when I was flipping through the TV channels late at night, and I stopped on a channel that was showing an Appalachian Trail documentary. I don't remember the title, but it's the one where someone gave several hikers video cameras and asked them to carry the cameras on their thru-hikes. Along the way, the hikers would sit down and talk to the camera and tell their stories. As I watched that program . . . . . I remembered . . . . back in college . . . . . I heard about the Appalachian Trail. All I knew was that it was a backpacking trip up the east coast.

I thought, "I can do that."

I guess that's how it started. I went to a big box outdoor store and picked out all the wrong gear. I had no idea what I was doing, but somehow it worked. On March 9, 1999, I stood on Springer Mountain and looked north to Katahdin. 196 days later, I stood on Katahdin. I walked from Georgia to Maine. I DID IT!!!

Okay, now what?

It didn't take long after thru-hiking the AT for me to realize what I had found. A different world. A world full of good things. Simplicity. Relaxation. Freedom. Self-confidence. Camaraderie. Before hiking the AT, "the trail" represented images of dirt paths, mountains, streams, backpacks, sleeping bags, tents, camping stoves, etc. Mostly physical things. After returning home, I quickly realized that "the trail" represents more of a feeling. A FEELING OF BEING INVINCIBLE.

I wanted that feeling again. I wanted to go back.

Only two months after summiting Katahdin, I decided to thru-hike again. Initially, I contemplated another Appalachian Trail thru-hike. Although I knew a second AT hike couldn't be the same as my 1999 hike, I missed the trail so much that I wanted to go back. I REALLY wanted to go back. My AT friend Soaring Eagle pointed out the obvious: I had already hiked the AT. She suggested that I tackle one of the other long trails instead of hiking the Appalachian Trail a second time. That sounded logical to me. The natural progression for AT thru-hikers is to head out west: to the Pacific Crest Trail. So that's where I went.

In May of 2001, I found myself in Southern California at the Mexican border. As I looked north, I knew that Canada was out there somewhere. That first day on the Pacific Crest Trail, I remember thinking over and over "what have I gotten in to?" This was DEFINITELY not the Appalachian Trail. It was HOT. Crazy hot. I was carrying too much weight, I had the wrong clothes and shoes, and I was totally unsure of what to expect for the next 2658 miles (2001 mileage).

Planning for that 2001 PCT hike was confusing. I wasn't sure what books to buy, what gear to carry, when to start the trail, NOTHING was clear. My hiking partners and I arbitrarily picked a starting date and headed north, using the same gear that worked for us on the AT.

I made it about halfway to Canada before a leg injury forced me to get off the trail. I returned home, where I spent the winter HAUNTED by the Pacific Crest Trail. It had beat me. And I'm a terrible loser.

April 2002 found me back in Southern California. I once again stood at the Mexican border looking north to Canada. This time, I knew what I was doing. I hiked with a vengeance, and completed the 2658-mile PCT in 140 days with only 12 zero days. No blisters, no injuries, just 140 days of pure hiking bliss. I completed the PCT. It beat me once, but this time victory was mine.

I was prepared to spend the entire year of 2003 working. I had a plan. I planned to work two jobs for a year, get completely out of debt, and save for a 2004 Continental Divide Trail hike. That plan was working perfectly until one Sunday night in late March 2003 when my friend Gottago called me. She started talking about the PCT, I started pacing back and forth, and my mind began to race. In about

10 minutes, Gottago convinced me to thru-hike the PCT again. Less than 4 weeks later, I was once again in Southern California walking north from the Mexican border.

I took the trail slower in 2003. I had nothing to prove to myself. This time, I knew I could do it. 151 days later, I was again in Manning Park. I had walked from Mexico to Canada a second time. It was another amazing summer on the PCT.

2004 found me on the Continental Divide Trail, searching for that elusive Triple Crown. The CDT is not an easy trail. It's a given that the CDT is a physically tough trail. But the huge difference between the PCT and the CDT is that on the CDT you have to be constantly aware of where you are. Gone are the hours and days of mindless walking, lost in thought. The instant you remove yourself from your surroundings and get lost in conversation with a hiking buddy, lost in a song on the radio, or lost in your mind, THAT'S when things go wrong.

I was never so proud as I was on November 7, 2004. That's the day I finished the CDT, the day I completed the Triple Crown. I was lucky to share that day with two close Triple Crown buddies. We survived 146 CDT days of route-finding, terrible weather, and compromises. 146 CDT days of walking on the top of the world, laughing, remembering PCT stories, talking about the AT, learning about each other and ourselves. It was a fantastic trip that I will always cherish.

In 2007, I returned to my favorite trail — the Pacific Crest Trail — and enjoyed perhaps my most rewarding hike to date.

From mid-July to mid-August 2010, I hiked the 500-mile Colorado Trail.
That's an absolutely stunning hike, one I highly recommend.

Returning to my thru-hiking roots, I hiked the Appalachian Trail again in 2012, followed by a southbound hike of the CDT from Canada to Grand Lake, CO. In 2013-2016, I completed the CDT from Grand Lake to Mexico.

People ask me all the time: WHY do you hike year after year?

Because the scenery is amazing.
Because the best people in the world walk long trails.
Because I can't call those people friends unless we have shared experiences.
Because I'm in the BEST shape ever when I'm thru-hiking.
I'm physically fit. I have legs of steel.
I'm mentally at peace. I have no stress. I'm free.

I understand when non-thru-hikers ask me why I hike every year. They couldn't possibly understand why I would do this ONE time. So of course they don't understand thru-hiking year after year after year — 20,000 miles so far. But what I DON'T get is when thru-hikers ask me the same question.

We'll be somewhere on the trail laughing and cooking dinner.
Or taking a break at the top of a pass.
Or telling stories on a porch in town.
ALWAYS, a thru-hiker will ask me the question: Why do you hike year after year?

And I just want to SHAKE him.

HELLO?!? How could you NOT get it?
Aren't you having the time of your life?
Aren't these the BEST people?
Isn't this FUN?
Don't you feel GREAT?

THAT'S why.

And as Billy Goat once said: "If you have to ask, then you'll never understand."

THE EVOLUTION OF
YOGI'S PCT HANDBOOK

In the spring of 2003, I got an email from someone who wanted to know the locations of the water caches in Southern California. I got out my 2002 Data Book (yep, I still had it) and started to make a list. I have a very strange mind for strange details. I can't remember where I put my car keys, yet I can remember specific curves of the trail, where the secret climbs are, and which streams were flowing or not. And, of course, the locations of the water caches.

So I made this water cache list. But I couldn't stop there. I mean, REALLY, what good is a water cache list? The caches aren't always full, and you're not supposed to count on them anyway. So I went through my Data Book again, this time noting which streams were/were not flowing in 2001 and 2002.

This was a pretty good water list. But I couldn't stop there, either. My mind was on a roll. And I had nothing better to do on a Sunday afternoon in Overland Park, Kansas. So I sat at my computer and, by sheer memory, added information for all the towns I'd been to, noted the confusing trail junctions, and then solicited tips from other 2002 PCT thru-hikers. When it was finished, I posted this information on my journal site.

That's when I realized that the PCT needs a book with detailed trail, town, and water information. The AT has books like this, why doesn't the PCT? It's obviously needed, as evidenced by the fact that many 2003 thru-hikers took the time to print the information off of my journal site and carry it with them. In 2003, this became known on the trail as "Yogi's Notes."

During my subsequent PCT thru-hikes, I did a lot of research. I noted the water sources, bear box locations, and confusing trail junctions, and collected detailed information about each town's services.

During non-hiking years, I take long road trips, visiting all the trail towns to update town services/maps.

From the time this book was first published in February 2004, it has gone through several evolutions. This is because the trail is constantly changing. Although the book is based on my own observations while hiking the PCT, I had a little help from my friends. Hikers from 2002 - 2019 contributed their thoughts on the towns and many aspects of thru-hiking. What I've ended up with is a collection of different opinions from people who have thru-hiked the PCT. They've been where you're going. They've done what you're about to do.

YOGI'S PCT HANDBOOK is written from the point of view of a bunch of hikers who got together to talk about the trail. It's the kind of talk you might hear while taking a zero in Warner Springs, while eating lunch on Mather Pass, or while enjoying the pies at Bob's in Etna. It's trail talk. It's intentionally contradictory. It's NOT grammatically correct. But it IS fun and it IS honest.

I hope that this book is helpful while you plan your hike and when you are hiking.
I had fun putting it together, and I look forward to keeping it alive for years to come.
And just think, this all started with an innocent question in an email!

TABLE OF CONTENTS

OVERVIEW

THEY'LL NEVER UNDERSTAND

Why do you want to thru-hike? Why do you like backpacking? Why do you like hiking? These questions always floor me. People can't understand WHY we like this stuff because it's all foreign to them. In their minds, we are walking into the UNKNOWN, to a place where a maniac will kill us, a bear will eat us, a rattlesnake will bite us, and where we will no doubt die of starvation, dehydration, heat stroke, and frostbite. All at the same time.

Non-trail people will never understand WHY we want to thru-hike. I think it's because this idea is so far removed from EVERYTHING we are taught as we're growing up: go to college, get a good job, get married, have kids, and then wait until you retire or die. You want to have fun? You can do that two weeks per year on your vacation. Don't be irresponsible and take six months off work to hike. Are you crazy?

You're stepping out, ignoring what society says you're SUPPOSED to do, and that scares them. They will NEVER understand us. All you can ask is that they recognize that this is something that is important to you and that you want their support. But, you have to do some work. You have to educate them about thru-hiking. Show them a map of the PCT. Direct them to your favorite online trail journals/blogs and PCT documentaries. Give them some information, and then they can form an educated opinion on whether or not you're truly crazy.

I like hiking for the same reasons someone else likes golfing, or playing softball, or running, sewing, reading, skating, skiing, surfing, biking, WHATEVER. I like hiking because I enjoy it. It gives me satisfaction. It makes me happy. It's fun. And I can't explain it to them any better than they can explain to me why they like to sew or skate or golf. I can't fathom why anyone would like golfing. So why would I expect them to understand why I like thru-hiking?

THE PACIFIC CREST TRAIL

The Pacific Crest Trail from the US-Mexican border to Manning Provincial Park, British Columbia, Canada is 2661.9 miles long (2019 mileage). "The Pacific Crest National Scenic Trail" (2653.1 miles)is entirely within the United States, from border to border. Most hikers complete 8.8 more miles into Canada on "The Pacific Crest Trail."

As you head north, you'll walk the length of California, Oregon, and Washington. You'll cross a corner of the Mojave desert. You'll embrace the High Sierra. You'll pass within 8 miles of Mt. Whitney, the highest point in the 48 contiguous States — and you'll most likely take the day-long side trip to summit Whitney. You'll reach a high elevation of 13,180 feet as you cross Forester Pass in California. In Oregon, you'll walk along the Rim of Crater Lake. As you enter Washington, you'll drop to 140 feet in elevation, the lowest point on the trail. You'll see snakes, lizards, deer, elk, bear, and marmots. Also ants, mosquitos, hornets, flies, and numerous other biting/stinging freaks of nature. You'll have some rain and snow, but usually your days will be gorgeous. You will meet the most incredible people in the world.

And you will change.

You won't know it when it's happening, and it's impossible to explain with words, but it's definitely there. You'll see it in your pictures, and you'll feel it. The level of confidence and sense of accomplishment is overwhelming. Thru-hikers have a certain "look," and it's not all about being dirty. It will show on your face and in how you carry yourself. It's not an easy look to achieve. It comes from within. And you don't get it until you've been there. Well guess what? You're about to go there. You are about to experience a world that others only dream about.

YOU CAN DO THIS

When I first looked into hiking the PCT, I wasn't sure I could do it. I had hiked the Appalachian Trail, but this was going to be different. I'd heard all these horrible things about the PCT:

- 30-mile waterless stretches
- The MOJAVE DESERT
- Rattlesnakes, scorpions, and bears, Oh My!
- 25-mile days, every day
- Snow travel with an ice axe

I thought, "I'm not sure I can do this. I certainly can't do it alone. What if I get lost?"

It can be done. You're not alone. Five thousand other people attempt a PCT thru-hike every year. You know all those horrible things? You'll get through them. It's not that bad. The "Water Report" will give you current information on the SoCal water sources. The Mojave Desert isn't very long. You'll soon be looking for rattlesnakes, scorpions, and bears because you want to snap a picture of one. 25-mile days on the PCT are nothing like 25-mile days on the AT. You simply have to get up a little earlier. You can learn how to use an ice axe, and chances are you'll NEVER need that skill.

But you can't just show up at the Mexican border and start walking north. You've got to do some research. You need a basic understanding of desert hiking and what to do in the snow, where to resupply, what gear is needed, how to treat water, and when to start and finish the trail.

The goals of this book are to make planning for your PCT hike easier and to remove the nightmare of on-trail logistics. We offer opinions on many hiking issues from PCT legends and veterans. You'll quickly realize that there are some issues that everyone agrees on, and others that no one agrees on. This is not a "Yogi says" book. I'm not telling you what to do or how to hike your hike. Instead, we present differing opinions from people who've been there: people who have thru-hiked the Pacific Crest Trail. This is the stuff we wish we knew before we hiked. Read our thoughts, then form your own opinion on what sleeping bag to carry, how to treat your water, what kind of stove to use, etc.

Anish: Before my first PCT hike, I was really worried about snow in the Sierra. It was a crazy snow year and I was really inexperienced, as was my partner. I was also worried about rattlesnakes and heat in the desert. I expected the PCT to really kick my ass.

The second time I thru-hiked the PCT, I was still worried about heat in the desert and various potential animal encounters. I still expected the PCT to kick my ass.

My fears have always proven to be far bigger pre-hike than what actually occurs. Both times I thru-hiked I saw rattlesnakes and never felt threatened. I encountered four mountain lions on my 2013 trek, and they were all easy to scare away. I ran into dozens of bears between the two hikes and again, they all ran. Animals really, really don't want anything to do with you unless they have been habituated. You aren't going to get eaten or bitten!

The snow in the Sierra is not to be taken lightly, especially if it's a big year – but with proper preparation you will be fine. Be smart, know when you're over your head (not just with snow, but anything), and use good judgment.

The PCT is tough and challenging, but it isn't impossible. Embrace it as an opportunity to grow and make yourself stronger, and you'll appreciate the difficulties.

BINK: Prior to my first hike, my biggest expectation was of hiking in mountains and having time to explore and get to really know the areas I was traveling through. My biggest fear was probably hiking in the desert.

The trail seemed to vary greatly from all of my expectations, but many times in good ways. In many cases, the problems I feared turned out not to be as much of an issue as I had imagined. On the other hand, many factors I had never even considered turned out to be real problems once out on the trail. This was all in 1992 in the days of very little trail information, so planning was not as easily done back then. Many unexpected challenges occurred for me that I had never anticipated. However, these moments of having to figure things out on the fly are what made this first of many PCT hikes to follow so magical.

<u>Hiker Box Special</u>: I was afraid of injuring myself or getting really dehydrated in SoCal. I honestly wasn't sure if I could make it to the Sierra let alone the Canadian Border. I definitely had plenty of injuries but was able to Just Keep Walking (JKW) and they all went away. Mostly blisters were the worst. The dehydration issue came up once or twice, but the PCT Water Report was far more important than I could have possibly imagined. Eventually you stop thinking about 2650 and just concentrate on getting to the next resupply. That kind of mentality will get you to Canada.

<u>Scrub</u>: Ever since I'd done most of the AT in 2011, I'd been reading about the PCT from a lot of sources – WhiteBlaze.net forums, YouTube videos, a friend who kept a very thorough blog on her 2012 hike, later on Yogi's guide (this book is crazy accurate, don't let anyone tell you otherwise) – and distilling that information. I felt that I came into the hike very, very well-informed, maybe too well-informed. I wasn't afraid of the things that people are normally afraid of: wild animals, being alone, snow in the Sierra. The first two are not rational and the last didn't apply to me, starting in May of 2013.

I was still definitely afraid of my two problems from the AT: injury (I got a tibia stress fracture in Pennsylvania that knocked me off the trail for a while) and, consequently, not finishing. I would have been seriously pissed off, maybe even depressed, if either of two things had happened to me again. Not finishing the AT had gnawed at me a surprising amount, so I REALLY wanted to finish the PCT. I came very well-prepared to do so, but I still knew that even my best-laid plans could get derailed by a problem at home or a freak accident on trail or some such thing. I'm very thankful that none of that happened.

What I'd read turned out to be largely accurate, and only a few small things about the trail really surprised me. There were surprisingly few people around in my first two weeks – I expected a bigger social scene but I learned I would've had to start in April to see that (I started May5). Certain weather events were also surprising. For instance, it absolutely pissed cold rain for 36 hours starting at about 4 pm on my very first day on trail, May 5th. It wasn't actually warm and sunny until the fifth day of the desert. I thought that was only supposed to happen to people who started in early/mid April. Then it stormed on me for two days near Lake Tahoe, July 2nd and 3rd. Then in Southern Oregon in the beginning of August, I had several days with hard rain and storms, which I know from living in Oregon is pretty uncommon that time of year. And then it was 90 degrees leaving Snoqualmie Pass on September 14th. None of those things are supposed to happen, but hey, they happened.

CONTRIBUTORS

Successful hikers come in many shapes and sizes, and they have conflicting viewpoints on most hiking-related topics. What works for one hiker could be the exact opposite of what works for the next hiker, yet both hikers are correct. So, in order to give you, the reader, more than one viewpoint, I present this book to you with a little help from my friends. These folks devoted several hours responding to a lengthy 92-item questionnaire covering topics from choosing gear, to preparing mail drops, to hiking in the desert/snow, to the disposal of toilet paper. They gave honest, insightful answers to many questions you may have now as you prepare for your own journey on the Pacific Crest Trail. Keep in mind that these are personal biased opinions. No two hikers have EXACTLY the same experience.

Since you may be basing your hiking decisions on what you read here, I thought you'd like to meet everyone.

(✱✱✱ Indicates Triple Crown Hikers)

	Male or Female?	Where are you from?	What year did you hike the PCT?	How old were you when you hiked the PCT?	What other trails have you hiked?	How many long-distance miles have you hiked?
"Yogi" Jackie McDonnell	Female	Shawnee, KS	2002 2003 2007	37 38 42	½ PCT 2001 Appalachian Trail 1999 & 2012 Continental Divide Trail 2004 Colorado Trail 2010 Continental Divide Trail 2012/2103/2016	20,000
"Anish" Heather Anderson	Female	Bellingham, WA	2005 2013 2018	24 32 37	Appalachian Trail 2003 & 2012 Continental Divide Trail 2006 & 2017 Wonderland Trail 2011 Arizona Trail 2016 Calendar Year Triple Crown 2018 ** Anish holds the fastest known times for female unsupported PCT, AT and overall AZT thru-hikes! She is also the first female Triple Triple Crowner!	23,000+
"BINK" Scott Williamson	Male	Truckee, CA	1993, 1996, 1997, 1998, 2000, 2004 (Yo-Yo), 2006 (Yo-Yo), 2007, 2008, 2009, 2011	First time 18 years old	Continental Divide Trail 1994 Florida Trail 1995 Appalachian Trail 1995 Many huge chunks of the PCT ** Bink held the fastest known time on the PCT several times, was the first person to Yo-Yo the PCT, and he has Yo-Yo'd twice!	50,000+
"Hiker Box Special" Michael Henrick	Male	Boston, MA	2013	28	None!	2,600-ish
"Scrub" Christopher Burke	Male	Eugene, OR	2013	25	85% Appalachian Trail 2011	4,500

YOGI ★★★, ★★★
(Yogi is a Double-Triple Crowner)

Here in this other world, this off-trail world, there are so many choices: food, clothes, entertainment, etc. It's very busy. So different from the simplistic thru-hiker lifestyle, from the world where all that really matters is finding the next water source. Transitioning from trail life to the other world is tough. After every hike, it gets harder. I've discovered that the trail is where I belong. Great people, great scenery, great living!

BILLY GOAT ★★★

My hero Billy Goat has hiked over 40,000 miles.
Once I asked Billy Goat, "where do you live?"
He pointed down to the trail and replied, "right here."

ANISH ★★★, ★★★, ★★★
(Anish is a Triple-Triple Crowner)

Thru-hiking made me aware of how deep I can truly dig mentally and physically. It taught me that I am stronger, braver, smarter, and more competent than I ever thought before.

I was terrified of night hiking and mountain lions before I began. In reality, when faced with hours and hours of night hiking and four mountain lions, I wasn't scared. I just did what I had to do and kept going.

Anish's unsupported speed records:

PCT in 2013: 2668.8 miles, 60 days, 17 hours, 12 minutes.

AT in 2015: 2189.2 miles, 54 days, 7 hours, 48 minutes.

AZT in 2016: 800 miles, 19 days, 17 hours, 9 minutes.

BINK ★★★

The PCT has in many aspects been my life, and man oh man has it been a blast!

My ideas around the PCT have really evolved over the years: what it means, what it is, and why it is so important to me. I feel so blessed to have spent so much time out there. Of course my off trail life is far from ideal because of this, but I would not trade any of it. I have not grown tired of it. Every hike is an entirely new learning experience for me.

I was 18 when I started my first long PCT hike. I am now 41 years old! I have seen crazy things on the trail many will never see:

◆ I have seen it snow in every single section of trail.

◆ I have seen fires radically alter the landscape.

◆ I have seen the bark beatles decimate many areas of southern California, areas that formerly had thick forest now with no trees.

◆ I have seen clear cuts in Washington grow in to the point that they no longer look like a clear cut.

◆ I remember when in most trail towns people thought that you were a homeless person and knew nothing of the trail, including places like Seiad Valley and Agua Dulce (towns where the trail goes right down main street).

◆ The year of my first PCT hike there were only 13 thru-hikers. Now the attempts are a few thousand a year.

I could tell stories forever about "how it used to be," but the important thing is that it has become what it is now. It's been 22 amazing years of experience and I have no plans to end it yet. I feel that I have still not seen and experienced all that the PCT offers; my journey continues.

1992   Mexico to Oregon
1993   Mexico to Canada
1994   Mexico to Tuolumne Meadows
         (training for CDT hike later that summer)
1995   Mexico to Kennedy Meadows
         (training for Florida to Canada hike later that summer)
1996   Mexico to Canada to Reds Meadow (first Yo-Yo attempt)
1997   Mexico to Canada (Yo-Yo attempt where I did not turn around),
         then I section hiked in the fall from Tuolumne Meadows to Mexico
1998   Canada to Mexico
1999   Mexico to Big Bear (section hike)
2000   Mexico to Canada to Selden Pass
         (another Yo-Yo attempt)
2003   Mexico to Cedar Grove (unintended section hike)
2004   Mexico to Canada to Mexico (first Yo-Yo)
2006   Mexico to Canada to Mexico (second Yo-Yo)
2007   Canada to Mexico
2008   Mexico to Canada (71 day hike)
2009   Mexico to Canada (65 day hike)
2011   Canada to Mexico (64 day hike)
2012   Canada to Timothy Lake in Northern Oregon
         (speed hike aborted due to fires)
2013   Canada to Belden CA (speed hike aborted due to illness)
2014   Canada to Crater Lake
         (828 miles in 18 days, speed hike aborted due to fires)

That comes out to 46,197 PCT miles give or take, including:
13 border-to-border continuous thru-hikes, and
2 separate section hikes never using anything twice.

HIKER BOX SPECIAL

I learned I can basically do anything I put my mind to. Hiking 2668 miles is incomprehensible, and it shows a lot of determination. I learned I need to spend more time in nature, surrounded by mountains. I learned it's okay to be alone. You don't have to feel like you should be around people all the time. I feel a lot more confident and have more perspective on the world around me. Things seem less important.

The incredible beauty of Washington astounded me. You think you're in the home stretch and it's in the bag only the trail just gets better and better. By the time you get to Manning Park you almost don't want to leave.

SCRUB

I had hiking partners most of the way on the AT, and I figured it would be the same on the PCT. Instead, I was a lone wolf for most of the PCT and enjoyed it. I learned I could be alone and sort of feed my brain on its own thoughts for a lot longer than I previously thought possible.

I was surprised by how much time I spent alone and how much I generally enjoyed that time. I was surprised to find myself not caring that much when people that I liked got ahead of or behind me.

I was totally flying solo, and I was cool with that.

RESOURCES

MAPS AND APPS

Guthook　　　　Smartphone app. [www.atlasguides.com]

NatGeo　　　　NatGeo is in the process of releasing a full PCT map set.
　　　　　　　　As of November 2019, Oregon and Washington are complete.
　　　　　　　　This map set will be available at [www.yogisbooks.com].

THRU-HIKING

Andrew Skurka　　Andrew is an exceptionally accomplished long-distance hiker.
　　　　　　　　His site is full of great info. [www.andrewskurka.com]

Cam Honan "Swami"　Backpacker Magazine dubbed Swami "the most traveled hiker on earth." If
　　　　　　　　you get the opportunity to see him speak, do not miss it! Check out his
　　　　　　　　website for articulate and hilarious tips, tales, and trip reports.
　　　　　　　　[www.thehikinglife.com]

Facebook　　　There is a page for each thru-hiking class, as well as a general Pacific Crest
　　　　　　　　Trail Page. [www.facebook.com]

Craig's PCT Planner　A great little program for figuring out how many days of food is needed
　　　　　　　　between resupply points. [www.pctplanner.com]

Thru-hiker　　　Store, make-your-own-gear projects, articles for lightweight and long
　　　　　　　　distance hikers, lightweight gear reviews, and a message forum.
　　　　　　　　[www.thru-hiker.com]

The Trail Show　Hosted by d-low, Speshul, POD, and Disco.
　　　　　　　　Prepare to be entertained! [www.thetrailshow.com]

Wizards of the PCT　Jester's most excellent PCT documentary.
　　　　　　　　Highly recommended! [www.tbwproductions.com]

SNOW SITES

The California snow page　　Information on snow levels. [http://cdec.water.ca.gov/snow/]

California Snow Water Content　Historical graphs.
　　　　　　　　　　　　[http://cdec.water.ca.gov/cgi-progs/products/PLOT_SWC.pdf]
　　　　　　　　　　　　[https://cdec.water.ca.gov/snow/current/snow/index.html]

Mountain Snowpack Maps　　Maps of the Western United States.
　　　　　　　　　　　　[http://www.wcc.nrcs.usda.gov/cgibin/westsnow.pl]

LIGHTWEIGHT GEAR

Triple Crown Outfitters   Located at the 702.2 mile mark on the PCT, in Kennedy Meadows CA. [https://triplecrownoutfitters.com/]

AntiGravityGear   Ultralight backpacking gear. [www.antigravitygear.com]

Enlightened Equipment   Lightweight quilts. [www.enlightenedequipment.com]

Gossamer Gear   Packs, shelters, accessories. [www.gossamergear.com]
If you're an ultralighter, this site is for you.

Hyperlite Mountain Gear   Cuben Fiber gear. [www.hyperlitemountaingear.com]

Lightheart Gear   Lightweight shelters. [www.lightheartgear.com]

LW Gear   Lynne Whelden's hiking videos and lightweight backpacking gear. [www.lwgear.com]

Mountain Laurel Designs   Super Ultra Lite backpacking wilderness travel gear. [www.mountainlaureldesigns.com]

Six Moon Designs   Ron "Fallingwater" Moak's lightweight packs and tents. [www.sixmoondesigns.com]

Superior Wilderness Designs   Handmade Ultralight Backpacking Gear. [www.swdbackpacks.com]

Tarptent   Henry Shires' lightweight shelters. [www.tarptent.com]

Ultralight Adventure Equipment   The most popular PCT packs. [www.ula-equipment.com]

ZPacks   Ultralight backpacking gear. [www.zpacks.com]

OTHER GEAR

Triple Crown Outfitters   Located at the 702.2 mile mark on the PCT, in Kennedy Meadows CA. [https://triplecrownoutfitters.com/]

Backcountry   Lots of gear. [www.backcountry.com]

Backcountry Gear   Lots of gear. [www.backcountrygear.com]

Campmor   Lots of gear. [www.campmor.com]

Dirty Girl Gaiters   Um, yeah, gaiters here. [www.dirtygirlgaiters.com]

Feathered Friends   Down sleeping bags and garments. [www.featheredfriends.com]

Frogg Toggs   Lightweight rain wear. [www.froggtoggs.com]

Hiker Trash   Super cool hiker souvenirs. [www.wearehikertrash.com]

Joe Trailman Gaiters   Yep, gaiters again. [www.joetrailmangaiters.com]

O2 Rainwear from Rainshield   Lightweight rain gear. [www.O2rainwear.com]

REI	Lots of gear. [www.rei.com]
Roadrunner Sports	Shoes. [www.roadrunnersports.com]
StickPic	An ultra-cool device for taking self-photos. [www.thestickpic.com]
Western Mountaineering	The very best down sleeping bags and clothing. [www.westernmountaineering.com]
Zappos	Shoes. [www.zappos.com]

SIERRA FOOD STORAGE

Sequoia & Kings Canyon National Park [www.nps.gov/seki]

Yosemite National Park [www.nps.gov/yose]

Sierra Wild Bear Info on Sierra bears and food storage. [www.sierrawild.gov]

Bear Box Locations [www.climber.org/data/BearBoxes.html]

Bear Canister Purchase or Rental [https://triplecrownoutfitters.com/]

FOOD

Pack Light, Eat Right	Food advice for thru-hikers, written by Dr. Brenda Braaten, Registered Dietitian and Belden CA Trail Angel. [http://thru-hiker.com/articles/pack_light_eat_right.php]
Thru-hiker Nutrition	[http://philmaffetone.com/healthy-hiking/]
Minimus	Individual packets of food and toiletries. [www.minimus.biz]
Harmony House Foods	Dehydrated veggies, soups, meals. [www.harmonyhousefoods.com]
Just Tomatoes	Dried fruits and veggies. [www.justtomatoes.com]
Mary Jane's Farm	Organic backpacking food. [www.maryjanesfarm.org]
Zero Day Resupply	Mail-order hiking food. Fantastic selection. Owned by Triple Crowner Chris Solinsky. [www.zerodayresupply.com]

REPAIR

Rainy Pass Repair	Repair for all types of backpacking gear. They do an excellent job cleaning down sleeping bags. [www.rainypass.com]

MISCELLANEOUS

Peak To Peak   Links to several backpacking websites. [www.peaktopeak.net]

Elevation Profiles   PCT by state and section. [www.bearcant.org/elevation.php]

BackpackGearTest   The Consumer Reports of backpacking. You want honest reviews about gear? This is the place to go. [www.backpackgeartest.org]

ALDHA   Appalachian Long Distance Hikers Association holds a hiker gathering each fall. [www.aldha.org]

PCT Days   A PCT hiker gathering in August every year. [www.pctdays.com]

Soft Paths   An excellent Leave-No-Trace book by David Cole and Rich Brame.

Backpacking Light   Lightweight backpacking tips. [www.backpackinglight.com]

The Lightweight Backpacker   Lightweight backpacking tips. [www.backpacking.net]

DOCUMENTARIES

Wizards of the PCT   Directed and edited by Shane "Jester" O'Donnell, "Wizards of the PCT" allows viewers to experience the joys, pains, and unusual amounts of dancing on a PCT hike without having to, you know, actually go outside. Jester shows a great combination of all aspects of trail life – from the social aspect, to the extreme weather, to hitchhiking, to hiker obsession with food and blisters. WHY are we hikers so fascinated with blisters?!? Finally! A PCT movie about HIKING!! Come along for the ride! [www.tbwproductions.com]

Embrace the Brutality   Jester did it again! Four years after "Wizards of the PCT," Team Bad Wizard returned to tackle the Continental Divide Trail. Don't miss this! [www.tbwproductions.com]

The Walkumentary   Directed and edited by Lawton "Disco" Grinter. Disco says: One of my goals with this film was to kind of unravel the mystery that is the CDT. I know that when I was finishing up my thru-hike of the Pacific Crest Trail, my fellow hikers were already talking about "doing the CDT," but no one had any real idea of what a CDT hike was all about, including myself. I think that video footage goes a long way, even more so than a trail journal or slide show, in showing a hiker what the Continental Divide Trail looks like, sounds like, and feels like. Hopefully I captured this in "The Walkumentary." [www.thewalkumentary.com]

Squatch Films   Documentaries for the Pacific Crest Trail, Appalachian Trail, and Camino de Santiago. [www.squatchfilms.com]

LOGISTICS

NORTH or SOUTH ?

The majority of PCT thru-hikes are northbound.
Because of that, this Handbook is written from the perspective of a northbound hiker.

What direction will you hike? Here are some considerations:

Weather Window

There are two major snow areas on a PCT thru-hike:
The Sierra (mile 720-ish to 1100-ish), and
Northern Washington (mile 2400-ish to Canada).
These areas are the boundaries of the PCT weather window.

Northbound hikers are concerned with leftover snow from the previous winter in the Sierra, and new snow for the coming winter in Washington.

Southbound hikers have exactly the opposite concerns: leftover snow from previous winter in Washington, and new snow for the coming winter in the Sierra.

The northbound weather window is approximately 3.5 months, spanning the trail from Kennedy Meadows (mile 702.2) to Manning Park (mile 2661.9).

The southbound weather window is approximately 2.5 months, spanning the trail from Manning Park (mile 2661.9) to Forester Pass (mile 779.5).

Start Date

Nobo: Start date from the Mexican border is dictated by the "enter the Sierra date." It's not advisable to enter the Sierra prior to June 1. Start at Campo late-April or early-May. Aim to reach Kennedy Meadows June 10-15.

Northbound hikers also have snow concerns in the Laguna Mountains (around mile 42), near San Jacinto (mile 160-ish to 190-ish), near Baden-Powell (mile 374-384).

Sobo: Start at Canadian border in early- to mid-July, based upon the snowmelt in the North Cascades.

Finish Date

Nobo: Finish date is dictated by winter in Washington, which can shut down the trail as early as mid-September, or as late as late-October. Aim to finish in Canada in late-September.

Sobo: Finish date is dictated by early season snow in the Sierra. Southbounders should shoot for crossing Forester Pass (mile 779.5) mid-September (no later than October 1). Finish at Campo no later than mid-November.

Water

Nobo: Southern California water sources are flowing in the spring.

Sobo: Many Southern California water sources dry up in the fall.

Water Caches

Nobo:
Water caches are (usually) stocked.

Sobo: Empty water caches with trash left behind by the nobos.

SoCal Water Report

Nobo: The Water Report is frequently updated, and will contain current information.

Sobo: You'll most likely have a Water Report which was last updated in May.

Daylight

Nobo: Begin with 13.5-hour days in SoCal, ending with 12-hour days in Washington.

Sobo: Begin with 15.5-hour days in Washington, end with 11-hour days in SoCal, lose a few minutes of daylight every single day.

Sun Position	Nobo: Sun at your back.	Sobo: Sun in your face.
Weather	Nobo: Warmer weather, sometimes unbearably hot weather.	Sobo: Not impacted by summer heat as much, but you are in the mountains during the COLD fall months.
Bugs	Nobo: Terrible mosquitos in Central California and Oregon.	Sobo: Not as many bug problems.
Trail Legs	Nobo: 700 miles to get in shape before reaching the Sierra.	Sobo: Begin in the North Cascades, which is some of the most physically demanding hiking of the whole trail.
Trail Community	Nobo: 5000+ thru-hikers per year.	Sobo: <500 thru-hikers per year.
Resorts	Nobo: The mountain resorts are open (to pick up packages, eat, shower, stay overnight).	Sobo: Many resorts are closed by the time sobos get there.
Canadian Border	Nobo: It is LEGAL to cross from the US into Canada on the PCT, provided you have your *Canada Pacific Crest Trail (PCT) Entry Permit.* Nobo hikers hike from Mexico to the Canadian border (mile 2653.1), continue for 8 more miles into Canada, finishing at Manning Park (mile 2661.9).	Sobo: It is ILLEGAL to cross from Canada into the US on the PCT. See the letter on [www.yogisbooks.com] in the LINKS tab. Sobo hikers start either at Rainy Pass (mile 2591.6) or Harts Pass (mile 2622.5), hike north to the border monument (mile 2653.1), then turn around and hike south on the PCT to Mexico. Some sobo hikers start at Ross Lake, hike over to the border monument, then hike south on the PCT to Mexico. See Anish's comments in Town Guide Section 28.

START and FINISH DATES

If you hiked the Appalachian Trail, you might have started that hike in February, March, or even early April. That works great on the AT; not so much on the PCT. Sure, you start in Southern California, but it's important to understand that the PCT in SoCal is not all desert. You'll be in the Laguna Mountains by mile 40, and you'll be at 9000 feet on the side of Mt. San Jacinto by mile 181.2. The PCT crosses many mountain ridges all the way to Kennedy Meadows (702.2 miles). 20 miles north of Kennedy Meadows, the PCT goes above 10,000 feet and stays at/near that elevation for 300 miles.

Starting the PCT prior to mid-April is not advisable. The concern should not be "is it difficult." Rather, the concern should be "is it dangerous." My opinion is that YES, it's dangerous. An experienced hiker died in 2005 when he got lost in the snow near PCT mile 181.2 (San Jacinto). It isn't advisable to hike north from Kennedy Meadows before early June anyway, so starting in March won't really get you anywhere. The end of April or beginning of May is the best time to start. Once you're on the trail, try to watch your mileage so you don't reach Kennedy Meadows too early.

You're fighting snow. IF YOU START TOO EARLY, you'll hit the Sierra too soon. By waiting until mid-June to enter the Sierra, you give the snow a chance to melt. Shoot for a June 10-15 Kennedy Meadows date. It takes most thru-hikers 5-6 weeks to cover the first 702.2 PCT miles (Mexican border to Kennedy Meadows). So, estimate how long 702.2 miles will take you, then work backwards from a June 10-15 Kennedy Meadows date to determine what date to begin your PCT hike.

IF YOU FINISH TOO LATE, you'll hit snow in Washington. So, after you make it through the Sierra, you can't simply take it easy. You must keep moving. Try to finish before October 1.

So you see, unlike the AT, the PCT has a very short thru-hiking window.

TRAIL NAME	PCT	Nobo Sobo Yo-Yo	Start Date	Finish Date	How many zeros	Kennedy Meadows Date	Dd you do Mt. Whitney?
Yogi	2002	Nobo	Apr 25	Sep 12	12	June 4	Yes
	2003	Nobo	Apr 26	Sep 22	21	June 11	No
	2007	Nobo	Apr 25	Sep 3	12	June 3	Yes
Anish	2005	Nobo	May 4	Sep 22	7	June 15	Yes
	2013	Nobo	June 8	Aug 7	0	June 24	No
BINK	13 thru hikes	Nobo Sobo Yo-Yo	varies	varies	varies	earliest 3/27 latest 6/30	Yes
Hiker Box Special	2013	Nobo	May 2	Sep 20	11	June 16	Yes
Scrub	2013	Nobo	May 5	Sep 23	14	June 12	Yes

BINK: Depends on the year, but take it from me: unless you like snow, you are better off starting later (May) than earlier if you can help it. I have observed snow melt rates of 1-3 feet a day! A week later can make all the difference!

TRAIL CLOSURES and REROUTES

In recent years, California has been engulfed by wildfires, while Washington has endured heavy rains and flooding. The PCT was hit hard in both areas. For current information on trail closures and reroutes, watch the PCTA website [www.pcta.org].

Each year seems to have a different sprinkling of trail closures. If a section of trail is closed, look at maps and try to find a detour route that does not involve interrupting a continuous hike. Don't make a quick decision to skip ahead. The PCT is not the only trail in the woods. You may not be able to walk the "official PCT," but you should be able to find other trails or roads that can get you back to the PCT further up the trail.

Mother Nature doesn't care if we walk the actual PCT. Fires, snow, and rain may force a detour. When that happens, THE DETOUR BECOMES YOUR PCT. It's the trail that you had when you were at that spot. If you could walk the "official PCT," you would. But when you can't, you make the best informed choice, and take another trail. Try to find a detour route that will not interrupt your continuous Mexico-to-Canada hike.

ALTERNATE ROUTES

Don't miss: Crater Lake, Eagle Creek, or San Jacinto. Don't feel like you have to stay on THE PCT just because it is THE Pacific Crest Trail. The PCT was built to accommodate horses. Many of the alternates are very cool hiker-only trails.

Anish: Whitney is definitely worth it! Eagle Creek is a beautiful hike, but the Wathum Lake Route is definitely not bad. I took the official equestrian route around Crater Lake in 2013. It was COVERED in blowdowns. It's nasty. The only redeeming quality is that there is a lot of water, which is nicer than schlepping water all the way from Mazama to Thielsen Creek.

In 2012 I hiked the OR/WA PCT and climbed Mt. McLaughlin. It was a great climb. I recommend it! Just be prepared and carry a LOT of water.

ALTERNATE ROUTES			Yogi	Anish	BINK	HBS	Scrub
San Jacinto Peak	mile 181.2	Took this route?	Yes	No	No	No	Yes
		Take it next time?	Yes	Yes	No	Yes	Yes
Mt. Whitney	mile 766.3	Took this route?	Yes	Yes	Yes	Yes	Yes
		Take it next time?	Yes	Yes	No	Yes	Yes
JMT to Thousand Island Lake	mile 909.0	Took this route?	Yes	No	No	No	No
		Take it next time?	Yes	Yes	No	No	Yes
JMT Tuolumne to Yosemite Valley	mile 942.5	Took this route?	No	Yes	No	No	No
		Take it next time?	Yes	No	No	Yes	Yes
Half Dome	mile 942.5	Took this route?	No	Yes	No	No	No
		Take it next time?	No	No	No	Yes	Yes
Mt. Lassen	mile 1351.3	Took this route?	No	No	No	No	No
		Take it next time?	Yes	Yes	No	Yes	No
Crater Lake Rim	mile 1823.0	Took this route?	Yes	Yes	Yes	Yes	Yes
		Take it next time?	Yes	Yes	Yes	Yes	Yes
Eagle Creek	mile 2128.1	Took this route?	Yes	Yes	Yes	Yes	Yes
		Take it next time?	Yes	Yes	Yes	Yes	Yes

BINK: I have taken many of the alternate routes at some point or another in the last twenty years. Mt. Whitney is fun if you have never been up it. If you have never seen Yosemite Valley, it's worth a look, but be prepared for many thousands of people. Crater Lake Rim is more than worth it, and depending on who you ask it is "official" PCT anyway. If you are only going to do one alternate, the Eagle Creek Trail has my vote. In my opinion, it should have been the route of the PCT. However, the stretch of PCT you would be on if not on the Eagle Creek Trail is also pretty nice, and you will have it mostly to yourself. It seems almost everyone is taking the Eagle Creek Trail these days. There are many old alternates in the old Wilderness Press guides that I don't really hear about people taking anymore. Some of these routes are worthy of consideration, such as the Indian Valley cross country alternate just north of Ebbetts Pass, which was once considered for the route of the PCT.

Hiker Box Special: I did a hike to Clouds Rest, which overlooks Half Dome, and is almost as amazing.

Scrub: Yogi said I couldn't curse too much in this, but I've got to say Mt. San Jacinto is the %&@ing $@%. One of the best places on the whole hike! I heard it gets very crowded on the afternoons and weekends with goofers from the Palm Springs tram, but if you get there in the morning, it might be all yours. Everyone around me came up with a reason to skip it, so I went up alone. It comes at a bad place in the hike – 180 miles in and everyone is whipped from climbing up into the San Jacinto range with no water – so an extra 1800 feet of climbing sounds like murder. But you should still do it, it's awesome. It was a wake-up call for me for exactly how mind-blowingly spectacular the PCT can be.

CONTINUOUS HIKE

This is a clear violation of the "Hike Your Own Hike" philosophy, but I can't help myself. Very few PCT hikers actually walk the entire PCT. Here's why:

- It's impossible in the Sierra. You'll lose the snow-covered trail. You'll glissade down the passes. Switchbacks will be covered with snow and ice, so you'll cut up or down the slope where it's safer. HUGE blowdowns will force you to cut up or down the slope.

- You'd be crazy to miss Crater Lake. The official PCT (aka the Stock PCT) does not go to the Crater Lake Rim. The Hiker PCT does. Are you really going to walk 1823.0 miles from Mexico to Crater Lake and then NOT walk along the Rim? Really?

- You'd be crazy to miss the Eagle Creek Trail (just before Cascade Locks, Oregon). This isn't even a Hiker PCT. It's an alternate route. The Eagle Creek Trail is littered with beautiful waterfalls, including Tunnel Falls, which you walk behind through a tunnel.

So you're not walking every step of the PCT, but you ARE walking from Mexico to Canada. Make sure you do just that: walk from Mexico to Canada. <u>Don't skip sections</u>.

✔ It's easy to skip 27.65 miles near Idyllwild. Hitch into Idyllwild on Pines-to Palms Highway, and return to the PCT via the Devil's Slide Trail.

✔ It's easy to skip 9 miles near Big Bear City. Hitch into Big Bear City on Highway 18 and return to the PCT on Van Dusen Canyon Road.

✔ It's easy to skip 8 miles near Tehachapi/Mojave. Get off the trail at Tehachapi-Willow Springs Road, go to Tehachapi/Mojave, and return to the trail at Hwy 58.

✔ It's easy to skip 4.4 miles from Mazama Village to the Crater Lake Rim. Just hitch up to the Rim. There are several opportunities like these to skip sections of the trail. Some hikers even skip larger sections of 50 or more miles. Don't do it. Stick out the hard parts. Walk from Mexico to Canada. You may be forced off the official PCT onto another trail for a fire or flood detour, but make every effort to walk a continuous hike. When your hike is over, you shouldn't have to clarify your hike. You don't want to have to say "yes, I walked from Mexico to Canada . . . . . well, there was that section near Mojave that I skipped, but that doesn't REALLY count because it was an ugly section through a windmill farm . . . . . and then I missed a few miles near Crater Lake when I got a ride up to the Rim . . . . . but it was ONLY 4.4 miles, that doesn't REALLY count . . . . . So technically, I guess I didn't walk ALL the way from Mexico to Canada."

Don't be a wimp. Don't take the easy way out. Just walk. It's not that hard.

Anish: It really depends on what you're there to do. I have always been out there to hike and so I walk everything. Connecting my footsteps has always been very important to me. If you skip a section, even a tiny one, it breaks up your hike and makes the temptation to skip again easier.

BINK: I am glad to see someone take a stand on this issue. We have all heard the saying "hike your own hike," but I feel that people who spend the summer skipping sections here and there degrade the overall accomplishment of others who have hiked the entire PCT Mexico to Canada.

I get asked about this subject all the time. Back in the 1990's, it seemed everyone was at least trying to walk the entire way from border to border and those who were skipping around were not considered to be thru-hikers. Nowadays it has become more common for people to hitchhike when they do not want to hike a section for whatever reason. In fact, from what I know or at least perceive, quite a few people are now having thru-hikes where they skip sections of trail at some point. For me personally, a continuous line of steps from border to border is a very important part of my hike, not so I can tell anyone about it but as a part of my journey. Staying 100% on official PCT has also been a part of the speed record hikes I have done and attempted. This is all for myself, my own rules I have made for myself. I am going out to hike the PCT border to border and if I were to skip a section it would sort of take the drive out of me.

As for what others are doing on their hikes? I don't really concern myself too much with that. My hikes take enough energy to keep things rolling without worrying about what others are doing. I can't really compare a continuous hike to a non-continuous hike because my only non-continuous hikes ended due to illness or injury or in one case sheer lack of mentally being "into" the hike (2003 Yo-Yo attempt). I hear many people commenting on the fact that people who have skipped large parts of the trail reach Canada and say they have "hiked" the PCT. This seems to have become a very fluid statement as compared to the past. I think that a PCT hike is different things to different people, and although I cannot imagine skipping sections on a PCT "thru" hike, I suppose it makes sense to some people. If you were injured and summer was rapidly going by and you wanted to see the "highlight" sections, this would be one way to do it, as I have seen people do in the past. Although skipping is something that has never been a part of my hiking experience, I like the fact that people have the freedom to choose that option. After all, there is enough structure/rules back in many people's off-trail lives.

On the PCT, I feel like we have a choice to set the structure and "rules" for ourselves. Don't want to wake up and hike until 10pm? Why not? My point here is that I would never consider skipping on a thru-hike, I think it takes part of the journey away when you do this. But that's me, my thinking; others might not feel that way. Are people who reach the Canadian or Mexican borders having skipped trail along the way "thru-hikers"? I feel that's for them to decide. It has been said that if you skip trail sections someone else will always somehow know and they always seem to. Outside of the trail community, the world at large does not care anyway. Most importantly, I don't want anyone telling me how I should conduct my PCT hike, and I am not about to tell anyone else how to conduct theirs.

<u>Hiker Box Special</u>: Do whatever you want, but explain to people that you're hiking most of the trail if you skip. They won't care.

<u>Scrub</u>: "Hike your own hike" is a misused phrase. To me, it means this: you can do WHATEVER you want to do with your time on the trail. Everyone has their own constraints (money, time) and their own goals, so you can flip, skip, race or goof around to your heart's content, because it's your time in this world that you're responsible for.

However, "Hike your own hike" does not mean you can do whatever you want and call it a thru-hike at the end. There are arguments, of course, over what "thru-hike" means, but I'm confident that skipping open and accessible sections of trail does not fall into any of them. Thru-hiking for the average reasonably fit person isn't a physical challenge (beyond the first few weeks), but a mental one, and when you skip a section of the trail because you don't feel up to it – welp, you failed the challenge. You're not a thru-hiker anymore. I'm not saying you're inferior to thru-hikers, because HYOH, but you're not a thru-hiker.

Why even skip? You shouldn't pay attention to what other nobo hikers say about an upcoming section of trail, because THEY HAVEN'T BEEN THERE EITHER. You have no idea before you get to a place what it's going to be like, what mood you're going to be in that day, what cool animal you're going to see, how the light is going to be glancing off the hills just right, etc. You may get to the end of the trail and find that one of your happiest memories wasn't in the High Sierra (which everyone sees), but on some warm evening in the Mojave (which too many people skip). You just don't know until you get there, and no one else knows any better than you.

No part of the trail has more intrinsic value than any other part. All of it comprises the PCT. You can't remove a piece and pretend that you've known and seen the whole thing. If your goal is to thru-hike, just man up, don't listen to the haters and fear-mongers, and do as much of it as you possibly can with the circumstances in your control.

IDENTIFICATION

You'll need a government-issued ID to <u>pick up mail at Post Offices</u>.

If you continue into Canada and finish your hike in Manning Park, you need to get back to the USA. As of November 2019, all travelers entering the US from Canada by air are required to have a passport book or Trusted Traveler Program Card; US citizens entering the US by land or sea are required to have either a passport book, a passport card, enhanced Driver's License, or Trusted Traveler Program Card. Passport information: [www.travel.state.gov] and [www.usps.com/passport].

PERMITS

Read this section very carefully. Then read it again. And maybe a third time.

Contrary to popular belief, the *PCT Long Distance Permit* (issued by the PCTA) is NOT required to hike the PCT. There are areas where permits are required, but those permits could be obtained from local agencies. Repeat: THERE ARE AREAS WHERE PERMITS ARE REQUIRED. However, the permit does not have to be the *PCT Long Distance Permit.*

PERMITS for MILE 0 (MEXICO) to 704 (KENNEDY MEADOWS)

As of November 2019, anyone can hike the first 704 miles of the PCT without a permit of any kind, with two exceptions:

(1) **CLEVELAND NATIONAL FOREST -** Quoted from the Cleveland NF website: "Permit is required to disperse camp within the Hauser Wilderness and on all Cleveland National Forest lands outside of the Laguna Mountain Recreation Area. Dispersed camping outside of a developed campground is not allowed in the Laguna Mountain Recreation Area . . . . . . Day users of the PCT, or hikers camping in developed campgrounds, do not require a visitor's permit." [https://www.fs.usda.gov/detail/cleveland/home/?cid=FSEPRD488307]

Okay, great. What is dispersed camping? Well, "dispersed camping" refers to the practice of camping anywhere you want. You see a nice flat spot, you're ready to stop for the day, you set up your shelter or cowboy camp. That's "dispersed camping." A permit is required to disperse camp in the Cleveland National Forest. That permit could be the *PCT Long Distance Permit*, or it could be a permit from the Cleveland National Forest.

What does this mean for PCT hikers? The PCT enters Cleveland National Forest at approximately mile point 13.8, and departs at approximately mile point 53.2. Within those 39.4 miles, Cleveland National Forest requires a permit for dispersed camping, but it does NOT require a permit for day hiking, and it does not require a permit for overnight hikers who camp in developed campgrounds.

If you have a printed, valid *PCT Long Distance Permit*, you are covered for dispersed camping. If you do not have a printed, valid *PCT Long Distance Permit*, you must use developed campgrounds for overnight camping. Hikers may camp without a permit at these developed campgrounds (some are fee campgrounds): Lake Morena (mile 20.0), Boulder Oaks (mile 26.0), Cibbets Flats (mile 32.6), and Burnt Rancheria (mile 41.5).

(2) **SAN JACINTO STATE PARK WILDERNESS -** Quoted from the California State Parks website: "Everyone entering the wilderness area for the day or for camping must have a permit in their possession. Day use wilderness permits are free and are available 24 hours a day at the State Park Headquarters office in Idyllwild." [https://www.parks.ca.gov/?page_id=636]

What does this mean for PCT hikers? The PCT is in the San Jacinto State Park Wilderness Area from mile 183.1 to mile 189.0. The San Jacinto State Park Wilderness requires a permit for day use and for camping. So, you must have a permit any time you are in the Wilderness. If you have a printed, valid *PCT Long Distance Permit*, you are covered. If you do not have a printed, valid *PCT Long Distance Permit*, you must obtain a permit from San Jacinto State Park Wilderness in Idyllwild CA (northbound hikers are in Idyllwild prior to mile 183.1).

PERMITS for MILE 704 (KENNEDY MDWS) to MILE 2661 (MANNING PARK)

If you have a printed, valid *PCT Long Distance Permit* (issued by the PCTA), you are covered for *most* of the PCT (see below). If you do not have a printed, valid *PCT Long Distance Permit*, you will need to do extensive research to find out where/how to get permits from local agencies. A very broad generalization of PCT permitting is this: permits are generally required in Wilderness Areas, National Parks, and California State Parks; in addition, some areas of Oregon have strict limitations on the number of hikers allowed on the PCT.

For more information, go to [www.pcta.org], click on [Discover The Trail], click on [Permits], click on [Permits for trips under 500 miles]. Please note that the title of that page is a bit misleading.

It does not apply only to trips under 500 miles. Rather, it gives information on permits issued by local agencies. Those permits available to anyone, regardless of the length of their hike.

What does this mean for PCT hikers? For areas north of Kennedy Meadows (mile 704), either obtain individual permits from every area which requires a permit, or get the *PCT Long Distance Permit.*

PCT LONG DISTANCE PERMIT

The *PCT Long Distance Permit* is NOT required to hike the PCT. I'll say that again:
The *PCT Long Distance Permit* is NOT required to hike the PCT.

However, permits ARE required in some areas, including California State Parks, National Parks and Wilderness Areas. You could obtain individual permits in each area which requires a permit. That would be a huge hassle. To simplify the permit process, the PCTA issues one permit which covers you for *most* of the PCT: *PCT Long Distance Permit.*

For more information, go to [www.pcta.org], click on [Discover The Trail], click on [Permits], click on [Permits for trips over 500 miles]. Go to the PCTA website RIGHT NOW. Fifty northbound thru-hiker permits are issued for each start date from the Mexican border. Fifteen southbound thru-hiker permits are issued for each start date from the Canadian border. Permit application day is always a circus. Be sure you know what day the permit system opens up.

If you have a printed, valid *PCT Long Distance Permit,* you also must have the *California Campfire Permit* and possibly permits for the North Cascades National Park and also the Obsidian and Pamelia Limited Entry Areas. Details are below.

500-mile distinction. The permit page on the PCTA website has links for trips over 500 miles and trips under 500 miles. There is a misconception in the hiking community that hikers do not need any permits if their trip is under 500 miles. THAT IS INCORRECT. Whether or not a permit is required is determined by the area you are hiking in, not by the length of your hike.

If a hiker is planning a hike over 500 miles, then the hiker may apply for the *PCT Long Distance Permit.* That permit covers the hiker for *most* permit-required areas (exceptions: North Cascades National Park, and Obsidian and Pamelia Limited Entry Areas).

If a hiker is planning a hike under 500 miles, that hiker may NOT apply for the *PCT Long Distance Permit.* That hiker must figure out what permits are required for the section of trail they are hiking. The hiker then must contact all the local agencies to obtain individual permits.

CALIFORNIA CAMPFIRE PERMIT

Quoted from the USFS website: "You can help protect the National Forests from wildfires by knowing and following the rules for the safe use of fire. You must have a *California Campfire Permit* to use a stove, lantern, or campfire outside a developed campground or recreation area. The permit is your agreement to follow the campfire restrictions and regulations in effect."

For more information, go to [http://www.preventwildfireca.org/Permits/]

What does this mean for PCT hikers? Even if you have a printed, valid *PCT Long Distance Permit,* you must also have the *California Campfire Permit.*

NORTH CASCADES NATIONAL PARK

An additional permit is required to camp in North Cascades National Park (PCT mile 2572.1 to 2588.2). This additional permit is required for CAMPING only. If you hike through the area without camping, then you do not need this additional permit. The *PCT Long Distance Permit* does NOT cover you to camp in this section; you MUST obtain the additional permit if you want to camp in this area.

Northbound hikers can get the permit at the Golden West Visitor Center in Stehekin WA, or call the North Cascades National Park Wilderness Info Center (360-854-7245) from Stevens Pass.

Southbound hikers can get the permit at the North Cascades National Park Wilderness Information Center in Marblemount WA or the Methow Valley Ranger Station in Winthrop WA.

For more information, go to [www.pcta.org], click on [Discover The Trail], click on [Permits].

What does this mean for PCT hikers? If you camp from 2572.1 to 2588.2, you need this permit even if you have a printed, valid *PCT Long Distance Permit.* If you hike through 2572.1 to 2588.2 without camping in that section, you do not need this permit.

OBSIDIAN and PAMELIA LIMITED ENTRY AREAS

An additional permit required to camp in the Obsidian Limited Entry Area (PCT mile 1971.4 to 1973.3) and Pamelia Limited Entry Area (PCT mile 2022.3 to 2023.7). This additional permit is required for CAMPING only. If you hike through the area without camping, then you do not need this additional permit. The *PCT Long Distance Permit* does NOT cover you to CAMP in these sections; you MUST obtain the additional permit if you want to camp in these areas.

For more information, go to [www.pcta.org], click on [Discover The Trail], click on [Permits].

What does this mean for PCT hikers? If you camp from 1971.4 to 1973.3 or 2022.3 to 2023.7, you need this permit even if you have a printed, valid *PCT Long Distance Permit.* If you hike through those areas without camping, you do not need this permit.

CENTRAL OREGON

Mt. Jefferson, Mt. Washington, and the Three Sisters Wilderness areas are implementing a new permit system in 2020 or 2021. Due to increasing popularity of these areas, entry will be limited. Hikers who have a printed, valid *PCT Long Distance Permit* are covered for these areas.

For current information, go to [www.pcta.org], click on [Discover The Trail], click on [Permits], click on [Permits for trips under 500 miles].

What does this mean for PCT hikers? If you have a printed, valid *PCT Long Distance Permit*, you are covered. If you do not, you must obtain permits from local agencies.

US-MEXICO BORDER

At the California-Mexico border, the PCT does not go into Mexico. The PCT monument is on the US side of the giant border wall. Because you stay in the US, no special permits are required.

US-CANADA BORDER - NORTHBOUND HIKERS

The **PCNST** (**P**acific **C**rest **N**ational **S**cenic **T**rail) Northern Terminus monument is at the US-Canada border. However, the **PCT** (**P**acific **C**rest **T**rail) continues 8.8 more miles into Canada. This US-Canada border crossing is unmanned. All hikers (including Canadians) who continue northbound into Canada must obtain permission from the Canadian government to enter Canada at the PCT unmanned border crossing. Permission is in the form of the *Canada Pacific Crest Trail (PCT) Entry Permit*, which is issued by the Canadian government. Processing takes up to 8 weeks, so apply for the entry permit before your hike. It is illegal to enter Canada via the PCT without this permit. Hikers must have a printed copy of this permit with them at all times while in Canada. Although this permit is issued by the Canadian government, in recent years US Border Patrol Agents have asked to see hikers' *Canada Pacific Crest Trail (PCT) Entry Permit* as hikers returned to the US.

If you have any blemishes on your legal record, Canada could deny your application. You certainly do not want to be caught in Canada if you have been denied entry.

Specific denial information is here: [www.travel.state.gov]:

> "Anyone with a criminal record (including misdemeanors or alcohol-related driving offenses) may not be able to enter Canada without first obtaining an approval for rehabilitation well in advance of any planned travel. To determine whether you may be inadmissible and how to overcome this finding, please refer to the CIC website:
>
> [www.cic.gc.ca/english/information/applications/guides/5312ETOC.asp#overview]
>
> Entry into Canada is solely determined by Canada Border Services Agency (CBSA) officials in accordance with Canadian law. Please see the CBSA's website for full details: [http://www.cbsa.gc.ca/] "

If you think you will be denied entry, or if you already have been denied entry into Canada, do not worry. You can hike in the US up to the Northern Terminus at the US-Canada border, turn around and hike south back to Rainy Pass, then hitch west to the Sedro-Woolley WA area near Interstate 5. From there, you can go north to Bellingham WA or south to Seattle WA. Both cities have airports and Amtrak. Details are in the Town Guide portion of this Handbook at milepoint 2591.6 and 2661.9.

For more information, go to [www.pcta.org], click on [Discover The Trail], click on [Permits].

US-CANADA BORDER - SOUTHBOUND HIKERS

The only legal way to cross into the US is at a manned border crossing. The US-Canada border crossing on the PCT is unmanned. Therefore, it is illegal to cross southbound from Canada into the US using the trail. If you are southbounding, you must hike in the United States up to the Northern Terminus monument, then turn around and hike south on the PCNST. In the Logistics chapter of this Handbook, see the "North or South?" section. Also, in the Town Guide portion of this book, see the shaded box in the "Manning Park" section (at mile point 2661.9).

GUIDEBOOKS, MAPS, and APPS

The PCT is easy to follow, but trail junctions are usually not signed "PCT that-a-way." It's important to carry actual paper maps, rather than relying solely on apps, PDF downloads, and GPS. Electronics fail all the time on the trail. Batteries run out. Using paper maps can literally save your life.

HALFMILE'S MAPS

[www.pctmap.net] Halfmile's Pacific Crest Trail maps were the gold standard for PCT hikers for many years. In 2019, Halfmile stopped releasing a new map set each year because he is working with NatGeo to create a new map set based upon Halfmile's research.

NATGEO PCT MAP SET

The brand new NatGeo PCT Map Set is in the process of being completed. Washington and Oregon are ready now; California is slated to be completed by the end of 2019. NatGeo worked in concert with Halfmile to create a great new resource for PCT'ers. This map set will be available at Yogi's Books [www.yogisbooks.com] and Triple Crown Outfitters [www.triplecrownoutfitters.com].

GUTHOOK APP (Atlas Guides)

Everyone uses Guthook's phone app. [www.atlasguides.com]. The best part of Guthook is the crowdsourced information regarding water sources and snow conditions. You can find out exactly what is going on from hikers who are in front of you. Atlas Guides usually runs a hiker special over Black Friday weekend.

PEOPLE

HIKING ALONE OR WITH OTHERS

If you want to hike by yourself, you can. But you don't have to. Most PCT hikers begin solo. That's because most of us don't know anyone at home who is crazy enough to walk from Mexico to Canada. You may be tempted to try to hook up with another PCT hiker before the trip, perhaps through one of the online forums. I don't recommend that. Until you meet someone and walk with them on the trail, you simply don't know if you'll be compatible hiking partners.

If you start your trip from mid-March to early-May, you will be in a big wave of hikers from Campo to at least Kennedy Meadows (702.2 miles). It will be easy to fall into a group or a partnership with other hikers.

Anish: I hiked in 2013 solo (I was attempting to set the self-supported speed record). I ran into a few hikers along the way that would hike with me for a few miles (or a couple days). Otherwise, it was a completely solo adventure. I enjoyed the distraction of company, but I really enjoyed hiking by myself.

BINK: I have hiked the PCT both solo and with others, although a bit more as a solo hiker. If hiking with others, be prepared to compromise at some level. I do feel that hiking with others makes the mentally difficult times easier because you are sharing the experience with someone else. I cannot say I prefer solo over hiking with others; they both have their merits. You will see much more wildlife hiking solo.

Stehekin is my favorite place in America! – Billy Goat

Hiker Box Special: Like most people, I started solo. I tended to either hike too fast or take too many breaks to keep me from hiking much with other people. Also, everyone is on a different schedule as far as zeros and neros and whatever. I usually camped with other people, but often solo, and I enjoyed both. Walking solo gives you a chance to take things in at your own pace, and you're quieter and see more wildlife.

Scrub: I started the hike alone, and because it was raining the first night and everyone was stuck in their tents, I did not really meet anyone until I got going the next day. I hiked with (by which I mean we sometimes walked together and definitely camped together) other individuals several times, but not nearly as often as I walked alone. I feel like I know my good hiking buddies really well, but looking back on it I was never with any one person for longer than about two weeks total, or one week consecutive.

Twice I lost people for good when they left town two hours ahead of me, and I never caught up. It didn't really matter . . . . I was content to be alone most of the time. Even if I was stuck in a trough between hiker waves for a few days, I knew that when I got to the next town I'd run into new and old faces and the scene would totally change for the next stretch. I ended up being surprised by how alone I was a lot of the time, and what little effort I made to hang with other people.

HIKING AS A COUPLE

Hiking with a partner is completely different from hiking solo. It REALLY does take commitment and compromise. Prior to the CDT in 2012, my boyfriend and I had always hiked solo. He had 20,000 solo miles; I had 17,000 solo miles. We had our independence dialed in. Our solo hiking styles were NOT the same: He hiked about 4 mph; I hiked 2-2.5mph. He liked to night-hike; I liked to sleep. He occasionally hiked marathon "days," going 30-ish hours straight; I liked to sleep. He often stopped a couple hours before sunset; I liked to hike until the sun went down. He ate dinner, then fell right to sleep; I ate dinner, then spent an hour or so looking over the next day's maps. He liked to wing it; I'm a planner. He liked to pick up a resupply box and move on; I liked to stay in town overnight. We both like bacon. Yum.

It could have been a recipe for disaster. Somehow, it worked out. It really came down to him modifying his hiking style to fit mine. For us, the relationship was more important than the hike.

We each carried our own food. Sometimes we would share/trade snacks, but otherwise our food was independent. Our resupply boxes were packed individually, but the mailing label address showed both our names. With both names on every package, one person could pick up mail for the other person.

Sometimes he would hike ahead of me, but we usually hiked together. That meant he had to alter his pace to match mine.

We shared a tent, the Big Agnes Copper Spur 3. We chose the three-person tent instead of a two-person tent because we didn't want to feel cramped inside our trail home. This was one of the best decisions we made. The Copper Spur 3 has a door on each side, so we could each get in/out of the tent without bothering the other person. We bought Western Mountaineering sleeping bags which zip together. Our NeoAir pads were strapped together each night with a coupler kit.

Setting up camp was quick. One person would set up the tent and blow up the sleeping pads, while the other person sourced water (we shared one water filter). Then we'd get into the tent, change into our sleeping clothes, cook/eat dinner, and go to sleep.

I moved slower in the mornings than he did, so while I was packing up my pack, he would take the tent down. Then he'd warm the handles of my hiking poles. That's a great hiking partner!

Anish: In 2005 I hiked as part of a couple. It was our first hike together aside from a few day hikes and there were a LOT of growing pains. We made a good team, however, and by the time we got through the Sierra we had an excellent system in place. It helps to establish camp chores and systems before the hike, but be willing to adapt them on trail if they aren't working. Also, be realistic about what each person can reasonably carry while maintaining pace. If you are not evenly matched in ability, that is going to cause a lot of problems. Discuss this before the hike, but again, be willing to adapt. If one partner is much slower or stronger, then there is going to be friction. You have likely never been with your partner 24/7 for several months before.

BINK: Hiking as a couple could be the most challenging of all ways to thru-hike the PCT. I thru-hiked twice with a significant other. We did not share food on either hike; on one hike we shared a shelter and stove. I hear of people going as far as sharing toothbrushes! As with any love relationship: BE PREPARED TO COMPROMISE!! I have seen some real disasters in this category of hikers. I have also seen some real inspiring love stories as well. My advice is GOOD LUCK!

TRAIL NAME

A thru-hike is a wonderful, crazy, unique experience. We take trail names to recognize this experience as a special time. Some hikers name themselves before hiking. Others wait to "get named" on the trail. I think a trail name should be just that: a TRAIL name. In my opinion, people who name themselves before setting foot on a trail do not have a TRAIL name. They have a NICK name. More importantly: by naming yourself, you cheat yourself out of a great story and memory.

Gottago was named on a PCT training hike. She had to pee. She thought she was alone, started to take care of business, then some guys on mountain bikes rolled by. One of them smiled and said, "When you gotta go, you gotta go."

Let your name represent who you are on the trail. Believe me, you'll be a different person, and I think that if you want to be called by a different name than the one you use back in the other world, it should have ties to your trail experience. Let your trail name happen. It will find you.

I remember on my Appalachian Trail hike when I got to Daicey Pond in Maine, a few miles before Katahdin, there was a representative of the Appalachian Trail Conference who was taking data from thru-hikers: when we started, where we were from, our opinions of the trail, etc. The ATC representative asked me the coolest question. First, he asked for my trail name. Then, he asked for my "other name." He didn't say "real name," he said "other name." He didn't spell it out in so many words, but by choosing his words carefully, he recognized that my TRAIL NAME is just as REAL as the name I was given at birth. Think about that.

So what about keeping your AT trail name for the PCT? Many hikers keep their AT trail names. Others take different trail names for their PCT hikes. I thought about this when I was planning my first PCT hike. Should I be "Jackie" until a new trail name found me, or should I stick with "Yogi," the name I got on the AT? The deciding factor was this: I was planning to hike the PCT with Paranoid, a fellow AT'er. I simply couldn't call Paranoid by her given name of Lizzie, and she couldn't call me Jackie. So, we agreed to stick with our AT names. Once we were on the PCT, Paranoid's name morphed into P-noid, and finally to simply "Noid." I remained "Yogi." Later, I thought about our decision. In my opinion, my trail name represents who I am IN THE HIKING WORLD. That world includes spending a night in a shelter on Grayson Highlands, postholing in the High Sierra, talking to a trail buddy on the phone, attending a hiker Gathering, or visiting a friend in Kentucky a year after the trail. It's who I am in the hiking world. And that world doesn't always happen on a trail.

Diesel and Hammer on Forester Pass

UNDOCUMENTED IMMIGRANTS

I've hiked north from Campo five times. I've never had any problems with undocumented immigrants, and I've seen plenty of them. Or maybe I should say I've heard plenty of them. They travel at night. Much like PCT hikers, they travel fast and light. Much like PCT hikers, they simply want to walk north as fast as possible. I've never heard of any hikers having any problems. If you're really that concerned, just camp out of sight of the trail, and keep all your gear inside your tent with you.

Common sense tells you to not camp alone anytime you are in an area that is easily accessed by non-thru-hikers. Just as you would not want to camp alone near a road anywhere else on the trail, you also would not want to camp alone near the Mexican border. If you can get to the border in the morning, you can easily walk the 20 miles into Lake Morena in 8 hours. There is a dedicated PCT hiker site at the Lake Morena Campground.

Anish: I've never been concerned and never encountered anyone that seemed threatening.

BINK: My very first time down there I was a little concerned, but nothing happened. Up until 1996, there was no wall at the border, just a three-strand barbed wire fence. Starting in the late 1990's, due to operation "gate keeper," Border Patrol enforcement was enhanced quite a bit in the San Diego area, and it seems since then the area around the PCT has become much more active. I have seen large groups of undocumented people traveling at night and dusk on a few occasions, but I have never had any problems or felt threatened. I have been woken up in the middle of the night a few times by the activities of the Border Patrol. I have heard all kinds of crazy stories that supposedly happened to other hikers, but never any that I could confirm.

Hiker Box Special: It wasn't a concern. They don't want to be seen.

Scrub: I didn't see any illegal activity. I saw Border Patrol trucks everywhere in the first 20 miles but did not have to talk to anyone.

MISCELLANEOUS TOPICS

AT vs PCT

Each year, the PCT attracts a large number of former Appalachian Trail hikers. It seems to be the natural progression for those of us who fell in love with long-distance hiking on the Appalachian Trail. Former AT hikers must understand that the PCT is an entirely different beast.

- 12,000-foot passes covered with ice and snow. 'Nuff said.

- 25+ mile days are common.

- Distance between resupply points is longer. 100 miles between resupply points is typical.

- There are no white blazes. You must always carry maps.

- Hot is hotter. Cold is colder. You can hike in 100+ degree weather during the day, then shiver in your 20-degree sleeping bag that very same night.

- In one afternoon in the Sierra, you will ford more streams than you forded on your entire AT hike.

- Most important is the shorter hiking window. Thru-hikers are on the AT every month of the year. The PCT has about a 6-month thru-hiking window, approximately April thru September.

Anish: The Appalachian and Pacific Crest Trails really don't have a lot in common other than they are both over 2,000 miles long.

+ The AT has a lot of people on it, thru-hikers, sectioners, day hikers, etc. It also has a lot of road crossings and towns for resupply. The shelters provide gathering points along the way that concentrate use. It's wet and humid. The trail tread is rough, rutted, rocky, and very steep in places.

+ The PCT has much less human activity except in popular day/week use areas (such as the desert high points, the Sierra, Goat Rocks, etc.). The road crossings are far less frequent, which means you need to be accurate with your logistics before you walk out of town. Water is sparse along the whole PCT, and there are frequent stretches where you will have to carry half a day (or more) of water with you. It isn't humid, and you are at considerably higher elevations, which can affect your respiration, perspiration, and your thirst rate. The trail tread is very graded and nice to walk on.

BINK: The two stand out comparisons are:

    (1) The AT mile per mile seemed more physically difficult.
    (2) The PCT is more mentally taxing and requires more endurance.

    Other differences:

✔ Fresh food seems more frequently accessible on the AT.

✔ Town stops and restaurant meals along the way cost a lot less along the AT than they do on the PCT.

✔ I never remember feeling the sun much on the AT, although the humidity combined with the heat was a real force. On the PCT, the direct sun is a real force to be reckoned with. I remember sweat poring out of my forehead all day long each day on the AT. On the PCT, you never sense all the sweat you are losing, but in many ways you are losing water more rapidly even on cool days.

✔ Water seemed much more plentiful on the AT. I hardly ever carried more than a liter or two. On the PCT, you must constantly pay attention to water.

✔ Although the PCT is a much drier trail than the AT, when you do have weather on the PCT it is usually more challenging to deal with, because temperatures are much cooler when there is weather at higher elevations. You can get snowstorms even in the summer on many parts of the PCT. I had 8 inches of snow on July 4th of 2000 in Central Oregon. I have been snowed on even in the Mojave Desert.

Scrub: This is a very common question once people find out that you've done the AT, and pretty soon it became clear to me that the easiest (and most correct) answer to give was: they're so different that they're not worth comparing. I thought that in MY years on MY hikes, the PCT was easier than the AT, but for every one of me there's two people who think the opposite. It's an academic discussion.

I will say that having done a long hike before was extremely helpful at the beginning of the PCT. It helped me to be relaxed, very go-with-the-flow, not to mention quite happy and grateful to be out hiking again. A lot of the newbies around me were stress cases at the beginning – blisters, water, fatigue. All the things that I knew from experience just aren't worth worrying about in the long term do seem much more overwhelming when you face them for the first time, and in the middle of the freaking desert to boot.

The first-timers around me were also very rigorous about their schedule. When we got to Julian, they were all like, "Umm, I don't want to go to Julian, because, like, I was planning to be at the Warner Springs PO Thursday morning, and if I went to Julian, I'd be there, like, Thursday afternoon." Meanwhile, myself and a fellow former ATer (Tree-Boo) were like, "Wait, there's FREE PIE down there!?!? Show me where!!" We were the only PCTers in Julian all day. It was crazy. Everyone else came up with some reason to skip out, even though they'd all heard about the free pie, too.

JOURNAL or BLOG

I highly recommend keeping a journal/blog. Whether you have an online journal/blog or a personal journal/blog, it's a great way to remember your trip after you're done.

- **Write several pre-hike entries.** This will get you used to writing.

- **Write what YOU want to remember,** not only what you think others will find interesting. It's great that others read it and live vicariously through you. But ultimately this is for YOU.

- **You do have some responsibility to your readers.** Explain things that non-thru-hikers would not understand. For example, when you say "I took a zero day," be sure to explain what a zero day is.

- **Avoid writing about annoying people and trail romances.** Two common themes that most online authors practice is to NOT write about trail romances, and to NOT mention other hikers by name/trail name when writing negatively about that person. Online journals/blogs are very popular, and you don't want to hurt someone because of what you wrote. You have no idea who is reading your journal/blog. You can always write what happened, just make up fictitious names for the people you're writing about.

- **There will be nights when you don't feel like writing.** When that occurs, write a few notes about what went on that day, so that when you eventually write about that day, you'll easily remember the details.

- **Be honest.** Don't sugar-coat your experiences. If the day sucked, write that. If your blisters hurt, write about that. There will be way more good things than bad things, but it's important to write about your complete experience.

- **Keep your online journal/blog 7-10 days behind,** especially if you're a woman. Readers get really involved in hiker journals/blogs, and they will come looking for you. You might not want to be found.

- **Don't expect to compose your journal/blog at the library computer in town.** Town time is important for relaxing, eating, resupplying, eating, showering, eating, doing laundry, and eating. Journaling/blogging in town is too much work, your journal/blog will quickly become a low priority, and you'll eventually stop posting it. Instead, use your phone to compose your thoughts when you are in your sleeping bag at night. Then email/post your journal/blog to your website when you have cell coverage.

- **Your electronic device could fail.** Protect it from water damage and from getting smashed. Store it inside two ziplocks, and then in a small Tupperware-style container. Get an OtterBox or LifeProof case for your phone.

Anish: There is a lot of cell phone coverage along the trail now, so it's much easier to share your journey as you go. It's up to you how much time you want to spend online. I like walking away from the constant stream of media and going into the mountains, so I keep my postings to a minimum. I journal for myself along the way, but it's not something I put online.

Hiker Box Special: Journaling/blogging is a chore. Your friends and relatives will love it, but you will probably learn to hate it. I updated every few weeks when I got to a real PC. It's nice to look back on, but not necessary.

Scrub: I set up a blog a few months before I left for the hike. On the trail, every night before going to bed, I wrote a journal entry on the notepad on my phone. When I got to town, I updated the entries to my blog using the Blogger app and added a few pictures. I didn't miss a day, and I liked doing it. It was never a chore, it was just something I had to do to make the day complete. On days when I didn't see many other people and was camping alone, I thought of it as a way of telling someone how my day had gone. I kept the blog 5-7 days behind real life because of the Hikin' Burke Uncertainty Principle: I didn't want anyone to know my movements and location at the same time.

I tried to get the major events and interactions of the day down, tried to describe briefly what the trail was like that day, then I'd add a little bit about whatever else happened to have occupied my thoughts. I didn't hold much back, meaning I employed tasteless and/or sardonic humor sometimes because that's just me, or I mentioned drugs and alcohol because that was an integral part of some days/nights. I wanted to be honest with myself if nothing else. I was thinking that years down the line, I myself might be looking back at the journal almost like a new and unfamiliar reader because I will have forgotten so many small details about the trip, so I'd better get them right.

Some people wrote incredibly thorough and complex blogs because they had tablets and typing was easier, and the options for embedding video and pictures were more robust than what was possible on a smartphone. But many more people start out with well-intentioned blogs and let them basically die off. I'd encourage you not to do that. The novel starts to become the routine for everyone a month or two into your hike, but what happens to you each day, even the dullest, hottest day somewhere in Northern California, is definitely still interesting to your readers who are not hiking, and will seem really interesting to you to look back on six months after you're done. So I'd put real effort into keeping a blog alive all the way through the hike if that's what you choose to do, and what you tell your friends and family you'll do.

ELECTRONICS

Technology in the electronics arena changes much too quickly to include specific recommendations in this book. Cameras, phones, email devices, GPS, and audio equipment are constantly improving to be lighter and less expensive with more features. Three key features to look for in all trail electronics: **weight, durability, battery life.**

When **weighing** each device, include the weight of the charger/cord, backup batteries, and solar charger. You'll need to charge them up frequently. The last thing you want to carry in your pack is a broken piece of gear, so make sure that your electronics are **durable**. **Battery life** is important. If you use your phone constantly and you're on a 4-5 day stretch between towns, you could be carrying dead weight for 2-3 days at a time.

PROTECT YOUR ELECTRONICS

The gear in your pack could get wet, banged up, or smashed. Pack your electronics in a water-tight Tupperware-style plastic container. In addition, put screen protectors on all your electronics screens.

This will protect the screens from scratches. No matter how careful you are, your electronics will get scratched on a hike.

Protect your cell phone with an OtterBox or LifeProof case. This is essential. No matter how much you THINK you'll be careful with your phone, chances are very good that you will drop it or bang it up during your hike. Choose a brightly-colored case, something that will jump out at you when you leave your phone on the ground. Avoid black, white, and green colored cases. Trust me. Get a brightly-colored phone case.

LABEL YOUR ELECTRONICS

Using a permanent Sharpie marker, write this on all your electronics: your trail name, your legal name, "If found, please call (your cell phone plus the phone number of someone at home)." Find some way to attach this information to all your power cords. Change the opening screen on your phone to "If found, please contact . . . ."

PICTURES and VIDEO

This trip is life-changing. Your life will quickly become defined as "before the PCT" and "after the PCT." You will look back on your pictures and video for the rest of your life, so take LOTS of pictures and video.

Be sure to make your camera/phone accessible while hiking. You are less likely to take pictures if you must take off your pack to access your camera/phone.

Many packs have pockets on the hip belt which seem ideal for holding a camera/phone. I advise against that, because when you take your pack off, those pockets quickly smack into the ground. You could easily break your camera/phone (been there, done that). Those pockets are better suited for holding snacks, maps, and data pages. Store your camera/phone in a side pocket or shoulder strap pocket which you can easily reach while wearing your pack.

Most smartphones take excellent pictures. However, your phone will quickly lose battery power if you constantly use it to take pictures.

Anish: I used the camera on my iPhone.

Hiker Box Special: I carried a point and shoot. Instead, I recommend taking your biggest, heaviest, most awesomest camera. The PCT is incredible, and it's worth having amazing photos. If you're weight conscious (which you should be), use a bounce box and bounce it forward to scenic areas (the Sierra, the Marble Mountains, the Three Sisters, and almost all of Washington).

Scrub: My smartphone had an okay camera, but I cared enough about picture quality that I carried a separate point-and-shoot digital camera for much of the way. Both of these were always within reach in my shoulder-strap pockets; the people I know who carried cameras in their packs unsurprisingly ended up not using them very often.

I started out with a decent Panasonic Lumix that permanently stopped working the day I left Wrightwood (mile 370ish). At South Lake Tahoe, I borrowed an old Nikon point-and-shoot from my dad and carried it the rest of the way, using it mostly for video and shots on cloudy days when my phone's camera really struggled to make anything look good. On future hikes, I will probably have a better smartphone with a better camera and more memory, and use that exclusively.

PHONES

Most hikers nowadays carry smartphones. You won't get coverage everywhere on the trail, but it sure is nice to have a phone handy in town. Many resorts and towns have removed pay phones, due to the fact that pretty much everyone has cell phones now.

Anish: I'd never carried a phone before. However, there are no pay phones anymore. I'd say that if there is anyone at home you'd like to be in contact with, a cell phone is going to make life a lot easier. If you just need a couple minutes to call or text and say "I'm OK" then you can probably just borrow one, since almost every hiker (and people in towns) have one. A smartphone of some sort is a pretty fantastic ultralight piece of gear. If you'd otherwise carry a camera, a GPS, a journal, an iPod, etc., instead you can carry just this one thing and do all of those (and a lot more).

BINK: I remember when no one had cell phones and now nearly everyone carries them. I carried a phone on my last few hikes, but just an old TDMA phone (does not do internet or such). I would like to not carry one, but it seems many towns along the PCT have removed their pay phones in recent years.

Scrub: There are still people out there who genuinely believe that phones don't belong in the wilderness, but I don't think they grasp the enormous range of traditional hiking uses that a smartphone has. I downloaded Halfmile's maps for free and viewed them only on my phone – didn't bother printing them. I used Google Drive to get new updates of the Water Report and then view it offline, and set up a resupply spreadsheet that I shared with my ground control person, complete with ETAs, mail drop addresses, and instructions. I wrote in my journal on the phone every night. I had a compass app on the phone. I used the camera heavily. I made to-do lists for the next town stop. I downloaded a few books of poetry for the Kindle app and sometimes read those at night or tried to memorize lines as I walked. I read the news on it in town or just out of town. I listened to music on it. And of course I used it as a normal old phone.

I have no problem saying that, with the setup I chose, my phone was just as essential to me as my sleeping bag or shelter. I took extra good care of it: bought a nice hard-rubberized case and screen protectors before the hike, was careful not to drop it or bang it around, double-Ziploc-bagged it when it was raining (touch screens work through Ziploc bags), made recharging the two spare batteries in town a top priority, etc. I never had all three batteries run out (I was on airplane mode 99% of the time outside of towns). Even with all that, I knew there was still a slight risk of electronics failure, but no more than, say, your pack accidentally rolling down a cliff.

GPS - GLOBAL POSITIONING SYSTEM

A GPS is absolutely not needed on the PCT. In my opinion, it would be a waste of money and weight. The PCT is easy to follow. Use apps, carry maps, look at them often, and you'll be fine.

PERSONAL LOCATOR

Spot Satellite Messenger and Garmin inReach electronically track your location via satellite.

Spot:	By pressing a button, you can send an "I'm Okay" message, or an "SOS (9-1-1) emergency" message. You can also leave the Spot turned on to create a track of your hike. The "I'm Okay" messages create link coordinates to Google Maps, so your friends/family can know exactly where you are in the world. The "SOS" message sends Search-And-Rescue out to find you.
Garmin inReach:	Send and receive text messages or emails Track your trip, share your location, let others follow your journey Pairs with your smartphone Interactive 2-way SOS in case of emergency Weather forecast

Anish: I carried a Spot. I think it's completely unnecessary on the PCT unless you are trying to set a record and want documentation. Even then I'm not really sure it's that important. That said, I would carry it again solely for the fact that my parents didn't worry about me nearly as much as they did on my previous adventures. Knowing that they could just go online and see my little "I'm OK" messages moving up the trail and be reassured was priceless to me.

Lithium AAA's are impossible to find in the small towns. They are also illegal to mail, therefore I did not have tracking enabled (tracking burns through batteries). However, I checked in 2-4 times per day manually.

Hiker Box Special: I used a Spot 2 in conjunction with spotwalla.org, which collects your Spot points and plots them on a map. You can link the map to your blog to show people where you are. I thought it was cool; some hikers were afraid of stalkers. Warning though, when the batteries run low, the Spot will tell you it sent and received a signal – but it didn't. It also won't tell you the batteries are running low.

MUSIC WHILE HIKING

Many hikers enjoy listening to music while hiking. Phones hold a lot of music, but the battery doesn't last long if you use it a lot. I carry a small AM-FM Radio which takes one AAA battery. I'm never without tunes.

An interesting advantage of a radio over recorded music comes from d-low. When he was on the CDT, he sent me an email regarding his decision to record all his favorite songs for that trip. He was looking forward to hiking along with his favorite tunes. After about six weeks, he realized that the recorded songs were a mistake. You see, on his other hikes, he had carried a little FM radio. After those hikes were over, he would often hear the songs which were popular during the summers of those hikes. Hearing those songs brought back memories of the hikes. Now, by not listening to the radio during his thru-hike, d-low was denying himself the creation of new song-influenced memories.

Anish: I don't listen to music while hiking, but a lot of people do. It can definitely help with the monotony of road walks (Seiad Valley) or distract you from buggy sections (Oregon).

BINK: Seems a lot of people these days hike with music. I have never been able to hike while listening to music, at least during the day. On recent speed record attempts, I have occasionally listened to the radio at night while hiking, using a cheap FM radio that takes one AAA battery.

I remember one year many years back there was a thru-hiker who had a very sizable old school style stereo system attached to his external frame pack. How it was powered I do not know. I remember standing under a blazing sun in the Mojave desert having a yelling conversation over the music with him as his large speakers, mounted on the pack frame facing forward, blasted out ZZ Top as he stood there wearing his "mobile marshal stack" as he called it. It was a surreal moment. I had that song stuck in my head the rest of that summer.

Hiker Box Special: I went music-free and just listened to my feet crunch the earth and my pack squeak against my back. I liked listening to the world around me and being okay with my boredom. People thought I was crazy.

Scrub: I always had music on my phone, but I rarely listened to it in the first 1,000 miles. Past that, though, I averaged an hour or so a day, usually in times of low motivation and/or obnoxious uphills. Walking through the solitary forest belting out Joni Mitchell or Too Short or the Let the Bodies Hit the Floor song or whatever music is in your headphones is one of the best parts about hiking, period.

CASH ON HAND

Many stores, restaurants, motels, and some Post Offices do not accept credit cards. Those that do accept credit cards often do not accept American Express. Some motels offer lower rates for those paying cash. Many small towns and resorts do not have ATMs. So, it's a good idea to always carry around $200 cash. Check the Handbook Town Guide section for specific information for each resupply location.

THRU-HIKE COST

Hikers typically spend $4000-$7000 on a thru-hike. Towns are where you'll spend your money. Every time you go to town, you'll have 2-3 restaurant meals, stay in a hotel, do laundry, buy snacks and beer. It adds up. I budget $100 for every day in town.

An alternative to a restaurant meal is to buy a rotisserie chicken and bagged salad from the grocery store. You'll get a LOT of food for little money, plus you don't have to tip.

Anish: You can make a hike as expensive or as cheap as you want. Make some of your gear. Buy inexpensive or used clothes to hike in (they're going to get trashed anyway). Scour internet discount gear sites for shoe sales. I got six pairs of shoes (enough for the whole trail and a new pair for when I got home) for $300. Use what you have. If you send resupply boxes, make and dehydrate your own meals. Buy bulk fruit and nuts and make your own trail mixes . . . . you get the idea.

When you're on the trail, set a budget for town and stick to it. A key to keeping it cheap: don't stay in town overnight. Camp just outside, hitch to town in the morning. Eat a big town breakfast (usually the cheapest meal to eat out, and often big portions). Do your chores, drink a beer or two if that's your thing, and hitch back out. Camp a short way down the trail. It will save you tons.

BINK: I have done PCT hikes with nearly no money and PCT hikes where I had enough. It seems like spending a lot of time in towns eats through money. On the speed hikes where I have not spent more than an hour or so in town stops, with no zeros for the entire trail, I typically spend very little money compared to hikes where I am taking zero days in town.

Scrub: Before my hike, I set up a joint checking account with my girlfriend specifically for the PCT. She and I each had a debit card for the account, so she could pay for mail drop food and postage or emergency gear orders.

Everything I did on the trail, including the trips to/from the termini, was paid for with that debit card. I had monthly installments of $1000 automatically put in from my real-life bank account, which ended up being more than enough. When I got home, I looked back at all the charges for the past five months and came up with an expenditure breakdown, which went like this:

        $1700 - Resupply costs, including mail drop postage and fees
        $1000 - Town food and drink
        $ 500 - Lodging
        $ 600 - New gear (mostly shoes, also a new jacket and pants) purchased on-trail
        $ 650 - Miscellaneous cash expenditures from ATM withdrawals
                (probably mostly went toward town food and drink)
        $ 350 - To/from trail transportation, including meals

No one ever talks about money in much detail, so I have no idea whether this is typical or not. You can definitely do it a lot cheaper than I did.

$$$ SPENT	Gear and clothing	Everything Else	Total
Yogi	$1000	$5000	$6000
Anish	< $1000	$2500	$3500
BINK	< $1000 I make a lot of my gear	$4000	$5000
Hiker Box Special	$1000	$4500	$5500
Scrub	$1250 pre-trail $ 650 on trail	$4200	$6100

THRU-HIKING DOGS

Dogs don't sit at home and think: "Gee, I think I'd like to walk the 2661.9-mile Pacific Crest Trail next summer. It will be okay, because I'll take breaks when *I* need to rest. I'll walk when *I* want to walk. I'll take a zero day when *I* want to take a zero day. I don't mind extreme heat and cold, because I'm prepared for that both mentally and physically. I run around at the park for an hour every Saturday, that's a lot like hiking. I know what I'm getting into."

There's a great scene at the end of a PCT documentary which shows two hikers with their dog at the Canadian border. The dog is running around, barking, and wagging his tail. Everything changes when the hikers put the dog's backpack onto his back. The dog stands as still as a statue. The dog won't move. One of the hikers says, "Every morning for two months we've been doing this and every morning he just stands there." It's painfully obvious that the dog does NOT want to go backpacking.

LEAVE YOUR DOG AT HOME.

BIKES ON THE PCT

From the United States Forest Service: *"The trail is open to the public for foot and equestrian travel only; bicycles and motorized vehicles are not permitted."*

The PCT is a trail for hikers and stock only. Bikes are not allowed. That is a fact.

One of the many reasons that bikes don't belong on the PCT is that it's not safe for the people on foot. Have you ever been walking along a trail and out of nowhere a bike comes barreling around the bend and almost takes you out? It's not fun.

There are signs at every trailhead indicating that bikes are not allowed on the PCT. The people on the bikes see those signs when they get on the trail, yet every bike person I've met has denied any knowledge that bikes aren't permitted. When I encounter a person on a bike, I ask if he/she knows they are on the PCT. They say yes. Then I ask if they know that bikes aren't allowed on the PCT. They say no. So I explain that bikes are not allowed. Then they ask me to move out of the way so they and their bike can get around me. NOPE. I'm not moving. You don't belong here, so I'm not going out of my way to make this easy for you. I can stand here all day if necessary. I've got a pack full of food, and Canada ain't goin' anywhere.

This could be a dangerous thing to do. It's what I do, and I'm not suggesting you do the same thing. I do think it's important that hikers let bikers know that this is the PCT and bikes are not allowed. All too many times, the PCT hikers I've been with step aside and passively let the bike rider go by. As soon as the biker is gone, the hikers complain about how pissed they are, that bikes don't belong on the PCT, etc. I can't be that passive. I've got to stand up for what I believe in. I think that if I cause the bike person to slow down for long enough for me to voice my opinion (and thus disrupt their fast bike ride), then maybe JUST MAYBE next weekend that bike rider will choose a different trail.

THRU-HIKE TRAINING

Many hikers every year start and finish thru-hikes without making a serious attempt to get fit before their hikes started. But it makes sense, doesn't it, to prepare your body for hiking a marathon every day? You'll make conscious decisions to go with one shelter over another, or one pack over another, etc., and a huge factor in making those choices is the weight of the gear. We're talking OUNCES here. Ask yourself this question: if you are putting so much thought into choosing between two shelters which have a weight difference of 10 OUNCES, shouldn't you put some thought into losing 10 POUNDS off your mid-section before your hike starts?

Most aspiring thru-hikers simply do not have the time to train for several hours each week, nor do we have access to mountain trails! We have jobs and families and responsibilities here in this "civilized world." But you CAN train for your thru-hike, and you SHOULD train for your thru-hike. If you increase your fitness level before stepping on the trail, you will enjoy your hike much more than if you start off cold.

First off, I'll say that I have absolutely no background in fitness. I only know what works for me. I'm a relatively active person, simply due to the fact that I do not spend 40 hours per week sitting at a desk.

Beginning about four months prior to a thru-hike, I begin exercising more. I have a TV in my exercise room. I spend at least an hour a day watching TV, so I get on the treadmill! An hour long show without commercials (love that DVR!) is usually right at 40 minutes long. That's the perfect length of time to put in a cardio workout. Next to my treadmill is a cheap stepper/climber. I alternate between the treadmill and the stepper during that 40-minute workout. I do this twice per day if the weather is cold/bad. If the weather is nice, I replace one of the daily treadmill/stepper workouts with a 4-mile walk outside. If you have access to trails, great! If you are in an area with sidewalks, walk in the grass next to the sidewalk. Walking in the grass works your legs/ankles completely differently than the repetitious movement of a treadmill or sidewalk.

During my workouts, I wear a heart rate monitor and try to keep my heart rate to an appropriate level to improve oxygen delivery to my muscles. "Training should maximize oxygen delivery and utilization. The more oxygen, the more efficiently energy is produced. That's what training is all about – how to improve the oxygen delivery system to your muscles." That's a quote from Dr. Brenda Braaten, from her sabbatical research on thru-hiker nutrition and training. A thru-hiker herself, Brenda has both the practical backpacking experience and the education to back up her research.

I highly recommend that you spend a substantial amount of time reviewing Brenda's hiking nutrition and training article: *"Pack Light, Eat Right – Nutritional recommendations for backpackers and other endurance exercise enthusiasts."* In the Snacks chapter, Brenda outlines "The Ideal Training Program" for thru-hikers. [www.thru-hiker.com/articles/pack_light_eat_right.php]

Be sure to strengthen your core. Hiking efficiently isn't all about leg strength.
A strong core strengthens your back, helps you keep up your pace, and also helps with balance.

A final thought on training: Nail-down all your gear at least two months before your hike starts. Load your pack, then wear it during your cardio exercises. After your workout is over, unload your pack. The next day, load your pack and do your cardio workout. Then unload the pack again. As you load/unload your pack, you will find the perfect way to load YOUR pack. Pretty soon, you will load your pack the exact same way every time. That's your goal. Everything should have its place in your pack. Efficient packing leads to less stress on the trail.

A good resource for thru-hike training is [www.backpacker.com].
Type "thru-hike training" into the search line.

Anish offers hiker training programs. Search "Training By Anish" on Facebook.

Don't put off your training until tomorrow. Start today!!

Anish: I run ultramarathons, mainly 100 mile mountain races. I train with a lot of trail mileage. Running, especially on trails, gets your foot/eye coordination ready, and it also primes your body for lots of impact. Do core work: abs and back. You are going to spontaneously gain 20+ pounds overnight and ask your body to walk all day. It needs every advantage it can get. Keep in mind, though, that nothing will get you in shape for a thru-hike, except a thru-hike. Be realistic about how fast you'll be able to go at the beginning, and don't push yourself into torn ligament, plantar fasciitis, or Achilles Tendinitis 200 miles in.

BINK: I have done hikes where I trained extensively and ones where due to working right up until leaving I have trained not at all. I cannot recommend training enough! Carry a pack when training. If you can train, do it!! If you cannot train prior to leaving, plan some extra zeros to help ease into the hike. Or just plan to suffer it out. But if you can train, you'll be glad you did.

Scrub: I walked a moderately difficult 9-mile route with my pack on maybe a dozen times in the month before I started my hike. Those few walks were good enough to make sure my shoes fit and my pack setup worked. Otherwise, the first 150-ish miles of the PCT aren't particularly punishing, and I was able to keep the hand brake on and let my body ease into it out there. That worked fine; I never had a musculoskeletal issue on the trail, and I was at full strength after 300 miles.

IF I HIKED THE PCT AGAIN . . . .

<u>Anish</u>: I'd have a brighter headlamp and a different pack. You can get away with anything for a headlamp if you don't night hike. But if you plan to night hike, use something light and bright. Make sure your pack doesn't hurt you. It's essential.

<u>BINK</u>: Well, that's the problem, I keep coming up with things I want to do differently, so I have to keep going out and hiking it again and again. I wish my employer understood that there are some important changes I need to make in my thru-hiking of the PCT, and it is critical I get out there to try them out this coming season! I know if I keep trying, eventually I will have the perfect PCT hike! Seriously, my enduring goal when hiking the PCT is to be more in the moment each day as I hike. This is easier said than done when there is fresh food awaiting a few days down the trail, or ice cold water 20 miles away and you have two liters left and it's 105 degrees.

<u>Hiker Box Special</u>: I think I would have done more running, possibly barefoot style running to get my feet stronger. There really isn't much you can do to replicate hiking all day every day, but you can sure try. The trail will get you in shape as long as you give it enough time.

<u>Scrub</u>: I would start earlier and goof around more. I goofed off plenty on the AT, but I also hadn't finished the whole trail. That bothered me SO MUCH for two years that I wasn't going to let the PCT slip away. Don't get me wrong, I had a ton of fun on the PCT. But if I were to do it again, I'd make a conscious effort to spend more time goofing off both in town and on the trail – swimming holes especially. There are no guarantees on being able to finish after about September 20, so I'd need to start earlier if I wanted to go slower.

IF YOU GO MISSING

You've planned, researched, asked questions, read books, looked at maps, downloaded apps, watched weather patterns, lurked (or participated) on the PCT social media sites. You're ready. You're confident. Knowledge is power, and you are now invincible.

Terrific.

But guess what? Your friends and family are not so sure. They think you are at least a little bit nuts to go on this 4-5 month, 2700-mile hike. They care about you. They love you. They are excited for you. But they're also concerned for your safety.

Hopefully your hike goes as planned, you have a fantastic time, and you never encounter any trouble. But what if you do have trouble? What if you go missing? What if you say you'll call on Tuesday, but now it's Thursday and your Mom hasn't heard from you? Should she call the authorities? Or will she be worried that she's overreacting, that you would be upset if she sent Search And Rescue out to find her invincible, experienced, capable son/daughter?

You planned and researched gear, clothing, maps, and apps. You owe it to your friends and family to also plan for unfortunate circumstances and provide them with the necessary information they will need in case of an emergency. Help your family and friends help you. Plan for the worst, hope for the best.

BAD THINGS HAPPEN TO EXPERIENCED HIKERS

Every year hikers go missing on the PCT.
Every year hikers disappear forever on the PCT.
Every year hikers die on the PCT.
The percentages are not high, but it does happen.

Before you blow this off as just a bunch of fearmongering, let me tell you: THIS IS REAL. You're probably thinking "that won't happen to me." The hikers on the list below probably thought the same thing. This list is by no means a comprehensive list of hikers who got into trouble. It is not presented to be disrespectful. Rather, it is presented so you can Google search their stories and learn from their mistakes.

Kris "Sherpa" Fowler	Missing from the PCT near White Pass WA, 2016. Still missing.
David O'Sullivan	Missing from the PCT near Idyllwild CA, 2017. Still missing.
Rika Morita	Died trying to cross a strong creek alone in the Sierra, 2017.
Chaocui Wang	Died trying to cross a strong creek alone in the Sierra, 2017.
Marvin Novo	Died of heat stroke in Southern California, 2017.
John Donovan	Used ultralight gear, no map, no compass. Warned to stay in Idyllwild CA until a blizzard passed. Left town anyway. Lost in that blizzard on San Jacinto in May, 2005. Body found one year later.
Katharina Groene	Unprepared for October 2018 weather in Washington. A chance encounter with a woman a few days earlier led to that woman following her gut feeling regarding a snowstorm, she contacted SAR, Katharina was rescued from almost certain death.
Marcus Mazaferri	Tried to cross a strong creek alone in the Sierra, 2017. Fell in creek, pack was swept away, he spent the night with wet clothes, no gear, no food, no way to start a fire, in freezing temperatures. The next day, without any form of navigation, Marcus tried to retrace his steps, wandered for eight miles, then heard bulldozers in the distance. He followed the sound and survived.
Alexandra Wilson	Was warned by a retired Forest Ranger to not leave Trout Lake WA in September 2013. Left town anyway. Got caught in rain/snow storm. Spent seven days waiting for weather to break. Eventually rescued herself by following an old road shown on her paper map. Yes, a PAPER MAP. Two other thru-hikers were rescued by helicopter from the same storm. (See TrailJournals website under Rocket Llama.)

HIKER'S RESPONSIBILITIES

- **Legal issues.** Because of HIPPA and privacy laws, your family cannot make medical decisions for you or obtain information unless you have given them legal authority to do so.

  Give someone Durable Power of Attorney and Medical Power of Attorney.

  - ▸ Durable Power of Attorney authorizes another person to engage in business, financial, and legal transactions on your behalf.

  - ▸ Medical Power of Attorney designates another person to make medical decisions for you in the event that you are unable to make those decisions for yourself.

  Make a Living Will and a Last Will and Testament.

  - ▸ A Living Will focuses on health care decisions while you are alive.

  - ▸ A Last Will and Testament outlines your preferences after you have died.

- **Designate one responsible person as the individual who contacts authorities if you are "missing."** Your "home contact person" is NOT someone who would get upset if you don't call exactly when you say you will. This is someone who you have had DETAILED conversations with regarding your hike, the terrain, your experience, the possibility of no cell signal, etc. This person is level headed, but also follows their gut, their intuition.

- **Login and password information.** Make a list of all your login names and passwords: email, Facebook, Instagram, Twitter, bank accounts, credit cards, student loans, etc., plus the passwords for your phone, laptop, tablet, desktop computer, etc. Place that list in a sealed envelope. Give the envelope to a trusted friend or family member. In the unfortunate event that you go missing, your home contact person can use this information to track you, to track your credit card activity, etc. If nothing bad happens to you, then you go back home to a sealed envelope, and nobody will ever have your passwords. But – god forbid – if you go missing, this information could be crucial to help find you.

- **Hiker-specific information.** Make sure the home contact person has all these details:

  - ▸ Gear - Give your home contact person a list and photos of your gear and clothing (color and style/brand of your pack, clothing, sleeping bag, etc.). This information helps the authorities determine if you have been seen. Be specific! Believe it or not, fellow hikers know the difference between a the bearded man wearing the red Black Diamond Rain Jacket and the bearded man wearing the red RAB Rain Jacket.

  - ▸ Trail name - Hikers usually do not know your name is Patty Johnson. But they do know you as Twinkle Toes. Your home contact person needs to know your trail name.

  - ▸ Hiking buddies - Your home contact person should know the trail names and legal names of the people you are hiking with. This is a fluid group; it constantly changes. Be sure to frequently update your home contact person with current information.

  - ▸ Current photo - Every couple weeks or so, send a current photo to your home contact person. This is important for all hikers, but more so for men than for women. Men often look completely different with facial hair.

  - ▸ Itinerary - Yes, we get it. You don't want to stick to a schedule. However, you do have an idea of where and when you will resupply. Be sure to keep your home contact person up-to-date on this information. If you do not pick up a resupply package, that could be reason for concern.

- **Consistent check-ins.** The hiker and the home contact person should develop a consistent check-in procedure. You might want to check in using your inReach or Spot once or twice per day. Or maybe you only check in when you are in town. Or maybe you always notify your home contact person of the next sure time you think you will have signal. One day it could be, "I'll call in three days." The next time it could be "I'll call in five days." Whatever procedure you decide on, be consistent. Stick to the check-in plan. If the hiker misses one check-in, it may or may not be cause for alarm. If the hiker misses three check-ins, it could be time for the home contact person to contact the authorities.

- **Trail Registers.** Sign every register. EVERY REGISTER. Signing in helps to narrow a search area, if a search is warranted.

- **Use Credit Cards.** Even if it is just for a small purchase, use a credit card every day you are in a town. This leaves a digital trail of your progress, which could be very helpful if you go missing.

- **Call Home.** Your Mom wants to hear from you. Call her often. (Mom, significant other, sibling, best friend – you know who the important people are in your life.)

- **Hitchhiking.** Take a photo of the license plate before you get in the car. Immediately text that to your home contact person. State where you get picked up from and where you are going to. Then put your phone in your pocket or pack so you don't accidentally leave it in the vehicle.

- **Personal Locator Device.** Are you carrying a SPOT? inReach? Some other PLB? Your home contact person should monitor your activity/checkins/status EVERY SINGLE DAY. If there are any changes in your activity, that could be cause for alarm. Let's say you typically check in every single day, then there are three days without a checkin. Hmmm. Perhaps this is a problem, or perhaps you are simply in an area without signal.

- **Google Tracking.** Add your home contact person to the "Location Sharing" function on Google. This allows them to see the real-time location of your phone, which is usually the same place you are.

- **YOU ARE SMART, SO BE SMART.** If the forecast calls for bad weather, stay in town until the storm passes. Sounds simple, doesn't it? Problem is that hikers think they are invincible, that nothing bad will happen. **You are NOT invincible. Mother Nature does not care about you.**

HOME CONTACT PERSON'S RESPONSIBILITIES

Worst case scenario: The home contact person thinks the hiker is missing. What happens next?

- ✔ **Call the hiker's cell phone**, send messages to inReach or SPOT, search for the hiker's phone using Google Tracking.

- ✔ **Use Facebook and Instagram.** Post a current trail photo of the missing hiker and his/her hiking companions. Tag "Pacific Crest Trail", "PCT Class of XXXX", etc. Include name, trail name, description/photo of pack, shelter, and clothing, plus trail names of their hiking companions.

- ✔ **Contact law enforcement and file a missing persons report.** Do not wait. Start with your local 9-1-1, or contact authorities near the last known location of the hiker. This is why constant checkins are important. The authorities need a place to start.

  Provide details: Missing hiker's name, trail name, physical description, current trail photo, photo and description of gear and clothing; names and trail names of fellow hikers; missing hiker's last known location; location where the missing hiker was supposed to call from or arrive at; reason why you think the hiker is truly missing.

- ✔ **Stay on top of law enforcement.** This is not their only case. As the home contact person, your job is to make sure law enforcement makes finding your hiker a priority. Check and double-check to make sure all potential areas are searched. Ask questions. Demand action. **Your hiker is counting on you.**

Moral of the story:

Hikers, be smart. Do not take unnecessary risks. You are NOT invincible.

Call your Mom. Call your girlfriend. Call your brother. Call your roommate. They care about you. They want to hear from you frequently. They will do everything in their power to save you.

GEAR

Thru-hikers are very passionate about gear. Everyone thinks that THEIR gear is the best. And it is. It's the best gear for that one person. But not everyone is the same, and what worked for someone else might not work for you. And what worked for you on the AT (or some other trail) might not work for you on the PCT.

On my first PCT thru-hike, I was in Stehekin (the last PCT town) with seven other thru-hikers. We were among the first 20 to finish the trail that year. There we were, eight Pacific Crest Trail thru-hikers. We'd just walked 2569 miles in four months. We had 89 miles to go. And we had eight different sleeping bags, eight different packs, eight different styles of shoes, eight different types of socks, eight different shorts, eight different rain jackets, etc. Yet we each had the PERFECT gear.

Do your research, choose your gear, and start the trail. But don't be afraid to change. Through trial and error, you'll find the perfect gear for you.

Anish: Choose what works for you and is the lightest, well-made piece you can afford. Save weight on big items (tent, pack, sleeping bag) and save money one the small ones (headlamp, stove, ziplocks instead of stuff sacks).

BINK: Try to go light if you can. Carry whatever you feel is a positive addition to your hike: things that make the hike and connection to nature better for you.

Hiker Box Special: Check out [www.linkhikes.com]; he's got some good advice. Look at Six Moon Designs and Gossamer Gear mostly. ZPacks makes great sleeping bags, but that cuben fiber stuff is expensive and unnecessary. Getting my base weight to 10-11 pounds was the most amazing feeling. You'll be hiking 10+ hours a day, so forget the luxuries, they don't matter.

Scrub: There's no good way to learn what gear will work for you without backpacking first. It was only after the AT that I was capable of making smart gear decisions. I did a lot of research online through WhiteBlaze and BackPackingLight. I also read Andrew Skurka's "The Ultimate Hiker's Gear Guide," which I highly recommend.

ULTRALIGHT PHILOSOPHY

I'm by no means an ultralight hiker, but I do make careful choices with my gear. I choose the lightest, most durable gear for my style of hiking.

In addition to spending money on gear, I also look at "spending ounces" on gear. Sometimes spending ounces is a good thing. For example, when I hiked the CDT with a partner, we spent the extra ounces on the Big Agnes Copper Spur 3 tent instead of the Copper Spur 2. Prior to this hike, my partner had over 20,000 solo miles, and I had over 17,000 solo miles. We weren't used to sharing gear. The extra floor area of the Copper Spur 3 allowed us to each have our own space, while enjoying spending time together. Many solo hikers make a similar choice by choosing a 2-person shelter over a 1-person shelter. Often, the difference is just a few ounces.

That said, most of your gear choices should be to OMIT ounces. "Ounces add up to pounds." You can easily fill an ultralight pack to the seams with every ultralight gadget on the market – and end up with a very heavy pack. REALLY THINK about everything you put in your pack.

Anish: Learn what you can do without. You'll be surprised. Carry items that serve more than one purpose.

BINK: I try to cut weight as much as I can, but also pride myself on being an all-weather hiker. It seems like the 4-pound base weight guys are running for town when the weather really gets going, but when it's nice they are moving with less effort. I feel there is no set formula as to what a person should have in their pack. The best way to find out what you need is to be flexible and willing to try out new things.

Hiker Box Special: The PCT has over 300,000 feet of elevation gain, and every step you take raises your torso a few inches. Every pound you take out of your pack will make your hike so much more enjoyable. Having a stove that boils water in under three minutes doesn't really matter. Walking out of town for 100 mile hike with 20 pounds or less on your back matters.

If you're worried about being uncomfortable, that's a myth. I was never too cold, too wet, or too uncomfortable. Think of it like a big scary roller coaster, everyone else went for a ride and loved it, so why don't you?

Scrub: If you put in good prep work and make smart choices with your gear, it's very possible to hike the entire PCT in relative comfort, physically and psychologically. If you can walk from Mexico to Canada and do it with ease because you prepared well and chose your gear intelligently, well done! That's a real achievement.

ON YOUR BACK

BASE WEIGHT

Your base weight is the weight of all your gear not including consumables (food, water, and fuel). This includes the weight of your empty backpack. Lightweight experienced hikers can get their base weight down under 10 pounds.

Make very careful choices on THE BIG THREE: backpack, shelter, and sleeping bag. These three pieces of gear will cost you both in dollars and weight. If you choose a 6-pound pack, a 3-pound sleeping bag and a 4-pound tent, you're already up to 13 pounds and you haven't even loaded your socks yet.

WHAT'S IN YOUR PACK ?

Following is a list of possible items to carry in your pack.   DO NOT take all this stuff.

THE BIG 3
Backpack
Shelter (including stakes, poles, ground cloth)
Sleeping Bag & Sleeping Pad

CLOTHES WORN WHILE HIKING
Shoes
Socks
Gaiters
Shirt (short-sleeved and/or long-sleeved)
Shorts
Underwear
Bandana
Sunglasses
Sun Hat
Watch

CLOTHES IN PACK
Long Pants
Wind Shirt
Warm Top
Warmer Top
Extra Bandana(s)
Gloves
Extra Socks
Camp Shoes

WHILE SLEEPING
Bag Liner
Sleeping Clothes
Sleeping Socks
Warm Hat

FIRST AID
Sunscreen
Neosporin
Tinactin
Vaseline
Zanfel or Calamine
Creamy Desitin
Vitamins
Ibuprofen
Benadryl
Imodium
Leukotape, Band-Aids, Medical Tape
Duct Tape (wrapped around water or fuel bottle)
Ace Bandage/Gauze
Second Skin
New-Skin Liquid Bandage
Moleskin
Sewing Needle
DEET

ELECTRONICS
Cell Phone (plus power cord)
Radio/Music Player
Camera
Solar Charger (or other power source)

RAIN GEAR
Jacket
Pants or Skirt
Rain Hat
Rain Gloves
Pack Cover
Garbage Bag (as pack liner)
Umbrella

COOKING
Stove
Pot
Pot Cozy
Fuel
Lighter / Matches
Spoon (2) ★
Small Pocket Knife

WATER
Bottles
Water filter/treatment

OTHER GEAR
Headlamp (2) ★
Hiking Poles
Rope
Compass
Bug Head Net
Bug Pants

PERSONAL ITEMS
Large Safety Pins
Little Scissors
Nail Clippers
Hair Ties
Comb/brush
Razor
Soap
Pack Towel
Lotion
Lip Balm
Toothbrush
Toothpaste
Dental Floss (use as sewing thread)
Earplugs
Baby Wipes
Purell
Trowel
Toilet Paper

★ I have lost my spoon and light before. Never again. Now I carry two spoons and two lights (a headlamp and a backup tiny photon light).

PAPER

Yogi Book Pages
Maps
Journal
Pen
Sharpie (for making hitchhiking signs)
Money
Credit Cards
Photo ID

EYE CARE

Glasses
Extra Contacts
Contact Solution
Eyedrops
Small Mirror

BACKPACK

Wayne Gregory (of Gregory Packs) uses interesting wording regarding backpacks. He says that you do not "carry" a pack, you "wear" a pack. You wear it like a pair of jeans. If you think about your pack in that regard, I believe you will make the correct pack choice. A pack that is perfect for another hiker might be completely wrong for you. You must wear your pack comfortably.

Capacity is a major concern when choosing a pack. Too small and you won't fit all your gear and food into the pack. Too large and you will fill it with too much stuff. Choose your gear first, then choose your pack. Your gear determines your pack capacity.

For most sections of the PCT, you won't need to carry more than five days of food. Gear plus five days of food can fit into a relatively small pack. However, two sections (Mojave to Kennedy Meadows, and Kennedy Meadows to Kearsarge Pass or VVR) require a larger-capacity pack. You

will carry a substantial amount of water north from Mojave, requiring more pack capacity. Then, leaving Kennedy Meadows, you will have 6-11 days of food PLUS a bear canister.

If you think you will lose weight during your hike, look for a pack that has a removable hip belt. Once you do lose weight, you can get a smaller hip belt and keep the same pack.

Check out these pack manufacturers (former PCT thru-hikers): ULA-Equipment, GossamerGear, Six Moon Designs, ZPacks, Hyperlite Mountain Gear, and Mountain Laurel Designs. They know EXACTLY what thru-hikers need.

Yogi: I've carried many different packs, and I'm always on the lookout for my next favorite pack! I'm a big fan of Osprey packs. The smaller shoulder straps work well with my female body, and the ventilated back panel helps prevent back rash (something I've struggled with while wearing other brands). My current pack is the Osprey Exos. Weighing only 2 pounds, the Exos carries my load very comfortably. The suspension is great, the back panel is highly ventilated, and the hip belt has small pockets which easily carry my maps and snacks.

Anish: I wore a ULA CDT, which didn't fit me. I had a lot of problems with my back and shoulders. Make sure your pack fits well before hand. Seriously. Load it up and wear it for a day before you go.

BINK: I have used homemade packs, ULA packs, and Six Moon Designs packs. I have always had pretty good luck with luck with all the packs I have used. I used my first homemade pack on my 1994 CDT hike and continued to use homemade packs all through my 1990's thru-hikes. I used some commercial packs on some of my hikes up into the mid 2000's. I went back to the homemade packs not because of any problems, but more for the fact that I like the process of sewing a pack, working hard to make it (if I can sew anyone can!), and then carrying that pack for thousands of miles. It is a very meaningful cycle.

It seems like no matter what the pack volume is, it is always full. So use a small pack if possible. Regardless of how many days of food it has my pack is a perpetual "Lead Sled." It never seems light to me no matter what.

Hiker Box Special: I used a ULA Circuit (which is big enough, don't get a Catalyst). The Circuit gave me pack rash, which nothing seemed to help with. I switched to a Six Moon Designs Starlite, which weighs a pound less but is waaay too big. The Starlite was great, although the suspension took some figuring out. I basically stuffed my sleeping bag in the bottom, put my pad in the pack's pad holder/pocket, put my tent on the big side pocket, threw my food bag in, and I was ready to go.

As my base weight lowered, my need for an overbuilt pack was gone. I switched to frameless rucksack style packs, and they just got smaller and lighter as my overall pack weight decreased. I HIGHLY recommend Mountain Laurel Designs. They offer many different models, suitable for a variety of base weights. They're strong, comfortable, and made right here in the USA.

Scrub: I used the Kalais by Elemental Horizons, a cottage manufacturer based in North Carolina. It's similar in size and design to the ULA Circuit. I loved it. It felt like it was glued to my back except under the heaviest loads (30+ pounds). The hip belt has four adjustable straps instead of two, so it was very easy to comfortably adjust the hip belt. I tested it on training walks without the removable aluminum stay, which is sort of like an internal frame, and found it much more comfortable with the stay left in. I'd encourage anyone else who wants a 45-50L pack with a 12-15 pound base weight to have a look at it online or talk to Matt, the owner, directly.

A PCT Documentary by Triple Crown hiker Shane "Jester" O'Donnell.

Available here: [https://www.tbwproductions.com/]

SHELTER

ALWAYS CARRY A SHELTER

Hiking through Southern California with NO SHELTER is asking for trouble. Be sure to have something, even if it is just a tarp that you might set up once or twice in those first 702.2 miles. It can and does rain/snow in Southern California. If you're not carrying a tent, be sure to have some mosquito netting and a way to rig it up so you can sleep at night. The mosquitos are bad, even in Southern California. You definitely need a weather-tight shelter with bug protection beginning at Kennedy Meadows (mile 702.2).

STAKES IN HARD OR SOFT GROUND

If you can't get your tent stakes into hard ground or if soft sand won't hold the stakes, use rocks instead. But don't simply place the rocks on top of the stakes. Instead, slide your trekking pole (or a sturdy stick) through the loop that normally holds your tent stake. The loop should be near the center of the pole. Lay the pole on the ground. Now place large rocks on top of the pole on either side of the tent loop. You may need two rocks on each side of the pole/stick. This method of "staking" out your tent is very secure and works much better than simply placing rocks on top of the stakes.

HIKING POLES AS TENT POLES

There are many lightweight shelter designs which use a trekking pole or poles as tent poles. This is a great way to save weight — two uses for everything! There is one potential challenge with this design. When setting up the shelter, usually the trekking pole is placed up-side-down (handle on the ground). The tip of the trekking pole then fits into a grommet on the shelter. Guy lines are used to hold the trekking pole erect. The challenge occurs when the trekking pole tips wear down. Not IF, but WHEN. Eventually, the pole tip gets shoved up into the plastic casing at the bottom of the trekking pole. It WILL happen. This occurs due to pressure put on the pole while hiking. The tip is still there.

It's just crammed into the plastic. After a few days, the plastic wears down and the tip emerges again. In the meantime, the plastic is too big to fit in the grommet on your shelter. When this happens, you can still set up your shelter, you just have to be creative. I'm not trying to discourage you from using this type of shelter, because the designs are GREAT! But you should be aware of this potential challenge.

COWBOY CAMPING

"Cowboy Camping" is when you don't use a shelter. Instead, you put your ground cloth down, lay out your sleeping bag, and sleep under the stars. I can't do it. I sleep much better knowing that bugs don't have the opportunity to get me. Plus, the netting on my Big Agnes Copper Spur allows for perfect night-sky viewing. When the weather is good, I simply do not set up the tent fly.

Anish: I hate bugs and looking like a little burrito for anything walking by.

BINK: I cowboy camp whenever possible, and yes I have had all manner of insects crawl onto me. But mice have probably been the biggest annoyance when cowboy camping. Carpenter ants can also be a nuisance. I have yet to have any snakes crawl over me in the desert, but I seem to always hear rumors of this happening. I have also awoke in the middle of the night with deer and bears sniffing my face, but they are usually much more alarmed than I am.

Hiker Box Special: Coming from the East it was amazing! I almost never cowboyed before, but loved waking up to the stars.

Scrub: I am a big fan of cowboy camping; I did it about 2/3 of the nights on the PCT, including a stretch of 30 straight nights in the desert. I know people who cowboyed more often than that, but their tolerance for bugs was higher than mine (I busted out the tent as soon as I reached a 3-mosquito quorum). I think the high prevalence of cowboy-camping opportunities is one of the best things about the PCT compared to the AT. You could be sleeping in the most badass place in the world, but if you wake up inside a tent, it looks just like everywhere else. Cowboy camping is also a lot faster than setting up a tent, especially if you have the kind of tent that I did (ZPacks Hexamid).

HIKER OPINIONS

Yogi: I want to be that hiker who cowboy camps most of the time, while carrying an ultralight silnylon shelter to use only when the weather is bad. I REALLY want to be that hiker. I've come to realize that I'm not. I've tried several ultralight silnylon shelters, and I've hated them all. I once showed Gottago the ultralight hybrid tarp/shelter I had just purchased. This was the fourth ultralight silnylon shelter I had purchased over the years. The previous three had been disasters. I'm still not sure why I kept trying. I was giddy with excitement showing Gottago this new shelter. With a dead-pan look, Gottago said: "You're going to hate that." She was right. It was awful. I hated it for many reasons:

- I like a bathtub floor, and it needs to be an ACTUAL bathtub floor, not just two inches of wall coming up from the ground. The bathtub floor needs to be taller than my face when I lay down. The trail can be very windy and sandy. A tall bathtub floor prevents sand from blowing on my face. In addition, a tall bathtub floor prevents water from splashing on my face when it rains.

- Single-wall and hybrid shelters take a LONG time to set up properly. Then when the temperature changes, you need to get out and tighten the guylines. I'd rather have a free-standing double wall tent which sets up in about a minute and needs no tightening later on.

- I need to be able to sit up and move around inside my shelter.
  I don't want the shelter walls or ceiling to touch my head.

- Condensation collects inside single-wall and hybrid shelters causing my sleeping bag to get wet.

- I want to lay in my shelter and still see the stars on clear nights. With a double-wall tent, I can do that (just not attach the fly). With single-wall or hybrid shelter, I cannot.

- The most important reason: single-wall and hybrid shelters flap in the wind.
  Flap, flap, flap, flap, flap = NO SLEEP.

I currently carry the Big Agnes Copper Spur HV UL. I love the height created by the cross bar at the top; it allows me to sit up in the tent without the walls smashing against my head, which happens in tents with an "A" shaped ceiling. The crossbar on the Copper creates MUCH more head room than the "A" shaped tents. The Copper Spur has a side door, which is MUCH easier to get out of a side door than a front door. With the side door, you just swing your legs out and stand up. No crawling.

These ceiling features ("A" vs crossbar) and door styles (front vs side) are found on shelters from many manufacturers, not just Big Agnes. Go to the nearest outdoor store and "try on" your shelter before purchasing. Set it up, get inside with a sleeping bag and a pack. Lay down, sit up, crawl in and out.

Anish: ZPacks Hexamid. I love it more than any other piece of gear I own.

BINK: Hiking through SoCal with no shelter is asking for trouble. I have seen it snow in EVERY section including the Mojave desert.

Since the 1992 hike, I used tarps for all of my PCT, FT, CDT, and AT hikes. I use a homemade silnylon tarp and a small homemade bug net tent for the buggy sections. Both cheap, simple, and relatively lightweight. I only sleep under it when I have to.

Hiker Box Special: I used a Henry Shires Tarptent Notch. It was great, but I would have used a Six Moon Designs Wild Oasis since it's a pound lighter and costs way less than those Z-packs Hexamids that everyone was using.

Scrub: I used a cuben fiber ZPacks Hexamid Solo without the extended beak. Normally this pitches with a trekking pole, but since I don't use those, I bought a very light dedicated tent pole from the ZPacks site. The whole setup with stakes weighed 14.5oz, and the tent was pretty roomy inside. When it's pitched taut, cuben fiber is awesome in rain and wind compared to nylon – it feels like there's an actual wall over you instead of some loose fabric. I think it's worth the extra dough.

All that said, I don't think I'd use the Hexamid again. Having a mesh door open to the elements was not a problem most of the time, because either (a) there were no elements to speak of, or (b) I had anticipated the wind/rain direction correctly. But when I got it wrong, holy shit was it a pain in the ass to turn the tent around in the middle of the night! The tent pole snapped on me in a windstorm in the Goat Rocks in Washington, then I splinted it a few days later, then it snapped again under a snow load at 6 a.m. on my very last morning on the PCT. It takes an eternity to set up compared to other tents, especially if the ground is not very stake-compatible. It also takes up quite a large footprint, and does not squeeze into nooks and crannies (say, under a bower of trees, where you might want to be in a storm) very well because of all the guylines. I think either a tarp-and-bivy, or a tiny, simple, double-walled tent like a Big Agnes Fly Creek that sets up in 30 seconds would be a better bet.

SLEEP SYSTEM

In order to stay warm at night, you need to look at your entire sleep system, not just the temperature rating of your sleeping bag. If you're a cold sleeper, you may think that a zero-degree bag will do the trick. For the PCT, a zero-degree sleeping bag most likely will be plenty warm enough (actually, it will usually be too warm), but creating a sleep system is much more practical.

With every gear choice you make, think about weight and function. A zero degree bag from Western Mountaineering weighs 2 pounds 12 ounces, and costs more than $700. Overkill? Probably. $700 is a lot of money, zero degrees is too warm, and the sleeping bag only serves one function. How about choosing a 20-degree bag, and adding a sleeping bag liner or wearing long underwear? If you're carrying a tent, the tent will add about 10 more degrees of warmth. If you're using a tarp, you most likely also have a bivy or sleeping bag cover; both of those will provide extra warmth. A silk sleeping bag liner will add warmth and keep your bag clean. Long underwear, a hat, and socks not only keep you warm, but they also protect your down bag from body oils and foot gunk. The loft in your bag will compress when dirty. Keeping it clean is part of your sleep system.

Your sleep system is a combination of many factors: sleeping bag, sleeping pad, sleeping clothes, food/water, campsite location, and shelter.

SLEEPING BAG

Western Mountaineering bags are the best bags available. You can learn a lot about sleeping bags by listening to Practical Backpacking's podcast interview with Gary Peterson of Western Mountaineering. [www.practicalbackpacking.com]

Sleeping bags are interesting. You start off cold. The sleeping bag starts off cold and not-so-fluffy. You slide into the bag. Your body heat warms up the down, which causes the sleeping bag to fluff up, and then the fluffy down insulates you from the cold. It's magic.

The PCT is cold – yes, even in the desert. Southern California is blistering hot in the daytime but cold at night. You need a good quality down sleeping bag.

Get a down bag. Just do it. Down bags weigh less, insulate better, and are more comfortable than synthetic bags. You'll read all this stuff on the internet about how down is bad because when it gets wet it does not have any insulation properties. Okay, great. The thing is, in over 20,000 miles of hiking I've never had my bag get wet. The PCT is usually a very dry trail - not humid like the AT. You will often get condensation on the top of your bag overnight, but this is quickly dried out during your lunch break. I use a pack towel to wipe the beads of condensation off the top of my bag.

Think about how your body regulates temperature. Most women get cold easier than most men. If you get cold easily, then carry a bag that has a lower temperature rating and is a few ounces heavier. You will be happier and have more energy if you sleep well. The PCT is always cold at night.

A 20° bag is perfect for a PCT hike. Keep the same bag for the entire trail. Many hikers use the Western Mountaineering UltraLite (1 pound 13 ounces, 20°); I used that bag for several hikes. Now I use the Western Mountaineering Sycamore (2 pounds, 25°). The semi-rec Sycamore has more space than the mummy UltraLite. I'm a side sleeper, and when I lay on my side in the UltraLite, my butt presses to the edge of the UltraLite, leaving zero loft between my butt and the cold outside air. There is more space in the Sycamore, which leaves loft all around me. So, when choosing your bag, think about your preferred sleeping position.

You may have noticed that I said "a 20° bag is perfect for a PCT hike," yet I use a 25° Sycamore. Why the difference? Well, when I need more warmth, I can cheat the Sycamore a bit. Because the Sycamore has continuous baffles, I can unzip the bag completely and then shake the down from the bottom of the bag to the top. Down under my body does not help with warmth; my sleeping pad keeps me warm from below. Shaking all the down to the top of the bag gives me about 2 more inches of down on top. That's really warm!

Look at your sleeping bag features. A mummy bag keeps you warm because it limits the amount of air space that needs to be heated by your body. A draft tube stops cold air from seeping in at the zipper. Continuous baffles allow you to shake most of the down to the top of the bag. Get inside the sleeping bag at the store. Lay on the floor and zip all the way up. Turn over, and over, and over. You should be comfortable, but not claustrophobic. The bag should be long enough for you, but not too long. If it is too long, then there is too much air space, and you won't stay as warm.

When packing your sleeping bag, ALWAYS use a waterproof dry bag, EVEN in the desert. Yes, the desert. It most likely will not rain in the desert, and there definitely are no fords, but what if your water bottles leak? You'll have a wet sleeping bag, and the desert nights are COLD. I pack my down bag in a waterproof 13 liter Sea-To-Summit eVAC Dry Bag.

Body oils and dirt will severely impact the loft/warmth of your sleeping bag. To clean your down sleeping bag, use the largest front-loading washer at the laundromat, and put a bunch of tennis balls (help break up clumps of down) in the washer and dryer with the sleeping bag. Wash the bag once with down soap, then wash it again with no soap to make sure everything is rinsed out. Put the bag and the tennis balls in the largest dryer, alternating between low heat and fluff. It takes FOREVER to dry the bag correctly and completely – usually 6+ hours. Take the bag out of the dryer every ~20 minutes to manually redistribute the clumps of down.

An alternative would be to have your bag professionally cleaned. Send it to someplace that is familiar with outdoor gear, such as Rainy Pass Repair in Washington. They will clean your bag and put a DWR (Durable Water Repellent) treatment on the shell. Rainy Pass Repair does excellent work, and they are very fast. [www.rainypass.com]

Billy Goat: Whatever the temperature rating of the bag, that is the temperature where you will die! Hee, hee, hee! Sleeping bags are never as warm as they're rated, and they're rated for men — who sleep considerably warmer than women. Subtract 10-15 degrees from the stated rating. For example, if a bag is rated to 10 degrees, I believe it will keep you warm when the outside temperature is 20-25 degrees. If you special order a bag, request an extra 4 ounces of down. Order the bag your own size, so extra bag isn't being carried.

Anish: Go Lite 20-degree down mummy. I love down. I'd recommend a colder rated bag, because there can be some really cold nights. You can always vent when it's warmer.

BINK: I currently use a down Western Mountaineering Highlite, highly modified with the zipper cut off. I have also used homemade synthetic fill quilts. The Highlite (a 35-degree bag) and is probably only best for mid-summer on the PCT. If going with only one bag, I feel that a 20-degree bag (like the Western Mountaineering UltraLite) would be better for the entire trail, especially in the spring and fall seasons. I have swapped out bags for a warmer bag on Yo-Yo hikes of the PCT, when hiking back into the High Sierra in late fall when temperatures are often in the low teens (and occasionally colder) in the mornings. Keep your body clean when possible. Even a rough sponge bath before bed will keep your sleeping bag cleaner. Put it in the sun during lunch breaks when possible, it really helps to puff it back up as well as sterilize it to some degree.

Hiker Box Special: I started with a down Marmot Helium 15-degree bag, which was super warm. Too warm. When I changed my pack, I changed my sleeping bag to a Feathered Friends Vireo, which weighs a pound less than the Marmot. I also had a really warm down jacket, which the Vireo was designed to work with, so now the jacket could do double-duty as part of my sleep system. The Vireo is great! Just get it a size longer if you have big feet. There's no zipper, but it's just like using a bag liner. I stayed warmish in it with all my clothes and jacket down to the mid 20's.

Scrub: I used a GoLite 3-season down quilt (20-degree) the whole way. It was perfect. Wayyy more comfortable than any mummy bag I've ever slept in. On the rare occasions that it was cold at night (the Sierra, a few nights in Washington), I slept with jackets on and their hoods up, since the quilt does not have anything to cover the head. This is the one gear item I would not change in a million years for the PCT.

SLEEPING PAD and GROUND CLOTH

A sleeping pad isn't so much about comfort – it's more about insulation. Your sleeping bag provides warmth on top of your body via loft from the down. Your sleeping pad protects your from the cold ground. For example, if you pair a zero-degree sleeping bag with a thin sleeping pad, you'll still be cold. Think about your SYSTEM. Perhaps a 20-degree bag paired with a higher-R-value sleeping pad will result in a warmer SYSTEM.

There are many styles of sleeping pads to choose from. When choosing your pad, you have to balance the weight, cost, and R-value of each option, then decide which pad is best for you. The R-value is a measure of insulation. The higher the R-value, the warmer you will sleep. An inflatable pad will always have the same R-value, assuming you inflate it fully. Non-inflatable pads compress over time, which will reduce the R-value.

If you use an inflatable sleeping pad, treat it with care or it WILL get a hole in it. You may have done the AT with an inflatable pad, but the PCT is different. We've got cacti and stickers on the PCT. Those stickers are everywhere.

3/4 length is long enough. Use your pack for the other 1/4 length. Two uses for everything, even your pack. Also, with your gear inside your pack, you've created a way to elevate your feet overnight.

Tyvek (the white stuff you see stapled up to buildings on construction sites) works great as a lightweight ground cloth.

Many hikers use Gossamer Gear's 1.6-ounce 40" x 96" Polycryo ground cloth.

BINK: I pack my sleeping pad inside my pack against my back to keep stuff from poking me as I hike. With proper campsite selection, the 1/8" thick pad works well for me. I was told that once over 40 years old that I would be upgrading to a thick pad, but at 41 still have not done so yet! On my 2006 Yo-Yo hike, I swapped for a ½" thick closed cell foam pad for the trip back through the High Sierra southbound to Kennedy Meadows, where I swapped back to my thin pad.

I have variously used sheets of Tyvek and very thin heat shrink plastic sheets from Gossamer Gear. Tyvek can be used as journal paper with a sharpie marker, thus you can sleep on your journal!

Scrub: I used a Tyvek ground cloth that was made by the guy who sold me my tent online. It was sized to fit inside a Hexamid Solo. I liked the white Tyvek because it lasted the whole way without any fraying or punctures, and I could find a clean square of it and use my Sharpie and write hitchhiking signs on it whenever needed. By the end of the trail, my groundsheet was a little scrapbook of hitchhiking destinations.

SLEEPING PAD COMPARISON	L	W	H	Weight	R-value	Cost
Gossamer Gear Nightlight Torso	29"	19"	3/4"	5-6 oz		$ 24
Gossamer Gear Thinlight	59"	19"	1/8"	2.9-3.4 oz		$ 18
Ridge Rest SOLite Short	48"	20"	5/8"	9 oz	2.8	$ 20
Ridge Rest SOLite Regular	72"	20"	5/8"	14 oz	2.8	$ 30
Z-Lite (aka Z-Rest) Short	51"	20"	3/4"	10 oz	2.6	$ 35
Z-Lite (aka Z-Rest) Regular	72"	20"	3/4"	14 oz	2.6	$ 45
Therm-a-Rest ProLite self-inflating Short	47"	20"	1"	11 oz	2.4	$ 80
Therm-a-Rest ProLite self-inflating Regular	72"	20"	1"	16 oz	2.4	$ 90
Therm-a-Rest NeoAir XLite Short	47"	20"	2.5"	8 oz	3.2	$130
Therm-a-Rest NeoAir XLite Regular	72"	20"	2.5"	12 oz	3.2	$170
Therm-a-Rest NeoAir XLite Long	77"	25"	2.5"	16 oz	3.2	$200
Therm-a-Rest NeoAir All Season SV Regular	72"	20"	2.5"	24 oz	4.9	$160
Therm-a-Rest NeoAir Trekker Regular	72"	20"	2.5"	19 oz	3.0	$130

SLEEPING CLOTHES

It's a good idea to carry clothes which you use only for sleeping: lightweight underwear (both tops and bottoms) and a pair of warm socks. Two reasons for sleeping clothes: (1) prevent body oils and dirt from impacting the loft/warmth of your sleeping bag, and (2) sweaty hiking clothes are cold to sleep in. You want your sleeping clothes to always be dry, so you never hike in them. While hiking you don't get wet only from rain. You will frequently be soaked from sweat. It's hot during the day, and cold at night. Sleeping in wet clothes is COLD. Always sleep with a hat on.

Scrub: Unless I was only a few hours outside of town and hence not very dirty yet, I ALWAYS slept in dedicated sleeping clothes that covered my whole body from the neck down. Thin liner socks on my feet, Montane Featherlite wind pants (lighter than long johns, similar fit) on my legs, and whatever shirt I happened to not be hiking in on my upper body (this changed a lot).

It takes a lot to disgust me, and still I was very often disgusted by how dirty I was, especially my lower legs and feet. There is no way I would consider putting those dirty bare legs and feet inside my sleeping bag. It's nothing like the AT, where I slept naked most of the time because I wasn't actually dirty, just sweaty. You're goddamn FILTHY a lot of the time on the PCT from all the dust. The sleeping clothes system worked: at the end of the hike, my bag was still clean and it barely had a smell.

FOOD and WATER

Food and water are part of your sleep system. Eat a high-calorie, fat-dense food before bed. Peanut butter, GORP, and Snickers are all good choices. Digesting the food takes calories, which in turn makes you warmer. If you wake up cold in the middle of the night, eat a snack. It will warm you up.

If your feet are cold, you will have trouble sleeping. A quick fix for cold feet is to boil water, pour it in a water bottle, screw the lid on really tight, put the water bottle in a sock, and put that in the foot of your sleeping bag.

Be sure to pee before going to bed. Your body uses energy to keep a full bladder warm. That energy could better be used to warm other parts of your body. If you wake up cold at night and you feel you need to pee, GO PEE! Don't hold it! Sure, it's cold out there and you don't want to get out of your bag, but you will be much warmer once you get rid of all that urine.

SLEEP SYSTEM	Shelter	Sleeping Bag	Sleeping Pad	Sleeping Clothes	Warm Hat
Yogi	Big Agnes Copper Spur	25° Western Mountaineering down Sycamore	NeoAir all season full length	Patagonia long underwear, SmartWool socks	Chicadoo ponytail hat
Anish	ZPacks Hexamid	20° GoLite down mummy	Therm-a-Rest Z-Rest full length	Icebreaker base layers and SmartWool socks	Patagonia beanie
BINK	Homemade silnylon tarp with bug net	35° Western Mountaineering down Highlite	Gossamer Gear Thinlight 3/4 length	Hiking clothes and clean socks	Wool watch cap
Hiker Box Special	TarpTent Notch	Feathered Friends down Viero, upper half 45°, lower half 20°	Gossamer Gear Nightlight 1/2 length	Stoic poly long underwear bottoms and Patagonia Capilene 3 top	Down jacket with hood. Added fleece hat in WA.
Scrub	ZPacks Hexamid	20° GoLite down quilt	Therm-a-Rest Z-Lite Sol 3/4 length	Montane Featherlite wind pants, clean hiking shirt, thin liner socks	Merino balaclava only on the coldest nights

CAMPSITE LOCATION

Choose your campsite carefully. One of the coldest nights of your PCT hike will most likely be at Lake Morena (PCT mile 20.0). The campground is next to a big lake with ridges surrounding the area. Cold air settles, and moist air from the lake causes all your gear to get covered in condensation. It's a better idea to hike out 2-3 miles and camp up on the next ridge. It's much warmer and drier on the ridge, rather than on grass next to a lake. This is a lesson many hikers learn the hard way on their first PCT night!

It's always tempting to sleep on a soft bed of grass. It's great when you set up camp, but grass collects condensation overnight, causing your gear to get wet, causing you to get cold. Camping under trees is great – the trees will keep condensation away from you (but some trees will drop sap onto your gear). To stay warm, the ideal spot to camp is AWAY from water, ON dirt/needles/duff, and UNDER tree cover.

SHELTER

Your shelter (or lack thereof) has a major impact on your sleep system. Cowboy camping has its benefits, but you will be exposed to the elements (dew and wind). A tarp will help with dew and provide some warmth. A tent can provide 10+ degrees of warmth.

TRICKS TO SLEEP WARMER

- Always wear a hat.

- If your bag has continuous baffles, you can shake most of the down to the top of the bag, leaving little fill underneath you. That will add warmth to the bag. You don't need the down underneath you, because your sleeping pad will insulate you from the cold ground. Sleeping bag warmth comes from the loft on top of you.

- You could lay your breathable rain jacket on top of your sleeping bag to add warmth.

- If you know it's going to be cold/wet, before leaving town make sure that your trail dinners are mashed potatoes. When they are cooked, mashed potatoes are a solid substance, not liquid-based like noodle or rice dinners. So there you are all cold and rainy on the trail. You set up your shelter and crawl into your sleeping bag. You're still cold. Cook up your dinner — mashed potatoes — and before eating them, put the pot (with the lid on) inside your sleeping bag for several minutes. This will warm up your bag. It will also get food smells on your bag, which is a bad thing. Don't do this with any food with liquid in it. No matter how careful you are, you will spill your pot full of food and liquid inside your sleeping bag. I witnessed another hiker doing this in the middle of a snowstorm. It was funny and sad at the same time!

Anish: Choose a campsite where no one has camped and away from water. Don't clear off the duff. Get into your sleep clothes and bag as soon as you can to maximize the residual heat from walking. Eat something high in fat and protein for dinner.

BINK: Avoid places that tend to collect katabatic air; read up on it. Avoid meadows; they are cold, the air sinks, and the air has higher humidity (often reaching dew point at night), meaning you get soaked. Knowing what vegetation grows in what climate zones can aid in detecting warmer areas to camp. Keep yourself clean. Salts on your skin from sweating all day will suck moisture out of the air and cause a sticky cold clammy feeling on your skin.

Billy Goat: ✔ Quickly change into warm, dry clothes when ending the day's hike. Get into the sleeping bag as quickly as possible before getting chilled.

✔ Use mittens as shoulder pads at night to increase shoulder warmth.

✔ Wear head cover and DRY socks.

✔ Fluff up the sleeping bag before climbing in.

✔ A tarp or tent helps retain body heat.

✔ Sleep under a tree, preferably on a bed of needles or leaves for softness and insulation from the ground. Piles of squirrel nut husks work, also. The tree keeps the cold, dampness, and even rain at bay.

✔ If it's windy, find wind protection like trees, bushes, rocks. Sleep feet into the wind and off the cold ground.

✔ Never sleep in a low spot where the cold will settle, especially not near water. Streams, lakes, or ponds will raise humidity in the area.

✔ Drink hot beverages before sleeping.

WATER TREATMENT

It's your decision:
> Don't treat your water
> Use chemicals (iodine, AquaMira, bleach)
> Use a water filter

Do whatever works for you. If you choose to not carry a water treatment method, and then you end up at a really gross water source — and there are PLENTY of these on the PCT — and your next water source is 10 miles away, and you're out of water, then you're screwed.

WHAT MAKES YOU SICK ?

Many people are afraid of bears. I'm more afraid of Giardia. Giardia is a tiny varmint that can take you off the trail. You can get Giardia from drinking untreated water, from not cleaning your hands after pooping and then eating with your hands, or from sharing food with people who haven't cleaned their hands properly. You don't want Giardia. If you get it, you will have diarrhea for 1-2 weeks or longer. This is explosive diarrhea, the kind that gives no warning.

Treatment Method	Packed Weight	Cost	Gallons
Sawyer Squeeze Filter	3 ounces, including bags	$40	unlimited
Sawyer Mini Filter	2 ounces, including bags	$25	unlimited
2 replacement pouches		$ 9	
Katadyn Hiker Filter	11 ounces	$70	200
replacement cartridge		$50	200
Aquamira	3.5 ounces	$15	30
Potable Aqua (iodine)	small bottle, 3 ounces	$ 7	6
SteriPEN	Several models, ranging from 2.6 ounces to 5.7 ounces (plus batteries). Many hikers have trouble with this device.	$50 to $165	varies

You can also get severe diarrhea from drinking snowmelt from the pink snow up high in the Sierra. The pink snow is sometimes referred to as "watermelon snow." Google it!

Many hikers do not treat their water, and they have no problems. There are also many hikers who do not treat their water, and they get sick. The people who advocate NOT treating water claim that hikers get sick because of not cleaning their hands properly after pooping, or from sharing food with others, NOT because of drinking untreated water. It's difficult to determine why thru-hikers get sick. We get water from too many different sources and eat food from too many different places to track back the source of our illness.

AQUAMIRA

Aquamira is a combination of two solutions which come in small plastic bottles. Mix 7 drops of each solution in a little mixing cap, wait 5 minutes, then add the mixture to your water. Shake. Wait 15 more minutes, then drink. Aquamira leaves a slight aroma/flavor in the water.

Aquamira hints: One package of Aquamira comes with one mixing cap. Every time you get a new package of Aquamira, keep your old mixing caps. It's good to have two (or more) mixing caps.

Screw the lids on REALLY TIGHT.
Screw the lids on REALLY TIGHT.
Screw the lids on REALLY TIGHT.

As extra protection against puncturing the bottles, keep the plastic display packaging; store the bottles in the packaging in your pack.

POTABLE AQUA

Potable Aqua is little iodine tablets. Add one or two iodine tablets to each quart, wait 20-30 minutes before drinking. Potable Aqua leaves a distinct flavor in the water.

STERIPEN

The SteriPEN is a handheld UV water purifier. It uses UV light to destroy bacteria, viruses, and protozoa. Turn it on, immerse it in one liter of water and stir for 90 seconds, then drink! Requires batteries, which vary depending upon the model: integrated, AA, or CR123 batteries (hard to find on the trail, and very expensive when you do find them).

WATER FILTER

There are many different styles/brands of water filters. The most popular are the Sawyer Squeeze followed by the Katadyn BeFree water filter.

WATER SYSTEM	Treatment	Type of Bottles	Capacity
Yogi	Sawyer Squeeze Filter	Smartwater	8 liters in the desert, 4-6 liters everywhere else
Anish	SteriPEN until it broke. Aquamira sometimes. MSR Aquatabs until I ran out. Nothing after that.	Platypus hose Gatorade bottles	8 liters in the desert, 4 liters from Tuolumne north
BINK	Nothing	Bottled water bottles	7-8 liters because I categorically avoid using water caches
Hiker Box Special	Usually nothing. Aquamira sometimes.	Gatorade	7 liters
Scrub	Nothing	Gatorade or Vitamin Water	7 liters in the desert, 4 liters after that

Sawyer Water Products introduced the Sawyer Squeeze filter in 2012, and it quickly became the most-used filter in long-distance hiking. This filter is fantastic. The Squeeze Filter system weighs 3 ounces. The filter screws onto the water bag; no pumping, no chemicals, no waiting, no worries! Incredibly fast flow rate, simple to use, and each filter can be backwashed to extend its life. Another key to extending the life of this system is to treat the bags with care. Don't squeeze too hard; if you squeeze too hard, you'll blow out the seams of the bag. Also, the filter comes with a syringe; use the syringe to backwash your filter at every town stop. EVERY TOWN STOP (this means carrying the syringe in your pack). When your bags need to be replaced, you can get two 2-liter (64 oz) bags for only $9.

I *highly recommend* the Sawyer Squeeze Filter system. It's fast and efficient. No chemicals. Sure, you'll need to replace the bags, but $9 to replace bags is cheaper than $50 to replace a cartridge.

HIKER OPINIONS

BINK: I do not treat any of my water. Yes, I have been sick on many occasions, so this comes with great risk. Use your own judgement. Although I have done many PCT thru-hikes without treating my water, I feel that treating water for biological contamination may be a more important factor in the near future due to the heavier use among day hikers, weekenders, and thru-hikers. If you do not want to risk getting sick at all, then treat your water!

Hiker Box Special: Hikers who treat get cavalier, drink anything, then get sick – or their filter freezes and doesn't work anymore. Hikers who don't treat have a more discerning eye and drink better water, but still might get sick. Pick your poison.

Scrub: I started with Aquamira , but I only used it three times in the first 400 miles of desert. After that I never treated anything except to strain nasty lake water in Oregon through a bandanna to get macro particles out. If you go this route, be forewarned: more annoying than having Giardia is the fact that everyone who sees you drinking straight from the streams will start a conversation about it. Some of them, especially section-hikers, will prophesy certain death on you. Seriously. Expect people to actually be upset with you for how you choose to drink water. Most of the time, my face was smiling politely but my mind was telling them to $%#& right off and leave me alone.

I got a pretty mild confirmed case of Giardia in Oregon that was easily vanquished with a 10-day course of Flagyl. Like everyone else who's ever gotten Giardia, I don't know where I got it from. Even making the assumption that it was from water, the experience was still worth it for the refreshing simplicity of drinking straight from natural sources the whole way. I will continue not to treat my water while hiking unless I'm someplace where it will be unavoidable to drink from sources that are known to be polluted.

WATER CONTAINERS

CONTAINER SIZE

Water is precious on the PCT, especially in Southern California. Your water sources could be 25+ miles apart. It's smart to have several small-capacity containers rather than one or two large-capacity containers. If you've got a gallon of water in one container, then it leaks, you're screwed. If you have four one-liter containers, and one of those leaks, it's not as bad.

TYPE OF CONTAINER

If you use a soft plastic bladder, odds are that it WILL get holes in it. The desert plants are very hostile. They attack bladders and inflatable sleeping pads. I personally wouldn't consider carrying a bladder – the soft ones get holes, the heavier ones (like MSR DromLite) make water taste like a tire.

Most thru-hikers carry their water in Gatorade or Smartwater bottles. A 1-liter Smartwater bottle weighs 1.3 ounces. Gatorade/Smartwater bottles seem to be indestructible. I've NEVER had one get a hole. They can be easily replaced when they get that black funk on them (if you've hiked, you know what I'm talking about). Just buy a new one. The best part is that when you buy your new water bottle, you get a bonus liter of Gatorade or Smartwater!!

Gatorade/Smartwater bottles are very versatile. You can add/subtract from your water capacity at every town stop. Just look at your data/maps for the longest waterless stretch between the town you're in and the next town. Then carry enough bottle capacity for that longest waterless stretch. If you have too many bottles, throw them away before leaving town. If you need more, chances are you're going to buy some Gatorade or soda when you're in town anyway, just save the bottle.

Scrub: I had used a bladder-and-hose hydration system on the AT, but I wasn't thrilled with it because it took too much fuss to refill. Moreover, those things are extremely break-prone. I ditched the whole bladder thing on the PCT. Instead, I used two plastic quart-sized Gatorade or Vitamin Water bottles in the side pockets of my backpack for drinking out of as I hiked. I replaced them whenever I felt like buying a cold Gatorade in town. It's like you pay $2 for a clean new bottle and get some free Gatorade as a bonus!

For storage in my pack, I used two 1-Liter Platypus SoftBottles. In the desert, I used an additional 2-Liter Source water bladder with the hose disconnected. I never drank straight out of the collapsible bladders/bottles, just used them for storage. I liked having multiple storage bottles instead of one big bladder/reservoir, because it was nice to adjust weight distribution in the pack. The SoftBottles weigh only 0.7 ounce each and roll up to the size of a few pencils when they're not in use. I've heard they also make good pillows blown up.

WATER CAPACITY

A rule of thumb for water capacity is one liter for every four miles, PLUS one liter for lunch and one liter for dinner. More water for hot sections, less water for cooler sections. In the extreme heat of the Mojave and some sections of Northern California, I drank one liter for every 2-3 miles. I wished for more, but that's all I could carry!

The most water I've carried was 8 liters, which is not uncommon in SoCal in dry years. Through SoCal on other hikes, a full load was usually 6 liters, sometimes 7. Pay attention to the Yogi Book pages, Guthook app, and the Water Report. You want to carry enough water, but not overdo it. Going thirsty sucks, and water is heavy. One liter weighs two pounds.

COOK SYSTEM

ALCOHOL STOVES

Lightweight alcohol stoves have been the thru-hiker standard for many years. They're easy to make. They're cheap and lightweight. They boil water fast. There aren't any mechanical parts which could break. Just don't step on it. You can use tent stakes or rocks for a stove stand. Heavy foil could serve as a windscreen. Many hikers make windscreens out of disposable roasting pans.

In recent years, fire restrictions were in effect for most of the PCT during the extremely dry thru-hiker seasons. This meant that open flames were not allowed, and stoves without a shut-off valve were not allowed. Therefore, alcohol stoves were banned. Most hikers switched from alcohol stoves to canister stoves. Many hikers went stoveless.

Make an alcohol stove:	Google "homemade alcohol stove."
Purchase an alcohol stove:	AntiGravityGear, Brasslite, Mini Bull Design, Trail Designs, Trangia Stoves, Vargo Triad Stove.
Fuel for alcohol stoves:	Denatured alcohol (hardware stores and paint stores) or HEET (a gas-line antifreeze, found at grocery stores, gas stations, auto parts stores, and C-stores). Regular HEET in the yellow bottle is best. Store your denatured alcohol or HEET in a plastic water bottle or soda bottle.

CANISTER STOVES

Canister stoves boil water much faster than alcohol stoves. In addition, canister stoves have a shut-off valve, so they can be used when fire restrictions are in effect. There are many good canister stoves from MSR, Snow Peak, and Primus. Fuel for canister stoves comes in – you guessed it – canisters. Many of the PCT trail towns have stores which stock canister fuel. However, it's a real possibility that they will be sold out if a bunch of hikers pass through town before you.

STOVE ACCESSORIES

Cook pot: Many PCT hikers use titanium cook pots.
Walmart sells a "grease pot," which is really cheap and lightweight.

Windscreen: Using a windscreen will greatly increase the efficiency of your stove.

Pot cozy: Buy or make a pot cozy! I used to think that a pot cozy was just fluff. Not true. It *really* keeps your food warm for a LONG time. AntiGravityGear offers a cozy collection, custom made to fit many different pots.

Spoon: Do not buy the "Light My Fire Spork." First of all, you don't need a fork. You're eating noodles, rice, mashed potatoes, stuffing. A spoon is perfect. Second, and most important, the "Light My Fire Sporks" ALWAYS BREAK.

Titanium sporks are lightweight, and you definitely won't break them, but it's REALLY hard to scoop liquid with a spork.

A Lexan spoon, a long-handle titanium spoon, or a plain ol' white plastic spoon are the way to go.

Clean-up: Just rinse your stuff with water, then air dry.
You do not need soap/sponge. Use water and your fingers.

HIKER OPINIONS

BINK: I have used a no-cook trail diet since 1998. When hiking in very early spring or late fall, I sometimes use a canister stove. On winter PCT section trips on snowshoes, I use white gas stoves due to them not being affected by the cold.

I carry a lidded container to cold-soak my dinners in as part of my no-cook system. I used to use plastic lidded containers, but many of the newer BPA-free plastic formulations are more prone to easily cracking or breaking. On my recent speed record attempt hikes, I used the titanium "BOT" (a lidded cook pot), which although slightly heavier, is 100% fail proof (an important consideration when no gear failures can happen).

I use a long-handled titanium spoon because the container I soak my dinners in is deep, and it's nice to not have my not-always-clean-hands in my dinner. I used plastic spoons for years, but grew tired of breaking them in peanut butter on cold days. You can, however, "weld" them back together with a lighter. I have hiked thousands of miles with spoons repaired this way.

Hiker Box Special: I used a homemade PBR can stove. It was fine. I made a stand out of wire mesh. My cook pot was a Snow Peak 0.5L pot. It was comically small. Get something 0.7L or bigger. I went stoveless in NorCal since it was too hot to eat hot food. I liked the change, and it made resupplying easier because I never had to worry about food.

Scrub: I went stoveless. My "cook pot" was a 28oz peanut butter jar with screw-on lid. Some stoveless people are really into cold-soaking meals for hours that you would normally just boil in a pot, but I'm not. I mostly grazed on snack food all day, sometimes also for dinner. The only thing I used the jar for was cold-soaking Idahoan mashed potatoes, which was a typical dinner for me.

COOK SYSTEM	Stove	Cook Pot	Spoon	Pot Cozy
Yogi	Yes	0.8 L MSR Titan Kettle	Orange Lexan spoon	Yes
Anish	None	None	Lexan spoon	No
BINK	None	1 L Titanium BOT	Long-handled titanium spoon	No
Hiker Box Special	Yes	0.5 L Snow Peak	Plastic spoon	No
Scrub	None	28-oz peanut butter jar	Spoon from my silverware drawer	No

Pros about going stoveless:

+ Eat in your tent, sleeping bag, while walking, wherever, whenever (awesome when it's rainy/snowy or buggy)

+ Don't have to worry about fuel resupply

+ Don't have to worry about your stove breaking

+ Don't have to worry about starting a forest fire with your alcohol stove in the windy desert (this was the biggest concern for me)

+ No dishwashing

+ Potential for weight savings (although that's not really why I do it and that tends to be cancelled out by the relative heaviness of snack food in general, compared to dehydrated/freeze-dried foods)

Cons (according to the haters):

- No coffee (except this isn't true, because Starbucks Via has delicious cold blends)

- No psychological boost on cold days. Personally, all calories warm me up physically and mentally, not just hot ones. Also, it's not cold very often on the PCT.

- Emergency blah, blah, blah. Emergency, my ass. I would not pack a stove just to account for the infinitesimal chance of getting hypothermia all by myself on what is a predominantly warm-weather, well-traveled trail.

I used a spoon from my silverware drawer at home. It fit snugly in my jar with the lid closed, which was the #1 spoon criterion for me (#2 was not breaking, like all those shitty plastic Light My Fire spoon/fork/knife combos do). All anyone really needs is a spoon, I think. Camping sporks tend to be the worst of both worlds: a fork that can't pick anything up and a spoon that can't hold any liquid. Just find a spoon somewhere, and don't sweat the decision too hard.

COOKING DINNER

Long-distance hikers don't exactly COOK. Here's what you do: boil your water, then add your rice/noodles/potatoes. Stir. For rice and noodles, keep your pot over the heat for about a minute. Remove the pot from the stove. Extinguish the stove. Put the lid on your pot. Wrap your windscreen or pot cozy around the outside of the pot as insulation. Let the pot sit for about 10 minutes with the lid on, stirring halfway through. After 10 minutes, your food is ready to eat!

Since we are not simmering our noodles or rice, there is no opportunity for water to evaporate. Therefore, you should use less water than the package indicates. For example, a package of Knorr noodles requires 2 cups of liquid. On the trail, only use 1.5 cups water. This works for foods that are meant to simmer. It does not work for foods like mashed potatoes or stuffing, which are simply quickly rehydrated with hot water. Use the full amount of water for these types of foods.

Your hike.

Your food.

Keep it yours.

Bewildering

bears...

for

the

long

haul.

BearVault

To keep your pot/food hot longer, use a pot cozy. You could build your own out of mylar insulation, or you could purchase a cozy from AntiGravityGear.

Many hikers stop in the evening to cook dinner, then put in a few more miles before camping. My favorite time of day to hike is after dinner. It's not as hot and the sun is lower, which creates amazing shadows. All the folds of the landscape are visible. And the sunsets are amazing, especially if smoke has blown into your area from forest fires.

There are many advantages to cooking dinner, then walking on:

- You don't carry your cooking water to camp. Instead, cook at the water source.

- You use the energy from your dinner, rather than wasting that energy while sleeping.

- When you get to your campsite for the evening, there are no "chores" to do. Just crawl into your warm sleeping bag!

- In theory, your chance encounters with bears are diminished. The bears will be attracted to the food odor where you cooked dinner, not where you're sleeping.

OVERNIGHT FOOD STORAGE

What should you do with your food while you sleep? There are a few options, including:

(1) Sleep with it.
(2) Use an Ursack.
(3) Hang a bear bag.
(4) Use odor-resistant bags such as an OPSAK.
(5) Use a bear canister – most hikers use the BearVault.

My answer to that question applies to myself only: I put my food bag into my pack with all my other gear. Then I put my pack under my feet as I sleep. I like to elevate my feet; it helps my feet and legs feel better the next day. Could a bear, a mouse, a marmot, or something else come into my tent looking for my food? Sure. Has it ever happened? Nope. Is this dangerous? Probably. But it's what I've always done – with these exceptions: (1) Bear canisters are required on some sections of the Pacific Crest Trail. I use a canister there. (2) Hanging food is required in grizzly country in Montana and Wyoming on the Continental Divide Trail. I hang my food there.

You decide for yourself what you want to do. I'm not suggesting you sleep with your food. If you want to know how to hang your food, Google this: "how to hang a bear bag." You'll find lots of websites with bear-bagging techniques. REI has an interesting article regarding bear canisters here: [www.rei.com/expertadvice/articles/bear+resistant+canisters.html]

According to the Pacific Crest Trail Association: "Approved bear canisters are required in parts of Sequoia and Kings Canyon (SEKI) National Parks, Inyo, Sierra and Humboldt-Toiyabe National Forests, and in all of Yosemite and Lassen National Parks. Basically, PCT hikers and horseback riders should, at the minimum, carry canisters between Kennedy Meadows (mile 702.2) and Sonora Pass (mile 1016.9) and then again in Lassen National Park (mile 1346.3 to 1365.5)."

See the "Sierra Food Storage" section of this Handbook for specific SEKI and Yosemite information. See mile 1346.3 in the Town Guide section of this Handbook for specific Lassen information.

Anish: Bear canister in the Sierra, otherwise it's in an OPSAK under my feet.

BINK: Outside of bear canister required areas, I sleep with it next to me.

Hiker Box Special: Bear can in the Sierra. Slept with it everywhere else, no problemo.

Scrub: Except for in the Sierra, when it went in a bear canister, at night my food always went in my Ursack Minor, which is a rodent-proof food bag that I also used on the AT. It hasn't been infiltrated yet, so I trust it. I put this bag right next to me (when cowboy camping) or right outside my tent door(when tenting). If I had hung my food in a tree or stashed it far away from me every night, I would have had problems all the time.

NPS ALLOWED BEAR CANISTERS - November 2019

BEAR VAULT
110b, 200, 250, 300, 350, 400, 450, 500
[www.bearvault.com] 866-301-3442

BEARIKADE Weekender MKII and
Expedition MKII (both 1766 and higher)
[www.wild-ideas.net] 805-693-0550

GARCIA - Backpacker Model 812
[www.backpackerscache.com]
559-732-3785

THE BEAR KEG - Counter Assault
[www.counterassault.com]
800-695-3394

The Bare Boxer Contender (101)
and Champ (202) [www.bareboxer.com]

UDAP No-Fed-Bear
[www.udap.com] 800-232-7941

LIGHTER1 Big Daddy and Little Sami
[www.lighter1.com]

See the "Bear Can Purchase / Rental" section of this Handbook, in the chapter "The Sierra".

PACK COVER

It can and does rain and snow in Southern California. And in the Sierra. And in Northern California. And in Oregon. And most definitely in Washington. Protect your pack. You can buy a pack cover. Or you can cover the outside of your pack with a sturdy garbage bag. Or you can line the inside of your pack with a sturdy garbage bag. Choose a method to protect your gear, but please do SOMETHING.

To further protect your sleeping bag, keep it in a waterproof stuff sack. This is especially important if you pack your sleeping bag at the bottom of your pack. Every time you set your pack down on the wet ground, the bottom will get wet. You don't want a wet sleeping bag.

OTHER GEAR	Trekking Poles	Compass	DEET	Headnet
Yogi	Sierra and Washington only	Yes	Yes	OR Spring Ring
Anish	No	Yes	Yes	OR Spring Ring
BINK	Never	Yes	Yes	OR Spring Ring with additional netting flaps sewn on
Hiker Box Special	No	No	Yes	OR Spring Ring
Scrub	No	Yes	No	OR Spring Ring

TREKKING POLES

I expend less energy without poles than with them. I only use poles on the PCT from Kennedy Meadows to Echo Lake (for snow and fords), then again from Snoqualmie Pass to Stehekin (for fords).

Scrub: I do not like trekking poles because I have this ideal that backpacking should feel like a normal old walk in the woods (or mountains, or desert, etc.). The minute there are poles in my hands, it stops feeling like a Walk and instead feels like some other activity – a Trek, a Slog. I've been lucky not to have chronic leg injuries in my life, and I keep a light-ish pack, so I really don't need them for hiking in normal conditions. They'd just be one more thing for me to lose or accidentally stab someone in the face with.

That said, poles really do have a bajillion potential uses: pitching tarps/tents, crossing rivers, hiking on snow, fending off dogs, taking pictures or video with the StickPic, digging catholes, saving your knees/shins/feet if you've had problems with them before . . . . they are a pretty multi-faceted piece of gear. I would've considered investing in some, say, for the Sierra section if I had been there in a higher snow year. But if you've never needed them before, don't feel like they are ESSENTIAL for a long hike just because you see all those pictures of thru-hikers with them. You'll get by without them just fine.

BINK: I have tried poles a few times over the years but could not get used to them. I'm considering trying them again.

Hiker Box Special: The people that used poles generally had poor balance and weak ankles. Whether that was from using poles or they were using poles because of poor balance and weak ankles is a tough call. Try hiking without them; you'll be surprised.

COMPASS

Always carry a compass, and know how to use it. Stay found!

Anish: I used my compass to find a spring in the desert and to make sure I turned the correct way on a road. I could have figured both of those out without it. However, if the snow is high in the Sierra, having a compass and the ability to use it is paramount.

BINK: I have used a compass many times on the PCT in snowy sections down in the trees (the southern end of Crater Lake National Park, for example). In the spring of 1994, I was training for my CDT hike by doing the first 1000 miles of the PCT. In mid-April, I was caught in a horrible snowstorm white out on Mt. San Jacinto in Southern California. I could not see more than 10 feet in the snow-covered (from the previous winter) terrain. I became very lost and hypothermic. Finally, I pulled out my compass and took a bearing off my map to get me to Saddle Junction. I was shocked to find the compass leading me off in what I thought was the opposite direction of where I sensed I needed to go and had been going for hours. I trusted the compass, and with an hour I was at Saddle Junction headed lower down into town and warmth and shelter. I am firmly convinced that compass saved my life that day.

Scrub: I had a compass on my phone that I could've used for actual backcountry navigation, but that issue never arose (2013: no Sierra snow navigation). I also had a little ping-pong-ball-sized compass that someone gave me in Big Bear City and I clipped on my shoulder strap. I looked down at that often just to get a general orientation. Sometimes on switchbacks or something I would tell my hiking buddies, "Wait, wait, wait guys, I think we're going south." It was this sense of humor that led to me hiking alone most of the trail.

BUG PROTECTION

DEET

As you sit at home planning your trip, you might think you would NEVER use DEET. You're wrong. Words cannot describe how bad the mosquitos can be on the PCT. They will make you insane. I would not hike north of Kennedy Meadows without DEET. The only stuff that works against these blood-thirsty freaks of nature is 95% DEET. The bottles that say "100" on the packaging are really 95% DEET. The brand of DEET doesn't seem to matter, as long as it's 95% DEET. Be sure to double-bag your bottle of DEET inside two ziplock bags. You do not want this stuff to get on your synthetic clothes.

To further preserve your sanity, be sure to have a mosquito headnet. Many hikers use the Outdoor Research Spring Ring Headnet (with a metal ring which goes around your head at mouth level, holding the headnet away from your face.

Jerry Goller (BackpackGearTest.org): To shorten a long story, the military proved that anything over about 30% DEET was wasted. The reason that 100% seems to work better is that it can take more degradation. The controlled release stuff actually works much better and much longer than the straight 100% DEET does because the controlled release stuff encapsulates the DEET. The encapsulating molecules break down at different rates causing the controlled release. It not only works better, it is also much more comfortable to wear. And it works. The two brands we worked with at BackpackGearTest.org were Sawyer Controlled Release and 3M Ultrathon. Try 'em.

WHERE ARE THE BUGS ?

Mosquitos swarm in the High Sierra and Oregon. But it's not just the mosquitos that will push you over the edge. There's something that looks like a fly-bee mutant. Yellowish-brown wings. Their bites are the worst. You'll see these monsters between Mojave and Kennedy Meadows; they don't react very fast, so you can always kill them. You'll get stung by yellow jackets, and that sting will stick with you for a week. They're very painful. Southern California has little fly-gnats which do everything in their power to get inside your head — through your ears, nose, mouth, eyes. The little biting flies in Washington are horrible. And of course, the entire PCT is smack dab in the middle of GIANT ANT WORLD.

Just exactly where will the mosquitos be bad? It depends. Depends on when the snow starts to melt. Depends on when you are there. I've had bad bugs in Southern California. Typically, the really bad bugs begin in the Sierra around mile 716.5. Bugs are terrible going north from Tuolumne (mile 942.5). Bugs continue to be bad for the rest of California. Bugs get terrible again north of Highway 140 in Oregon (mile 1773.4). Bugs are often bad through Oregon up to Snoqualmie Pass in Washington (mile 2393.6). So, carry bug protection beginning at Kennedy Meadows (mile 702.2). Keep it until the bugs go away somewhere in Washington.

HIKER OPINIONS

Anish: I HATE mosquitoes. I would have gone crazy without a headnet.

BINK: I do carry DEET but use it sparingly. I also pick up and carry my homemade net tent for the worst of the buggy section. Typically I have not seen mosquitos on my Yo-Yo attempts until Oregon. If you are entering Oregon in early July, beware!!

Hiker Box Special: Headnets are essential since I don't like putting DEET on my face.

Scrub: Much like with sun protection, I preferred to fight the bugs with clothes rather than chemicals. I never used a drop of DEET. I had been in shorts, but in Mammoth I bought some long pants and a headnet to go with my long-sleeve shirt. When the shit was hitting the fan, I just covered up all my skin, shoved my hands in my pockets, and kept moving. Occasionally they bit through my clothes, but that was rare. It sucked to have to deal with them like that, and yes it was the nadir of fashion, but I don't think it would've been any more bearable with DEET.

FAVORITE GEAR

My favorite pieces of gear are: Osprey Exos pack, Marmot DriClime Windshirt, and Western Mountaineering sleeping bags.

Anish: My ZPacks Hexamid tent and my Patagonia Houdini Jacket. They are both uber-light, functional, and do what they needed to do perfectly with no frills or waste.

BINK: I cannot say I have a favorite piece of gear. I suppose I really like anything that I have made. I do carry a small P38 military can opener attached to my knife that has some history behind it. That little can opener is the only piece of gear that has been on every single one of my PCT hikes, everything else has been worn out, lost, replaced or otherwise exchanged over the years. Maybe that little unassuming but well traveled can opener is my favorite piece of gear. Well that's it – now I'll probably lose it on the next hike!

Scrub: My GoLite 3-Season down quilt was probably my favorite piece of gear, with my Elemental Horizons Kalais backpack a close second. They are both infinitely comfortable, well-conceived, and well-made.

LUXURY ITEMS

I carry a little bottle of lotion. The dry air in the west makes my skin crack, especially on my fingertips. This can be very painful.

Anish: iPhone. Wet wipes (showers are not frequent).

BINK: Well let's see, that can opener is a luxury item. Is a full-handled toothbrush a luxury item?

Scrub: At two points in the hike, I had a cotton T-shirt specifically for town. For a week in NorCal, I also had a pair of cutoff jean shorts, also just for town. Eventually I got rid of both because I realized that I had enough clothes to go round, even while I was doing laundry in town. Also, putting on a clean shirt and shorts when your skin is just filthy doesn't make you feel that much cleaner.

In the desert, I was carrying a merino wool hoodie as my base layer for sleeping and sometimes town, and that was totally luxurious and overkill. It weighed upwards of 10oz, but damn was it comfortable, and kind of stylish to boot (not hiker stylish, but real-world stylish). Jettisoned it after Kennedy Meadows, I think.

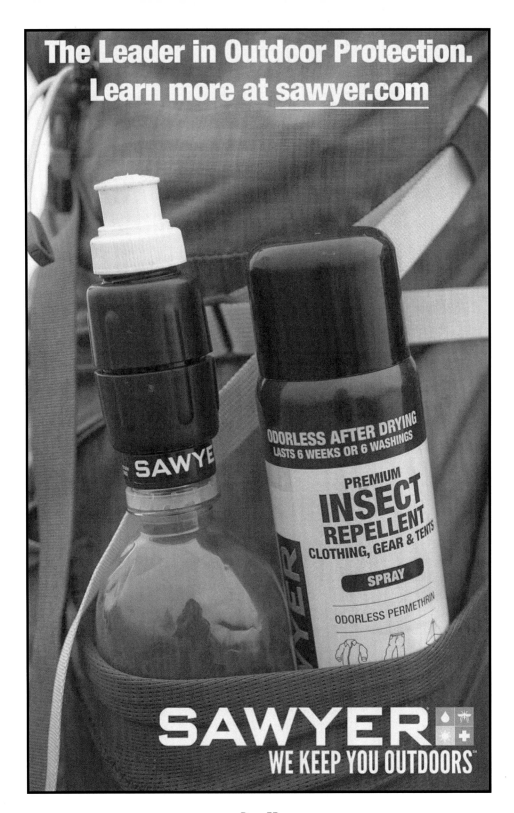

UNIQUE GEAR

In 2007, I carried an umbrella. I had watched Joe Moon with his umbrella on the CDT, and Scott Williamson had told me he uses an umbrella. I figured I'd give it a try. LOVED IT!! It was wonderful in the hot sun and even more crucial in the rain. Now I take my umbrella on every hike. On the AT in 2012, everyone thought I was nuts for carrying an umbrella . . . . except for the days it rained. On those days I was a genius!

My warm hat is unique: it's from Chicadoo (Google it!), and has a hole in the back for my ponytail to escape.

GEAR CHANGES FROM AT TO PCT

I pretty much changed everything, due to:

(1) The PCT was my second thru-hike. I knew nothing about gear when I bought my AT gear. For the PCT, I was more experienced, and I knew what to look for.

(2) Gear gets lighter every year. For example: the lightest double-wall tent on the market for my AT hike was completely different from the lightest double-wall tent on the market two years later when I hiked the PCT.

The PCT environment has a major impact on your AT-to-PCT gear changes:

- The PCT rarely has shade. The California sun is HOT.
  You will stay MUCH cooler if you wear a long-sleeved shirt, which keeps the sun off of your skin.

- You must wear a sun hat and sunglasses.

- You DO NOT need boots. Boots are heavy, hot, and will never dry after being wet.
  Get lightweight breathable running shoes.

- Do not wear liner socks paired with thicker socks. Instead, wear one pair of thin breathable socks. Carry two extra pair of socks. Rinse them out often.

- You will actually wear rain gear on the PCT. Many AT hikers do not wear rain gear because the AT is humid – wearing rain gear on the AT makes you soaked from sweat. The PCT is not humid. When it rains on the PCT, it is usually also cold and windy. Rain gear will help prevent hypothermia.

- You actually need maps on the PCT. Most AT hikers don't carry maps, because the trail is well marked. Not so on the PCT. You need maps.

Anish: Warmer clothing for the PCT. I carried maps and guides for the PCT, which I didn't do on the AT. I carried water treatment on the PCT. I also carried a warmer sleeping bag and a tent on the PCT. I went shelterless on the AT.

BINK: I hiked the AT with a little less warm clothing and a lighter sleeping bag, but otherwise the same gear for the most part.

Scrub: I changed almost everything, because I knew I could go a lot lighter and still be within my comfort zone. I got way more into gear research after the AT and would get a specific idea of what I wanted, then wait until I saw a good deal online and pounce. I also sold a few of my AT things online. For the PCT, I got a new down quilt, new smaller pack, new ultralight shelter, trail runners instead of boots, bottles instead of hydration system, different style hiking shirt and hat . . . . the list goes on. I would have barely recognized my current self two years ago on the AT.

CLOTHING and FOOTWEAR

CLOTHING

On the AT, you may have had summer gear and winter gear. On the PCT, you'll most likely carry the same gear for the whole trip, maybe adding a warmer top and rain gear in the Sierra and Oregon-Washington. The PCT is always cold at night. The colder sections are Kennedy Meadows to Sierra City (mile 702.2 to mile 1195.4) and Oregon-Washington (mile 1691.7 to 2661.9). No cotton clothes! Look for moisture-wicking material.

When you finally reach Ashland Oregon, the last thing you think you'll need are your warm clothes. Northern California was hot, and you've decided to bounce your sleeping clothes, gloves, hat, and warm top up to Cascade Locks. DON'T DO IT. Oregon nights are cold. Layering is important. With several layers, you can add/remove items as you cool down or warm up.

Anish: The things you wear day-to-day are going to be trashed. You don't have to spend a lot on them. Invest your money in good jackets (a warm jacket and a rain jacket). Those items need to be quality, because when you need them, you REALLY need them.

CLOTHING FOR THE ENTIRE PCT

SUN HAT   Something with a brim. You must shade your face and nose.

SUNGLASSES   Gotta have 'em.

SHORTS   Running shorts or hiking-style shorts.
Some hikers use the shorts from pants that have zip-off legs.

PANTS   Most hikers have synthetic pants, because they dry fast.
Many have convertible zip-off leg pants.

SOCKS   Injinji toe socks are fantastic! Thick wool or wool-type socks are a bad idea. It's usually too hot for that. Wrapping your feet in insulating socks is asking for blisters. If you need more cushioning under your feet, then replace your shoe insoles with something thicker. Have at least two pair of socks. I use three. Rinse your socks whenever you get to water. Hang them on the back of your pack to dry. Change them often.

HIKING SHIRT   Some hikers wear short-sleeved shirts or tank tops. Others wear synthetic long-sleeved shirts. Your hiking shirt should be white or some other very light color. Yes, it's going to show dirt. You don't care about that. The sun is hot, and a light-colored shirt will be more comfortable to wear.

LONG-SLEEVED SHIRT - Sometimes it's cold, even in the desert. You might want a long-sleeved shirt to hike in. Also, when you get sunburned, you'll need something with long sleeves to wear while you hike. Make sure this shirt is white or light-colored so you don't bake in the hot desert sun.

WARM TOP   Fleece, down jacket, or wind proof top.
Many thru-hikers wear the Marmot DriClime Windshirt.

RAIN JACKET   It rarely rains in Southern California. But it does rain sometimes. And it snows sometimes. Keep your rain jacket with you for the entire PCT. It's good not only for rain, but for warmth, too.

RAIN PANTS OR RAIN KILT   Most hikers don't carry them. I like rain pants in Washington (because it's cold), and a ULA rain kilt everywhere else.

WARM HAT Make sure it covers your ears. It should not be bulky, because you'll wear it almost every night while you sleep.

GLOVES Yes! For the whole trail.

SLEEPING CLOTHES Lightweight long-sleeved underwear tops and bottoms. Warm socks. These clothes are NEVER worn while hiking.

ADD THESE FOR THE SIERRA AND OREGON-WASHINGTON

EXTRA PAIR OF LINER GLOVES To sleep in if your hiking gloves are wet.

ANOTHER WARM TOP Fleece, down jacket, etc.

RAIN PANTS OR KILT It rains a lot in Washington.

SLEEPING BAG LINER Adds 5-10 degrees warmth.

CLOTHING	Yogi	Anish
Hiking Shirt	Long-sleeved poly/nylon shirt similar to the Mountain Hardwear Canyon. Your shirt should be light-colored. I like brighter colors rather than tan (looks better in pictures). I also wear a Marmot tank top with no seams in the back.	I hike in a thrift store dress. It's cheap, lasts a long time, is quick drying, and lighter than two pieces. I also wear a bikini top instead of a sports bra for the same reasons. Bonus to wearing a skirt or dress: you can pee standing up!!!
Hiking Shorts	Moisture-wicking running shorts with a liner. I look for shorts with a longer inseam (no booty shorts!).	
Hiking Pants	Any brand of nylon pants like the REI Sahara.	
Hiking Hat	A regular floppy sun hat with a hole in the back like a ball cap. My ponytail goes through the hole.	I started with a Peal Izumi visor but lost it. I always lose my hats, so I don't even try anymore.
Warm Hat	Chicadoo ponytail hat.	Patagonia beanie.
Warm Top	Marmot DriClime Windshirt.	Patagonia Houdini Jacket.
Base Layer or Sleeping Clothes	Top: Icebreaker 200 zip neck. Bottom: Patagonia Capilene 2. SmartWool socks.	Icebreaker base layers. SmartWool socks.
Underwear	No. My running shorts have a liner.	No.
Gloves	CAMP G Comp Wind or CAMP G Comp Warm	Cheap fleece thrift store gloves.
Sierra changes	Extra gloves, warmer long underwear bottoms, add down jacket (either Western Mountaineering Flight or Montbell UL).	Extra layers, rain jacket.
Washington changes	Extra gloves, warmer long underwear bottoms, add down jacket (either Western Mountaineering Flight or Montbell UL).	Extra layers, rain jacket.

CLOTHING	Scrub	Hiker Box Special
Hiking Shirt	Long-sleeved button-down nylon shirts. Used both ExOfficio Air Strip Lite and Mountain Hardwear Canyon.	Campo to KM, a Columbia fishing shirt (got torn up by my pack), then a $2 poly thrift store dress shirt from KM to Canada. I like a long sleeve button-down since it keeps sun of your arms and neck, but you can roll the sleeves and open the buttons for venting.
Hiking Shorts	Columbia PFG fishing shorts for most of the trail. Running shorts for Nor Cal and part of Oregon. The only thing I require for hiking shorts is that they have pockets (for tent stakes when I set up the tent, and for money/phone/Yogi maps in town), are synthetic (for swimming), and don't look exceptionally dweeby or molestery.	The North Face running shorts with a liner.
Hiking Pants	ExOfficio convertible hiking pants for the buggy stretch from Mammoth to Echo Lake and mid-Oregon to Canada (I don't use DEET).	Started with pants, but didn't need them. I was hesitant to give up hiking pants and underwear, but running shorts with a liner were much more comfortable and cooler. My legs didn't really get sun burned since I used an umbrella.
Hiking Hat	OR Sun Runner.	OR sun hat. I preferred no hat with my umbrella.
Warm Hat	Merino wool balaclava in the Sierra and Northern Washington only.	No.
Warm Top	Very old Campmor 1/4-zip fleece. Also a wind jacket (started with Marmot Trail Wind Hoodie, switched to Patagonia Houdini).	Marmot Guides Jacket. Pairs well with a lighter weight sleeping bag like the Feathered Friends Vireo.
Base Layer	Merino wool top. Montane Featherlite wind pants. Thin liner socks.	Stoic long underwear bottoms. Patagonia Capilene 3 top.
Underwear	ExOfficio boxer-briefs (the official underwear of male PCT hikers). Worth the $25, because one will last the whole way.	No.
Gloves	Fleece liners only in the Sierra and Northern Washington.	MSR wool blend.
Sierra changes	Balaclava, liner gloves, and a GoLite Bitterroot hooded down coat. I wore these every night for 150 miles.	Hat and gloves.
Washington changes	At Snoqualmie Pass, I had a raincoat, my warm down coat, balaclava, gloves, and a second pair of sleeping clothes mailed to me. I used every single thing and was very happy to have it all. Heading into both Stehekin and Manning pretty much all of it was wet. I would err on the side of having tons of layers to cycle through at that point in the hike.	Hat and gloves.

CLOTHING	BINK
Hiking Shirt	I have used many different types of hiking shirts over the years, but the one thing they have all had in common has been their 100% polyester fabric. You don't need to spend a fortune for this, on my first Yo-Yo hike of the PCT, I hiked the entire 5300 mile trip in the same $3 thrift store shirt.
Hiking Shorts	I prefer running shorts made of a lighter weight polyester material. The downside to these is that they tend to get holes in them pretty easily. However the lighter weight material shorts rub on my legs less as I walk.
Hiking Pants	I rarely carry pants. When I do, they are extremely lightweight breathable ripstop nylon pants.
Hiking Hat	I have mostly worn a baseball style cap with deserts flaps. I have recently decided to go back to the wide brim all around style because my ears have been getting burned with the cap with flaps.
Warm Hat	Wool synthetic blend watch cap.
Warm Top	Long-sleeved polypro.
Base Layer or Sleeping Clothes	None during summer months. In early spring, late fall, or winter trips, I use thin polypro base layers. Clean socks.
Underwear	No. My running shorts have a liner.
Gloves	Very lightweight fleece mittens.
Sierra changes	More clothing.
Washington changes	Umbrella and rain kilt if I don't already have them.

RAIN GEAR

Many hikers use Frogg Toggs, O2 Rainwear, or the Marmot PreCip. Get breathable fabric. Pit-zips are a great rain jacket feature, because they allow you to vent your body heat. If you've got a lot of hair that requires a ponytail, make sure that when your hair is up, and you have your rain jacket on, the rain jacket hat covers your head and the hat bill extends over your face. I've tried 'em all. My current favorite is an old Integral Designs eVent. I pair that with GoLite rain pants or a ULA rain kilt. I always carry an umbrella.

BINK: My latest jacket has been a very lightweight anorak style polyester jacket which is not entirely water proof. I find with days and days of rain and hiking in the rain I end up soaked anyway. GORE-TEX can be overrated, but is nice to have in certain conditions. The brush in Washington will soak you as much as the rain. I found that with many back-to-back days of rain, I (and all of my gear) tend to become progressively wetter as the days go on. The umbrella allows me to endure the rain much easier than I could without one, at least when it is not really windy. If you carry an umbrella, on a northbound trip you will probably rarely use it for rain. But it is good for sun as well as using as a wind break on one end of a tarp.

Scrub: I made a bomb-proof pack cover out of a trash compactor bag. Anyone can do this and I'm surprised more people don't. I cut out two holes to feed the pack's shoulder straps through, then put the trash bag on over the pack. The only downside is that you have to undo the shoulder straps each time you put the cover on or take it off, but the upside is that, unlike almost every other pack cover known to man, it actually stays on and works at keeping the pack dry, and it's cheap as well. My important stuff (sleeping bag and sleeping/down clothes) stayed in their own dry storage inside the pack: the sleeping bag at the bottom in another trash compactor bag, and the clothes in a Sea To Summit silnylon dry sack. Never had a problem with these items getting wet.

RAIN SYSTEM		Rain Jacket	Rain Pants		Pack Liner	Pack Cover	Umbrella
Yogi		Any jacket with eVent fabric.	GoLite pants in Washington. ULA rain kilt everywhere else.		Trash Bag	Yes	Yes
Anish		OR Helium	No		Yes	No	Yes
BINK		Anorak style polyester jacket and ultralight silnylon glove shells.	Used my windpants.		Yes	No	Yes
HBS		No rain jacket. Used my wind jacket and umbrella.	Cheap Columbia rain pants.		Trash Bag	No	Yes
Scrub		Outdoor Research conventional rain jacket only from Snoqualmie Pass to Canada.	No. For the cold rainy days in Washington, I wore long johns underneath my long hiking pants and that worked fine, provided I had a dry layer (my wind pants) to change into for sleeping.		No	Yes	No

FOOTWEAR

The vast majority of thru-hikers wear running shoes. Some hikers wear trail runners. Very few hikers wear traditional heavy hiking boots, but some do! Running shoes are lightweight, breathable, and don't need to be broken in. Look for shoes with a wide base, especially at the ball of the foot, which I believe helps to prevent you from turning your ankle.

Your hiking shoes should be at least one size bigger than you wear now. Your feet will swell a lot!! If your feet swell so much that your feet are crammed into the shoes, don't be afraid to cut your shoes. They're not doing you any good the way they are. I've often had to cut away the part of the shoe that rubs against my ankle. I wear mens shoes, and sometimes they are taller at the ankle than I'd like. So, I trim them down, then repair the cut section with duct tape. I've watched many hikers cut the toes out of their shoes after 100-200 miles 'cause their shoes didn't fit anymore.

The "one size bigger" concept works for normal human beings.
If you are an athlete, your shoe size may not increase during a thru-hike.

Do not get shoes with waterproofing or water resistant materials.
They WILL NOT prevent your feet from getting wet.
They WILL prevent your shoes from drying AFTER getting wet.

ZERO DROP FOOTWEAR

"Zero Drop" describes footwear with the ball of the foot at the same height as the heel, and very little arch support. This type of footwear has become very popular among thru-hikers in the last few years. In theory, it sounds good: the human body wasn't created with heel/arch support, so shoes also should not have heel/arch support. I suppose if you started walking as a toddler without heel/arch support, then this theory would hold true as you grow. But if you've lived for 20, 30, 40, 50 years with heel/arch support, then take away the support while adding the weight of a pack, the result is usually arch, ankle, knee, or hip problems. Your entire body has developed structurally assuming you have heel/arch support. Taking that away is like taking away fence posts and hoping the fence stays up.

This vast majority of thru-hikers solve the "no support" problem by putting expensive insoles into zero drop shoes. O-K-A-Y. What's the point of buying expensive zero drop shoes just to put expensive insoles inside for support? Doesn't make sense. So now they've spent $120 on shoes and $50 on insoles. Podiatrists recommend replacing running shoes every 350 miles; thru-hikers tend to stretch that to 600-700 miles. That means hikers are spending at least $800 on footwear just because everyone else is wearing a certain brand.

Don't think you have to wear a certain brand of shoes just because it's what other hikers wear. Instead, find a brand which supports YOUR body, which feels good on YOUR feet.

HOT WEATHER SHOES

For Campo CA to Kennedy Meadows CA (mile 0 to mile 702.2) and Sierra City CA to Cascade Locks OR (mile 1195.4 to mile 2147.1), you need the lightest-weight, lightest-colored, most breathable shoes possible. The tread is not all that important, because you won't see much snow. You might have some snow near Baden-Powell (mile 377.9) or Fuller Ridge (mile 188.0), but it will only be for a few miles.

When you take off your shoes and socks, your feet should be filthy dirty black (from the sand). If you haven't hiked in SoCal, I can't begin to describe to you how hot the days are. And you're walking on hot sand, so your shoes are doubly hot. So hot, in fact, that when you stop for a break and feel the bottom of your shoes, sometimes they're too hot to touch.

SNOW / WET WEATHER SHOES

For Kennedy Meadows CA to Sierra City CA (mile 702.2 to mile 1195.4) and for Washington (mile 2147.5 to mile 2661.9), you also want lightweight breathable shoes, but pay close attention to the tread. Kennedy Meadows to Sierra City will be covered with snow, and Washington will have wet rocks, rain, and possibly snow and ice. Be sure these shoes have tread with good nubs. No waterproofed shoes! It won't matter. Your feet will be wet most of the time. Wet from fording, wet from postholing, wet from the trail that turns into a stream. The only thing waterproof shoes will do differently from other shoes is that the waterproof shoes will never dry out.

BUYING SHOES

Salespeople will try to sell you shoes which are heavier than you need. They think backpacking with running shoes is a bad idea. They'll also push the waterproof/breathable shoes. Don't buy into the hype. Don't assume that the salespeople know more than you do. Unless they've thru-hiked the PCT or CDT in the last few years, you know way more than they do. You've done your research and you know what you want. State what features you need, then try on as many models of lightweight, breathable shoes as possible. You don't want ANY waterproofing, water resistance, or water protection of any kind. In a strong wind, you should feel the wind blow into your shoes. If running shoes pinch when you try them on at the store, do not buy them. The pinch will not go away. You do not "break in" running shoes like you would "break in" a traditional boot.

The shoes you start the trail with will NOT last the whole hike. You'll go through 4-6 pair of shoes during one thru-hike. Pay close attention to the tread. Look for tread with nubs that can grab snow and rocks. Some of the treads are pretty flat, and looking closely you can see how they would wear down quickly.

ABSOLUTELY do not buy a bunch of shoes now, even if they're on sale. You won't know if they actually work until you get on the trail and hike in them. The one exception would be if you are buying your shoes from Zappos. Zappos offers a 365-day return policy on unworn shoes.

Whenever you need new shoes, order them online and have them delivered to the next town, and pay close attention to where the shoes will be delivered. If it is a General Delivery Post Office addresses, MAKE SURE the box is mailed via Priority Mail through the US Postal Service. NOT UPS, NOT FEDEX. You must be very clear about this when you order your shoes.

Before my first thru-hike, I was a perfect women's size 9.5. Now, I'm a WOMEN'S size 10. While hiking, I wear MEN'S size 10 running shoes (men's shoes have a much wider toe box than women's shoes). I wear one pair of Injinji toe socks. I carry two extra pair of socks and change them often. I rinse the socks out whenever possible. I get new shoes about every 350-400 miles. And I NEVER GET BLISTERS.

GAITERS

From 1999 to 2003, I wore gaiters. They kept dirt/rocks out of my shoes, but my feet didn't breathe well, so I stopped wearing gaiters. Dirty Girl Gaiters hit the hiking scene around 2011. Dirty Girls are fantastic! They breathe well, and they look cool. I now wear gaiters in desert areas where the hostile plants attack my shoes and socks.

CAMP SHOES

Some hikers like to have a lightweight shoe to wear around camp: something that will let your feet breathe or to wear when your hiking shoes are soaked. Many hikers carry Crocs or flip-flops. Chacos and Tevas are great but are too heavy to carry on a thru-hike as camp shoes. I pick up cheap flip-flops if I will be in a section where my feet get wet a lot. Otherwise, my hiking shoes serve as camp shoes.

HIKER OPINIONS

BINK: On my very first long PCT hike in 1992, along with my 70-pound pack (yes it was heavy!), I hiked in a pair of boots that weighed 7 pounds per pair! My pack base weight is now around that.

I have tried many brands of running shoes over the years. The most important consideration is that the shoe must be wide enough for my foot. Many brands of shoes are entirely too narrow for thru-hikers whose feet swell considerably over time. It is not uncommon that people end up jumping a size or even two sizes during the course of their hike. My recommendation is a high quality running shoe that is somewhat wide and not too snug. I consider running shoes or trail runners (not lightweight boots) that have a plastic plate under the forefoot (known as a rock guard) to be better for my feet. I am a heavier hiker (typically 180+ pounds at the start), and the ultralight running shoes do not last for me. Different shoes work for different people, and some folks feel more comfortable in a pair of boots, especially if they have had past ankle injuries, so I recommend trying several kinds on pre-hike training hikes to find what is best for you.

I change shoes any time I have a recurring repetitive stress-type injury. Switching to new shoes or even to a different shoe often helps.

I typically will get about 400 miles at best per a pair of shoes. Many people are surprised to hear this, as it seems many folks get 700+ miles per pair. I find that although the shoes appear fine on the outside, they are broken down internally by this point, especially if you have been hiking a lot of miles in rain or snow.

Hiker Box Special: I switched shoes every time they wore out and never found anything I loved. The first pair was too small so they only lasted 43 miles. SIZE UP! I tried everything, they all suck when your feet are worn out. The best fitting shoes were Altra Lone Peaks, but they had zero stiffness and I could feel every rock.

Scrub: I wore Vasque Mindbender trail runners, size 10.5 (I wear size 10 at home) the whole way. Never looked back, never changed models or sizes, never had a blister. When I finished, I was on my fourth pair, each one lasting 700-800 miles. I wore Darn Tough Hike/Trek 1/4-crew merino wool socks the whole way. I got exactly 900 miles out of my first pair before holes started showing up. Flip-flops are more like "town shoes" or "just got done swimming" shoes. I didn't use them much in camp, because the minute I stop to camp, I'm not getting back up again. However, it's a whole lot safer to walk around, say, the balcony of your motel room in Mojave, CA, in flip-flops than barefoot.

FOOTWEAR	Shoes	Pairs of Shoes	Socks	Gaiters	Camp Shoes
Yogi	Running shoes	6	Injinji	No	No
Anish	Altra Lone Peak	5	Injinji	No	No
BINK	Running shoes	6	Nylon men's dress socks for summer, snow-free trail. Medium weight wool blend socks for snowy sections.	No	No
Hiker Box Special	Running shoes	6	Thin poly running	No	No
Scrub	Vasque Mindbender	4	Darn Tough Hike/Trek 1/4 crew merino wool	No	Yes

PERSONAL CARE

FIRST AID

Thru-hikers take so much Ibuprofen that it is commonly referred to as "Vitamin I."
Check out Leukotape. It's amazing for preventing/curing blisters and back/hip chafe.

First aid options: Ibuprofen, Tinactin, Neosporin, Pamprin, Imodium, Benadryl, Blistex, duct tape, Vaseline, creamy Desitin (for chafing), baby wipes, dental floss, tweezers and scissors (both are on the mini Swiss Army knife), sewing needle, Band-Aids, medical tape, athletic tape, moleskin, Aspirin, antibiotics, Flagyl, alcohol wipes, scissors, super glue.

HYGIENE

Carry a small bottle of Purell hand sanitizer and/or some baby wipes to sanitize your hands after pooping and before eating. This is very important in the prevention of illness.

I clean my feet each time I get to a stream, and I wipe down my entire body with a dedicated body bandana at the end of each day. I take special care to make sure that the chafe-prone areas are always free of sweat and dirt. I carry three pair of hiking socks and two pair of running shorts (with a liner). Each day I rinse one pair of shorts so that I have a "clean" pair for the next day. Truthfully, the shorts are not really clean; they're just cleaner than they were before, plus now they're sweat-free! I rinse my socks every time I get to a stream, attach the wet socks onto my pack with safety pins, and put on a "clean" pair of socks. I try to change my socks at least every 10 miles.

Anish: I wash up once a day with wet wipes or a bandana. Don't use soap or let the dirty water get into the water source.

BINK: I take water bottle showers and swim when possible. Sponge baths do the job in the drier sections when water is scarce. I carry disposable razor heads, which I attach to a stick and shave with out on the trail.

Hiker Box Special: Bandana baths! You don't need soap, just wet your bandana and scrub away the dirty bits. Everyone stinks, so don't bother worrying about it.

Scrub: I was bad at staying clean. The PCT gets you shockingly, revoltingly dirty, and somehow I always ended up with more dirt glommed onto my legs than anybody else. I took foot and leg baths in ponds and streams sometimes, but probably not as often as I could have. I didn't carry soap. No matter how biodegradable it says it is on the label, there's no way it's LNT to use that shit in a natural water source. Hand sanitizer is worthless except to work the dirt on your hands into a permanent film.

DEODORANT

If you think that the only part of your body that will stink is your underarms . . . . well . . . just wait. Hikers sweat EVERYWHERE, and it all smells . . . . like . . . . sweat. Putting deodorant on your underarms won't help. There are other parts of your body that smell WAY worse than your underarms. Think about it, you'll understand. After a few weeks, you won't notice your smell, and everyone around you smells the same – except the day hikers. You will soon acquire the ability to smell them (and their soap) BEFORE you see them.

Packing Slip

YOGI'S BOOKS

Yogi's Books, LLC
98953 Sacatar Ranch Road
Inyokern, CA 93527

Ship To: Emaline Lubinger
2305 Monte Vista Drive
PINOLE, CA 94564 US

Order # 13090
Date 1/22/2021
User emalinelubinger@gmail.com
Ship Date

Description	Price	Qty	Ext. Price
PCT Handbook Books: Yogi's PCT Handbook	$39.95	1	$39.95

	Sub Total:	$39.95
	Tax:	$3.10
	Shipping:	$10.26
	Total:	$53.31

CHAFE

Chafe sucks. I had BAD butt chafe on my second PCT thru-hike. I tried everything to make it better: powder, Vaseline, diaper rash cream, Neosporin. I even tried six different shorts. The only thing that helped, believe it or not, was Vagisil. It lubes your cheeks without being greasy. Men may be hesitant to buy this stuff, but I'm telling you, it cured my problem.

Chafe also happens on your back, shoulders, hips, anyplace where your sweaty clothes rub against your skin. The miracle cream for curing normal chafe is CREAMY DESITIN. Rub it in real good.

Many hikers use Anti Monkey Butt powder or Leukotape.

The best way to handle chafe is to STAY CLEAN. I find that if I frequently wash the sweat/dirt off my chafe-prone areas and my clothing, then I usually don't get chafe. Whenever you feel the chafe coming on, stop immediately and rinse that area with water.

BINK: I have a personal theory that the dirt and salt from sweat on skin and in clothes combined with bacteria makes this problem worse. I feel that staying as clean as practical and cleaning your clothes frequently helps reduce chafing.

Hiker Box Special: I had chafe on and off, treated it with Neosporin. That stuff is a wonder drug. After I switched to running shorts, getting chafe was rare.

Scrub: I only had butt chafe a few times, always during a cool and gentle afternoon (when I wasn't sweating much) that had been preceded by a hot morning (when I had sweated a lot). Body Glide worked in almost all cases, except one really bad day which came before Sierra City when I had to make myself a chew toy out of a Gatorade cap just to get the last 10 miles done. But that was an extreme case.

TOILET PAPER

Pack it out. Dig your hole to poop, but please pack out your toilet paper. It's really not that messy. Trail poop is different from off-trail poop. It must have something to do with the food we eat while hiking. Cleaning yourself after pooping requires very little toilet paper, cause you're just not very messy. Pack out your toilet paper in a ziplock bag. If you bury your TP, it might biodegrade in a few months, but in the meantime animals are digging it up. Nobody wants to see your used toilet paper.

Anish: You don't need toilet paper. Use natural substances, leaves, sticks rocks, etc. If you do use TP, pack it out!

BINK: On one of my Yo-Yo hikes, I did an experiment when I went back south from Canada: I dug up (and re-buried of course) many of the catholes that I had used on my way north to check on their decomposition. I could find no sign of feces in holes more than three weeks old. The toilet paper, however, seemed to take much more time to degrade. Not until I checked a hole almost two months old did I find the paper was degraded.

I noticed that holes where I used peroxide whitened, "natural" toilet paper (rather than standard chlorine bleach whitened toilet paper), the "natural" toilet paper was breaking down 2-3 times faster. This proved to me what I have heard for years, that bacteria has a very difficult time attacking the cellulose fibers in standard toilet paper due to the PH from the bleaching process. The "natural" brands of toilet paper cost more, but you might consider the environmental effects of different types of TP. All this might seem a bit overboard to you. But the PCT is my second home, and I am always trying to lessen my impact upon it. And no, I do not re-dig my catholes as a normal course, but that one year it was an interesting experiment.

Hiker Box Special: BURY IT DEEP! I saw way too many rocks with TP and shit under them, GROSS. I went ultralite, but still carried a trowel.

Crater Lake, Oregon

<u>Scrub</u>: I used natural sources when I could find them (there are big leafy plants all over California north of the desert). If those weren't readily available, I used TP and buried it. Packing out TP sounds pretty gross to me, and I don't think I'd do it unless it were required.

I had always dug respectable catholes, but one thing happened that changed my mind about that: I was in Northern California when I rounded a bend and saw an enormous buck standing five feet off the trail digging at something in the ground. Unlike the other deer in the area, he really did not care about my presence at all. I was in such awe at the presence of this majestic creature, who was letting me get so close to him, but I wondered what it was that he could possibly be so focused on in the ground? And then the TP and poop started flying up and he started snacking on it as I looked on in horror. It changed the way I thought about cute little deer forever, and it also made me dig my catholes REALLY REALLY deep from then on.

MENSTRUATION

Ladies, always be prepared. Many women are not regular while thru-hiking. Always carry tampons/pads, a piece of foil, and whatever medication you use for cramps. You cannot bury tampons or pads in the ground. You cannot put them in privys/outhouses. You MUST pack them out. Place the used tampon/pad in a ziplock bag. Wrap the bag in a piece of foil. The foil will mask any odor.

<u>Anish</u>: Pads are safer than tampons from a hygiene standpoint. Regardless of what you choose, pack it out!!!

CONTACTS AND GLASSES

Many hikers wear contacts while thru-hiking. Contacts are no more work on the trail than they are at home. If you wear contacts, choose your sunglasses carefully. There is fine, fine, fine sand on the entire PCT. It blows and gets everywhere. If you can find sunglasses that wrap around the side of your face a bit, this will help keep the sand out of your eyes. But you don't want your sunglasses to be snug against your face. If they're too close to your cheeks, they'll fog up when you get hot and sweaty. You don't need the sunglasses with the leather pieces at the temple. Just get some dorky aviator-type glasses – something with a little side protection.

Get the one-day disposable contacts for your hike. You put a new pair of contacts in every morning, take them out at night and throw them away. With a new pair of contacts each day, you will get very little irritation. Plus, carrying extra contacts is much lighter than carrying contact solution.

POISON OAK

Know what it looks like and avoid it. Google "Poison Oak Images" and you'll get itchy just staring at the computer screen.

You'll find Poison Oak in Southern California and also from Sierra City to Oregon.

When you are traveling in areas with Poison Oak, be very careful to NOT touch the bottoms of your shoes and hiking poles. Your shoes and poles could have the Poison Oak oils on them. Many hikers use their hiking poles to scratch mosquito bites on their legs. If your pole has been in Poison Oak, then you scratch your leg with your pole, you could spread the Poison Oak oils onto your skin.

Calamine will help with the itching, but Zanfel will heal the rash. Although Zanfel is expensive, I wouldn't hike without it. Why? Because Zanfel STOPS the itch and STOPS the Poison Oak from spreading all over your body. From the Zanfel website: "Zanfel is the only product known to remove urushiol, the toxin responsible for the reaction, from the skin after bonding, enabling the affected area to immediately begin healing. After using Zanfel, the itching and pain are the first things to be relieved, usually within 30 seconds."

POODLE-DOG BUSH

Yeah, the name sounds silly, but this is no joke. Do not touch it!

Poodle-Dog Bush rash (worse than Poison Oak) has sent MANY hikers to the hospital.
Poodle Dog Bush is all over Southern California in areas which have recently burned.

Poodle-Dog Bush has many different appearances, depending upon if the plant is flowering (lavender, purple, blue) or not. The plant ranges in size from an small shrub to over six feet tall. It grows in the trail, on the side of the trail, and hangs over the trail.

Wear long pants and long-sleeved shirts, and wash those clothes separately from your other clothes. If there is a detour around a Poodle-Dog Bush area, TAKE IT!

BINK: On my 2011 southbound hike, I started showing symptoms of poodle-dog bush itching a week before I finished. I was itching HEAD TO TOE EVERYWHERE, even the soles of my feet, for a month after I got off the trail! It was quite an experience, to say the least. If I had been northbounding, this would have really negatively affected my hike. Luckily, I was finished hiking by the time it became really bad. I really didn't treat it except with anti-itch cream. It seems like most people don't react this way, but man oh man I sure had it!

Scrub: Poodle-Dog Bush reeks of weed and you will probably smell it before you see it. It really pisses everybody off after awhile, but it's not something to get overly worried about, because there are thorough warnings about it in Halfmile's notes, Yogi's Book, and the Water Report.

THE DESERT

DESERT HIKING ADVICE

♦ Arrive at Campo fully hydrated. That doesn't mean that you drink a gallon of water the day that you leave home. You've got to start earlier. It takes several days to fully hydrate your body. A few weeks before your trip, start hydrating. Water, water, water. All day long.

♦ A big part of managing your water in the desert is making sure your body uses the water you drink. An umbrella goes a long way to help with this. The umbrella keeps the sun's rays from directly hitting your body, which keeps your body cooler, which decreases the amount of water you lose through sweat.

♦ Every time — and I mean EVERY TIME — you take a break, remove your shoes and socks, and elevate your feet. Let your feet breathe. Rinse your socks every time you get to a stream. Change your socks frequently.

♦ Get up early in the morning. Begin hiking shortly after dawn. Don't hike between noon and 4 p.m. Find a shady spot and park yourself for the entire afternoon. Take a nap. Eat your dinner for lunch. You've got plenty of time to cook.

♦ Don't store your water at the very top of your pack. It will get very hot up there.
Pack it a little lower, with your jacket or other insulating gear on top of the water.

♦ Carry electrolyte drinks (Gatorade powder, Propel, NUUN tablets, MIO drops).

♦ Tank up. I try to drink at least one liter at every source.

Anish: Drink! Take electrolytes, B vitamins and vitamin C. Wear long sleeves, sunglasses, a visor, etc. Carry an umbrella. Be prepared for COLD. I had advanced stage hypothermia in the Anza-Borrego Desert (Scissors Crossing area).

BINK: Carry and consume lots of water when it is very hot (100+ degrees), have some type of electrolyte replacement drink or product available. I use an umbrella because much of the mountainous areas of Southern California lack shade now, due to the many fires in the last 12 years or so. Loose-fitting lightweight clothing helps a lot. I have hiked on days that were as hot as 118 degrees. I find anything over 110 degrees, which is rare, demands careful attention to your body and its needs throughout the day.

Hiker Box Special: UMBRELLA, UMBRELLA, UMBRELLA! It will extend your hiking hours and save you water and weight in sunscreen.

Early morning in the Mojave

Scrub: People hate on the desert way too much. I really enjoyed it and thought it was stunningly beautiful the whole way through (with the exception of the burn areas). No one likes the constant looming threat of running out of water, though, and it takes a psychological toll after a while, especially at the end in the Mojave where the water situation is at its worst and the Sierra is so tantalizingly close. Just play it cool, be smart but not stressed about the water and the midday heat, and I can almost promise you'll like the desert.

It rained on me on four out of my first five days in the desert, starting May 5. When I got into Mt. Laguna on the end of the second day, it had rained all day and I hadn't layered properly and was borderline hypothermic. I needed 30 minutes in the hot showers to revive. So you should be ready for anything, no matter when you start.

I would say that about 50% of my days in the desert were hot enough that I was forced into some kind of afternoon break. This ranged from a little 1.5-2 hour siesta in the shade, to 7 hours utterly alone under a solitary Joshua tree at Bird Spring Pass (mile 630.8) on a 105-degree day. I didn't have a hard-and-fast rule about when or when not to break, but if you pay attention to how you're feeling, you can tell if you're operating at a loss and your strength and hydration is being sapped unsustainably fast. I was usually able to tell by noon what kind of day it was in that regard.

I tried to eat a little something every time I got to a water source so that I wouldn't pig out on water alone and become hyponatremic, which has happened to me before in Arizona and it SUCKS. I would err on the side of carrying more water than you think you need, at least until you get very confident in judging your water consumption in all conditions. If you have too much water, you will *always* be able to find someone thirstier than you, on whom you can offload a liter. Everyone wins.

There is a huge difference in how you dress for the dry, direct heat of the desert than the humid heat of the East Coast. On the AT, everyone's strategy was wear as little as possible – shirts off, short shorts, etc. If you did that in the desert on the PCT, you'd turn into a human tortilla chip. I personally found that, counterintuitively, wearing long sleeves and covering up my neck in the heat of the day kept me cooler, not to mention prevented sunburn.

In the desert with the really intense sun, I walked with the sleeves rolled down most of the time – I wanted my skin to be in the shade and my sweat to hang out on my arms as long as possible and not evaporate instantly. This would only work, I think, if you had a shirt made of loose, high-performance wicking fabric, otherwise your shirt would just stick to you and suffocate you. I did side-by-side tests with one sleeve down and one sleeve rolled up and found that I felt cooler with the sleeves down. For the rest of the trail, where there wasn't quite such dry and direct heat, I hiked with sleeves rolled up most of the way.

I did a similar experiment with my hiking hat. I hiked in an Outdoor Research Sun Runner, which is a baseball hat with mesh venting on the sides and a removable neck flap for sun protection. I ran tests in the desert to decide whether I was cooler with the neck flap down or up, and it was definitely cooler down. You want to shade as much of your head and neck as possible in SoCal. My hat was synthetic, so I could throw it in the washing machine in town and it came out looking good as new. I used the neck flap a lot in the desert and then mailed the flap home after the Sierra when I realized I wasn't using it at all anymore.

SUNSCREEN

The PCT is definitely not a "long green tunnel" like the AT. The PCT is rarely in the trees. Instead, the trail is almost always exposed. The sun is constant on the PCT. Try to have some sort of base tan before starting the trail. And you've got to use sunscreen. I've always kept it until Central Oregon.

BINK: I generally only will use sunscreen on my nose, and only in the High Sierra.

Hiker Box Special: No sunscreen, just a big hat and my umbrella. If you use poles, keep some sunscreen for your hands.

Scrub: Clothes are better than chemicals. I never used a drop of sunscreen. I wore shorts, so my calves got a little burned the first day. Because I was in long sleeves and had my sheik hat on whenever it was bright and sunny, the rest of my body was allowed to tan pretty gently over a few weeks.

SUNGLASSES

You need sunglasses for the entire trail. You don't have to spend a fortune on sunglasses. Target and Walmart sell polarized sunglasses for about $10.

Anish: I wear polarized sunglasses.

BINK: I would not consider hiking the PCT without sunglasses.
Unlike the AT, I consider sunglasses a necessary piece of equipment on any PCT hike.

Hiker Box Special: Sent my sunglasses home, the hat and umbrella worked fine.

Scrub: I normally dislike sunglasses, but I had old-school glacier goggles through the desert and Sierra that I wore maybe every one out of four days. In the desert and Sierra, there are some places where the rocks around you are so bright-white, and the midday sunlight is so direct overhead (think of the latitude and the time of year), that you feel like you're in a reflector oven even if it's not especially hot out. If you hike through the Sierra in snow, then you need sunglasses even more. I'd consider sunglasses essential for the first 1000 miles (I sent them home after that and never wanted them again).

SUN HAT

You need a good sun hat with a brim to shade your face. Most hikers use a wide-brim hat. Other hikers use a ball cap style hat combined with a bandana to shade the neck area.

If you've got a lot of hair that requires a ponytail, try to find a hat with a wide brim PLUS a hole in the back (like a ball cap has) for your ponytail. If you try to stuff all your hair up inside your hat, you will roast from the heat. I know. I've got a lot of hair.

Your sun hat should have a chin strap. The trail is very windy. You don't want to lose your hat to the wind. The chin strap might have a small leather piece which can be used to cinch the strap under your chin. Cut the leather piece off (but don't cut through the chin strap) and add a cord lock. The leather pieces don't cinch the strap very well. The cord lock works much better. After adding the cord lock, tie a small knot at the center of the chin strap. The knot will prevent the cord lock from slipping off the strap.

Gottago at the Southern Monument

WATER CACHES

DON'T COUNT ON WATER CACHES. If they're there, great. But you shouldn't rely on them. The one time you do, that cache will be dry. Don't drink directly out of the water bottles at the caches – that is DISGUSTING. You are leaving your germs on the bottle for the next person. Instead, pour the water into your own water bottle, and drink from that. Take only what you need.

The dramatic increase in the number of hikers in recent years had a dire effect on the water caches: the Trail Angels who stock them simply cannot keep up with demand. Some caches go through 100+ gallons of water a day, and that isn't enough. I personally spoke with several hikers who arrived without water and found empty caches. They counted on the caches; they were then stuck in the desert without water, with the next natural water 10+ miles away. This can be life-threatening.

Water caches were easy to maintain a few years ago. A Trail Angel could go to a road crossing with 50 gallons of water, return to restock the cache a week later and the cache wouldn't be empty yet. That was do-able back when there were only 300 or so hikers on the PCT each year. Now there are well over 4000 thru-hikers each year. It's simply not possible to keep up with the demand for water at the caches.

For this reason, we have decided to remove all notes regarding water caches from the "Trail Tips and Town Guide" section of this book. We feel that by advertising the location of water caches, we are all contributing to life-and-death situations that hikers find themselves in by relying on caches. By not advertising the caches, we hope that hikers will rely on themselves to find and carry water from natural sources, rather than rely on retired Trail Angels to haul water for physically fit hikers.

Anish: Don't count on water caches. Ever.

BINK: Up until the early 2000's, water caches did not exist and people did just fine without them. Water caches have become a massive intrusion on the PCT. Piles of broken up water bottles now line many sections of the trail. We have a choice NOT to utilize them. However, we do not appear to have a choice that they appear out on the PCT to begin with.

I understand that the people who put these out are trying to help out, but in reality they are placing a man-made element out on the PCT that is detrimental to the wilderness character of the PCT itself. Ask any southbounder about the water caches and see what they found upon arriving at them: in many cases, empty water bottles scattered in the wind and associated trash scattered about.

The same can be said for much of the "trail magic" that people put out onto the trail. After the coolers are empty, they become trash barrels overflowing with hikers' trash bags. I categorically avoid the use of the water caches. Unfortunately, they are too convenient for most folks; after all, most people will utilize whatever resources are available to them. I have a feeling the water caches are here to stay.

There are now a few individuals who have taken it upon themselves to destroy the caches in the first 300 miles. I am aware that one of them is a Park Ranger for the Anza-Borrego State Park and is destroying the caches as part his job of protecting the Park. I AM NOT ASSOCIATED with the destruction of them and do not condone these acts. Far too many people rely upon the caches now, and someone could be put into a dangerous situation by these actions.

Hiker Box Special: Water caches enable lazy hikers to feel entitled to special treatment. Hikers freaked out when the caches were empty. Just carry extra water.

Scrub: Some of the caches are unbelievable feats of volunteer work – you get to a dirt road, and you are Out There in the Middle of Nowhere, and there are 75 gallons of water sitting in the shade for you to drink just because you've decided you're going to try to hike some stupid trail for five months of your life. It's kind of nonsensical when you think about it.

I used caches as little as possible. It was pretty easy to plan for natural sources because I usually had a recently updated Water Report on my phone. Only once did I take more than a liter. I treated the caches as helpful but inessential supplements to the natural sources in the area.

WATER REPORT

The PCT Water Report contains first-hand information from people who have recently been on the PCT. One of the last things you should do before leaving home is to print the Water Report. Take it with you as you begin your hike. [www.pctwater.com].

Scrub: In Southern California, you should find some way to have the Water Report accessible. I was able to view it on my phone offline with Google Drive, but you could also have it printed out and use computers in town to get updates. It's worth way more than a map for the first 750 miles.

THE SIERRA

SIERRA HIKING ADVICE

Be prepared for your mileage to drop in the Sierra. If you've been doing 25 miles per day or more prior to Kennedy Meadows, you'll drop to 17 or 18 miles per day through Tuolumne. You'll be slowed down by stream crossings, postholing, snow/ice-covered passes, higher elevation, and losing/finding the trail. And, of course, by the constant beauty. Wow. This place is amazing.

BINK: Hiking the Sierra is no different than any other part of the PCT except for the facts that in many years it will hold snowpack well into the summer, and there are regulations we are required to adhere to. Other than that, I would say things are really no different than most of the rest of the trail. The one bonus is that water is usually readily available. Be aware that if you enter the Sierra early in the season before the snowpack begins to melt, your daily mileage will be significantly lower. I typically have a 40 mile per day average for the rest of the trail, but my average mileages over the years in the High Sierra are:

April	7-15 miles per day
Early May	10-18 miles per day
Late May to June	15-25 miles per day

SIERRA SNOW LEVELS

Everybody panics. You've decided to hike the PCT. You started by purchasing books, researching gear, picking out our shoes, backpacks, and sleeping bags. Should you take a filter or use Aquamira? Tent or tarp? Why don't any previous thru-hikers have underwear on their gear lists?

You get all that figured out and then it hits you — OH, MY GOD!!! There is SNOW in the Sierra! It's not melting! Another storm is about to hit Southern California! Doesn't that mean it will also snow in the Sierra? What do I do? HELP ME!!!

Here's the thing with the snow: EVERY year this snow panic happens PCT social media sites. Everyone freaks out. Eventually, there will be a year when all the scary snow predictions are correct — and that could happen the year YOU decide to hike. But the truth is that you have decided to hike the PCT THIS YEAR. You've given notice at work, you've made arrangements to put your stuff in storage or sublease your apartment/house, you've convinced your friends/family that you're not insane, and you're excited for your hike to begin. You've planned and researched and all you think about now is standing at the Mexican border looking north to Canada.

Now it's January, and you've discovered a graph which shows the Sierra has more snow than ever before. Maybe you should postpone your hike for another year.

DON'T DO IT!!! Don't postpone. Continue with your plans. Go to Campo and hike north. You have six weeks from the time you start your hike until you reach Kennedy Meadows (the beginning of the Sierra). A lot can happen in six weeks. There could be a huge melt (Yay!), there could be huge late spring storms (Oh, No!), or things could be "normal" (huh?). The truth is that nobody knows what the Sierra will be like when the thru-hikers get there in June. Don't let December-to-April snow predictions freak you out. If the Sierra IS impassable, then you and all the other thru-hikers will figure out what to do. You will not be alone.

My favorite comment about PCT snow predictions comes from Little John. He says:

*When I met Freefall the year before my thru-hike, I was curious about the amount of snow in the High Sierra. He left Kennedy Meadows early and spent a lot of time hiking in the snow. Here is what he told me: "You are going to hear at least a dozen times between now and the time you get to Kennedy Meadows about the **record snowfall, the most snow in history, and the worst year to hike the PCT ever.** Don't pay any attention to any of it. Because you will be hearing it from people who will NOT be standing with you at the top of Forester Pass. There WILL be snow and you WILL hike over it to get to where you need to go. It's not that bad." He was right on all counts.*

Mather Pass: 12,100 feet

SNOW WEBSITES

Whew! Glad I was able to convince you to continue with your plans.
If you're still feeling brave, check out these snow websites:

The California Snow Page	Information on snow levels [http://cdec.water.ca.gov/snow/]
California Snow Water Content	Historical graphs [http://cdec.water.ca.gov/cgi-progs/products/PLOT_SWC.pdf] [https://cdec.water.ca.gov/snow/current/snow/index.html]
Mountain Snowpack Maps	Maps for the Western United States [www.wcc.nrcs.usda.gov/cgibin/westsnow.pl]

SIERRA SNOW TRAVEL

You may not have a good idea of what we're talking about when we mention the passes. Imagine a ski slope like you'd see in the Olympics for downhill ski racing. The REALLY steep slopes. Okay, now imagine that it's covered with snow/ice and you're traveling across the slope, while angling either up to the crest or down from the crest. Where would you go if you slipped? You'd fly hundreds of feet down the icy slope. How would you stop? Well, that would happen when you slam into a boulder or a tree or a frozen lake. You could break a bone or worse. The passes are damn scary when they're covered with snow and ice.

Try to plan your days in the Sierra so you are NOT crossing a pass early in the morning. You MUST give the snow time to soften. If you're there too early in the day, you will be walking on ice. But don't wait too long. In the afternoon the snow gets very soft, causing you to posthole. Postholing is where you are walking on top of soft, deep snow and your foot (or both feet) sink into the snow. You often sink up to your knee, thigh, or butt. Sometimes you can recover easily, other times you have to dig out your legs. Not easy to do, especially wearing a backpack. Sometimes, after digging out one leg, you put all your weight on the other leg to try to get out of the hole, and guess what? The other leg sinks all the way in. Postholing is exhausting.

While hiking on sketchy steep slopes, we're NEVER sure that ANY step we take will hold. It's very tense. And scary. And nerve-wracking. And dangerous. Hikers have died in the Sierra from slipping on icy slopes and from getting swept away in fast-moving creeks.

As Billy Goat climbed up the steep snow steps between the first and second switchbacks on Mather Pass, one of his legs postholed and he flipped back, ending with his back against the snow and his head upside down looking out into space. The only thing that kept him from sliding down the pass was his leg which had postholed up past his knee.

This is serious stuff.

You might first see snow on Mt. Whitney or Forester Pass. Take time on the approach to Whitney or Forester and practice with your ice axe. It will be good practice and probably a lot of fun!! Once snow starts melting, it melts FAST. The longer you can put off your Kennedy Meadows date, the better the snow situation will be. Of course, you'll also have more mosquitos and deeper creek crossings. Pick your poison. Aren't choices great?

Anish: Stay calm. It's never as bad as you think it will be.

BINK: There really is nothing tricky to snow travel, just do not plan on doing the kinds of daily mileages that you had been doing prior to hitting the snow. Ascending the passes early in the morning before it heats up will save you tons of effort. On the other hand, the north sides will be icy, and I recommend carrying an ice axe and knowing how to use it. Hiking poles? I have seen many snapped hiking poles from people attempting to self arrest with them. In many years you can get away without an ice axe through the High Sierra, it just depends on conditions. Don't be daunted by the snow! It is taxing, and it presents navigation issues, but in general it can be quite an adventure. Don't like the snow? Wait a few weeks. The melt rate is incredible by late June of most years. A week or two of melt can mean many more miles of dry trail in a big snow season.

ICE AXE and TRACTION DEVICES

ICE AXE

An ice axe is a tool used on both the ascent and descent of steep terrain in frozen conditions. The adze is used to cut footsteps in ice (also great for catholes!). The pick is used to plunge into ice/snow to stop a person from sliding down a steep snowy/icy slope.

Used properly, the ice axe could save your life. Don't just buy an ice axe, and then hope you'll figure it out. Get some training. Do a web search or check with your local outfitter. You might find an ice axe class.

Google this: "how to self-arrest." There are many self-arrest videos online.
Learn how to use the axe BEFORE you begin your hike.

But here's the problem: You won't know if you need the ice axe until you are close to the Sierra. That's several weeks AFTER you begin your northbound hike. So, DON'T BUY AN ICE AXE YET. If you need one, you can pick one up in Kennedy Meadows at Triple Crown Outfitters. If you buy it before your hike, you have to pay to ship it to Kennedy Meadows. There is a chance you won't even need it so you'll have to pay to ship it back home. Just wait to see if you need it, and if you do, then buy it in Kennedy Meadows.

Early season hikers will have TONS of snow. I only know about the snow situations I encountered during early June in 2001-2002-2003-2007. I've walked the Sierra both with and without an ice axe. I am not an expert on traveling over snow and ice. I had no training. I was there, and had to keep moving forward. None of the hikers who've commented in this book are experts. We're simply presenting what we did and saw on our thru-hikes.

Here's the thing: hikers rarely take their ice axes off their packs. They cross the passes using their poles. If you carry an ice axe, be sure to learn how too self-arrest, and put the axe in your hands. It will not help you if it is strapped to the back of your pack.

Should you carry an ice axe or not? This is a personal decision. If you know how to self-arrest, and you've got your ice axe in your hands when you slip, the ice axe could save your life. But you MUST know how to use it.

TRACTION DEVICES: CRAMPONS and MICRO SPIKES

Traction devices attach to your shoes, giving you extra traction on ice. Crampons strap onto your shoes, micro spikes stretch over your shoes. Crampons are more sturdy, and provide more traction. Micro spikes weigh less and provide less traction than crampons.

I did not use traction devices on my four trips through the Sierra on the PCT. On the CDT in 2012, I used crampons in Glacier National Park. REAL crampons, not micro spikes. Holy cow! Crampons are fantastic. I was much more confident, and more important, my steps were secure. Crossing icy terrain isn't scary when every step is a sure step. I'll definitely carry crampons on future PCT hikes.

WHERE DO YOU NEED AN ICE AXE AND/OR TRACTION DEVICES ?

If you hike during a thru-hiker season (leaving Kennedy Meadows before July), and if you're going to carry an ice axe and traction devices, you need them from Kennedy Meadows (mile 702.2) to Echo Lake (mile 1092.3). Some people say you can get rid of your axe/traction devices at Tuolumne or Sonora Pass. I disagree, because there is still substantial snow north of Tuolumne, including "Elephant's Back" just before Carson Pass (only 15 miles before Echo Lake). Elephant's Back has snow conditions similar to the Sierra passes.

You might encounter snow on Fuller Ridge (mile 188.0) or going up Baden-Powell (mile 377.9). Some people suggest having an ice axe and traction devices for these sections.

Anish: In 2005, I sent my ice axe and crampons to Kennedy Meadows and mailed them home from Tahoe. For that year it was the right stretch. Other years are different. I self-arrested glissading near Sonora Pass in 2005.

BINK: I have had serious self-arrest incidents on numerous occasions on PCT hikes, both in the High Sierra and on southbound hikes in the North Cascades. I consider an ice axe an absolute necessity for any southbounder starting the PCT before mid-July. The North Cascades contain some treacherous places when snowbound. Just north of Snoqualmie Pass (I-90) is a place known as Chickamin Ridge. The traverse in this section in early season contains numerous high angle snow chutes where an unchecked slide could be lethal. There have been several deaths in this area from such slides, although none of PCT hikers that I am aware of. On several occasions, I have self- arrested here from falls that could have resulted in serious injury or death. Look up pictures of the "cat walk." Imagine that filled in with snow. You will want an ice axe here.

As for the High Sierra, I consider the north side of Glen Pass to be one of the more dangerous slopes to be on in icy conditions. But all of this depends on timing and the type of year it is. Some years carrying an ice axe would be a waste of time, so don't take my "carry an ice axe" advice as absolute. It seems most northbounders these days do not carry axes, but the last few seasons have been very dry.

Where you need an ice axe all depends on the year. On a northbound hike, I pick up my ice axe at Kennedy Meadows (the southern one) and carry it to Echo Lake. On southbound trips starting in June, I have started the hike with one and carried it through all of Washington. Oregon can have a few nasty spots as well if you are there early. In the Mt. Jefferson area, there are several areas where the tread (when snowbound) can present many miles of very high angle (40 degrees plus) traversing on snow slopes. I have been unfortunate enough to have been here in heavy snow years in early July without an ice axe, and the slow crawl that became my hiking pace was frustrating and nerve wracking on some of the exposed areas.

WHERE SHOULD YOU PICK UP SNOW/ICE GEAR?

Some years, you may want snow/ice gear on Fuller Ridge (just north of Idyllwild), and on Mt. Baden-Powell (just north of Wrightwood).

The vast majority of PCT hikers pick up their snow/ice gear in Kennedy Meadows (mile 702.2). This is the last on-trail resupply spot prior to entering the High Sierra. No matter what your start date is from Campo, you have no way to know what date you will arrive in Kennedy Meadows, or what the snow conditions will be in the Sierra when you get there. It's impossible to predict when and how fast the snow will melt out in the Sierra. Because of this, we recommend you do not purchase snow/ice gear until one-two weeks before you get to Kennedy Meadows, using one of three options:

- When you are in Mojave/Tehachapi, order your ice axe and traction devices from Triple Crown Outfitters website [https://triplecrownoutfitters.com/] and have your gear waiting for you at Triple Crown Outfitters' physical location when you get to Kennedy Meadows.

- Wait until you get to Kennedy Meadows, and purchase at Triple Crown Outfitters right in Kennedy Meadows.

- Order from another online dealer and have your gear shipped to Grumpy Bear's Retreat in Kennedy Meadows [http://www.grumpybearsretreat.com/].

GLISSADING

I love to glissade! It's my reward for the tough climb up the pass. It's also not really very smart. Glissading is when you sit on your butt and slide down a snowfield, like you would do if you had a sled. Problem is that when you glissade, you don't know what's at the bottom or even where the bottom is. But it's a quick fun way to get down off a pass. For me, it's also less exhausting and scary than trying to gently step across an icy slope. I look at glissading as a controlled slide, rather than the out-of-control experience I'm sure I would have if I slipped from a standing position.

There are dangers when glissading:

- It's possible to go out of control. To avoid that, I tend to dig my heels in.
  Consequently, I don't glissade as fast as everyone else. Fear. It gets me every time.

- Make sure you can see where you're going.
  You don't want to glissade over a cliff or into a lake.

- You can't see what's under the snow. Imagine if there was an air pocket under the snow on your glissade path. If you fell into that butt-first, you could be really stuck.

- Do not push your pack in front of you. Why? Because it can't stop itself.

SUNSCREEN and SUNGLASSES

When you are walking on snow, don't forget to put sunscreen on your neck, the bottom of your chin, your ears, the underneath part of your arms, and the part of your face that is normally shaded by your hat. Because in the snow, you are getting attacked by sun rays from all directions, not just from above. Don't forget sunglasses! They are more important on snow than in the desert. Grasshopper (2002) hiked without sunglasses and went snowblind in the Sierra.

Mt. Whitney summit

MT. WHITNEY

The Mt. Whitney side trip is only 17 miles round trip from Crabtree Meadow. Don't miss it!! You are only 8.5 miles from the top of the tallest mountain in the 48 contiguous states, and you are in the best shape of your life. Don't pass this up. You may never get the chance to summit Whitney again. Leave Kennedy Meadows with an extra day of food to account for your Whitney trip.

Anish: I hiked Mt. Whitney in 2005. It was well worth it. I recommend camping at Crabtree or Guitar Lake and summiting early in the day.

BINK: In 1992 I hiked up Mt. Whitney and slept on top. The view of the stars up there at night is amazing! Although it involves plenty of regulations and crowds of people on top, this side trip is worth it. Like any highest mountain, people want to see it for that reason alone, and I suppose this is the main drive for many to visit it.

Hiker Box Special: DO IT! The views are amazing and when else will you be in the best hiking shape of your life and a stone's throw from the highest peak in the lower 48? The Whitney side trip was basically the turnaround of the hike for me. By the time I got to Whitney, I was frustrated at still being footsore, still having pack rash, and being 60 miles into the most talked about part of the trail without much in the way of scenery. I was questioning how much further I wanted to continue. Once I hit the summit of Whitney, I felt so much joy at being there that I knew I had to go on. After Crabtree Meadow the trail just got more and more incredible and I never looked back.

Scrub: I started the PCT not very enthusiastic about the idea of climbing Whitney, because every other big mountain I'd climbed in my life up til that point had led to me feeling half-dead at the summit from altitude sickness. But as a thru-hiker, I was in such good shape and so acclimated by that point that I felt fantastic at the top. In fact, all the thru-hikers up there did. Meanwhile, nearly every single day-hiker looked abjectly miserable (understandably so, when you consider what they just put themselves through, coming straight up the other side from Lone Pine).

I would encourage all thru-hikers to go up Mt. Whitney, conditions permitting. People hike Whitney at all times of the day – for sunset with a hike down afterward, camping at the summit overnight, night-climbing for sunrise at the top, or a daylight trip like my friends and I did. You won't be alone no matter when you do it.

FORDING CREEKS

In the Sierra, your feet are constantly wet from fording, postholing, and from walking in the wet trail. And I mean CONSTANTLY wet. Don't even bother taking off your hiking shoes when fording. You've probably got another ford within the next two miles anyway. Stopping to take off your shoes just slows you down and allows the mosquitos to feast on you.

Cupcake and I called wet feet "freedom." Why? Because "freedom's just another word for nothin' left to lose." Once your feet are wet, you can step anywhere.

The depth of most of the fords ranges from ankle deep to mid-thigh deep. I'm 5'10" and the deepest creeks I've forded were up to my hips. The bad fords usually hit me mid-thigh. I've never got my pack wet, and I've never fallen in. The two worst fords are usually Bear Creek (mile 869.1) and Rancheria Creek in Kerrick Canyon (mile 979.8). You'll hear about how bad Evolution Creek (mile 850.9) is. I've never had trouble with Evolution.

- Leaving your shoes on when fording will give you more traction on the slippery rocks in the creek. Even if it wasn't helpful, it would still be pointless to remove your shoes. Your feet will be wet all day anyway.

- Hiking poles will help you keep your balance. If you don't have poles, try to find large sticks.

- Don't always cross the creek at the point where the PCT goes into the water. That's not always the best spot.

- Calm water isn't always best, because calm water is usually deep water.

- If the water is fast, face upstream and shuffle to your side. You will have MUCH MORE strength in your legs to fight the water if you are facing upstream.

- Creek bottoms are not flat. You could be up to your knees with one step, up to your hips with the next step.

- Small short women: DO NOT give your pack to someone else to carry across the stream for you. The weight of your pack will help hold you down in strong water.

- To keep your gear dry, line the inside of your pack with a heavy trash bag, double-ziplock-bag anything electronic, and always pack your sleeping bag in a waterproof dry bag. ALWAYS.

- During the day, the snow melts and the water flows downhill, causing the creeks to rise. Therefore, the best time to ford is early in the morning when the creeks are at their lowest level for the day. However, thru-hikers do not have the luxury of always being at the right place at the right time.

Anish: Use trekking poles or sticks to stabilize yourself if the water is strong or very deep. Don't be afraid to go up or downstream looking for a safer crossing. Camp and wait for the lower morning water levels if you need to.

BINK: Creek fording can be the single most dangerous part of a typical PCT hike. My advice is hit them early in the morning. If you don't feel comfortable fording, search for a log or a better spot. You may lose many miles this way, but beats what I like to call "involuntary swimming." I am no whitewater expert, and creeks have caused me much grief on PCT hikes, so I'll leave it at that. Be careful!

Scrub: Don't ford barefoot. There is too much risk of abrasion or entrapment/mangling. If you have water/camp footwear and want to use that, great. If not (and assuming you're in meshy trail runners), take your socks off and your insoles out, then put the shoes back on your bare feet and go through that way. Your feet and shoes will get wet, but they will dry out so much faster if you can put dry socks and dry insoles back on after crossing. In some years, there will be so many crossings that the effort won't be worth it every time, but in a dry-ish year with low creeks, it's a nice system to use.

CHOOSING A CAMPSITE

LEAVE NO TRACE

Tha Wookie: When you are camping near the trail at an established campsite, make sure to camp in the already impacted area or any other durable surface (i.e., don't camp on fragile vegetation, or expand the site looking for a softer pad). Avoid sites that have only been used a few times or that appear to have a chance of recovering. When stealth (or "pristine site") camping, find an area that is resistant to trampling (no forbs, herbs, or soft soils), do not have a fire, and cover the site with sticks and pine needles when you leave. Leaving no trace means just that. It's the best way to protect the forest resources and your rights as a recreational lands user.

AVOID ANIMALS

Many hikers stop near a water source between 5-6 p.m., cook dinner, walk until it's almost dark, then find some place to camp which looks like nobody has camped there before. We try to avoid established campsites. Bears, marmots, mice, and other animals are attracted to established campsites because they know they can find food there. By choosing your campsite carefully, you can (in theory) avoid problems with animals, especially bears.

AVOID CONDENSATION

If you camp on grass or out in the open, you will most likely get a lot of condensation. This condensation forms on top of your sleeping bag and on the inside of your tent or tarp. To prevent this, camp AWAY from water, ON dirt/needles/duff, and UNDER tree cover. This is true whether you sleep out in the open, in a tent, or under a tarp.

TIME YOUR DAY

The Weathercarrot: There are three factors to think about when strategizing your campsite location, and they often conflict: (1) avoiding bears, (2) avoiding high passes first thing in the morning when they are frozen, and (3) avoiding high passes in the afternoon during a persistent daily thunderstorm pattern (which varies tremendously from year to year). It can be hard to choose a spot when all three of these factors are occurring at once. I find that when bear boxes are not available, it's best to camp right around tree line, where snow is fairly plentiful and late spring has not fully taken hold; the bears seem to come to these elevations after the June thru-hiker time. But this also gives you the dilemma of being on your way up to the pass first thing the next morning, unless you did it at the end of the previous day in order to camp high, in which case you had timing problems with lightning. This was the dilemma we faced when almost 12 days in a row featured a lot of lightning, from Forester Pass all the way to the north end of Yosemite.

HIKER OPINIONS

Anish: Camp in established locations to minimize impact in the very popular Sierra. In other locations, disperse your use and make your site invisible to people behind you to avoid it becoming an established impacted site.

BINK: I avoid any place that looks like an established campsite (this greatly reduces bear problems). By avoiding established sites, I often find myself on soft beds of duff at night, as well as experiencing fewer rodent and other animal problems in the middle of the night.

SIERRA FOOD STORAGE - November 2019

"Proper food storage" is required from Kennedy Meadows (mile 702.2) to Sonora Pass (mile 1016.9). That includes SEKI and Yosemite National Parks. "Proper food storage" is open to interpretation by individual agencies, and at times by individual Rangers (whom you may encounter along the trail). Some areas allow hanging food. Others specifically prohibit hanging. Some areas require bear canisters. Sleeping with your food, defending your food, posting a guard for your food are all NOT proper food storage methods, and these practices violate the food storage requirements.

Sierra Food Storage requirements are confusing to figure out, and the regulations change without notice. Quite often, a website will contradict itself from one page to the next. In fact, the SEKI Food Storage map states "Information is subject to rapid and unannounced change."

According to the Pacific Crest Trail Association: "Approved bear canisters are required in parts of Sequoia and Kings Canyon (SEKI) National Parks, Inyo, Sierra and Humboldt-Toiyabe National Forests, and in all of Yosemite and Lassen National Parks. **Basically, PCT hikers and horseback riders should, at the minimum, carry canisters between Kennedy Meadows (mile 702.2) and Sonora Pass (mile 1016.9)."**

Sierra Wild:	[www.sierrawild.gov]
Bear Box locations:	[www.climber.org/data/BearBoxes.html]
Bear Box and Canister Info:	[http://onthetrail.org/faq/bear-box/]
Bear canister article:	[www.rei.com/expertadvice/articles/bear+resistant+canisters.html]

SEQUOIA and KINGS CANYON (SEKI) NATIONAL PARKS

The PCT enters SEKI at PCT mile 753.9, and departs SEKI at PCT mile 855.9 (Piute Pass Trail). Park-allowed Portable Food Storage Containers (bear canisters) are required for part of this length of trail, and recommended for all of it. See the SEKI Wilderness Trip Planner:
[https://www.nps.gov/seki/planyourvisit/upload/NoYear-Wilderness-Trip-Planner-Final.pdf]

From that document: "The PCT passes through the Rock Creek and Rae Lakes Loop animal-resistant food-storage container requirement areas where all travelers are required to use animal-resistant containers. You must use the animal-resistant containers or boxes to store all your food, garbage, and scented items. "

This map shows the PCT passing through two areas in SEKI where Portable Food Storage Containers (canisters) are required:

[https://www.nps.gov/seki/planyourvisit/upload/FoodStorageRequirements_8x11_20150729-2.pdf]

From looking at that map, it appears that the canister-required areas in SEKI are:
(1) Mile 753.9 (PCT enters SEKI) to mile 762.9 (Guyot Pass)
(2) Mile 779.5 (Forester Pass) to mile 807.1 (Pinchot Pass)

Additional SEKI information: [https://www.nps.gov/seki/planyourvisit/bear_bc.htm]

YOSEMITE NATIONAL PARK

The PCT enters Yosemite National Park at PCT mile 929.5 (Donohue Pass),
and departs Yosemite National Park at PCT mile 997.1 (Dorothy Lake Pass).
From the Yosemite National Park website [www.nps.gov/yose]:

"You are required by federal regulations to store all your 'food' properly throughout Yosemite National Park. You must have your food stored unless it's within arm's reach (so, don't go for a swim or take a nap while leaving food out). 'Food' includes all food and drinks, regardless of packaging, along with trash, toiletries, and other scented items. These items **must** be stored in either an allowed bear-resistant food canister or food locker. Hanging food is illegal throughout Yosemite."

"Bear resistant food containers (bear canisters) are required for overnight hikers throughout the Wilderness (counterbalance food hangs are no longer legal)."

"Please note that these food storage regulations have the force and effect of federal law: Failure to store your food properly may result in impoundment of your food or car and/or a fine of up to $5,000 and/or revocation of your camping permit."

"Allowed bear canisters are required throughout Yosemite National Park.
Hanging food is not permitted anywhere in Yosemite.
There are no exceptions for Pacific Crest Trail through-hikers."

NPS ALLOWED BEAR CANISTERS - November 2019

BEAR VAULT
110b, 200, 250, 300, 350, 400, 450, 500
[www.bearvault.com] 866-301-3442

BEARIKADE Weekender MKII and
Expedition MKII (both 1766 and higher)
[www.wild-ideas.net] 805-693-0550

GARCIA - Backpacker Model 812
[www.backpackerscache.com]
559-732-3785

THE BEAR KEG - Counter Assault
[www.counterassault.com]
800-695-3394

The Bare Boxer Contender (101) and
Champ (202)
[www.bareboxer.com]

UDAP No-Fed-Bear
[www.udap.com] 800-232-7941

LIGHTER1 Big Daddy and Little Sami
[www.lighter1.com]

BEAR CAN PURCHASE or RENTAL

Triple Crown Outfitters located in Kennedy Meadows south (mile 702.2) offers canisters for purchase or rent, both for northbounders and southbounders. [www.triplecrownoutfitters.com]

Canisters for purchase: Bear Vault 500, Bear Vault 450
Canisters for rent: Bear Vault 500, Bear Vault 450, Garcia, Bear Keg

NORTHBOUNDERS

From the PCTA website: **"Hikers and horseback riders should, at the minimum, carry canisters between Kennedy Meadows (mile 702.2) and Sonora Pass (mile 1016.9)."**

Purchase: If you purchase a canister elsewhere, you have to pay postage to ship it to yourself at Kennedy Meadows south. Makes more sense to save the postage $$ and purchase your canister in Kennedy Meadows south at Triple Crown Outfitters.

Rental: Northbound hikers pick up their rental canister at Triple Crown Outfitters in Kennedy Meadows south. Hikers can return the canister for no charge at Kennedy Meadows Resort and Pack Station (Kennedy Meadows north), which is 10 miles west of Sonora Pass, nobo mile 1016.9. Alternatively, hikers can mail the canister back to Triple Crown Outfitters.

SOUTHBOUNDERS

The sentence above from the PCTA website lists northbound mileage. Using southbound mileage, that sentence would read: **"Hikers and horseback riders should, at the minimum, carry canisters between Sonora Pass (southbound mile 1636.2) and Kennedy Meadows (southbound mile 1950.9)."**

Purchase: Order a canister from [www.triplecrownoutfitters.com], ship it to Kennedy Meadows Resort and Pack Station (Kennedy Meadows north), which is 10 miles west of Sonora Pass.

Rental: Triple Crown Outfitters has rental canisters available at Kennedy Meadows Resort and Pack Station (KM north). It's possible to show up at KM north and rent a canister on the spot. However, to guarantee there will be a canister for you, it is best to place your rental order on TCO's website. Southbound hikers return their rented canister to Triple Crown Outfitters in Kennedy Meadows south. For details, click on the BEAR CANISTERS link at [www.triplecrownoutfitters.com].

SIERRA BEAR BOX LOCATIONS

A bear box is a large, heavy metal box which a bear cannot open or move.

753.9	No Bear Box - ENTER SEQUOIA & KINGS CANYON NATIONAL PARK
760.5	Bear Box - Rock Creek Crossing
766.3	Bear Box - Crabtree Meadows
	Bear Box - Crabtree Ranger Station (this is on the Mt Whitney side trip)
770.3	Bear Box - Wallace Creek and High Sierra Trail Junction
774.1	Bear Box - Bear box is10-15 minutes before Tyndall Creek
774.7	Bear Box - Shepherd Pass Trail / Tyndall Creek
784.3	Bear Box - Center Basin Trail
786.1	Bear Box - Upper Vidette Meadow
787.0	Bear Box - Vidette Meadow
787.3	Bear Box - Junction Up Bubbs Creek
788.9	Bear Box - Charlotte Lake (one mile off the PCT)
793.5	Bear Box - Rae Lakes
795.2	Bear Box - Arrowhead Lake
799.8	Bear Box - Woods Creek
855.9	No Bear Box - LEAVE SEQUOIA & KINGS CANYON NATIONAL PARK
929.5	No Bear Box - ENTER YOSEMITE NATIONAL PARK - Donohue Pass
942.5	Bear Box - Tuolumne Meadows Campground
948.3	Bear Box - Glen Aulin
997.1	No Bear Box - LEAVE YOSEMITE NATIONAL PARK - Dorothy Lake Pass

BINK: The bear "problem" was, in my opinion, mostly created by the National Park Service. Until the late 1950's, black bears roamed the Yosemite Valley garbage dump at will (this was a spectator event encouraged by the Park). Starting in the late 1960's, the Park Service quit allowing bears access to the dump. Bears then became a nuisance in Yosemite Valley, raiding camps, breaking into cars, etc. Starting in the 1970's, the Park Service began capturing and relocating the worst offenders from Yosemite Valley to the backcountry areas in Yosemite and SEKI National Parks. By the 1980's, the backcountry areas had serious bear problems.

The Park Service loves to blame backpackers for this, and no doubt they were not helpful. Unfortunately, we are now stuck with a decades-long wildlife mismanagement problem mostly created by the early policies of the National Park Service who refuse to take any responsibility for this issue.

Have bear canisters helped? Absolutely. Prior to them being required, I never had any bear problems on 8+ PCT thru-hikes in the High Sierra, but I attribute this to my not cooking in camp and not camping near any of the "hot spots" or any established campsites. While I feel the regulations surrounding the canisters are a bit draconian, I also feel that they have generally helped matters. It is with some reluctance that I now carry a canister where required, but this is easier than trying to fight it. I would rather focus on my hike than being upset by Park Service mismanagement and misguided policies. I don't want to make it sound like I am all against the National Park Service, because the reality is that they have been the primary reason that the Parks they oversee have been protected and preserved to the degree that they have been. Like any bureaucratic agency, they have their good points and their shortcomings. Overall, they have done much to help preserve some of the most beautiful areas in the world.

Hiker Box Special: Don't be a jerk, just carry the canister. Pick it up at Independence, and mail it home from Kennedy Meadows North.

Scrub: I wish everyone would carry a bear canister where they're supposed to, not for their sake but for the bears'. Some people skip out and get away with it. I would say the majority of people I knew, 80% maybe, were following the rules. Most people, myself included, had actually gotten used to having them by the end of the canister-required stretches, and we thought that at the very least it was nice to have psychological security about our food at night.

SIERRA RESUPPLY STRATEGY

Upon leaving Kennedy Meadows, some hikers choose to hike straight through to Vermilion Valley Resort without exiting the Sierra to resupply. That's a long haul (176.5 miles) and it isn't easy hiking. If you add in a Whitney side trip, that brings the distance to 193.5 miles. The Sierra terrain, snow, and creek crossings combine to slow down your daily mileage. The physical exertion requires more calories per day just to keep you going. It's extremely challenging both mentally and physically, but it is also magical.

I've hiked through the Sierra many times. The first time I exited at Kearsarge Pass and resupplied in Bishop. The other times I hiked straight through from Kennedy Meadows to VVR. The hike out over Kearsarge Pass is stunning. However, I prefer to do the long resupply and stay in the Sierra for 11 days. By the time I hit Kennedy Meadows, it feels like the whole hike has been building up to something, and for me, that something is an eleven-day hike through some of the most stunning scenery on the planet.

SUGGESTED SIERRA RESUPPLY STRATEGY					
This shows how we would resupply for the 240.3 miles from Kennedy Meadows to Tuolumne Meadows if we hiked again.					
M = Pick up a mail drop B = Buy food Mt. Whitney adds 17.0 miles, for a total of 257.3 miles from KM to Tuolumne.	YOGI	ANISH	BINK	HBS	SCRUB
702.2 Kennedy Meadows	B	B	B	B	B
745.3 Trail Pass to Lone Pine					
750.2 Cottonwood Pass to Lone Pine					
766.3 Would you do Mt. Whitney?	Yes	Yes	Yes	Yes	Yes
788.9 Kearsarge Pass to Lone Pine				M	
788.9 Kearsarge Pass to Independence			M		
788.9 Kearsarge Pass to Bishop					B
857.7 Muir Trail Ranch					
878.7 Vermilion Valley Resort	M		M	B	
906.7 Reds Meadow				B	
906.7 Mammoth Lakes	M	B			B
942.5 Tuolumne Meadows	M	M	M	M	B

TRAIL TOWNS

HITCHHIKING

If you've never hitched before, it probably sounds scary. The fact is that on a thru-hike, hitching is usually the only way to get from the trail to town. It's usually a lot of fun, and you'll meet some really interesting people.

Use common sense. Don't hitch alone. There are always other hikers around, and everyone goes into the same towns.

If you don't want to get into a car that stops for you, make some excuse like: "Oh!! Damn, I think I left my jacket about a mile back. Thanks for stopping, but I'll have to go back and get my jacket." Never had to use that, but I will if the ride looks sketchy.

TRAIL TO TOWN

Make sure your pack looks good. Don't have a bunch of dirty socks hanging off your pack. In fact, make absolutely sure that the only thing you'll be putting into the car is your pack. Attach all your miscellaneous items to your pack (hiking poles, fanny pack, whatever else). This is VERY important, because when you get dropped off in town, you'll reach into the car for your pack and forget the hiking poles, jacket, phone, and fanny pack that you put on the floor or the back seat.

Choose your hitching spot carefully. Make sure the cars can see you and have room to slow down and stop. If there is a sign that says "trailhead" or "PCT," stand near that sign.

Take off your sunglasses and sunhat. Smile. Hold a sign which indicates where you want to go. If the people in the car know they're not going to be stuck with you for several hours, they're more likely to pick you up.

Smile and wave at EVERY CAR that passes you, including the people driving the other direction. Many, many times I've had cars turn around and come back to pick me up.

I will not say that hitchhiking is safe. You're getting in a car with someone who chose to pick you up. This is EXACTLY what our mothers warned us to not do. I am not telling you to hitchhike. It's your choice to hitchhike or not. You could walk into town.

TOWN TO TRAIL

There is an art to getting FROM town back TO the trail. It begins the very moment you arrive in town. BE NICE. Say please and thank you. Tip big at restaurants and bars. That means 20-25% of your bill. It's usually only a couple dollars more than a 15% tip, and it builds karma. More importantly, restaurant servers and bartenders know a lot of people, especially in small towns. You treat them well, and they'll spread the word that hikers are good people. The person who tips well is remembered kindly. The person who tips poorly is remembered poorly. Word will spread – either good or bad – depending upon how you tip.

Talk to the locals. Take every opportunity to educate the locals about the trail. Tell them where the trail crosses the highway, and that if they ever see someone with a backpack, that person is harmless. It's probably another hiker who would love a short ride into town.

Smile and say hello when you pass people on the street and in the stores. If you have the opportunity to strike up a conversation, DO IT. Talk about the trail. Talk about how you needed to come into town to resupply and get cleaned up. Follow that with something like "we're not sure how we'll get back to the trail tomorrow. It's only 10 miles by car, but we don't have a car." By phrasing things this way, you give the town person the opportunity to help you, to do something nice. They like that. I've found that people are much more "willing" to drive me to the trail when it's THEIR idea, rather than when I blatantly ask for a ride (but, of course, that was my plan all along).

Anish: Be safe and listen to your gut. If something feels off, don't take the ride.

BINK: I have avoided hitchhiking on my last five hikes of the PCT because it is easier for me to just go to the next town along the trail that is a short walk away. In the past, I hitchhiked into and out of some resupply towns and never really had any problems. These days with the awareness by local people of the PCT, it seems to have become pretty easy for most folks to hitchhike into town to resupply. I have heard of some funny/interesting hitchhike stories from PCT hikers, but to date no negative ones.

Scrub: I love hitchhiking; it makes me feel so vagabondish even though deep down I know I'm just an overly educated, upper-middle-class kid from the East Coast suburbs. I hitched as often as possible – pretty much anything over a mile off-trail. I would always change into a cleanish, non-hiking shirt and take off my hat. I put my wallet and phone on my person in case my pack got left behind/ejected from a truck bed/stolen along the way. In tricky places, I would also make a sign for my destination out of some region of my Tyvek groundsheet – I always made sure that "PCT HIKER" was in lettering equally as big as the destination, because that's actually what people are stopping for.

ZERO DAYS

A "zero" is a day that you do not hike. Not at all. It's a zero-mile day. You hiked into town yesterday. Today is a day off, or a "zero" day. Tomorrow, you'll hike out.

Zeros are very important. Don't think that you're being lazy by taking a zero. Look at your life back home. You get two days off from work each week, right? That's 44 days off in 5 months. During your 5-month PCT hike, you'll take between 10-30 zeros. 10-30 days off. You need them. You need to relax, eat, go to a movie, watch TV, eat, read a book, call your Mom, eat, hang out with trail buddies, do nothing, eat.

Some people like to take zeros on the trail. Others like to take zeros in towns with a lot of activity (Ashland OR, South Lake Tahoe CA). Still others like to take zeros in towns with not much to do (Kennedy Meadows CA, Castella CA, Cascade Locks OR). Review the town descriptions in this book and form an idea of where you might want to take a zero day. Most zero days are unplanned. You'll take a zero when your body tells you to. Or when a bunch of your friends are together. Or for no reason other than to relax.

Similar to a zero day, a nero is "nearly a zero." Taking a nero helps to save money. Here's how it works: Camp close to town – say 3-5 miles before the road to town. Hitch in early in the morning, get your town chores done early, then relax in the motel all afternoon. You'll only pay for one night in a motel, yet you'll take the majority of the day off. Nearly a zero. You could also take a nero on the way out of town. Leave town late in the day, only put in a few miles, then camp.

Anish: Take zeros to stay healthy and happy, but don't overdo it.

BINK: Zero days can be really restorative, but they can also be exhausting whirlwinds of trying to get "town chores" done. I have had "zero" days where I felt like I was walking all day around town running errands. Sometimes it can be a real relief to get back out on the trail! I am also very convinced that time speeds up in town. Zero days seem to go by in a flash, whereas time spent out on the trail seems to pass at a more sedate pace. I have had several thru-hikes with zero zeros where I did not spend more than an hour or two in any one town. I actually have enjoyed these hikes and their continuous nature. But really, do you want to hike that 4000-foot climb out of town at 1 pm when it's 101 degrees? When the alternative is another round of cold drinks and ice cream spent in the shade the rest of the afternoon?

Hiker Box Special: Take plenty of zero days in SoCal. Then when you're in the groove, try to stick to nero days. I always felt worse after a zero than a nero until I was really really exhausted.

Scrub: I didn't take very many zero days, only 11 out of the 139 days I was on the trail. Two of them were planned long in advance as meet-ups with my girlfriend, three of them were planned a section in advance because I knew I needed a break physically, and the other half-dozen were more spur-of-the-moment. But the spur-of-the-moment ones are always the best. I would take more next time, it's just that I was very set on finishing and any time I stayed in one place too long, even in SoCal, I started to think of the winter rains in Washington.

HIKER BEHAVIOR

This topic is a tough one, but something needs to be said. Thru-hiking is a great experience, and we've got some incredible Trail Angels and trail towns along the way. All it takes is one bad seed to cause Trail Angels or town businesses to stop welcoming hikers. We have a responsibility to future hikers to be outstanding trail ambassadors.

Smile. Say "please" and "thank you." ALWAYS tip 20% at restaurants, especially when you ask for separate checks. If you stay at a hostel or a private home, always ask permission before drinking alcohol or smoking.

When you check into a motel, ask for a trash bag. Hikers accumulate an unbelievable amount of trash while in town. Put all your trash in the trash bag. DO NOT trash any motel room. Before checking out, place all your dirty towels in a pile in the bathroom.

Never sneak extra hikers into a motel room. Never let another hiker take a shower in your motel room. Those are both considered "theft of services," and you could be arrested.

RESUPPLY

RESUPPLY STRATEGY

There are three broad schools of thought concerning resupply:

- Mail all your food
- Buy all your food in trail towns
- Hybrid – a combination of mail drops and buying in town

A mail drop resupply strategy is only recommended for experienced hikers who are 100% sure they will not tire of mail drop food or for hikers with special dietary restrictions.

There are some stops where there simply are not any stores, or where resupply options are extremely limited. Using a resupply strategy where you buy along the way could result in much longer carries.

A hybrid resupply strategy is perfect for the PCT. Buy at most resupply locations; send food packages to a few select locations. You do not need a home resupply person to send your food packages. You could prepare them from a previous town stop, then ship them ahead to yourself. Or, you could use a trail resupply company such as Zero Day Resupply [www.zerodayresupply.com].

USPS, UPS, or FEDEX

Usually the most economical shipping method is USPS Priority Mail. Post Offices are located in even the smallest trail towns, so shipping USPS mail is easy. Priority Mail typically takes 2-3 business days to travel from the shipping location to the destination location. However, the because some locations are extremely remote, it's best to allow 1-2 extra days.

Some locations do not have street delivery of USPS mail. For these locations, use UPS or FedEx to ship your packages. Pay careful attention to the addresses listed in the Town Guide section of this book. Some are labeled as USPS addresses, others are labeled as UPS or FedEx addresses. If you are using a General Delivery address, that must ship via USPS.

BOUNCE BOX

A bounce box contains items you need in town, but not on the trail. You pick it up in town, take things out of / put things into the box, then ship it ahead (bounce it) to yourself further up the trail. This may sound like a great idea, but managing a bounce box can be a pain in the ass. You'll constantly be modifying your hike to be in town during Post Office hours. Plus, you'll spend a fortune on postage.

Be careful when choosing where you send your bounce box, because there are places along the PCT where you CANNOT mail out packages. If you send your bounce box to someplace with no outgoing mail for packages, you're stuck with it. Don't send your bounce box to these locations:

151.8	Paradise Café		1742.7	Hyatt Lake Resort
341.9	Cajon Pass Inn		1773.4	Fish Lake Resort
517.6	Hikertown / Wee Vill Market		1820.9	Crater Lake (Mazama)
857.7	Muir Trail Ranch		1906.6	Shelter Cove Resort
906.7	Reds Meadow		1952.6	Elk Lake Resort
1016.9	Kennedy Meadows Resort (north)		1995.1	Big Lake Youth Camp
1349.7	Drakesbad Guest Ranch		2097.4	Timberline Lodge
1419.0	Burney Falls State Park		2295.4	White Pass WA
1718.7	Callahan's Lodge		2393.6	Snoqualmie Pass WA
1735.3	Green Springs Inn		2464.7	Stevens Pass Ski Area

HYBRID RESUPPLY STRATEGY

Using a hybrid resupply strategy, you'll buy food at most locations, and pick up packages at places where there is inadequate food available. You don't need a resupply person at home to do food drops for you. You can do them yourself from the trail.

Prepare your package at these locations	Mail your packages to these locations
Home	109.5 Warner Springs CA
558.5 or 566.5 Mojave/Tehachapi	857.7 Muir Trail Ranch 878.7 Vermilion Valley Resort
906.7 Mammoth Lakes CA or 1092.3 South Lake Tahoe CA	1286.9 The Braatens (Belden CA) 1419.0 Burney Falls State Park
1718.7 Ashland OR	1820.9 Crater Lake 1906.6 Shelter Cove Resort 1952.6 Elk Lake Resort 1995.1 Big Lake Youth Camp 2097.4 Timberline Lodge
2147.1 Cascade Locks OR	2295.4 White Pass WA (limited resupply) 2393.6 Snoqualmie Pass WA (limited resupply) 2464.7 Stevens Pass/Skykomish/Leavenworth 2572.4 Stehekin WA

DETAILED RESUPPLY INFORMATION

A good step-by-step guide for choosing food, preparing mail drops, and navigating the USPS system is the book "Hold for Hiker", available at [www.yogisbooks.com]

IF WE HIKED THE PCT AGAIN, THIS IS HOW WE WOULD RESUPPLY

Following is a chart of resupply locations along the PCT. The information contained in this chart shows how previous hikers would resupply if we hiked the trail again. Knowing what we know now, knowing what we can find in the towns, this shows the places where we would send a mail drop or buy food.

If we hiked again, this is how we would resupply

		YOGI	ANISH	BINK	HBS	SCRUB
B =	Buy food					
M =	Pick up a mail drop					
41.5	Mt. Laguna CA	M	B	B	B	
77.0	Julian CA					B
109.5	Warner Springs CA	M	M	M	M	
151.8	Paradise Café			M		
151.8	Idyllwild CA from Pines-to-Palms Hwy					B
179.4	Idyllwild CA from Saddle Junction	M	B	M	B	
209.5	Cabazon CA					
266.1	Big Bear City CA from Highway 18	M	B		B	B
275.1	Big Bear City CA from Van Dusen Canyon Road			B		
341.9	I-15 Cajon Pass	B	M	B		B
363.4	Wrightwood CA from Acorn Trail					
369.3	Wrightwood CA from Highway 2	M	B		B	B
444.3	Acton KOA	M	M	M	M	M
485.8	Lake Hughes CA					
517.6	Hikertown or Wee Vill Market		M	M		M
558.5	Mojave CA from Tehachapi-Willow Springs Rd			M		B
566.5	Mojave CA from Highway 58	B				
558.5	Tehachapi CA from Tehachapi-Willow Springs Rd		B		B	
566.5	Tehachapi CA from Highway 58					
652.1	Onyx CA					
652.1	Lake Isabella CA		B		M	
702.2	Kennedy Meadows (Triple Crown Outfitters)	B	B	B	B	B
745.3	Lone Pine CA (Trail Pass)					
750.2	Lone Pine CA (Cottonwood Pass)					
788.9	Lone Pine CA (Kearsarge Pass)				M	
788.9	Independence CA from Kearsarge Pass			M		
788.9	Bishop CA from Kearsarge Pass					B
857.7	Muir Trail Ranch					
878.7	Vermilion Valley Resort	M		M	B	
878.7	Mono Hot Springs					
906.7	Reds Meadow				B	

If we hiked again, this is how we would resupply

		YOGI	ANISH	BINK	HBS	SCRUB
B =	Buy food					
M =	Pick up a mail drop					
906.7	Mammoth Lakes CA	M	B			B
942.5	Tuolumne Meadows	M	M	M	M	B
942.5	Lee Vining CA					
1016.9	Kennedy Meadows Resort (North)				B	M
1016.9	Bridgeport CA					
1016.9	Walker CA					
1048.4	Markleeville CA					
1092.3	Echo Lake CA	B		B		B
1092.3	South Lake Tahoe CA		B		B	
1124.8	Tahoe City CA					
1153.4	Truckee CA					
1153.4	Soda Springs CA				B	B
1195.4	Sierra City CA	M	B	M	B	M
1263.5	Bucks Lake	B				
1286.8	Belden Town	M		M	M	
1286.9	Quincy CA					B
1331.3	Chester CA		B		B	B
1349.7	Drakesbad Guest Ranch		M	M		
1373.4	Old Station CA	M			B	
1409.7	Burney Guest Ranch (not open when the hikers on this table hiked)					
1411.3	Burney CA (town)					B
1419.0	Burney Falls State Park	M	M	M	M	
1501.2	Dunsmuir CA					
1501.2	Castella CA	M	M	M	M	
1501.2	Mt. Shasta CA					B
1599.7	Etna CA		B	M	B	B
1655.9	Seiad Valley CA	M	B	M	B	B

If we hiked again, this is how we would resupply

		YOGI	ANISH	BINK	HBS	SCRUB
	B = Buy food					
	M = Pick up a mail drop					
1718.7	Ashland OR		B		B	B
1718.7	Callahan's Lodge	M		M		
1735.3	Green Springs Inn					
1742.7	Hyatt Lake Resort					
1773.4	Fish Lake Resort					
1820.9	Crater Lake Mazama Village	M	M	M	M	M
1848.0	Diamond Lake Resort					
1906.6	Shelter Cove Resort	M		M	M	M
1907.9	Crescent Lake OR					
1952.6	Elk Lake Resort	M		M		
1952.6	Bend OR from Elk Lake Resort					
1983.7	Sisters OR from McKenzie Pass					
1983.7	Bend OR from McKenzie Pass					
1995.1	Big Lake Youth Camp	M	M	M		M
2000.9	Sisters OR from Santiam Pass					
2000.9	Bend OR from Santiam Pass				B	
2092.2	Government Camp OR					
2097.4	Timberline Lodge	M	M	M	M	
2147.1	Cascade Locks OR	B	M	M	B	M
2147.1	Hood River OR					
2147.1	Stevenson WA					
2229.4	Trout Lake WA				M	
2295.4	White Pass WA	M	M	M	M	M
2295.4	Packwood WA					
2393.6	Snoqualmie Pass WA	M	M	M	M	M
2464.7	Stevens Pass Ski Area	M	M	M	M	M
2464.7	Skykomish WA					
2572.4	Stehekin WA	M	M	M	M	M
2572.4	Chelan WA					
2591.6	Winthrop WA					

TOWN SERVICES: Border to Big Bear City

Legend:
- ⌂ = C-Store
- ▥ = Grocery
- ★ = Supermarket
- M = Available for motel guests only

Mile Point	Location	Miles From Trail (H = Hitch, W = Walk)	Post Office	Mail Drops	Resupply	Outfitter	Lodging	Camp	Meals	Laundry	Shower	ATM	Computer	Alcohol Fuel	Canister Fuel
20.0	Lake Morena CA	on trail			⌂				✶		⚿	$			✓
26.0	Pine Valley CA	8 H	☏		▥		⚑		✶			$			✓
41.5	Mt. Laguna CA	0.4 W	☏	✉	▥	⚒	⚑	◭	✶		⚿			✓	
77.0	Stagecoach Trails RV Park	4 H			⌂		⚑	◭	✶	⌂	⚿				
77.0	Julian CA	13 H	☏		▥				✶	M ◁			⊡		
109.5	Warner Springs Resource Center	on trail	☏		⌂		⚑	◭	✶	M ◁			⊡		✓
109.5	Warner Springs PO/Resort	1.2 W	☏				⚑		✶		⚿				
109.5	Lake Henshaw Resort	13 H	☏		▥		⚑	◭	✶	◁					
109.5	Santa Ysabel CA	15 H	☏						✶						
151.8	Paradise Valley Café	1 W		✉					✶						
151.9	Anza CA	7 H	☏		▥		⚑		✶			$			
151.9	Idyllwild CA		☏	✉	▥	⚒	⚑	◭	✶	◁	⚿	$	⊡	✓	✓
	via Pines-to-Palms Hwy	19 H													
179.4	via Devils Slide Trail	2.5 W + 2.6 H													
209.0	Cabazon CA	4.5 H	☏		⌂				✶			$	⊡	✓	
266.1	Big Bear City CA (Hwy 18)	5 H	☏	✉	★		⚑	◭	✶	◁		$	⊡	✓	✓
275.1	Big Bear City CA (Van Dusen)	4 W	☏						✶	◁		$	⊡	✓	✓

TOWN SERVICES: Big Bear City to Mojave / Tehachapi

Legend: 🏪 = C-Store 🛒 = Grocery ★ = Supermarket M = Available for motel guests only

Mile Point	Location	Miles From Trail (H = Hitch / W = Walk)	Post Office	Mail Drops	Resupply	Outfitter	Lodging	Camp	Meals	Laundry	Shower	ATM	Computer	Alcohol Fuel	Canister Fuel
266.1	Big Bear City CA (Hwy 18)	5 H	✓	✉	★		✓	▲	✓	✓		$	🖥	✓	✓
275.1	Big Bear City CA (Van Dusen)	4 W	✓		🛒		✓		✓	✓		$	🖥	✓	✓
298.5	Cedar Glen CA	3.6 H	✓		🛒				✓	✓					✓
298.5	Lake Arrowhead CA	5.6 H	✓		★		✓		✓			$			
341.9	Cajon Pass	0.4 W		✉	🏪				✓	M ✓			M 🖥		
363.4	Wrightwood CA (Acorn Trail)	3.6 W	✓	✉	★		✓		✓	M ✓		$	🖥	✓	✓
369.3	Wrightwood CA (Hwy 2)	5.5 H	✓	✉	🛒		✓	▲	✓	M ✓	≋	$	🖥	✓	✓
444.2	Acton CA	5.7 H	✓	✉			✓			✓		$	🖥	✓	✓
444.3	Acton KOA	0.2 W			🏪			▲		✓	≋			✓	✓
454.5	Agua Dulce CA	on trail		✉	🛒		✓		✓			$			✓
485.8	Lake Hughes CA	2.3 W	✓	✉	🛒		✓		✓			$			
517.6	Hikertown	on trail		✉	🏪			▲			≋				
517.6	Wee Vill Market	8 ride		✉	🏪			▲	✓		≋				
558.5	Mojave CA (Willow Spgs Road)	9 H	✓	✉	★		✓		✓	✓		$	🖥	✓	✓
566.5	Mojave CA (Hwy 58)	11 H	✓				✓			✓		$	🖥	✓	✓
558.5	Tehachapi CA (Willow Spgs Rd)	9 H	✓	✉	★		✓	▲	✓	✓	≋	$			
566.5	Tehachapi CA (Hwy 58)	9 H	✓				✓					$			

TOWN SERVICES: Mojave / Tehachapi to Muir Trail Ranch

Legend: ⊕ = C-Store ◫ = Grocery ★ = Supermarket M = Available for motel guests only

Mile Point	Location	Miles From Trail (H = Hitch, W = Walk)	Post Office	Mail Drops	Resupply	Outfitter	Lodging	Camp	Meals	Laundry	Shower	ATM	Computer	Alcohol Fuel	Canister Fuel
558.5	Mojave CA (Willow Spgs Road)	9 H	✉	⊠	★		✓		✓	✓		$	✓	✓	✓
566.5	Mojave CA (Hwy 58)	11 H	✉	⊠	★		✓		✓	✓	✓	$		✓	✓
558.5	Tehachapi CA (Willow Spgs Road)	9 H	✉		★		✓		✓	✓		$	✓	✓	✓
566.5	Tehachapi CA (Hwy 58)	9 H	✉	⊠	★		✓	✓	✓	✓		$		✓	✓
652.1	Kernville CA	38 H	✉		★	✓	✓		✓	✓		$	✓	✓	✓
652.1	Ridgecrest CA	25 H	✉		★	✓	✓		✓	✓	✓	$	✓	✓	✓
652.1	Lake Isabella CA	36 H	✉	⊠	★		✓	✓	✓	✓	✓	$		✓	✓
652.1	Inyokern CA	15 H	✉		⊕										
652.1	Onyx CA	17 H	✉		⊕ ★				✓						
652.1	Weldon/South Lake CA	24 H			★		✓	✓	✓	M ✓	✓	$			✓
702.2	Kennedy Meadows CA	0.7 W		⊠	◫	✓		✓	✓	✓				✓	✓
Lone Pine CA			✉	⊠	◫	✓	✓	✓	✓		✓	$	✓	✓	
745.3	from Trail Pass	2.5 W + 20 H													
750.2	from Cottonwood Pass	3.8 W + 20 H													
788.9	from Kearsarge Pass	7.5 W + 29 H													
788.9	Independence CA	7.5 W + 13 H	✉	⊠	⊕ ★		✓ ✓		✓	M ✓	✓	$	✓	✓	✓
788.9	Bishop CA	7.5 W + 55 H	✉		★	✓	✓ ✓		✓	✓	✓	$	✓	✓	✓
857.7	Muir Trail Ranch	1.5 W		⊠									✓	✓	✓

Page 117

TOWN SERVICES: Muir Trail Ranch to South Lake Tahoe CA

Legend: M = Available for motel guests only
⌂ = C-Store 且 = Grocery ★ = Supermarket

Mile Point	Location	Miles From Trail (H = Hitch, W = Walk)	Post Office	Mail Drops	Resupply	Outfitter	Lodging	Camp	Meals	Laundry	Shower	ATM	Computer	Alcohol Fuel	Canister Fuel
857.7	Muir Trail Ranch	1.5 W		✉										✓	✓
878.7	Vermilion Valley Resort	1.5W + boat	☎	✉	且		✓	✓	✓	✓	🚿		💻	✓	✓
878.	Mono Hot Springs	1.5W + boat + H		✉			✓	✓	✓						✓
906.7	Reds Meadow	0.3 W	☎	✉	且		✓	✓	✓	✓	🚿		💻	✓	✓ ✓
906.7	Mammoth Lakes CA	0.3 W + bus			★	✓	✓	✓	✓	✓	🚿	$	💻	✓ ✓	✓ ✓
942.5	Tuolumne Meadows CA	on trail	☎	✉	且		✓	✓	✓		M		💻		✓ ✓
942.5	Lee Vining CA	19 bus or H	☎	✉	且		✓	✓	✓	✓	🚿	$	💻	✓	✓ ✓
1016.9	Kennedy Meadows Resort (North)	10H	☎	✉	⌂ 且		✓	✓	✓	✓	🚿	$	💻	✓	✓
1016.9	Bridgeport CA	32H			且		✓		✓			$			
1016.9	Walker CA	29H			且		✓		✓	✓		$			
1048.4	Markleeville CA	18 H	☎		且		✓		✓						
1092.3	Echo Lake CA	on trail			★ 且		✓	✓	✓						
1092.3	South Lake Tahoe CA	9 H	☎	✉	★	✓	✓	✓	✓	✓	🚿	$	💻	✓	✓

TOWN SERVICES: South Lake Tahoe CA to Old Station CA

Legend:
⊕ = C-Store 具 = Grocery ★ = Supermarket
M = Available for motel guests only

Mile Point	Location	Miles From Trail (H = Hitch, W = Walk)	Post Office	Mail Drops	Resupply	Outfitter	Lodging	Camp	Meals	Laundry	Shower	ATM	Computer	Alcohol Fuel	Canister Fuel
1092.3	Echo Lake CA	on trail		⊠	⊕		🛏🛏		🍴					✓	✓
1092.3	South Lake Tahoe CA	9 H	⌂	⊠	★	⚒	🛏🛏	⛺	🍴🍴	🧺	🚿	$	💻	✓	
1124.8	Tahoe City CA	12 H	⌂	⊠	★	⚒	🛏		🍴	🧺		$	💻	✓	
1153.4	Truckee CA	8 H	⌂	⊠	具 ★	⚒	🛏🛏	⛺	🍴🍴	🧺	🚿	$	💻	✓	✓
1153.4	Soda Springs CA	3.4 H	⌂	⊠	具		🛏		🍴🍴	🧺		$			
1195.4	Sierra City CA	1.5 H or W	⌂	⊠	具 ★		🛏🛏	⛺	🍴	🧺	🚿	$	💻	✓	✓
1263.5	Bucks Lake	3 H or W			⊕		🛏	⛺	🍴						
1286.8	Belden CA	on trail		⊠	⊕		🛏	⛺	🍴🍴	🧺	🚿	$			
1286.9	Caribou Crossroads	1.1 H or W		⊠	⊕		🛏	⛺	🍴🍴		🚿				
1286.9	Quincy CA	30 H	⌂		★	⚒	🛏	⛺	🍴	🧺	🚿	$	💻	✓	✓
1331.3	Chester CA	8 H	⌂	⊠	★		🛏		🍴	🧺	🚿	$	💻	✓	
1349.7	Drakesbad Guest Ranch	0.5 W		⊠					🍴						
1373.4	Old Station: PO & Hat Cr. Rst.	0.3 W	⌂		⊕		🛏	⛺	🍴	🧺	🚿			✓	
1377.3	Old Station: Fill-Up, JJ's Café, & Rim Rk Ranch	0.4 W		⊠	⊕		🛏		🍴		🚿			✓	

TOWN SERVICES: Old Station CA to Ashland OR

Legend: ⊕ = C-Store 🛒 = Grocery ★ = Supermarket M = Available for motel guests only

Mile Point	Location	Miles From Trail (H = Hitch, W = Walk)	Post Office	Mail Drops	Resupply	Out fitter	Lodging	Camp	Meals	Laundry	Shower	ATM	Computer	Alcohol Fuel	Canister Fuel
1373.4	Old Station: PO & Hat Cr. Rst.	0.3 W	☎		⊕		🛏	⛺	🍴	🧺	🚿			✓	
1377.4	Old Station: Fill-Up, JJ's Café, & Rim Rk Ranch	0.4 W		✉	⊕		🛏		🍴		🚿			✓	
1409.7	Burney Mtn Guest Ranch	0.1 W		✉	⊕		🛏				🚿				
1411.3	Burney CA	7 H	☎	✉	★		🛏		🍴	🧺	🚿	$	▯	✓	✓
1419.0	Burney Falls State Park	on trail		✉	⊕		🛏	⛺			🚿				
1501.2	Castella CA	2.5 H or W	☎	✉	⊕ 🛒		🛏	⛺	🍴		🚿			✓	
1501.2	Dunsmuir CA	4.5 H	☎	✉ M	🛒 ★		🛏	⛺	🍴	🧺		$	▯	✓	✓
1501.2	Mt. Shasta CA	12 H	☎		🛒 ★	🎒	🛏	⛺	🍴			$	▯	✓	✓
1560.2	Callahan CA	8.3 H	☎		🛒				🍴						
1599.7	Etna CA	10.4 H	☎	✉	🛒		🛏	⛺	🍴	🧺	🚿	$	▯	✓	✓
1655.9	Seiad Valley CA	on trail	☎	✉	★			⛺	🍴	🧺	🚿			✓	
1718.7	Ashland OR	13 H	☎	✉	🛒 ★	🎒	🛏	⛺	🍴	🧺		$	▯	✓	✓
1718.7	Callahan's Lodge	1 H or W		✉			🛏		🍴	🧺	🚿			✓	✓

TOWN SERVICES: Ashland CA to Bend/Sisters OR

Legend: ⛪ = C-Store, 🏪 = Grocery, ★ = Supermarket M = Available for motel guests only

Mile Point	Location	Miles From Trail (H = Hitch, W = Walk)	Post Office	Mail Drops	Resupply	Outfitter	Lodging	Camp	Meals	Laundry	Shower	ATM	Computer	Alcohol Fuel	Canister Fuel
1718.7	Ashland OR	13 H	✓	✓	★	✓	✓		✓	✓		$	✓	✓	✓
1735.3	Green Springs Inn	1.8 H or W		✓			✓	✓	✓						
1742.7	Hyatt Lake	Resort 1.4W, Camp 0.3 W		✓			✓	✓	✓		✓				
1773.4	Fish Lake Resort	2 W or H		✓			✓	✓	✓	✓	✓				✓
1773.4	Lake of the Woods Resort	3.7 H		✓			✓	✓	✓						
1820.9	Crater Lake Mazama Village	0.8 W		✓	⛪		✓	✓	✓	✓	✓	$	✓	✓	✓
1820.9	Crater Lake OR Post Office	4 H or W	✓	✓			✓		✓			$			
1820.9	Crater Lake Rim Village	on hiker PCT			⛪		✓		✓						
1848.0	Diamond Lake Resort	alternate	✓	✓	⛪		✓	✓	✓	✓	✓	$		✓	✓
1906.6	Shelter Cove Resort	1.4 W		✓	⛪		✓	✓	✓	✓	✓	$		✓	✓
1907.9	Crescent Lake OR	7 H		✓	🏪		✓		✓			$			✓
1952.6	Elk Lake Resort	1 W		✓			✓	✓	✓		✓				✓
1952.6 / 1983.8 / 2000.9	Bend OR — from Elk Lake / from McKenzie Pass / from Santiam Pass	1 W + 32 H / 37 H / 37 H	✓	✓	★	✓	✓	✓	✓	✓		$	✓	✓	✓
1983.8 / 2000.9	Sisters OR (McKenzie Pass) / Sisters OR (Santiam Pass)	15 H / 15 H	✓	✓	★	✓	✓	✓	✓	✓	✓	$	✓	✓	✓

TOWN SERVICES: Bend/Sisters OR to Cascade Locks OR

Legend: 🏠 = C-Store 異 = Grocery ★ = Supermarket M = Available for motel guests only

Mile Point	Location	Miles From Trail (H = Hitch, W = Walk)	Post Office	Mail Drops	Resupply	Out fitter	Lodging	Camp	Meals	Laundry	Shower	ATM	Computer	Alcohol Fuel	Canister Fuel
	Bend OR														
1952.6	from Elk Lake	1 W + 32 H	☎	✉	★	✓	✓		✓	✓		$	✓	✓	✓
1983.8	from McKenzie Pass	37 H													
2000.9	from Santiam Pass	37 H													
1983.8	Sisters OR (McKenzie Pass)	15 H	☎	✉	★	✓	✓		✓	✓	✓	$	✓	✓	✓
2000.9	Sisters OR (Santiam Pass)	15 H	☎	✉			✓		✓	✓	✓			✓	
1995.1	Big Lake Youth Camp	0.7 W			異			▲	✓						
2046.0	Olallie Lake Resort	on trail			異		✓	▲							
2092.2	Government Camp OR	4.8 H	☎				✓		✓	✓		$		✓	
2092.2	Sandy OR	32 H	☎		★		✓		✓	✓		$	✓	✓	
2097.4	Timberline Lodge	on trail		✉	異		✓	▲	✓	M ✓	✓	$	M ✓	✓	
2147.1	Cascade Locks OR	on trail	☎	✉			✓		✓	✓	✓	$	✓	✓	
2147.1	Stevenson WA	3.2 W	☎	✉	★		✓		✓	✓		$	✓	✓	
2147.1	Hood River OR	20 bus or H	☎		★		✓		✓	✓		$	✓	✓	✓

TOWN SERVICES: Cascade Locks OR to Manning Park

Legend: ⛪ = C-Store ⵚ = Grocery ★ = Supermarket M = Available for motel guests only

Mile Point	Location	Miles From Trail (H = Hitch, W = Walk)	Post Office	Mail Drops	Resupply	Outfitter	Lodging	Camp	Meals	Laundry	Shower	ATM	Internet	Alcohol Fuel	Canister Fuel
2147.1	Cascade Locks OR	on trail	PO	✉	ⵚ		🛏	⛺	🍴		🚿	$	💻	✓	✓
2147.1	Stevenson WA	3.2 W	PO		★		🛏		🍴	⧖		$	💻	✓	
2147.1	Hood River OR	20 bus or H	PO		★		🛏		🍴	⧖		$	💻	✓	
2229.4	Trout Lake WA	13 H	PO	✉	⛪		🛏	⛺	🍴	M ⧖	🚿			✓	
2295.4	White Pass WA	0.5 W	PO	✉	ⵚ		🛏		🍴	⧖		$	💻	✓	✓
2295.4	Packwood WA	20 H					🛏	⛺	🍴	⧖	🚿	$		✓	✓
2393.6	Snoqualmie Pass WA	0.3 W		✉	⛪		🛏		🍴	M ⧖	🚿	$	M 💻	✓	
2464.7	Stevens Pass Ski Area	on trail		✉			🛏		🍴					💻		
2464.7	Skykomish WA	16 H	PO		⛪		🛏	⛺	🍴	⧖		$	💻	✓	✓
2464.7	Dinsmores / Baring WA	24 H					🛏	⛺	🍴	⧖	🚿		💻		✓
2464.7	Leavenworth WA	35 H	PO		★		🛏		🍴	M ⧖	🚿	$	💻	✓	✓
2572.4	Stehekin WA	11.1 bus	PO	✉			🛏	⛺	🍴	⧖	🚿	$	💻	✓	✓
2572.4	Chelan WA	bus + ferry	PO		★		🛏	⛺	🍴	⧖		$		✓	✓
2591.6	Mazama WA	18 H		✉	⛪	🎣	🛏		🍴						
2591.6	Winthrop WA	35 H	PO	✉	★	🎣	🛏		🍴	⧖	🚿	$	💻	✓	✓
2661.9	Manning Park	0.9 W		✉	⛪		🛏		🍴	⧖		$	M 💻		

LANDMARKS and TOWNS by MILE POINT

Mile Point	Yogi Book Section	Location
0.0	1	La Mesa CA
0.0	1	El Cajon CA
0.0	1	US-Mexico border
1.4	1	Campo CA
20.0	1	Lake Morena County Park
26.0	1	Boulder Oaks Campground / Pine Valley CA
26.6	1	Interstate 8
41.5	1	Mt. Laguna CA
77.0	2	Scissors Crossing/Julian CA/Stagecoach RV Park
91.2	2	Third Gate
106.2	2	Eagle Rock
109.5	2	Warner Springs CA
109.5	2	Lake Henshaw Resort
109.5	2	Santa Ysabel CA
151.8	3	Pines-to-Palms Highway
151.8	3	Paradise Valley Café / Anza CA
151.8	3	Idyllwild CA via Pines-to-Palms Hwy
179.4	3	Saddle Junction
179.4	3	Devils Slide Trail
179.4	3	Idyllwild CA via Devils Slide Trail
181.2	4	San Jacinto Alternate
188.0	4	Fuller Ridge
209.5	4	Interstate 10
209.5	4	Cabazon CA
209.5	4	Banning CA
218.5	4	Whitewater Preserve
266.1	4	Big Bear City CA via Highway 18
275.1	4	Van Dusen Canyon Road
275.1	4	Big Bear City CA via Van Dusen Canyon Road
298.5	5	Cedar Glen CA / Lake Arrowhead CA
307.9	5	Deep Creek Hot Springs
328.7	5	Silverwood Lake
341.9	5	Cajon Pass
341.9	5	Interstate 15
363.4	5	Acorn Trail
363.4	5	Wrightwood CA via Acorn Trail
369.3	5	Wrightwood CA via Highway 2
377.9	6	Mt. Baden-Powell
386.1	6	Endangered Species Detour
444.2	6	Acton CA
444.3	6	Acton KOA
454.5	6	Agua Dulce CA

Mile Point	Yogi Book Section	Location
485.8	7	Lake Hughes CA
517.6	7	Hikertown / Wee Vill Market
558.5	7	Tehachapi-Willow Springs Road
558.5	7	Mojave CA via Tehachapi-Willow Springs Road
558.5	7	Tehachapi CA via Tehachapi-Willow Springs Road
566.5	7	Highway 58
566.5	7	Mojave CA via Highway 58
566.5	7	Tehachapi CA via Highway 58
652.1	8	Walker Pass
652.1	8	Kernville CA / Onyx CA
652.1	8	Lake Isabella CA / Weldon CA & South Lake
652.1	8	Inyokern CA / Ridgecrest CA
702.2	8	Triple Crown Outfitters
702.2	8	Kennedy Meadows CA
745.3	9	Trail Pass
745.3	9	Lone Pine CA via Trail Pass
750.2	9	Cottonwood Pass
750.2	9	Lone Pine CA via Cottonwood Pass
766.3	9	Mt. Whitney
779.5	9	Forester Pass
788.9	9	Kearsarge Pass Trail
788.9	9	Bishop CA via Kearsarge Pass
788.9	9	Independence CA via Kearsarge Pass
788.9	9	Lone Pine CA via Kearsarge Pass
791.1	10	Glen Pass
807.1	10	Pinchot Pass
816.9	10	Mather Pass
838.6	10	Muir Pass
850.9	10	Evolution Creek
857.7	10	Muir Trail Ranch
865.6	10	Selden Pass
878.7	10	Vermilion Valley Resort
878.7	10	Mono Hot Springs
884.9	10	Silver Pass
906.7	10	Reds Meadow CA
906.7	10	Mammoth Lakes CA
929.5	10	Donohue Pass
941.7	10	Tuolumne Meadows Lodge
942.5	10	Tuolumne Meadows PO/Store
942.5	10	Lee Vining CA
942.5	10	Yosemite Valley

Mile Point	Yogi Book Section	Location
1016.9	11	Sonora Pass
1016.9	11	Bridgeport CA
1016.9	11	Kennedy Meadows Resort
1016.9	11	Walker CA
1048.4	11	Markleeville CA
1076.6	11	Carson Pass
1092.3	11	Echo Lake CA
1092.3	11	South Lake Tahoe CA
1124.8	12	Tahoe City CA
1153.4	12	Donner Pass
1153.4	12	Donner Ski Ranch
1153.4	12	Soda Springs CA
1153.4	12	Truckee CA
1157.1	12	Interstate 80
1195.4	12	Sierra City CA
1263.5	13	Bucks Lake
1286.8	13	Belden Town
1286.9	13	Caribou Crossroads
1286.9	13	Quincy CA
1331.3	14	Chester CA
1349.7	14	Drakesbad Guest Ranch
1373.4	14	Old Station CA
1409.7	15	Burney Mountain Guest Ranch
1411.3	15	Burney CA
1419.0	15	Burney Falls State Park
1501.2	16	Castella CA
1501.2	16	Dunsmuir CA
1501.2	16	Interstate 5
1501.2	16	Mount Shasta CA
1599.7	17	Etna CA
1599.7	17	Alderbrook Manor
1599.7	17	Hiker Hut
1655.9	18	Seiad Valley CA
1691.7	19	California-Oregon border
1718.7	19	Callahan's Siskiyou Lodge
1718.7	19	Ashland OR
1718.7	19	Interstate 5
1735.3	20	Green Springs Inn
1742.7	20	Hyatt Lake Resort
1773.4	20	Fish Lake Resort
1773.4	20	Lake of the Woods Resort
1820.9	20	Crater Lake Mazama Village
1820.9	20	Crater Lake Post Office
1820.9	20	Crater Lake Rim Village

LANDMARKS and TOWNS by MILE POINT

Mile Point	Yogi Book Section	Location
1848.0	21	Diamond Lake Resort
1906.6	21	Shelter Cove Resort
1907.9	21	Crescent Lake OR
1907.9	21	Willamette Pass
1952.6	22	Elk Lake Resort
1983.7	22	McKenzie Pass / Hwy 242
1983.7	22	Sisters OR via Hwy 242
1983.7	22	Bend OR via Hwy 242
1995.1	22	Big Lake Youth Camp
2000.9	22	Santiam Pass / Hwy 20
2000.9	22	Sisters OR via Hwy 20
2000.9	22	Bend OR via Hwy 20
2046.0	23	Olallie Lake Resort
2092.2	23	Sandy OR
2092.2	23	Government Camp OR
2097.4	23	Timberline Lodge OR
2128.1	23	Eagle Creek Alternate
2147.1	23	Cascade Locks OR
2147.1	23	Hood River OR
2147.1	23	Portland OR
2147.1	23	Stevenson WA
2147.1	23	Interstate 84
2147.5	24	Oregon-Washington border
2229.4	24	Trout Lake WA via Road 23
2229.4	24	Mount Adams Zen Buddhist Temple
2295.4	24	White Pass WA
2295.4	24	Packwood WA
2393.6	25	Snoqualmie Pass WA
2393.7	25	Interstate 90
2464.7	26	Stevens Pass
2464.7	26	Skykomish WA
2464.7	26	Baring WA
2464.7	26	Dinsmore, Jerry
2464.7	26	Leavenworth WA
2541.1	27	Suiattle River
2572.4	27	Stehekin WA
2572.4	27	Chelan WA
2591.6	28	Rainy Pass
2591.6	28	Mazama WA
2591.6	28	Winthrop WA
2622.5	28	Harts Pass
2653.1	28	US-Canada border
2661.9	28	Manning Park

Mile Point	Yogi Book Section	
363.4	5	Acorn Trail
444.2	6	Acton CA
444.3	6	Acton KOA
454.5	6	Agua Dulce CA
1599.7	17	Alderbrook Manor
151.8	3	Anza CA
1718.7	19	Ashland OR
209.5	4	Banning CA
2464.7	26	Baring WA
1286.8	13	Belden Town
2000.9	22	Bend OR via Hwy 20
1983.7	22	Bend OR via Hwy 242
266.1	4	Big Bear City CA via Highway 18
275.1	4	Big Bear City CA via Van Dusen Canyon Road
1995.1	22	Big Lake Youth Camp
788.9	9	Bishop CA via Kearsarge Pass
26.0	1	Boulder Oaks Campground
1016.9	11	Bridgeport CA
1263.5	13	Bucks Lake
1411.3	15	Burney CA
1419.0	15	Burney Falls State Park
1409.7	15	Burney Mountain Guest Ranch
209.5	4	Cabazon CA
341.9	5	Cajon Pass
1691.7	19	California-Oregon border
1718.7	19	Callahan's Siskiyou Lodge
1.4	1	Campo CA
1286.9	13	Caribou Crossroads
1076.6	11	Carson Pass
2147.1	23	Cascade Locks OR
1501.2	16	Castella CA
2572.4	27	Chelan WA
1331.3	14	Chester CA
750.2	9	Cottonwood Pass
1820.9	20	Crater Lake Mazama Village
1820.9	20	Crater Lake Post Office
1820.9	20	Crater Lake Rim Village
1907.9	21	Crescent Lake OR
308.0	5	Deep Creek Hot Springs
179.4	3	Devils Slide Trail
1848.0	21	Diamond Lake Resort
2464.7	26	Dinsmore, Jerry
1655.9	12	Donner Ski Ranch
1655.9	12	Donner Pass
929.5	10	Donohue Pass
1349.7	14	Drakesbad Guest Ranch
1501.2	16	Dunsmuir CA

Mile Point	Yogi Book Section	
2128.1	23	Eagle Creek Alternate
106.2	2	Eagle Rock
1092.3	11	Echo Lake CA
0.0	1	El Cajon CA
1952.6	22	Elk Lake Resort
386.1	6	Endangered Species Detour
1599.7	17	Etna CA
850.9	10	Evolution Creek
1773.4	20	Fish Lake Resort
779.5	9	Forester Pass
188.0	4	Fuller Ridge
791.1	10	Glen Pass
2092.2	23	Government Camp OR
1735.3	20	Green Springs Inn
2622.5	28	Harts Pass
1599.7	17	Hiker Hut
517.6	7	Hikertown
2147.1	23	Hood River OR
1742.7	20	Hyatt Lake Resort
179.4	3	Idyllwild CA via Devils Slide Trail
151.9	3	Idyllwild CA via Pines-to-Palms Hwy
788.9	9	Independence CA via Kearsarge Pass
1501.2	16	Interstate 5
1718.7	19	Interstate 5
26.6	1	Interstate 8
209.5	4	Interstate 10
341.9	5	Interstate 15
1157.1	12	Interstate 80
1202.6	23	Interstate 84
2393.7	25	Interstate 90
652.1	8	Inyokern CA
77.0	2	Julian CA
652.1	8	Kernville CA
788.9	9	Kearsarge Pass Trail
702.2	8	Kennedy Meadows CA
1016.9	11	Kennedy Meadows Resort
1773.4	20	Lake of the Woods Resort
0.0	1	La Mesa CA
109.5	2	Lake Henshaw Resort
485.8	7	Lake Hughes CA
652.1	8	Lake Isabella CA
20.0	1	Lake Morena County Park
2464.7	26	Leavenworth WA

Mile Point	Yogi Book Section	
942.5	10	Lee Vining CA
750.2	9	Lone Pine CA via Cottonwood Pass
788.9	9	Lone Pine CA via Kearsarge Pass
745.3	9	Lone Pine CA via Trail Pass
906.7	10	Mammoth Lakes CA
2661.9	28	Manning Park
1048.4	11	Markleeville CA
816.9	10	Mather Pass
2591.6	28	Mazama WA
1983.7	22	McKenzie Pass / Hwy 242
566.5	7	Mojave CA via Highway 58
558.5	7	Mojave CA via Tehachapi-Willow Springs Road
878.7	10	Mono Hot Springs
2229.4	24	Mount Adams Zen Buddhist Temple
1501.2	16	Mount Shasta CA
377.9	6	Mt. Baden-Powell
41.5	1	Mt. Laguna CA
766.3	9	Mt. Whitney
838.6	10	Muir Pass
857.7	10	Muir Trail Ranch
2046.0	23	Olallie Lake Resort
1373.4	14	Old Station CA
652.1	8	Onyx CA
2147.5	24	Oregon-Washington border
2295.4	24	Packwood WA
151.8	3	Paradise Valley Café
807.1	10	Pinchot Pass
26.0	1	Pine Valley CA
151.8	3	Pines-to-Palms Highway
2147.1	23	Portland OR
1286.9	13	Quincy CA
2591.6	28	Rainy Pass
906.7	10	Reds Meadow CA
652.1	8	Ridgecrest CA
179.4	3	Saddle Junction
181.2	4	San Jacinto Alternate
2092.2	23	Sandy OR
109.5	2	Santa Ysabel CA
2000.9	22	Santiam Pass / Hwy 20
77.0	2	Scissors Crossing
1655.9	18	Seiad Valley CA
865.6	10	Selden Pass
1906.6	21	Shelter Cove Resort
1195.4	12	Sierra City CA

LANDMARKS and TOWNS ALPHABETICALLY

Mile Point	Yogi Book Section	
884.9	10	Silver Pass
328.7	5	Silverwood Lake
2000.9	22	Sisters OR via Hwy 20
1983.7	22	Sisters OR via Hwy 242
2464.7	26	Skykomish WA
2393.6	25	Snoqualmie Pass WA
1153.4	12	Soda Springs CA
1016.9	11	Sonora Pass
1092.3	11	South Lake Tahoe CA
77.0	2	Stagecoach Trails RV Park
2572.4	27	Stehekin WA
2464.7	26	Stevens Pass
2147.1	23	Stevenson WA
2541.1	27	Suiattle River
1124.8	12	Tahoe City CA
566.5	7	Tehachapi CA via Highway 58
558.5	7	Tehachapi CA via Tehachapi-W Springs Road
558.5	7	Tehachapi-Willow Springs Road
91.2	2	Third Gate
2097.4	23	Timberline Lodge OR
745.3	9	Trail Pass
702.2	8	Triple Crown Outfitters
2229.4	24	Trout Lake WA via Road 23
1153.4	12	Truckee CA
941.7	10	Tuolumne Meadows Lodge
942.5	10	Tuolumne Meadows PO/Store
2653.1	28	US-Canada border
0.0	1	US-Mexico border
275.1	4	Van Dusen Canyon Road
878.7	10	Vermilion Valley Resort
1016.9	11	Walker CA
652.1	8	Walker Pass
109.5	2	Warner Springs CA
517.6	7	Wee Vill Market
652.1	8	Weldon CA
2295.4	24	White Pass WA
218.5	4	Whitewater Preserve
1907.9	21	Willamette Pass
2591.6	28	Winthrop WA
363.4	5	Wrightwood CA via Acorn Trail
369.4	5	Wrightwood CA via Highway 2
942.5	11	Yosemite Valley

Mail Drop Addresses

Number of days indicates how long the location holds mail after it arrives at the location. If no time limit mentioned, hiker mail typically held until end of hiker season (no promises!).

26.0 Pine Valley

Post Office, USPS only, 15 days:
Hiker's Legal Name
PCT Hiker, ETA: MM/DD/YY
General Delivery
Pine Valley, CA 91962

41.5 Mount Laguna

Post Office, USPS only:
Hiker's Legal Name
PCT Hiker, ETA: MM/DD/YY
General Delivery
Mount Laguna, CA 91948

Store/Lodge USPS address:
Hiker's Legal Name
PCT Hiker, ETA: MM/DD/YY
c/o Laguna Mountain Lodge
PO Box 146
Mt. Laguna, CA 91948

Store/Lodge,
UPS or FedEx address:
Hiker's Legal Name
PCT Hiker, ETA: MM/DD/YY
c/o Laguna Mountain Lodge
10678 Sunrise Highway
Mt. Laguna, CA 91948

77.0 Julian

Post Office, USPS only, 30 days:
Hiker's Legal Name
PCT Hiker, ETA: MM/DD/YY
General Delivery
1785 Highway 78
Julian, CA 92036

109.5 Warner Springs

Post Office, USPS only, 30 days:
Hiker's Legal Name
PCT Hiker, ETA: MM/DD/YY
General Delivery
Warner Springs CA 92086

109.5 Santa Ysabel

Post Office, USPS only, 30 days:
Hiker's Legal Name
PCT Hiker, ETA: MM/DD/YY
General Delivery
Santa Ysabel CA 92070

151.8 Paradise Valley Café

USPS, UPS, FedEx:
Hiker's Legal Name
PCT Hiker, ETA: MM/DD/YY
c/o Paradise Valley Café
61721 State Highway 74
Mountain Center, CA 92561

151.8 Anza

Post Office, USPS only, 30 days:
Hiker's Legal Name
PCT Hiker, ETA: MM/DD/YY
Anza CA 92539

151.8 Idyllwild

Post Office, USPS only, 3 weeks:
Hiker's Legal Name
PCT Hiker, ETA: MM/DD/YY
General Delivery
Idyllwild, CA 92549

Idyllwild Inn, USPS address:
Hiker's Legal Name
PCT Hiker, ETA: MM/DD/YY
c/o Idyllwild Inn
PO Box 515
Idyllwild, CA 92549

Idyllwild Inn
UPS or FedEx address:
Hiker's Legal Name
PCT Hiker, ETA: MM/DD/YY
c/o Idyllwild Inn
54300 Village Center Drive
Idyllwild, CA 92549

209.5 Cabazon

Post Office, USPS only, 30 days:
Hiker's Legal Name
PCT Hiker, ETA: MM/DD/YY
General Delivery
Cabazon CA 92230

266.1 Big Bear City

Post Office, USPS only, 30 days:
Hiker's Legal Name
PCT Hiker, ETA: MM/DD/YY
General Delivery
Big Bear City, CA 92314

Trail Angels
USPS, UPS, FedEx:
Hiker's Legal Name
PCT Hiker, ETA: MM/DD/YY
c/o Steve & Sandy Teutschman
840 E Angeles Blvd
Big Bear City, CA 92314

266.1 Big Bear Lake

Post Office, USPS only, 30 days:
Hiker's Legal Name
PCT Hiker, ETA: MM/DD/YY
General Delivery
472 Pine Knot
Big Bear Lake, CA 92315

Big Bear Hostel, USPS address:
Hiker's Legal Name
PCT Hiker, ETA: MM/DD/YY
c/o Big Bear Hostel
PO Box 1951
Big Bear Lake, CA 92315

Big Bear Hostel
UPS or FedEx address:
Hiker's Legal Name
PCT Hiker, ETA: MM/DD/YY
c/o Big Bear Lake Hostel
541 Knickerbocker Rd (office)
Big Bear Lake, CA 92315

298.5 Cedar Glen

Post Office, USPS only, 15 days:
Hiker's Legal Name
PCT Hiker, ETA: MM/DD/YY
General Delivery
Cedar Glen CA 92321

298.5 Lake Arrowhead

Post Office, USPS only, 15 days:
Hiker's Legal Name
PCT Hiker, ETA: MM/DD/YY
General Delivery
Lake Arrowhead, CA 92352

Mail Drop Addresses

Number of days indicates how long the location holds mail after it arrives at the location. If no time limit mentioned, hiker mail typically held until end of hiker season (no promises!).

341.9 Cajon Pass

Cajon Pass Inn
USPS, UPS, FedEx:
Hiker's Legal Name
PCT Hiker, ETA: MM/DD/YY
c/o Cajon Pass Inn
8317 US Hwy 138
At the 15 Freeway
Phelan, CA 92371

363.4 Wrightwood

Post Office, USPS only,
hiker mail held until ETA:
Hiker's Legal Name
PCT Hiker, ETA: MM/DD/YY
General Delivery
Wrightwood, CA 92397

Hardware Store, USPS address:
Hiker's Legal Name
PCT Hiker, ETA: MM/DD/YY
c/o Mountain Hardware
PO Box 398
Wrightwood, CA 92397

Hardware Store prefers hikers
ship using UPS or FedEx.
UPS or FedEx address:
Hiker's Legal Name
PCT Hiker, ETA: MM/DD/YY
c/o Mountain Hardware
1390 Highway 2
Wrightwood, CA 92397

444.2 Acton

Post Office, USPS only, 15 days:
Hiker's Legal Name
PCT Hiker, ETA: MM/DD/YY
General Delivery
Acton, CA 93510

444.3 Acton KOA

USPS, UPS, FedEx:
Hiker's Legal Name
PCT Hiker, ETA: MM/DD/YY
c/o Acton KOA
7601 Soledad Canyon Road
Acton, CA 93510

485.8 Lake Hughes

Post Office, USPS only, 30 days:
Hiker's Legal Name
PCT Hiker, ETA: MM/DD/YY
General Delivery
16817 Elizabeth Lake Road
Lake Hughes, CA 93532

517.6 Hiker Town

USPS, UPS, FedEx:
Hiker's Legal Name
PCT Hiker, ETA: MM/DD/YY
c/o Hikertown
26803 W. Ave C-15
Lancaster, CA 93536

517.6 Wee Vill Market

USPS, UPS, FedEx:
Hiker's Legal Name
PCT Hiker, ETA: MM/DD/YY
c/o Wee Vill Market
18348 W. Avenue D
Lancaster, CA 93536

517.6 Wind Farm

USPS, UPS, FedEx:
Hiker's Legal Name
PCT Hiker, ETA: MM/DD/YY
c/o Avangrid Renewables -
Manzana Wind
17890 Champagne Ave
Rosamond, CA 93560

558.5 Mojave

Post Office, USPS only,
hiker mail held for 3 months:
Hiker's Legal Name
PCT Hiker, ETA: MM/DD/YY
General Delivery
2053 Belshaw St
Mojave, CA 93501

Original Motel 6
USPS, UPS, FedEx:
Hiker's Legal Name
PCT Hiker, ETA: MM/DD/YY
c/o Motel 6
SR 58 / Sierra Hwy @ SR 14
16958 State Route 58
Mojave CA 93501

558.5 Tehachapi

Post Office, USPS only, 30 days:
Hiker's Legal Name
PCT Hiker, ETA: MM/DD/YY
General Delivery
1085 Voyager Drive
Tehachapi, CA 93581

Trail Angels
USPS, UPS, FedEx:
Hiker's Legal Name
PCT Hiker, ETA: MM/DD/YY
c/o Dalton Steele Reed
115 S. Mojave Street
Tehachapi CA 93561

652.1 Onyx

Post Office, USPS only,
hiker mail held for 60 days:
Hiker's Legal Name
PCT Hiker, ETA: MM/DD/YY
General Delivery
8275 Easy Street
Onyx, CA 93255

652.1 Weldon

Post Office, USPS only,
hiker mail held for 30 days:
Hiker's Legal Name
PCT Hiker, ETA: MM/DD/YY
General Delivery
Weldon, CA 93283

652.1 Lake Isabella

Post Office, USPS only, 30 days:
Hiker's Legal Name
PCT Hiker, ETA: MM/DD/YY
General Delivery
Lake Isabella, CA 93240

Lake Isabella Motel
USPS address:
Hiker's Legal Name
PCT Hiker, ETA: MM/DD/YY
c/o Lake Isabella Motel
PO Box 2134
Lake Isabella, CA 93240

Lake Isabella Motel
UPS or FedEx address:
Hiker's Legal Name
PCT Hiker, ETA: MM/DD/YY
c/o Lake Isabella Motel
400 Highway 155
Lake Isabella, CA 93240

65210   Kernville

Post Office, USPS only, 30 days:
Hiker's Legal Name
PCT Hiker, ETA: MM/DD/YY
General Delivery
Kernville, CA 93238

652.1   Inyokern

Post Office, USPS only, 30 days:
Hiker's Legal Name
PCT Hiker, ETA: MM/DD/YY
General Delivery
HOLD IN INYOKERN !!
Inyokern, CA 93527

652.1   Ridgecrest

Post Office, USPS only, 30 days:
Hiker's Legal Name
PCT Hiker, ETA: MM/DD/YY
General Delivery
Ridgecrest, CA 93555

702.2 Kennedy Meadows

Triple Crown Outfitters
is a new gear and resupply shop
in KM! Full hiker resupply, no
need to send a box. See resupply
photos in the Town Guide section
of this book, mile 702.2.

Grumpy Bear Retreat
in Kennedy Meadows
USPS, UPS, FedEx:
Hiker's Legal Name
PCT Hiker, ETA: MM/DD/YY
c/o Grumpy Bear Retreat
   in Kennedy Meadows
98887 Kennedy Meadows Road
Inyokern, CA 93527

745.3   Lone Pine

Post Office, USPS only, 30 days:
Hiker's Legal Name
PCT Hiker, ETA: MM/DD/YY
General Delivery
Lone Pine, CA 93545

Whitney Portal Hostel UPS or
FedEx only, 2 weeks after ETA:
Hiker's Legal Name
PCT Hiker, ETA: MM/DD/YY
c/o Whitney Portal Hostel
238 Main Street
Lone Pine, CA 93545

788.9   Bishop

Post Office, USPS only, 30 days:
Hiker's Legal Name
PCT Hiker, ETA: MM/DD/YY
General Delivery
Bishop, CA 93514

788.9   Independence

Post Office, USPS only,
30 days after ETA date:
Hiker's Legal Name
PCT Hiker, ETA: MM/DD/YY
General Delivery
Independence, CA 93526

Courthouse Motel
USPS address:
Hiker's Legal Name
PCT Hiker, ETA: MM/DD/YY
c/o The Courthouse Motel
157 N Edwards St.
PO Box 29
Independence, CA 93526

Courthouse Motel
UPS or FedEx address:
Hiker's Legal Name
PCT Hiker, ETA: MM/DD/YY
c/o The Courthouse Motel
157 N Edwards St.
Independence, CA 93526

857.7   Muir Trail Ranch

Instructions on website:
www.muirtrailranch.com

878.7   Vermilion Valley Resort

UPS or FedEx only, 30 days:
Hiker's Legal Name
PCT Hiker, ETA: MM/DD/YY
Vermilion Valley Resort
c/o Rancheria Garage
62311 Huntington Lake Road
Lakeshore, CA 93634

878.   Mono Hot Springs

USPS only, summer address,
held until ETA date:
Hiker's Legal Name
PCT Hiker, ETA: MM/DD/YY
General Delivery
Mono Hot Springs, CA 93642

906.7   Reds Meadow

Instructions on website:
www.redsmeadow.com

906.7   Mammoth Lakes

Post Office, USPS only:
Hiker's Legal Name
PCT Hiker, ETA: MM/DD/YY
General Delivery
Mammoth Lakes, CA 93546

942.5   Tuolumne Meadows

Post Office, USPS only:
Hiker's Legal Name
Hiker's Trail Name
PCT Hiker, ETA: MM/DD/YY
General Delivery
c/o Tuolumne Meadows
      Post Office
Yosemite National Park, CA
                    9 5389

942.5   Lee Vining

Post Office, USPS only, 30 days:
Hiker's Legal Name
PCT Hiker, ETA: MM/DD/YY
General Delivery
121 Lee Vining Ave
Lee Vining, CA 93541

Mail Drop Addresses

Number of days indicates how long the location holds mail after it arrives at the location. If no time limit mentioned, hiker mail typically held until end of hiker season (no promises!).

1016.9 Kennedy Meadows Resort

This is NOT the Kennedy Meadows before the Sierra. The other Kennedy Meadows is at mile 702.2. BE SURE you send your box to the correct location.

UPS only:
Hiker's Legal Name
PCT Hiker, ETA: MM/DD/YY
c/o Kennedy Meadows Resort
    and Pack Station
42421 State Highway 108
Pinecrest, CA 95364

1016.9 Bridgeport

Post Office, USPS only, hiker mail held until end of Sept:
Hiker's Legal Name
PCT Hiker, ETA: MM/DD/YY
General Delivery
29 Kingsley Street
Bridgeport, CA 93517

1016.9 Walker

Post Office, USPS only, 30 days:
Hiker's Legal Name
PCT Hiker, ETA: MM/DD/YY
General Delivery
Coleville, CA 96107

1048.4 Markleeville

Post Office, USPS only, 15 days:
Hiker's Legal Name
PCT Hiker, ETA: MM/DD/YY
General Delivery
Markleeville, CA 96120

1092.3 South Lake Tahoe

Post Office, USPS only, 15 days unless arrival date is later:
Hiker's Legal Name
PCT Hiker, ETA: MM/DD/YY
General Delivery
South Lake Tahoe, CA 96150

Mellow Mountain Hostel USPS, UPS, FedEx:
Hiker's Legal Name
PCT Hiker, ETA: MM/DD/YY
c/o Mellow Mountain Hostel
4081 Cedar Ave
South Lake Tahoe, CA 96150

1124.8 Tahoe City

Post Office, USPS only, 30 days:
Hiker's Legal Name
PCT Hiker, ETA: MM/DD/YY
General Delivery
950 N Lake Tahoe Blvd, Suite 12
Tahoe City, CA 96145

1153.4 Soda Springs

Post Office, USPS only, 30 days:
Hiker's Legal Name
PCT Hiker, ETA: MM/DD/YY
General Delivery
Soda Springs, CA 95728

Clair Tappaan Lodge USPS address:
Hiker's Legal Name
PCT Hiker, ETA: MM/DD/YY
c/o Clair Tappaan Lodge
PO Box 36
Soda Springs, CA 95728

Clair Tappaan Lodge UPS or FedEx address:
Hiker's Legal Name
PCT Hiker, ETA: MM/DD/YY
c/o Clair Tappaan Lodge
19940 Donner Pass Road
Norden, CA 95724

1153.4 Truckee

Post Office, USPS only, 15 days:
Hiker's Legal Name
PCT Hiker, ETA: MM/DD/YY
General Delivery
10050 Bridge Street
Truckee, CA 96161

Office Boss accepts packages, must call to make arrangements.
530-587-1620

1195.4 Sierra City

Post Office, USPS only:
Hiker's Legal Name
PCT Hiker, ETA: MM/DD/YY
General Delivery
215 Main Street
Sierra City, CA 96125

Store, USPS:
Hiker's Legal Name
PCT Hiker, ETA: MM/DD/YY
c/o Sierra Country Store
PO Box 196
Sierra City, CA 96125

Store, UPS or FedEx address:
Hiker's Legal Name
PCT Hiker, ETA: MM/DD/YY
c/o Sierra Country Store
213 Main Street
Sierra City, CA 96125

Red Moose Inn, USPS:
Hiker's Legal Name
PCT Hiker, ETA: MM/DD/YY
c/o Red Moose Inn
PO Box 213
Sierra City, CA 96126

Red Moose Inn, UPS or FedEx:
Hiker's Legal Name
PCT Hiker, ETA: MM/DD/YY
c/o Red Moose Inn
224 Main Street
Sierra City, CA 96126

1286.8 Belden

Belden Town Resort UPS or FedEx only:
Hiker's Legal Name
PCT Hiker, ETA: MM/DD/YY
c/o Belden Town Resort
14785 Belden Town Road
Belden, CA 95915

Mail Drop Addresses

Number of days indicates how long the location holds mail after it arrives at the location. If no time limit mentioned, hiker mail typically held until end of hiker season (no promises!).

1286.9 Quincy

Post Office, USPS only, 15 days unless you call to hold longer:
Hiker's Legal Name
PCT Hiker, ETA: MM/DD/YY
General Delivery
Quincy, CA 95971

PCIRC, USPS, UPS, FedEx:
Hiker's Legal Name
PCT Hiker, ETA: MM/DD/YY
c/o PCIRC
591 Main Street
Quincy, CA 95971

1331.3 Chester

Post Office, USPS only, 30 days:
Hiker's Legal Name
PCT Hiker, ETA: MM/DD/YY
General Delivery
Chester, CA 96020

1349.7 Drakesbad

USPS, UPS, FedEx:
Hiker's Legal Name
PCT Hiker, ETA: MM/DD/YY
c/o Drakesbad Guest Ranch
End of Warner Valley Road
Chester, CA 96020

1373.4 Old Station

Post Office, USPS only:
Hiker's Legal Name
PCT Hiker, ETA: MM/DD/YY
General Delivery
Old Station, CA 96071

1377.3 Old Station Fill-Up

UPS or FedEx only:
Hiker's Legal Name
PCT Hiker, ETA: MM/DD/YY
c/o JJ's Café
13385 Hwy 89
Old Station, CA 96071

1411.3 Burney

Post Office, USPS only, 30 days:
Hiker's Legal Name
PCT Hiker, ETA: MM/DD/YY
General Delivery
Burney, CA 96013

Word of Life Church USPS, UPS, FedEx:
Hiker's Legal Name
PCT Hiker, ETA: MM/DD/YY
c/o Word of Life
    Assembly Church
37341 Main Street
Burney, CA 96013

1419.0 Burney Falls State Park

USPS, UPS, FedEx:
Hiker's Legal Name
PCT Hiker, ETA: MM/DD/YY
c/o Burney Park Camp Store
McArthur Burney Falls State Pk
24900 State Highway 89
Burney, CA 96013

1501.2 Castella

Post Office, USPS only, 30 days:
Hiker's Legal Name
PCT Hiker, ETA: MM/DD/YY
General Delivery
Castella, CA 96017

Store, USPS address:
Hiker's Legal Name
PCT Hiker, ETA: MM/DD/YY
c/o Ammirati's Market
PO Box 90
Castella, CA 96017

Store, UPS or FedEx address:
Hiker's Legal Name
PCT Hiker, ETA: MM/DD/YY
c/o Ammirati's Market
20107 Castle Creek Road
Castella, CA 96017

1501.2 Dunsmuir

Post Office, USPS only, hiker mail held for 30 days, unless you call to ask to hold longer:
Hiker's Legal Name
PCT Hiker, ETA: MM/DD/YY
General Delivery
Dunsmuir, CA 96025

Dunsmuir Lodge USPS, UPS or FedEx:
Hiker's Legal Name
PCT Hiker, ETA: MM/DD/YY
c/o Dunsmuir Lodge
6604 Dunsmuir Ave
Dunsmuir, CA 96025

1501.2 Mount Shasta

Post Office, USPS only:
Hiker's Legal Name
PCT Hiker, ETA: MM/DD/YY
General Delivery
301 S. Mt Shasta Blvd
Mount Shasta, CA 96067

1560.2 Callahan

Post Office, USPS only:
Hiker's Legal Name
PCT Hiker, ETA: MM/DD/YY
General Delivery
Callahan, CA 96014

1599.7 Etna

Post Office, USPS only:
Hiker's Legal Name
PCT Hiker, ETA: MM/DD/YY
General Delivery
119 Diggles Street
Etna, CA 96027

Alderbrook Manor Hiker Hut USPS, UPS, FedEx:
Hiker's Legal Name
PCT Hiker, ETA: MM/DD/YY
c/o Alderbrook Manor
836 Sawyers Bar Road
Etna, CA 96027

Mail Drop Addresses

Number of days indicates how long the location holds mail after it arrives at the location. If no time limit mentioned, hiker mail typically held until end of hiker season (no promises!).

1655.9 Seiad Valley

Post Office, USPS only:
Hiker's Legal Name
PCT Hiker, ETA: MM/DD/YY
General Delivery
44717 State Highway 96
Seiad Valley, CA 96086

Store
USPS, UPS, FedEx:
Hiker's Legal Name
PCT Hiker, ETA: MM/DD/YY
c/o Seiad Valley Store
44719 State Highway 96
Seiad Valley, CA 96086

RV Park
USPS address:
Hiker's Legal Name
PCT Hiker, ETA: MM/DD/YY
c/o Mid River RV Park
PO Box 707
Seiad Valley, CA 96086

1718.7 Callahan's Lodge

USPS, UPS, FedEx:
Hiker's Legal Name
PCT Hiker, ETA: MM/DD/YY
c/o Callahan's Lodge
7100 Old Highway 99 South
Ashland, OR 97520

1718.7 Ashland

Post Office, USPS only, hiker mail held 30 days or until ETA:
Hiker's Legal Name
PCT Hiker, ETA: MM/DD/YY
General Delivery
Ashland, OR 97520

Rodeway Inn
USPS, UPS, FedEx:
Hiker's Legal Name
PCT Hiker, ETA: MM/DD/YY
c/o Rodeway Inn
2359 Ashland Street
Ashland, OR 97520

1735.3 Green Springs Inn

USPS, UPS, FedEx:
Hiker's Legal Name
PCT Hiker, ETA: MM/DD/YY
c/o Green Springs Inn
11470 Highway 66
Ashland, OR 97520

1742.7 Hyatt Lake Resort

UPS or FedEx only:
Hiker's Legal Name
PCT Hiker, ETA: MM/DD/YY
c/o Hyatt Lake Resort
7900 Hyatt Prairie Road
Ashland, OR 97520

1773.4 Fish Lake Resort

UPS only:
Hiker's Legal Name
PCT Hiker, ETA: MM/DD/YY
c/o Fish Lake Resort
State Hwy 140, Mile Marker 30
Eagle Point, OR 97524

1820.9 Crater Lake

Mazama Village Store
USPS address:
Hiker's Legal Name
PCT Hiker, ETA: MM/DD/YY
c/o Mazama Village Camp Store
Mazama Village
Crater Lake, OR 97604

Mazama Village Store
UPS or FedEx address:
Hiker's Legal Name
PCT Hiker, ETA: MM/DD/YY
c/o Mazama Village Camp Store
569 Mazama Village Drive
Crater Lake, OR 97604

1848.0 Diamond Lake Resort

USPS, UPS, FedEx:
Hiker's Legal Name
PCT Hiker, ETA: MM/DD/YY
c/o Diamond Lake Resort
340 Resort Drive
Diamond Lake, OR 97731

1906.6 Shelter Cove Resort

USPS, UPS, FedEx:
Hiker's Legal Name
PCT Hiker, ETA: MM/DD/YY
c/o Shelter Cove Resort
27600 West Odell Lake Road
Highway 58
Crescent, OR 97733

1907.9 Crescent Lake

Willamette Inn, USPS only:
Hiker's Legal Name
PCT Hiker, ETA: MM/DD/YY
c/o Willamette Pass Inn
PO Box 1035
Crescent Lake OR 97733

1952.6 Elk Lake Resort

UPS or FedEx only:
Hiker's Legal Name
PCT Hiker, ETA: MM/DD/YY
c/o Elk Lake Resort
60,000 Century Drive
Bend, OR 97701

1952.6 Bend

Post Office, USPS only, 2 weeks:
Hiker's Legal Name
PCT Hiker, ETA: MM/DD/YY
General Delivery
Bend, OR 97701

REI
USPS, UPS, FedEx:
Hiker's Legal Name
PCT Hiker, ETA: MM/DD/YY
c/o REI #96
380 SW Powerhouse Drive
Bend, OR 97702

Trail Angel
USPS, UPS, FedEx:
Hiker's Legal Name
PCT Hiker, ETA: MM/DD/YY
c/o Brian Douglass
1686 NE Tucson Way
Bend, OR 97701-6235

Mail Drop Addresses

Number of days indicates how long the location holds mail after it arrives at the location. If no time limit mentioned, hiker mail typically held until end of hiker season (no promises!).

1983.7 Sisters

Post Office, USPS only, 15 days:
Hiker's Legal Name
PCT Hiker, ETA: MM/DD/YY
General Delivery
Sisters, OR 97759

Sisters Inn, USPS address:
Hiker's Legal Name
PCT Hiker, ETA: MM/DD/YY
c/o Sisters Inn
PO Box 938
Sisters, OR 97759

Sisters Inn
UPS or FedEx address:
Hiker's Legal Name
PCT Hiker, ETA: MM/DD/YY
c/o Sisters Inn
605 N. Arrowleaf Trail
Sisters OR 97759

1995.1 Big Lake Camp

USPS or UPS only:
Hiker's Legal Name
PCT Hiker, ETA: MM/DD/YY
c/o Big Lake Youth Camp
26435 Big Lake Road
Sisters, OR 97759

2092.2 Gov't Camp

Post Office, USPS only, 2 weeks or ETA, whichever is later:
Hiker's Legal Name
PCT Hiker, ETA: MM/DD/YY
General Delivery
88331 E Govt Camp Loop
Government Camp, OR 97028

2092.2 Sandy

Post Office, USPS only, 15 days:
Hiker's Legal Name
PCT Hiker, ETA: MM/DD/YY
General Delivery
Sandy, OR 97055

2097.4 Timberline Ldg

USPS or UPS only:
Hiker's Legal Name
PCT Hiker, ETA: MM/DD/YY
c/o Timberline Lodge Ski Area
27500 E Timberline Road
WY'East Store
Timberline Lodge, OR 97028

2147.1 Cascade Locks

Post Office, USPS only, hiker mail held until end of October:
Hiker's Legal Name
PCT Hiker, ETA: MM/DD/YY
General Delivery
Cascade Locks, OR 97014

Cascade Locks Ale House
USPS address:
Hiker's Legal Name
PCT Hiker, ETA: MM/DD/YY
c/o Cascade Locks Ale House
PO Box 388
Cascade Locks OR 97014

Cascade Locks Ale House
UPS or FedEx address:
Hiker's Legal Name
PCT Hiker, ETA: MM/DD/YY
c/o Cascade Locks Ale House
500 WaNaPa Street
Cascade Locks OR 97014

Port Marine RV Park
USPS only:
Hiker's Legal Name
PCT Hiker, ETA: MM/DD/YY
c/o Port Marine RV Park
355 WaNaPa Street
Cascade Locks, OR 97014

2147.1 Stevenson

Post Office, USPS only, 15 days:
Hiker's Legal Name
PCT Hiker, ETA: MM/DD/YY
General Delivery
Stevenson, WA 98648

Rodeway Inn accepts mail drops.
509-427-5628

2147.1 Hood River

Post Office, USPS only,
hiker mail held for 30 days:
Hiker's Legal Name
PCT Hiker, ETA: MM/DD/YY
General Delivery
Hood River, OR 97031

2229.4 Trout Lake

Post Office, USPS only:
Hiker's Legal Name
PCT Hiker, ETA: MM/DD/YY
General Delivery
2393 Highway 141
Trout Lake, WA 98650

Grocery, USPS:
Hiker's Legal Name
PCT Hiker, ETA: MM/DD/YY
c/o Trout Lake Grocery
PO Box 132
Trout Lake, WA 98650

Grocery, UPS or FedEx:
Hiker's Legal Name
PCT Hiker, ETA: MM/DD/YY
c/o Trout Lake Grocery
2383 Highway 141
Trout Lake, WA 98650

2295.4 White Pass

USPS, UPS, FedEx:
Hiker's Legal Name
PCT Hiker, ETA: MM/DD/YY
c/o White Pass Rural Branch PO
    at the Kracker Barrel Store
48851 US Highway 12
Naches, WA 98937

2295.4 Packwood

Post Office, USPS only, 30 days:
Hiker's Legal Name
PCT Hiker, ETA: MM/DD/YY
General Delivery
Packwood, WA 98361

Mail Drop Addresses

Number of days indicates how long the location holds mail after it arrives at the location. If no time limit mentioned, hiker mail typically held until end of hiker season (no promises!).

2393.6 Snoqualmie Pass

Chevron
USPS, UPS, FedEx, 3 weeks:
Hiker's Legal Name
PCT Hiker, ETA: MM/DD/YY
c/o Chevron Station
521 State Route 906
Snoqualmie Pass, WA 98068

Summit Inn
USPS, UPS, FedEx:
Hiker's Legal Name
PCT Hiker, ETA: MM/DD/YY
c/o Summit Inn Hotel
603 SR 906
PO Box 163
Snoqualmie Pass, WA 98068

2464.7 Stevens Pass

UPS or FedEx only:
Hiker's Legal Name
PCT Hiker, ETA: MM/DD/YY
c/o Stevens Pass
93001 NE Stevens Pass Hwy, US2
Skykomish, WA 98288

2464.1 Skykomish

Post Office, USPS only, hiker mail held until end of hiker season:
Hiker's Legal Name
PCT Hiker, ETA: MM/DD/YY
General Delivery
Skykomish, WA 98288

2464.7 Leavenworth

Post Office, USPS only, 30 days:
Hiker's Legal Name
PCT Hiker, ETA: MM/DD/YY
General Delivery
Leavenworth, WA 98826

2572.4 Stehekin

Post Office, USPS only:
Hiker's Legal Name
PCT Hiker, ETA: MM/DD/YY
General Delivery
Stehekin, WA 98852

2572.4 Chelan

Post Office, USPS only, 30 days:
Hiker's Legal Name
PCT Hiker, ETA: MM/DD/YY
General Delivery
Chelan, WA 98816

2591.6 Mazama

USPS, UPS, FedEx:
Hiker's Legal Name
PCT Hiker ETA: MM/DD/YY
c/o Goats Beard Mountain
    Supplies
50 Lost River Road
Mazama WA 98833

2591.6 Winthrop

Post Office, USPS only, 30 days:
Hiker's Legal Name
PCT Hiker, ETA: MM/DD/YY
General Delivery
Winthrop, WA 98862

Hostel, USPS address:
Hiker's Legal Name
PCT Hiker, ETA: MM/DD/YY
North Cascades Mountain Hostel
PO Box 1338
Winthrop, WA 98862

Hostel, UPS or FedEx address:
Hiker's Legal Name
PCT Hiker, ETA: MM/DD/YY
North Cascades Mountain Hostel
209 Castle Ave
Winthrop, WA 98862

2661.9 Manning Park

Hiker's Legal Name
PCT Hiker, ETA: MM/DD/YY
c/o Manning Park Lodge
7500 Highway #3
Manning Provincial Park, BC
V0X IR0   CANADA

USING YOGI'S PCT HANDBOOK

The second half of this Handbook contains trail and town information. Don't carry the whole book on the trail. Just take the pages you need for each section. The trail and town information is organized in 28 separate sections. Each section begins with a summary box similar to this:

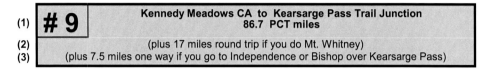

(1) **# 9** — Kennedy Meadows CA to Kearsarge Pass Trail Junction — 86.7 PCT miles

(2) (plus 17 miles round trip if you do Mt. Whitney)

(3) (plus 7.5 miles one way if you go to Independence or Bishop over Kearsarge Pass)

This summary box tells you:

(1) This is Handbook Section #9. From Kennedy Meadows CA to the PCT junction with the Kearsarge Pass Trail, you will walk 86.7 PCT miles.

(2) If you choose to go up Mt. Whitney — which is a side trip OFF the PCT — you must ADD 17 miles (8.5 miles from the PCT to the top of Whitney, then 8.5 miles back down to the PCT).

(3) If you leave the PCT via Kearsarge Pass (to Independence , Bishop, or Lone Pine), you must ADD 7.5 miles (7.5 miles ONE WAY from the PCT-Kearsarge Pass Trail junction, over Kearsarge Pass, ending at the trailhead parking lot).

If you turn to the actual Section # 9 "Kennedy Meadows CA to Kearsarge Pass Trail Junction" in the Handbook, you'll notice that information for Kennedy Meadows is NOT included in this section. Instead, Kennedy Meadows is described in Section #8 "Mojave or Tehachapi CA to Kennedy Meadows CA." Why? Because as you hike out of Kennedy Meadows into the Sierra with your "Kennedy Meadows to Kearsarge" data, you don't care what you can find in Kennedy Meadows. You've already been there. However, as you were hiking into Kennedy Meadows from Mojave or Tehachapi, you wanted to know what you'd find in Kennedy Meadows when you got there. You had that information in your pack, because it was included in your "Mojave or Tehachapi to Kennedy Meadows" Handbook section.

So you see, *"YOGI'S PACIFIC CREST TRAIL HANDBOOK"* is organized into sections which are logical for thru-hikers and easy for mail drops.

Radar: I really liked the way you have town information at the END of a section so that I didn't have to carry the beginning of the next section. You also repeat information as necessary. Excellent design on your part.

Little John: I really like the summary boxes at the beginning of each section, especially when there are two ways out of one town and into the next. There were several points on the trail that I jumped off at a different location than I had planned (including both Big Bear City and Wrightwood). Using the summary boxes, I was able to look at the section in advance and plan my hike much better.

TRAVEL TO THE TERMINUS

SOUTHERN TERMINUS

PUBLIC TRANSPORTATION

Taxi fare from the San Diego airport to Campo is $200+. Instead, you could take public transportation for less than $20. You'll take a bus from the airport to downtown, then a trolley from downtown to El Cajon, then another bus from El Cajon to Campo. Bus-Trolley-Bus information is in the Town Guide section of this Handbook.

PREVIOUS HIKERS and TRAIL ANGELS

Many people are willing to help PCT hikers get from San Diego to Campo. Your chances of finding a ride with a previous hiker or a Trail Angel are very good. If you can get a ride with someone, TAKE IT. The bus-trolley-bus combination works, but it takes a long time. If you take the afternoon bus, you will arrive in Campo after 5pm.

The best way to start the trail is to contact one of the many San Diego Trail Angels (see below). The San Diego Trail Angels use a coordinated effort to make sure that all hikers have a relaxing, welcoming start to their hikes.

BARNEY and SANDY MANN

We (Scout and Frodo) host Pacific Crest Trail hikers before their permit start date: U.S. hikers for one night and international hikers for up to three nights. We also host section hikers. We pick hikers up when they arrive in San Diego, give them a place to sleep, feed them home-cooked meals, and drive them to the southern terminus of the PCT early in the morning. Many PCT supporters volunteer time to help us.

Please read over our website at [www.sandiegopct.com]. It includes instructions on how to sign up to be hosted by us.

There is a special tab on our website for non-US hikers.

We're looking forward to meeting you all, and hope our hospitality can make things a bit less stressful.

2020 will be our last year hosting hikers.

Barney and Sandy Mann
sandiegopct@gmail.com

NORTHERN TERMINUS

The PCNST (**P**acific **C**rest **N**ational **S**cenic **T**rail) is border to border within the United States. The Northern Terminus monument is at the US-Canada border. Most hikers continue 8.8 more miles into Canada on the PCT (**P**acific **C**rest **T**rail), finishing at Manning Park.

US-CANADA BORDER

Northbounders entering Canada. It is legal to cross from the US into Canada on trail only if you have your "Application to enter Canada via the PCT" with you as you enter Canada. See the "Logistics" chapter.

Northbounders returning to the US. The closest major airports to Manning Park are in Vancouver (British Columbia), Bellingham (Washington), and Seattle (Washington). As of November 2019, all travelers entering the US from Canada by air are required to have a passport book or a Trusted Traveler Card; US citizens entering the US by land or sea are required to have either a passport book, a passport card, an enhanced Driver's License, or a Trusted Traveler Card.
Passport information: [www.travel.state.gov] and [www.usps.com/passport].

Northbounders who do not go into Canada. If you think your "Application to Enter Canada via the PCT" will be denied, or if you already have been denied entry into Canada, do not worry. You can hike up to the Northern Terminus at the US-Canada border, then turn around and hike south using the options shown in shaded boxes in Section 28 of the Town Guide portion of this Handbook.

Southbounders beginning at the Northern Terminus. It is illegal to cross from Canada into the US using the trail. You must enter the US at a manned border crossing. If you are southbounding, you must hike in the United States up to the Northern Terminus monument, then begin hiking south on the PCT. See the "Logistics" chapter of this book and the shaded boxes in Section 28 of the Town Guide portion of this Handbook.

TRANSPORTATION INFORMATION

Transportation options for travel from Manning Park to the US are outlined on the last two pages of the Town Guide portion of this Handbook.

POST-HIKE THOUGHTS

At the end of every hike, I wonder:
Since my hike is over and I have completed this hike, am I NOW a thru-hiker?
Or, since my hike is over and I am off the trail, am I NO LONGER a thru-hiker?
Different perspectives. I guess we all have to decide for ourselves.

BINK: The one thing that surprised me on my first hike was how difficult it was both mentally and physically! It never seemed to be "easy." I was taken a bit off guard by how important food and water became in my day-to-day life out on the trail. I was surprised with how connected I became to my environment, meaning I began to really feel as if the nature I was living in each day was my home.

My first hike changed who I was as a person to a great degree. It left me feeling that much of the fairly conventional life I had led up to that point was unnecessary, and that I wanted to spend as much of the rest of my life in nature as practical. Of course that was the ideal, but the reality has been I still lead a work a day life and never seem to have as much time in nature as I would like. My thinking, however, was forever altered after that first PCT hike, and it is difficult for me to express it in words. I suppose it made me realize what the really important things were in my life and what parts of it were unnecessary fluff. I feel that for many people who thru-hike the PCT, it is not necessarily a life-changing experience, but it does seem that everyone comes out of the experience with some positive insight about themselves and life in general that they did not have prior to their hike. After all, it sure beats work!

I never really re-enter the regular world after a hike; I just keep having these longs spells of zero days where I work to make more money so I can hike again! Seriously, re-entry can be difficult, but it can also be wonderful. I enjoy certain aspects of the "man-made" world as I like to call it as much as I do the experience of a PCT thru-hike. Obviously, the PCT experience contains some aspect that I cannot obtain from my daily life back in civilization working and just as caught up in the rat race as anybody. When a hike is over, I try to focus and all the points of the man-made world that I feel are great to have after being on the trail, such as being with my loved ones, unlimited clean water available at all times, fresh food, etc. Of course, after a few weeks the novelty wears off, and I am already planning my next hike! So really, I feel that I handle it as well as anyone can.

Scrub: It's impossible to say how the hike changed me. Six years on might be a better time to ask that question. I would caution anyone against believing the Cheryl Strayed narrative, that a long hike tidily cleans up all the big problems within one's life or personality. I'm not even sure of the less bold and seemingly universally accepted assumption that hiking changes you/me for the better. It could turn out to be a completely maladaptive behavior in the larger arc of my life. I just don't really know now. All I know is that, for me, it's fun and I like it.

When my hike ended, I went straight home to the apartment that I already shared with my (non-thru-hiking) girlfriend, and two weeks to the day after reaching Canada I was walking into an office building dressed in business clothes, back at the job I had before I left. This didn't and doesn't bother me. The trail was always going to be a self-contained adventure and I didn't expect it to have immediate broad implications on the direction of my life. Some people really struggle with re-entry or it is a long, drawn-out itinerant process for them. My circumstances, for better or worse, were pretty stable, and I figured that once I got home I might as well get on with it.

The only re-entry problem I had was that, for about the first five days after coming home, I was exhausted by being around more than two people at once for any sustained amount of time. I had gotten very used to being alone or hiking with just one person for a few hours at most. But after a week of being home, I felt like I'd never left.

FINAL THOUGHTS

Drink a lot of water. Especially in the desert. Even in cold weather.

Don't try to keep up with anybody. I cannot stress this strongly enough!! If you try to walk even 1/4 mile per hour faster than your comfortable pace, that makes every single step a strain. That's every step, every day, for weeks and weeks. This is more than your body can handle, and eventually this WILL lead to injury and blisters. Walk at the pace that is comfortable for you.

Do not view this trip as a walk from Mexico to Canada. That's a LONG way. Looking at the big picture can be overwhelming, especially when you're in the Mojave, it's hot, you're carrying six liters of water, you feel like you've been on the trail forever, then you realize that you have TWO THOUSAND more miles to walk. No, no, no. Don't look at Canada as your goal. If you want to go to Canada, get on a plane and fly there.

Instead, look at your thru-hike as a bunch of back-to-back shorter trips. For example, when you leave Campo, you're walking to Lake Morena. That's only 20.0 miles. No problem. Then, you're walking from Lake Morena to Mt. Laguna. 21.5 miles. You can do that. Your next "trip" is Mt. Laguna to Warner Springs. 68.0 miles. Cool. Before you know it, you're relaxing in Warner Springs. Woo! Hoo! You've just walked 109.5 miles!! Small trips at your own pace. That's the key.

If you're considering quitting your hike, wait a week. Then re-think your decision. The PCT is an incredible trail. Every difficult situation is followed by something great. The scenery alone is enough to keep you amazed day after day after day.

When you go to bed at night on the trail, think about where you woke up yesterday morning. Think about how many miles, how many passes, how many ridges, how many fords, how many friends, how many conversations about everything and absolutely nothing, how many beautiful views happened in those two days. You'll experience more in two days on the trail than in an entire month at home. THAT's why we hike the Pacific Crest Trail. Have fun everyone!

TRAIL TIPS and TOWN GUIDE

The Town Guide begins following this page.

Use a utility knife to remove the Town Guide pages from this book. Place the appropriate pages in your mail drops, and carry them with you on the trail.

WHAT?!?!? Carry actual paper information?

Yep.

It's less than one-half of an ounce per one hundred miles. I'm pretty sure that won't kill any PCT hiker. You're tough.

All information in this Handbook
could change without notice.

All Information – That means Post Office hours,
motel rates, phone numbers, mail drop information,
town services, store hours of operation, trail
conditions, bear canister requirements, border
crossing requirements, water sources, etc. –
EVERYTHING

IMPORTANT

Before your hike, be sure to get the most current
information. We post an update file to our website
each spring. This file shows major trail/town
changes which have occurred since the printing of
this edition. To find the update file, go to
www.yogisbooks.com, then click UPDATES & LINKS.

TRAIL TIPS AND TOWN GUIDE

SOUTHERN CALIFORNIA

CENTRAL CALIFORNIA

NORTHERN CALIFORNIA

Handbook Section	Distance in miles	Trail Section
# 14	86.5	Belden to Old Station. . . . . Page 305
# 15	45.6	Old Station to Burney Park . . . . Page 311
# 16	82.2	Burney Park to Castella-Dunsmuir-Mt. Shasta . . . Page 317
# 17	98.5	Castella-Dunsmuir-Mt. Shasta to Etna . . . . Page 327
# 18	56.2	Etna to Seiad Valley . . . . Page 331
# 19	62.8	Seiad Valley to Ashland. Page 333

OREGON

Handbook Section	Distance in miles	Trail Section
# 20	102.2	Ashland to Crater Lake . . . . Page 343
# 21	87.0	Crater Lake to Willamette Pass . . . . Page 353
# 22	93.0	Willamette Pass to Santiam Pass . . . . Page 359
# 23	146.2	Santiam Pass to Cascade Locks.. . . . . Page 367

WASHINGTON

Handbook Section	Distance in miles	Trail Section
# 24	148.3	Cascade Locks to White Pass. . . . . Page 384
# 25	98.2	White Pass to Snoqualmie Pass. . . . . Page 391
# 26	71.1	Snoqualmie Pass to Stevens Pass . . . . Page 395
# 27	107.7	Stevens Pass to Stehekin. . . . . Page 401
# 28	89.5	Stehekin to Manning Park. . . . . Page 409

THE TOWN GUIDE DETAILS

This Handbook is written from the perspective of a NORTHBOUND PCT hiker. If I say to turn right on a road to get to a town, this means that if you're walking from Mexico to Canada, you should turn right. If you're SOUTHBOUND, you'll have to reverse all directions.

Scott Williamson provided his personal historical perspective on PCT water sources gained while completing his 13+ PCT thru-hikes, numerous section-hikes, and LASH-hikes, totaling 50,000+ PCT miles!

Nothing is set in stone. You may plan to get water at a source which was good in the past. Now it's 2019, and when you get there, it's dry. I cannot promise that what we found at any water source, trail junction, or town stop will be exactly what you find when you get there. I've done my best to make sure that this book is as accurate as possible. However, things change from year to year.

TRAVELING BY PLANE

Protect your backpack on the plane. Put it inside a large duffle bag or plastic bag. Many airlines have great big strong plastic bags. Call the airline desk at the airport you're flying out of and ask if they've got bags available. Many people put baby car seats, strollers, etc., in bags like this. They also work great for backpacks. Tie an address tag both on your pack and also on the outside of the plastic bag.

Make sure you do not have ANY gear strapped to the outside: sleeping pad, tent poles, etc. Gear strapped to the outside of your pack could disappear. Make sure all pack straps are tied down. If not, these could catch on the conveyer belts used to move luggage. Strap the hip belt around the pack.

Do not have any perishable food in your backpack (checked luggage). No fruit, lunch meat, cheese, etc. The plane could spend some time on a hot runway, and your food would spoil. Do not have any prohibited items with you as you go through airport security. For a very clear and precise list of what you can / cannot have on your person or in your luggage, see this website:

[https://www.tsa.gov/travel/security-screening/whatcanibring/all-list]

Be prepared to be chosen for inspection at the airport. Every time I fly to or from the trail, I'm chosen. I finally asked why I always get picked. The person with the magic metal-detecting wand told me it's because I've got a one-way ticket.

SHUTTLE TO CAMPO

WTT Transportation. [http://www.shuttlesd.com/] [shuttlesandiego@gmail.com] 760-789-7252. Service throughout SoCal, including San Diego, Los Angeles, PCT Southern Terminus, Lake Morena, Boulder Oaks, Kitchen Creek Road, Mt. Laguna, Sunrise Highway trailhead, Scissors Crossing, Julian, Warner Springs, Idyllwild, Palm Springs.

SAN DIEGO AIRPORT TO CAMPO

DO NOT let your pack out of your sight. Keep it with you at all times.

BUS - TROLLEY - BUS

DATA IN THIS SECTION IS CURRENT AS OF November 2019

Bus and trolley route maps: Go to [https://www.sdmts.com/].
Choose [SCHEDULES & REAL TIME], then use the Trip Planner.

Airport to Downtown:	MTS Bus Route #992
Downtown to El Cajon:	Trolley - Green or Orange Line (Downtown to El Cajon)
El Cajon to Campo:	MTS Bus Route #894

The Green Line goes through a much nicer section of San Diego (Mission Valley), which has lots of restaurants and shopping.

San Diego to Campo via public transportation takes about 3.5 hours. Have EXACT CHANGE, cash only for bus. Trolley ticket vending machines take credit/debit cards and cash, but give maximum $5 change. Call Southeast Rural Transit about 2 weeks early to make a reservation on Bus #894 from El Cajon to Campo. Reservations on Bus #894 are recommended, but not required. No reservations needed for airport Bus #992.

STEP 1: Bus # 992 - Airport to American Plaza Trolley Station - 15-30 minutes

Information for Step 1:   Regional Transit Operator   619-233-3004

Go out to the sidewalk in front of the airport terminal and look for the bus sign. Bus #992 picks up at both terminals. Bus #992 runs approximately every 15 minutes. Sit near the front of the bus and tell the bus driver you need to get off at the American Plaza Trolley Station at Broadway & Kettner.

Get off the bus at Broadway & Kettner.
Walk one block north on Kettner to the American Plaza Trolley Station.

STEP 2: Eastbound Green or Orange Trolley from American Plaza Trolley Station to El Cajon Transit Center - 50 minutes

Information for Step 2:   Regional Transit Operator   619-233-3004

The eastbound Green and Orange Trolley both leave American Plaza approximately every 15 minutes (30 minutes on weekends). There are THREE trolleys here. Whatever you do, DO NOT get on the BLUE Line.

The Orange Line goes through La Mesa, which is a good place to stop if you need to stay overnight. See the La Mesa map on the following page.

STEP 3: Bus #894 - El Cajon Transit Center to Campo - 2 hours

Information for Step 3:   Southeast Rural Transit   800-858-0291

November 2019 Schedule:

Take Southeast Rural Bus #894 from the
El Cajon Transit Center to Campo CA.
Bus #894 makes four trips per day Mon - Fri.
Bus #894 does not run on Saturday or Sunday.
Bus schedule: [https://www.sdmts.com/].

El Cajon	Campo	Lake Morena
8:30a	10:12a	
11:45a	1:27p	
3:00p	4:51p	5:11p
5:45p	7:30p	

SUPPLYING OR STAYING OVERNIGHT IN SAN DIEGO

LA MESA	EL CAJON

BUS SERVICE: San Diego Metropolitan Transit System (MTS). [https://www.sdmts.com/]
Website has a route planner. MTS is the bus and trolley system.

AIRPORT TO LA MESA:

Take Bus #992 from airport to downtown.
Then the Orange Trolley eastbound.
Get off the Trolley at the La Mesa Blvd stop, which is 3 stops before the El Cajon Transit Center.

LA MESA TO CAMPO:

Take the Orange Trolley from La Mesa to the El Cajon Transit Center, then take bus #894 to Campo.

AIRPORT TO EL CAJON:

Take Bus #992 from airport to downtown.
Then take the Orange or Green Trolley eastbound. Get off the Trolley at the El Cajon Transit Center.

EL CAJON TO CAMPO:

Take bus #894 from the El Cajon Transit Center to Campo.

CAR RENTAL:

| Enterprise | 619-698-2505 |
| Hertz | 619-469-1834 |

CAR RENTAL:

| Enterprise | 619-444-4744 |

POST OFFICE:

619-460-4659
Mon-Fri 9a-5p, Sat 9a-1p
Does not accept PCT General Delivery

POST OFFICE:

619-588-8665
Mon-Fri 8:30a-5p, Sat 8:30a-noon
Does not accept PCT General Delivery

RESUPPLY:

Vons. 619-464-1011. 5a-midnight every day.

RESUPPLY:

Walmart. 619-440-2009. 6a-midnight every day.

LODGING:

Lodge of La Mesa 619-466-5988 $$

Minimum age to check in is 21 years old.
No cash accepted, no smoking.
Laundry, free breakfast, free WiFi.
Microwave and refrigerator in rooms.

LODGING:

Relax Inn	619-442-2576	$$
Travelodge	619-441-8250	$$
Super 8	619-627-0647	$$
Motel 6	619-588-6100	$$
Courtyard	619-334-6999	$$$

RESTAURANT: Several

RESTAURANT: Several

COMPUTER: Library   619-469-2151

COMPUTER: Library   619-588-3718

ATM: Yes

ATM: Yes

CANISTER FUEL: Dick's Sporting Goods
619-447-0191

Rates: $ = usually less than $50
$$ = usually $50-$80
$$$ = usually $80-$110
$$$$ = usually greater than $110

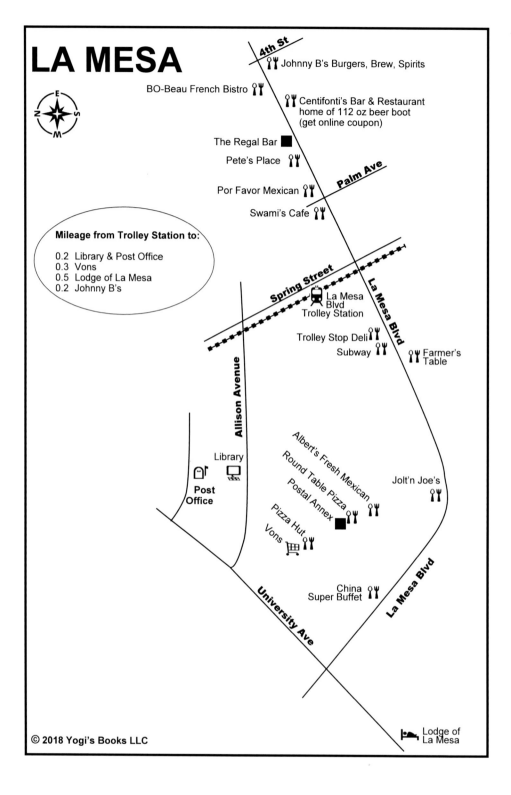

LA MESA

Johnny B's Burgers, Brew, Spirits

BO-Beau French Bistro

Centifonti's Bar & Restaurant
home of 112 oz beer boot
(get online coupon)

The Regal Bar

Pete's Place

Por Favor Mexican

Swami's Cafe

4th St

Palm Ave

Mileage from Trolley Station to:

0.2 Library & Post Office
0.3 Vons
0.5 Lodge of La Mesa
0.2 Johnny B's

Spring Street

La Mesa Blvd

La Mesa Blvd Trolley Station

Trolley Stop Deli

Subway

Farmer's Table

Allison Avenue

Library

Post Office

Albert's Fresh Mexican

Round Table Pizza

Postal Annex

Pizza Hut

Vons

Jolt'n Joe's

China Super Buffet

University Ave

La Mesa Blvd

Lodge of La Mesa

© 2018 Yogi's Books LLC

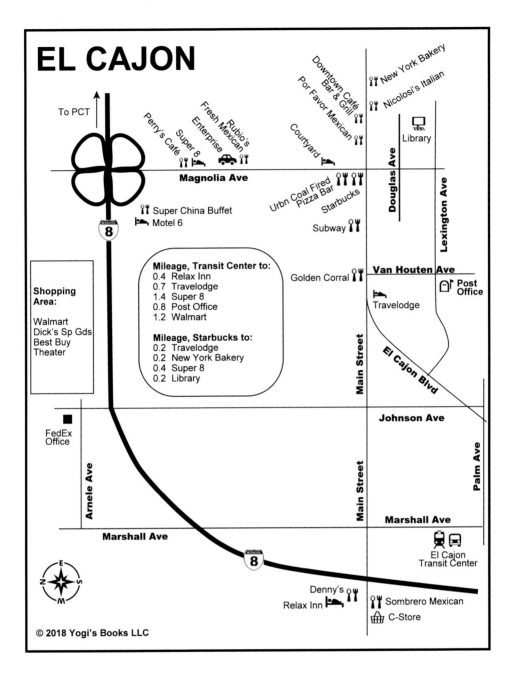

EL CAJON

To PCT

Perry's Café
Super 8
Enterprise
Fresh Mexican
Rubio's

Downtown Café Bar & Grill
Por Favor Mexican
Courtyard

New York Bakery
Nicolosi's Italian

Library

Douglas Ave

Lexington Ave

Magnolia Ave

Super China Buffet
Motel 6

Urbn Coal Fired Pizza Bar
Starbucks

Subway

Mileage, Transit Center to:
0.4 Relax Inn
0.7 Travelodge
1.4 Super 8
0.8 Post Office
1.2 Walmart

Mileage, Starbucks to:
0.2 Travelodge
0.2 New York Bakery
0.4 Super 8
0.2 Library

Golden Corral

Van Houten Ave

Post Office

Travelodge

El Cajon Blvd

Shopping Area:

Walmart
Dick's Sp Gds
Best Buy
Theater

Main Street

FedEx Office

Johnson Ave

Arnele Ave

Main Street

Palm Ave

Marshall Ave

Marshall Ave

El Cajon Transit Center

N E S W

Denny's
Relax Inn

Sombrero Mexican
C-Store

© 2018 Yogi's Books LLC

20.0 Lake Morena County Park - on trail

Resupply: Oak Shores Grocery (C-Store) 619-478-5845, 0.3 mile away.

26.0 Pine Valley CA - 8 mile hitch

Post Office: 619-473-8680, USPS only
Mon-Fri 8:30a-noon, 1p-5p
Sat 10:30a-12:30p
General Delivery held for 15 days

Hiker's Legal Name
PCT Hiker, ETA: MM/DD/YY
General Delivery
Pine Valley, CA 91962

Resupply: Large Grocery Store: Mountain Market 619-473-0038

41.5 Mount Laguna CA - 0.4 mile walk

Post Office: 619-473-8341, USPS only
Mon-Fri noon-4p, Sat 9a-11a
As soon as mail drops arrive, Postmaster will "scan
delivered to agent for General Delivery." She will keep
mail until hiker arrives, or until end of hiking season.
Mail drops MUST have a valid domestic return address.
Phone number on return address is appreciated.

Hiker's Legal Name
PCT Hiker, ETA: MM/DD/YY
General Delivery
Mount Laguna, CA 91948

Mail Drops: Store (619-473-8533) accepts mail drops, $10 fee, held for 3-4 weeks only.
Mail drop must have ETA and hiker's phone number.
Store open 9a-5p every day.

USPS Address:
Hiker's Legal Name
PCT Hiker, ETA: MM/DD/YY
c/o Laguna Mountain Lodge
PO Box 146
Mt. Laguna, CA 91948

UPS or FedEx Address:
Hiker's Legal Name
PCT Hiker, ETA: MM/DD/YY
c/o Laguna Mountain Lodge
10678 Sunrise Highway
Mt. Laguna, CA 91948

Resupply: Small Grocery Store: 619-473-8533.

77.0 Stagecoach Trails RV Park - 4 mile hitch

Resupply: Small C-Store, snacks only. 760-765-3765.

77.0 Julian CA - 13 mile hitch

Post Office: 760-765-3648, USPS only
Mon-Fri 9a-4p. Sat 10a-noon.
General Delivery held for 30 days

Hiker's Legal Name
PCT Hiker, ETA: MM/DD/YY
General Delivery
1785 Highway 78
Julian, CA 92036

Resupply: Small Grocery Store: Jack's Grocery Store 760-765-3200

109.5 Warner Springs Resource Center - on trail

Resupply: Store at Resource Center is loaded with hiker food. 760-782-0670.

109.5 Warner Springs Post Office - 1.2 miles off trail

Post Office: 760-782-3166, USPS only
Mon-Fri 8a-4p, Sat 8a-1:30p
PO is very small; don't send your package
too far before your arrival.
General Delivery held for 30 days

Hiker's Legal Name
PCT Hiker, ETA: MM/DD/YY
General Delivery
Warner Springs, CA 92086

Resupply: C-Store: Warner Springs Ranch Gas Mart 760-892-7133 Snacks, beer

Grocery store: Sunshine Summit Store 760-782-3529
8.8 miles north of Warner Springs Post Office

109.5 Lake Henshaw Resort - 11 mile hitch

Resupply: C-Store: 760-782-3501

RESUPPLY SUMMARY

109.5 Santa Ysabel CA - 15 mile hitch

Post Office: 760-765-0441, USPS only
Mon-Fri 9a-11a and 11:30a-3:30p
Sat 9a-11a
General Delivery held for 30 days

Hiker's Legal Name
PCT Hiker, ETA: MM/DD/YY
General Delivery
Santa Ysabel, CA 92070

Resupply: Grocery store: Don's Market 760-765-3272

151.8 Paradise Valley Café - 1 mile off trail

Mail Drops: Paradise Valley Café (951-659-3663)
Accepts mail drops, no fee, USPS, UPS,
or FedEx. No outgoing mail.
Café open every day. Hours vary.
Mon-Tue close at 3p. 951-659-3663.

Hiker's Legal Name
PCT Hiker, ETA: MM/DD/YY
c/o Paradise Valley Café
61721 State Highway 74
Mountain Center, CA 92561

151.8 Anza CA - 7 mile hitch

Post Office: 951-763-2074, USPS only
Mon-Fri 9a-4p
Sat 10a-1p
General Delivery held for 30 days

Hiker's Legal Name
PCT Hiker, ETA: MM/DD/YY
General Delivery
Anza, CA 92539

Resupply: Large grocery store: Anza Village Market 951-763-4321

151.8 Idyllwild CA - Pines to Palms Highway - 18 mile hitch
179.4 Idyllwild CA - Devils Slide Trail - 2.5 mile walk plus 2.6 mile TH hitch

Post Office: 951-659-1969, USPS only
Mon-Fri 9a-5p
Sat closed, but usually hikers can
pick up packages on Sat 1:30p-3p.
Knock on white dutch door.
General Delivery held for 3 weeks.

Hiker's Legal Name
PCT Hiker, ETA: MM/DD/YY
General Delivery
Idyllwild, CA 92549

Mail Drops: Idyllwild Inn (951-659-2552) accepts mail drops for guests only, no fee:

USPS Address:	UPS or FedEx Address:
Hiker's Legal Name	Hiker's Legal Name
PCT Hiker, ETA: MM/DD/YY	PCT Hiker, ETA: MM/DD/YY
c/o Idyllwild Inn	c/o Idyllwild Inn
PO Box 515	54300 Village Center Drive
Idyllwild, CA 92549	Idyllwild, CA 92549

Resupply: Grocery store: Village Market 951-659-3169
Small supermarket: Fairway Foods 951-659-2737

209.5 Cabazon CA - 4.5 mile hitch on frontage road (very little traffic)

Post Office: 951-849-6233, USPS only
Mon-Fri 8:30a-11:30a and 12:45p-4p
Sat closed
If mail drop is not picked up 15 days after
arrival, PO will scan as "Unclaimed" or
"Delivered", but PO will hold for another
15 days. If not picked up after a total of
30 days, mail will be returned to sender.

Hiker's Legal Name
PCT Hiker, ETA: MM/DD/YY
General Delivery
Cabazon, CA 92230

Resupply: Small Grocery Store: 951-849-6422

RESUPPLY SUMMARY

| 266.1 | **Big Bear City via Highway 18 - 5 mile hitch** |
| 275.1 | **Big Bear City via Van Dusen Canyon Road - 4 mile walk** |

Post Office: There are TWO Post Offices which accept General Delivery.

Big Bear CITY Post Office:	Hiker's Legal Name
909-585-7132, USPS only	PCT Hiker, ETA: MM/DD/YY
Mon-Fri 9a-4:30p	General Delivery
Sat package pick up only 1p-2p	Big Bear City, CA 92314
General Delivery held for 30 days	
Big Bear LAKE Post Office:	Hiker's Legal Name
909-866-1035, USPS only	PCT Hiker, ETA: MM/DD/YY
Mon-Fri 8:30a-5p	General Delivery
Sat 10a-noon	472 Pine Knot
General Delivery held for 30 days	Big Bear Lake, CA 92315

Mail Drops: Big Bear Hostel (909-866-8900) in Big Bear LAKE
Accepts mail drops, no fee for guests, $5 fee for non-guests.

USPS Address:	UPS or FedEx Address:
Hiker's Legal Name	Hiker's Legal Name
PCT Hiker, ETA: MM/DD/YY	PCT Hiker, ETA: MM/DD/YY
c/o Big Bear Hostel	c/o Big Bear Lake Hostel
PO Box 1951	541 Knickerbocker Rd (office)
Big Bear Lake, CA 92315-1951	Big Bear Lake, CA 92315-1951

Mail Drops: Trail Angels Steve & Sandy Teutschman (909-800-7028)
accept mail drops, no fee, USPS, UPS, FedEx:

Hiker's Legal Name
PCT Hiker, ETA: MM/DD/YY
c/o Steve & Sandy Teutschman
840 E Angeles Blvd
Big Bear City, CA 92314

Resupply: Big Bear City Grocery Store: Community Market 909-585-2641

Big Bear Lake Supermarkets:	Vons	909-866-8459
	Stater Brothers	909-866-5211

| 298.5 | **Cedar Glen CA - 3.6 mile trailhead hitch** |

Post Office: 909-337-4614, USPS only   Hiker's Legal Name
Mon-Fri 8:30a-5p   PCT Hiker, ETA: MM/DD/YY
Sat 9a-11a   General Delivery
General Delivery held for 15 days   Cedar Glen, CA 92321

Resupply: Grocery store: Jensen's Minute Shoppe 909-337-3500

| 298.5 | **Lake Arrowhead CA - 2 mile hitch or bus from Cedar Glen** |

Post Office: 909-337-2673, USPS only   Hiker's Legal Name
Mon-Fri 9a-4:30p   PCT Hiker, ETA: MM/DD/YY
Sat closed   General Delivery
** DO NOT include the physical   Lake Arrowhead, CA 92352
address of the Post Office on the
General Delivery address **
General Delivery held for 15 days

Resupply: Supermarket: Stater Brothers 909-377-5854

RESUPPLY SUMMARY

341.9	Cajon Pass / Interstate 15 - 0.4 mile walk to Chevron

Mail Drops: Cajon Pass Inn   Hiker's Legal Name
(760-249-6777)   PCT Hiker, ETA: MM/DD/YY
is one mile from the PCT.   c/o Cajon Pass Inn
Accepts mail drops, no fee,   8317 US Hwy 138
USPS, UPS, FedEx.   At the 15 Freeway
Outgoing mail is letters only.   Phelan, CA 92371

Resupply: Large C-Store: Chevron 760-249-4574. Great snack selection.

363.4	Wrightwood via Acorn Trail - 3.6 mile walk
369.3	Wrightwood via Highway 2 - 5.5 mile hitch

Post Office: 760-249-8882, USPS only   Hiker's Legal Name
Mon-Fri 8:45a-5p   PCT Hiker, ETA: MM/DD/YY
Sat package pick up only 8a-11a   General Delivery
Hiker mail held until ETA.   Wrightwood, CA 92397

Mail Drops: Mountain Hardware (760-249-3653) accepts mail drops.
Open Mon-Sat 8:30a-5:30p, Sun 8:30a-4:30p. UPS/FedEx is preferred.

USPS Address: UPS or FedEx Address:
Hiker's Legal Name   Hiker's Legal Name
PCT Hiker, ETA: MM/DD/YY   PCT Hiker, ETA: MM/DD/YY
c/o Mountain Hardware   c/o Mountain Hardware
PO Box 398   1390 Highway 2
Wrightwood, CA 92397   Wrightwood, CA 92397

Resupply: Supermarket: Jensen's Foods 760-249-3322.

444.2	Acton CA - 5.7 mile hitch

Post Office: 661-269-8618, USPS only   Hiker's Legal Name
Mon-Fri 10a-5p   PCT Hiker, ETA: MM/DD/YY
Sat package pick up only 8a-10a   General Delivery
General Delivery held for 15 days   Acton, CA 93510

Resupply: Two large grocery stores:
Acton Market Country Store   661-269-1522
The Original Acton Market   661-441-0454

444.3	Acton KOA - 0.2 mile walk

Mail Drops: Acton KOA (661-268-1214)   Hiker's Legal Name
Accepts mail drops,   PCT Hiker, ETA: MM/DD/YY
$2 fee for guests, $5 fee for non-guests.   c/o Acton KOA
USPS, UPS, FedEx.   7601 Soledad Canyon Road
     Acton, CA 93510

Resupply: Little store has minimal snacks and ice cream. 661-268-1214.

454.5	Agua Dulce CA - on trail

Resupply: Small C-Store.

478.2	Green Valley Market - 2 miles off trail

Resupply: Large C-Store: Green Valley Market 661-270-0444

RESUPPLY SUMMARY

485.8 Lake Hughes CA - Store is 2.3 miles from trail, PO is 0.7 mile farther

Post Office: 661-724-9281, USPS only
Mon-Fri 8a-12:30p and 1:30p-5p
Sat package pickup only 10a-noon
General Delivery held for 30 days

Hiker's Legal Name
PCT Hiker, ETA: MM/DD/YY
General Delivery
16817 Elizabeth Lake Road
Lake Hughes, CA 93532

Resupply: Grocery Store: Papa's Country Store 661-724-1634.

517.6 Hikertown - on trail

Mail Drops: Hikertown accepts mail drops,
$5 fee. No outgoing mail.
USPS, UPS, FedEx.

Hiker's Legal Name
PCT Hiker, ETA: MM/DD/YY
c/o Hikertown
26803 W. Ave C-15
Lancaster, CA 93536

Resupply: 4 miles east of Hikertown (rides usually available)
is a large C-store: Centennial Market 661-724-1100

517.6 Wee Vill Market - 8 miles off trail, call for ride

Mail Drops: Wee Vill Market. 661-724-2200.
Accepts Mail Drops, no fee.
USPS, UPS, FedEx.

Hiker's Legal Name
PCT Hiker, ETA: MM/DD/YY
c/o Wee Vill Market
18348 W. Avenue D
Lancaster, CA 93536

Resupply: C-Store.

536.9 Wind Farm - 1.2 miles off trail

Mail Drops: 661-256-2122, 4321.
Mail drops accepted, but the
package MUST include a
conspicuous phone number.
UPS or FedEx only! Pick up
packages during office hours
Mon-Fri 6:30a - 5p.

Hiker's Legal Name
PCT Hiker, ETA: MM/DD/YY
c/o Avangrid Renewables - Manzana Wind
17890 Champagne Ave
Rosamond, CA 93560

558.5 Mojave via Tehachapi-Willow Springs Road - 11 mile hitch
566.5 Mojave via Highway 58 - 9 mile freeway hitch

Post Office: 661-824-3502, USPS only
Mon-Fri 9a-1p, and 2p-4p
Sat closed
Hiker mail held for 3 months

Hiker's Legal Name
PCT Hiker, ETA: MM/DD/YY
General Delivery
2053 Belshaw St
Mojave, CA 93501

Mail Drops: Original Motel 6 (661-219-0784)
Accepts mail drops for guests, no fee,
USPS, UPS, FedEx:

Hiker's Legal Name
PCT Hiker, ETA: MM/DD/YY
c/o Motel 6
SR 58 / Sierra Highway @ SR 14
16958 State Route 58
Mojave, CA 93501

Resupply: Stater Brothers Supermarket 661-824-2719

RESUPPLY SUMMARY

| 558.5 | Tehachapi via Tehachapi-Willow Springs Road - 9 mile hitch |
| 566.5 | Tehachapi via Highway 58 - 9 mile freeway hitch |

Post Office: 661-822-0279, USPS only
Mon-Fri 9a-5p
Sat 10a-2p
General Delivery held for 30 days

Hiker's Legal Name
PCT Hiker, ETA: MM/DD/YY
General Delivery
1085 Voyager Drive
Tehachapi, CA 93581

Mail Drops: Tehachapi Trail Angels (661-750-4852)
accept mail drops, no fee,
USPS, UPS, FedEx:

Hiker's Legal Name
PCT Hiker, ETA: MM/DD/YY
c/o Dalton SteeleReed
115 S. Mojave St
Tehachapi, CA 93561

Resupply:
Albertsons Supermarket	661-823-7090
Dollar General Market	661-750-0121
Walmart	661-825-2258

HELPFUL RESUPPLY INFORMATION

"Town Services" and "Resupply Summary" tables are strategically placed within the "Trail Tips and Town Guide" section of this Handbook at five locations:

Mile point	Location
0.0	Campo CA
566.5	Mojave/Tehachapi CA
1092.3	South Lake Tahoe CA
1718.7	Ashland OR
2146.9	Cascade Locks OR

These tables contain consolidated, basic information regarding town services. It's helpful to have this information with you in case you want to know what's ahead, but you don't want to carry the detailed pages with you just yet. For example, you may need to call your home resupply person from Idyllwild and ask them to mail you a package to Mojave. Or you may want to ship your own mail drops ahead from one trail town to another. It's nice to have this information readily available.

The addresses contained in the "Resupply Summary" tables are duplicated in the "Mail Drops and Resupply" chapter of this Handbook, on the table titled "Mail Drop Addresses". This duplication is intentional. The idea is for the hiker to tear the Town Guide pages out of this Handbook and carry them on the trail. Leave the front section of the Handbook with your home resupply person so that person will have access to all the addresses of the resupply locations. Please note that the "Mail Drop Addresses" list is simply a list of addresses. It does NOT contain phone numbers, mail drop holding fees, special instructions, etc.

This applies to all listings in this Handbook:

Lodging rate estimate:
$	usually less than $50
$$	usually $50-$80
$$$	usually $80-$110
$$$$	usually greater than $110

0.0 - US-Mexico Border - PCT Register is in the box on the back side of the monument.

1.4 - Campo CA

OVERVIEW:	Bus #894 (from El Cajon) will drop you off at the Campo Store. You can get water from the fire station or the store.
GETTING HERE:	On trail.
SHUTTLE:	WIT Transportation. 760-789-7282. [shuttlesandiego@gmail.com]
POST OFFICE:	619-478-5466, USPS only Mon-Fri 8:30a-11:30a, 12:30p-4:30p Sat 9:30-noon. USPS only. If not picked up 15 days after mail arrives, PO will scan as delivered, but will keep mail at PO until hiker arrives.
	Hiker's Legal Name PCT Hiker, ETA: MM/DD/YY General Delivery 951 Jeb Stuart Road Campo, CA 91906

RESUPPLY:	Limited resupply at the Campo Trading Post Store (large C-Store). 619-478-5494. Usually open every day 8a-8p.
ATM:	At the store.
FUEL:	Canister fuel at the Campo Trading Post Store.

4.4 - Creeklet - Usually has water.

15.4 - Hauser Creek - Usually dry. Good water in wet years.

20.0 - Lake Morena County Park

OVERVIEW:	Open year-round. The PCT skirts the east edge of the campground.
GETTING HERE:	On trail.
SHUTTLE:	WIT Transportation. 760-789-7282. [shuttlesandiego@gmail.com]
BUS:	[https://www.sdmts.com/] San Diego MTS busses 894 and 888 stop in Lake Morena. Both go to the El Cajon Transit Center. Bus 888 stops in Pine Valley, where there is a motel. See the Pine Valley page of this Handbook.
RESUPPLY:	Oak Shores Grocery. 619-478-5845. The store is smaller than a small grocery store, larger than a large convenience store. Good selection of beer and wine. Usual store hours: 7a-9p every day. Located in Morena Village.
RESTAURANT:	Oak Shores Grocery sells burgers, sandwiches, scooped ice cream, and gigantic breakfast burritos. Usually open 7a-9p every day.
CAMPING:	Lake Morena County Park 619-579-4101. PCT site: $5/person. Must check in at the Ranger Station or Entry Booth. This is the first reliable water north of Campo.
SHOWER:	Coin-operated showers at the campground. Bring quarters.
FUEL:	Usually canister fuel at Oak Shores Grocery.
ATM:	ATM at Oak Shores Grocery. You can get up to $40 at a time. There is a normal ATM at a gas station 3 blocks away.

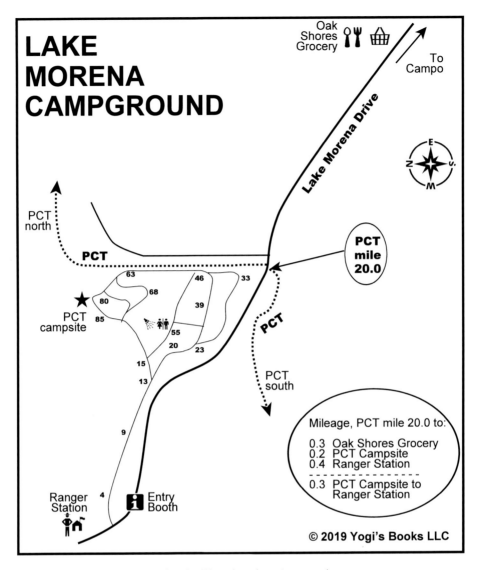

LAKE MORENA CAMPGROUND

Oak Shores Grocery

To Campo

Lake Morena Drive

PCT north

PCT

PCT mile 20.0

63

46

33

68

80

39

PCT campsite

85

55

20

23

15

13

PCT

PCT south

9

Mileage, PCT mile 20.0 to:

0.3 Oak Shores Grocery
0.2 PCT Campsite
0.4 Ranger Station
- - - - - - - - - - - - - - -
0.3 PCT Campsite to Ranger Station

4

Ranger Station

Entry Booth

© 2019 Yogi's Books LLC

24.1 - Bridge Over Cottonwood Creek - Water here in wet years only.

25.5 - Cottonwood Creek - Usually flowing, but lots of horse/cow crap.

26.0 - Boulder Oaks Campground - Spigots, trash, privy, picnic tables. Water is usually shut off here in fall, and sometimes shut off for northbound season. Leaving the campground, head for Old Hwy 80 (the next paved road). When you reach the road, turn left on the PCT, which parallels the road for a while, then the PCT crosses the road. Hitch left to go to Pine Valley (8 miles), or to Interstate 8 Exit 51 (2.4 miles), where there is a rest area. San Diego MTS bus #888 stops at the rest area and continues on to Pine Valley and San Diego. WIT Transportation serves Boulder Oaks. 760-789-7252.

26.6 - Interstate 8

30.2 - Kitchen Creek Road - Water usually in the creek WAY down below the trail.
WIT Transportation serves Kitchen Creek Road. 760-789-7252.

32.0 - Fred Canyon - No water. Good camping.

26.0 - Pine Valley

GETTING HERE: (1) PCT mile 20.0 (Lake Morena) – Take MTS bus #888.

(2) PCT mile 26.0 (Boulder Oaks Campground) – Hitch 8 miles on Old Hwy 80.

(3) PCT mile 26.0 (Boulder Oaks Campground) – walk or hitch 2.6 miles north on Old Hwy 80 until you get to the rest area at I-8 exit 51. MTS bus #888 stops here. Take bus to Pine Valley.

BUS: [https://www.sdmts.com/]   San Diego MTS bus 888 stops in Pine Valley.

POST OFFICE:
619-473-8680, USPS only
Mon-Fri 8:30a-noon, 1p-5p
Sat 10:30a-12:30p
General Delivery held for 15 days

Hiker's Legal Name
PCT Hiker, ETA: MM/DD/YY
General Delivery
Pine Valley, CA 91962

RESUPPLY: Mountain Market   619-473-0038
Full resupply.
Oct-May: M-F 7a-7p, Sa 8a-7p, Su 9a-5p
June-Sep: Mon-Sat 7a-7p, Sun 8a-6p

LODGING: Pine Valley Inn   619-473-8560
Microwave & refrigerator in rooms
Rates $$

RESTAURANT: Yes.

COMPUTER: Library   619-473-8022   Closed Sun-Mon

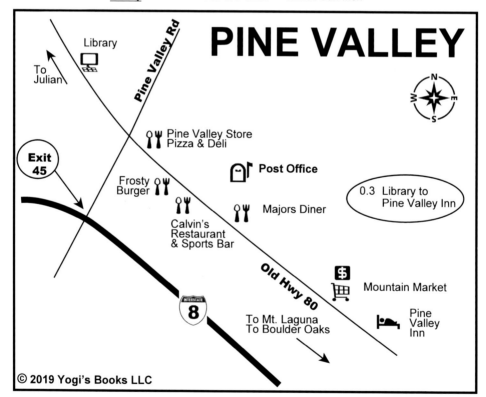

© 2019 Yogi's Books LLC

32.6 - Fred Canyon Road - Cibbets Flat Campground is 0.8 off trail down road to left. $15 per site, 8 people max. Water spigots, privy, fire pits, picnic tables.

36.9 - Long Canyon - The creek is to your left, and you'd have to 'shwack down to it. Wait to get water until the "ford" 0.8 mile farther.

37.7 - Long Canyon Creek Ford - This "ford" is a reliable stream about a foot across.

41.8 - approximately - There is a nice wooded area up on this ridge. Way better camping up here than back at Long Canyon Creek, which gets COLD at night because cold air settles in canyons.

41.5 - Burnt Rancheria Campground - Water from spigots, showers.

42.1 - Burnt Rancheria Campground Drinking Fountain - Water here.

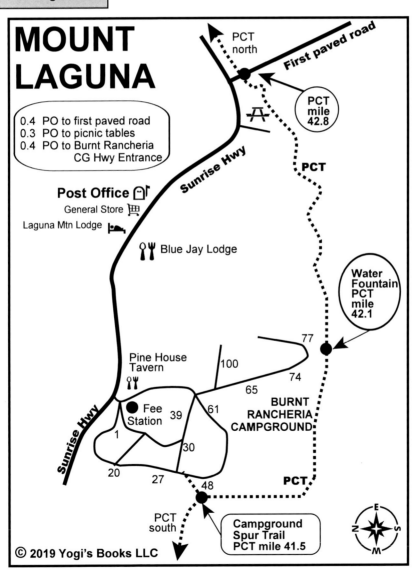

41.5 - Mt. Laguna CA

MOUNT LAGUNA

0.4 PO to first paved road
0.3 PO to picnic tables
0.4 PO to Burnt Rancheria
      CG Hwy Entrance

PCT north

First paved road

PCT mile 42.8

PCT

Post Office
General Store
Laguna Mtn Lodge

Sunrise Hwy

Blue Jay Lodge

Water Fountain PCT mile 42.1

Pine House Tavern

77

100

74

65

BURNT RANCHERIA CAMPGROUND

Fee Station

39   61

1

30

20   27

48

Sunrise Hwy

PCT south

PCT

Campground Spur Trail PCT mile 41.5

© 2019 Yogi's Books LLC

OVERVIEW:	Hiker-friendly. PO and Store are in same building.

GETTING HERE: Three options:

(1)   At PCT mile 41.5 (campground spur trail), or PCT mile 42.1 (water fountain), cut through Burnt Rancheria Campground. Make your way over to Sunrise Highway. Turn right (north) on the highway.

(2)   At PCT mile 45.1, you'll see picnic tables up in the trees on the left side of the trail. Cut up past the picnic tables through the picnic area to Sunrise Highway. Turn left on the highway, go about 0.3 mile to the store/PO.

(3)   When the PCT hits the first paved road (PCT mile 42.8), turn left, walk about a minute to the next paved road (Sunrise Highway), turn left, walk about 0.4 mile and you'll see the store/PO on the right. It's the building with the large porch. Water is at the restroom building.

SHUTTLE: WTT Transportation. [www.shuttlesd.com] [shuttlesandiego@gmail.com] 760-789-7252. Service throughout SoCal, including San Diego, Los Angeles, PCT Southern Terminus, Lake Morena, Boulder Oaks, Kitchen Creek Road, Mt. Laguna, Sunrise Highway trailhead, Scissors Crossing, Julian, Warner Springs, Idyllwild, Palm Springs.

POST OFFICE: As soon as mail arrives, Postmaster will "scan delivered to agent for General Delivery." She will keep mail until hiker arrives, or until end of hiking season. Mail MUST have a valid domestic return address. Phone number on return address is appreciated.

619-473-8341   USPS only
Mon-Fri noon-4p, Sat 9a-11a

Hiker's Legal Name
PCT Hiker, ETA: MM/DD/YY
General Delivery
Mt. Laguna, CA 91948

MAIL DROPS: General Store accepts mail drops, $10 fee, held for 3-4 weeks only.
Mail drop must have ETA and hiker's phone number.
Open 9a-5p every day. 619-473-8533.

USPS Address:
Hiker's Legal Name
PCT Hiker, ETA: MM/DD/YY
c/o Laguna Mountain Lodge
PO Box 146
Mt. Laguna, CA 91948

UPS or FedEx Address:
Hiker's Legal Name
PCT Hiker, ETA: MM/DD/YY
c/o Laguna Mountain Lodge
10678 Sunrise Highway
Mt. Laguna, CA 91948

RESUPPLY: Possible resupply at the General Store. 619-473-8533.
This is a small grocery store with decent hiker resupply.
Open 9a-5p every day. No ATM. Accepts credit cards, $10 minimum.

LODGING: Laguna Mountain Lodge. 619-473-8533. Inquire at the store (open 9a-5p every day). Rates $$ - $$$$ Weekend rates are higher. Satellite TV. Motel rooms have microwave and refrigerator, cabins have kitchenettes.

CAMPING: Burnt Rancheria Campground 0.4 mile south of PO/Store.
This is a pay campground. Reservations: [www.recreation.gov]

SHOWER: Burnt Rancheria Campground 0.4 mile south of PO/Store.

RESTAURANT: Blue Jay Lodge   619-473-8844   Open weekends.
Pine House Tavern   619-473-8857   Usually open every day during high hiker season.

ATM: No.

FUEL: Usually canister fuel at the General Store.

47.5 - Mt. Laguna Campground - Campground Host 619-473-2082. This is a pay campground. Reservations 877-444-6777 or [www.recreation.gov]. This is a campground, NOT the store/PO. You'll see a big wooden overlook deck on the left side of the PCT. That's where you get off the PCT and go up the road to the campground. The campground is 0.2 mile off the PCT (turn left on the road) and has coin-operated showers. Campground entrance to showers = 0.4 mile.

48.7 - G.A.T.R. Road - Spigot (100 feet down the trail on the right) *usually* on, but not always.

52.6 - Pioneer Mail Picnic Area - Privy, trash, picnic tables. Picnic area water spigots are usually turned off. There is a disgusting horse trough behind the big trailhead sign.

59.5 - Sunrise Trailhead Junction - Follow side trail 0.25 mile to Sunrise Highway rest area parking lot and privy. To the west a well is visible. Follow old road to the well.
WIT Transportation serves Sunrise Highway Trailhead. 760-789-7252.

62.4 - Mason Valley Fire Tank - Usually dry.

63.7 - Upper Chariot Canyon - No water here. Some hikers have found water 20 minutes down the road. BINK: I have only seen water run at the trail a few times. Usually water can be found until mid-June about 3-5 minutes down canyon. Listen and look for it as you walk.

68.4 - Rodriguez Spur Truck Trail - When you get to the gate, follow the road northwest 1.1 miles. Look for rust colored tank. BE SURE TO TREAT THIS WATER.

77.0 - Highway S2

77.3 - Highway 78 / Scissors Crossing - There is a stream here, but it is reported to be horse/cow contaminated, and is often dry. Scissors Crossing may be the last water until Barrel Spring, 23.8 miles north. The hike north from Scissors Crossing is long, hot, and dry.

BINK: 0.5 mile downstream there is often water when it is dry at the trail, but consider it polluted.

Bus # 891 westbound passes through Scissors Crossing on FRIDAYS ONLY, between 8:15a and 8:25a. Call for information 619-233-3004.

SHUTTLE: WIT Transportation. 760-789-7282. [shuttlesandiego@gmail.com]

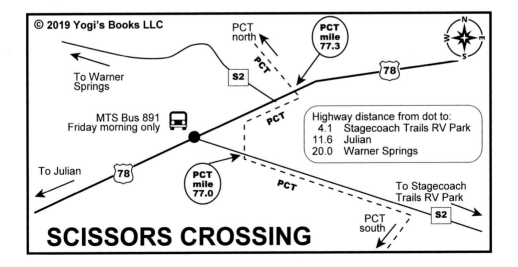

77.0 - Stagecoach Trails RV Park

CONTACT: 760-765-3765. [www.stagecoachtrails.com]
GETTING HERE: 4 miles east on Hwy S2.
BUS: MTS Bus #891 stops here and at Scissors Crossing.
[https://www.sdmts.com/]
RESUPPLY: Small C-Store with possible hiker resupply. Usually open 9a-5p.
LODGING: Cabins $ - $$$$
CAMPING: Camping $
DAY USE: $, includes shower.
FOOD: Small store has deli, pizza, and ice cream bar. No beer.
LAUNDRY & SHOWERS: Yes.
OTHER SERVICES: Shuffleboard, volleyball, horseshoe pits, and a swimming pool!

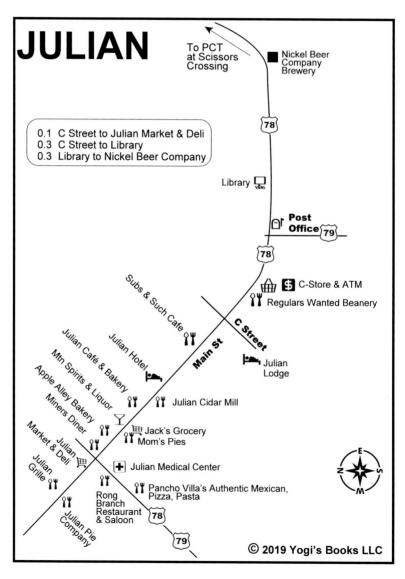

JULIAN

To PCT at Scissors Crossing

Nickel Beer Company Brewery

0.1 C Street to Julian Market & Deli
0.3 C Street to Library
0.3 Library to Nickel Beer Company

Library

Post Office

C-Store & ATM
Regulars Wanted Beanery

Subs & Such Cafe

Julian Hotel

Julian Café & Bakery

Mtn Spirits & Liquor

Apple Alley Bakery

Miners Diner

Market & Deli

Julian Grille

Julian Lodge

Julian Cidar Mill

Jack's Grocery
Mom's Pies

Julian Medical Center

Pancho Villa's Authentic Mexican, Pizza, Pasta

Rong Branch Restaurant & Saloon

Julian Pie Company

© 2019 Yogi's Books LLC

Page 170

OVERVIEW: Touristy. Excellent food.

GETTING HERE: 11.6 miles west (left) of Scissors Crossing.

SHUTTLE: WTT Transportation. [www.shuttlesd.com] [shuttlesandiego@gmail.com]
760-789-7252. Service throughout SoCal, including San Diego, Los Angeles, PCT Southern Terminus, Lake Morena, Boulder Oaks, Kitchen Creek Road, Mt. Laguna, Sunrise Highway trailhead, Scissors Crossing, Julian, Warner Springs, Idyllwild, Palm Springs.

POST OFFICE: 760-765-3648, USPS only
Mon-Fri 9a-4p
Sat 10a-noon
General Delivery held for 30 days

Hiker's Legal Name
PCT Hiker, ETA: MM/DD/YY
General Delivery
1785 Highway 78
Julian, CA 92036

RESUPPLY: Julian Market 760-765-2606 Full resupply. 8a-7p every day.
Jack's Grocery 760-765-3200 Full resupply, good hiker food. 9a-8p daily.

LODGING: Ask for hiker rates. Weekday rates:

Julian Lodge 760-765-1420 $$$
Julian Hotel 760-765-0201 $$ (ask for hiker rate)

Rates: $$ = usually $50-$80. $$$ = usually $80-$110

RESTAURANTS: Possible free lunch for hikers at Mom's Pies.
Possible free fruit at Granny's Kitchen.

LAUNDRY: Free laundry for guests at Julian Hotel.

COMPUTER: Library. 760-765-0370.

MEDICAL: Julian Medical Center. 760-765-1223.

91.2 - Third gate after Scissors Crossing - When you get to the Third Gate (that's the third metal gate north of Scissors Crossing, with a number "3" on it!), immediately past the gate there is a trail going right/east. There is a large "WATER" sign pointing down the side trail.

101.1 - Barrel Spring - Good piped water. Watch for poison oak and ticks in this area.
BINK: If no water from pipe, obtain water from spring box uphill from trough.

101.2 - Montezuma Market - 4 miles east on Hwy S22 (Montezuma Valley Road). Big white Yeti in front of store. 760-282-4428. Very small C-Store, with beer.

105.0 - San Ysidro Creek - Usually flowing, but there are cows everywhere.

106.2 - Eagle Rock - Walk behind a rock outcropping to see the eagle. From the other side of the rocks, the arrangement of the rocks looks like an eagle with outstretched wings. Very cool.

109.5 - Highway 79 - Several options for resupply/rest.

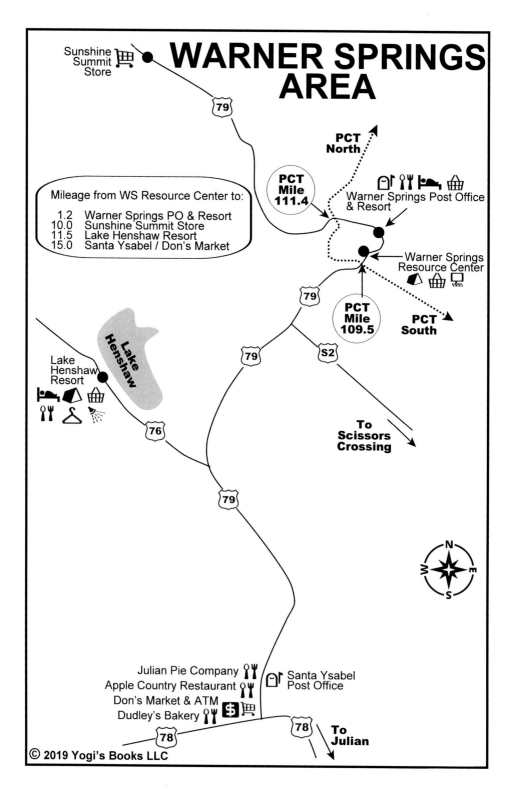

WARNER SPRINGS AREA

Sunshine Summit Store

79

PCT North

PCT Mile 111.4

Warner Springs Post Office & Resort

Mileage from WS Resource Center to:

1.2 Warner Springs PO & Resort
10.0 Sunshine Summit Store
11.5 Lake Henshaw Resort
15.0 Santa Ysabel / Don's Market

Warner Springs Resource Center

79

PCT Mile 109.5

PCT South

Lake Henshaw

79

S2

Lake Henshaw Resort

To Scissors Crossing

76

79

N
W · E
S

Julian Pie Company
Apple Country Restaurant
Don's Market & ATM
Dudley's Bakery

Santa Ysabel Post Office

78

78 To Julian

© 2019 Yogi's Books LLC

Warner Springs Resource Center 0.1 mile from PCT mile 109.5	Warner Springs CA 1.2 mile from PCT mile 109.5

CONTACT:

[www.wscrcenter.org]
Office 760-782-0670.
Email: [WarnerResourceCenter@gmail.com]

RESORT:

The Warner Springs Resort closed a few years ago. It is in the process of reopening.
Some services have resumed.
[www.warnerspringsranchresort.com]

GETTING HERE:

Resource Center is 0.1 mile east of the first PCT crossing of Highway 79 (PCT mile 109.5). It's across Hwy 79 from the Fire Station. Open every day 8a-4p during peak hiker season.

NOTICE:

Camping, restrooms, and showers are not available while school is in session.

GETTING HERE:

You can usually get a ride to the PO. Just ask at the Resource Center. If not, there are three options to get to the Post Office:

(1) Side Trail - As you approach the first crossing of Highway 79, watch for this trail near the second gate.

(2) PCT mile 109.5 - Turn right on Hwy 79, hitch or walk 1.2 miles.

(3) PCT mile 111.4 - Turn right on Hwy 79, hitch or walk 1.4 miles.

MAIL DROPS: No.

POST OFFICE:
760-782-3166, USPS only
Mon-Fri 8a-4p, Sat 8a-1:30p
This post office gets thousands of hiker mail drops. Postmaster requests that hikers do not send packages too early. General Delivery held for 30 days.

Hiker's Legal Name
PCT Hiker, ETA: MM/DD/YY
General Delivery
Warner Springs, CA 92086

RESUPPLY:

Full resupply includes dry food, cheese sticks, tortillas, foot care products, sunscreen, OTC pain killers, duct tape, toilet paper, batteries.

RESUPPLY:

Warner Springs Gas Mart. 760-892-7133.
Small C-Store: beer, lots of snacks, very limited dinner selection. 7a-7p every day.

On Hwy 89, 8.8 miles north of the Post Office is the Sunshine Summit Store (760-782-3529). ATM inside. It's an easy hitch, and full resupply. 7a-8p every day.

LODGING: No.

LODGING: Warner Springs Cottages with AC, no TV. Rates $$$. 760-782-4220.

CAMPING: Yes.
Restrooms open 24 hours.

CAMPING: No.

MEALS: No.

RESTAURANT:

Golf Course Grill next to the Post Office has great food and pizza. 760-782-4271. Open 8a-8p.

LAUNDRY: No.
SHOWERS: No.
COMPUTER: Yes.

LAUNDRY: No.
SHOWERS: No.

ATM: No ATM, but credit cards are accepted.

ATM: No.

Lake Henshaw Resort **11.5 miles from PCT mile 109.5**	**Santa Ysabel CA** **15.0 miles from PCT mile 109.5**
OVERVIEW: Lakeside resort.	**OVERVIEW:** Basic services, but no lodging.
CONTACT: Information: 760-782-3501 [http://lakehenshawresort.com/]	
GETTING HERE: From Warner Springs, hitch Hwy 79 south for 7 miles to the intersection of Hwy 76 and 79, turn right on Hwy 76, go 4 miles.	**GETTING HERE:** From Warner Springs, hitch Highway 79 south for 15 miles to the intersection with Highway 78.
POST OFFICE: No.	**POST OFFICE:** 760-765-0441, USPS only Mon-Fri 9a-11a, 11:30a-3:30p Sat 9a-11a Gen Delivery held for 30 days Hiker's Legal Name PCT Hiker, ETA: MM/DD/YY General Delivery Santa Ysabel CA 92070
RESUPPLY: C-Store.	**RESUPPLY:** Don's Market. 760-765-3272. Good grocery store. 6a-8p every day.
LODGING: Cabins with kitchens sleep up to 7 people. Rates $$+ Cabins usually full the first weekend in May. Rollaways available.	**LODGING:** No.
CAMPING: $	**CAMPING:** No.
RESTAURANT: Yes.	**RESTAURANT:** Yes.
LAUNDRY: Yes.	**LAUNDRY:** No.
SHOWERS: Yes.	**SHOWERS:** No.
LAKE DAY USE: 2017: $7.50 **MOTORBOAT RENTAL:** 2017: $35/day. $30/day after 1pm.	**ATM:** Yes.

SHUTTLE: WTT Transportation. [http://www.shuttlesd.com/] [shuttlesandiego@gmail.com] 760-789-7252. Service throughout SoCal, including San Diego, Los Angeles, PCT Southern Terminus, Lake Morena, Boulder Oaks, Kitchen Creek Road, Mt. Laguna, Sunrise Highway trailhead, Scissors Crossing, Julian, Warner Springs, Idyllwild, Palm Springs.

Rates: $ = usually less than $50
$$ = usually $50-$80
$$$ = usually $80-$110
$$$$ = usually greater than $110

111.4 - Highway 79

112.6 - Agua Caliente Creek just past picnic tables - Good water.

114.9 - Campsite - DOUBLE TAP: Watch for Poison Oak.

115.6 - Agua Caliente Creek last crossing - You cross it five times. Good water. When you start gaining elevation, make sure you've already got water, 'cause the creek soon disappears as you go uphill.

119.6 - Lost Valley Spring - There is a sign on the left side of the PCT directing you to water 0.2 mile down in Lost Valley. BINK: Easy to locate, always has water, but has strong sulfur taste.

126.9 - Short cut to water tank - DOUBLE TAP: Look for a signed trail to the right of the PCT that goes up. This is a short cut to the tank at Mike Herrera's place.

127.3 - Chihuahua Valley Road - Go 0.2 mile to a left-branching 0.1-mile dirt spur road leading to Mike's house (with water and a bunkhouse). Water should be filtered/treated.

136.5 - Tule Canyon Creek - Usually no creek here. When it has water, it usually tastes like a pipe. BINK: Has water in wet years.

137.0 - Tule Canyon Road - Tule Spring is 0.3 East. Look for a big spigot which looks like something you could hook a fire hose to. The water tastes like a pipe.
If spigot is not working, look for a seep in the high grass to the left of the tank.

139.5 - Guzzler - Important water source - Cistern is underground. Looks like a 12' x 24' old broken parking lot. This is directly on the left side of the trail. Be sure to treat this water.
DOUBLE TAP (2014): Concrete is crumbling; don't put too much weight on it.

140.2 - Nance Canyon seasonal creeklet - No creek here.

BINK: In WET years there is water here. Check downstream 100 yards. In dry years sometimes there are pools. Had water in June 2008! There are several homesteads just upstream, possibly this was irrigation run off? This stream is rarely reliable.

143.1 - Table Mountain Truck Trail

151.8 - Pines-to-Palms Highway 74 - Turn left to <u>Paradise Valley Café</u> and/or to <u>hitch to Idyllwild</u>.

151.8 - Paradise Valley Café

GLORY: The Jose Burger at the Paradise Café is a MIRACLE. It's enough to inspire a following of cultish fanaticism to be rivaled only by politics, football, religion and, well, thru-hiking.

SUGE: The Jose Burger at Paradise Café is the best burger on the trail. Swiss cheese, bacon, avocado, mushrooms, green chiles, tomato, onion, lettuce, pickles. I've got a fuzzy, out of focus picture of one. Glory and I were in shock and awe when they came out. Quite literally, I had to eat the burger in sections: work on the top part, then in the middle, then attack a corner of the bottom, etc.

Are you hungry yet? Keep reading . . . . .

Paradise Valley Café (951-659-3663) is about one mile west (left) of the PCT on Pines-to-Palms Highway. Good food. PCT Register.

If the Café is closed, water is available from the hose on the side of the restaurant.
Outside hose faucet will not be on for early-season hikers. After the last freeze, the hose will be on.

Open 7 days a week, but close early (3p) on Mondays and Tuesdays. Hours vary!

Accepts hiker mail drops USPS, UPS, or FedEx. No fee. Mail drops can be picked up anytime the Café is open. Mail drop MUST have your name and ETA on all sides of the box. Be sure to make your box look unique (color, stripes, etc.). No outgoing mail.

Hiker's Legal Name
PCT Hiker, ETA: MM/DD/YY
c/o Paradise Valley Café
61721 State Highway 74
Mountain Center, CA 92561

151.8- Anza CA

GETTING HERE: From PCT mile 151.9, hitch down to Paradise Café, then hitch 6 miles west on Highway 371.

POST OFFICE: 951-763-2074, USPS only
Mon-Fri 9a-4p
Sat 10a-1p
General Delivery held for 30 days

Hiker's Legal Name
PCT Hiker, ETA: MM/DD/YY
General Delivery
Anza , CA 92539

RESUPPLY: Anza Village Market   951-763-4321   Excellent resupply. 10a-6:30p daily.

RESTAURANTS: Yes.

ATM: Yes.

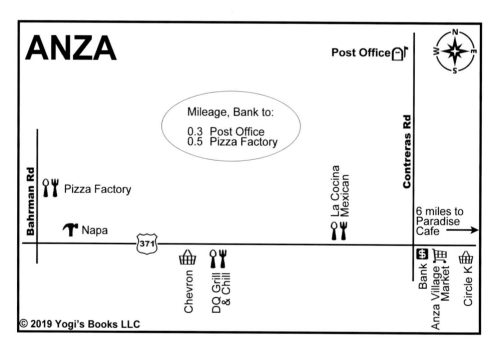

ANZA

© 2019 Yogi's Books LLC

OVERVIEW: Full-service tourist town, small enough to get around easily on foot.

GETTING HERE:
(1) Pines-to-Palms Highway (mile point 151.8): Walk left one mile to the Paradise Café and hitch to Idyllwild from there (hitch is 18 miles). At the Café, there is a highway junction, hitching is easier there than at the trail. Take Hwy 74 to Mountain Center (13.5 miles), then Hwy 243 to Idyllwild (4.5 miles).

(2) Devils Slide Trail (mile point 179.4): Leave the PCT at Saddle Junction take the 2.5 mile Devils Slide Trail down to the Humber Park Trailhead, then hitch 2.6 miles down to Idyllwild. The Devils Slide Trail is easy. The 27.5 PCT miles between Pines-to-Palms and Devils Slide are not easy.

SHUTTLE: Idyllwild Shuttle Bus. [www.forestfolk.org] 951-426-9688
Serves local area and also goes to Cabazon. Does not operate every day.

WTT Transportation. [http://www.shuttlesd.com/] 760-789-7252.
[shuttlesandiego@gmail.com] Service throughout SoCal, including San Diego, Los Angeles, PCT Southern Terminus, Lake Morena, Boulder Oaks, Kitchen Creek Road, Mt. Laguna, Sunrise Highway trailhead, Scissors Crossing, Julian, Warner Springs, Idyllwild, Palm Springs.

POST OFFICE:
951-659-1969, USPS only
Mon-Fri 9a-5p. Sat closed,
but usually hikers can pick up
packages on Sat from 1:30p-3p.
Knock on the white dutch door.

Hiker's Legal Name
PCT Hiker, ETA: MM/DD/YY
General Delivery
Idyllwild, CA 92549

General Delivery held for 3 weeks.

MAIL DROPS: Idyllwild Inn (888-659-2552) accepts mail drops for guests, no fee.
Mail drop MUST have an ETA and your name on all sides of the box.

USPS Address:
Hiker's Legal Name
PCT Hiker, ETA: MM/DD/YY
c/o Idyllwild Inn
PO Box 515
Idyllwild, CA 92549

UPS or FedEx Address:
Hiker's Legal Name
PCT Hiker, ETA: MM/DD/YY
c/o Idyllwild Inn
54300 Village Center Drive
Idyllwild, CA 92549

RESUPPLY: Full resupply. Two grocery stores. Fairway Foods is bigger.

Village Market	951-659-3800	Sun-Th 7a-6p, Fri-Sat 7a-7p
Fairway Foods	951-659-2737	Sun 9a-7p, Mon-Sat 9a-8p

OUTFITTER: Nomad Ventures 951-659-4853 During hiker season, open 7:45a-6:15p every day.

RESTAURANTS: Many restaurants. Jan's is great.

LAUNDRY: Yes.

SHOWER: Showers at Mount San Jacinto State Park 951-659-2607

ATM: Yes.

COMPUTER: Idyllwild Public Library 951-659-2300

FUEL: Denatured alcohol by the ounce at Village Hardware 951-659-4457
Canister fuel and white gas at Nomad Ventures 951-659-4853

MEDICAL:
Fern Creek Medical Center 951-659-9912
Idyllwild Health Center 951-659-4908

IDYLLWILD LODGING	Rates	TV	frig	micr	other
Idyllwild Inn 888-659-2552	$$$ +	Y	Y	Y	laundry service, accepts mail drops, some kitchenettes, rides to Humber Park and Deer Springs
	Motel-type rooms and large cabins which sleep 1-8 people. One free load of laundry for hikers staying two or more nights, otherwise $5/load. Rate depends upon the size of the room and if it's a weekday or weekend. Location is ideal – across the street from the PO and a block from Jan's Red Kettle.				
Silver Pines Lodge 951-659-4335	$$$ +	TV DVD	Y	Y	historic Lodge computer, laundry service, free DVD movies ride to Humber Park
Idyllwild Bunkhouse 951-659-2201	$$$ +	Y			all kitchenettes
Still House Hostel	New for 2018: Still House Hostel. 26500 Hwy 243. @StillHouseHostel Search "Still House Hostel" on Facebook. Floor Space, hot shower, laundry, full kitchen access.				
Mount San Jacinto State Park 951-659-2607	Pay camping. Restroom and shower for registered campers. Register at the Idyllwild Ranger Station (building with big porch). 2019: $5 per person. [www.parks.ca.gov/msjsp]				
	$ = usually less than $50 $$ = usually $50-$80 $$$ = usually $80-$110 $$$$ = usually greater than $110				

Map Symbols

David "Awol" Miller has given us permission to use the map symbols he created for his excellent book "The AT Guide". These map symbols allow you to easily find town services with a quick glance at the town maps.

- Airport
- ATM or Bank
- Boat
- Bowling
- Bus
- Camping
- Car Rental
- Computer
- C-Store
- First Aid
- Grocery Store
- Hardware Store
- Hostel
- Hotel
- Information
- Internet/WiFi
- Laundry
- Light Rail
- Lounge/Bar
- Outfitter
- Outgoing Mail
- Pay Phone
- Pharmacy
- Picnic Table
- Pool
- Post Office
- Ranger Station
- Restaurant
- Restroom/Privy
- Shoe Store
- Shower
- Ski Lift
- Theater
- Train Station

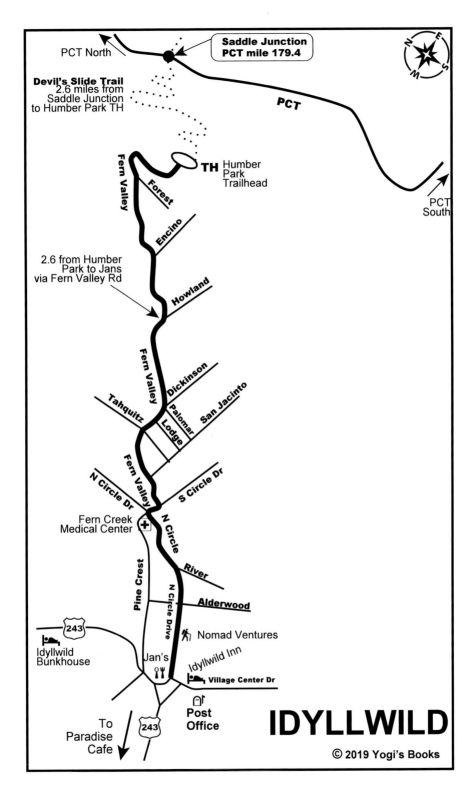

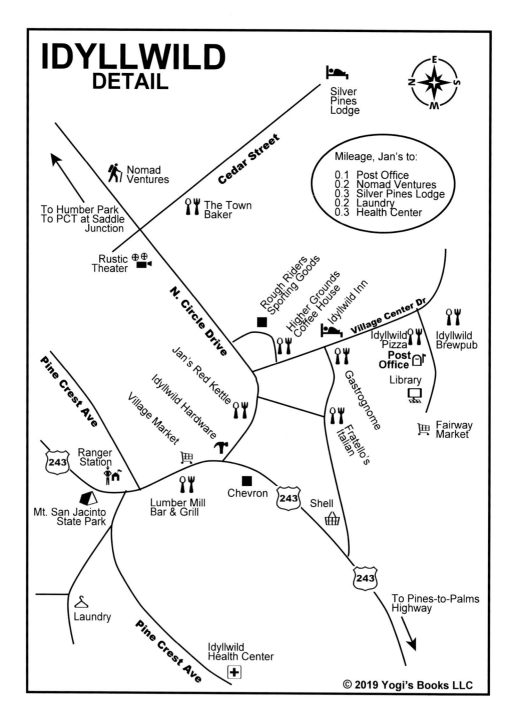

IDYLLWILD
DETAIL

Silver Pines Lodge

Cedar Street

Nomad Ventures

The Town Baker

To Humber Park
To PCT at Saddle Junction

Rustic Theater

Mileage, Jan's to:
0.1 Post Office
0.2 Nomad Ventures
0.3 Silver Pines Lodge
0.2 Laundry
0.3 Health Center

N. Circle Drive

Rough Riders Sporting Goods

Higher Grounds Coffee House

Idyllwild Inn

Village Center Dr

Idyllwild Pizza

Idyllwild Brewpub

Post Office

Library

Jan's Red Kettle

Idyllwild Hardware

Village Market

Pine Crest Ave

Gastrognome

Fratello's Italian

Fairway Market

Ranger Station

243

Mt. San Jacinto State Park

Lumber Mill Bar & Grill

Chevron

243

Shell

243

To Pines-to-Palms Highway

Laundry

Pine Crest Ave

Idyllwild Health Center

© 2019 Yogi's Books LLC

There are two ways out of Idyllwild: Hitch to Pines-to-Palms Highway
Walk the Devils Slide Trail up to Saddle Junction

There are two ways into Big Bear City: Hitch on Highway 18
Walk on Van Dusen Canyon Road

Pines-to-Palms Hwy	to Hwy 18	114.3 PCT miles	
Devils Slide Trail	to Hwy 18	86.7 PCT miles	plus 2.5 miles Devils Slide
Pines-to-Palms Hwy	to Van Dusen Cyn Rd	123.3 PCT miles	plus 2.8 miles Van Dusen
Devils Slide Trail	to Van Dusen Cyn Rd	95.7 PCT miles	plus 2.5 miles Devils Slide
			plus 2.8 miles Van Dusen

158.4 - Tunnel and Live Oak Springs - Tunnel Spring is 0.3 off PCT, water sometimes tastes like sulfur. Live Oak Spring has ice cold water, but it is a mile off PCT with a lot of elevation loss.

162.7 - Cedar Spring - Spring is 1.0 mile off trail. Quite an elevation drop, but great water

163.3 - Eagle Spring - Seasonal spring, 0.3 mile off trail.

166.6 - Fobes Ranch Trail Junction

168.6 - Spitler Peak Trail Junction

177.3 - Tahquitz Valley Trail - Seasonal creek 0.1 mile before.

178.0 - Tahquitz Peak Trail - Alternate joins PCT here.

179.4 - Saddle Junction - Devils Slide Trail goes to Idyllwild from here.

181.2 - Wellmans Cienaga Trail - Be careful here. Many hikers take the wrong trail. The PCT makes a left U-turn. The Wellmans Cienaga Trail goes straight. You will see a sign welcoming you to the San Jacinto Wilderness Area. This sign is on the Wellmans Cienaga Trail, not the PCT.

181.2 - San Jacinto Alternate Loop

The Wellmans Cienaga Trail is the beginning of the side trail to the top of San Jacinto Peak. Leave the PCT here and make a 6.5-mile loop over the top of San Jacinto, then rejoin the PCT near mile 185.7, which is 4.5 PCT miles north of where you got off the PCT at the Wellmans Cienaga Trail. If you're going to the top, take Halfmile's San Jacinto map. There are a few trail junctions that might be confusing without the map. [www.pctmap.net]

San Jacinto is 10,800 feet tall. From the top, you look directly down to the desert floor 9600 feet below you at 1200 feet. AWESOME. Don't miss it.

185.6 - North Fork San Jacinto River / Deer Springs - Spring/stream/runoff. Not really a river.
Fill up here. This is the last water until Snow Canyon Road, 20.1 miles north.
Fuller Ridge and the walk down to Snow Canyon Road can be dry and hot.

185.7 - Watch where you're going just north of the water at Deer Springs. There are two junctions. The second junction (I think) is where the San Jacinto loop trail rejoins the PCT, and I know of many hikers who took the wrong trail here. The junction looks like a switchback. The PCT goes left, toward Fuller Ridge. The more prominent trail is the San Jacinto trail, obviously going up the ridge to the right. This uphill trail will take you to the top of San Jacinto. Be careful here. Pay attention. There is usually water flowing across the trail just after this junction.

188.0 - Fuller Ridge - SOCKS: On snow-covered trail, many hikers descended too soon and came out way down on Black Mountain Road. Keep contouring near the ridge - the trail does not descend rapidly. JOKER: If you hit the road, head UP. You'll encounter the trail after you start descending on the other side.

190.7 - Black Mountain Road - BINK: Water about 1-2 miles west on road, not worth the walk.

205.7 - Snow Canyon Road - Spigot with good water.

209.5 - Interstate 10 / Banning CA

Banning has lots of lodging, restaurants, resupply, etc. There is a bus from Cabazon to Banning, where you can connect to other busses which service Banning and Beaumont. Banning Transit 951-922-3252.

[www.ci.banning.ca.us/], then click on Living in Banning, City Services, Banning Transit.

209.5 - Interstate 10 / Cabazon CA

OVERVIEW:	Cabazon is small.
GETTING HERE:	From the PCT crossing of I-10, Cabazon is 4.5 miles west (left). Hitching on the interstate is illegal. Railroad Ave (south of the interstate, between the railroad tracks and I-10), has very little traffic. Hard hitch. Tamarack Road (north of the interstate) does not go to Cabazon.
TAXI:	Banning/Beaumont/Cabazon Taxi 951-233-7708
SHUTTLE:	Idyllwild Shuttle Bus. [www.forestfolk.org] 951-426-9688 Cabazon to Idyllwild. Does not operate every day.

POST OFFICE: 951-849-6233, USPS only   Hiker's Legal Name
Mon-Fri 8:30a-11:30a, 12:45p-4p   PCT Hiker, ETA: MM/DD/YY
Sat closed.   General Delivery
If mail is not picked up 15 days after arrival,   Cabazon, CA 92230
PO will scan as "Unclaimed" or "Delivered",
but PO will hold for another 15 days. If not
picked up after a total of 30 days, mail will be
returned to sender.

RESUPPLY:	Possible resupply at the little grocery: Cabazon Country Store. 951-849-6422. Usually open Mon-Fri 6a-9p, Sat-Sun 7a-9p.
RESTAURANTS:	Burger King.
	Morongo Casino Resort & Spa. 888-667-6646. Located at I-10 exit 104 (1.5 miles west of exit 106) AYCE buffets and expensive lodging. Also, a California favorite: In-N-Out Burger ! ! !
ATM:	At Circle K.
FUEL:	HEET at Shell.
COMPUTER:	Library. 951-849-8234.

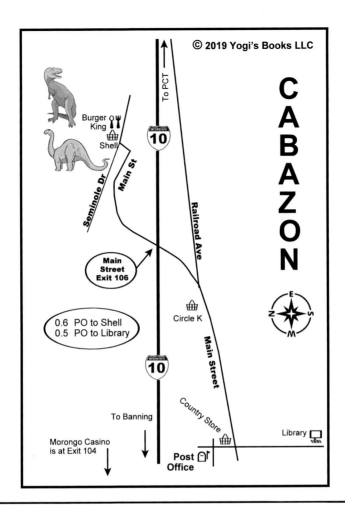

© 2019 Yogi's Books LLC

C A B A Z O N

To PCT

INTERSTATE **10**

Burger King

Shell

Seminole Dr

Main St

Main Street Exit 106

Railroad Ave

Circle K

0.6 PO to Shell
0.5 PO to Library

INTERSTATE **10**

Main Street

To Banning

Country Store

Morongo Casino is at Exit 104

Library

Post Office

214.0 - approximately - DOUBLE TAP (2014): Good camping.

218.5 - Old Jeep Road in Whitewater Canyon - The Whitewater Preserve (760-325-7222), is 0.6 mile off trail. Free camping, water, picnic tables, flush toilets, wading pool. No fires or alcohol.

220.1 - Whitewater Creek - The most water you've seen yet! JOKER: Good water, but not a good lunch spot. NO shade once you get here. A nice tree about a mile before, though.

226.2 - East Fork Mission Creek - Good water, and you'll cross the creek about 20 more times. Many hikers have a tough time with the trail up Mission Creek. This section is hot and mentally tough. Many hikers hitch into Big Bear City early.

235.5 - Creekside Camp - Usually there is water here. BINK: Many of the live oaks here have died and fallen into the campsite, but spots can still be found. DOUBLE TAP: Watch out for Poodle Dog Bush from here for a mile or so up the trail.

238.6 - approximately - Nice, reliable stream here in a cool canyon. The next on-trail water is at Arrastre Trail Camp, 17.6 miles north.

239.9 - Mission Creek Trail Camp - BINK (2004): There is a very good spring here that always has water, but most people have a very difficult time locating it. When you arrive to the dirt road, backtrack 50 yards, cross dry creek bed over to the south side, continue walking southeast, pass a camping area. You will see water spigots here; they are dry. Continue past a horse corral keeping it to your left. Angle slightly right and toward the hillside. You will soon locate a rough trail and if you start to listen you can hear the water. It is a spring, located in a somewhat brush-choked area, but is easily accessed. Total approximate distance off-trail is about 0.2 - 0.3 mile. I have had people tell me this spring does not exist, but trust me I have used it many times. It can be tricky to locate, but should be considered a reliable water source.

BINK (2006): People continue to have trouble finding the very reliable spring here. Again head south east 80 yards into the campground. Look for the horse corrals, slight down hill to the east. From them head level about 50 yards to the south, then look up to the brush to your right, you should pick up a faint trail which goes 10 yards into the green brush to a very good flowing spring. Listening for it helps. Don't give up, it does exist!

250.3 - Animal cages just after "four roads and a trail" - Lions, tigers, and bears, oh my!!

252.1 - Onyx Summit - Take side road left (west) 0.1 mile over to Highway 38.
Hitch right (north) to Big Bear City.

256.2 - Arrastre Trail Camp at Deer Spring - This is an established campsite with picnic tables and fire pits. If there is no water at the campsite, go about 0.1 - 0.2 mile farther north on the PCT, and you'll find a little stream.

256.7 - Spring - BINK: A spring runs across the trail appearing to be a small creek (not the creek in the canyon bottom you are following). This spring seems to have become a very reliable water source in recent years and if running is much better than Deer Spring.

266.1 - Highway 18 - Hitch left to Big Bear City.

268.6 - Doble Trail Camp - BINK: Water here is sporadic. Check metal catchment in grass uphill of spigot. Remove lid, sometimes you can turn the valves here to turn the camp spigot on.

275.1 - Van Dusen Canyon Road - Dirt road with very little traffic. Go left to Big Bear City.
BINK: Creek 0.1 mile before the road usually fairly reliable in spring.

266.1 or 275.1 - Big Bear City CA

OVERVIEW: There are two towns here: Big Bear CITY and Big Bear LAKE.
                      Big Bear LAKE is larger than Big Bear CITY, and they're both full service.
                      Public bus transportation runs between the two towns.

GETTING HERE: (1) PCT mile 266.1 - Hitch 5 miles left on Highway 18.
                          Do not road walk along Highway 18. There is no shoulder. Dangerous!

                      (2) PCT mile 275.1 -Turn left on Van Dusen Canyon Road,
                          walk 4.0 miles from PCT to Big Bear City Post Office.

RIDE: From April 1 until mid-Nov, Steve and Sandy Teutschman give rides.
                      Papa Smurf 909-800-7028 or Mtn Mama 909-800-7029.

TAXI SERVICE: Big Bear Cab 909-866-8294
                      Ride-Cali   909-338-3471

CAR RENTAL: Enterprise (inside Northwoods Resort). 909-866-1156. Mon-Fri 8a-5p.

BUS SERVICE: Mountain Transit public bus. 909-878-5200.
                      Busses run every day approximately once per hour from 5:30a-7p.
                      The last return trip to Big Bear CITY is around 6p.

TRAIL ANGELS: From April 1 until mid-Nov, Steve and Sandy Teutschman provide camping and
                      3 bunks inside, plus space as needed inside when the weather is bad. Other
                      services: laundry, showers, food, loaner clothes, computer, accept mail drops.
                      Papa Smurf 909-800-7028 or Mtn Mama 909-800-7029.

POST OFFICE:	Post Office in Big Bear CITY: 909-585-7132, USPS only Mon-Fri 9a-4:30p Open Sat from 1p-2p for package pick up only General Delivery held for 30 days	Hiker's Legal Name PCT Hiker, ETA: MM/DD/YY General Delivery Big Bear City CA, <u>92314</u>
	Post Office in Big Bear LAKE: 909-866-1035, USPS only Mon-Fri 8:30a-5p Sat 10a-noon General Delivery held for 30 days	Hiker's Legal Name PCT Hiker, ETA: MM/DD/YY General Delivery 472 Pine Knot Big Bear Lake CA, <u>92315</u>
	Branch PO near Vons: Does not accept General Delivery. Mon-Fri 10a-12:30, 1:30p-4p. Sat closed.	

MAIL DROPS: Big Bear Hostel (909-866-8900) accepts mail drops, no fee for guests, $5 fee for non-guests:

USPS Address: Hiker's Legal Name PCT Hiker, ETA: MM/DD/YY c/o Big Bear Hostel PO Box 1951 Big Bear Lake, CA 92315-1951	UPS or FedEx Address: Hiker's Legal Name PCT Hiker, ETA: MM/DD/YY c/o Big Bear Hostel 541 Knickerbocker Road (office) Big Bear Lake, CA 92315-1951
The Teutschmans accept mail drops, no fee, USPS, UPS, FedEx. Papa Smurf 909-800-7028 Mtn Mama 909-800-7029	Hiker's Legal Name PCT Hiker, ETA: MM/DD/YY c/o Steve & Sandy Teutschman 840 E Angeles Blvd Big Bear City, CA 92314

OUTGOING MAIL:	Kathy's Postal Plus 909-866-2344	Mon-Fri 10a-5p. Sat-Sun 10a-3p.
	The UPS Store 909-878-4747	Mon-Fri 8:30a-6p. Sat 9a-3p. Sun closed.
	Teutschmans 909-800-7028 or 7029	Trail Angels offer outgoing mail, including Regional Rate boxes.

RESUPPLY: BIG BEAR CITY has a mid-sized grocery store:

Community Market   909-585-2641
Mon-Thur 7:30a-9p, Fri-Sat 7:30a-10p, Sun 7:30a-9p

BIG BEAR LAKE has 2 large supermarkets. Bus stops at both.

Vons	909-866-8459	6a-midnight every day
Stater Brothers	909-866-5211	6a-11p every day

OUTDOOR STORE: Big 5 Sporting Goods   909-866-2730

RESTAURANTS: Many restaurants.
Thelma's and Grizzly Manor Café are hiker favorites.
Teddy Bear Café (near Hostel) has hiker breakfast special.

LAUNDRY:	Big Bear CITY:	Across from Community Market and at Motel 6.
	Big Bear LAKE:	Next to Vons and at both hostels.

ATM: Many, including one inside Thelma's restaurant.

COMPUTER: Library in Big Bear LAKE   Bus stops here   909-866-5571

FUEL:	Big Bear CITY:	HEET at Valero C-Store	
	Big Bear LAKE:	Denatured alcohol at K-Mart	909-866-9200
		Canister fuel at Big 5 Sporting Goods	909-866-2730

MEDICAL: Bear Valley Community Hospital   Bus stops here   909-866-6501

LODGING: Many lodging options. Rates:
                  $ = usually less than $50. $$ = usually $50-$80. $$$ = usually $80-$110.

                  These are hiker favorites:

                  Big Bear Hostel in Big Bear LAKE
                          909-866-8900   [www.bigbearhostel.com]
                          2019 rates: Dorm $25/person one night, $20 for the second night.
                                  Private rooms $$
                          Reservations: call ahead or reserve online.
                          One block from Big Bear LAKE Post Office.
                          Free ride to/from trail (Hwy 18) if they have time.
                          Lake view party deck, BBQ, and full kitchen.
                          Liquor store around corner. Bank and ATM next to Hostel.
                          Free internet computer.
                          Coin laundry with loaner clothes.
                          Free DVD movies, ping pong, foosball.
                          Many restaurant deals for Hostel guests.
                          The bus drops off across the street. You want the "Veteran's Park"
                          bus stop at the corner of Big Bear Blvd and Knickerbocker Road.

                  ITH Mountain Adventure Lodge in Big Bear LAKE. 909-866-2532.
                          Information in italics is from 2018, not confirmed for 2019.
                          Free hot breakfasts and home cooked dinners.
                          2018 rates: Dorm bunk $25 includes dinner and breakfast
                                  Private rooms $$
                                  Camping $15, includes dinner and breakfast
                          Free laundry from 6pm to 8am
                          iPad for guests to use
                          Free rides to PCT at Hwy 18
                          Use Marta bus stop at the JR Market/entrance to big Bear Village,
                          which is at the base of the street heading up to the Lodge.

                  Motel 6   Big Bear CITY   909-585-6666   Rates $$
                          TV in the rooms. Laundry at the motel.

                  Nature's Inn   Big Bear CITY   909-585-2226
                          Bunk room and private rooms. Rates: $ - $$$
                          Rooms have TV, refrigerator, microwave
                          Loaner clothes available
                          Common room has pool table, games, TV, internet

                  Best Western   Big Bear LAKE   909-866-6666
                          Ask for PCT rate.
                          Complimentary hot breakfast, pool, hot tub

                  Honey Bear Lodge   Big Bear LAKE   909-866-7825
                          Big rooms, great location
                          Outside shaded area with picnic tables and grills
                          Rates: $$+

                  Vintage Lakeside Inn   Big Bear LAKE. 909-866-4978
                          Rates: $$+
                          Ask for PCT hiker rate.

CAMPING: Teutschman's home
                  Papa Smurf 909-800-7028 or Mountain Mama 909-800-7029

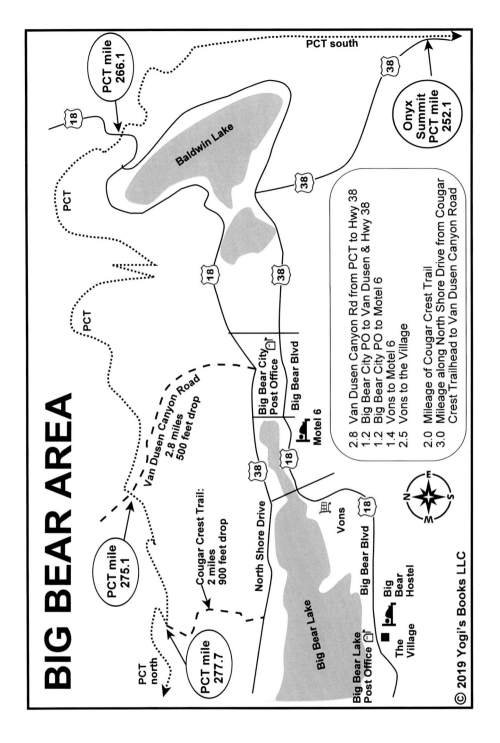

BIG BEAR AREA

PCT south

PCT mile 266.1

Baldwin Lake

18

38

Onyx Summit PCT mile 252.1

PCT

PCT

18

38

38

PCT

Van Dusen Canyon Road
2.8 miles
500 feet drop

Big Bear City Post Office

Big Bear Blvd

Motel 6

38

18

2.8 Van Dusen Canyon Rd from PCT to Hwy 38
1.2 Big Bear City PO to Van Dusen & Hwy 38
1.2 Big Bear City PO to Motel 6
1.4 Vons to Motel 6
2.5 Vons to the Village

2.0 Mileage of Cougar Crest Trail
3.0 Mileage along North Shore Drive from Cougar
     Crest Trailhead to Van Dusen Canyon Road

PCT mile 275.1

Cougar Crest Trail:
2 miles
900 feet drop

North Shore Drive

Vons

18

Big Bear Blvd

PCT north

PCT mile 277.7

Big Bear Lake

Big
Bear
Hostel

The Village

Big Bear Lake Post Office

© 2019 Yogi's Books LLC

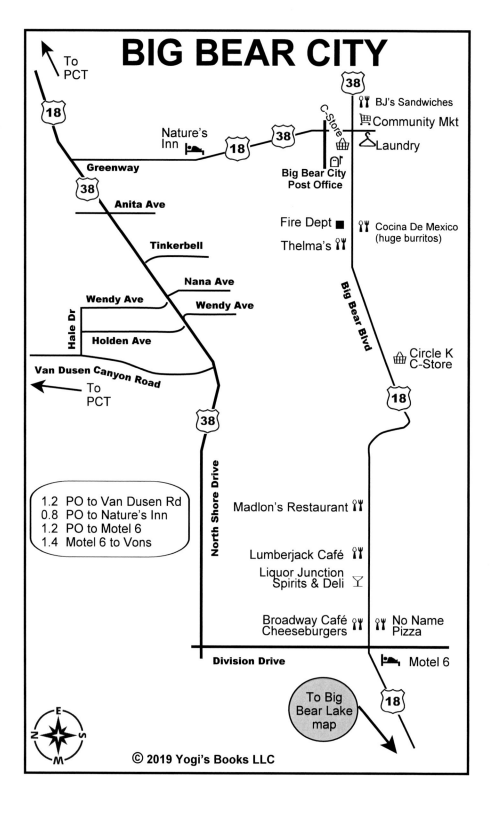

BIG BEAR CITY

To PCT

18

Nature's Inn

18   38   38

C-Store

BJ's Sandwiches
Community Mkt
Laundry

Greenway

38

Anita Ave

Big Bear City Post Office

Tinkerbell

Fire Dept ■   Cocina De Mexico
(huge burritos)

Thelma's

Nana Ave

Wendy Ave

Wendy Ave

Hale Dr

Holden Ave

Big Bear Blvd

Van Dusen Canyon Road

← To PCT

Circle K C-Store

38

18

North Shore Drive

1.2 PO to Van Dusen Rd
0.8 PO to Nature's Inn
1.2 PO to Motel 6
1.4 Motel 6 to Vons

Madlon's Restaurant

Lumberjack Café

Liquor Junction Spirits & Deli

Broadway Café   No Name
Cheeseburgers   Pizza

Division Drive   Motel 6

To Big Bear Lake map

18

N E S W

© 2019 Yogi's Books LLC

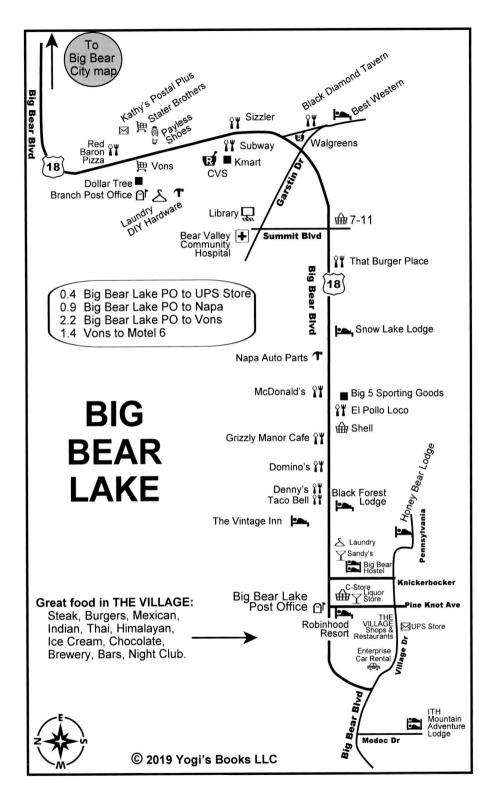

To Big Bear City map

Big Bear Blvd

18

Kathy's Postal Plus
Stater Brothers
Payless Shoes

Red Baron Pizza
Vons
Dollar Tree
Branch Post Office
Laundry
DIY Hardware

Sizzler

Subway

CVS   Kmart

Black Diamond Tavern

Best Western

Walgreens

Garstin Dr

Library

Bear Valley Community Hospital

Summit Blvd

7-11

That Burger Place

Big Bear Blvd

18

0.4 Big Bear Lake PO to UPS Store
0.9 Big Bear Lake PO to Napa
2.2 Big Bear Lake PO to Vons
1.4 Vons to Motel 6

Snow Lake Lodge

Napa Auto Parts

BIG BEAR LAKE

McDonald's

Big 5 Sporting Goods

El Pollo Loco

Shell

Grizzly Manor Cafe

Domino's

Denny's
Taco Bell

Black Forest Lodge

Honey Bear Lodge

The Vintage Inn

Pennsylvania

Laundry

Sandy's

Big Bear Hostel

Knickerbocker

C-Store
Liquor Store

Pine Knot Ave

Great food in THE VILLAGE:
Steak, Burgers, Mexican,
Indian, Thai, Himalayan,
Ice Cream, Chocolate,
Brewery, Bars, Night Club.

Big Bear Lake Post Office

Robinhood Resort

THE VILLAGE Shops & Restaurants

UPS Store

Village Dr

Enterprise Car Rental

Big Bear Blvd

ITH Mountain Adventure Lodge

Modoc Dr

N E S W

© 2019 Yogi's Books LLC

TRIPLE CROWN OUTFITTERS

Need gear or food shipped to you on the trail? TCO has you covered! Owners Worldwide and Yogi know that gear fails just when you need it the most.

Order from our website, and we will ship your package promptly.

Need a bear canister or snow gear for the Sierra? It doesn't make sense to purchase canisters or snow gear ahead of time and then pay to ship it to Kennedy Meadows. Instead, get that gear from TCO right in Kennedy Meadows.

We highly recommend pre-ordering your bear canister from the Triple Crown Outfitters website, and we will hold it in Kennedy Meadows for you until you arrive.

Prefer to rent a bear canister? Canisters are needed from Kennedy Meadows to Sonora Pass. Rent from TCO in Kennedy Meadows south, return to Kennedy Meadows Resort and Pack Station (KM north) 10 miles west of Sonora Pass. If you don't go to KM north, you can mail the rental canister back to TCO.

Triple Crown Outfitters is known as **"the best resupply on the PCT."** This great selection is also available for online shipping.

Questions?   jackie@triplecrownoutfitters.com
                      matt@triplecrownoutfitters.com

Visit us online at **www.triplecrownoutfitters.com**

Visit our **physical location in Kennedy Meadows, CA.**

Two ways out of Big Bear City: Hitch on Highway 18 or walk on Van Dusen Canyon Road
Two ways into Wrightwood: Walk on the Acorn Trail or hitch on Hwy 2 (highway might not be open)

Big Bear City Hwy 18	to	Wrightwood Acorn Trail	97.3	miles
Big Bear City Hwy 18	to	Wrightwood Hwy 2	103.3	miles
Big Bear City Van Dusen	to	Wrightwood Acorn Trail	88.3	miles
Big Bear City Van Dusen	to	Wrightwood Hwy 2	94.3	miles

268.6 - Doble Trail Camp - BINK: Water here is sporadic. Check metal catchment in grass uphill of spigot. Remove lid, sometimes you can turn the valves here to turn the camp spigot on.

275.1 - Van Dusen Canyon Road - Dirt road with very little traffic. Go left to Big Bear City.
BINK: Creek 0.1 mile before the road usually fairly reliable in spring.

277.7 - Cougar Crest Trail - BE CAREFUL HERE!! Many hikers mistakenly go left down the Cougar Crest Trail. The PCT makes a U-turn to the right.

285.6 - Little Bear Springs Trail Camp -
BINK: Spigot almost always turned off. Water 95% time at creek nearby camp.

285.9 - Holcomb Creek - Good water.

298.5 - Deep Creek Bridge / Splinters Cabin - Pavilion, privy, picnic table, trash cans.
From the trailhead, hitch to Cedar Glen or Lake Arrowhead.

298.5 (bridge) to 313.4 (ford) - BINK: There is a road above the Deep Creek canyon all through here. When driving on it in the off season, I was shocked at how much garbage dumping occurs in all of the drainages through here which later flow over the PCT. I would consider Deep Creek and all of these seasonal streams through as fairly polluted.

298.5 (bridge) to 341.9 (Cajon Pass) -
This is a totally exposed, extremely hot section. Take plenty of water.

301.3 - DOUBLE TAP: Watch for an unpaved road which goes down and to the right of the creek bed. There a few campsites in this area.

307.9 - Deep Creek Hot Springs - Cold creek, hot springs, and naked people.

310.0 - Footbridge - DOUBLE TAP: Don't climb down the steep slope on the south side of the bridge (which also has Poison Oak) to get water here. You'll cross Deep Creek again at mile 313.6 and it's MUCH easier to get water there.

313.0 - Mojave River Forks Reservoir Dam -
PCT tread drops down below the dam (to the left). Follow the PCT markers.

313.4 - Deep Creek Ford - BINK: After crossing the creek, the trail continues to be overgrown and without any true trail tread for quite a distance. Careful navigation helps here.

314.3 - Hwy 173

316.2 - Trailside Spring - Doesn't always have water.

317.3 - Piped Spring - About 200 yards before Grass Valley Road, watch for a piped spring on the right side of the trail, down off the trail about 8 feet. Watch for this! Not flowing in 2016, 2017, 2018.

317.9 - Grass Valley Creek - Usually flows. Watch out for hornets.

319.9 - Campsite - Trail to the right leads to a small campsite.

298.5 - Cedar Glen

OVERVIEW: Small mountain town, no lodging. Lake Arrowhead is accessible by bus/hitch.

GETTING HERE: 3.6 mile trailhead hitch from Splinters Cabin (a popular day use area).
                Any cars leaving Splinters Cabin will go to Cedar Glen.

BUS: Mountain Transit RIM Route 4 serves Cedar Glen and Lake Arrowhead.
                There are connecting busses to Big Bear City/Lake and San Bernardino.
                [https://mountaintransit.org/]

POST OFFICE: 909-337-4614, USPS only   Hiker's Legal Name
                Mon-Fri 8:30a-5p, Sat 9a-11a   PCT Hiker, ETA: MM/DD/YY
                General Delivery held for 15 days   General Delivery
                                                         Cedar Glen CA 92321

RESUPPLY: Jensen's Minute Shoppe   909-337-3500   Full resupply, limited dinner choices
                                                         Sun-Thur 6a-10p, Fri-Sat 6a-11p

RESTAURANTS: Yes.
LAUNDRY: Yes.
CANISTER FUEL: Jensen's usually has canister fuel.

298.5 - Lake Arrowhead

OVERVIEW: Touristy, located on the lake.

GETTING HERE: Trailhead hitch from Splinter's Cabin, then hitch or bus 2 miles on Hwy 173.

BUS: Mountain Transit RIM Route 4 serves Cedar Glen and Lake Arrowhead.
                There are connecting busses to Big Bear City/Lake and San Bernardino.
                [https://mountaintransit.org/]

POST OFFICE: 909-337-2673, USPS only   Hiker's Legal Name
                Mon-Fri 9a-4:30p, Sat closed   PCT Hiker, ETA: MM/DD/YY
                ** DO NOT include the physical   General Delivery
                address of the Post Office on the   Lake Arrowhead, CA 92352
                General Delivery address **
                General Delivery held for 15 days

OUTGOING MAIL: Postal Connection   909-337-5199   Mon-Fri 9a-6p. Sat 10a-4p. Sun closed.

RESUPPLY: Stater Brothers   909-337-5854   6a-11p every day

RESTAURANTS: Yes.

LAUNDRY: No.

ATM: Yes.

LAKE ARROWHEAD LODGING		Rates	TV	frig	micr	other
Arrowhead Lake Inn	909-337-6633	$$$$	Y	Y	Y	continental breakfast
Saddleback Inn	909-336-3571	$$$$	Y	Y	some	
Lake Arrowhead Resort	909-336-1511	$$$$	Y	no	no	

There are many other lodging options around Lake Arrowhead. Mountain Transit bus system services this area.	$ = usually less than $50 $$ = usually $50-$80 $$$ = usually $80-$110 $$$$ = usually greater than $110

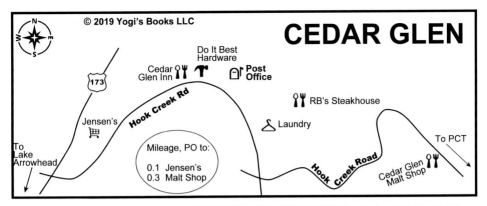

CEDAR GLEN

© 2019 Yogi's Books LLC

173

Hook Creek Rd

Do It Best Hardware

Cedar Glen Inn

Post Office

RB's Steakhouse

Laundry

Jensen's

To Lake Arrowhead

Mileage, PO to:

0.1 Jensen's
0.3 Malt Shop

Hook Creek Road

To PCT

Cedar Glen Malt Shop

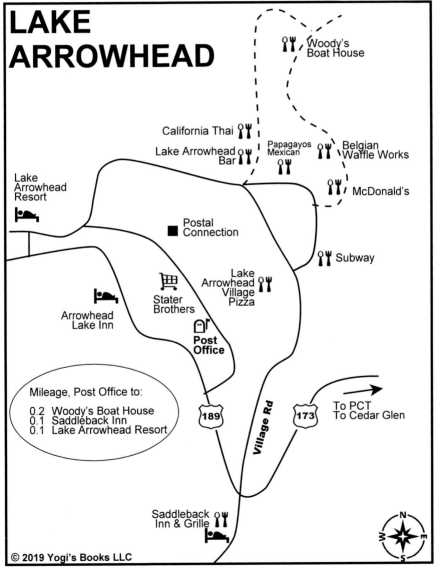

LAKE ARROWHEAD

Woody's Boat House

California Thai

Lake Arrowhead Bar

Papagayos Mexican

Belgian Waffle Works

McDonald's

Lake Arrowhead Resort

Postal Connection

Subway

Stater Brothers

Lake Arrowhead Village Pizza

Arrowhead Lake Inn

Post Office

Mileage, Post Office to:

0.2 Woody's Boat House
0.1 Saddleback Inn
0.1 Lake Arrowhead Resort

189

Village Rd

173

To PCT
To Cedar Glen

Saddleback Inn & Grille

© 2019 Yogi's Books LLC

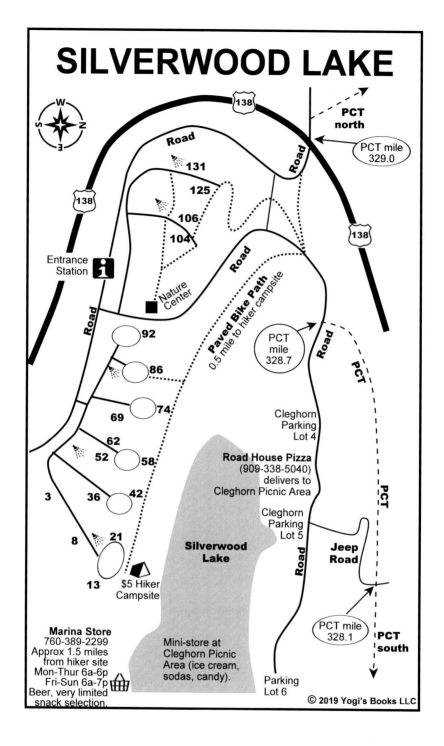

SILVERWOOD LAKE

138

PCT north

PCT mile 329.0

Road

131

125

106

104

138

138

Entrance Station

Nature Center

Road

Paved Bike Path
0.5 mile to hiker campsite

PCT mile 328.7

Road

PCT

92

86

74

69

62

52

58

42

36

3

8

21

13

$5 Hiker Campsite

Cleghorn Parking Lot 4

Road House Pizza
(909-338-5040)
delivers to
Cleghorn Picnic Area

Cleghorn Parking Lot 5

Jeep Road

Silverwood Lake

Road

PCT

PCT mile 328.1

PCT south

Marina Store
760-389-2299
Approx 1.5 miles
from hiker site
Mon-Thur 6a-6p
Fri-Sun 6a-7p
Beer, very limited
snack selection.

Mini-store at
Cleghorn Picnic
Area (ice cream,
sodas, candy).

Parking Lot 6

© 2019 Yogi's Books LLC

323.8 - Highway 173 - At mile 323.8, the trail gets a little confusing. Go out to Highway 173, turn left, walk along the highway for 0.6 mile to cross a bridge, then the trail tread continues on the SAME SIDE of the highway. <u>Don't cross the highway.</u>

326.3 - DOUBLE TAP: Watch for a steep trail on the left which leads down to covered concrete picnic tables.

328.1 - Cross Jeep Road - To get water, take this left-descending jeep road down to the <u>Silverwood Lake Recreation Area</u> (see Handbook "Silverwood Lake" map). Get plenty of <u>water here</u>, because the next water is at Cajon Pass, 14.0 very hot miles north of here. If you're not pure, after getting water you can walk the road out of the Recreation Area and pick up the PCT again at the bike path. If you're not sure where to go, just head toward the highway. The PCT uses the underpass to cross Highway 138.

Road House Pizza (909-338-5040) delivers to Cleghorn Picnic Area.

328.7 - Bike Path to Silverwood Lake Cleghorn Picnic Area - You can backtrack to the Recreation Area now on the bike path. This takes you back to Silverwood Lake Recreation Area, to the same place you could have got to via the jeep road at mile 328.0. See Handbook "Silverwood Lake" map.

329.0 - Highway 138 Overpass - After walking under Highway 138, go left for about 500 feet to the Park Office. There is a spigot across from the mailboxes.

333.1 - Small Stream - Usually good water.
BINK: Southbounders take note: there is a smaller barely-flowing stream about 0.25 mile north of this one which could be confused with it. Keep going.

341.4 - Crowder Canyon - You'll see a tiny stream. Walk another mile and get water at McDonald's.

341.9 - Interstate 15 / Cajon Pass

OVERVIEW:	Typical interstate exit. You could buy snacks to take you from here to Wrightwood.
GETTING HERE:	When you emerge at I-15, you'll see a PCT sign with "McDonald's 0.4 mile" and an arrow pointing right.

MAIL DROPS:	Cajon Pass Inn 760-249-6777 Accepts mail drops, no fee USPS, UPS, or FedEx. Outgoing mail is letters only	Hiker's Legal Name PCT Hiker, ETA: MM/DD/YY c/o Cajon Pass Inn 8317 US Hwy 138 At the 15 Freeway Phelan, CA 92371

RESUPPLY:	<u>Chevron</u> (760-249-4575) is open 24 hours. C-Store with great snack selection. Do not count on this store for trail dinners.
LODGING:	Hiker-friendly <u>Cajon Pass Inn</u> 760-249-6777. Rates: $$ Rooms have microwave, refrigerator, TV. Rate includes hot breakfast. Laundry, hot tub, and pool on site.
CAMPING:	<u>Don't camp anywhere near the Interstate.</u> Trains go through Cajon Pass all night long blaring their horns. Get at least to Swarthout Canyon Road (5.3 PCT miles north of Cajon Pass) before camping. At Swarthout Canyon Road, you'll have a ridge between you and the Cajon Pass train tracks.
RESTAURANT:	<u>McDonald's</u> next to Chevron on this side of the interstate. <u>Subway</u> and <u>Del Taco</u> over by Cajon Pass Inn. Amazing real ice cream milkshakes at the <u>Chevron</u>!
ATM & HEET: COMPUTER:	At Chevron. Available for guests at Cajon Pass Inn.
WATER:	<u>Fill up with water at McDonald's.</u> This is the last on-trail water until Wrightwood CA.

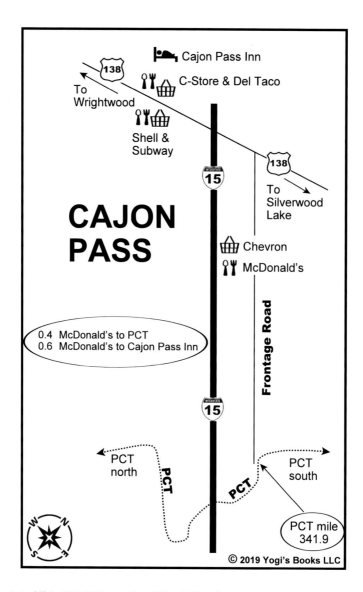

138

To
Wrightwood

🛏 Cajon Pass Inn

🍴🧺 C-Store & Del Taco

🍴🧺
Shell &
Subway

INTERSTATE 15

138

To
Silverwood
Lake

CAJON
PASS

🧺 Chevron

🍴 McDonald's

Frontage Road

0.4 McDonald's to PCT
0.6 McDonald's to Cajon Pass Inn

INTERSTATE 15

PCT
north

PCT

PCT

PCT
south

PCT mile
341.9

© 2019 Yogi's Books LLC

341.9 (Interstate 15) to 358.7 (Sheep Creek Truck Road) -
This is a very hot, exposed, waterless section.

347.3 - Swarthout Canyon Road -
There are very few chances to camp until you get all the way up on the ridge.

358.7 - Sheep Creek Truck Road

357.2 - approximately - Gobbler's Knob -
DOUBLE TAP: Good campsites at junction of multiple unpaved jeep roads.

363.4 - Acorn Canyon Trail - If you go to Wrightwood from here, you walk 3.6 miles off trail, down out of the mountains to Wrightwood, then walk the same 3.6 miles back up to the PCT when you leave town. Instead, you could walk only 6.0 more miles north on the PCT and hitch to Wrightwood on Angeles Crest Highway 2 (at PCT mile 369.4).

364.3 - Guffy Campground - Bears here. BINK: Have never seen this spring dry.
DOUBLE TAP: Trail to the spring is on the right of the PCT after an extremely steep 0.1 mile.

367.1 - Blue Ridge Campground - DOUBLE TAP: Nice picnic tables here.

369.3 - Angeles Crest Highway 2 - The PCT crosses Hwy 2 at Inspiration Point.
This is a highway overlook area with privy. Hitch to the right to go to Wrightwood.
Hwy 2 is often closed. California Highway Information (Caltrans) 1-800-427-7623.

363.4or 369.3 - Wrightwood CA

OVERVIEW: Wrightwood is a nice compact town. Good place for a zero day.
Great grocery store, internet, restaurants.

GETTING HERE:
(1)   PCT mile 363.4 - walk the 3.6 mile Acorn Trail.
(2)   PCT mile 369.3 - hitch 5.5 miles on Highway 2.

TRAIL ANGELS: Check the PCT Register at the Hardware Store for a list of Trail Angels.

POST OFFICE:
760-249-8882, USPS only   Hiker's Legal Name
Mon-Fri 8:45a-5p   PCT Hiker, ETA: MM/DD/YY
Sat package pick up only 8a-11a   General Delivery
Hikers can pick up mail drops at the   Wrightwood, CA 92397
Post Office as early as 7a Mon-Fri.
Ring the bell in the lobby.

MAIL DROPS:
760-249-3653   Mon-Sat 8:30a-5:30p, Sun 8:30a-4:30p
Hiker-friendly Mountain Hardware accepts mail drops, no fee.
Be sure to put name on all sides of box, and "Hold for PCT Hiker" on top.
Must have valid domestic return address. **UPS/FedEx is preferred.**

USPS Address: UPS or FedEx Address:
Hiker's Legal Name   Hiker's Legal Name
PCT Hiker, ETA: MM/DD/YY   PCT Hiker, ETA: MM/DD/YY
c/o Mountain Hardware   c/o Mountain Hardware
PO Box 398   1390 Highway 2
Wrightwood, CA 92397   Wrightwood, CA 92397

HIKER SERVICES:
Mountain Hardware takes care of hikers !!
- Official PCT Register with list of Trail Angels.
  When you register, ask for your free PCT trail memento while supplies last.
- Charging station (bring your charging cord and adapters)
- Pack parking station: leave your pack while you check out town.
  Be sure to pick it up before closing time.
- $20 purchase gets you a100g canister fuel for ONE CENT !!
- Denatured alcohol, white gas by the ounce.
- Gear: Sawyer Squeeze filters, Katadyn BeFree, Leukotape by foot or roll,
  Tyvek, Dirty Girl Gaiters, Altras, Injinji's, Merrell Moab 2, Microspikes, Sea To
  Summit products, Mountain House freeze dried food, Darn Tough exchange.

RESUPPLY:
Full resupply at Jensen's Finest Foods (small supermarket).
760-249-3322. Sun-Thur 7a-9p. Fri-Sat 7a-10p.

OUTDOOR STORE:
Mountain Hardware (760-249-3653) has a camping section (gloves, warm hats,
                                   Tenacious Tape, canister fuel, Tyvek).

Mini-Mart (760-249-6115) carries Darn Tough Socks, warm hats, gloves.

RESTAURANTS:
Yodeler	760-249-6482	Great burgers, salads, music
Grizzly Café	760-249-6733	Ask for PCT discount
Mile High Pizza	760-249-4848	EXCELLENT, delivers to motels
Evergreen Café	760-249-6393	Huge delicious breakfasts

LAUNDRY:
There is NO public laundry in Wrightwood.
The Pines Motel allows guests to use the motel's laundry machines.

SHOWER: At Camp Wrightwood. 760-249-3453.

ATM:	At Jensen's Finest Foods.
COMPUTER:	Wrightwood Public Library. 760-249-4577.
FUEL:	Denatured alcohol by the ounce, canister fuel, and white gas at Mountain Hardware. 760-249-3653.
DETOUR AHEAD:	The Endangered Species Detour begins at PCT mile 386.0.

WRIGHTWOOD LODGING		Rates	details
Cedar Lodge	760-249-4673	$$$	No laundry
Mt. View Cabins & Motel	760-249-5578	$$ - $$$	Small and large rooms which accommodate up to 8 people. No laundry.
Grand Pine Cabins	760-249-9974	$$$	Ask for hiker rate. No laundry.
Canyon Creek Inn	760-249-4800	$$$	Cable TV, DVD player, refrigerators. Laundry $10/load.
Camp Wrightwood	760-249-3453	$ bunk	This is a kids camp. Space available most weekends. No walkins! You must call first to check on availability. No alcohol, no drugs. Party crowd is not welcome here. Bunk and a shower for $10 donation.
Bear With Us Lodging 1474 Betty Street contact Janet: cell 909-965-7483 home 760-249-3457 bearwithuslodging@hotmail.com			$ per person, hostel-style shared lodging. Call before arriving to check on availability. Hiker-friendly Janet runs a beautiful cabin! A full service homes (no laundry) open exclusively for PCT hikers during hiker season. Fully equipped kitchen, cable TV, DVD and VCR, game room, outdoor BBQ hut. No camping. Bear With Us sleeps up to 10 people. [http://wrightwoodcalif.com/accommodations/BearWithUs.htm] Shuttles available to/from PCT at Inspiration Point/Highway 2 (for guests only, when Janet has time).
Holistic Health Day Spa and Lodging	760-249-6600		Three miles west past the Mountain View Motel. Bunk room $, private rooms $+, shower, free laundry, free ride into Wrightwood and to trail, free fruit when you leave.
The Bud Pharm	text or call 760-963-4306 bar phone 760-249-8020		Dave & The Bud Pharm have been hosting PCT hikers, travelers & Mountain High employees since 2008. We offer a shady camp area under some pines with a community fire pit and wood. BBQ's, fridge, showers, coin op laundry ($1.00 wash $1.00 Dry) TV, outside wet bar area, WiFi, pool, great company, long term parking and rides. No charge for spending a zero or two here! *The Bud Pharm says: NO TWEEKERS, ASSHOLES, OR HARD DRUGS PERMITTED! ISSUES LIKE THIS WILL BE REMOVED!* *DO NOT ASK ABOUT SCORING BAGS ON THE PHONE!*
		$ = usually less than $50 $$ = usually $50-$80 $$$ = usually $80-$110 $$$$ = usually greater than $110	

WRIGHTWOOD

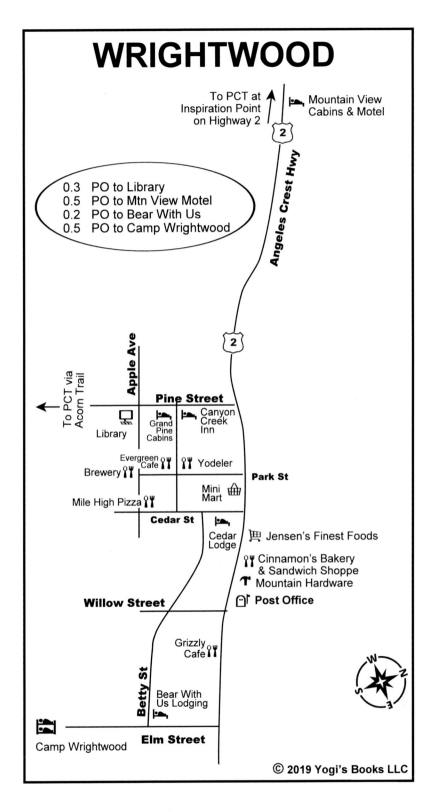

To PCT at
Inspiration Point
on Highway 2

Mountain View
Cabins & Motel

2

Angeles Crest Hwy

0.3 PO to Library
0.5 PO to Mtn View Motel
0.2 PO to Bear With Us
0.5 PO to Camp Wrightwood

2

Apple Ave

To PCT via
Acorn Trail

Pine Street

Library

Grand
Pine
Cabins

Canyon
Creek
Inn

Evergreen
Cafe

Yodeler

Brewery

Park St

Mile High Pizza

Mini
Mart

Cedar St

Cedar
Lodge

Jensen's Finest Foods

Cinnamon's Bakery
& Sandwich Shoppe

Mountain Hardware

Willow Street

Post Office

Grizzly
Cafe

Betty St

Bear With
Us Lodging

Camp Wrightwood

Elm Street

© 2019 Yogi's Books LLC

Map Symbols

David "Awol" Miller has given us permission to use the map symbols he created for his excellent book "The AT Guide". These map symbols allow you to easily find town services with a quick glance at the town maps.

✈	Airport	➕ First Aid	⚟ Lounge/Bar	🏕 Ranger Station
💲	ATM or Bank	🛒 Grocery Store	🚶 Outfitter	🍴 Restaurant
🚤	Boat	🔨 Hardware Store	✉ Outgoing Mail	🚻 Restroom/Privy
👥	Bowling	🛏 Hostel	📞 Pay Phone	👟 Shoe Store
🚌	Bus	🛌 Hotel	℞ Pharmacy	
⛺	Camping	ℹ Information	⛱ Picnic Table	🚿 Shower
🚗	Car Rental	📶 Internet/WiFi	🏊 Pool	🚡 Ski Lift
🖥	Computer	🧥 Laundry	📮 Post Office	🎦 Theater
🧺	C-Store	🚈 Light Rail		🚂 Train Station

Need gear shipped to you on the trail? TCO has you covered!

Questions?   jackie@triplecrownoutfitters.com
              matt@triplecrownoutfitters.com

Visit us today: **Physical location in Kennedy Meadows**
                 Online: www.triplecrownoutfitters.com

Two ways out of Wrightwood CA: Walk on the Acorn Trail or Hitch on Hwy 2.

Wrightwood Acorn Trail	to	Agua Dulce	91.1 miles
Wrightwood Hwy 2	to	Agua Dulce	85.1 miles

364.3 - Guffy Campground - Bears here. BINK: Have never seen this spring dry.
DOUBLE TAP: Trail to the spring is on the right of the PCT after an extremely steep 0.1 mile.

367.3 - Blue Ridge Campground - DOUBLE TAP: Nice picnic tables here.

369.3 - Angeles Crest Highway 2 - The PCT crosses Highway 2 at Inspiration Point (highway overlook area with privy and trash cans). Hitch to the right to go to Wrightwood. Highway 2 is often closed. California Highway Information (Caltrans) 1-800-427-7623.

370.4 - Grassy Hollow Visitor Center - Water & bathrooms, water not always turned on.

374.0 - Vincent Gap / Highway 2 - Privy and trash cans.

375.7 - Lamel Spring - BINK: This is a good spring, but a very shallow pool. Bring something to scoop water out. Generally reliable year round.

377.9 - Mt. Baden-Powell - DEFINITELY go to the top. It's only 0.1 mile off the PCT.

383.7 - Little Jimmy Spring - Little side trail goes to this delicious spring.

383.9 - Little Jimmy Campground - This is an established campsite, and bears know they can find food here. There are stories of bear problems here every year. Use the bear boxes.

Access these files as often as possible:

(1) **Pacific Crest Trail Water Report -** Current status of water sources. Frequently updated during hiker season. [www.pctwater.com]

(2) **Yogi's PCT Handbook update file -** Changes to trail/town information which have occurred between the time your book was printed and now. Frequently updated during hiker season. [www.yogisbooks.com], then click UPDATES & LINKS

Do you have changes/updates to report?
If so, send them here: yogisbooks@gmail.com

Endangered Species Closure - Halfmile maps are here: [www.pctmap.net]

386.1 - Highway 2 / Islip Saddle - 8.0 miles of the PCT are closed. This begins at PCT mile 386.1 (Islip Saddle), and ends at PCT mile 394.0 (Burkhart Trail). **You have two options** to get from PCT mile 386.0 (Islip Saddle) to PCT mile 398.0 (Cloudburst Summit).

   (1) **Detour: 24.5 miles**. See Halfmile California maps D5, D5A, D5B, and D6.

      0.0 Islip Saddle (PCT mile 386.1) - Privy, tables, trash. Leave PCT here, take trail.

      5.0 Big Rock Creek.

      5.3 South Fork Campground.

      7.7 Holcomb Canyon Creek.

     10.5 Punchbowl Canyon Creek.

     13.6 Cruthers Creek.

     19.0 Little Rock Creek tributary.

     20.5 Burkhart Trail - Soak your feet in this COLD creek. Join PCT mile 394.0 here.

     21.7 Cooper Cyn Trail CG - Campground creek is sometimes dry. Turn left from PCT into the campground, walk all the way to the back of the campground, creek is down a small hill. Cannot see or hear creek from PCT. Next water is 15.8 miles ahead at Fountainhead Spring.

     24.5 Cloudburst Summit (PCT mile 398.0). No services.

   (2) **Highway: 8.9 miles**. See Halfmile California maps D5 and D6.

      0.0 Islip Saddle (PCT mile 386.1) - Privy, picnic tables, trash.

      4.3 Eagle's Roost (PCT mile 390.2) - Privy, picnic tables, trash.
                                   Leave PCT here, take highway.

      6.9 Buckhorn Campground exit (water).

      7.7 Buckhorn Campground entrance (water).

         Next water is 14.2 miles ahead at Fountainhead Spring.

      7.9 Buckhorn Day Use Area - Privy, picnic tables, trash.

      8.9 Cloudburst Summit (PCT mile 398.0). No services. Join PCT here.

398.0 - Cloudburst Summit / Highway 2

398.8 - Highway 2

400.6 - Camp Glenwood - Water is usually turned off.

    BINK: Water here is always a crap shoot. A much more reliable option is to continue north on the PCT/dirt road past the camp building, about 100 yards up you will see a water tank. This tank feeds the spigots near the building. At the base of it is a valve without a handle. The handle is usually hidden under the insulation and boards. Find it and you can turn the valve and obtain water even when the water system is off. Make sure to put it back, they do this so no vandals will drain the tank.

401.1 - Highway 2 - Privy, picnic tables, trash.

403.0 - Three Points on Angeles Crest Highway 2 - Cross highway, continue on PCT uphill to a privy and trash. Or, you could hitch Highway 2 to the left (hard hitch) to "Newcomb's Ranch." This is 2 miles south of Three Points. From their website: "Newcomb's Ranch offers casual dining with a wonderful selection of beers (including local draft beers) and wines. We serve wholesome breakfast favorites, appetizers, salads & soups, hamburgers and sandwiches, sumptuous entree specials, with several delicious vegetarian options, as well as delectable desserts." 626-440-1001.

406.6 - Signed trail junction - About 0.1 mile before Sulphur Springs Campground, the PCT splits into a Stock PCT (right) and a Hiker PCT (left). The Stock PCT goes down to the campground and the water. The Hiker PCT stays up on the ridge away from the water. The two PCT's meet again 0.6 mile after the split. If you take the Stock PCT down to the campground, the easiest way to get back to the Hiker PCT and avoid backtracking is to continue on the Stock PCT, which follows the road to the left. Watch for the Hiker PCT to cross the road. It's an obvious crossing.

406.6 - Sulphur Springs Campground - The spigots are usually not working. Privy here.
BINK: Large water tank/spring area located on far east side of the camp sometimes has water.

410.4 - Fiddleneck Spring - Usually dry.

411.0 - Fountainhead spring - BINK: Appears as a small creek crossing the trail.

418.5 - Signed spur trail to Pacifico Mountain Road -
This trail goes to the Mill Creek Ranger Station (water here).

418.6 - Mill Creek Summit - Cross the road (not the highway), and you'll find a picnic area with tables and a privy. No water. Go up to the Ranger Station and you can get water there. It's maybe a 5 minute walk. Remember the road you just crossed? If you would have turned left on the road instead of crossing it to the picnic area, you would have found the Ranger Station up the hill. PCT crosses highway after the picnic area.

Acton Pizza Place delivers here. 661-269-0096.

TAKE PLENTY OF WATER FROM THE MILL CREEK RANGER STATION.
The next sure water is at North Fork Ranger Station, 17.4 extremely hot miles ahead.

421.2 - Mount Gleason Road

425.8 - Shady campsite - In a shady ravine is an on-trail creek. BINK: Reliability seems to vary from year to year. Always dry in fall. 2011 was the only time I have ever seen this drainage have water after June in 20 years of coming through here. It could be the Station Fire helped it to become more reliable. The campsite itself seemed overgrown with new grass and brush.

430.4 - Messenger Flats Campground - Camping, privy, trash cans.
BINK: Water here seems to never be turned on.

431.9 - Moody Canyon Road - Seasonal stream is often dry.

433.1 - Lots of poison oak 2-3 miles before the Ranger Station.

436.1 - North Fork Ranger Station - Camping. Water from a spigot on the side of the building. Hot dogs, sodas, snacks, ice cream for purchase.

North Fork to Agua Dulce 18.4 miles) is totally exposed and very hot.

444.1 - Soledad Canyon Trailhead - Privy and trash.

444.2 - Soledad Canyon Road - Acton KOA is 0.2 mile to the right. Acton is 5.7 miles to the right.

444.2 - Acton CA

OVERVIEW: Good grocery, PO, and places to eat. No lodging.

GETTING HERE: 5.7 mile hitch on Soledad Canyon Road (go right).

POST OFFICE: 661-269-8618, USPS only
Mon-Fri 10a-5p
Sat open 8a-10a for package pick up only
General Delivery held for 15 days

Hiker's Legal Name
PCT Hiker, ETA: MM/DD/YY
General Delivery
Acton, CA 93510

OUTGOING MAIL: Acton Business Center. 661-269-1190. FedEx, UPS, USPS shipping.

RESUPPLY: Acton Market Country Store   661-269-1522. 7a-10p every day.
Scooped ice cream, milkshakes, breakfast bar.
Bigger than the "Original" Market.

The Original Acton Market   661-441-0454. 7a-10p every day.
Good resupply. Giant pizzas.

RESTAURANTS: 49'er Saloon 661-526-4414   Mexican and American food.

Pizza Place   661-269-0096   Pizza, chicken, sandwiches, pasta, salads.

Wence's Bistro   661-269-1888   American, Chinese, Italian, & Mexican food.

LODGING: No.

LAUNDRY: No.

ATM: Yes.

COMPUTER: Library. 661-269-7101.

444.3 - Acton KOA

OVERVIEW: 661-268-1214. Hiker-friendly, swimming pool.
Campground will be full on Memorial Day weekend - don't count on staying here.

GETTING HERE: Mile 444.2 - Turn right on Soledad Canyon Road, go 0.2 mile.
Mile 444.3 - Take trail to the right, go 0.2 mile.

MAIL DROPS: Accepts mail drops,
USPS, UPS, or FedEx
$2 fee for guests
$5 fee for non-guests

Hiker's Legal Name
PCT Hiker, ETA: MM/DD/YY
c/o Acton KOA
7601 Soledad Canyon Road
Acton, CA 93510

RESUPPLY: No resupply. Little C-Store with ice cream. 8a-8p in summer.

CAMPING: Pay camping.

RESTAURANTS: Restaurants in Acton which deliver to the KOA:

Pizza Place   661-269-0096   Pizza, chicken, sandwiches, pasta, salads.

Wence's Bistro   661-269-1888   American, Chinese, Italian, & Mexican food.

LAUNDRY: Yes.

SHOWER: Yes.

FUEL: Canister fuel and HEET.

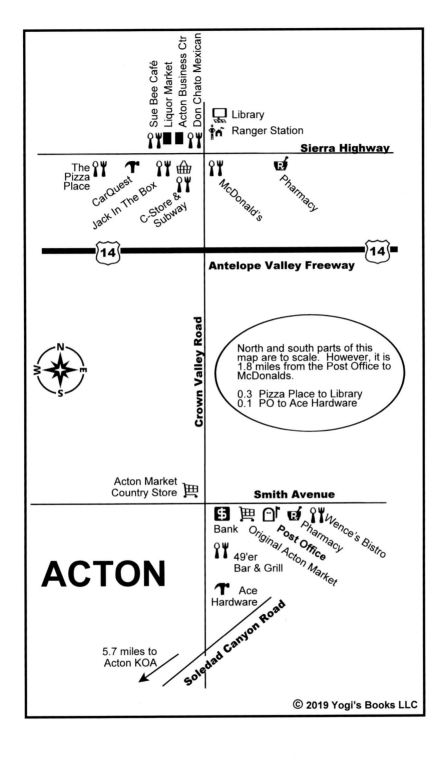

ACTON

North and south parts of this map are to scale. However, it is 1.8 miles from the Post Office to McDonalds.

0.3 Pizza Place to Library
0.1 PO to Ace Hardware

Sue Bee Café
Liquor Market
Acton Business Ctr
Don Chato Mexican

Library
Ranger Station

Sierra Highway

The Pizza Place
CarQuest
Jack In The Box
C-Store & Subway

McDonald's
Pharmacy

14   Antelope Valley Freeway   14

Crown Valley Road

Acton Market
Country Store

Smith Avenue

Bank
Original Acton Market
Post Office
Pharmacy
Wence's Bistro

49'er
Bar & Grill

Ace Hardware

Soledad Canyon Road

5.7 miles to
Acton KOA

© 2019 Yogi's Books LLC

444.4 - Polluted Creek - BINK: Some of the most polluted water on the entire trail. Do not drink! This area near the trailer park is the least scenic of the entire PCT, but don't despair once you are a half mile farther it is all left behind!

YOGI: The 10.1 miles from here to Agua Dulce can be very hot. It's totally exposed. Take a lot of water. There are two places where you can get out of the sun. The first is a really cool cave in a large rock on the left side of the trail. You'll see the cave for about a mile before you get there. The second place is in the tunnel under Antelope Valley Freeway 14.

451.1 - Antelope Valley Freeway 14 - PCT crosses under this major freeway.

453.6 - Vasquez Rocks Interpretive Center

453.6 - Escondido Canyon Road

454.5 - Agua Dulce CA

OVERVIEW: Good grocery store, restaurants, ATM.

GETTING HERE: The trail goes right through town.

RESUPPLY: General Store (C-store).

RESTAURANTS: Yes.

ATM: At the General Store.

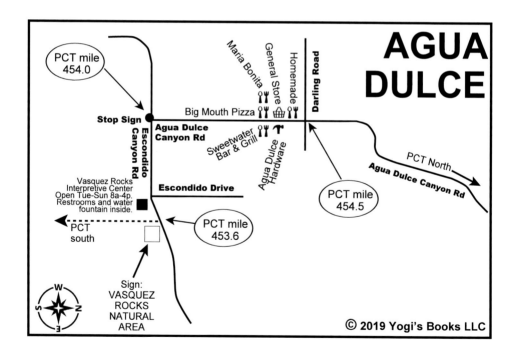

Two ways into Mojave and Tehachapi: Hitch on Tehachapi-Willow Springs Road
Hitch on Highway 58

| Agua Dulce | to | Tehachapi-Willow Springs Road | 104.0 miles |
| Agua Dulce | to | Highway 58 | 112.0 miles |

WARNING!!! The hike out of Agua Dulce is <u>dreadfully hot</u>. Take 4 liters of water.

458.5 - Mint Canyon - Map shows a creek. There is NOT a creek here.

463.2 - Bear Spring - Usually this is dry or barely flowing. Tastes nasty.
In 2017 and 2018, however, good flow and good water.

465.6 - Bouquet Canyon Road

478.2 - San Francisquito Canyon Road - Water at Ranger Station 0.1 mile to the left.

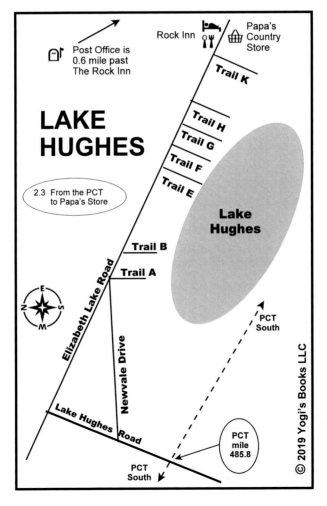

Rock Inn

Papa's Country Store

Post Office is 0.6 mile past The Rock Inn

Trail K

LAKE HUGHES

Trail H

Trail G

Trail F

Trail E

2.3 From the PCT to Papa's Store

Lake Hughes

Trail B

Trail A

Elizabeth Lake Road

PCT South

Newvale Drive

Lake Hughes Road

PCT mile 485.8

© 2019 Yogi's Books LLC

PCT South

485.8- Lake Hughes CA

GETTING HERE: See handbook map.

POST OFFICE: 661-724-9281, USPS only
Mon-Fri 8a-12:30p and 1:30p-5p
Sat closed. Usually hikers can pick up
packages on Saturday from 10a-noon.

General Delivery held for 30 days.

Hiker's Legal Name
PCT Hiker, ETA: MM/DD/YY
General Delivery
16817 Elizabeth Lake Road
Lake Hughes, CA 93532

RESUPPLY: Papa's Country Store. 661-724-1634.
This is a small grocery store, usually open Mon-Sat 6a-9p, Sun 7a-9p.
The store has a trail register from back when the trail came through town.

LODGING: Rock Inn. 661-724-1855. Rates $$$. Rooms have AC and TV.

RESTAURANT: The Rock Inn (661-724-1855) features Harley-Davidson memorabilia on the
walls, friendly atmosphere, and a Philly steak and cheese sandwich to die for.
Mon-Wed 8a-10p, Thur 8a-midnight, Fri 8a-1a, Sat 8a-2a, Sun 8a-10p.

ATM: At store.

487.1 - Trailside wet-season spring - Usually dry. BINK: Some years this has a fair amount of flow,
but do not count on it. In the fall of 2011 there was a rope in place to assist in climbing above
the trail to the source of the spring; I was able to fill bottles with a little effort.

493.0 - Maxwell Trail Camp Guzzler - Look for a concrete slab. Easy to miss. Water tastes strange.

493.4 - Upper Shake Campground - Privy and trash. Water not reliable in 2017 and 2018. BINK:
Creek always flows here but can be difficult to locate. BATTERIES: Down to campground
about 0.6 mile, when at campground, water is about 0.25 mile southeast from info kiosk down
hill, great water still running on June 4.

502.4 - Red Rock Water Tank - A HUGE round concrete water tank on top of the hill. Watch for the
tank up on the right, just a few minutes after you crest the hill. Fill up here. The next water is
at Highway 138, which is 15.2 very hot miles ahead.

502.4 - Guzzler behind oak shrubs

502.4 (Red Rock Tank) to 517.6 (Hwy 138) - Area burned. Very exposed.

504.5 - Guzzler near Liebre Mountain Truck Trail - Look for cistern north of dirt road.

510.9 - BINK: Approximately 100 yards before crossing Pine Canyon Road you cross a streambed,
which is often dry. Bushwhack over to where it goes under the road (visible from trail) to obtain
ice cold water.

517.6 - Highway 138

Hikertown When you hit Highway 138, Hikertown is   Hiker's Legal Name
the house across the highway on the right.   PCT Hiker, ETA: MM/DD/YY
Water and rustic bunk room available   c/o Hikertown
Accepts mail drops, $5 fee, USPS, UPS, FedEx. 26803 W. Ave C-15
[http://www.hikertown.org/] [Highway138@gmail.com] Lancaster, CA 93536

Neenach   On Hwy 138, 4 miles east of Hikertown. 661-724-1100.
Café and 8a-8p everyday. Hikertown provides a shuttle.
Market   Bacon cheeseburgers, black bean burgers, pizza, salad,
breakfast burritos, hoagie sandwiches, deep fried food,
beer. Picnic tables outside. Inside seating area with big
screen and NetFlix. Store 7a-8p every day; kitchen
closes earlier than store.

Wee Vill   On Hwy 138, 8.5 miles east of Hikertown.   Hiker's Legal Name
Market   661-724-2200. Free camping on green grass, free   PCT Hiker, ETA: MM/DD/YY
shower, shaded porch with tables, air-conditioned   c/o Wee Vill Market
seating inside with grilled food and ice cream.   18348 W. Avenue D
Call between 5a-8p for a ride. Store Mon-Fri 5a-9p, Lancaster, CA 93536
Sat-Sun 6a-9p. Kitchen closes earlier than store.
Accepts mail drops, no fee, USPS, UPS, FedEx.

534.9 - Cottonwood Creek Bridge - No creek. There us usually a spigot where hikers can get water from the aqueduct (spigot turned off in dry years). Check PCT water report for status of spigot. BINK: On the northwest side of the wash near the metal lean-to is a pipe with flowing water. If it is not flowing, check the valve uphill on the aqueduct down in a concrete hole.

536.9 - Wind Farm - 1.2 miles off trail. 661-256-2122, 4321. Per email in Feb 2019: "We accept packages. We prefer that hikers NOT consider our office as a rest stop, but if they need help, we can try to assist. We have a big bench in front of the office where hikers can sit and rest."

Mail drops accepted, but the package MUST include a conspicuous phone number.
Pick up during office hours only Mon-Fri 6:30a - 5pm. UPS or FedEx only !

Hiker's Legal Name
PCT Hiker, ETA: MM/DD/YY
c/o Avangrid Renewables - Manzana Wind
17890 Champagne Ave
Rosamond, CA 93560

541.5 - Tylerhorse Canyon - Nice stream here.

558.2 - Oak Creek - The water smells funny here. Horse/cow contaminated.
This is the last on-trail water until Golden Oaks Spring, 25.1 miles ahead.

558.5 - Tehachapi-Willow Springs Road - Paved, not much traffic. Tehachapi left, Mojave right.

566.5 - Highway 58 / Tehachapi Pass - Highway 58 is a major freeway. Tehachapi left, Mojave right.

MOJAVE - TEHACHAPI AREA

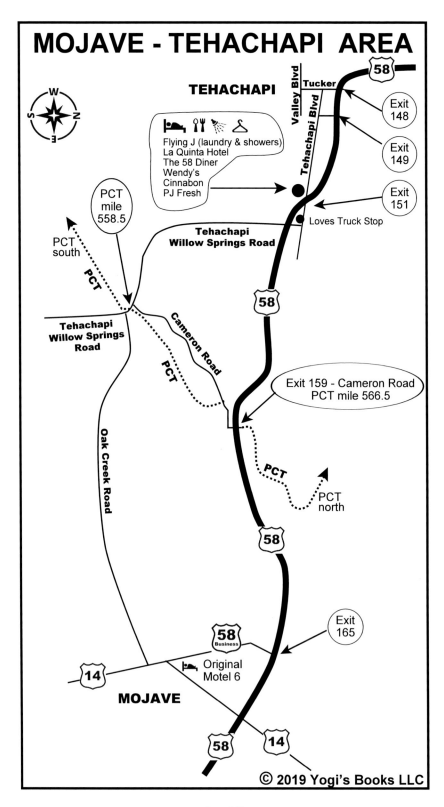

	MOJAVE	TEHACHAPI
OVERVIEW:	It's HOT here. You do less walking in Mojave than in Tehachapi. Restaurants are mostly fast-food style.	It'S HOT here, too. Nice town, but it's very spread out. Better restaurant options than Mojave. Trains go through town all night long blaring their horns REAL LOUD.
GETTING HERE:	(1) PCT mile 558.5 - Take Tehachapi-Willow Springs Road to the right for about 0.2 mile until you reach Oak Creek Road. Then hitch Oak Creek road 9 miles east (left) to Mojave. (2) PCT mile 566.5 - Hitch to the right approximately 11 miles: Highway 58 east to Exit 165, then go south on CA-58 BR. You'll be on CA-58 BR for 4 miles.	(1) PCT mile 558.5 - Hitch 9 miles to the left on Tehachapi-Willow Springs Rd. (2) PCT mile 566.5 - Hitch 9 miles to the left on Highway 58.
TRAIL ANGELS:	Lots of Trail Angels in Mojave/Tehachapi. See the Facebook group: "Tehachapi Pass (Tehachapi and Mojave) PCT Trail Angels"	

BUS:	KERN TRANSIT 800-323-2396
	    Reservations required at least one day in advance to guarantee a ride.
	
	    Round trip Mojave Carl's Jr. to Cameron Road, continuing to Tehachapi Kmart.
	    Mon-Fri: 9 trips per day. Sat-Sun: 3 trips per day.
	    When boarding, you must tell the driver you are going to Cameron Rd.
	    Call one hour in advance to be picked up at Cameron Road.
	
	    "Dial A Ride" bus service. No service Sundays or holidays.
	    Mojave: Mon-Sat 7a-6p. Tehachapi: Mon-Fri 5:45a-7p. Sat 7:30a-5:30p.	

TAXI:	661-600-2771	661-600-2771

CAR RENTAL:	Enterprise 661-824-5437
	    Mon-Fri 8a-5p. Sat-Sun closed.
		Enterprise 661-823-0500
		    Mon-Fri 8a-5p. Sat-Sun closed.

POST OFFICE:	661-824-3502, USPS only Mon-Fri 9a-1p, and 2p-4p. Sat closed. Hiker mail is held for 3 months Hiker's Legal Name PCT Hiker, ETA: MM/DD/YY General Delivery 2053 Belshaw St Mojave, CA 93501	661-822-0279, USPS only Mon-Fri 9a-5p. Sat 10a-2p. General Delivery held for 30 days Hiker's Legal Name PCT Hiker, ETA: MM/DD/YY General Delivery 1085 Voyager Drive Tehachapi, CA 93581
MAIL DROPS:	Original Motel 6 (661-219-0784) Accepts mail drops for guests, no fee, USPS, UPS, FedEx: Hiker's Legal Name PCT Hiker, ETA: MM/DD/YY c/o Motel 6 SR 58 / Sierra Highway @ SR 14 16958 State Route 58 Mojave CA 93501	Wits End Tehachapi Trail Angels (661-750-4852) accept mail drops, no fee, USPS, UPS, FedEx: Hiker's Legal Name PCT Hiker, ETA: MM/DD/YY c/o Dalton SteeleReed 115 S. Mojave St Tehachapi, CA 93561
OUTGOING MAIL:		Postal ASAP 661-822-7508 UPS Store 661-823-4940 Wits' End 661-750-4852 (Trail Angels)
RESUPPLY:	Stater Brothers Supermarket 661-824-2719, 6a-11p daily	Albertsons Supermarket 661-823-7090, 6a-midnight daily Dollar General Market 661-750-0121,7a-10p daily Walmart 661-825-2258, 5a-11p daily

	MOJAVE	TEHACHAPI
OUTDOOR STORE:		Big 5 Sporting Goods 661-822-4197
RESTAURANTS:	Many restaurants, mostly fast-food.	Many.
LAUNDRY:	Yes, also at some motels.	Laundromats in town, laundry at some motels, laundry at Flying J Truck Stop.
SHOWER:		Airport and Flying J Truck Stop.
ATM:	Yes.	Yes.
COMPUTER:	Kern County Library 661-824-2243	Kern County Library 661-822-4938
FUEL:	HEET: Napa Auto Parts 661-824-4796 Denatured alcohol: Carl's Hardware store 661-824-3422	Denatured alcohol: K-Mart 661-822-7496 HEET: AutoZone 661-823-1294 Canister fuel: Big 5 Sp Gds 661-822-4197
MEDICAL:	Adventist Health Community Care 661-824-4511	Tehachapi Hospital 661-823-3000 Omni Family Health Medical/Dental Clinic Walk-in clinic Mon 9a-6p, Tue-Fri 8a-5p. 800-300-6664
GET SOME CASH:	Kennedy Meadows and Vermilion Valley Resort do not have ATMs. If you need cash for KM or VVR, get it in Mojave or Tehachapi.	

MOJAVE LODGING more motels shown on map ask for PCT hiker rates		Rates	TV & AC	micr frig	laundry	computer	pool hot tub	other
Original Motel 6	661-219-0784	$	Y	ask	Y	no	pool	accepts mail drops
Airport Motel 6	661-824-2421	$$	Y	ask $	Y	no	pool	
America's Best Value Inn	661-824-9317	$$	Y	Y	no	no	pool	cont bkfst
Best Western	661-824-3601	$$$	Y	Y	Y	Y	pool	hot breakfast

TEHACHAPI LODGING ask for PCT hiker rates		Rates	TV & AC	micr frig	laundry	computer	pool hot tub	other
Best Western Plus	661-823-1800	$$$$	Y	ask	Y	Y	Y	hot bkfst
Sure Stay Hotel	661-822-5591	$$$	Y	Y	Y	Y	Y	hot bkfst
Fairfield Inn	661-822-4800	$$$$	Y	frig	Y	Y	Y	hot bkfst
Holiday Inn Express	661-822-9837	$$$$	Y	Y	Y	Y	Y	Denny's and PO across street
La Quinta 2 miles out of town restaurant & C-store adjacent to hotel	661-823-8000	$$$$	Y	Y	Y	Y	pool	cont bkfst with waffles, restaurant on site, see "Mojave-Tehachapi Area" Handbook map
Ranch Motel	661-822-4283	$$	Y	Y	no	no	no	not individual AC
Santa Fe Motel	661-822-3184	$$	Y	ask	Y	no	no	accepts mail drops
Tehachapi Airport CAMPING		2019: $5 camping on grass. Shower, bathroom, trees, picnic tables, BBQ grill, water. Enter at pedestrian gate just to the left of the main auto gate. Camp east of hangars at SE part of airport by trees.						
		$ = usually less than $50 $$ = usually $50-$80 $$$ = usually $80-$110 $$$$ = usually greater than $110						

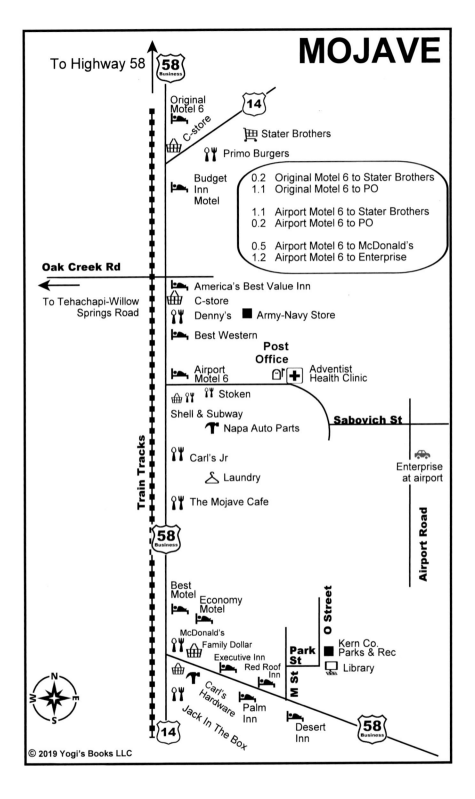

MOJAVE

To Highway 58

58 Business

14

Original Motel 6

C-store

Stater Brothers

Primo Burgers

Budget Inn Motel

0.2 Original Motel 6 to Stater Brothers
1.1 Original Motel 6 to PO

1.1 Airport Motel 6 to Stater Brothers
0.2 Airport Motel 6 to PO

0.5 Airport Motel 6 to McDonald's
1.2 Airport Motel 6 to Enterprise

Oak Creek Rd

To Tehachapi-Willow Springs Road

America's Best Value Inn

C-store

Denny's   Army-Navy Store

Best Western

Post Office

Airport Motel 6

Adventist Health Clinic

Stoken

Shell & Subway

Napa Auto Parts

Sabovich St

Carl's Jr

Enterprise at airport

Laundry

The Mojave Cafe

58 Business

Airport Road

Best Motel

Economy Motel

O Street

McDonald's

Family Dollar

Park St

Kern Co. Parks & Rec

Executive Inn

Red Roof Inn

Library

Carl's Hardware

M St

Palm Inn

Desert Inn

58 Business

Jack In The Box

14

© 2019 Yogi's Books LLC

Train Tracks

N W E S

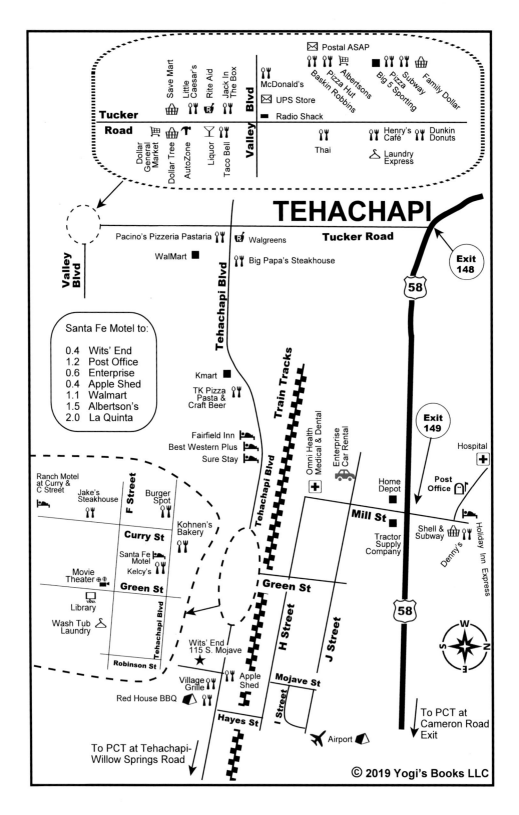

TEHACHAPI

Tucker Road

Exit 148

58

Save Mart
Little Caesar's
Rite Aid
Jack In The Box

Tucker Road

McDonald's
UPS Store
Radio Shack

✉ Postal ASAP
Albertsons
Baskin Robbins
Pizza Hut
Big 5 Sporting
Pizza
Subway
Family Dollar

Valley Blvd

Dollar General Market
Dollar Tree
AutoZone
Liquor
Taco Bell

Thai
Henry's Café
Dunkin Donuts
Laundry Express

Valley Blvd

Pacino's Pizzeria Pastaria
Walgreens
WalMart
Big Papa's Steakhouse

Tehachapi Blvd

Santa Fe Motel to:

0.4 Wits' End
1.2 Post Office
0.6 Enterprise
0.4 Apple Shed
1.1 Walmart
1.5 Albertson's
2.0 La Quinta

Kmart

TK Pizza Pasta & Craft Beer

Train Tracks

Fairfield Inn
Best Western Plus
Sure Stay

Omni Health Medical & Dental

Enterprise Car Rental

Exit 149

Hospital

Ranch Motel at Curry & C Street

Jake's Steakhouse

F Street

Burger Spot

Kohnen's Bakery

Curry St

Santa Fe Motel
Kelcy's

Movie Theater

Green St

Library

Wash Tub Laundry

Home Depot

Mill St

Post Office

Tractor Supply Company

Shell & Subway

Denny's

Holiday Inn Express

Green St

H Street

J Street

58

Wits' End
115 S. Mojave

Apple Shed

Robinson St

Tehachapi Blvd

Village Grille
Red House BBQ

Mojave St

I Street

Hayes St

Airport

To PCT at Tehachapi-Willow Springs Road

To PCT at Cameron Road Exit

© 2019 Yogi's Books LLC

RESUPPLY SUMMARY

652.1 Inyokern CA - hitch 15 miles

Post Office: 760-377-5125, USPS only
Mon-Fri 11a-4p, Sat closed
Must write "Hold in Inyokern" on box.
If not, your box will automatically be
sent to Kennedy Meadows.
General Delivery held for 30 days.

Hiker's Legal Name
PCT Hiker, ETA: MM/DD/YY
General Delivery
HOLD IN INYOKERN !!
Inyokern, CA 93527

Resupply: C-Store: Inyokern Market   760-377-3298

652.1 Onyx CA - hitch 17.6 miles

Post Office: 760-378-2121, USPS only
Mon-Fri 9a-noon and 1p-4p
Sat package pickup only 7:30a-9:15a
Hiker mail held for 60 days

Hiker's Legal Name
PCT Hiker, ETA: MM/DD/YY
General Delivery
8275 Easy Street
Onyx, CA 93255

Resupply: Very small C-Store: Onyx Store (snacks only) 760-378-3299

652.1 Weldon CA - hitch 25 miles

Post Office: 760-378-2175, USPS only
Mon-Fri 8:30a-12:30p and 1p-4p
Sat closed
General Delivery held for 30 days

Hiker's Legal Name
PCT Hiker, ETA: MM/DD/YY
General Delivery
Weldon, CA 93283

Resupply: Large Grocery Store: Sierra Gateway Supermarket 760-378-2207

652.1 Kernville CA - hitch 38 miles

Post Office: 760-376-6418, USPS only
Mon-Fri 9a-12:30p, 1p-3p
Sat closed
General Delivery held for 30 days

Hiker's Legal Name
PCT Hiker, ETA: MM/DD/YY
General Delivery
Kernville, CA 93238

Resupply: Large Grocery Store: Sierra Gateway Market 760-376-2424

652.1 Lake Isabella CA - hitch 35 miles

Post Office: 760-379-2553, USPS only
Mon-Fri 10a-4p
Sat closed, but usually hikers can
pick up packages on Sat from 9a-10a.
Ring buzzer on door in lobby.
General Delivery held for 30 days

Hiker's Legal Name
PCT Hiker, ETA: MM/DD/YY
General Delivery
Lake Isabella, CA 93240

Mail Drops: Lake Isabella Motel (760-379-2800) accepts mail drops, no fee.

USPS Address:
Hiker's Legal Name
PCT Hiker, ETA: MM/DD/YY
c/o Lake Isabella Motel
PO Box 2134
Lake Isabella, CA 93240

UPS or FedEx Address:
Hiker's Legal Name
PCT Hiker, ETA: MM/DD/YY
c/o Lake Isabella Motel
400 Highway 155
Lake Isabella, CA 93240

Resupply: Supermarkets: Vons Supermarket   760-379-4461
Lake Isabella Supermarket   760-379-8222

652.1 Ridgecrest CA - hitch 25 miles

Post Office: 760-375-1939, USPS only
Mon-Fri 10a-5p
Sat 10a-2p
General Delivery held for 30 days

Hiker's Legal Name
PCT Hiker, ETA: MM/DD/YY
General Delivery
Ridgecrest CA 93555

Resupply: Supermarkets: Walmart Supercenter   760-371-4974
Stater Brothers   760-375-5557
Albertsons   760-384-4015

RESUPPLY SUMMARY

702.2	Kennedy Meadows CA - TCO & Grumpy Bear Retreat 3 miles off trail, call for ride

Mail Drops: Grumpy Bear's Retreat 559-850-2327 accepts USPS, UPS, FedEx
packages, no fee:
Hiker's Legal Name
PCT Hiker, ETA: MM/DD/YY
c/o Grumpy Bear's Retreat in Kennedy Meadows
98887 Kennedy Meadows Road
Inyokern, CA 93527

The mail carriers in Kennedy Meadows often mis-deliver mail. To make sure
your package is delivered properly, write this in GREAT BIG LETTERS next
to the address: DELIVER TO GRUMPY BEAR

Resupply: Triple Crown Outfitters (559-302-9943) is stocked with full hiker resupply,
great selection at great prices. No need to send yourself a mail drop. See
resupply photos in the Kennedy Meadows section of this book (mile 702.2).
See Triple Crown Outfitters Facebook page for current information.
Contact: jackie@triplecrownoutfitters.com or matt@triplecrownoutfitters.com
[https://triplecrownoutfitters.com/]

744.5	Lone Pine via Mulkey Pass Trail -	2.0 mile trail + 20 mile TH hitch
745.3	Lone Pine via Trail Pass Trail -	2.5 mile trail + 20 mile TH hitch
750.2	Lone Pine via Cottonwood Pass Trail -	3.8 mile trail + 20 mile TH hitch
766.3	Lone Pine via Whitney Portal -	14.6 mile trail + 12 mile TH hitch
788.9	Lone Pine via Kearsarge Pass Trail -	7.5 mile trail + 29 mile TH hitch

Post Office: 760-876-5681, USPS only   Hiker's Legal Name
Mon-Fri 9:30a-12:30p and 1:30p-4:30p   PCT Hiker, ETA: MM/DD/YY
Sat closed, but possible package   General Delivery
pickup from 10:30a-noon.   Lone Pine, CA 93545
General Delivery held for 30 days

Mail Drops: Whitney Portal Hostel (760-876-0030)   Hiker's Legal Name
Accepts mail drops, UPS and FedEx only.   PCT Hiker, ETA: MM/DD/YY
Mail MUST have a throw away date (ETA).   c/o Whitney Portal Hostel
If mail is not picked up within 2 weeks   238 Main Street
of ETA, it will be thrown away.   Lone Pine, CA 93545

Resupply: Large Grocery Store: Joseph's Bi-Rite Market   760-876-4378

788.9	Independence CA - 7.5 mile hike plus 13 mile TH hitch

Post Office: 760-878-2210, USPS only   Hiker's Legal Name
Mon-Fri 9:30a-12:45p and 1:15p-4p   PCT Hiker, ETA: MM/DD/YY
Sat closed, but possible package pickup   General Delivery
from 8:30a-10:30a. Knock on door.   Independence, CA 93526
Normal Gen Delivery held for 30 days.
Hiker mail held for 30 days after ETA.

Mail Drops: Courthouse Motel (760-878-2732)
Accepts mail drops, free for guests, $5-$10 for non-guests.

USPS Address: UPS or FedEx Address:
Hiker's Legal Name   Hiker's Legal Name
PCT Hiker, ETA: MM/DD/YY   PCT Hiker, ETA: MM/DD/YY
c/o The Courthouse Motel   c/o The Courthouse Motel
157 N Edwards St.   157 N Edwards St.
PO Box 29   Independence, CA 93526
Independence, CA 93526

Resupply: Large C-Store: Valley Market Chevron   562-277-7171
Local Market: Owens Valley Growers Co-Op   760-915-0091

RESUPPLY SUMMARY

788.9   Bishop CA - 7.5 mile hike plus 53 mile TH hitch

Post Office: 760-873-3526, USPS only
Mon-Fri 9a-4p
Sat 9a-1p
General Delivery held for 30 days

Hiker's Legal Name
PCT Hiker, ETA: MM/DD/YY
General Delivery
585 W. Line Street
Bishop, CA 93514

Resupply: Supermarkets: Vons   760-872-9811
Smart & Final   760-873-7181

857.7   Muir Trail Ranch - 1.5 mile hike

Mail Drops: See website for mail drop info: [www.muirtrailranch.com]
2019: $85 fee

Resupply: No resupply.

878.7   Vermilion Valley Resort - boat or 4.5 mile hike

New owners for 2020. Information below is for 2019.

Mail Drops: Mail drops can be picked during store hours, usually 8a-8p every day. This UPS address IS correct; however, the UPS system will say that it is not. Please have the UPS clerk override the system with this address. It WILL get delivered at this address. 559-259-4000. [info@edisonlake.com]

UPS or FedEx ONLY!
Be sure your mail arrives
10-14 days before YOU arrive!
2019: There is a $30 charge
PER BOX/BUCKET to pick up
($50 for May, Sep 15-October pick up).

25 pound limit per box or bucket.
$10 surcharge for overweight boxes.

Must have name and ETA on four
sides of package. The charge to mail
out boxes is postage PLUS $12/box/bucket.

2019: Packages can be picked up only from May 20 - Oct 20.

UPS only address:
Hiker's Legal Name
PCT Hiker, ETA: MM/DD/YY
Vermilion Valley Resort
c/o Rancheria Garage
62311 Huntington Lake Road
Lakeshore, CA 93634

Resupply: Very small store, but it's geared toward hikers.
You could resupply here only if hikers before you did not clean out the store.
559-259-4000. [info@edisonlake.com]

878.7   Mono Hot Springs - get to VVR, then hitch 6 miles

Post Office: 559-325-1710, USPS only
7:30a-9p every day
PO summer season: May 15-Nov 1

Mail must have "Hold Until" date.
If not, it will be held for only 10 days.

USPS summer address:
Hiker's Legal Name
PCT Hiker, Hold Until: MM/DD/YY
General Delivery
Mono Hot Springs, CA 93642

Resupply: Small C-Store, not good for resupply, geared toward car campers

---

906.7   Reds Meadow - 0.3 mile walk

Mail Drops: 760-934-2345.
Print mail drop form: [www.redsmeadow.com]
2019: Mail Drop fee is $40 plus $1/day.
Fee must be paid 2 weeks in advance.
Pick up your mail drop at the store between 7a-7p every day.
Outgoing mail is letters only.

Resupply: Campground Store: Sometimes the store has good resupply.
Sometimes it's just car camping items.

RESUPPLY SUMMARY

906.7 Mammoth Lakes CA - bus from Reds Meadow

Post Office: 760-934-2205, USPS only
Mon-Fri 8a-4p
Sat closed

Hiker's Legal Name
PCT Hiker, ETA: MM/DD/YY
General Delivery
Mammoth Lakes, CA 93546

Resupply: Supermarket: Vons   760-934-4536
Whole Foods Market: Sierra Sundance   760-934-8122

942.5 Tuolumne Meadows CA - on trail

Post Office: 209-372-8236, USPS only
Approximate hours:
Mon-Fri 9a until 4p or 5p.
Sat 9a-noon. Hours vary
and they close for lunch.
Mail drop must have ETA.

Hiker's Legal Name
Hiker's Trail Name
PCT Hiker, ETA: MM/DD/YY
General Delivery
Tuolumne Meadows
Yosemite National Park, CA 95389

Resupply: Grocery Store: 209-372-8609
Surprisingly good store, you could resupply here.

942.5 Lee Vining CA - 19 mile bus or hitch

Post Office: 760-647-6371, USPS only
Mon-Fri 9a-1p and 2p-4p
Sat closed
General Delivery held for 30 days

Hiker's Legal Name
PCT Hiker, ETA: MM/DD/YY
General Delivery
121 Lee Vining Ave
Lee Vining, CA 93541

Resupply: Small grocery store: Mono Market   760-647-1010
Large C-Store: Tioga Gas Mart   760-647-1088
C-Store: Chevron   760-647-6330

1016.9 (Northern) Kennedy Meadows Resort - 11 mile hitch

Call only between 8a-7:30p Pacific time
209-965-3900 or 209-965-3911 - Phone summer
209-965-3900 - Phone winter (owner)

This is NOT the Kennedy Meadows before the Sierra.
The other Kennedy Meadows is at mile 702.2.
BE SURE you send your box to the correct location.

Mail Drops: 2019: $15 fee, **UPS only.** Must have ETA on box.
Address your box EXACTLY like this:

Hiker's Legal Name
PCT Hiker, ETA: MM/DD/YY
c/o Kennedy Meadows Resort and Pack Station
42421 State Highway 108
Pinecrest, CA 95364

Resupply: Good hiker resupply at the small store.

RESUPPLY SUMMARY

1016.9 Bridgeport CA - 32 mile hitch

Post Office: 760-932-7991, USPS only
Mon-Fri 8a-noon and 1p-4p
Sat closed, but usually hikers can pick up
mail on Sat from 10:30a-1p. Knock on door.
When hiker mail arrives, Postmaster scans
it as "delivered." He then holds hiker mail
until the end of September.

Hiker's Legal Name
PCT Hiker, ETA: MM/DD/YY
General Delivery
29 Kingsley Street
Bridgeport, CA 93517

Resupply: Grocery store: General Store. 760-932-7224. Good resupply, but expensive.

1016.9 Walker CA - 29 mile hitch

Post Office: No Post Office in Walker. Coleville CA Post Office is 5 miles north of
Walker. Call Post Office BEFORE mailing your package. Postmaster
needs to know your mail is coming. General Delivery held for 30 days.

530-495-2133, USPS only
M-F 8a-11p and 11:30a-2:30p
Sat 9:30a-11:30a

Hiker's Legal Name
PCT Hiker, ETA: MM/DD/YY
General Delivery
Coleville, CA 96107

Resupply: Small grocery store: Walker Country Store and Deli 530-495-2945

1048.4 Markleeville CA - 18 mile hitch

Post Office: 530-694-2125, USPS only
Mon-Fri 8:30a-11a, noon-3:30p
Sat 8:30a-10:30a
General Delivery held for 15 days

Hiker's Legal Name
PCT Hiker, ETA: MM/DD/YY
General Delivery
Markleeville, CA 96120

Resupply: Grocery store: Markleeville General Store

530-694-2448
Good hiker resupply

1092.3 Echo Lake CA - on trail

Post Office: 530-659-7207. Mon-Sat 11a-2p. Outgoing mail only.
This Post Office does NOT accept incoming packages/mail.

Resupply: Small grocery store: 530-659-7207

1092.3 South Lake Tahoe CA - 19 mile hitch

Post Office: Main Post Office:
530-544-5867, USPS only
Mon-Fri 8:30a-5p
Sat noon-2p
General Delivery held for 15 days
unless arrival date is later.

Hiker's Legal Name
PCT Hiker, ETA: MM/DD/YY
General Delivery
South Lake Tahoe, CA 96150

Mail Drops: Mellow Mountain Hostel (530-600-3272)
Accepts mail drops, no fee if it arrives when
the guest is here, $5 fee if it arrives before
the guest, $7 fee for non-guests.
USPS, UPS, or FedEx.

Hiker's Legal Name
PCT Hiker, ETA: MM/DD/YY
c/o Mellow Mountain Hostel
4081 Cedar Ave
South Lake Tahoe, CA 96150

Resupply: Supermarkets: Raley's at the "Y"   530-541-5160
Raley's in Village Shopping Center   530-544-3417
Safeway   530-542-7740
Grocery Outlet   530-542-1077
Grass Roots Natural Foods   530-541-7788

Need gear or food shipped to you on the trail? TCO has you covered! Owners Worldwide and Yogi know that gear fails just when you need it the most.

Order from our website, and we will ship your package promptly.

Need a bear canister or snow gear for the Sierra? It doesn't make sense to purchase canisters or snow gear ahead of time and then pay to ship it to Kennedy Meadows. Instead, get that gear from TCO right in Kennedy Meadows.

We highly recommend pre-ordering your bear canister from the Triple Crown Outfitters website, and we will hold it in Kennedy Meadows for you until you arrive.

Prefer to rent a bear canister? Canisters are needed from Kennedy Meadows to Sonora Pass. Rent from TCO in Kennedy Meadows south, return to Kennedy Meadows Resort and Pack Station (KM north) 10 miles west of Sonora Pass. If you don't go to KM north, you can mail the rental canister back to TCO.

Triple Crown Outfitters is known as **"the best resupply on the PCT."** This great selection is also available for online shipping.

Questions?   jackie@triplecrownoutfitters.com
                      matt@triplecrownoutfitters.com

Visit us online at **www.triplecrownoutfitters.com**

Visit our **physical location in Kennedy Meadows, CA.**

Two ways out of Mojave & Tehachapi: Hitch to Tehachapi-Willow Springs Road
                                              Hitch to Highway 58

Tehachapi-Willow Springs Road	to	Kennedy Meadows	143.7	miles
Highway 58	to	Kennedy Meadows	135.7	miles

566.5 - Highway 58 - Major freeway crossing. Hot, hot, hot hike up the ridge from here.

575.1 - Unpaved Road - DOUBLE TAP: After you get on an unpaved road, there is a use trail to the left which leads to a few campsites.

583.3 - Golden Oaks Spring -
Fill up here. It's a hot, hot, hot hike to Robin Bird Spring, 18.8 miles ahead.

602.1 - Robin Bird Spring - Walk along the fence uphill about 20 yards and you'll see a place where you can open up the fence. Go inside, walk up the hill and you'll find nice water. Cattle contaminated, be sure to treat. BINK: The pipe uphill inside fenced area is fed from an enclosed catchment 15 yards uphill and seems to be mostly protected from cattle contamination.

603.1 - Good camp one mile north of Robin Bird Spring.

604.2 - Cottonwood Creek - Murky water. I wouldn't drink it.

607.1 - Landers Creek - Dry in 2013-2016. BINK: Usually has water.

607.5 - Waterhole Mine Spring - Campground with great flowing piped spring.
To find it, look for a road that parallels Landers Creek.

608.1 - Piute Mountain Road, first crossing - BINK: 0.25 mile east on this road is a small decrepit cabin to the right in a meadow. Nearby you will see an old horse corral, near this corral on the edge of the meadow emerges a wonderful spring with a pool to obtain water from. Not sure if this is private land or not, so please treat it with the according respect by not camping here.

608.9 - Unpaved NF Road 29SO5 - Water 0.3 mile off trail.
JOKER: This campground and spring is to the left at the next road AFTER the register box.
BINK: A pipe gushes ice cold water near the tank. Quite a walk off trail.

YOGI: The hike from here to Walker Pass is very hot, dry, and exposed, with no on-trail natural water. The next SURE water is at Yellow Jacket Spring, 28.1 miles north, then 0.7 mile downhill off the PCT.

615.9 - Kelso Valley Road

617.7 - Butterbredt Canyon Road (SC123) - Gross cow water 1.2 mile off the PCT here.
Hot, hot, hot walk from here to Walker Pass, 34.4 miles ahead.

620.0 - Willow Spring - This is a 670-foot elevation drop off the PCT. SCRUB (2013): Take the gully down to the left 1.5 miles to Willow Spring, which has serious cow traffic but is a reliable natural source nonetheless, with flat camping nearby. There was a trough on the west/left side of the fenced spring area and a kind of hard-to-find faucet way on the other side, the east/right. Both had lots of good looking water.

621.9 - Dove Spring Canyon Road - Willow Spring is 2 miles off trail via sandy jeep road.

630.8 - Bird Spring Pass

637.0 - Yellow Jacket Spring - Seasonal water 0.7 mile down the ridge to the left off the PCT.
This is a 140-foot elevation drop off the PCT.

643.8 - McIvers Spring - At mile 643.8, watch carefully for the PCT trail tread to resume on the left side of the road. This turn is not marked well. If you're going to McIvers Spring, continue straight on the road. From the poorly-marked PCT-jeep road junction, McIvers Spring and Cabin are only a 4-minute walk down the road. McIvers Spring was not great in 2013-2016: polluted and flowing slow. 2017-2018: flowing, but smelly.

644.5 - approximately - Good campsites here in the jeep turnout.

651.3 - Walker Pass Campground - Reliable water at spring (see map).

652.1 - Highway 178 / Walker Pass

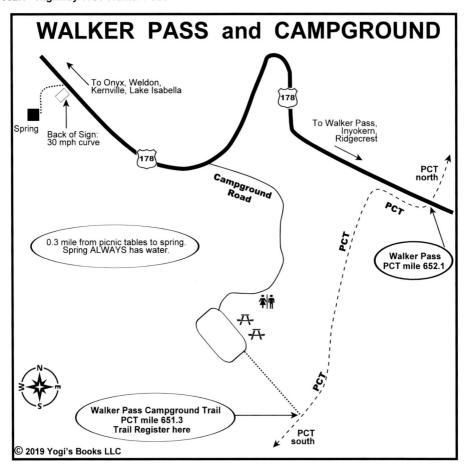

WALKER PASS and CAMPGROUND

To Onyx, Weldon, Kernville, Lake Isabella

178

Spring

Back of Sign: 30 mph curve

To Walker Pass, Inyokern, Ridgecrest

178

Campground Road

PCT north

PCT

0.3 mile from picnic tables to spring. Spring ALWAYS has water.

PCT

Walker Pass PCT mile 652.1

PCT

Walker Pass Campground Trail PCT mile 651.3 Trail Register here

PCT south

© 2019 Yogi's Books LLC

Bus from Lake Isabella to Ridgecrest, Mon-Wed-Fri. 2019 schedule is below. Kern Transit. 800-323- 2396. [kerntransit.org]   Bus will pick up hikers at Walker Pass, but you must flag the bus down. You can call for pickup, but there is NO CELL SERVICE from Tehachapi Pass (Highway 58) until about a mile north of Walker Pass on the PCT. Dang!

	Lake Isabella	Onyx	Ridgecrest	
Eastbound →	5:20a	5:35a	6:45a	
	8:30a	8:02a	7:05a	← Westbound
Eastbound →	12:40p	12:55p	2:05p	
	3:50p	3:22p	2:25p	← Westbound
Eastbound →	5:00p	5:15p	6:25p	
	8:10p	7:42p	6:45p	← Westbound

WALKER PASS AREA

Mileage indicates distance from Walker Pass.

TRAIL ANGELS
There is a huge Trail Angel network
serving all towns on this map.
Find the Facebook page for
"Walker's Pass Trail Angels".

RIDGECREST - 25 miles
Spread out by trail town standards.
Public bus system.
Many motels, restaurants.
Good town if you just want to stay in
motel. Not great town for walking
around. Canister fuel.

INYOKERN - 15 miles
Just a few blocks long.
One motel, C-Store, restaurant, bar,
Post Office.

ONYX - 17 miles
Only services are Post Office
and Store, which are one mile apart.
Store has snacks and
deli sandwiches.

WELDON - 24 miles
Post Office and KOA are about
1.5 mile apart. KOA has air
conditioned minimal cabins (no
TV, shared bath), swimming pool.

SOUTH LAKE - 27 miles
2 miles from Weldon. No lodging.
Great resupply at grocery store.
Canister fuel here.

LAKE ISABELLA - 36 miles
One motel, great shakes at
Nelda's Diner, great resupply at Vons.
Good town if you just want to stay in
motel. Not great town
for walking around. Canister fuel.

KERNVILLE - 38 miles
Great place to spend some time!
Small town, a few motels,
great brewery, great resupply
at grocery store. Canister fuel.

© 2019 Yogi's Books LLC

WALKER PASS: Towns with more services		
KERNVILLE	**RIDGECREST**	**LAKE ISABELLA**
POST OFFICE: 760-376-6418, USPS only Mon-Fri 9a-12:30p, 1p-3p Sat closed. Gen Delivery held for 30 days Hiker's Legal Name PCT Hiker, ETA: MM/DD/YY General Delivery Kernville, CA 93238	760-375-1939, USPS only Mon-Fri 10a-5p Sat 10a-2p. Gen Delivery held for 30 days Hiker's Legal Name PCT Hiker, ETA: MM/DD/YY General Delivery Ridgecrest, CA 93555	760-379-2553, USPS only Mon-Fri 10a-4p, Sat closed, package pickup only 9a-10a. Gen Delivery held for 30 days Hiker's Legal Name PCT Hiker, ETA: MM/DD/YY General Delivery Lake Isabella, CA 93240
OUTGOING MAIL: **MAIL DROPS:**	No.	OUTGOING MAIL: PackWrap. 760-446-3010. USPS and UPS shipping. Mon-Th 8a-6p. Fri 8a-5p. Sat-Sun closed. UPS Customer Center 760-375-7861 Mon-Fri 10a-1:30p, 2:30p-5p FedEx Ship Center 800-463-3339 Mon-Fri 10a-5:15p	MAIL DROPS: Lake Isabella Motel 760-379-2800. Accepts mail drops, no fee. USPS address: Hiker's Legal Name PCT Hiker, ETA: MM/DD/YY c/o Lake Isabella Motel PO Box 2134 Lake Isabella, CA 93240 UPS or FedEx address: Hiker's Legal Name PCT Hiker, ETA: MM/DD/YY c/o Lake Isabella Motel 400 Highway 155 Lake Isabella, CA 93240
CAR RENTAL:	No.	Enterprise 760-384-2816. Mon-Fri 7:30a-5p. Sat 9a-noon. Budget & Avis 760-446-1082, 760-446-5556 Mon-Fri 7:30a-5p, Sat 8a-1p. Sun noon-4p.	No.
RESUPPLY:	Sierra Gateway Market 760-376-2424 Sun-Th 6a-7p Fri-Sat 6a-8p	Stater Brothers 760-375-5557 6a-11p every day Walmart Supercenter 760-371-4974 6a-midnight every day Albertsons 760-384-4015 5a-midnight every day	Isabella Supermarket 760-379-8222 Mon-Sat 7a-7p, Sun 8a-6p Vons 760-379-4461 6a-midnight every day
OUTDOOR STORE:	Sierra Gateway Market Camping section, warm hats & gloves, canister fuel. 760-376-2424 Sierra South Sports Camping section, clothing. 760-376-3745 Shell Riverside One Stop Camping section, canister fuel. 760-376-1688	Big 5 Sporting Goods 760-384-4582 Mon-Th 10a-9p Fri-Sat 9:30a-9p Sun 9:30a-7:30p Todd's Outdoor Supply 760-375-7223 Mon-Fri 9a-6p. Sat 9a-4p. Sun closed.	Lake Isabella Supermarket has some camping supplies, including canister fuel.
RESTAURANTS:	Several.	Several.	Several. Excellent shakes at Nelda's Diner.
BREWERY:	Kern River Brewing Company 760-376-2337. Awesome!	Not a brewery, but Schooners has a huge selection of tap beer.	No.
SHOWER:	No.	Kerr McGee Community Center. 760-499-5151, Call for shower hours.	Haven RV Park.
LAUNDRY & ATM:	Yes.	Yes.	Yes.
COMPUTER:	No.	Library 760-384-5870	Library 760-549-2083

WALKER PASS: Towns with more services

	KERNVILLE	RIDGECREST	LAKE ISABELLA
CANISTER FUEL:	Sierra Gateway Market Shell Riverside One Stop	Big 5 Sporting Goods Todd's Outdoor Supply	Lake Isabella Supermarket
MEDICAL:	No.	Ridgecrest Regional Hospital 760-446-3551 Rural Health Clinic 760-499-3855	Kern Valley Health Center 760-379-2415 Mon-Sat 8a-5p, Sun closed

KERNVILLE LODGING		rates	AC	micr	frig	laundry	bkfst	pool	computer
Kern Lodge	760-376-2223	$$$+	Y	no	no	no	no	Y	no
Kernville Inn	760-376-2206	$$$+	Y	no	no	no	no	Y	no
Kernville Riverfront Lodge	760-376-1396	$$$+	Y	kitchens		no	no	no	no
Pine Cone Motel	760-376-6669	$$$$	Y	no	no	no	no	Y	Y
Sierra Gateway Cottages	800-888-8194	$$$$		kitchens		no	no		no

Look at room and online reviews before paying! Some motels in Ridgecrest are NASTY.

RIDGECREST LODGING		rates	AC	micr	frig	laundry	bkfst	pool	computer
American Inn	760-375-3020	$$	Y	no	some	no	cont	no	no
America's Best Value Inn	760-371-7454	$$	Y	no	no	no	no	no	no
Best Western	760-371-2300	$$$$	Y	Y	Y	Y	full	Y	Y
Budget Inn	760-375-1351	$$	Y	Y	Y	no	no	no	no
Clarion Inn	760-446-7910	$$	Y	Y	Y	no	order off menu	Y	Y
Econo Lodge	760-446-2551	$$	Y	Y	no	no	dlx cont	Y	no
Hampton Inn	760-446-1968	$$$$	Y	Y	Y	Y	cont	Y	Y
Motel 6	760-904-6979	$	Y	some	some	Y	no	Y	no
Oyo Hotel 1	760-375-1591	$$	Y	Y	Y		cont	Y	Y
Oyo Hotel 2	760-384-3575	$$	Y	Y	Y	Y	cont	no	no
Quality Inn	760-375-9731	$$	Y	Y	no	no	hot	Y	Y
Spring Hill Suites	760-446-1630	$$$$	Y	Y	Y	Y	hot	Y	Y
Super 8	760-375-2220	$$	Y	Y	Y	Y	cont	no	no

LAKE ISABELLA LODGING		rates	AC	micr	frig	laundry	bkfst	pool	computer
Lake Isabella Motel	760-379-2800	$$+	swamp cooler	no	some	Y	cont	Y	no
Haven RV Park camping	760-478-4310	Rides to/from trail. Shaded grass tent area, BBQ pits, picnic tables, rec room, showers, laundry.							
Kern Motel		Several hikers have reported terrible experiences at the Kern Motel (bugs, dirty sheets, rooms not clean, etc.). Do not pay for a room unless you look at it first.							

Lodging rate estimate:
$ usually less than $50
$$ usually $50-$80
$$$ usually $80-$110
$$$$ usually greater than $110

	INYOKERN	ONYX	WELDON–SOUTH LAKE
POST OFFICE:	760-377-5125, USPS only Mon-Fri 11a-4p. Sat closed. Gen Delivery held for 30 days Hiker's Legal Name PCT Hiker, ETA: MM/DD/YY General Delivery HOLD IN INYOKERN !! Inyokern, CA 93527 Must write "Hold in Inyokern" on box. If not, your box will automatically be sent to Kennedy Meadows.	760-378-2121, USPS only Mon-Fri 9a-noon and 1p-4p Hiker mail held for 60 days Hiker's Legal Name PCT Hiker, ETA: MM/DD/YY General Delivery 8275 Easy Street Onyx, CA 93255	760-378-2175, USPS only Mon-Fri 8:30a-12:30p,1p-4p. Sat closed Hiker mail held for 30 days Hiker's Legal Name PCT Hiker, ETA: MM/DD/YY General Delivery 5765 Vista Grande Weldon, CA 93283
RESUPPLY:	Inyokern Market is a C-Store. 760-377-3298 6:30a-9p every day	Onyx Store is a small C-Store. 760-378-3299. Usually 10:30a-6p every day. You could get snacks here, but not great resupply.	Sierra Gateway Supermarket 760-378-2207 7a-7p every day
OUTDOOR STORE:	No.	No.	Sierra Gateway Sporting Goods 760-378-1315 Mon-Thur 4a-7p Fri-Sat 4a-8p, Sun 5a-7p
LODGING:	Mayfair Motel 760-377-5700 $$. AC.	No.	Weldon KOA. 760-378-2001. Air conditioned camping cabins (use your sleeping bag), no TV. Rates $$ - $$$. Tent camping $.
RESTAURANTS:	Bernardino's Restaurant Five Fingers Pub	Great deli sandwiches at the Onyx Store.	Sierra Vista Restaurant next to KOA 760-378-2923. Wed-Sun 5p-8p. Buy food at the Supermarket and cook it in the outdoor kitchen at the KOA.
LAUNDRY:	No.	No.	At KOA.
SHOWER:	No.	No.	At KOA.
ATM:	At Inyokern Market.	No.	At Sierra Gateway
CANISTER FUEL:	No.	No.	Canister Fuel at Sierra Gateway Sporting Goods.
SWIMMING POOL:	No.	No.	At Weldon KOA. Non-guests can pay a day rate.

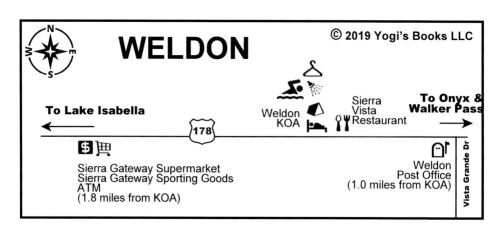

WELDON © 2019 Yogi's Books LLC

To Lake Isabella — 178 → To Onyx & Walker Pass

Weldon KOA — Sierra Vista Restaurant

$ 🛒 Sierra Gateway Supermarket Sierra Gateway Sporting Goods ATM (1.8 miles from KOA)

Weldon Post Office (1.0 miles from KOA)

Vista Grande Dr

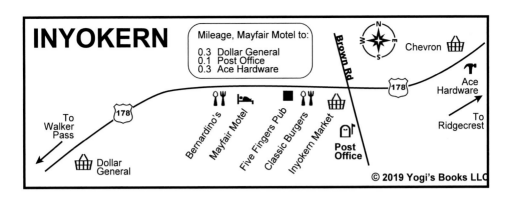

INYOKERN

Mileage, Mayfair Motel to:
0.3 Dollar General
0.1 Post Office
0.3 Ace Hardware

Brown Rd

Chevron

178

Ace Hardware

To Walker Pass

178

To Ridgecrest

Bernardino's

Mayfair Motel

Five Fingers Pub

Classic Burgers

Inyokern Market

Post Office

Dollar General

© 2019 Yogi's Books LLC

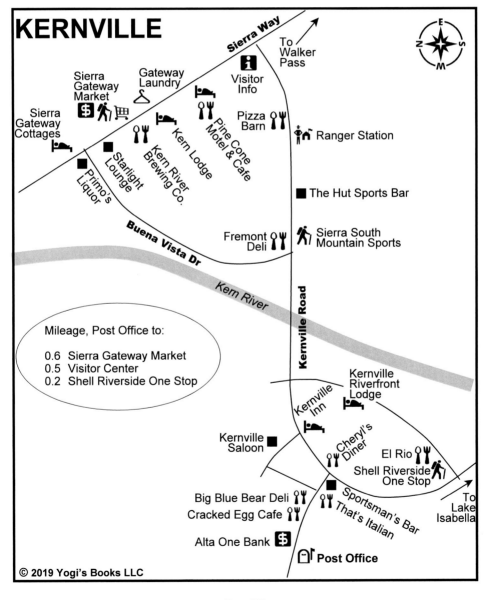

KERNVILLE

Sierra Way

To Walker Pass

Sierra Gateway Market

Gateway Laundry

Visitor Info

Sierra Gateway Cottages

Pine Cone Motel & Cafe

Pizza Barn

Ranger Station

Starlight Lounge

Kern River Brewing Co.

Kern Lodge

The Hut Sports Bar

Primo's Liquor

Buena Vista Dr

Fremont Deli

Sierra South Mountain Sports

Kern River

Kernville Road

Mileage, Post Office to:

0.6 Sierra Gateway Market
0.5 Visitor Center
0.2 Shell Riverside One Stop

Kernville Riverfront Lodge

Kernville Inn

Cheryl's Diner

El Rio

Kernville Saloon

Shell Riverside One Stop

Big Blue Bear Deli

Cracked Egg Cafe

Sportsman's Bar

That's Italian

To Lake Isabella

Alta One Bank

Post Office

© 2019 Yogi's Books LLC

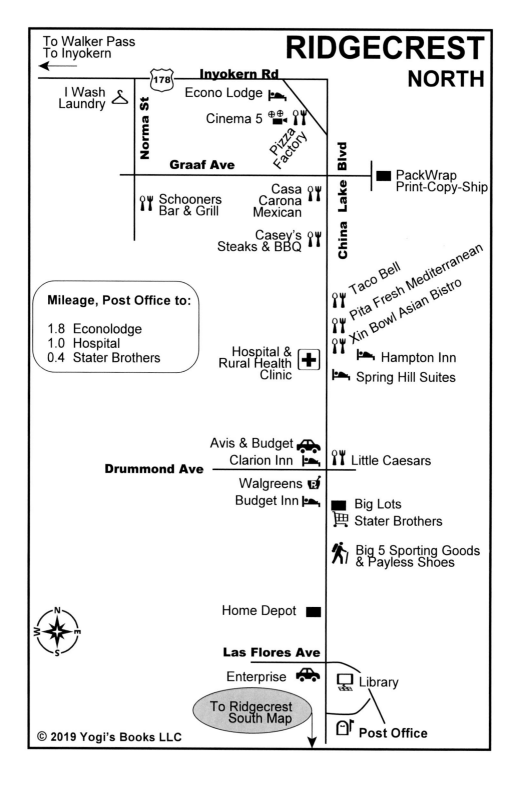

RIDGECREST
SOUTH

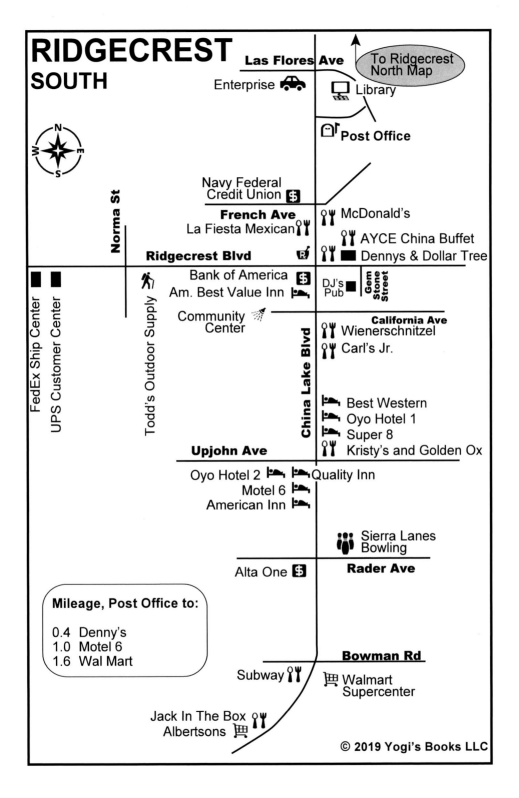

Las Flores Ave

Enterprise

To Ridgecrest North Map

Library

Post Office

Norma St

Navy Federal Credit Union $

French Ave

La Fiesta Mexican

McDonald's

AYCE China Buffet

Dennys & Dollar Tree

Ridgecrest Blvd

Bank of America $

Am. Best Value Inn

Community Center

DJ's Pub

Gem Stone Street

Todd's Outdoor Supply

China Lake Blvd

California Ave

Wienerschnitzel

Carl's Jr.

Best Western

Oyo Hotel 1

Super 8

Kristy's and Golden Ox

Upjohn Ave

FedEx Ship Center

UPS Customer Center

Oyo Hotel 2   Quality Inn

Motel 6

American Inn

Sierra Lanes Bowling

Alta One $ **Rader Ave**

Mileage, Post Office to:

0.4 Denny's
1.0 Motel 6
1.6 Wal Mart

Bowman Rd

Subway

Walmart Supercenter

Jack In The Box

Albertsons

© 2019 Yogi's Books LLC

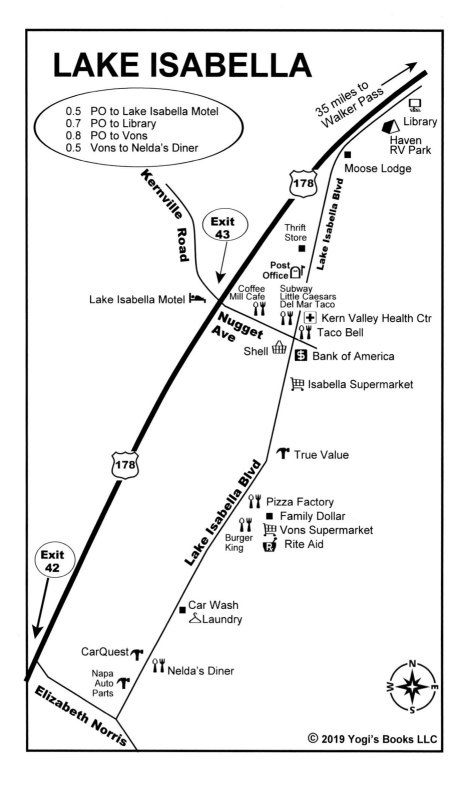

LAKE ISABELLA

0.5 PO to Lake Isabella Motel
0.7 PO to Library
0.8 PO to Vons
0.5 Vons to Nelda's Diner

35 miles to Walker Pass

Library

Haven RV Park

Moose Lodge

178

Kernville Road

Exit 43

Thrift Store

Post Office

Lake Isabella Blvd

Coffee Mill Cafe

Subway
Little Caesars
Del Mar Taco

Lake Isabella Motel

Nugget Ave

Kern Valley Health Ctr

Taco Bell

Shell

Bank of America

Isabella Supermarket

178

True Value

Pizza Factory

Family Dollar

Lake Isabella Blvd

Burger King

Vons Supermarket

Rite Aid

Exit 42

Car Wash

Laundry

CarQuest

Napa Auto Parts

Nelda's Diner

Elizabeth Norris

© 2019 Yogi's Books LLC

663.8 - Joshua Spring - 0.3 mile down off the PCT. Good water early in season, but usually dries up by June. Smelly, lots of bugs. There are bear problems here every year.

668.7, 669.4, 670.0, 670.2 - Spanish Needle Creek - All good water.
Second crossing is best, and has cool shade.

678.4 - Seasonal Creek - Dry.

680.9 - Unpaved Canebrake Road - Small stream 0.1 mile before the road.
Chimney Creek Campground is 0.2 to the right. No water at campground.

683.1 - Fox Mill Seasonal Spring - DOUBLE TAP (2014): Follow use trail to right of PCT to a trough about 50 ft down the trail. Walk past the trough (nasty water) about 20 ft and you will reach the flowing spring with good water. Cross the small flowing spring stream for several good campsites on top of the small hill. Load up with water here as next reliable water source is the Kern River in 14.6 miles at mile 697.7.

693.5 - Manter Creek - Usually good water. Dry in 2012-2016.

696.8 - Seasonal Creek - Always dry during PCT hiker season.

697.7 - South Fork Kern River - Most water you've seen yet. You could swim here.

699.9 - Stream - Has water.

700.4 - Alternate to Hiker Hangout (Triple Crown Outfitters and Grumpy Bear's Retreat).
See Guthook app or the Kennedy Meadows Yogi map below.

702.2 - Hiker Hangout in Kennedy Meadows

OVERVIEW: **Triple Crown Outfitters (TCO) and Grumpy Bear's Retreat comprise "Hiker Hangout in Kennedy Meadows."**

TCO is a full outfitter focused on PCT hikers: Great gear and awesome resupply. Grumpy Bear is a restaurant/bar with great food and ice cold beer.

GETTING HERE: **PCT mile 700.4** - Walk, hitch, or call for a ride. Follow the alternate shown on the map in this Yogi book, also listed on Guthook app. It's an easy shortcut from PCT mile 700.4 over to Hiker Hangout (Triple Crown Outfitters & Grumpy Bear). If you have a satellite phone, you can call Grumpy Bear for a ride. **Grumpy Bear will drive you back to mile 700.4 so you won't miss any PCT miles.**

PCT mile 702.2 - Walk 0.7 mile over to Tom's Place or the General Store, then hitch or call for a ride. Hitching to Hiker Hangout is easy. If you can't hitch, use the pay phone at the General Store to call for a ride Grumpy's (559-850-2327) or Triple Crown Outfitters (559-302-9943).

RESUPPLY: In previous years, hikers had to send resupply boxes to Kennedy Meadows. Not any more! **Triple Crown Outfitters is fully stocked with great hiker resupply** at great prices. See photos below. New items are frequently added. To save time shopping, you can pre-order your resupply, TCO will have it waiting for you. See comments on Guthook from previous hikers.
559-302-9943 [www.triplecrownoutfitters.com]

OUTFITTER: **Triple Crown Outfitters** 559-302-9943 [www.triplecrownoutfitters.com]. A full service outfitter: stoves, fuel, cook pots, spoons, stuff sacks, ice axes, crampons, bear canisters, socks, clothing, shoes, poles, pole tips, water filters, backpacks, tents, Tyvek, gaiters, sleeping bags, sleeping pads, sunglasses, ear buds, phone cords, solar chargers, toiletries and personal items, OTC medication, etc.

Triple Crown Outfitters is owned by Yogi (Double Triple Crowner) and Worldwide (Triple Crowner). We pride ourselves on being fully stocked with fair prices. Our extensive hiking experience and product knowledge are skills you just don't find in most retail or online locations.

BEAR CANISTER:	**Bear Vaults are in stock at Triple Crown Outfitters (TCO) to rent or buy.** Makes sense to buy or rent your bear canister in Kennedy Meadows, rather than pay to ship one from home. Most hikers pre-order from TCO's website and have their canister held at TCO for hiker pickup. [www.triplecrownoutfitters.com]
SIERRA GEAR:	**Triple Crown Outfitters** has everything you need to swap out gear for the Sierra. Ice axes and traction devices are in stock. See "Outfitter" section above.
MAIL DROPS:	**No need to ship a package to Kennedy Meadows.** Triple Crown Outfitters has full resupply, low prices, great selection. Triple Crown Outfitters also has ice axes, traction devices, bear canisters, and lots of other gear.

Grumpy Bear's Retreat accepts USPS, UPS, FedEx packages, no fee:
Hiker's Legal Name
PCT Hiker, ETA: MM/DD/YY
c/o Grumpy Bear's Retreat in Kennedy Meadows
98887 Kennedy Meadows Road
Inyokern, CA 93527

The mail carriers in Kennedy Meadows often mis-deliver mail. To make sure your package is delivered properly, write this in GREAT BIG LETTERS next to the address:

DELIVER TO GRUMPY BEAR

CAMPING:	At Hiker Hangout. **Camping at Hiker Hangout (Triple Crown Outfitters & Grumpy Bear) ensures you are at the beginning of the line for breakfast at Grumpy Bear,** and that is very important!
RESTAURANTS:	**Grumpy Bear's Retreat.** 559-850-2327 [www.grumpybearsretreat.com]

- Outdoor music every night until 9:30-10pm.
- Huge pizzas, burgers, veggie burgers, appetizers, milkshakes, banana splits, vegan menu, full bar with beer, wine, liquor.
- Breakfast is eggs, bacon, potatoes, and HUGE AYCE pancakes.
- **PCT tradition: THE GRUMPY BURGER -** Two 1/3 pound beef patties, cheese, bacon, avocado, egg, jalapeno, lettuce, tomato, pickle, onion
- **Hungry hikers attempt: THE TRIPLE CROWN BURGER -** Three 1/3 pound beef patties, three cheese slices, bacon, egg, jalapenos, lettuce, pickle, tomato, onion, topped with onion rings.

BEER:	In addition to serving beer in the restaurant, **Grumpy Bear has off-sale beer (a.k.a. "Beer To Go").** Ice available.
WiFi:	Varcomm Phone Company offers **great WiFi at Grumpy Bear's Retreat** for a daily fee (similar to paying for motel WiFi).

Free WiFi 24 hours a day at Triple Crown Outfitters.

TV:	Watch sports and anything else on the **TV at Grumpy Bear.**
SHOWER:	At Grumpy Bear, towel included.
LAUNDRY:	Free at Grumpy Bear.
FUEL:	Triple Crown Outfitters carries HEET and fuel canisters.
PCT REGISTER:	At Triple Crown Outfitters and Grumpy Bear.
DISC GOLF:	At Tom's Place.
MOVIES:	Every night at Tom's Place.
MT. WHITNEY:	The Mt. Whitney side trip is only 17 miles round trip from Crabtree Meadow (PCT mile 766.3). Don't miss it!! You are only 8.5 miles from the top of the tallest mountain in the 48 contiguous states, and you are in the best shape of your life. Don't pass this up. You may never get the chance to summit Whitney again. Leave KM with an extra day of food to account for your Whitney trip.

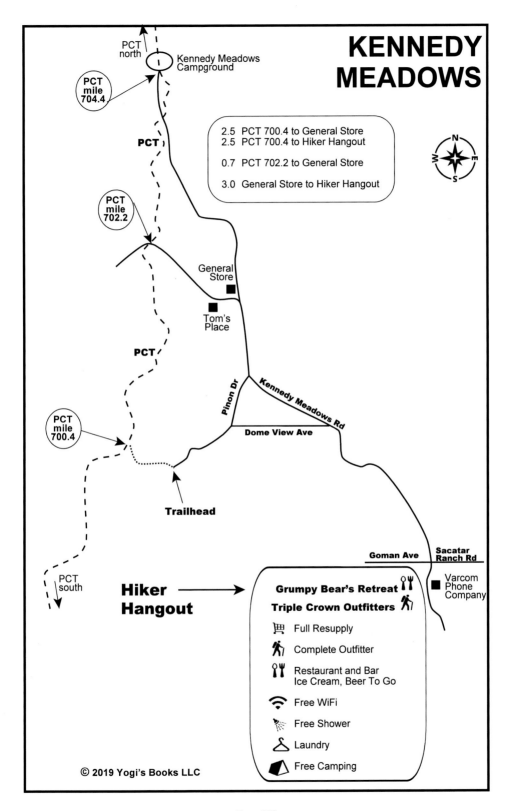

KENNEDY MEADOWS

PCT north

Kennedy Meadows Campground

PCT mile 704.4

PCT

2.5 PCT 700.4 to General Store
2.5 PCT 700.4 to Hiker Hangout

0.7 PCT 702.2 to General Store

3.0 General Store to Hiker Hangout

PCT mile 702.2

General Store

Tom's Place

PCT

Pinon Dr

Kennedy Meadows Rd

PCT mile 700.4

Dome View Ave

Trailhead

Goman Ave

Sacatar Ranch Rd

Varcom Phone Company

PCT south

Hiker Hangout →

Grumpy Bear's Retreat

Triple Crown Outfitters

Full Resupply

Complete Outfitter

Restaurant and Bar
Ice Cream, Beer To Go

Free WiFi

Free Shower

Laundry

Free Camping

© 2019 Yogi's Books LLC

Sample resupply items available at Triple Crown Outfitters in Kennedy Meadows. New items are frequently added.

Sample resupply items available at Triple Crown Outfitters in Kennedy Meadows. New items are frequently added.

Sample resupply items available at Triple Crown Outfitters in Kennedy Meadows. New items are frequently added.

**Sample resupply items available at Triple Crown Outfitters in
Kennedy Meadows. New items are frequently added.**

Sample resupply items available at Triple Crown Outfitters in Kennedy Meadows. New items are frequently added.

Sample resupply items available at Triple Crown Outfitters in Kennedy Meadows. New items are frequently added.

"Proper food storage" is required from Kennedy Meadows (mile 702.2) to Sonora Pass (mile 1016.9). That includes SEKI and Yosemite National Parks. "Proper food storage" is open to interpretation by individual agencies, and at times by individual Rangers (whom you may encounter along the trail). Some areas allow hanging food. Others specifically prohibit hanging. Some areas require bear canisters. Sleeping with your food, defending your food, posting a guard for your food are all NOT proper food storage methods, and these practices violate the food storage requirements.

Sierra Food Storage requirements are confusing to figure out, and the regulations change without notice. Quite often, a website will contradict itself from one page to the next. In fact, the SEKI Food Storage map states "Information is subject to rapid and unannounced change."

According to the Pacific Crest Trail Association: "Approved bear canisters are required in parts of Sequoia and Kings Canyon (SEKI) National Parks, Inyo, Sierra and Humboldt-Toiyabe National Forests, and in all of Yosemite and Lassen National Parks. **Basically, PCT hikers and horseback riders should, at the minimum, carry canisters between Kennedy Meadows (mile 702.2) and Sonora Pass (mile 1016.9)."**

NATIONAL PARK SERVICE ALLOWED BEAR CANISTERS

The following bear-resistant containers are allowed in SEKI and Yosemite National Parks.

GARCIA - Backpacker Model 812
[www.backpackerscache.com]
559-732-3785

THE BEAR KEG - Counter Assault
[www.counterassault.com]
800-695-3394

UDAP No-Fed-Bear
[www.udap.com]
800-232-7941

LIGHTER1 Big Daddy and Little Sami
[www.lighter1.com]

BEAR VAULT - 110b, 200, 250, 300, 350, 400, 450, 500
[www.bearvault.com]
866-301-3442

BEARIKADE - Weekender MKII and Expedition MKII (both 1766 and higher)
[www.wild-ideas.net]
805-693-0550

The Bare Boxer Contender (101) and Champ (202)
[www.bareboxer.com]

BEAR CANISTER PURCHASE or RENTAL

Triple Crown Outfitters located in Kennedy Meadows south offers canisters for purchase or rent, both for northbounders and southbounders. [www.triplecrownoutfitters.com]

Canisters for purchase:　　Bear Vault 500, Bear Vault 450
Canisters for rent:　　Bear Vault 500, Bear Vault 450, Garcia, Bear Keg

NORTHBOUNDERS

From the PCTA website: **"Hikers and horseback riders should, at the minimum, carry canisters between Kennedy Meadows (mile 702.2) and Sonora Pass (mile 1016.9)."**

Purchase: If you purchase a canister elsewhere, you have to pay postage to ship it to yourself at Kennedy Meadows south. Makes more sense to save the postage $$ and purchase your canister in Kennedy Meadows south at Triple Crown Outfitters..

Rental: Northbound hikers pick up their rental canister at Triple Crown Outfitters in Kennedy Meadows south. Hikers can return the canister for no charge at Kennedy Meadows Resort and Pack Station (Kennedy Meadows north), which is 10 miles west of Sonora Pass, nobo mile 1016.9. Alternatively, hikers can mail the canister back to Triple Crown Outfitters.

SOUTHBOUNDERS

The sentence above from the PCTA website lists northbound mileage. Using southbound mileage, that sentence would read: **"Hikers and horseback riders should, at the minimum, carry canisters between Sonora Pass (southbound mile 1636.2) and Kennedy Meadows (southbound mile 1950.9)."**

Purchase: Order a canister from [www.triplecrownoutfitters.com], ship it to Kennedy Meadows Resort and Pack Station (Kennedy Meadows north), which is 10 miles west of Sonora Pass.

Rental: Triple Crown Outfitters has rental canisters available at Kennedy Meadows Resort and Pack Station (KM north). It's possible to show up at KM north and rent a canister on the spot. However, to guarantee there will be a canister for you, it is best to place your rental order on TCO's website. Southbound hikers return their rented canister to Triple Crown Outfitters in Kennedy Meadows south. For details, click on the BEAR CANISTERS link at [www.triplecrownoutfitters.com].

SEQUOIA & KINGS CANYON (SEKI) NATIONAL PARKS

The PCT enters SEKI at PCT mile 753.9, and departs SEKI at PCT mile 855.9 (Piute Pass Trail). Park-allowed Portable Food Storage Containers (bear canisters) are required for part of this length of trail, and recommended for all of it. See the SEKI Wilderness Trip Planner:

[https://www.nps.gov/seki/planyourvisit/upload/NoYear-Wilderness-Trip-Planner-Final.pdf]

From that document: "The PCT passes through the Rock Creek and Rae Lakes Loop animal-resistant food-storage container requirement areas where all travelers are required to use animal-resistant containers. You must use the animal-resistant containers or boxes to store all your food, garbage, and scented items."

This map shows the PCT passing through two areas in SEKI where Portable Food Storage Containers (canisters) are required:

[https://www.nps.gov/seki/planyourvisit/upload/FoodStorageRequirements_8x11_20150729-2.pdf]

From looking at that map, it appears that the canister-required areas in SEKI are:

> (1)   Mile 753.9 (PCT enters SEKI) to mile 762.9 (Guyot Pass)
> (2)   Mile 779.5 (Forester Pass) to mile 807.1 (Pinchot Pass)

Additional SEKI information: [https://www.nps.gov/seki/planyourvisit/bear_bc.htm]

YOSEMITE NATIONAL PARK

The PCT enters Yosemite National Park at PCT mile 929.5 (Donohue Pass),
and departs Yosemite National Park at PCT mile 997.1 (Dorothy Lake Pass).

From the Yosemite National Park website [www.nps.gov/yose]:

"You are required by federal regulations to store all your 'food' properly throughout Yosemite National Park. You must have your food stored unless it's within arm's reach (so, don't go for a swim or take a nap while leaving food out). 'Food' includes all food and drinks, regardless of packaging, along with trash, toiletries, and other scented items. These items must be stored in either an allowed bear-resistant food canister or food locker. Hanging food is illegal throughout Yosemite."

"Bear resistant food containers (bear canisters) are required for overnight hikers throughout the Wilderness (counterbalance food hangs are no longer legal)."

"Please note that these food storage regulations have the force and effect of federal law: Failure to store your food properly may result in impoundment of your food or car and/or a fine of up to $5,000 and/or revocation of your camping permit."

"Allowed bear canisters are required throughout Yosemite National Park.
Hanging food is not permitted anywhere in Yosemite.
There are no exceptions for Pacific Crest Trail through-hikers."

Kennedy Meadows to Kearsarge Pass Tr Jct
86.7 PCT miles
(plus 17 miles round trip if you do Mt. Whitney)
(plus 7.5 miles one way if you go to Independence or Bishop over Kearsarge Pass)

EXTRA MILES: The <u>Mt. Whitney</u> side trip adds 17 miles round trip.

If you leave the Sierra via <u>Kearsarge Pass</u>, the hike from the PCT to the Onion Valley Trailhead adds 7.5 miles one way.

SIERRA PCT BEAR BOX LOCATIONS:

753.9	No Bear Box - ENTER SEQUOIA & KINGS CANYON NATIONAL PARK
760.5	Bear Box - Rock Creek Crossing
766.3	Bear Box - Crabtree Meadows
	Bear Box - Crabtree Ranger Station (this is on the Mt Whitney side trip)
770.3	Bear Box - Wallace Creek and High Sierra Trail Junction
774.1	Bear Box - Bear box is10-15 minutes before Tyndall Creek
774.7	Bear Box - Shepherd Pass Trail / Tyndall Creek
784.3	Bear Box - Center Basin Trail
786.1	Bear Box - Upper Vidette Meadow
787.0	Bear Box - Vidette Meadow
787.3	Bear Box - Junction Up Bubbs Creek
788.9	Bear Box - Charlotte Lake (one mile off the PCT)
793.5	Bear Box - Rae Lakes
795.2	Bear Box - Arrowhead Lake
799.8	Bear Box - Woods Creek
855.9	No Bear Box - LEAVE SEQUOIA & KINGS CANYON NATIONAL PARK
929.6	No Bear Box - ENTER YOSEMITE NATIONAL PARK - Donohue Pass
942.5	Bear Box - Tuolumne Meadows Campground
948.3	Bear Box - Glen Aulin
997.1	No Bear Box - LEAVE YOSEMITE NATIONAL PARK - Dorothy Lake Pass

<u>**"Proper food storage" is required**</u>   (canister, bear boxes, or hanging if allowed) from Kennedy Meadows (702.2) to Sonora Pass (1016.9).

704.4 - Kennedy Meadows Campground - Water from a creek and from spigots.

706.6 - Steel-girdered wooden bridge - Good water.

708.6 - Crag Creek - Gross, oily, and barely flowing.

716.5 - South Fork Kern River Bridge - Treat this water. Lots of swallow droppings.
Many established campsites uphill before crossing the bridge.

719.2 - Cow Creek - Usually good water. No water in 2014-2016 (extremely dry years).

720.7 - Olancha Pass 2nd Trail Junction - Usually good water.

728.1 - Seasonal creek - Usually good water.

730.8 - Death Canyon Creek - Usually good water. Dry in 2013-2016.
Trail leads to a spring 0.2 mile off PCT.

736.4, 738.3, 741.7 - Springs - Pay attention to your maps.

736.4 - Junction with a faint half mile long lateral to a spring -
Watch the right side of the PCT for a "corral" sign.
DOUBLE TAP: Tons of good camping in the trees to the left of the PCT at a saddle.

738.3 - Second saddle with path signed CORRAL - Careful, because these directions also fit the previous water (mile point 736.4). Pay attention to where you are and the saddles you've walked over, and look for a sign (partially hidden by branches) on a tree on the right of the PCT next to a faint right-branching trail. To find water here, take the trail off the PCT to the right down the hill. When you see the corral, veer to the right until you get to an open meadow. The creek is on the far side of the meadow. In 2002, we found a dry creek here which had one small pool of water. In 2003, it was strong-flowing and clear. In 2007, this source was bone dry, while the previous source (mile point 736.4) had good water. Go figure.

741.7 - Sierra crest at a low saddle to Diaz Creek - Again, pay close attention to where you are. There is a faint unsigned use trail to the right, as the PCT makes a curve to the left. We noticed this due to the rocks lined up along the PCT, which guided us to stay *on* the PCT and not veer *off* onto a different trail. The different trail is the trail to the water. Water is about 5 minutes off the PCT, with very little elevation drop. To find it, take the faint trail off the PCT. When this trail opens up to a meadow covered with sage, veer to the left – you'll notice where there is an obvious large depression (almost like a giant crack) where there would logically be water. The water was warm, but flowing well.

743.0 - Dutch Meadow Spring - Watch the right side of the PCT carefully. After a brief climb, at a left-turning switchback, watch for an unmarked trail on the right side of the PCT. This junction is sometimes marked with a cairn or a note.

SCRUB (2013): Dutch Meadow Spring is easily the best water source around. If you miss the usage trail, just head down to the meadow and angle to the left/west up its south side and you will find the creek soon enough.

744.5 - Mulkey Pass - Spring to the right about 0.25 mile down the trail (toward Horseshoe Meadows) near low scrubby bushes. There are signs on the tree.

745.3 - Trail Pass Trail - This goes down to Horseshoe Meadows Trailhead.

745.3 - Lone Pine CA

OVERVIEW: A compact town, with all the services hikers need.

GETTING HERE: Many options. Mulkey Pass Trail, Trail Pass Trail and Cottonwood Pass Trail all end up at Horseshoe Meadows Trailhead. This area is very popular when the road is open. From the trailhead, you have a 20-mile hitch down into Lone Pine. This could be a TOUGH hitch.

(1)   Mile 744.5 - Mulkey Pass - Take Mulkey Pass Trail approximately 2 miles to Horseshoe Meadows. 465-foot elevation loss.

(2)   Mile 745.3 - Trail Pass - Take Trail Pass Trail approximately 2.5 miles to Horseshoe Meadows. Gentle elevation descent of 600 feet.

(3)   Mile 750.2 - Cottonwood Pass -
Take Cottonwood Pass Trail approximately 3.8 miles to Horseshoe Meadows. Drops 1200 feet, much steeper than Trail Pass Trail.

(4)   Mile 766.3 - Crabtree Meadows to Trail Crest to Whitney Portal -
Leave PCT at Crabtree Meadow, hike up to Trail Crest, then down to Whitney Portal. Hitch 12 miles down to Lone Pine on the Portal Road. (NOT RECOMMENDED, because in order to return to the PCT via Whitney Portal, you need a Whitney Permit, and a fixed number of Whitney Permits are issued for each day.)

(5)   PCT mile 788.9 - Kearsarge Pass - 7.5 miles up and over Kearsarge Pass to the Onion Valley Trailhead. It's 13 miles from the trailhead parking lot to Independence. From Independence, hitch 16 miles south on Highway 395 to Lone Pine.

BUS SERVICE: See bus information after the Lone Pine Handbook section.

SHUTTLES: The outfitter offers shuttles. Elevation. 760-876-4560.

POST OFFICE:	760-876-5681, USPS only Mon-Fri 9:30a-12:30p & 1:30p-4:30p Sat closed, but usually hikers can pick up packages from 10:30a-noon. General Delivery held for 30 days	Hiker's Legal Name PCT Hiker, ETA: MM/DD/YY General Delivery Lone Pine, CA 93545
MAIL DROPS:	Whitney Portal Hostel (760-876-0030) Accepts mail drops, UPS or FedEx only. Mail MUST have a throw away date (ETA). If mail is not picked up within 2 weeks of ETA, it will be thrown away. [https://www.mountwhitneyportal.com/en-us]	Hiker's Legal Name PCT Hiker, ETA: MM/DD/YY c/o Whitney Portal Hostel 238 South Main Street Lone Pine, CA 93545

RESUPPLY: Full resupply at Joseph's Bi-Rite Market 760-876-4378 8a-8p every day

OUTFITTER: Elevation 760-876-4560 9a-7p every day
Big Willi Mountaineering 760-878-8325 9 -5p Thur-Mon. Closed Tue-Wed.

RESTAURANTS: Several.

LAUNDRY: Laundromat across the street from the Dow Villa.

SHOWER: At Whitney Portal Hostel, includes towel. 760-876-0030.

ATM: Yes.

COMPUTER: Lone Pine Branch Library 760-876-5031

FUEL: Elevation 760-876-4560 Denatured, canister fuel, white gas, Esbits

MEDICAL: Southern Inyo Hospital 760-876-5501

LODGING: Dow Villa MOTEL and HOTEL. 800-824-9317

Dow Villa Motel:	Rooms have private bath, TV/VCR, refrigerator, some have microwaves. Rates: $$$$
Dow Villa Hotel:	Less expensive than Dow Villa Motel Rooms with TV, private bath. Rates: $$$ Rooms with TV, shared bath. Rates: $$
Whitney Portal Hostel:	760-876-0030 Open 24 hours. Check in 3p, check out 10a. Bunks $, Rooms $$$ Hostel has computers, no charge Laundry across the street

LONE PINE LODGING Ask for hiker rates		Rates	frig TV	micr	laundry	other
Dow Villa Hotel/Motel	800-824-9317	see above				
Whitney Portal Hostel	760-876-0030	see above				
Mt. Whitney Motel	760-876-4207	$$$$	Y	Y	no	in-room spa
Lone Pine Budget Inn	760-876-5655	$$$	Y	Y	no	
The Portal Motel	760-876-5930	$$$	Y	Y	no	
The Trails Motel	800-862-7020	$$$	Y	Y	Y	pool
Timberline Motel	760-876-4555	$$$	Y	Y	no	
Best Western	760-876-5571	$$$$	Y	no	Y	hot bkfst, pool, computer
		$	= usually less than $50			
		$$	= usually $50-$80			
		$$$	= usually $80-$110			
		$$$$	= usually greater than $110			

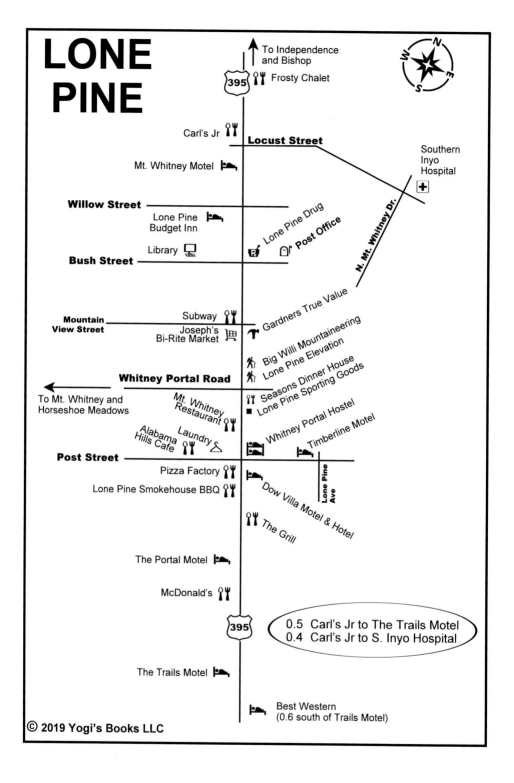

LONE PINE

To Independence and Bishop

395

Frosty Chalet

Carl's Jr **Locust Street**

Mt. Whitney Motel

Southern Inyo Hospital

Willow Street

Lone Pine Budget Inn

Lone Pine Drug

Post Office

Library

Bush Street

N. Mt. Whitney Dr.

Gardners True Value

Mountain View Street

Subway

Joseph's Bi-Rite Market

Big Willi Mountaineering

Lone Pine Elevation

Seasons Dinner House

Whitney Portal Road

Lone Pine Sporting Goods

To Mt. Whitney and Horseshoe Meadows

Mt. Whitney Restaurant

Whitney Portal Hostel

Timberline Motel

Alabama Hills Cafe

Laundry

Post Street

Lone Pine Ave

Pizza Factory

Lone Pine Smokehouse BBQ

Dow Villa Motel & Hotel

The Grill

The Portal Motel

McDonald's

395

0.5 Carl's Jr to The Trails Motel
0.4 Carl's Jr to S. Inyo Hospital

The Trails Motel

Best Western
(0.6 south of Trails Motel)

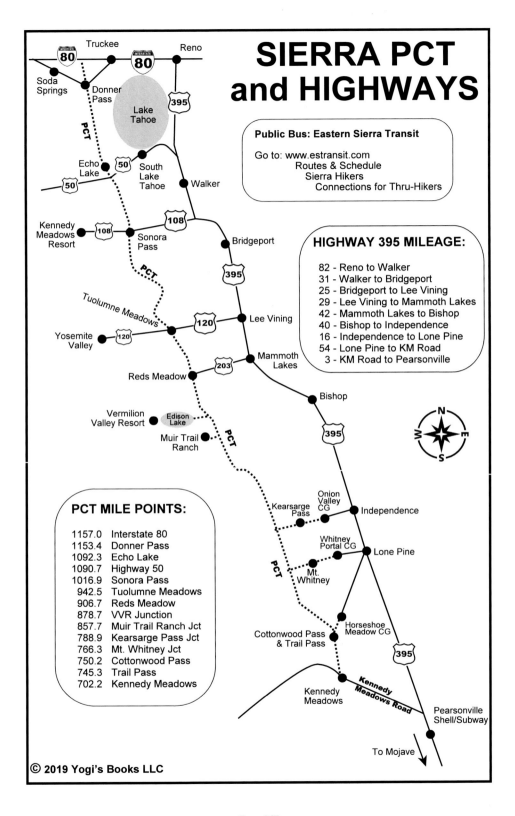

SIERRA PCT and HIGHWAYS

Truckee · Reno · Interstate 80 · Interstate 80

Soda Springs · Donner Pass · Lake Tahoe · 395

PCT

Echo Lake · 50 · South Lake Tahoe · Walker

50

Kennedy Meadows Resort · 108 · 108 · Sonora Pass · Bridgeport

PCT · 395

Tuolumne Meadows

120 · Lee Vining

Yosemite Valley · 120

Mammoth Lakes · 203

Reds Meadow · 203

Bishop

Vermilion Valley Resort · Edison Lake · 395

Muir Trail Ranch · PCT

N
W · E
S

Public Bus: Eastern Sierra Transit

Go to: www.estransit.com
Routes & Schedule
Sierra Hikers
Connections for Thru-Hikers

HIGHWAY 395 MILEAGE:

82 - Reno to Walker
31 - Walker to Bridgeport
25 - Bridgeport to Lee Vining
29 - Lee Vining to Mammoth Lakes
42 - Mammoth Lakes to Bishop
40 - Bishop to Independence
16 - Independence to Lone Pine
54 - Lone Pine to KM Road
3 - KM Road to Pearsonville

PCT MILE POINTS:

1157.0 Interstate 80
1153.4 Donner Pass
1092.3 Echo Lake
1090.7 Highway 50
1016.9 Sonora Pass
942.5 Tuolumne Meadows
906.7 Reds Meadow
878.7 VVR Junction
857.7 Muir Trail Ranch Jct
788.9 Kearsarge Pass Jct
766.3 Mt. Whitney Jct
750.2 Cottonwood Pass
745.3 Trail Pass
702.2 Kennedy Meadows

Onion Valley CG · Kearsarge Pass · Independence

Whitney Portal CG · Lone Pine

PCT · Mt. Whitney

Horseshoe Meadow CG

Cottonwood Pass & Trail Pass · 395

Kennedy Meadows · Kennedy Meadows Road · Pearsonville Shell/Subway

To Mojave

© 2019 Yogi's Books LLC

Eastern Sierra Transit Fixed Routes

760-872-1901   [www.estransit.com]

Service along Highway 395 from Reno to Lancaster.
Service is limited (only a few busses per day), and no service Saturday or Sunday.
The website has a trip planner which gives itineraries and fares

Eastern Sierra Transit Dial-a-Ride
Reservations are encouraged, but same-day service is available.

[www.estransit.com]

Lone Pine	760-614-0030	Mon-Fri	7:30a-3:30p
Bishop	760-873-1901	Mon-Thu Fri Sat Sun	7a-6p 7a-2a 8:30a-2a 8a-1p
Mammoth Lakes	760-924-3184	Mon-Fri	8a-5p
Walker	530-402-6832	Mon-Thur	8a-4:30p

Reds Meadow Shuttle

Eastern Sierra Transit Mammoth Lakes
office: 760-924-3184
[www.estransit.com]

Busses from the Reds Meadow store to Mammoth Mountain Lodge
Service depends upon snow. Usually runs from early-June to early-September.
Every day 8a-5p until late-June, then 7:30a-7:45p.
From 10a-4p, bus frequency is every 20 minutes. Other times every 30-45 minutes.

Mammoth Area Shuttle (MAS)
Bike Shuttle

760-934-2571, ext. 9238

Service between Mammoth Bike Park (located by the Mammoth Mountain Lodge) to the Village.
Usually runs from mid-June to mid-September.
Service from 9a-4:30p, frequency is approximately every 20-30 minutes.
Times and frequency are based on demand and are subject to change.
Paid Mountain Bike Park riders have seating priority.

Yosemite Area Transit (YARTS)

877-989-2787   [www.yarts.com]

2019 Schedule June, September, October

The Village	Mammoth Lakes Mammoth Mtn Inn	The Village	Mammoth Lakes Shilo Inn	Lee Vining Whoa Nellie	Tuolumne Mdws Store	Yosemite Valley Visitor Center
	8:00a	8:07a	8:20a	9:22a	9:57a	11:57a
8:30p	8:20p		7:57p	7:32p	6:50p	5:00p

2019 Schedule July and August

The Village	Mammoth Lakes Mammoth Mtn Inn	The Village	Mammoth Lakes Shilo Inn	Lee Vining Whoa Nellie	Tuolumne Mdws Store	Yosemite Valley Visitor Center
	6:45a	6:52a	7:05a	8:07a	8:42a	10:32a
	8:00a	8:07a	8:20a	9:22a	9:57a	11:47a
7:35p	7:25p		7:02p	6:37p	5:55p	4:05p
8:30p	8:20p		7:57p	7:32p	6:50p	5:00p

746.8 - Creek

750.2 - Cottonwood Pass - The Cottonwood Pass Trail goes down to Horseshoe Meadows Trailhead, where you can hitch into Lone Pine.

750.8 - Chicken Spring Lake - Water isn't a problem after Chicken Spring Lake.
    JOKER: Last good camping where bear cans are not required.

753.9 (enter Sequoia/Kings Canyon National Park) to 762.9 (Guyot Pass) -
    PCT hikers are required to use canisters or bear boxes.

760.5 - Rock Creek Crossing - Bear box here.

761.7 - Guyot Creek - Water here.

762.9 - Guyot Pass

766.3 - Crabtree Meadow - Bear box here.

766.3 - Mt. Whitney

The Mt. Whitney side trip is only 17 miles round trip from Crabtree Meadow. You are only 8.5 miles from the top of the tallest mountain in the 48 contiguous states, and you are in the best shape of your life. Don't pass this up. You may never get the chance to summit Whitney again.

HINT - If you go up Mt. Whitney, you don't have to backtrack to Crabtree Meadow to pick up the PCT again. From Crabtree Ranger Station, instead of going back downhill to Crabtree Meadow, you can stay on the JMT heading west and pick up the PCT again in about a mile.

Crabtree Ranger Station, 1.3 miles northeast of Crabtree Meadow (this is off the PCT, on the Whitney side trip) - Bear box here. JOKER: Stay at the Crabtree Meadows Ranger Station. Guitar Lake is COLD with terrible condensation because there's no trees. In snowy years or if you're early, you'll find wet, miserable ground.

767.0 - PCT and JMT merge - For the next 175.5 miles (to Tuolumne Meadows) the JMT and the PCT are the same, and the signs all indicate JMT, rather than PCT. North of Reds Meadow the two trails split for 13.9 miles.

770.3 - Wallace Creek and High Sierra Trail Junction - Bear box here.

774.1 - Creek - There is a bear box at the first creek after Bighorn Plateau.

774.7 - Shepherd Pass Trail / Tyndall Creek - Ford the creek, continue on the PCT for about a minute, and you'll see the bear box on the left.

779.5 (Forester Pass) to 807.1 (Pinchot Pass) -
    PCT hikers are required to use canisters or bear boxes.

779.5 - Forester Pass - As you're approaching Forester, look at that wall of rock in front of you. It forms a sort of wide "V." The notch of the "V" is Forester Pass. Really. I'm not kidding. That's it.

784.3 - Center Basin Trail - Bear box here. After crossing a side creek, watch the left side of the PCT. Bear Box is down from the PCT. You have to watch for it.

786.1 - Upper Vidette Meadow - Bear Box here.

787.0 - Vidette Meadow - Bear box here. There is usually bear activity here.

787.3 - Junction up Bubbs Creek Canyon - Bear box here.

787.9 - WATER - PCT crosses a major stream twice between Bubbs Creek Canyon trail junction and Charlotte Lake.

788.5 - Bullfrog Lake Junction - Gorgeous hike up to Kearsarge Pass.

788.9 - Charlotte Lake - Bear box at Charlotte Lake, which is about a mile off the PCT.

788.9 - Kearsarge Pass Trail - BEAUTIFUL side trail!! This is where you leave the PCT go to Independence CA or Bishop CA (hike 7.5 miles over Kearsarge Pass to Onion Valley, then hitch to Independence or Bishop).

788.9 - Independence CA

OVERVIEW: Compact and friendly.

GETTING HERE: Leave the PCT either at the PCT-Bullfrog Lake Junction (PCT mile 788.5) or the PCT-Kearsarge Pass Trail Junction (PCT mile 788.9). Walk 7.5 miles up and over Kearsarge Pass to the Onion Valley Trailhead. Take the time to talk to EVERY hiker you meet. You need a ride into town, and these people have cars. It's 13 miles from the trailhead parking lot to Independence. You're not really hitching. You're trying to get a ride from people with cars at the trailhead. This can be an easy thing on a weekend, not so easy during the week.

DOUBLE TAP: About a mile down from Kearsarge Pass you can get AT&T service. No AT&T service at Onion Valley.

BUS SERVICE: See bus information after the Lone Pine Handbook section.

SHUTTLES: Some motels offer pay shuttles.
East Side Sierra Shuttle: paul@inyopro.com 760-878-8047
Shuttle anywhere in the Sierra Nevada, including trailheads

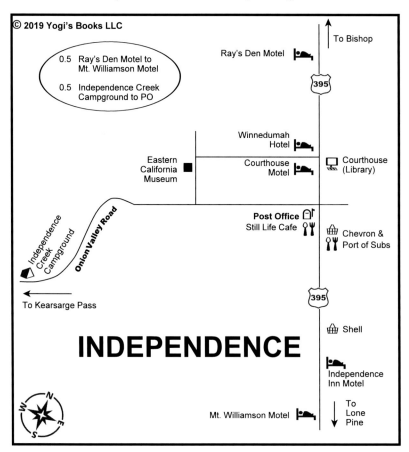

POST OFFICE:	760-878-2210, USPS only Mon-Fri 9:30a-12:45p and 1:15p-4p Sat closed, but possible package pickup from 8:30a-10:30a, knock on door.	Hiker's Legal Name PCT Hiker, ETA: MM/DD/YY General Delivery Independence, CA 93526

Normal Gen Delivery held for 30 days.
Hiker mail held for 30 days after ETA.

MAIL DROPS: Courthouse Motel (760-878-2732)
Accepts mail drops, free for guests, $5-$10 for non-guests

USPS address: Hiker's Legal Name PCT Hiker, ETA: MM/DD/YY c/o The Courthouse Motel 157 N Edwards St. PO Box 29 Independence, CA 93526	UPS or FedEx address: Hiker's Legal Name PCT Hiker, ETA: MM/DD/YY c/o The Courthouse Motel 157 N Edwards St. Independence, CA 93526

RESUPPLY: Two small C-Stores with snacks, but no dinners. No prices on anything.
Chevron   760-878-2618
Shell   760-878-2172

RESTAURANTS: Yes.

LAUNDRY: Some of the motels will let hikers use laundry machines.

SHOWER: At Courthouse Motel.

ATM: At Shell and at Chevron.

COMPUTER: Inyo County Library 760-878-0260 (Courthouse basement)

FUEL: Shell   760-878-2172   Canisters
Chevron   760-878-2618   Canisters

MUSEUM: TEATREE: I spent the afternoon at the Eastern California Museum checking out desert and Sierra history and artifacts. They had an extensive exhibit about Manzanar, the Japanese WWII internment camp, which was about five miles from here. Very interesting. Depressing, but interesting.

INDEPENDENCE LODGING ask for hiker rates		Rates		TV, frig micr, AC	$ shuttle	other
Courthouse Motel	760-878-2732	Rooms $$$ Bunkhouse 2018: $25		Y	for guests	drop-off laundry svc, clothesline
Ray's Den Motel	760-878-2122	$$$		Y	no	no laundry
Mt. Williamson Motel	760-878-2121	$$$ hot breakfast included (eggs, bacon, toast)		Y	Y	drop-off laundry $
Independence Inn	530-945-0103	$$ - $$$		Y	Y	coin laundry
Winnedumah Hotel	760-309-3770	$$$$	no TV, frig, micr does have AC		no	includes breakfast
Independence Creek Campground		$ camping				
	Rates: $ = usually less than $50 $$ = usually $50-$80 $$$ = usually $80-$110 $$$$ = usually over $110					

788.9 - Bishop CA

OVERVIEW:	Full service town.
GETTING HERE:	40 miles north of Independence on Hwy 395.
BUS SERVICE:	See bus information after the Lone Pine Handbook section.
SHUTTLE:	East Side Sierra Shuttle: paul@inyopro.com 760-878-8047 Shuttle anywhere in the Sierra Nevada, including trailheads
CAR RENTAL:	Enterprise 760-873-3704 Mon-Fri 8a-5p. Sat & Sun closed.

POST OFFICE:
760-873-3526, USPS only
Mon-Fri 9a-4p, Sat 9a-1p
General Delivery held for 30 days.
If you want to bounce a box ahead, the
Bishop Postmaster requires you to either file
a package intercept or go to the PO in person.
You cannot bounce a box by phone.

Hiker's Legal Name
PCT Hiker, ETA: MM/DD/YY
General Delivery
585 West Line Street
Bishop, CA 93514

RESUPPLY:
Vons Supermarket	760-872-9811	5a-1a every day
Smart & Final	760-873-7181	Mon-Sat 8a-8p, Sun 8a-6p
Grocery Outlet	760-872-1505	7a-9p every day

OUTFITTER:
Eastside Sports	760-873-7520	9a-9p every day
Sage To Summit	760-872-1756	9a-7p every day
Mammoth Gear Exchange	760-873-4300	9a-7p every day

RESTAURANTS:
Hiker favorites:
Jack's Restaurant and Bakery	760-872-7971	
Schat's Bakkery	760-873-7156	
Holy Smoke BBQ	760-872-4227	
Mountain Rambler Brewery	760-258-1348	Hiker/climber bar

LAUNDRY:	Yes.
ATM:	Yes.
SHOWER:	At Washtub Laundromat.
COMPUTER:	Bishop Branch Library 760-873-5115

FUEL:
K-Mart	760-872-7030	Denatured alcohol
Eastside Sports	760-873-7520	Canisters, white gas
Sage To Summit	760-872-1756	Canisters, denatured, Esbits

MEDICAL:	Northern Inyo Hospital 760-873-5811

BISHOP LODGING		Rates	frig	micr	TV	laundry	pool	hot tub	bkfst	computer
America's Best Value Inn	760-873-4912	$$$	Y	Y	Y	Y	Y	no	cont	no
Best Western	760-873-3543	$$$$	Y	Y	Y	Y	Y	Y	hot	Y
Cielo Hotel	760-873-6381	$$$$	some	some	Y	no	no	no	hot	Y
Creekside Inn	760-872-3044	$$$$	Y	Y	Y	Y	Y	Y	no	no
Comfort Inn	760-873-4284	$$$$	Y	no	Y	Y	Y	Y	hot	Y
Days Inn	760-872-1095	$$$	Y	Y	Y	Y	Y	Y	cont	no
Elms Motel	760-873-8118	$$$	no	no	Y	no	no	no	no	no
Holiday Inn Express	760-872-2423	$$$$	no	no	Y	Y	Y	Y	hot	Y
Motel 6	760-873-8426	$$$	Y	no	Y	Y	Y	no	no	no
Mountain View Motel	760-873-4242	$$	Y	lobby	Y	no	Y	no	cont	no
Red Roof Inn	760-873-3564	$$$	Y	Y	Y	no	Y	no	cont	Y
TraveLodge	760-872-1771	$$$$	Y	Y	Y	Y	Y	Y	cont	Y
Trees Motel	760-873-6391	$$$	Y	Y	Y	no	no	no	no	no
Town House Motel	760-872-4541	$$	Y	some	Y	no	Y	no	no	no
Vagabond Inn	760-873-6351	$$$$	Y	Y	Y	Y	Y	Y	hot	Y
Village Motel	760-872-8155	$$$	Y	Y	Y	no	Y	Y	no	no
Hostel California	760-399-6316	$ bunk, includes linens, towel, shower. $$ private rooms with private bathroom. Loaner bikes, skateboards, loaner clothes, full kitchen, ping pong table. No laundry.								
		$ = usually less than $50 $$ = usually $50-$80 $$$ = usually $80-$110 $$$$ = usually greater than $110								

Access these files as often as possible:

(1) **Pacific Crest Trail Water Report -** Current status of water sources. Frequently updated during hiker season. [www.pctwater.com]

(2) **Yogi's PCT Handbook update file -** Changes to trail/town information which have occurred between the time your book was printed and now. Frequently updated during hiker season. [www.yogisbooks.com], then click UPDATES & LINKS

Do you have changes/updates to report?
If so, send them here: yogisbooks@gmail.com

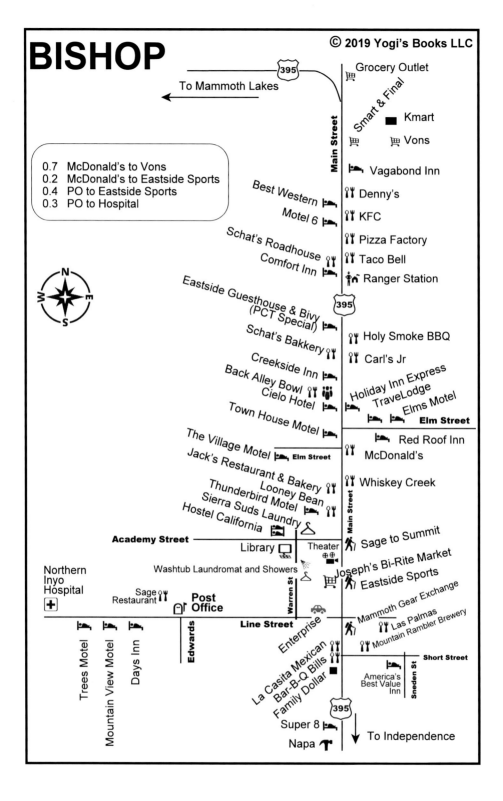

BISHOP

395

To Mammoth Lakes

Grocery Outlet

Smart & Final

Kmart

Vons

Main Street

Vagabond Inn

Best Western

Denny's

Motel 6

KFC

Pizza Factory

Schat's Roadhouse

Taco Bell

Comfort Inn

Ranger Station

Eastside Guesthouse & Bivy
(PCT Special)

395

Holy Smoke BBQ

Schat's Bakkery

Carl's Jr

Creekside Inn

Holiday Inn Express

Back Alley Bowl

TraveLodge

Cielo Hotel

Elms Motel

Town House Motel

Elm Street

The Village Motel

Red Roof Inn

Elm Street

McDonald's

Jack's Restaurant & Bakery

Whiskey Creek

Looney Bean

Thunderbird Motel

Sierra Suds Laundry

Hostel California

Academy Street

Library

Theater

Sage to Summit

Washtub Laundromat and Showers

Joseph's Bi-Rite Market

Northern
Inyo
Hospital

Eastside Sports

Sage
Restaurant

**Post
Office**

Mammoth Gear Exchange

Las Palmas

Enterprise

Mountain Rambler Brewery

Line Street

La Casita Mexican

Bar-B-Q Bills

America's
Best Value
Inn

Short Street

Family Dollar

Sneden St

Trees Motel

Mountain View Motel

Days Inn

Edwards

Warren St

395

Super 8

To Independence

Napa

0.7 McDonald's to Vons
0.2 McDonald's to Eastside Sports
0.4 PO to Eastside Sports
0.3 PO to Hospital

N
W   E
S

#10

Kearsarge Pass Trail Jct to Tuolumne Meadows
153.6 PCT miles
(plus 7.5 miles one way if you're coming back to the PCT
from Independence or Bishop over Kearsarge Pass)

EXTRA MILES - If you left the Sierra via Kearsarge Pass to go to Independence or Bishop, the return trip to the PCT adds 7.5 miles.

"Proper food storage" is required (canister, bear boxes, or hanging if allowed) from Kennedy Meadows (702.2) to Sonora Pass (1016.9).

779.5 (Forester Pass) to 807.1 (Pinchot Pass) -
PCT hikers are required to use canisters or bear boxes.

791.1 - Glen Pass - This is always the scariest pass for me. Going down is steep and icy. Do not do this pass very early in the morning. BINK: I agree.

Stay to the left of the bowl as you ascend.
When descending, look down between Rae Lakes, the trail goes over that spit of land.

793.5 - Rae Lakes - Bear box. After fording the connecting stream between upper and middle Rae Lakes, the PCT takes you along the shore. Watch for a sign indicating a bear box off the PCT to the left. Keep watching. You'll see it. Bad bear problems in the Rae Lakes Basin.

795.2 - Arrowhead Lake - Bear box.

798.5 - approximately - DOUBLE TAP: You will cross multiple smaller streams after turning to the west. There is a path that leads down to the north when crossing these streams that looks like the trail. It is not, keep going west and you will see a wooden fenced gate. This is the PCT and the PCT starts a short climb right after going through the gate. If you take the path to the right (north) when crossing the streams you will start heading down the valley via the streams which is the wrong way.

799.8 - Woods Creek - Bear box. Suspension bridge.
DOUBLE TAP: If there are no campsites available near the trail, head to the left (south) over a small hill where you will find plenty of campsites on the hill and behind it.

807.1 - Pinchot Pass - JOKER: When coming up the valley, you'll climb in a wooded area with no views of an obvious Pass. Once you crest above most of the timber, you may think the Pass is directly ahead. It isn't, it's 90 degrees to your left (initially). The trail makes a hard left somewhere near the timberline; pay attention to your maps to catch it. Once you're headed to the correct Pass, go high left above the basin filled with (possibly snow-covered) lakes, then swing around to the right at the top. The Pass is up there after a final gradual ascent above the basin with the lakes.

816.9 - Mather Pass - There is a lake just below the Pass. The Pass is up to the left of the lake. The PCT swings to the right of the lake, goes above the lake to the left, then switchbacks up to the actual Pass. Pay close attention to where you are. Some hikers choose to NOT take the PCT over on the right of the lake. Instead, they kick steps straight up the snow wall on the left of the lake.

831.0 - Bishop Pass Trail - There is a Ranger Station here via the use trail to the left of the PCT junction with the Bishop Pass Trail.

838.6 - Muir Pass - Watch your map on the way up and keep track of the lakes. Hikers have misjudged their location and gone up the wrong pass (the one south of Muir). Try to NOT go down Muir Pass in the afternoon. If you do, you'll be postholing for HOURS.

850.1 - Old crossing of Evolution Creek - Marked with a sign. DOUBLE TAP: Creek is wider here and the flow is not as strong as at the actual PCT crossing (mile 850.9) which makes this alternate a way better option early in the season when the creek is running strong. Later on in the season the PCT crossing at mile 850.9 is pretty EASY. Either way your feet are getting wet.

850.9 - Evolution Creek Crossing - The ford isn't that bad, but it does have some force to it. Do not cross at the trail. It's pretty deep there. Try crossing about 10 yards upstream.

855.9 - Piute Creek & Piute Pass Trail - Leave SEKI National Park.

856.7 - John Muir Cabin - BINK: A small cabin 30 yards to the south of the trail (on left of a northbounder). It is open to the public and offers some shelter in bad storms, but it is dark and somewhat dirty inside and is only about 10 x 20 feet in size.

857.7 - Florence Lake Trail - Take this trail to Muir Trail Ranch.

857.7 - Muir Trail Ranch

OVERVIEW: High Sierra Wilderness Ranch, catering to families and groups. From the MTR website: "Since we are primarily a guest ranch and our remote location makes it very difficult to receive supplies and maintain our facilities, we are only able to offer meals, hot spring baths/showers, restrooms, and laundry to guests who are staying with us overnight." [www.muirtrailranch.com]

JMT/PCT hikers are welcome to pick up mail drops, charge electronic devices, and stay overnight if space is available.

Open June-Sep (determined by snow), 8a-5p every day.

GETTING HERE: MTR is 1.5 miles off the PCT.

CONTACT:
Year-round   email [howdy@muirtrailranch.com]
October-May   call   209-966-3195

MAIL DROPS: MTR website has information on sending mail drops. 2019 fee to receive a resupply bucket is $85 for a 25-pound bucket, plus $2 per pound over 25 pounds. Fee must be prepaid. Only prepaid resupply buckets will be picked up from the Lakeshore Post Office and delivered to the Ranch. Read the VERY DETAILED INSTRUCTIONS on the website regarding sending a resupply bucket.

2017 pick up dates: 07-01-17 to 09-27-17
2018 pick up dates: 06-13-18 to 09-22-18
2019 pick up dates: Mid June to 09-30-19

OUTGOING MAIL: Priority Mail Flat Rate Boxes, pay postage plus $10 fee.

STORE: Store sells fuel canisters, batteries, matches, souvenirs.

LODGING: Short stays in tent cabins or log cabins *might* be available.
Meals are included in overnight stays. See "Short Stay" link on website for details.

COMPUTER: 2018: 15 minutes for $10

PHONE: No.

CHARGING: You can charge your electronic devices.

FUEL: Canister fuel, denatured alcohol, and white gas.

865.6 - Selden Pass - The easiest pass.

869.1 - Bear Creek - This ford can be hard. The water is deep and strong.

874.5 - Bear Ridge Trail - Alternate route to VVR (7.3 miles).

878.8 - Trail junction to Edison Lake Ferry - 1.5-mile side trail takes you to Edison Lake. There is a bear box at the lake near the spot where the ferry loads.

OVERVIEW: **Information in this Handbook from the VVR website in November 2019. New owners take over in 2020.**

559-259-4000. [info@edisonlake.com]
Open June-October (determined by snow).
Prices/services change each season.

No ATM here. **IT'S VERY EASY TO RACK UP A GIANT TAB.**
When you get your tab, be sure to carefully review all charges.

GETTING HERE: (1) Mile 878.7 - Take a 1.5 mile side trail from the PCT to Mono Creek Landing on Lake Edison, then take the ferry (2019: $13/person one way, $23 round trip). Pick up location is the flag on the beach. Pay for the ferry ride when you get to VVR.

2019: Plans are for the ferry to operate June 1 - Oct 8. Leave VVR at 9a & 4p, pick up at dock on beach near PCT at 9:45a & 4:45p. If lake is low, pickup times will be different.
Large groups with ATT service can call for pickup 559-259-4000.
The most current info is here: [www.edisonlake.com]

(2) Mile 878.7 - Walk the trail around the lake.
It is 4.5 trail miles from Mono Creek Landing to VVR.

(3) Mile 874.5 - Bear Ridge Trail - Alternate trail, 7.3 miles.

RESUPPLY: Very small store, but it's geared toward hikers.
You could resupply here only if hikers before you did not clean out the store.

Quoted from the VVR website: "Any packages left or not picked up by the specified date, will be held 30 days unless special arrangements are made. After that time period, at our discretion, we will place the food in a hikers box for other hikers in need of extra supplies at no charge. Unclaimed Hiker Resupply box contents at our discretion will be placed in the Hiker Barrels or sold in the store to offset transportation, handling and storage costs."

MAIL DROPS: Mail drops can be picked during store hours, usually 8a-8p every day.

This UPS/FedEx address IS correct; however, the UPS and FedEx systems will say that it is not. Please have the clerk override the system with this address. It WILL get delivered at this address.

UPS/FedEx only address:
Hiker's Legal Name
PCT Hiker, ETA: MM/DD/YY
Vermilion Valley Resort
c/o Rancheria Garage
62311 Huntington Lake Road
Lakeshore, CA 93634

★ **UPS or FedEx ONLY !!**
★ Be sure your mail drop arrives 10-14 days before YOU arrive!
★ Box/bucket fee is $30 each.
★ May or Sep 15-October pick up is $50 per box/bucket.
★ 25 pound limit per box or bucket. $10 surcharge for overweight boxes.
★ Must have name and ETA on four sides of package.
★ The charge to mail out boxes is postage PLUS $12/box.
★ Know how many boxes/buckets you'll have here.
★ If you don't know to ask for a package, you probably won't get it.
★ Unclaimed packages can be returned for $30 plus postage.
★ 2019: Mail available for pickup only from May 20 - October 20.

ALL SERVICES: Canvas-walled tents with wooden floors and bunk beds (use your sleeping bag).
There are also a few motel rooms available, rates $$$ +
Two nights in the Hiker Camping area for free.
Good restaurant, small store, laundry, showers, PCT Register, computer.

FUEL: Denatured alcohol by the ounce, canister fuel, white gas.

878.7 - Mono Hot Springs

OVERVIEW: 559-325-1710. Open May 15-Nov 1 (determined by snow).

GETTING HERE: (1) PCT mile 878.7 - Take VVR / Edison Lake Ferry, then hitch.
(See VVR Handbook page)

(2) PCT mile 857.7 - Take Florence Lake Trail to Florence Lake,
then take Florence Lake Ferry, then hitch.
Ferry on trail side of lake: 9a, 11a, 1p, 3p, 5p
2018: $13 one way, $25 round trip
[www.florence-lake.com]

(3) PCT mile 874.5 - Take the Bear Creek drainage trail.

POST OFFICE: 7:30a-9p every day, USPS only   USPS summer address:
PO summer season: May 15-Nov 1   Hiker's Legal Name
Mail must have "Hold Until" date.   PCT Hiker, Hold Until: MM/DD/YY
If not, it will be held for only 10 days.   General Delivery
Outgoing mail: June 1-Sep 15   Mono Hot Springs, CA 93642

RESUPPLY: Store is open 7:30a-9p every day: name-brand staples, fresh milk, fruits, vegetables, ice, frozen meats, ice cream, soft drinks, beer, wine, candy.

LODGING: Cabins sleep 1-5 people. No TV. Rates $$$ +
Tent Cabins sleep 1-7 people. Rates $$ +

CAMPING: Mono Hot Springs Campground (NFS Fee Campground) adjacent to the Resort. "Absolutely no personal tents are allowed on Resort property."

RESTAURANT: Hours vary depending upon time of year.
Generally open every day mid-June until Labor Day.
Memorial day to mid-June: Dinner only
Labor day to end of September: Lunch Fri-Sun, Dinner every day
Custom orders for killer breakfast burritos for next day/morning pickup.

OTHER SERVICES: Massages, hot springs, showers.

Leaving VVR - The PCT crosses Mono Creek three times. These crossings can be very strong late in the day. Think about this if you take the afternoon ferry out of VVR.

884.9 - Silver Pass - On the way down, keep looking ahead for a glimpse of the trail. This descent us usually pretty snow-covered. Pay attention to your map!

889.5 - Tully Hole - Watch for the turn! Hikers often miss this turn.

890.5-ish (above Tully Hole) to 895.9-ish (Duck Lake outlet) - Bear canisters required.

891.6 - Virginia Lake inflow - DOUBLE TAP: Right after crossing the inflow look to your right and you will see a group of trees a few hundred feet from the trail. Behind these trees are a few good campsites.

903.3 - Horseshoe Lake Trail to Mammoth Lakes - You could take this 3.4-mile side trail to Mammoth Lakes, then hitch or shuttle 5 miles. Or, you could stay on the PCT for 3.5 miles farther until you reach Reds Meadow, where there is a bus that can take you to Mammoth Lakes. The bus runs periodically through the day, but it doesn't start running until mid-June. It all depends on the snow.

903.9 - Mammoth Pass Trail Junction - Also goes to Mammoth Lakes.

906.7 - Reds Meadow

OVERVIEW:	Open approximately mid-June to October 1 (dates determined by snow). If you are early in the season, Reds Meadow may not be open AND the busses to Mammoth may not be running. Store phone 760-934-2345.
	The restaurant and the store open at 7a and close at 7p SHARP.
GETTING HERE:	Turn right on the Abandoned Stagecoach Road, walk 0.3 mile past several cabins and horse corrals. You will eventually reach the store and restaurant. You'll know it when you see it.
SHUTTLE:	East Side Sierra Shuttle: paul@inyopro.com 760-878-8047 Shuttle anywhere in the Sierra Nevada, including trailheads
MAIL DROPS:	Print mail drop form: [www.redsmeadow.com] 2019: Mail drop fee is $40. Fee must be paid 2 weeks in advance. Pick up your mail drop at the store between 7a-7p every day. Outgoing mail is letters only. Unclaimed packages are not returned or forwarded.
RESUPPLY:	Sometimes the store has good resupply. Store is open 7a-7p.
LODGING:	Cabins and motel rooms available. 760-934-2345. Rates: $$$$+ Two JMT/PCT hiker cabins. Each has one set of bunk beds. Rates: $$
CAMPING:	Fee Campground. Usually open mid-June to mid-Sept. There are two campsites reserved specifically for JMT/PCT hikers. Two tents per site.
RESTAURANT:	Diner-type restaurant. 7a-7p.
SHOWER:	Pay showers.
FUEL:	Canister fuel at store.

906.7 - Mammoth Lakes CA

OVERVIEW:	Hiker-friendly, good bus system, great places to eat.
GETTING HERE:	Mammoth Lakes is about 8 miles from Reds Meadow. Three options:

(1) Mile 903.3 - From Upper Crater Meadow, take the 3.4-mile Horseshoe Lake Trail over Mammoth Pass to Horseshoe Lake, then take the local shuttle 5 miles into town (or hitch).

(2) Mile 906.7 - From Reds Meadow, take the Reds Meadow Shuttle ($7) from to the Adventure Center (Mammoth Mountain Lodge). Shuttle operates from late June through 2 days after Labor Day. Service operates every 20 minutes or less from 10a to 4p, and every 45 minutes or less from 7:30a to 10a and from 4p to 7p. The last bus departs Reds Meadow Resort at 7:45p. Then take the free Mammoth bus from the Adventure Center to town. Bus info at the end of Mammoth Lakes section.

(3) Mile 914.9 - From Agnew Meadow, take the Reds Meadow Shuttle ($7) to the Adventure Center (Mammoth Mtn Lodge). Take the local shuttle from the Adventure Center to town (see #1 above).

BUS SERVICE:	See bus information after the Lone Pine Handbook section.
	Reds Meadow Shuttle bus: If you are early in the season, Reds Meadow may not be open AND the busses to Mammoth may not be running. Opening date is mid-June. It all depends on the snow. Info: Sierra Transit Authority Mammoth Lakes Office 760-924-3184.

TAXI SERVICE:	Mammoth Taxi/Backpacker Shuttle	760-934-8294
	Mammoth Cab	760-924-2227
	My Mammoth Shuttle	760-709-6459

CAR RENTAL:	Enterprise (airport)	760-924-1094
	Hertz (inside Kittredge Sports)	760-934-7004
	Hertz (airport)	760-934-2271

SHUTTLE: East Side Sierra Shuttle: paul@inyopro.com 760-878-8047
Shuttle anywhere in the Sierra Nevada, including trailheads

POST OFFICE:	760-934-2205, USPS only	Hiker's Legal Name
	Mon-Fri 8a-4p	PCT Hiker, ETA: MM/DD/YY
	Sat closed	General Delivery
		Mammoth Lakes, CA 93546

OUTGOING MAIL: Mammoth Business Essentials 760-924-2257 UPS, USPS, FedEx
Mon-Fri 8:30-5:30p. Sat 9a-3p. Sun closed.

RESUPPLY: Vons Supermarket 760-934-4536 Open 24 hours

Sierra Sundance Whole Foods Market 760-934-8122
Mon-Sat 9a-6p, Sun 9a-5p
In the Rite Aid shopping center

OUTFITTER: Mammoth Mountaineering Supply 760-934-4191
8a-8p every day
PCT discount

Kittredge Sports 760-934-7566 Mon-Th 7a-8p, Fri-Sat 7a-9p, Sun 7a-8p

Footloose Sports 760-934-2400 8a-8p every day. Get new shoes here.

RESTAURANTS: Many restaurants. Here are some favorites:

Latin Market	Behind Rite Aid. Best tacos in town.
Breakfast Club	Tasty breakfast. 6a-1p. Cash only.
Base Camp Café	Large breakfasts, reasonable prices.
John's Pizza	Delicious pizza.
Schat's Bakkery	Delicious bread, pastries, cookies, and a little sandwich restaurant in the back of the bakkery.

LAUNDRY: Yes.

SHOWER: At the Campground.

ATM: Yes.

COMPUTER: Mammoth Lakes Library 760-934-4777

FUEL:	Napa Auto Parts	760-934-3375	HEET
	DIY Home Center	760-924-7112	Denatured Alcohol
	Mammoth Mountaineering	760-934-4191	Denatured, canisters, white gas.

MEDICAL: Mammoth Hospital 760-934-3311

THEATER: Minaret Cinema 760-934-3131

SEAMSTRESS: Leslie's Alterations. Repairs backpacks, zippers, and clothing.
760-934-6027 or 760-937-0354 (cell). [mtnfrog1@verizon.net]

MAMMOTH LODGING		Rates	frig micr	TV	laundry	pool	hot tub	bkfst
Motel 6	760-904-6991	$$$	some	Y	Y	Y	no	no
Quality Inn	760-934-5114	$$$	Y	Y	Y	no	Y	hot
Alpenhof Lodge	760-934-6330	$$$$	Y	Y	Y	Y	Y	cont
Holiday Haus & Maderne Hostel	760-934-2414	rooms $$$$ hostel $	no	Y	no	no	no	cont for motel
Rodeway Inn	760-934-6855	$$$	most	Y	no	Y	Y	cont
TraveLodge	760-934-8892	$$	Y	Y	Y	no	Y	cont
Sierra Lodge	760-934-8881	$$	all kitchenettes	Y	Y	no	Y	cont
Davison Street Hostel	760-924-2188	$ dorm ask for PCT rate $$$ + private	Check in after 4:30p. Check out before 11a. Linens provided. Quiet time after 10p. Community kitchen.					
New Shady Rest Campground		Camping $	Bear boxes, picnic tables, bathrooms. Showers across the street.					
Mammoth Mtn RV Park	760-934-3822	Camping $	Camping, cabins, shower, laundry, indoor heated pool, spa, rec room.					
		$ = usually less than $50 $$ = usually $50-$80 $$$ = usually $80-$110 $$$$ = usually greater than $110						

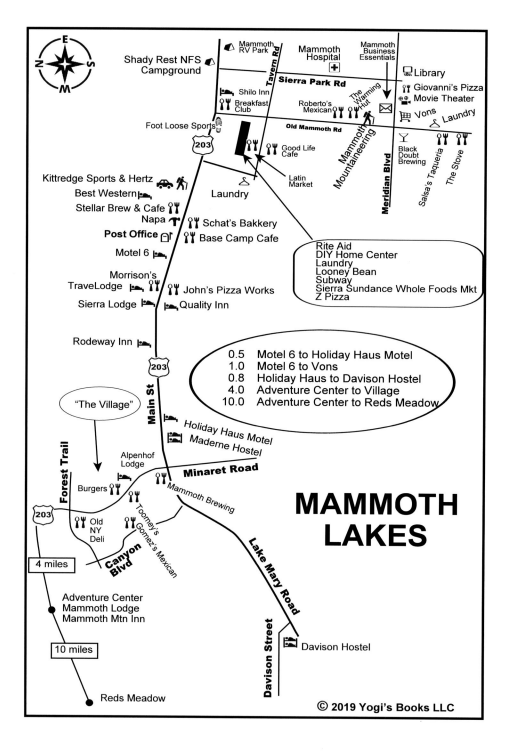

Shady Rest NFS Campground
Mammoth RV Park
Mammoth Hospital
Mammoth Business Essentials
Library
Sierra Park Rd
Giovanni's Pizza
Movie Theater
Shilo Inn
Breakfast Club
Roberto's Mexican
The Warming Hut
Vons
Laundry
Foot Loose Sports
Old Mammoth Rd
Mammoth Mountaineering
203
Good Life Cafe
Black Doubt Brewing
Salsa's Taqueria
The Stove
Meridian Blvd
Latin Market
Kittredge Sports & Hertz
Laundry
Best Western
Stellar Brew & Cafe
Napa
Schat's Bakkery
Post Office
Base Camp Cafe
Motel 6

Rite Aid
DIY Home Center
Laundry
Looney Bean
Subway
Sierra Sundance Whole Foods Mkt
Z Pizza

Morrison's
TraveLodge
John's Pizza Works
Sierra Lodge
Quality Inn

Rodeway Inn

203

0.5   Motel 6 to Holiday Haus Motel
1.0   Motel 6 to Vons
0.8   Holiday Haus to Davison Hostel
4.0   Adventure Center to Village
10.0   Adventure Center to Reds Meadow

"The Village"

Main St

Holiday Haus Motel
Maderne Hostel

Forest Trail

Alpenhof Lodge

Minaret Road

Burgers

Mammoth Brewing

203

Old NY Deli

Toomey's

Gomez's Mexican

Canyon Blvd

MAMMOTH LAKES

4 miles

Lake Mary Road

Adventure Center
Mammoth Lodge
Mammoth Mtn Inn

10 miles

Davison Street

Davison Hostel

Reds Meadow

© 2019 Yogi's Books LLC

LEAVING REDS MEADOW - Bear canisters are required from before Reds Meadow (906.7) until you leave Yosemite National Park at Dorothy Lake Pass (997.1).

906.8 - Rainbow Falls Trail Junction - DOUBLE TAP: Definitely go see Rainbow Falls as it is incredible and only a short 30 minute round trip hike.

909.0 - JMT and PCT diverge - The JMT is on the left side of a valley, the PCT is on the right. The JMT side (14.1 miles) has more ups-and-downs, and is more scenic than the PCT side. The PCT side (13.9 miles) climbs up the ridge, and mostly stays high.

914.9 - Agnew Meadow Trailhead - Spigot and privy.
Bus stop is 0.3 mile away. Bus goes to Reds Meadow and Mammoth Lakes.

922.9 - JMT and PCT merge - at Thousand Island Lake. Bad bear trouble some years.

929.6 - Donohue Pass - Enter Yosemite National Park. On the final approach to Donohue Pass, you're walking across a flat-ish area with a bunch of stream crossings. Ahead of you is a ridge with a few possible low points that could be THE PASS. Walk toward the ridge. When you can't go any further without climbing the ridge, veer left. You keep the flat-ish area to your left, and you hug the ridge to your right. Look for cairns marking the trail (which continues traversing below the ridge for a while). As you're looking up at the ridge, trying to figure out which low point is Donohue Pass, watch your map carefully. Donohue Pass is the farthest low point on the ridge, to the southwest. I think there were three low points that we thought could be Donohue, and it was the farthest one — maybe the third choice??? Each time I've been here, I've been confused.

931.2 - Lyell Fork Crossing - Don't camp any closer to Tuolumne than this. The farther you go down in elevation, the more active the bears are. Bear problems are common Lyell Canyon.

940.1 - APPROACHING TUOLUMNE -
After crossing the first bridge at mile 940.2, a trail sign indicates "Tuolumne 1.4 miles." Go right.

940.8 - Junction - Campground / PO / Store are to the left. Lodge and PCT to the right.

Yosemite Area Transit (YARTS)

877-989-2787 [www.yarts.com]

2019 Schedule June, September, October

The Village	Mammoth Lakes Mammoth Mtn Inn	The Village	Mammoth Lakes Shilo Inn	Lee Vining Whoa Nellie	Tuolumne Mdws Store	Yosemite Valley Visitor Center
	8:00a	8:07a	8:20a	9:22a	9:57a	11:47a
8:30p	8:20p		7:57p	7:32p	6:50p	5:00p

2019 Schedule July and August

The Village	Mammoth Lakes Mammoth Mtn Inn	The Village	Mammoth Lakes Shilo Inn	Lee Vining Whoa Nellie	Tuolumne Mdws Store	Yosemite Valley Visitor Center
	6:45a	6:52a	7:05a	8:07a	8:42a	10:32a
	8:00a	8:07a	8:20a	9:22a	9:57a	11:47a
7:35p	7:25p		7:02p	6:37p	5:55p	4:05p
8:30p	8:20p		7:57p	7:32p	6:50p	5:00p

Tuolumne Meadows CA

All services open mid-June to mid-September (dates determined by snow).
All resupply boxes will be at the PO/Store, not at the Lodge.

941.7 - The Tuolumne Lodge

OVERVIEW: Tent cabins with wood-burning stoves, restaurant.

GETTING HERE: When you reach the junction at mile 941.7, go right. You'll see a large parking lot. Stay to the right end of the parking lot, you'll see the Lodge. It's not an actual building. Not a lodge at all! It's a temporary building with white walls. You'll also see several white tent cabins. These aren't actual cabins. Not cabins at all! Nope, they're tents.

RESUPPLY: Only has chips, a little candy, and fresh fruit.

LODGING: If the Lodge is not already full, hikers can rent tent cabins (sleep 4 people), which have wood-burning stoves. Shower is included in your stay.
Lodge reservations: 888-413-8869
Rates: $$$$

RESTAURANT: The Lodge serves family-style dinner and breakfast, reservations are required for dinner. Direct line to the Lodge 209-372-8413 (for reservations).
Or, just ask at the Lodge. Getting a dinner reservation is easy.
Dinner served 5:30p-8p family style.
Breakfast served 7a-9a family style. Boxed lunches for purchase.

SHOWER: Showers are only for Lodge guests.

942.5 - Highway 120 / Tuolumne Post Office and Store

OVERVIEW: Snack bar, grocery store, outdoor store, Post Office, campground.

GETTING HERE: (1) PCT mile 940.8 - Go left at the junction. You'll stay in the woods, cross a creek, then walk along a campground road. When you reach Highway 120, turn left. You will be at the PO/Store within minutes.

(2) PCT mile 942.5 - Stay on the PCT until you reach Highway 120. Turn left on the highway. You will be at the PO/Store within minutes.

POST OFFICE: The opening date of the PO/Store is determined by the snowfall.
The PO/Store could open as late as July, but it usually opens sometime in June. Call the Yosemite Valley PO (209-372-4475) around May 1 to find out when the road is expected to be cleared of snow, and when the PO/Store will open. Don't send a box unless you know the PO/Store will be open when you get here.

If Tuolumne is not open, mail will be at the Yosemite Valley PO (209-372-4475).

Tuolumne PO: 209-372-8236. The Tuolumne Post Office is in the same building as the store. Approximate hours are Mon-Fri 9a-5p. Sat 10a-1p. Sunday pickup usually okay. Hours vary and they close for lunch!

USPS only. Allow a couple extra days for your box to get here. Per a phone call to Michael at the Tuolumne PO, you should address your box exactly like this:

Hiker's Legal Name
Hiker's Trail Name
PCT Hiker, ETA: MM/DD/YY
General Delivery
c/o Tuolumne Post Office
Yosemite National Park, CA 95389

Hikers can leave notes for other hikers at the Tuolumne Post Office.

For Search-and-Rescue assistance, Michael at the Tuolumne PO requests that hikers put BOTH their legal name and their trail name on packages.

If you've got an ETA on your box, they will hold your box for a month. With no ETA, it will be held for 2 weeks only. This is a tiny Post Office. Do something to make your box easily identifiable: colored paper, colored tape, stickers, something like that. The PO is attached to the store.

RESUPPLY:	Tuolumne Store 209-372-8609. Surprisingly good store, you could resupply here. However, in 2018 the only dinners were Ramen. Store hours are approximately 9a-5p before the High Sierra Camps open up. After the Camps open, the store hours are approximately 9a-8p. Hours vary!! When the road is first cleared, and the store first opens up, the store might be open for a few hours each afternoon.
CAMPING:	The Fee Campground is behind the PO/Store. Find the backpacker site. There are bear boxes at the campground. Be sure to use the bear boxes for all your smellables. Chances are very good that a bear will stroll through the campground. No showers at the campground.
RESTAURANTS:	Grill attached to the PO/Store. Usually open 8a-6p.
LAUNDRY:	No.
SHOWERS:	No.
ATM:	Yes, but out of order in 2018.
FUEL:	Denatured, canisters, and white gas usually at the Tuolumne Store.
MEDICAL:	Yosemite Medical Clinic in Yosemite Valley 209-372-4637 Mammoth Hospital in Mammoth Lakes 760-934-3311
BUGS & BEARS:	When you leave Tuolumne, BE SURE you have a lot of DEET. The next 150 miles are mosquito hell. Bears are active close to Tuolumne. Unless you're camping at Glen Aulin (where there are bear boxes), try to camp at least 15 miles north of Tuolumne.
SOUTH LAKE TAHOE:	Try to plan your days north of Tuolumne so that you do not arrive in South Lake Tahoe on Friday or Saturday. Weekend motel rates in South Lake Tahoe much more expensive than the weekday rates.

YOSEMITE VALLEY

- Many PCT hikers finish the JMT by hiking 22 miles down to Yosemite Valley.

- Permit required to hike down to the Valley and/or camp along the way. Per the YNP website: "Pacific Crest Trail through-hikers with a valid permit issued by the Pacific Crest Trail Association do not need an additional wilderness permit in order to camp in the Yosemite Wilderness while along the Pacific Crest Trail. However, if you plan to hike elsewhere in Yosemite (off of the Pacific Crest Trail) and camp overnight, you will need to get a separate wilderness permit. PCT through permits are also not valid to ascend the Half Dome cables or visit Yosemite Valley."
[https://www.nps.gov/yose/planyourvisit/jmt.htm]

What does this mean for a PCT hiker who wants to hike down to Yosemite Valley?
Your PCTA permit does NOT cover you for the JMT from Tuolumne to Yosemite Valley.

You're a PCT hiker. You can EASILY cover the 22 miles from Tuolumne to Yosemite Valley in one day without camping along the way. Because you are not camping, you might think you can hike from Tuolumne to the Valley without a permit. Nope. If you are carrying overnight gear, you must have a separate wilderness permit, issued at the Tuolumne Ranger Station. Why? Well, you have overnight gear. You could easily try to stealth camp without a permit. Because you are prepared to camp overnight, you must have a permit.

- Half Dome (special permit required to ascend Half Dome) is along the way.

- Tuolumne Wilderness Center issues permits (see Tuolumne Handbook map).
Open 8a-4:30p every day.

- Halfmile maps this route on the last four pages of California Section H [www.pctmap.net]

TUOLUMNE

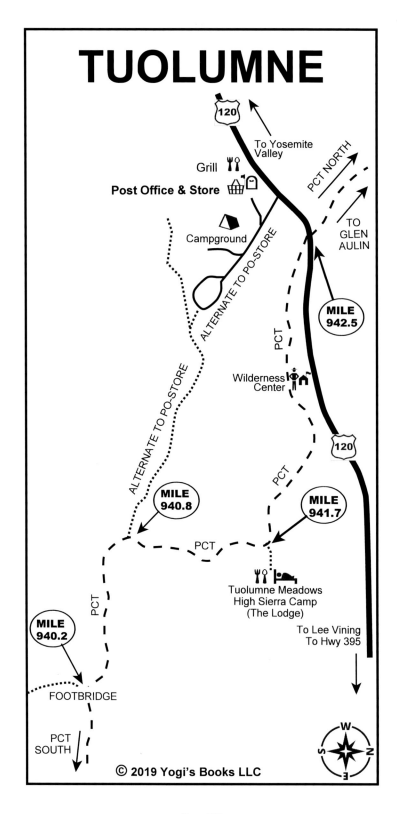

OVERVIEW: Touristy, but quiet. Good food and lodging.

GETTING HERE: Hitch or take the bus 19 miles from Tuolumne Meadows.

BUS SERVICE: See bus information in the Tuolumne Meadows Handbook section and after the Lone Pine Handbook section.

SHUTTLE: East Side Sierra Shuttle: paul@inyopro.com 760-878-8047
Shuttle anywhere in the Sierra Nevada, including trailheads

POST OFFICE:
760-647-6371, USPS only
Mon-Fri 9a-1p and 2p-4p
Sat closed
General Delivery held 30 days

Hiker's Legal Name
PCT Hiker, ETA: MM/DD/YY
General Delivery
121 Lee Vining Ave
Lee Vining, CA 93541

RESUPPLY:

Mono Market	760-647-1010	Small grocery store, beer No Knorr or Idahoan, just a few ramen
Tioga Gas Mart	760-647-1088	Large C-Store, beer & wine Snacks only, no dinners
Chevron	760-647-6330	C-Store, beer

OUTDOOR STORE: Beaver's Sporting Goods 760-647-6406 Mountain House, tenacious tape, canister fuel, lots of Coghlan's brand

LODGING:

Lake View Lodge	760-647-6543	Laundry on site. $$$$+ Motel Rooms with AC and TV. Cottages with kitchens and TV. Bare bones cabins, bed/bedding only, shared bathroom.
Lee Vining Motel	760-647-6440	Open from 4p-8p, does not take reservations. No AC.
Murphey's Lodging	760-647-6316	Must check in by 8p. Refrigerator, TV, AC.
Yosemite Gateway	760-647-6467	Some rooms have AC. $$$$+

CAMPING: Mono Vista RV Park 760-647-6401
Tent sites, shower, laundry, community room, game room, horseshoe pits.

RESTAURANTS: Whoa Nellie Deli 760-647-1088.
Don't miss this nationally renowned restaurant!

LAUNDRY: Yes.

SHOWER: At RV Park.

ATM: Yes.

COMPUTER: Library 760-647-6123

FUEL:

Tioga Gas Mart	760-647-1088	Quart denatured alcohol
Beaver's Sporting Goods	760-647-6406	Quart denatured alcohol, Esbits, canister fuel

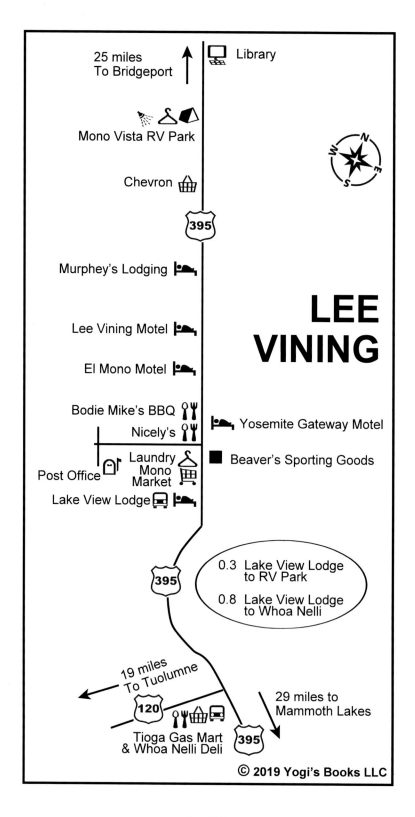

25 miles
To Bridgeport

Library

Mono Vista RV Park

Chevron

395

Murphey's Lodging

Lee Vining Motel

El Mono Motel

Bodie Mike's BBQ

Nicely's

Post Office

Laundry
Mono
Market

Lake View Lodge

LEE VINING

Yosemite Gateway Motel

Beaver's Sporting Goods

395

0.3 Lake View Lodge
     to RV Park

0.8 Lake View Lodge
     to Whoa Nelli

19 miles
To Tuolumne

120

Tioga Gas Mart
& Whoa Nelli Deli

395

29 miles to
Mammoth Lakes

© 2019 Yogi's Books LLC

LEAVING TUOLUMNE - With your back to the store, turn right on the highway and walk for 0.2 mile until you get to the PCT. Cross the highway. Take a gravel/dirt road that goes to Glen Aulin. Go past the gate. The road forks when you can see a bridge in the distance. Don't go to the bridge. Take the right fork of the road. Immediately there is another fork. Go left. Walk up the hill past the soda springs. A cabin is off to your left. The PCT does not go to the cabin. Stay to the right and follow the PCT up into the woods.

> **Bear canisters are required** from before Reds Meadow (906.7) until you leave Yosemite National Park at Dorothy Lake Pass (997.1).

948.3 - Glen Aulin - Bear boxes here. Bears here, too.

> DOUBLE TAP: Take the trail to the left at the Glen Aulin bridge junction to check out Waterwheel Falls which is ~3 miles down the Grand Canyon of the Tuolumne River. Waterwheel Falls is the most unique waterfall I have ever seen and there is a large horse camp at the bottom of the falls 0.1 mile off the trail to the left in a large grove of trees. You will go down ~1,000 ft in the process which you will have to climb back up, so keep that in mind.

956.2 - Virginia Canyon Trail - BINK: Return Creek in Virginia Canyon can be a dangerous ford.

962.0 - Matterhorn Canyon Trail Junction - DOUBLE TAP: Large horse camp after you cross Matterhorn Creek. After crossing the creek keep walking straight back for ~100ft and you will find it in a grove of trees that you can see from the PCT.

968.4 - Smedberg Lake - DOUBLE TAP: One of the few lakes that is not frigid as it gets a lot of direct sunlight. A great place to take a dip and a break.

972.7 - Benson Lake Trail - DOUBLE TAP: Follow the trail to the left for 0.5 mile for white sand beach Benson Lake. Lots of mosquitoes if it is not windy.

979.8 - Rancheria Creek in Kerrick Canyon - This was always the toughest creek crossing. VERY strong water. BINK: This can be a dangerous ford.

982.3 - Stubblefield Canyon - DOUBLE TAP: Terrible mosquitoes here.

997.1 - Dorothy Lake Pass - Depart Yosemite National Park.

1008.8 - Cross the crest - JOKER: Epic ridge walk. Camping from here until Sonora Pass is very exposed. Before Sonora Pass, there are sometimes glissades which will save a mile or two.

1016.9 - Sonora Pass / Highway 108

1040.8 - Wolf Creek Pass and 1044.1 Junction to Asa Lake -
Watch the trail junctions carefully.

1048.4 - Highway 4 near Ebbetts Pass

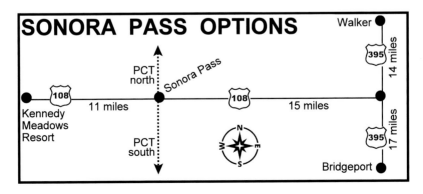

1016.9 - (Northern) Kennedy Meadows Resort

OVERVIEW: Excellent place for PCT'ers to stay/hang out.

Open from the last weekend in April to Columbus Day weekend in October.

Call only between 8a-7:30p Pacific time.
209-965-3900 or 209-965-3911 - Phone summer
209-965-3900 - Phone winter
[www.kennedymeadows.com]

GETTING HERE: Daily shuttle to/from Sonora Pass.

From Sonora Pass, hitch left on Hwy 108.
Best hitching from the trailhead (100 yards farther on the PCT).
Approximately 10 miles down the highway, you'll see a big "Kennedy Meadows" road sign here. Take this left. Go one mile down dirt road to Kennedy Meadows Resort.

MAIL DROPS: **There are TWO places called Kennedy Meadows.**
The other Kennedy Meadows is at PCT mile 702.2.
Make sure you send your box to the correct Kennedy Meadows.

2019: $15-$30 fee. Packages only received May 1 - October 1.
Unclaimed packages are discarded on October 15.
Must have ETA on box. **UPS only !!**

Hiker's Legal Name
PCT Hiker, ETA: MM/DD/YY
c/o Kennedy Meadows Resort and Pack Station
42421 State Highway 108
Pinecrest, CA 95364

OUTGOING MAIL: Outgoing mail via USPS. You can mail out your bear canister, ice axe, etc.

RESUPPLY: Camp store has good hiker resupply, snacks, ice cream, cheese, etc.

BEAR CANISTERS: Southbounders can pick up bear canister rentals here.
Return to Triple Crown Outfitters in KM south.
Prepay and information: [www.triplecrownoutfitters.com]

LODGING: PCT SPECIAL ($40/night) - includes a bed in a shared room with other hikers in the lodge, with shower, laundry, and Wi-Fi. Check out time 10am.

CAMPING: Yes.

There is also a campground adjacent to KM Resort. Usually $10/night. Possible free PCT camping in the overflow area. You must check in with the campground host first.

LAUNDRY: Yes.

SHOWER: Yes.

CELL SERVICE: No. Two pay phones available. Purchase phone cards in store.

COMPUTER: No.

RESTAURANTS: Restaurant offering breakfast, lunch and dinner from 6am to 9pm. We have a full breakfast, lunch and dinner menu with nightly specials including prime rib, baby back ribs, Italian night, many other dinners. Dinner menu also includes many steak, fish, and other options. Dinners include soup, salad and dessert. Prices are fair and portions are plentiful!

FUEL: Canister fuel.

OVERVIEW: Compact, very expensive, with a long 2-part hitch.
Kennedy Meadows Resort is a much better option.

GETTING HERE: From the PCT crossing at Sonora Pass, hitch to the right on
Highway 108 East, then Highway 395 South to Bridgeport.
It's approximately 32 miles.

BUS SERVICE: See bus information after the Lone Pine Handbook section.

SHUTTLE: East Side Sierra Shuttle: paul@inyopro.com 760-878-8047
Shuttle anywhere in the Sierra Nevada, including trailheads

Hill's Shuttle Service: 209-329-4745, leave message.
Serves PCT, Eastern Sierra, local airports

POST OFFICE: 760-932-7991, USPS only
Mon-Fri 8a-noon and 1p-4p. Sat closed, but
usually hikers can pick up packages on Sat
from 10:30a-1p. Knock on door.

Hiker's Legal Name
PCT Hiker, ETA: MM/DD/YY
General Delivery
29 Kingsley Street
Bridgeport, CA 93517

When hiker mail arrives, Postmaster scans it as
"delivered." He then holds hiker mail until the end
of September.

RESUPPLY: General Store 760-932-7224 Open usually 7a-10p every day in summer.
Terrible hiker resupply.
Very few snacks, no dinners.

OUTDOOR STORE: Ken's Sporting Goods 760-932-7707
Fishing store has canister fuel, Mountain House, bug spray

RESTAURANTS: Many.

LAUNDRY: No.

ATM: At General Store.

COMPUTER: Library 760-932-7482

FUEL: HEET at Napa Auto Parts 760-932-7043
Also at one of the gas stations.

BRIDGEPORT LODGING		Rates	AC	TV	micr	frig	other stuff
Bridgeport Inn 760-932-7380	Economy Rooms	$$$ +	no	no	no	no	shared bath
	Other Rooms		Y	Y	no	no	private bath
Redwood Motel 760-932-7060		$$$ +	Y	most	Y	Y	private bath
Ruby Inn 760-932-7241		$$$$	Y	Y	Y	Y	cont bkfst
Silver Maple Inn 760-932-7383		$$$$	Y	Y	no	Y	
Walker River Lodge 760-932-7021		$$$$	Y	Y	Y	Y	pool & spa. suites avail. cont bkfst
Rates: $$$ = usually $80-$110 $$$$ = usually greater than $110							

SIX MILES SOUTH OF BRIDGEPORT ON HIGHWAY 395:
Willow Springs Motel & RV Park 760-932-7725 Cabins, laundry, shower
Virginia Creek Settlement 760-932-7780 Tent cabins, cabins, motel rooms, camping, restaurant, shower

BRIDGEPORT

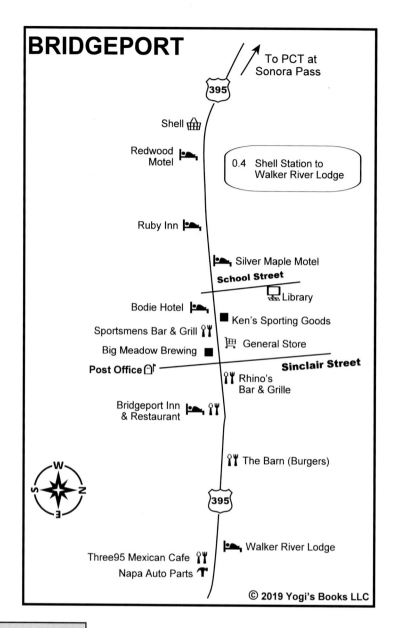

To PCT at Sonora Pass

395

Shell

Redwood Motel

0.4 Shell Station to Walker River Lodge

Ruby Inn

Silver Maple Motel

School Street

Library

Bodie Hotel

Ken's Sporting Goods

Sportsmens Bar & Grill

General Store

Big Meadow Brewing

Post Office

Sinclair Street

Rhino's Bar & Grille

Bridgeport Inn & Restaurant

The Barn (Burgers)

395

Walker River Lodge

Three95 Mexican Cafe

Napa Auto Parts

© 2019 Yogi's Books LLC

1016.9 - Walker CA

OVERVIEW: Compact, with a long hitch. Lodging is much cheaper here than in Bridgeport.

GETTING HERE: From the PCT crossing at Sonora Pass, hitch to the right on Hwy 108 East, then Hwy 395 North to Walker. It's approximately 29 miles.

BUS SERVICE: Walker Dial-a-Ride. 530-402-6832. [www.estransit.com] Mon-Thur 8a-4:30p.

There is a fixed bus route from Walker to Coleville Post Office, Mon-Wed-Fri only, one round trip per day. [www.estransit.com]

POST OFFICE:	NO POST OFFICE IN WALKER. Coleville CA Post Office is 5 miles north of Walker. 530-495-2133. Mon-Fri 8a-11p, 11:30a-2:30p. Sat 9:30a-11:30a. Call Post Office BEFORE mailing your package. Postmaster needs to know your mail is coming. USPS only. General Delivery held for 30 days. USPS only.	Hiker's Legal Name PCT Hiker, ETA: MM/DD/YY General Delivery Coleville, CA 96107

RESUPPLY: Walker Country Store and Deli   Small grocery store
530-495-2945. Mon-Sat 6a-9p. Sun 7a-8p.

Walker General Store. C-Store.

RESTAURANTS:	Yes.
LAUNDRY:	Yes.
ATM:	At General Store.

WALKER LODGING		Rates	AC	TV	micr	frig	other stuff
Andruss Motel	530-495-2216	$$$	Y	Y	Y	Y	kitchenette available. pool.
Sierra Retreat Motel	530-495-2213	$$	Y	Y	kitchens		
Toiyabe Motel	530-495-2280	$$	Y	Y	Y	Y	
West Walker Motel	530-495-2263	$$	Y	Y	Y	Y	
		Rates: $$ = usually $50-$80. $$$ = usually $80-$110					

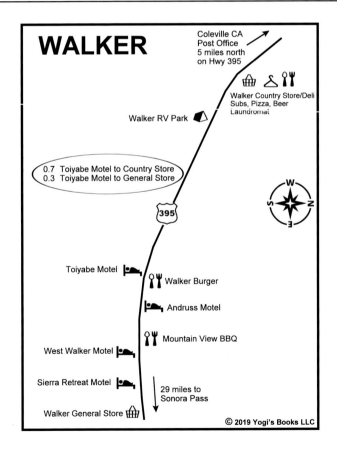

OVERVIEW: Tiny town only a few blocks long. Hiker-friendly with good resupply.

GETTING HERE: At Ebbetts Pass, hitch to the right 18 miles on Hwy 4 (which turns into Hwy 89).

POST OFFICE: 530-694-2125, USPS only
Mon-Fri 8:30a-11a, noon-3:30p
Sat 8:30a-10:30a
General Delivery held for 15 days

       Hiker's Legal Name
PCT Hiker, ETA: MM/DD/YY
General Delivery
Markleeville, CA 96120

RESUPPLY: Markleeville General Store   530-694-2448.
         Grocery store with good hiker resupply.

LODGING: Creekside Lodge   530-694-2511   Rates $$$

RESTAURANT: Yes.

LAUNDRY: No.

ATM   No.

COMPUTER: Library
530-694-2120

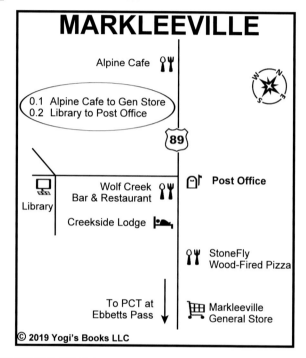

MARKLEEVILLE

Alpine Cafe

0.1 Alpine Cafe to Gen Store
0.2 Library to Post Office

89

Library

Wolf Creek
Bar & Restaurant

Post Office

Creekside Lodge

StoneFly
Wood-Fired Pizza

To PCT at
Ebbetts Pass

Markleeville
General Store

© 2019 Yogi's Books LLC

1060.4 - Campsite - DOUBLE TAP: Large campground with multiple campsites and a fire ring.

1067.1 - approximately - BINK: About a mile and a half (?) past Blue Lakes Road is a small stream that often runs across the trail, and if not is usually running just above the trail. It is probably snow-melt-fed and thus I would assume it dry by August. A nice flat camping area is located above the trail on the south side of the stream as well about 100 feet uphill.

1069.7 - Lost Lakes Spur Road - The PCT crosses the road, then goes slightly right. There is a faint path in front of you, with a PCT marker high up on a tree. The PCT does not go down the road. It crosses the road.

1071.1 - Muddy Pond - Sign on the left "No ATV's . . ." Don't take that road/trail. Go straight, kind of over a small rise. If this area is covered in snow, look carefully for cairns up on the rise.

     SOCKS: Pay attention to this small intersection and make your life easier. Go STRAIGHT. Not left. Not right. STRAIGHT.

1074.0 to 1075.0 - Elephant's Back - At the end of the climb, you may find a huge hunk 'o snow here on the east side of Elephant's Back.

1076.6 - Carson Pass / Highway 88 - Visitor Information Station has PCT Register and water for PCT hikers. No snack or soda machines.

> Sorensen's Resort   10 miles north on Highway 88. 800-423-9949.
> Restaurant. Rooms and cabins $$$$.

HINT - There are two parking lots here. To continue north on the PCT, walk down Highway 88 to the left until you reach the other parking lot. Go to the far northwest end of that parking lot and you'll see the PCT trailhead. Lots of mosquitos between Carson Pass and Echo Lake.

1090.0 - Trailhead Parking- The PCT emerges at a large parking lot and then you don't know where to go. Stay to the left side of the parking lot, walk along a service road, and keep watching the woods on your left. You soon will see the PCT again.

> JOKER: I say cut to the road and hitch to South Lake Tahoe from here.
> I've hitched here twice and never had trouble finding a ride.
> I prefer SLT over Echo Lake. SLT is one of the best stops on the entire trail.

1090.7 - Highway 50 - MINER: It's probably better to look for a ride to South Lake Tahoe from Echo Lake (mile 1092.3) rather than Hwy 50. I got hassled by two young deputies for hitchhiking on the highway. They had no knowledge or interest in the trail and had no idea what I was doing there and didn't care.

1092.3 - Echo Lake CA

OVERVIEW:	Open Memorial Day through Labor Day (weather permitting).
	Echo Lake is a destination resort at the end of a road. All services are in one building. Like all other Sierra resorts/resupply places, the opening and closing dates of Echo Lake are determined by the snow. All services are closed after Labor Day.
GETTING HERE:	The PCT comes out of the woods to a road with parking on both sides of the road. Cross the road, walk into the parking lot, veer to the left, and you'll see a sign indicating "trail." Walk this trail down the hill, and you'll arrive behind the bathrooms near the PO/Store.
POST OFFICE:	No incoming mail accepted.
	The Echo Lake Post Office is for outgoing mail only. Mail addressed to Echo Lake is kept at the Twin Bridges Post Office, 9 miles away.
	Echo Lake Post Office. 530-659-7207. Mon-Sat 11a-2p.
RESUPPLY:	Possible resupply at the Chalet Grocery Store. 530-659-7207 Usually open 8a-6:30p every day. Hours vary.
	Store is geared toward people with cars, but hikers could resupply here. It's like a small grocery store.
LODGING:	Echo Chalet offers rustic cabins, no TV. 530-659-7207 $$$ - $$$$ per night for 2 people, 2 night minimum.
RESTAURANT:	Deli inside the grocery store serves milkshakes, sandwiches, Panini's, and gourmet Hot Dogs.
ATM:	No.
WATER:	They will not allow you to fill up water bottles here.

OVERVIEW: MANY cheap motels and a bunch of casino all-you-can-eat buffets. PO, laundry, restaurants, K-Mart, Raley's and Safeway Supermarkets, Rite Aid, stove fuel, movie theater, EVERYTHING. This is a big town with a great bus system.

GETTING HERE: South Lake Tahoe is about 9 miles from Echo Lake.

(1)   Mile 1090.7 - Highway 50.
           A lot of traffic on Highway 50, but the cars are FLYING.

(2)   Mile 1092.3 - Echo Lake (a tourist destination at the end of a road). Strike up a conversation with the tourists near the Echo Lake PO/Store. Talk about your trip, then yogi or ask for a ride.

BUS SERVICE: When you get into SLT, there is a place called "the Y" where Highway 89 goes northwest and Highway 50 continues northeast into town where there are many motels and AYCE buffets. From the "Y" you can take the bus all over town.

BlueGo	530-541-7149	The local SLT bus.
TART	530-550-1212	Lake Tahoe's west and north shores plus Truckee.

SHUTTLE:

South Tahoe Airporter	866-898-2463	South Lake Tahoe to Reno
North Tahoe Express	866-216-5222	North Shore, Truckee, Reno

UNCONFIRMED: Shuttle Around Tahoe. Phone "not accepting calls."

Shuttle Around Tahoe	530-318-9294	Anyone, anywhere, anytime

BIKE RENTAL: Lime Bikes. Bike and scooter rentals located around town. If you ride without a helmet, you could get an expensive ticket. Download the Lime Bike app. Follow instructions.

CAR RENTAL:

Hertz	775-586-0041	M-F 7:30a-9:30p	Sat 9a-1p. Sun closed.
Avis	530-544-5289	M-F 8a-5p	Sat-Sun 8a-3p.
Enterprise	530-544-8844	M-F 8a-5p	Sat 8a-1p. Sun closed.

South Lake Tahoe is big. Rent a car to save time on town errands.

POST OFFICE: There are several Post Offices in South Lake Tahoe, but the ONLY Post Office that accepts General Delivery mail is the Main PO. General Delivery mail is held for 30 days only. Main PO not very hiker-friendly.

Main Post Office:	530-544-5867 USPS only	Mon-Fri 8:30a-5p, Sat noon-2p

Keep the tracking number from your package. This will help the SLT Post Office find your package. USPS only. Hiker mail held for 15 days unless ETA is later.

Hiker's Legal Name
PCT Hiker, ETA: MM/DD/YY
General Delivery
South Lake Tahoe, CA 96150

Tahoe Valley Branch PO:	530-541-4365	Mon-Fri 9a-5p Sat closed
Stateline Branch PO:	775-588-2623	Mon-Fri 10a-1:30p, 2:30p-5p Sat closed

MAIL DROPS: Mellow Mountain Hostel (530-600-3272) Accepts mail drops, no fee if the mail drop arrives when the guest is here, $5 fee if it arrives before the guest, $7 fee for non-guests. USPS, UPS, FedEx:

Hiker's Legal Name
PCT Hiker, ETA: MM/DD/YY
c/o Mellow Mountain Hostel
4081 Cedar Ave
South Lake Tahoe, CA 96150

RESUPPLY:	Raley's at the "Y"	530-541-5160	6a-11p every day
	Raley's in Village Sh Ctr	530-544-3417	6a-midnight
	Safeway	530-542-7740	open 24 hours
	Grocery Outlet	530-542-1077	7a-11p every day
	Grass Roots Nat Foods	530-541-7788	9a-8p every day

OUTFITTER:	Tahoe Sports Ltd	530-542-4000	
	Reno NV: REI	775-828-9090	
	Sierra Trading Post	775-828-8050	

RESTAURANTS: Many restaurants. AYCE buffets at the casinos.

LAUNDRY: Several laundromats. Also laundry at some motels.

SHOWER: At Mellow Mountain Hostel.

ATM: Many ATMs.

COMPUTER: Library. 530-573-3185.

FUEL:	K-Mart	530-541-8971	HEET
	Napa Auto Parts	530-541-1850	HEET
	Ace Hardware	530-543-6600	HEET
	Raley's	530-544-3417	HEET
	Tahoe Sports Limited	530-542-4000	Canisters

MEDICAL: Barton Memorial Hospital 530-541-3420

POISON OAK: There is a lot of poison oak north of here, all the way to Oregon. Know what it looks like and avoid it. Pick up some Zanfel (great stuff, but it's expensive) or calamine at Rite Aid (530-541-2530).

There are MANY motels in South Lake Tahoe. Online rates are cheapest.
Holiday and weekend rates (Fri-Sat) are much higher than the weekday rates.
Try the casinos for cheap rates and good food.

HIKER-FRIENDLY LODGING	Weekday Rates	TV AC	frig micr	laundry	other
Apex Inn 530-541-2940	$$	Y	some	no	great location, outside hot tub, BBQ & picnic area
Motel 6 530-542-1400	$$	Y	some	Y	possible PCT discount, pool and laundry,
Budget Inn 530-544-2834	$$	Y	some	Y	heated pool
Mellow Mountain Hostel 530-600-3272	2018: $30 per person	Each dorm room has a bathroom and 2 sets of bunk beds (sleep 4). Laundry, kitchen, computer, pool table.			

Harrah's Casino	775-588-6611	**Paradice Motel**	530-544-6800
Montbleu Casino	775-588-3515	**The Trailhead**	530-544-3642
Harveys Casino	775-588-2411	**Big Pines Mountain House**	530-541-5155
Hard Rock Casino	844-588-7625		

CAMPING:	"Campground by the Lake" operated by the City of South Lake Tahoe. Entrance is on Rufus Allen Boulevard, just past the Library. 530-542-6096. [www.cityofslt.us] then search [campground] Camping, $ sleeping cabins $$, and tent cabins $$.

Rates: $ = usually less than $50. $$ = usually $50-$80. $$$ = usually $80-$110

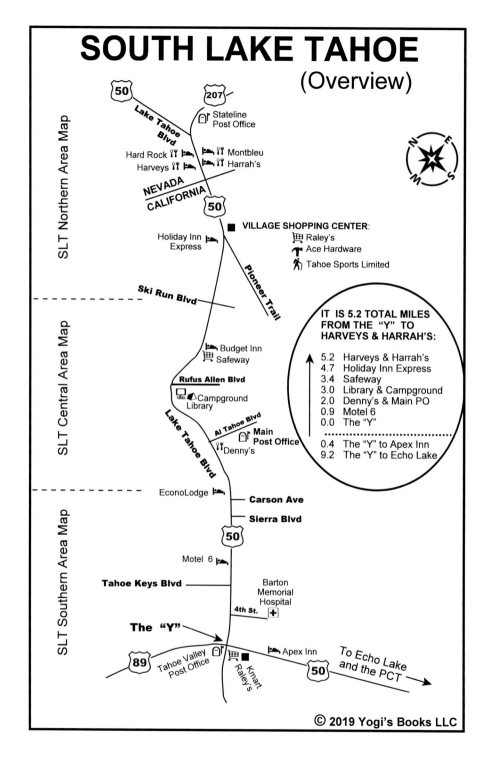

SOUTH LAKE TAHOE

(Overview)

SLT Northern Area Map

SLT Central Area Map

SLT Southern Area Map

50

207

Lake Tahoe Blvd

Stateline Post Office

Hard Rock — Montbleu
Harveys — Harrah's

NEVADA
CALIFORNIA

50

VILLAGE SHOPPING CENTER:
Raley's
Ace Hardware
Tahoe Sports Limited

Holiday Inn Express

Pioneer Trail

Ski Run Blvd

IT IS 5.2 TOTAL MILES FROM THE "Y" TO HARVEYS & HARRAH'S:

5.2 Harveys & Harrah's
4.7 Holiday Inn Express
3.4 Safeway
3.0 Library & Campground
2.0 Denny's & Main PO
0.9 Motel 6
0.0 The "Y"

0.4 The "Y" to Apex Inn
9.2 The "Y" to Echo Lake

Budget Inn
Safeway

Rufus Allen Blvd

Campground
Library

Al Tahoe Blvd

Main Post Office

Denny's

Lake Tahoe Blvd

EconoLodge

Carson Ave

Sierra Blvd

50

Motel 6

Tahoe Keys Blvd

Barton Memorial Hospital

4th St.

The "Y"

89

Tahoe Valley Post Office

Kmart
Raley's

Apex Inn

To Echo Lake and the PCT

50

© 2019 Yogi's Books LLC

SOUTH LAKE TAHOE
(Southern area)

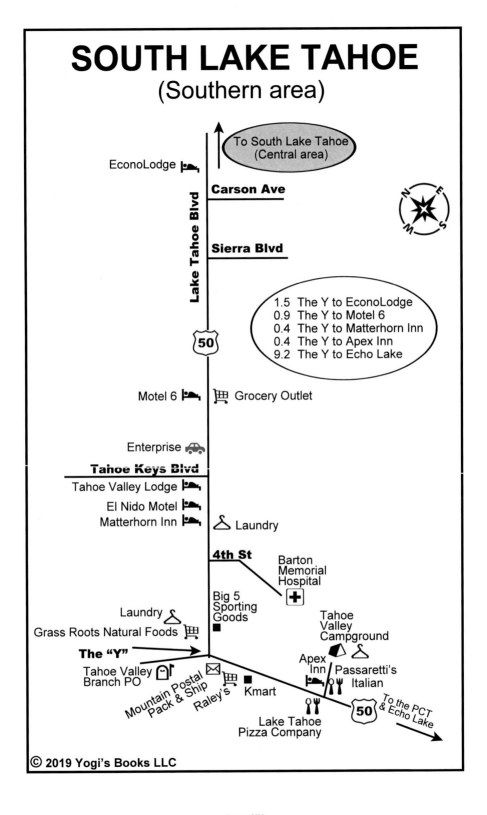

To South Lake Tahoe
(Central area)

EconoLodge

Carson Ave

Lake Tahoe Blvd

Sierra Blvd

50

1.5 The Y to EconoLodge
0.9 The Y to Motel 6
0.4 The Y to Matterhorn Inn
0.4 The Y to Apex Inn
9.2 The Y to Echo Lake

Motel 6   Grocery Outlet

Enterprise

Tahoe Keys Blvd
Tahoe Valley Lodge
El Nido Motel
Matterhorn Inn   Laundry

4th St
Barton
Memorial
Hospital

Big 5
Sporting
Goods

Laundry
Grass Roots Natural Foods

Tahoe
Valley
Campground

The "Y"
Tahoe Valley
Branch PO

Apex
Inn   Passaretti's
Italian

Mountain Postal
Pack & Ship
Raley's   Kmart

50

To the PCT
& Echo Lake

Lake Tahoe
Pizza Company

© 2019 Yogi's Books LLC

SOUTH LAKE TAHOE
(Central area)

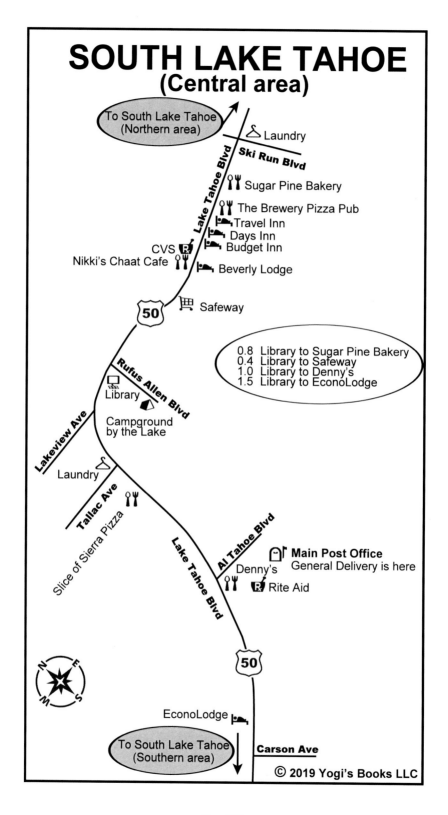

To South Lake Tahoe (Northern area)

Laundry

Ski Run Blvd

Lake Tahoe Blvd

Sugar Pine Bakery

The Brewery Pizza Pub

Travel Inn

Days Inn

CVS

Budget Inn

Nikki's Chaat Cafe

Beverly Lodge

50

Safeway

0.8 Library to Sugar Pine Bakery
0.4 Library to Safeway
1.0 Library to Denny's
1.5 Library to EconoLodge

Rufus Allen Blvd

Library

Campground by the Lake

Lakeview Ave

Laundry

Tallac Ave

Slice of Sierra Pizza

Lake Tahoe Blvd

Al Tahoe Blvd

Main Post Office
General Delivery is here

Denny's

Rite Aid

50

EconoLodge

To South Lake Tahoe (Southern area)

Carson Ave

© 2019 Yogi's Books LLC

SOUTH LAKE TAHOE
(Northern area)

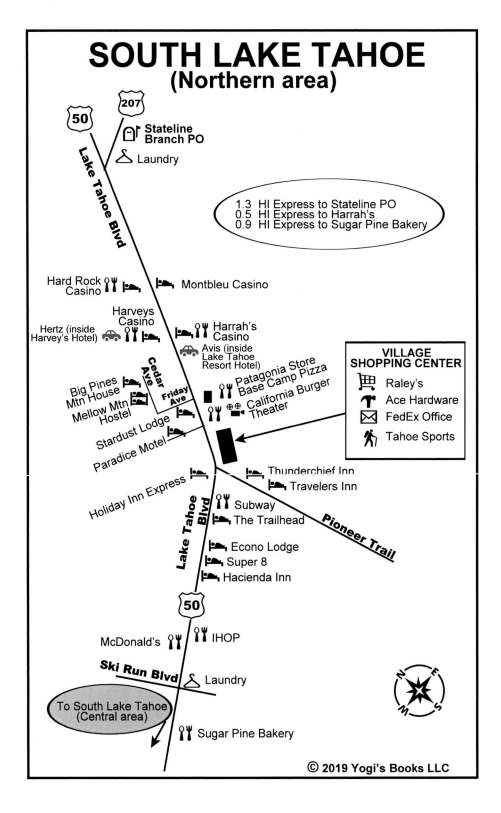

50

207

Stateline Branch PO

Laundry

Lake Tahoe Blvd

1.3 HI Express to Stateline PO
0.5 HI Express to Harrah's
0.9 HI Express to Sugar Pine Bakery

Hard Rock Casino

Montbleu Casino

Harveys Casino

Hertz (inside Harvey's Hotel)

Harrah's Casino

Avis (inside Lake Tahoe Resort Hotel)

Cedar Ave

Big Pines Mtn House

Friday Ave

Patagonia Store
Base Camp Pizza

California Burger
Theater

Mellow Mtn Hostel

Stardust Lodge

Paradice Motel

Holiday Inn Express

Lake Tahoe Blvd

VILLAGE SHOPPING CENTER

Raley's

Ace Hardware

FedEx Office

Tahoe Sports

Thunderchief Inn

Travelers Inn

Subway

The Trailhead

Pioneer Trail

Econo Lodge

Super 8

Hacienda Inn

50

McDonald's

IHOP

Ski Run Blvd

Laundry

To South Lake Tahoe
(Central area)

Sugar Pine Bakery

© 2019 Yogi's Books LLC

RESUPPLY SUMMARY

1124.8 Tahoe City - 12 mile trailhead hitch

Post Office: 530-583-4900, USPS only
Mon-Fri 8a-4:30p
Sat closed
General Delivery held for 30 days

Hiker's Legal Name
PCT Hiker, ETA: MM/DD/YY
General Delivery
950 N Lake Tahoe Blvd
Suite 12
Tahoe City, CA 96145

Resupply: Supermarkets: Safeway   530-583-2772
Save Mart   530-583-5231

1153.4 Soda Springs CA - 3.4 mile hitch to Post Office & Store
1.5 mile to Clair Tappaan

Post Office: 530-426-3082, USPS only
Mon-Fri 9a-1p, 1:30p-3:30p.
Sat closed, but usually hikers
can pick up packages on Saturdays
from 9:30a-noon. Knock on door.
General Delivery held for 30 days

Hiker's Legal Name
PCT Hiker, ETA: MM/DD/YY
General Delivery
Soda Springs, CA 95728

Mail Drops: Clair Tappaan Lodge accepts mail drops, no fee for guests, small fee for non-guests. 530-426-3632.

USPS address:
Hiker's Legal Name
PCT Hiker, ETA: MM/DD/YY
c/o Clair Tappaan Lodge
PO Box 36
Soda Springs, CA 95728

UPS or FedEx address:
Hiker's Legal Name
PCT Hiker, ETA: MM/DD/YY
c/o Clair Tappaan Lodge
19940 Donner Pass Road
Norden, CA 95724

Resupply: Grocery Store: Soda Springs General Store   530-426-3080
Excellent hiker resupply

1153.4 Truckee CA Exit 185 area - 8 mile hitch

Post Office: Branch PO does not accept
General Delivery mail.

530-587-4835.
Mon-Fri 9a-4:30p.
Sat closed.

Mail Drops: Office Boss (next to Safeway) accepts packages.
Must call to arrange. 530-587-1620. Open every day.

Resupply: Supermarkets: Safeway   530-582-7950
Save Mart   530-587-5522

1153.4 Truckee CA Old Towne area - 9.5 mile hitch

Post Office: 530-587-7158, USPS only
Mon-Fri 8:30a-5p
Sat 11a-2p
General Delivery held for 15 days

Hiker's Legal Name
PCT Hiker, ETA: MM/DD/YY
General Delivery
10050 Bridge Street
Truckee, CA 96161

Resupply: C-Store: Truckee Beacon   530-582-5529

RESUPPLY SUMMARY

1195.4 Sierra City CA - 1.5 mile walk or hitch

Post Office: 530-862-1152, USPS only
Mon-Fri 10a-2:30p
Sat 10:30a-12:30p
Hiker mail held until end of hiker season

Hiker's Legal Name
PCT Hiker, ETA: MM/DD/YY
General Delivery
215 Main Street
Sierra City, CA 96125

Mail Drops: Sierra City Country Store (530-862-1560) accepts mail drops, no fee.
9a until 7p or 8p every day.

USPS Address:
Hiker's Legal Name
PCT Hiker, ETA: MM/DD/YY
c/o Sierra Country Store
PO Box 196
Sierra City, CA 96125

UPS or FedEx address:
Hiker's Legal Name
PCT Hiker, ETA: MM/DD/YY
c/o Sierra Country Store
213 Main Street
Sierra City, CA 96125

Mail Drops: Red Moose Inn
(530-862-1024)
Accepts mail
drops, USPS only,
no fee.

USPS address:
Hiker's Legal Name
PCT Hiker, ETA:
MM/DD/YY
c/o Red Moose Inn
PO Box 213
Sierra City, CA 96126

UPS or FedEx address:
Hiker's Legal Name
PCT Hiker, ETA:
MM/DD/YY
c/o Red Moose Inn
PO Box 213
Sierra City, CA 96126

Resupply: Grocery store: Sierra City Country Store   530-862-1560

1263.5 Bucks Lake Alternate

Resupply: C-Store: Haskins Valley Store   530-283-9667   Good resupply
Small C-Store: Lakeshore Store   530-283-2848   Snacks only

1286.8 Mailing to Belden

Packages shipped to the Belden Zip Code via UPS, FedEx, and DHL often end up in
Oroville CA instead. If you have anything shipped to Belden using UPS or FedEx, be
sure the that it is shipped pure ground or USPS (not SmartPost, SurePost, or other
Ground to Post Office hybrids). *This is especially important when ordering from REI,
Amazon, etc.*

1286.8 Belden Town Resort - on trail

Mail Drops: Belden Town Resort (530-283-9662)
accepts mail drops, UPS or FedEx
only. Hiker mail service changes
from year to year. Sometimes they
take hiker mail, sometimes they
don't. There is usually a package
fee, sometimes up to $20/box.

Hiker's Legal Name
PCT Hiker, ETA: MM/DD/YY
c/o Belden Town Resort
14785 Belden Town Road
Belden, CA 95915

Resupply: Sometimes the small store has decent hiker resupply.
Resupply status seems to change from year to year.

1286.9 Caribou Crossroads - 1.5 mile walk or hitch

Resupply: Very small C-Store: Caribou Crossroads   530-283-1384

RESUPPLY SUMMARY

1286.9　Quincy CA - 30 mile hitch

Post Office: 530-283-3912, USPS only
Mon-Fri 8:30a-5p
Sat closed, but hikers can pick up
packages on Saturdays from 2p-3p.
Knock on the dutch door.
General Delivery held for 15 days,
unless you call to request longer hold
or request to forward.

Hiker's Legal Name
PCT Hiker, ETA: MM/DD/YY
General Delivery
Quincy, CA 95971

Plumas Crisis Intervention &
Resource Center (PCIRC) accepts
mail drops, no fee. Package must
have ETA. 530-283-5515.

Hiker's Legal Name
PCT Hiker, ETA: MM/DD/YY
c/o PCIRC
591 Main Street
Quincy, CA 95971

Resupply:　Supermarket:　　　Safeway　　　530-283-1404
Natural Foods Mkt:　Quincy Natural Foods　530-283-3528

1331.3　Chester CA - 8 mile hitch

Post Office: 530-258-4184, USPS only
Mon-Fri 8:30a-4p. Sat closed.
General Delivery held for 30 days.

Hiker's Legal Name
PCT Hiker, ETA: MM/DD/YY
General Delivery
Chester, CA 96020

Resupply:　Supermarket:　Holiday Foods Supermarket　530-258-2122

1349.7　Drakesbad Guest Ranch - 0.5 mile off trail

Mail Drops: Accepts mail drops, no fee.
USPS, UPS, FedEx.
Mail must have ETA.
No outgoing mail. Click-n-Ship
does not work for Drakesbad address.

Hiker's Legal Name
PCT Hiker, ETA: MM/DD/YY
c/o Drakesbad Guest Ranch
End of Warner Valley Road
Chester, CA 96020

Resupply:　No resupply.

1373.4　Old Station Post Office and Hat Creek Store - 0.2 mile off trail

Post Office: 530-335-7191, USPS only
Mon-Fri 11a-3p
Sat open 1p-2p for package pick up
and cash sales only. Mail must have
a valid domestic return address, and
a phone number is helpful. The Old
Station Postmaster goes to great
lengths to return unclaimed packages
to hikers, including making posts on
Facebook. If you provide your phone
number, her job will be easier.

Hiker's Legal Name
PCT Hiker, ETA: MM/DD/YY
General Delivery
12529 State Hwy 44-89
Old Station, CA 96071

Resupply:　Tiny C-Store:
Hat Creek Store　530-335-7121　Very limited snacks. No hiker resupply.

RESUPPLY SUMMARY

1377.4 Old Station Fill Up - 0.4 mile off trail, Rim Rock Store 0.4 mile farther

Mail Drops: JJ's Café (530-335-7225) Accepts UPS or FedEx packages, no fee. Open 7a-3p every day from late-April until mid-November. Email Chuck first so they can verify receipt: [chuck.woodman@gmail.com]

Hiker's Legal Name
PCT Hiker, ETA: MM/DD/YY
c/o JJ's Café
13385 Hwy 89
Old Station, CA 96071

Resupply: Small C-Stores: Old Station Fill-Up   530-335-3152

Rim Rock Ranch Store   530-335-7174
Best resupply in Old Station

1409.7 Burney Mountain Guest Ranch - 0.1 mile off trail

Mail Drops: 530-335-2544. Accepts mail drops, $5 fee. Outgoing mail is postage plus $2.

USPS address:
Hiker's Legal Name
PCT Hiker, ETA: MM/DD/YY
c/o Burney Mountain Guest Ranch
PO Box 2588
Burney, CA 96013

UPS or FedEx address:
Hiker's Legal Name
PCT Hiker, ETA: MM/DD/YY
c/o Burney Mountain Guest Ranch
22800 Guest Ranch Road
Cassel, CA 96016

Resupply: Decent hiker resupply in little store.

1411.3 Burney CA - 7 mile hitch

Post Office: 530-335-5430, USPS only
Mon-Fri 9:30a-4p
Sat closed
General Delivery held for 30 days

Hiker's Legal Name
PCT Hiker, ETA: MM/DD/YY
General Delivery
Burney, CA 96013

Mail Drops: Word of Life Assembly Church
530-335-4419. Accepts mail drops.
USPS, UPS, FedEx.

Hiker's Legal Name
PCT Hiker, ETA: MM/DD/YY
c/o Word of Life Assembly Church
37341 Main Street
Burney, CA 96013

Resupply: Supermarket: Safeway   530-335-3212

1419.0 Burney Falls State Park - on trail

Mail Drops: Store accepts mail drops.
USPS, UPS, FedEx.
Store phone 530-335-5713.
Store usually open 8a-8p during summer. Closes after Labor Day.
2017 package fee was
$7/box and $2.50/letter, cash only.

Hiker's Legal Name
PCT Hiker, ETA: MM/DD/YY
c/o Burney Park Camp Store
McArthur Burney Falls State Park
24900 State Highway 89
Burney, CA 96013

Resupply: Very small C-Store, geared to car campers. 530-335-5713

RESUPPLY SUMMARY

1501.2 Castella CA - 2.5 mile walk or hitch

Post Office: 530-235-4413, USPS only
Mon-Fri 11a-3p
Sat 8:40a-10a
General Delivery held for 30 days

Hiker's Legal Name
PCT Hiker, ETA: MM/DD/YY
General Delivery
20115 Castle Creek Road
Castella, CA 96017

Mail Drops: Ammirati's (530-235-2676) accepts mail drops, no fee. USPS is best !!

USPS Address:
Hiker's Legal Name
PCT Hiker, ETA: MM/DD/YY
c/o Ammirati's Market
PO Box 90
Castella, CA 96017

UPS or FedEx Address:
Hiker's Legal Name
PCT Hiker, ETA: MM/DD/YY
c/o Ammirati's Market
20107 Castle Creek Road
Castella, CA 96017

Resupply: C-Store: Ammirati's Market. 530-235-2676.
Sometimes has decent resupply; sometimes has bare shelves.
Lots of beer and liquor on shelves. Excellent beer selection.

1501.2 Dunsmuir CA - 4.5 mile Interstate hitch or taxi

Post Office: 530-235-0338, USPS only
Mon-Fri 8:30a-5p
Sat closed, but usually hikers can
pick up packages on Sat from 9a-11a.
Knock on back door inside lobby.

Hiker mail held for 30 days, unless
you call to ask to hold longer.

Hiker's Legal Name
PCT Hiker, ETA: MM/DD/YY
General Delivery
Dunsmuir, CA 96025

Mail Drops: Dunsmuir Lodge (530-235-2884)
Accepts mail drops for guests.
No fee. USPS, UPS, FedEx.

Hiker's Legal Name
PCT Hiker, ETA: MM/DD/YY
c/o Dunsmuir Lodge
6604 Dunsmuir Ave
Dunsmuir, CA 96025

Resupply: Grocery store: Dunsmuir Supermarket 530-235-4751

1501.2 Mount Shasta CA - 12 mile Interstate hitch or taxi

Post Office: 530-926-1343, USPS only
Mon-Fri 8:30a-5p
Sat closed
Hiker mail held until end of hiker season.

Hiker's Legal Name
PCT Hiker, ETA: MM/DD/YY
General Delivery
301 S. Mt. Shasta Blvd
Mount Shasta, CA 96067

Resupply: Supermarket: Ray's Food Place   530-926-3390

Natural Foods Mkt: Mountain Song   530-926-3391
                          Berryvale   530-926-1576

1560.2 Callahan CA - 8.3 mile hitch

Post Office: 530-467-5155, USPS only
Mon-Fri 11:30a-3:30p
Sat 10:30a-12:30p
Hiker mail held until end of hiker season.

Hiker's Legal Name
PCT Hiker, ETA: MM/DD/YY
General Delivery
Callahan, CA 96014

Resupply: Small C-Store, not good for resupply: Callahan Emporium 530-467-3395

RESUPPLY SUMMARY

1599.7 Etna CA - 11 mile hitch

Post Office: 530-467-3981, USPS only
Mon-Fri 9a-5p
Sat package pick up only 8a-10a.
General Delivery mail MUST have
a valid domestic return address.
If not picked up 15 days after mail
drop arrives at PO, Postmaster will
scan as "delivered to agent", then she
will keep hiker mail until the end of
hiker season.

Hiker's Legal Name
PCT Hiker, ETA: MM/DD/YY
General Delivery
119 Diggles Street
Etna, CA 96027

Mail Drops: Alderbrook Manor (530-467-3917)
Accepts mail drops,
no fee for guests, $5 for non-guests.
USPS, UPS, or FedEx.

Hiker's Legal Name
PCT Hiker, ETA: MM/DD/YY
c/o Alderbrook Manor
836 Sawyers Bar Road
Etna, CA 96027

Resupply: Large grocery store: Ray's Food Place 530-467-5235

1655.9 Seiad Valley CA - on trail

Post Office: 530-496-3211, USPS only
Mon-Fri noon-4p
Sat noon-1:30p
Put your name on every side of your
package. Hiker mail held until end
of hiker season.

Hiker's Legal Name
PCT Hiker, ETA: MM/DD/YY
General Delivery
44717 State Highway 96
Seiad Valley, CA 96086

Mail Drops: Store accepts mail drops,
no fee, USPS, UPS, or FedEx.
Must have real name on package,
must show photo ID to pick up.
Store open 6a-8p or 9p every day.
530-496-3399.

Hiker's Legal Name
PCT Hiker, ETA: MM/DD/YY
c/o Seiad Valley Store
44719 State Highway 96
Seiad Valley, CA 96086

Mail Drops: RV Park accepts hiker boxes. $5 fee. 530-496-3400.
If you camp here ($15-$20), the $5 package fee is waived.
UPS or FedEx are recommended.

USPS address:
Hiker's Legal Name
PCT Hiker, ETA: MM/DD/YY
c/o Mid River RV Park
PO Box 707
Seiad Valley, CA 96086

UPS or FedEx Address:
Hiker's Legal Name
PCT Hiker, ETA: MM/DD/YY
c/o Mid River RV Park
44701 State Highway 96
Seiad Valley, CA 96086

Resupply: Large C-Store: Seiad Valley Store 530-496-3399
Good hiker resupply, owner Rick knows what hikers want.

1718.7 Callahan's Siskiyou Lodge - 1 mile walk or hitch

Mail Drops: Accepts mail drops, $5 fee,
USPS, UPS, or FedEx.
Mail must have ETA.
No outgoing mail.

Hiker's Legal Name
PCT Hiker, ETA: MM/DD/YY
c/o Callahan's Lodge
7100 Old Highway 99 South
Ashland, OR 97520

Resupply: No resupply.

RESUPPLY SUMMARY

1718.7   Ashland OR - 13 mile hitch or shuttle

Post Office: 541-552-1622. Mon-Fri 9a-5p.
Sat closed, but usually hikers can pick
up packages on Saturdays from 8a-4p.
Knock on double white door in lobby.
USPS only.

Do not put PO street address on
General Delivery address.

Hiker mail held for 30 days or until ETA.

Hiker's Legal Name
PCT Hiker, ETA: MM/DD/YY
General Delivery
Ashland, OR 97520

Mail Drops: Rodeway Inn (541-482-5111)
Accepts mail drops, free for guests,
$5+ for non-guests. Clearly label
your mail drop as a hiker package,
must have ETA. USPS, UPS, FedEx:

Hiker's Legal Name
PCT Hiker, ETA: MM/DD/YY
c/o Rodeway Inn
2359 Ashland Street
Ashland, OR 97520

Resupply: Supermarkets:

Albertsons	541-482-6320
Shop 'n Kart	541-488-1579
Food Co-Op	541-482-2237

Access these files as often as possible:

(1)   Pacific Crest Trail Water Report - Current status of water sources.
Frequently updated during hiker season. [www.pctwater.com]

(2)   Yogi's PCT Handbook update file - Changes to trail/town information which have occurred
between the time your book was printed and now. Frequently updated during hiker season.
[www.yogisbooks.com], then click UPDATES & LINKS

Do you have changes/updates to report? If so, send them here: yogisbooks@gmail.com

Map Symbols

David "Awol" Miller has given us permission to use the map symbols he
created for his excellent book "The AT Guide". These map symbols allow
you to easily find town services with a quick glance at the town maps.

Airport	First Aid	Lounge/Bar	Ranger Station
ATM or Bank	Grocery Store	Outfitter	Restaurant
Boat	Hardware Store	Outgoing Mail	Restroom/Privy
Bowling	Hostel	Pay Phone	Shoe Store
Bus	Hotel	Pharmacy	Shower
Camping	Information	Picnic Table	Ski Lift
Car Rental	Internet/WiFi	Pool	Theater
Computer	Laundry	Post Office	Train Station
C-Store	Light Rail		

1098.4 - Lake Aloha - DOUBLE TAP: This lake is usually pretty warm and great for a dip if you hit it in heat of the day. At the Mosquito Pass Trail Junction, there is a great campsite with a rock cliff to jump in Lake Aloha about 0.5 mile to the west. To find this campsite, turn left at the mile 1099.9 junction and then stay along the lake (you will see a faint trail) after the junction up to Mosquito Pass. The campsite is few hundred feet down this faint trail.

1103.2 - Gilmore Lake Trail - DOUBLE TAP: Good camping at Gilmore Lake. Take the ~4 mile round trip up to Mount Tallac (9,738 ft), which has tremendous view of Lake Tahoe from the top.

1107.4 - Junction to Eagle Falls Picnic Area - Go left.

1107.6 - Spur Trail to Dicks Lake - Go right.

1109.9 - Middle Velma Lake - DOUBLE TAP: Plenty of good campsites at the south side of the lake near the shore but you have go off trail to find them. There is also a small use trail to the right near mile 1112.3.

1112.6 - Seasonal Phipps Creek - Water here.

1118.6 - Richardson Lake's northwest corner - BINK: On the south side of the lake, well hidden up in the woods is a Sierra Club ski hut. It is somewhat tricky to find, but a determined hiker could find it, if in need of good shelter.

SCRUB: To find the Ludlow Ski Hut at Richardson Lake, leave the PCT and head to the right around the north side of the lake. Stay close to the lake and you will cross a small concrete bridge; shortly after that there is a grassy camping area with a fire ring right on the lake. Head straight uphill from the grassy area, keep looking through the trees, and the hut is maybe 200 yards away.

1124.8 - Barker Pass - This is a dirt road with very little traffic.

1124.8 - Tahoe City CA

OVERVIEW:	Touristy town. with all hiker services.
GETTING HERE:	Barker Pass Road is a little-used dirt road. Easier to get rides on weekends. Take this road 7 miles east to Highway 89, then go 5 miles north on Highway 89.
BUS SERVICE:	TART 530-550-1212 Lake Tahoe's west and south shores.
	North Lake Tahoe & Truckee Transit 530-582-4964
SHUTTLE:	North Tahoe Express 866-216-5222 North Shore, Truckee, Reno
	UNCONFIRMED: Shuttle Around Tahoe. Phone "not accepting calls." Shuttle Around Tahoe 530-318-9294 Anyone, anywhere, anytime
POST OFFICE:	530-583-4900, USPS only Mon-Fri 8a-4:30p Sat closed General Delivery held for 30 days	Hiker's Legal Name PCT Hiker, ETA: MM/DD/YY General Delivery 950 N Lake Tahoe Blvd Suite 12 Tahoe City, CA 96145
RESUPPLY:	Safeway 530-583-2772 6a-10p every day Save Mart 530-583-5231 6a-11p every day

TAHOE CITY LODGING		Rates	TV	micr frig	laundry	bkfst	pool	other
America's Best Value Inn	530-583-3766	$$$$	Y	some	no	cont	Y	
Mother Nature's Inn	530-581-4278	$$$	Y	Y	no	no	no	
Pepper Tree Inn	530-583-3711	$$$$	Y	Y	Y	cont	Y	
Tahoe Marina Lodge	530-583-2365	$$$$	Y		Y	no	Y	1- and 2-bedroom condos full kitchens
Tahoe City Inn	530-581-3333	$$$	Y	Y	no	Sat-Sun cont	no	
		$$$ = usually $80-$110				$$$$ = usually greater than $110		

OUTDOOR STORE:
Alpenglow Sports
530-583-6917

RESTAURANTS: Yes.

LAUNDRY: Yes.

ATM: Yes.

COMPUTER:
Library. 530-583-3382.

FUEL:
Usually HEET at
the gas stations.

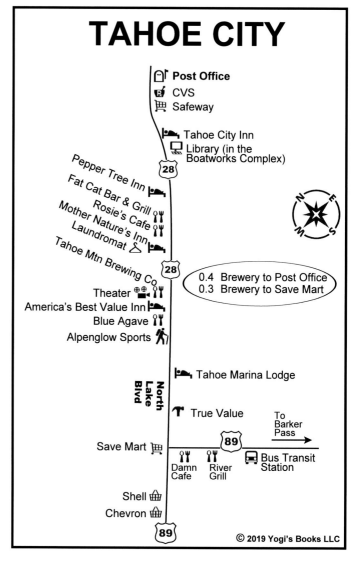

TAHOE CITY

Post Office

CVS

Safeway

Tahoe City Inn

Library (in the Boatworks Complex)

28

Pepper Tree Inn

Fat Cat Bar & Grill

Rosie's Cafe

Mother Nature's Inn

Laundromat

Tahoe Mtn Brewing Co

28

0.4 Brewery to Post Office
0.3 Brewery to Save Mart

Theater

America's Best Value Inn

Blue Agave

Alpenglow Sports

Tahoe Marina Lodge

North Lake Blvd

True Value

To Barker Pass

89

Save Mart

Damn Cafe

River Grill

Bus Transit Station

Shell

Chevron

89

© 2019 Yogi's Books LLC

1147.8 - Saddle north of Anderson Peak - BINK: 100 yards east uphill of here is the Benson/Anderson Sierra Club ski hut. This two story hut has a wonderful view. Water is obtained by going 0.25 mile north down the rough trail from the saddle at the PCT, to a year-round spring.

1153.4 - Donner Pass / Old Highway 40 - When you emerge into a parking lot, see the large gray building on the right. There is a water spigot behind shrubs above a rock retaining wall.

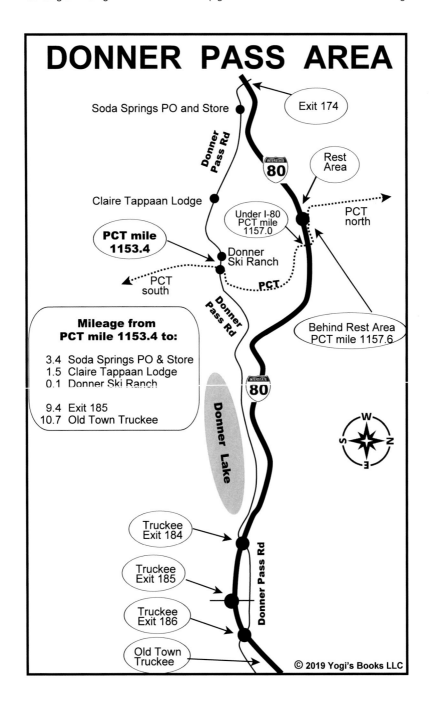

DONNER PASS AREA

Soda Springs PO and Store

Exit 174

Donner Pass Rd

INTERSTATE 80

Rest Area

Claire Tappaan Lodge

Under I-80 PCT mile 1157.0

PCT north

PCT mile 1153.4

Donner Ski Ranch

PCT south

PCT

Donner Pass Rd

Behind Rest Area PCT mile 1157.6

Mileage from PCT mile 1153.4 to:

3.4 Soda Springs PO & Store
1.5 Claire Tappaan Lodge
0.1 Donner Ski Ranch

9.4 Exit 185
10.7 Old Town Truckee

INTERSTATE 80

Donner Lake

Truckee Exit 184

Truckee Exit 185

Donner Pass Rd

Truckee Exit 186

Old Town Truckee

© 2019 Yogi's Books LLC

1153.4 - Soda Springs CA

OVERVIEW: Post Office, store, and restaurant. This is very close to I-80 exit 174. PO and store are in the same building.

GETTING HERE: Hitch 3.4 miles left (west) on Highway 40.

POST OFFICE: 530-426-3082, USPS only
Mon-Fri 9a-1p, 1:30p-3:30p
Sat closed, but usually hikers can pick up
packages on Saturdays from 9:30a-noon.
Knock on door.

Hiker's Legal Name
PCT Hiker, ETA: MM/DD/YY
General Delivery
Soda Springs, CA 95728

General Delivery held for 30 days.

MAIL DROPS: Clair Tappaan Lodge accepts mail drops (530-426-3632),
no fee for guests, small fee for non-guests, USPS, UPS, or FedEx.

USPS address:
Hiker's Legal Name
PCT Hiker, ETA: MM/DD/YY
c/o Clair Tappaan Lodge
PO Box 36
Soda Springs, CA 95728

UPS or FedEx address:
Hiker's Legal Name
PCT Hiker, ETA: MM/DD/YY
c/o Clair Tappaan Lodge
19940 Donner Pass Road
Norden, CA 95724

RESUPPLY: Soda Springs General Store. 530-426-3080. 8a-7p every day.
Store has excellent hiker resupply, including Idahoans.

LODGING: Sierra Club's Clair Tappaan Lodge. 530-426-3632.
Located 1.5 miles west of PCT crossing of Donner Pass Road
(between Donner Pass and Soda Springs).
Bunks with mattresses (use your sleeping bag).
Free ride to/from trail if they have time (arranged in advance).
Free laundry, hot drinks, hot tub, WiFi.
2019: $70 includes: bunk, laundry, shower, hot tub, dinner served at 6pm sharp,
pack your own lunch at 7:30am, and hot breakfast at 8am.

RESTAURANTS: Deli sandwich counter in the store.

LAUNDRY: At Clair Tappaan for guests.

SHOWER: Free for guests. $5 for non-guests.

ATM: Free for guests. $5 for non-guests.

1153.4 - Donner Ski Ranch

Donner Ski Ranch is only 0.1mile off the PCT. 530-426-3635. First beer free for PCT'ers.
Bar & Café open usually every day at 11am. Beer, cocktails, food, shower, laundry, bunk room.

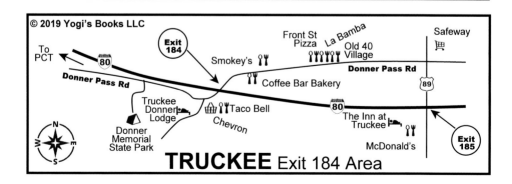

© 2019 Yogi's Books LLC

TRUCKEE Exit 184 Area

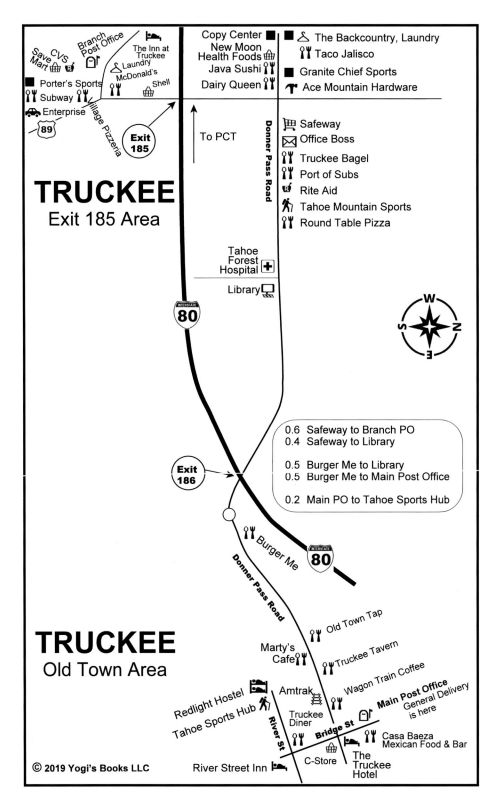

TRUCKEE
Exit 185 Area

Save Mart
CVS
Branch Post Office
The Inn at Truckee
Laundry
McDonald's
Shell
Porter's Sports
Subway
Enterprise
89
Village Pizzeria
Exit 185
To PCT

Copy Center
New Moon Health Foods
Java Sushi
Dairy Queen
The Backcountry, Laundry
Taco Jalisco
Granite Chief Sports
Ace Mountain Hardware

Donner Pass Road

Safeway
Office Boss
Truckee Bagel
Port of Subs
Rite Aid
Tahoe Mountain Sports
Round Table Pizza

Tahoe Forest Hospital
Library

INTERSTATE 80

Exit 186

0.6 Safeway to Branch PO
0.4 Safeway to Library

0.5 Burger Me to Library
0.5 Burger Me to Main Post Office

0.2 Main PO to Tahoe Sports Hub

Burger Me
INTERSTATE 80

Donner Pass Road

Old Town Tap
Marty's Cafe
Truckee Tavern
Wagon Train Coffee
Main Post Office
General Delivery is here

TRUCKEE
Old Town Area

Redlight Hostel
Tahoe Sports Hub
Amtrak
Truckee Diner
Bridge St
River St
Casa Baeza Mexican Food & Bar
C-Store
The Truckee Hotel
River Street Inn

© 2019 Yogi's Books LLC

Truckee - Exit 184 & 185 area	Truckee - Old Town

GETTING HERE: Hitch to the right from Donner Pass (Hwy 40 / Donner Pass Road). Exit 185 is 8 miles from Donner Pass (PCT mile 1153.4). Old Town Truckee is about 1.5 miles farther.

BUS SERVICE: TART Truckee Trolley runs Mon-Sat every hour from 9:15a-5:15p. Trolley stops at Safeway. 530-550-1212.

North Lake Tahoe & Truckee Transit 530-582-4964

North Lake Tahoe Express 866-216-5222

TAXI: High Sierra Taxi 530-412-1927
Bluebird Taxi 530-414-1547

CAR RENTAL: Enterprise
530-550-1550
Mon-Fri 8a-5p
Sat & Sun 9a-2p

POST OFFICE: Branch Post Office 530-587-4835 Mon-Fri 9a-4:30p Sat closed This PO does not accept General Delivery Mail.	**POST OFFICE:** Main Post Office 530-587-7158 Mon-Fri 8:30a-5p Sat 11a-2p USPS only General Delivery held for 15 days.
MAIL DROPS: Office Boss, open every day 530-587-1620. Accepts packages, call to arrange. UPS & FedEx outgoing mail.	Hiker's Legal Name PCT Hiker, ETA: MM/DD/YY General Delivery 10050 Bridge Street Truckee, CA 96161
RESUPPLY: Safeway 530-582-7950 Save Mart 530-587-5522	**RESUPPLY:** Truckee Beacon (C-Store) 530-582-5529
OUTFITTER: Mountain Ace Hardware and Sports has a reasonable supply of camping odds and ends including fuel and filters. 530-587-4844. The Backcountry Some hiking gear 530-582-0909 Tahoe Mountain Sports 530-536-5200. 10a-6p every day	**OUTFITTER:** Tahoe Sports Hub has some backpacking gear, canister fuel, plus a consignment area with slightly used gear. 530-582-4510. 9a-7p every day.
RESTAURANT: Yes. Trail Angel Freeloader says: Taco Jalisco is the best Mex in town.	**RESTAURANT:** Yes. Be sure to eat at The Truckee Diner!
LAUNDRY: Yes. **ATM:** Yes. **LIBRARY:** 530-582-7846	**LAUNDRY:** No. **ATM:** Yes.

Truckee - Exit 184 & 185 area	Truckee - Old Town
LODGING, weekday rates: The Inn at Truckee 530-587-8888, $$$ + Laundry Donner Memorial State Park: Camping Visitor Center 530-582-7892 Campground Kiosk 530-582-7894	**LODGING, weekday rates:** River Street Inn B & B 530-550-9290, $$$$ The Truckee Hotel 530-587-4444, $$$ + Redlight Hostel 530-536-0005, $+ Laundry
HEET: Denatured at Mountain Ace Hardware 530-587-4844. HEET maybe at Safeway 530-582-7950 HEET maybe at Shell 530-587-3853	**HEET:** HEET usually at Beacon C-Store 530-582-5529.
CANISTER FUEL: Mountain Ace Hardware 530-587-4844 The Backcountry 530-582-0909 Tahoe Mountain Sports 530-536-5200	**CANISTER FUEL:** Tahoe Sports Hub 530-582-4510
MEDICAL: Tahoe Forest Hospital 530-587-6011	

1157.0 - Interstate 80

1157.6 - Behind the Interstate 80 Rest Area - After you walk under the interstate, there is a signed junction with a left-branching side trail up to the rest area. Don't take this side trail. Continue on the PCT for maybe 5 minutes, and you will end up directly behind the rest area. From this spot, there is a short, unsigned side trail over to the rest area building. The side trail stays on the left (east) side of the little lake. The rest area has trash, picnic tables, bathrooms, water fountains, and electrical outlets, vending machines.

1160.8 - Peter Grubb Hut - PCT register here. Water on the PCT about 0.1 mile past the hut. Leaving the Peter Grubb Hut, at the junction after the water, the PCT goes right.

1168.9 - Snowbank Spring - Good water. Watch for sign on tree to right, easy to miss.

1179.3 - Descend to a creek - Creek does not cross trail. Get water the first time you hear the creek. You'll go off trail at a switchback to get to the creek. There is a signed, well-worn trail down to the creek.

1183.6 - Pass Creek Road - Pass Creek has good water. DOUBLE TAP: When you hit this paved road, turn right and follow the paved road over the bridge which you can see from here. You will see a PCT sign further down after crossing the bridge.

1192.9 - Alternate route into Sierra City - You could leave the PCT here and take a 3.1-mile alternate route into Sierra City. If you choose to stay on the PCT instead, you walk 2.5 PCT miles from here to Highway 49, then Sierra City is 1.5 highway miles to the left.

DOUBLE TAP: After turning left right before the bridge over Milton Creek and hiking a short distance on the use trail you hit an unpaved road. Turn RIGHT at this road to go down towards the campground and into Sierra City.

SMARTY: After walking through the campground, there is a great swimming hole along side of the road in 0.25 to 0.5 mile. Look for it on the left directly by the road. There are a couple of minor roads before you get there. These are not it. From the main road you can see a locally made dam and pool directly below the road. The pool has a nice waterfall and is deep enough to dive into.

1195.4 - Sierra City CA / Highway 49

OVERVIEW:	Very small town. Just a few blocks long. A few restaurants, small store, laundry, a couple motels, Post Office.
GETTING HERE:	PCT mile 1192.9: Walk the alternate route. PCT mile 1195.4: Walk or hitch 1.5 miles left on Hwy 49.

POST OFFICE:
530-862-1152, USPS only
Mon-Fri 10a-2:30p
Sat 10:30a-12:30p
Hiker mail held until end of hiker season

Hiker's Legal Name
PCT Hiker, ETA: MM/DD/YY
General Delivery
215 Main Street
Sierra City, CA 96125

MAIL DROPS:
Sierra City Country Store (530-862-1560)

Accepts mail drops, no fee,
9a until 7p or 8p every day.

USPS address:
Hiker's Legal Name
PCT Hiker, ETA: MM/DD/YY
c/o Sierra Country Store
PO Box 196
Sierra City, CA 96125

UPS or FedEx address:
Hiker's Legal Name
PCT Hiker, ETA: MM/DD/YY
c/o Sierra Country Store
213 Main Street
Sierra City, CA 96125

Red Moose Inn (530-862-1024)

Accepts mail drops, no fee.
Open Wed-Sun 8a-2p
After hours: 530-862-1136

USPS address:
Hiker's Legal Name
PCT Hiker, ETA: MM/DD/YY
c/o Red Moose Inn
PO Box 213
Sierra City, CA 96126

UPS or FedEx address:
Hiker's Legal Name
PCT Hiker, ETA: MM/DD/YY
c/o Red Moose Inn
224 Main Street
Sierra City, CA 96126

RESUPPLY:
Hiker-friendly Sierra City Country Store. 530-862-1560.
Open approximately 9a until 7p or 8p every day. Hours could vary.
This is a Grocery Store, you could resupply here.

Message from Store owner Larry Breed: "Our hiker-friendly Sierra Country Store has a full selection of meat, produce, dry goods, deli, beer/wine/hard liquor, sandwiches, and ice cream. We have water access and an area with tables for spreading out backpacks. We are a Verizon hot spot."
[www.sierracountrystore.com]

CAMPING:
Camping on the side of the church (not on Sundays).

RESTAURANTS:
A few restaurants.

The store has deli sandwiches, big burgers, burritos, grilled chicken, pastrami, BLT, grilled cheese. If you want something that's not on the menu, just ask!

LAUNDRY: No.

SHOWERS: At Visitor Center.

ATM: At the store.

FUEL: Canister fuel at the store.

MEDICAL CLINIC: Western Sierra Medical Clinic. 530-289-3298.
This is in Downieville, 13 miles west of Sierra City.

POISON OAK:
There is a lot of poison oak on the trail for the rest of California.
Know what it looks like and avoid it. Carry Zanfel or Calamine.

SIERRA CITY LODGING		Rates	TV	micr frig	AC	other
Buttes Resort	530-862-1170	$$$ +	Y	some	no	computer for guests, most rooms have DVD players, free DVD rental.
Herrington's	530-862-1151	$$$ +	Y	no	no	computer for guests, courtesy phone in lobby.
open May-October						Print a coupon from their website for: 10% discount Fri, Sat, Sun. 20% discount M-Tu-W-Th.
Red Moose Café/Inn 530-862-1024 after hours: 530-862-1136 [www.redmoosecafe.com]		$$$ +				Open Wed-Sun 8a-2p no laundry
River Haven 530-862-1549 [www.riverhaven.drivehq.com] Walk down the driveway. Don't need to call ahead. Owner Susan Jorjorian 218 Main Street (lower level behind another house)		$$ +				Three bedrooms for rent in a house. Guests have access to living room, dining room, kitchen. Laundry $5 for guests only. Computer available. Also available is an outdoor 10' x 20' tent space with one king bed, one rollaway, one twin bed, all with linens/bedspreads. Private swimming hole, WiFi, picnic tables.
Yuba River Inn 530-862-1122		$$$ +				Cabins sleep 1-6 people. BBQ, TV, most have full kitchens.
Church - camping						PCT hikers can camp at church, but not on Sundays
		$ = usually less than $50 $$ = usually $50-$80 $$$ = usually $80-$110 $$$$ = usually greater than $110				

Easy Food Resupply

Triple Crown Outfitters in Kennedy Meadows is known as "the best resupply on the PCT." This great selection is also available for online shipping.

www.triplecrownoutfitters.com

- Huge selection

- Fast shipping

- Relax in town instead of shopping

- Quickly pick up a box and get back on trail

- Perfect for international hikers

Questions? Call or email:
559-302-9943
jackie@triplecrownoutfitters.com

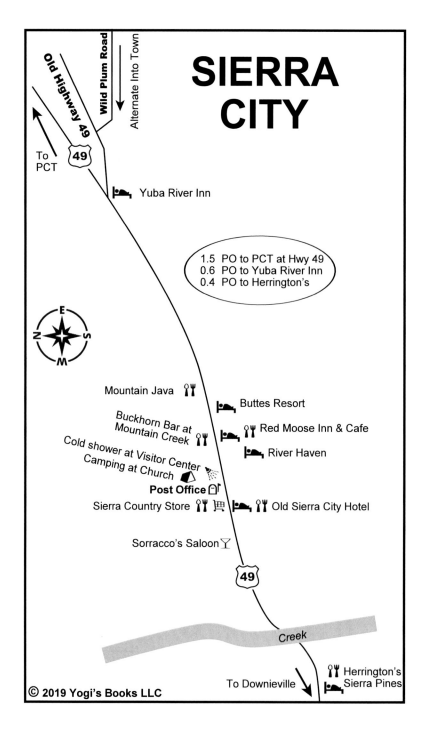

SIERRA CITY

Old Highway 49

Wild Plum Road

Alternate Into Town

To PCT

49

Yuba River Inn

1.5 PO to PCT at Hwy 49
0.6 PO to Yuba River Inn
0.4 PO to Herrington's

Mountain Java

Buttes Resort

Buckhorn Bar at Mountain Creek

Red Moose Inn & Cafe

Cold shower at Visitor Center

River Haven

Camping at Church

Post Office

Sierra Country Store

Old Sierra City Hotel

Sorracco's Saloon

49

Creek

To Downieville

Herrington's
Sierra Pines

© 2019 Yogi's Books LLC

1197.2 - Water at switchback - You will hear water at one switchback and access at the next. There is a wooden "water" sign on the PCT.

1202.6 - Spring after Sierra Buttes Jeep Trail - About 5 minutes after the jeep road is a gushing spring on the left side of the trail. Take the side trail up to the tower. Great amazing views. You can see forever and get a glimpse of Lassen. Take the loop trail back to the PCT.

1207.3 - Packer Lake Lodge - 530-862-1221. Lodge is 0.7 mile off the PCT. Turn left on Packer Lake Road. At the next junction, go right. Cabins with a 2-night minimum. Restaurant with grab-and-go style food. Beer. Italian style family dinner on Wednesday nights.

1211.7 - Summit Lake Road - Water and camping at Summit Lake.

1216.0 - Little Jamison Creek - There is a 6-foot-tall post near the jeep road on the right. Walk this road to the right a few yards, and you'll find a stream. Piped spring up hill.

1219.7 - The "A" Tree - GREAT spring here. Walk down the road to the left. You'll see the spring on your right. Exactly what is the "A" Tree?

Meadow Ed: "A few years ago, 2001 I think, I got picked up in Truckee and went out to the area where my friends were doing trail work. For years there was a big tree at the crossing that had a bee's nest in it. So someone said 'well, if we've got a B Tree, we need an A tree too!' So there it is. We put a sign on The 'A' Tree that very day."

Go about a mile north on the PCT up the ridge, you'll find decent camping.

1224.0 - West Branch Nelson Creek - Good water. DOUBLE TAP: Good flow off trail, look for campsites to the right of the PCT and you should be able to hear it from there and bushwhack down to it which isn't too hard.

1231.3 - Duck Soup Pond - Way down off the PCT. Gross water.

1232.1 - Second saddle next to seasonal spring - Watch carefully for an old, old, overgrown road at the second saddle with tent sites and a fire ring. From the PCT, take the old road to the right. Go downhill. You'll see a good dirt road and a 2-track below you. Take 2-track to the right, go past a mossy area, ICE COLD spring is just after the mossy area.

1234.8 - Quincy-LaPorte Road - You could go into Quincy CA from here (hitch right), but it's a HARD HITCH. I don't suggest it. No cars on this deserted road. To get water here, go left 0.25 mile down the road to a spot where the highway goes over a creek. Go down on the left side of the highway to filter from the creek.

1236.9 - Alder Spring - BINK: Signed side trail "Alder Spring 800 feet," about a 4 minute walk north off the PCT. Halfway along you cross a paved road and continue on the trail to the ice cold spring with good flow out of metal trough. The area around the junction of the PCT and spring trail has possible camping.

1241.4 - Black Rock Creek Road 22N56 at a saddle - Paved road. Follow a signed trail to the spring. Easy 5-minute walk to ICE COLD WATER.

1244.5 - Fowler Creek - Off PCT.

1249.3 - Delicious Spring - Sometimes this spring is only trickling. Easier to get water here than from Middle Fork Feather River.

1249.7 - Middle Fork Feather River - Big river, good water, great swimming. BUCKEYE & SWIFT: Cross the bridge and follow a side trail right down to the river. The water is the perfect temperature for swimming. DOUBLE TAP: No good campsites from here until around 1258.8.

1253.0 - Bear Creek - Usually good water. Camping here. Watch for poison oak.

1253.7 - Small Creek - Usually good water.

1257.9 - Seasonal spring - Usually good water.

1259.8 - Seasonal spring just before Lookout Rock - Usually good water.

1263.5 - Big Creek Road - Turn left to go to Bucks Lake.

1264.6 - McFarland Spring - BINK: A wooden "Spring" sign on a tree. Always has water.

1265.6 - Creeklet - Usually has water.

1267.9 - Bucks Summit / Bucks Lake Road - This is where the Bucks Lake alternate loop returns to the PCT. You could hitch (go right) to Quincy CA from here. Hitch 3 miles left to the Lakeshore Resort (530-283-2848). Half-pound burgers, homemade pizza, 18 beers on tap.

> DOUBLE TAP: Campsites west of the PCT just before Bucks Lake Road.

1269.1 - Bucks Creek - Usually has water.

1276.2 - Clear Creek Springs - Good water.

1277.6 - Clear Creek - Usually good water.

1278.0 - Pond - Usually has water.

1281.7 - Canyon View Spring - BINK: Small metal trough with water flowing into it.

1286.8 - Belden Town Resort

1286.9 - Highway 70 -   1.5 miles to the right: Caribou Crossroads
30.0 miles to the right: Quincy CA

1263.5 - Bucks Lake Alternate   The Bucks Lake alternate begins on Big Creek Road. This is a 6.8-mile alternate loop, returning to the PCT at Bucks Summit. There are three resorts along the way. If you stay on the PCT instead, the distance to Bucks Summit is only 4.4 miles.

	Haskins Valley Inn and Store	Bucks Lake Lodge Timberline Inn	Lakeshore Resort and Store
CONTACT:	530-283-9667	530-283-2262	530-283-2848
RESUPPLY:	C-Store with good hiker resupply. Canister fuel. 8a-8p every day	No	Snacks only Small C-Store Weekday 9a-7p Weekends 8a-8p
LODGING:	Haskins Valley Inn B&B No TV Includes full hot bkfst Rates: $$$$	Cabins and motel rooms No TV Rates: $$$	Cabins for weekly rent No TV Rates: $$$$
CAMPING:	Fee campground across road.	Free camping.	
RESTAURANT:	Deli sandwiches Breakfast burritos Soups	Open weekends, 8a-9p. Free drink or ice cream for hikers.	Half-pound burgers Homemade pizza 18 beers on tap Sun-Thur 10a-10p Fri-Sat 10a-midnight
ATM:	No	No	No

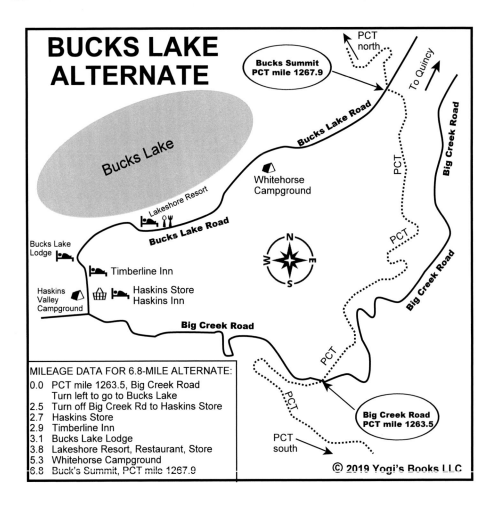

BUCKS LAKE ALTERNATE

Bucks Lake

Bucks Summit
PCT mile 1267.9

PCT north

To Quincy

Bucks Lake Road

Big Creek Road

Whitehorse
Campground

Lakeshore Resort

Bucks Lake Road

PCT

PCT

Bucks Lake
Lodge

Timberline Inn

Haskins
Valley
Campground

Haskins Store
Haskins Inn

Big Creek Road

Big Creek Road

PCT

PCT

Big Creek Road
PCT mile 1263.5

PCT
south

MILEAGE DATA FOR 6.8-MILE ALTERNATE:

0.0 PCT mile 1263.5, Big Creek Road
    Turn left to go to Bucks Lake
2.5 Turn off Big Creek Rd to Haskins Store
2.7 Haskins Store
2.9 Timberline Inn
3.1 Bucks Lake Lodge
3.8 Lakeshore Resort, Restaurant, Store
5.3 Whitehorse Campground
6.8 Buck's Summit, PCT mile 1267.9

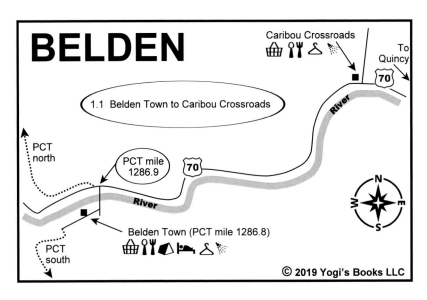

BELDEN

Caribou Crossroads

To
Quincy

70

River

1.1 Belden Town to Caribou Crossroads

PCT
north

PCT mile
1286.9

70

River

Belden Town (PCT mile 1286.8)

PCT
south

BELDEN	Belden Town	Caribou Crossroads
SUMMARY:	Belden Town prices, resupply items, and policies seem to change from year to year.	Caribou Crossroads Store/Restaurant 2018: 6a-6p every day in high season Closed Tuesdays during off season.
CONTACT:	530-283-9662	530-283-1384 [www.cariboucrossroads.com]
GETTING HERE:	On trail.	Use caution walking Hwy 70 (dangerous). Braatens offer shuttles for guests.
RESUPPLY:	Sometimes the small store has decent hiker resupply. However, this seems to change from year to year. Usually open Mon-Thur 8a-8p, Fri-Sun 8a-9p.	Caribou: New owners for 2019. 2018: 6a-6p every day in high season Closed Tuesdays during off season.
SHIPPING TO BELDEN:	Packages shipped to the Belden Zip Code via UPS, FedEx, and DHL often end up in Oroville CA instead of Belden CA. If you have anything shipped to Belden using UPS or FedEx, be sure that it is shipped pure UPS or FedEx (not SmartPost, SurePost, or other Ground to Post Office hybrids). *This is especially important when ordering from REI, Amazon, etc.*	
MAIL DROPS:	2018: Accepts mail drops, **UPS OR FEDEX ONLY.** Mail Drop fee is $10-$20, depending upon the size. **UPS or FedEx only:** Hiker's Legal Name PCT Hiker, ETA: MM/DD/YY c/o Belden Town Resort 14785 Belden Town Road Belden, CA 95915	2017 and earlier: The Caribou Village Post Office accepted USPS mail drops, no fee. Outgoing mail was letters and Priority Mail Flat Rate boxes only. Stamps for sale. Sounds good, but it didn't work well. The store was typically understaffed. Hikers arrived to find the store closed during the day, or their mail drops could not be found when the store was open. If the store is closed when mail is delivered, mail will NOT be left at the store; instead it will be sent to Quincy (30 miles from Belden). If you want to risk it, here are the Caribou addresses:
	USPS only: Hiker's Legal Name PCT Hiker, ETA: MM/DD/YY c/o Caribou Crossroads PO Box 1 Belden CA 95915	**UPS or FedEx only:** Hiker's Legal Name PCT Hiker, ETA: MM/DD/YY c/o Caribou Crossroads 16242 State Hwy 70 Belden CA 95915
LODGING:	Motel Rooms. Rates: $$$ CAMPING: Near the river. Sometimes free, sometimes there is a fee. USFS land nearby; camp there for free.	Camping space for up to six tents.
RESTAURANT:	Restaurant usually 8a-8p. Bar usually 8a-10p.	Diner with good food. Excellent milkshakes!! Usually open 8a-5p every day. The grill closes at 4:30p.
LAUNDRY:	Yes. Inquire at the store.	Yes.
SHOWER:	Yes. Inquire at the store.	Yes.
PAY PHONE:	Across from store.	No.
FUEL:	Store usually stocks canister fuel.	New owners for 2018. 2017: Canisters and HEET at store.
ATM:	ATM inside bar.	No.
	Looking ahead: No ATM at Old Station, Burney Falls State Park, or Castella. Castle Crags State Park (campground at Castella) does not take credit cards.	

OVERVIEW: Typical small trail town.

GETTING HERE: (1) PCT mile 1234.8 - Quincy-LaPorte Road - Hitch to Quincy (go right). Not recommended. Extremely little traffic on this road.

                (2) PCT mile 1267.9 - Bucks Lake Road - Hitch to Quincy (go right).

                (3) PCT mile 1286.9 - Highway 70/Belden - Take Highway 70 East (right) from Belden to Quincy. This is approximately 30 miles.

BUS SERVICE: Plumas County Transit (530-283-2538) local bus service in Quincy. Bus runs Mon-Fri only, 7a-10p. Also service from Quincy to Chester.

HIKER SERVICES: Plumas Crisis Intervention & Resource Center (PCIRC) accepts packages, hot showers, laundry, internet access, cell phone charging.

POST OFFICE: 530-283-3912, USPS only   Hiker's Legal Name
Mon-Fri 8:30a-5p   PCT Hiker, ETA: MM/DD/YY
PO closed on Saturday, but hikers can pick General Delivery
up packages on Saturdays from 2p-3p.   Quincy, CA 95971
Knock on the dutch door.

General Delivery held for 15 days, unless you call to ask them to hold longer or to forward.

MAIL DROPS: Plumas Crisis Intervention & Resource   Hiker's Legal Name
Center (PCIRC) accepts mail drops, no fee. PCT Hiker, ETA: MM/DD/YY
Package must have ETA.   c/o PCIRC
530-283-5515   591 Main Street
                                   Quincy, CA 95971

RESUPPLY: Safeway Supermarket   530-283-1404   Open 24 hours
                Quincy Natural Foods   530-283-3528   Mon-Sat 7a-8p. Sun 8a-7p.

OUTFITTER: Feather River Outdoors   530-283-0455   Mon-Fri 10a-6p. Sat 9:30a-4:30p. Sun closed.

RESTAURANTS: Many restaurants.
Free supper every Wednesday at 6pm at Methodist Church.

LAUNDRY: Yes.
ATM: Yes.
COMPUTER: Plumas County Library   530-283-6310
MEDICAL: Plumas District Hospital   530-283-2121
FUEL: HEET at hardware store by Safeway.

QUINCY LODGING		Rates	TV, micr, frig, AC	laundry
Gold Pan Lodge	530-283-3686	$$	Y	no
Spanish Creek Motel	530-283-1200	$$ ask for PCT rate	Y	no
Quincy Courtyard Suites	530-283-1401	$$$$	TV, kitchens	Y
Pine Hill Motel	530-286-1670	kitchenette cabins		
There are also several motels in East Quincy, 3 miles from Quincy.				

                    $ = usually less than $50
                    $$ = usually $50-$80
                    $$$ = usually $80-$110
                    $$$$ = usually greater than $110

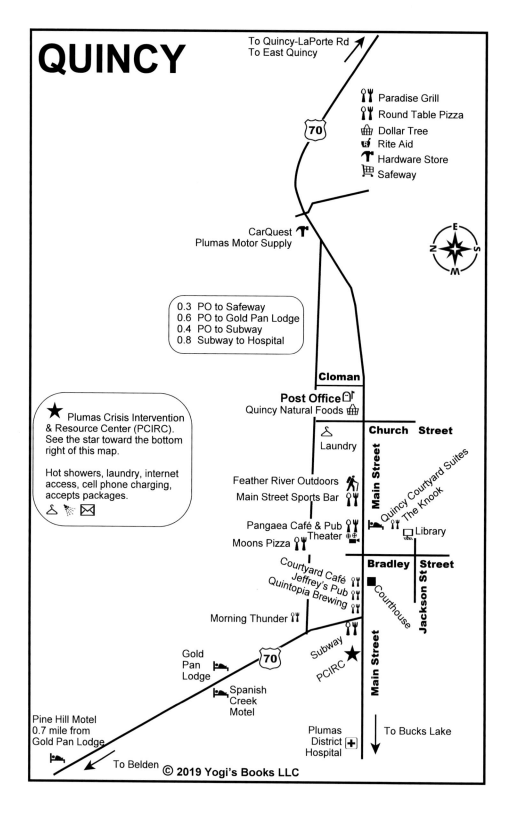

QUINCY

To Quincy-LaPorte Rd
To East Quincy

70

- 🍴 Paradise Grill
- 🍴 Round Table Pizza
- 🏬 Dollar Tree
- Rite Aid
- 🔨 Hardware Store
- 🛒 Safeway

CarQuest
Plumas Motor Supply

0.3 PO to Safeway
0.6 PO to Gold Pan Lodge
0.4 PO to Subway
0.8 Subway to Hospital

Cloman

Post Office 📪
Quincy Natural Foods 🏬

★ Plumas Crisis Intervention
& Resource Center (PCIRC).
See the star toward the bottom
right of this map.

Hot showers, laundry, internet
access, cell phone charging,
accepts packages.

Laundry

Church   Street

Feather River Outdoors
Main Street Sports Bar

Quincy Courtyard Suites
The Knook

Pangaea Café & Pub
Theater
Moons Pizza

Main Street

📖 Library

Courtyard Café
Jeffrey's Pub
Quintopia Brewing

Bradley   Street

Courthouse

Jackson St

Morning Thunder

Subway

Gold
Pan
Lodge

70

★
PCIRC

Spanish
Creek
Motel

Main Street

Pine Hill Motel
0.7 mile from
Gold Pan Lodge

Plumas
District
Hospital ✚

To Bucks Lake

To Belden © 2019 Yogi's Books LLC

DOUBLE TAP: It's a big ~4,800 ft climb out of Belden. The first 5 miles out of Belden is exposed and very hot, start early in the morning. Once you get to Rattlesnake Spring at mile 1291.8 you get good tree coverage for the rest of the big climb.

1287.9 - Indian Creek - Water here. Campsite below the trail before crossing the bridge.
Several creeks between 1287.9 (Indian Creek) and 1292.7 (Williams Cabin).

1291.8 - Rattlesnake Spring - Usually good water.

1292.7 - Williams Cabin Site - Water on trail. No cabin here.

1293.6 - Myrtle Flat Camp - Water here.

1293.6 (Myrtle Flat Camp) to 1297.3 (creek fed by Poison Spring) - Several creeks here.

1297.3 - Creek fed by Poison Spring -
Usually good water, but it's off trail to the left and can be hard to get to.

1299.6 - Poison Spring headwater (Andesite Spring) - Water here.

1301.1 - Frog Spring - Good cold water.

1305.4 - Humbug Road 27N01 at Cold Springs - Cross the road, then the spring is to the left about 0.1 mile. Look for a big 'ol trough. Piped water. Many good campsites.

1313.2 - Robbers Spring - BINK: Sign on post reads "Spring 0.3 mile" marks a side trail which drops to the right. Good water, but steep 300 feet elevation loss to get to the spring. DOUBLE TAP (2014): Get water here. Many hikers could not find the water at 1318.0 (Carter Meadow).

1318.0 - Carter Meadow Trail Junction - Flowing in 2016, 2017, 2018. Many hikers have trouble finding this water. Water 0.5 mile down the hill. NOCONA (2004): Just a puddle, but clear and cold. You have to keep your eyes open — it's on the right side of the trail as you descend. HOT SISTER (2006): I did not find the pond, but there was a small stream off to the left in a meadowy area about a half mile down the side trail.

1328.0 - Soldier Creek Springs - Good cold water.

1331.3 - Highway 36 - Chester CA is 8 miles to the right.

1333.1 - Marian Creek - Dry.

1334.8 - Stover Camp spring - Great water. Look for gushing piped spring.

1340.7 - North Fork Feather River - Water here.

1346.0 - Descend NW to an abandoned road - Sometimes a creek crosses the PCT just after this road, which is just before the boundary to Lassen Volcanic National Park.

1346.3 - Boundary Spring - BINK: At the southern boundary of Lassen Volcanic Nat'l Park, a side trail signed "Boundary Spring 400 feet" drops to the right.

1346.3 to 1365.5 - PCT passes through Lassen National Park - According to the Lassen NP website below, "Overnight backcountry users must use a bear canister." *You do not need a canister if you hike through this area during the day (do not stay overnight). One exception: Warner Valley Campground is at mile 1350.3. You can legally camp at Warner Valley Campground WITHOUT a bear canister as long as you put your food in the bear boxes. Everything here in italics was confirmed via phone call to Lassen National Park in July, 2018.*
[https://www.nps.gov/lavo/planyourvisit/wilderness-permit-information.htm]

1346.6 - Swampy Little Willow Lake -
PCT crosses the outlet, which is rarely flowing. Lots of mosquitos here.

1347.5 - Terminal Geyser - It's worth the trip!!

OVERVIEW: Compact, all services (except no outfitter). The only drawback is that most of the motels do not have air conditioning, and you'll probably be here in July. It's hot.

GETTING HERE: Hitch 8 miles to the right where the PCT crosses Highway 36. Pay close attention to where the PCT crosses the highway. It can be hard to spot the PCT from a car going 55 mph, and you need to know where to stop on your hitch back out.

POST OFFICE: 530-258-4184, USPS only
Mon-Fri 8:30a-4p
Sat closed
General Delivery held for 30 days

 Hiker's Legal Name
PCT Hiker, ETA: MM/DD/YY
General Delivery
Chester, CA 96020

RESUPPLY: Holiday Foods Supermarket 530-258-2122 7a-10p every day

OUTDOOR STORE: The Sports Nut 530-258-3327

RESTAURANTS: Yes.

LAUNDRY: Yes.

SHOWER: At the laundromat and RV Park.

ATM: Yes.

COMPUTER: Library 530-258-2742

FUEL: Denatured and canisters at Ayoobs Ace Hardware 530-258-2611
Denatured at Chester True Value Hardware 530-258-3955
HEET at Napa Auto Parts 530-258-3151
Canister Fuel at The Sports Nut 530-258-3327

MEDICAL: Seneca Hospital 530-258-2151

GET SOME CASH: Old Station, Burney Falls State Park, and Castella do not have ATMs.
Castle Crags State Park (campground at Castella) does not take credit cards.

CHESTER LODGING ask for hiker rates	Rates	TV	frig	micr	AC	laundry	other
Antlers Motel 530-258-2722	$$$	Y	Y	no	Y	no	fireplaces
Best Western 530-258-2002	$$$$ ask for hiker rate	Y	Y	Y	Y	Y	cont bkfst, hot tub, computer for guests
Cedar Lodge 530-258-2904	$$ - $$$$ ask for hiker rate	Y	Y	Y	no	no	3 miles out of town Pool, BBQ. Bakery next door.
Seneca Motel 530-258-2815	$$	Y	some	some	no	no	ask for hiker rate
Leisure RV Park 530-258-2302	$ camping					Y	showers & laundry
Lutheran Church	*UNCONFIRMED:* *Camping at the church. No response to phone messages.* *Camping was allowed in 2018.*						
	$ = usually less than $50 $$ = usually $50-$80 $$$ = usually $80-$110 $$$$ = usually greater than $110						

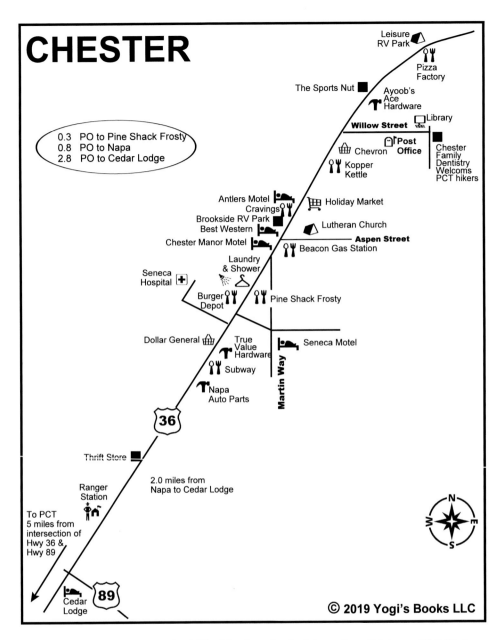

CHESTER

Leisure RV Park

Pizza Factory

The Sports Nut

Ayoob's Ace Hardware

Library

Willow Street

0.3 PO to Pine Shack Frosty
0.8 PO to Napa
2.8 PO to Cedar Lodge

Chevron

Post Office

Chester Family Dentistry Welcoms PCT hikers

Kopper Kettle

Antlers Motel
Cravings

Holiday Market

Brookside RV Park
Best Western

Lutheran Church

Chester Manor Motel

Aspen Street

Beacon Gas Station

Laundry & Shower

Seneca Hospital

Burger Depot

Pine Shack Frosty

Dollar General

True Value Hardware

Seneca Motel

Martin Way

Subway

Napa Auto Parts

36

Thrift Store

2.0 miles from Napa to Cedar Lodge

Ranger Station

To PCT
5 miles from intersection of Hwy 36 & Hwy 89

Cedar Lodge **89**

© 2019 Yogi's Books LLC

Leaving Chester, returning to the PCT - 5.0 miles after the intersection of Highways 36 & 89, there is a "Soft Shoulder" road sign on the right. The highway crests a little hill. The PCT is at the crest, near green highway signs for Highways 36 and 89. On the left (south) side of the highway are stairs leading up to the sobo trail. On the right (north) side is a vehicle turnaround.

Bus: Susanville Indian Rancheria Public Transit Program (530-257-1128) leaves Chester at 8:35am Mon, Wed, Fri, in front of the Holiday Market back to the PCT. $3 in 2018.

1350.0 - Drakesbad Guest Ranch

CONTACT:	Drakesbad is open from early-June to Columbus Day. Drakesbad is under new management for 2019: Snow Mountain, LLC. Contact: 209-763-2850. PCT page on the website states that hikers have these amenities: Swimming pool, warm showers, evening meals, restrooms, mail service. [http://lassenlodging.com/pct/]
GETTING HERE:	From the junction at PCT mile 1349.7, look downhill and you'll see the swimming pool. Do not bushwhack down to Drakesbad from here. There is a decent sized stream to cross, and there are posted signs at Drakesbad deterring people from cutting up to the PCT from the pool. <u>There are two ways to get to Drakesbad:</u>

    (1) <u>Mile 1349.7</u> - Follow the signs which lead you to the left, and eventually you'll circle back around to Drakesbad.

    (2) <u>Mile 1350.0</u> - When you reach the dirt road near Warner Valley Campground, take the road to the left to Drakesbad.

MAIL DROPS:	Accepts mail drops, no fee. USPS, UPS, FedEx. Mail must have ETA. No outgoing mail. Click-n-Ship does not work for Drakesbad address.	Hiker's Legal Name PCT Hiker, ETA: MM/DD/YY c/o Drakesbad Guest Ranch End of Warner Valley Road Chester, CA 96020
	Mail is not delivered to Drakesbad; it is picked up in town by Drakesbad staff. So, overnight, Amazon 2-day shipping, and other express shipping will probably not arrive at Drakesbad quickly. Send your package early!	
CAMPING:	<u>Warner Valley Campground</u> on the PCT, 0.25 mile from Drakesbad.	
RESTAURANT:	Beer available here!	
	Evening meals are available for PCT'ers. No mention of breakfast or lunch.	
LAUNDRY:	No.	
SHOWER:	Yes.	

1350.3 - Warner Valley Campground - Water spigots and bear boxes. Proper overnight food protection (bear canister or use of bear boxes) is required within Lassen National Park (mile 1346.3 to 1365.5). Per the Lassen NP website below, "Overnight backcountry users must use a bear canister." *You do not need a canister if you hike through this area during the day (do not stay overnight). One exception: Warner Valley Campground is at mile 1350.3. You can legally camp at Warner Valley Campground WITHOUT a bear canister as long as you put your food in the bear boxes. Everything here in italics was confirmed via phone call to Lassen National Park in July, 2018.* https://www.nps.gov/lavo/planyourvisit/wilderness-permit-information.htm

1351.3 - Trail to Mt. Lassen

1352.9 - Campsites - Kings Creek always has water.

1355.3 - Junction to Horseshoe Lake - Water here.

1357.0 - Swan Lake outlet creek - No water.

1363.5 - East end of Badger Flat - No water.

1365.5 - Depart Lassen National Park

1369.6 - Campsites and water - Water on the left of the PCT in Hat Creek.

OLD STATION	PO & Hat Creek Resort PCT mile 1373.4	Fill-Up, JJ's Café, & Rim Rock Ranch, PCT mile 1377.3
GETTING HERE:	At mile 1373.4, follow the gated road (instead of the PCT which goes to the right). You'll soon see a horse corral on the left. Walk past the horse corral. The Post Office, tiny C-Store, and Hat Creek Resort are to the right of the big grassy open area. The shower/laundry building is to the left of the grassy area.	At mile 1377.3, turn left on Hwy 44, walk 0.2 mile till you get to the intersection of Hwy 44 & Hwy 89. Turn left on Hwy 89. Walk 0.2 mile farther, and you'll reach the Old Station Fill-Up C-Store. Rim Rock Ranch is 0.4 mile past the Fill-Up.
MAIL:	**POST OFFICE:** 530-335-7191, USPS only, Mon-Fri 11a-3p Sat 1p-2p for package pick up & cash sales only. Mail must have a valid domestic return address, and a phone number is helpful. The Old Station Postmaster goes to great lengths to return unclaimed mail to hikers, including making posts on Facebook. If you provide your phone number, her job will be easier. Hiker mail held until end of hiker season. Hiker's Legal Name PCT Hiker, ETA: MM/DD/YY General Delivery Old Station, CA 96071	**MAIL DROPS:** JJ's Café accepts UPS/FedEx packages, no fee. Open 7a-3p every day from late-April until mid-November. Email Chuck first so they can verify receipt: [chuck.woodman@gmail.com] Hiker's Legal Name PCT Hiker, ETA: MM/DD/YY c/o JJ's Café 13385 Hwy 89 Old Station, CA 96071
RESUPPLY:	Hat Creek Store 530-335-7121 This is a tiny C-Store with very limited snacks. No hiker resupply. Usually opens at 8a, closes between 5p and 8p. Hours vary.	Old Station Fill-Up 530-335-3152 Small C-Store. Summer hours usually 7a-7p. Rim Rock Ranch Store. 530-335-7174. Best hiker resupply in Old Station. Small C-Store, carries Idahoans and Pasta Roni.
RESTAURANT:	No, but there are sandwiches and scooped ice cream at the store.	JJ's Café (530-335-7225) Usually 7a-3p every day. Sometimes open for dinner from Memorial Day until mid-August. Call to find out. Breakfast, burgers, beer, and more!
LODGING:	Hat Creek Resort. 530-335-7121. Check in at the Store. Motel rooms, and cabins with cable TV, microwave, frig. Rates: $$$ + Yurts available.	Rim Rock Ranch. 530-335-7114. Housekeeping cabins, motel units, B & B.
CAMPING:	Hat Creek Resort 530-335-7121. Pay camping, 5 people per site, includes showers.	No, but you can camp back along the PCT.
SHOWER:	Yes.	Yes, at JJ's Café whenever the Café is open in Spring/Summer/Fall. $4 for 6min.
LAUNDRY: **ATM:**	Yes, at the shower building. No.	No. No.
FUEL:	Usually HEET at Hat Creek Store.	Usually HEET at Old Station Fill-Up.

OLD STATION

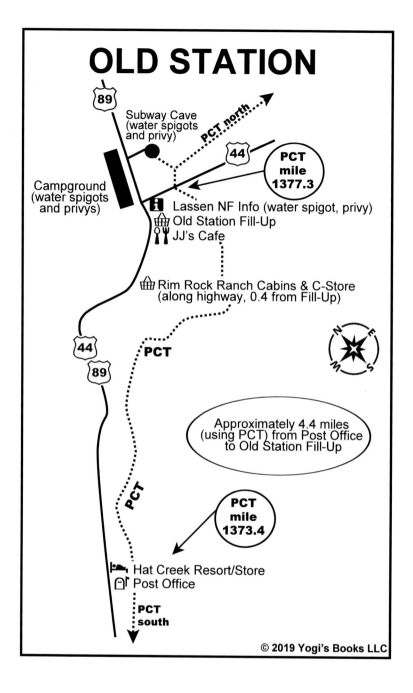

89

Subway Cave
(water spigots
and privy)

PCT north...

44

PCT
mile
1377.3

Campground
(water spigots
and privys)

Lassen NF Info (water spigot, privy)
Old Station Fill-Up
JJ's Cafe

Rim Rock Ranch Cabins & C-Store
(along highway, 0.4 from Fill-Up)

44

89

PCT

N
E
S
W

PCT

Approximately 4.4 miles
(using PCT) from Post Office
to Old Station Fill-Up

PCT
mile
1373.4

Hat Creek Resort/Store
Post Office

PCT
south

© 2019 Yogi's Books LLC

1377.3 - Cross Highway 44 - To reach the Old Station Fill-Up C-Store: Turn left on Hwy 44, walk 0.2 mile till you get to the intersection of Hwy 44 & Hwy 89. Turn left on Hwy 89. Walk 0.2 mile farther, and you'll reach the Old Station Fill-Up.

1377.5 - Subway Cave A few minutes after crossing Highway 44, you'll see an unmarked left-branching trail. This goes to Subway Cave. Cool cave, be sure to take your headlamp and a jacket. It's dark and cold in there. Water spigots near Subway Cave.

1385.5 - Lost Creek - Good, cold water. BINK: As you walk along the south side of Lost Creek Canyon, there is a new trail with a sign on a post reading "Lost Creek" with newly cut trail going down to the spring which is the source of this creek (1/3 mile down to the creek on the switchbacking trail. Many years ago in 1997 I had left Subway Cave with not enough water and bushwhacked down to that spring. I remember it having a very high flow (probably in the hundreds of gallons a minute) and being very ice cold, and for all these years wondered why they did not build a side trail down to it. Well now they have.

1393.5 - Road 22 - Water tank next to the old corral visible from where the PCT crosses FR22.

1406.9 - Rock Spring Creek - Has water, sometimes gross water.

1407.3 - PG & E Road - 0.2 miles to the right is the PG&E campground. Water, privy trash cans.

1407.4 - Crystal Lake State Fish Hatchery Road - Shortly after this road is a junction which is signed "Meadow Loop Trail." The PCT goes left at this junction.

1407.7 - Baum Lake - DOUBLE TAP: Nice spot to take a dip in the lake and to get some water to the right of the PCT after crossing the lake for the 2nd time.

1409.7 - Burney Mountain Guest Ranch - See below.

1411.3 - Highway 299 - Burney CA is 7 miles to the left.

1418.0 - Highway 89 - Shortly after crossing the highway, you'll see a trail junction on the right. This is an alternate route into Burney Falls State Park. In a geeky way, this is a super cool alternate route because you pass the springs that create Burney Creek. In less than a mile, you watch a dry creek bed become raging Burney Falls.

CONTACT: [www.burneymountainguestranch.com]
                [BurneyMountainGuestRanch@integrity.com]
                530-335-2544

GETTING HERE: 0.3 miles off the PCT.
                Turn left on the power line road, go 0.1 mile to the gravel road and turn left.

MAIL DROPS: Accepts mail drops, $5 fee. Outgoing mail is postage plus $2.

USPS address:	UPS or FedEx address:
Hiker's Legal Name	Hiker's Legal Name
PCT Hiker, ETA: MM/DD/YY	PCT Hiker, ETA: MM/DD/YY
c/o Burney Mountain Guest Ranch	c/o Burney Mountain Guest Ranch
PO Box 2588	22800 Guest Ranch Road
Burney, CA 96013	Cassel, CA 96013

RESUPPLY: Decent hiker resupply and ice cream

LODGING: Bunk Room: $$$$ per bunk per night

                Private Room: $$$$ per night, $20 each additional person.

                Rate for Bunk Room or Private Room includes mail drop receipt, one load of
                laundry, shower, breakfast, dinner, swimming pool access.

RESTAURANT: Breakfast, lunch, and dinner are available.

CAMPING: 2018: $25 includes camping, shower, laundry, pool, breakfast.

LAUNDRY: Washer, no dryer.

SHOWER: Yes.

WiFi: Yes.

Access these files as often as possible:

(1) **Pacific Crest Trail Water Report -** Current status of water sources.
     Frequently updated during hiker season. [www.pctwater.com]

(2) **Yogi's PCT Handbook update file -** Changes to trail/town information which have
     occurred between the time your book was printed and now. Frequently updated during
     hiker season. [www.yogisbooks.com], then click UPDATES & LINKS

Do you have changes/updates to report?
If so, send them here: yogisbooks@gmail.com

1411.3 - The Town of Burney CA

OVERVIEW: This is the <u>TOWN</u> of Burney, not Burney Falls State <u>PARK</u>.

GETTING HERE: Hitch 7 miles to the left on Hwy 299.

TAXI: <u>Burney Taxi</u>. 530-605-7950

TRAIL ANGELS: Search "Burney PCT Angels" on Facebook.

POST OFFICE: 530-335-5430, USPS only
Mon-Fri 9:30a-4p. Sat closed.
General Delivery held for 30 days

Hiker's Legal Name
PCT Hiker, ETA: MM/DD/YY
General Delivery
Burney, CA <u>96013</u>

MAIL DROPS: <u>Word of Life Assembly Church</u>
530-335-4419. Accepts mail drops.
USPS, UPS, FedEx.

Hiker's Legal Name
PCT Hiker, ETA: MM/DD/YY
c/o Word of Life Assembly Church
37341 Main Street
Burney, CA 96013

RESUPPLY: <u>Safeway Supermarket</u>   530-335-3212 6a-11p daily.

SPORTS STORE: <u>Burney Sporting Goods</u>   530-335-4033 Limited clothing and shoes.
Has hiking poles and DEET.

LODGING: The check-in for The Charm Motel and Green Gables Motel is called
"Burney Falls Lodging" (see town map).

RESTAURANTS: Yes.

LAUNDRY: Yes.

SHOWER: At Word of Life Church.

ATM: Yes.

COMPUTER: <u>Library</u> 530-335-4317

FUEL: No HEET at gas stations.
Sometimes HEET at Napa Auto Parts   530-335-4544
Canister fuel usually at Burney Sporting Goods   530-335-4033

MEDICAL: <u>Burney Health Center</u>   530-335-5457

BURNEY LODGING Ask for hiker rates		Rates	Cable TV, pool, AC	frig micr	laundry
Charm Motel	530-335-3300	$$$	Y	Y	Y
Green Gables Motel	530-335-3300	$$$	Y	Y	use laundry at Charm Motel
Burney Motel	530-335-4500	$$$	Y	Y	Y
Shasta Pines Motel	530-335-2201	$$	Y	some	no
Word of Life Assembly Church	530-335-4419	Maximum 20 people per night. Sleep in gym. Showers. Free WiFi. Use of kitchen. Usually give rides to trail.			
		$ = usually less than $50 $$ = usually $50-$80 $$$ = usually $80-$110 $$$$ = usually greater than $110			

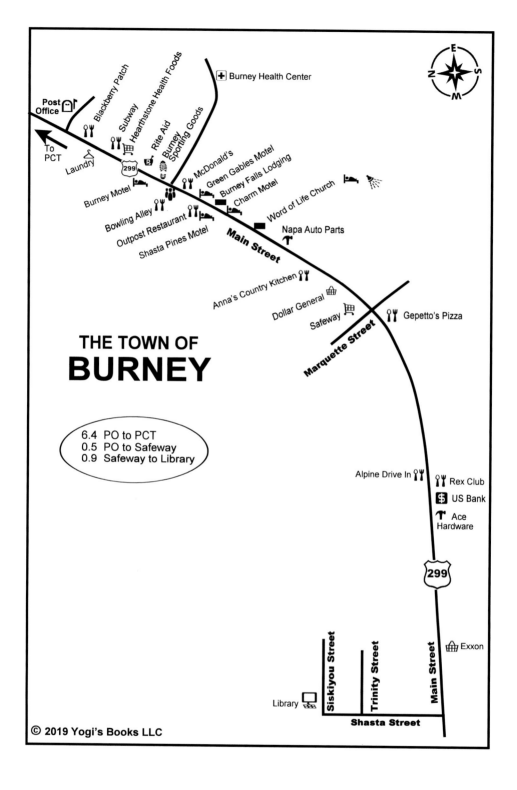

THE TOWN OF
BURNEY

6.4 PO to PCT
0.5 PO to Safeway
0.9 Safeway to Library

© 2019 Yogi's Books LLC

1419.0 - Burney Falls State Park

OVERVIEW:
Burney Falls State Park   530-335-2777
Burney Falls Camp Store   530-335-5713

This is the State PARK, not the TOWN of Burney (mile point 1411.3).
The Park caters to shiny, happy, car-driving tourists, not PCT Hikers.

[www.parks.ca.gov] search "McArthur-Burney Falls Memorial State Park"

GETTING HERE:
See Handbook map for "Burney Falls State Park"

(1) If you come into the Park on the PCT, you'll leave the PCT at mile 1419.0, then cross the creek via a large bridge. Then veer to the left and find your way to the Park entrance kiosk (where the cars drive in). Enter the Park, stay on the road, and the store will be on the right.

(2) If you took the alternate route (PCT mile 1418.0) into the Park past the springs, you do not cross the bridge. Near the bridge, you'll see the paved roads. Veer to the left along the road and find your way to the park entrance kiosk (where the cars drive in). Enter the Park, stay on the road, and the store will be on the right.

IMPORTANT! If you want to take a shower, stop at the entrance gate to get quarters. The store will only make change for $2 of quarters.

MAIL DROPS:
The store accepts mail drops, USPS, UPS, FedEx. Store phone 530-335-5713.

Store usually open 8a-8p during summer. Closes after Labor Day.

2018 mail fee is $7/box and $2.50/letter, cash only. No outgoing mail.

Make your box very unique-looking. Many hikers (myself included) were told that our boxes were not here, when they actually were. We had to ask the staff to go look for our boxes again – they found our boxes the second time.

Hiker's Legal Name
PCT Hiker, ETA: MM/DD/YY
c/o Burney Park Camp Store
McArthur Burney Falls State Park
24900 State Highway 89
Burney, CA 96013

RESUPPLY:
Store usually open 8a-8p every day during high season,
8a-6p toward the end of the summer, 9a-5p after Labor Day.
You cannot resupply here.
Food selection is less than a C-Store, and it is expensive.

LODGING:
Primitive cabins: bunks, covered porch, propane heat. No electricity or plumbing.
Bath house nearby with bathrooms and showers. 2018: $65-$105

CAMPING:
Yes. $ hiker/biker site.

RESTAURANTS:
No restaurant. Store has frozen food, veggie burgers, sandwiches, hot dogs, pretzels, soft serve ice cream.

SHOWERS:
Clean coin-operated showers at the campground. Inquire at the store.
Store will only make change for $2 of quarters.
You can get more quarters back at the entrance gate.

ATM:
No.

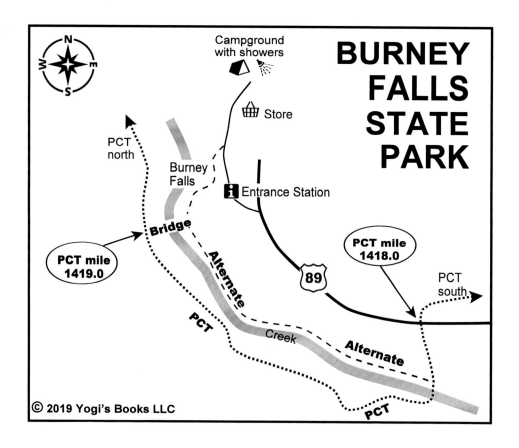

POISON OAK - Section "O," which is the next 82.2 miles, is crawling with poison oak.
LEAVING BURNEY FALLS - Go back to the big bridge, cross the creek, turn right.

1424.5 - Rock Creek - Water here. BANDANA: The best swimming on the entire trail. STRAIGHT
JACKET: Don't try sliding from the upper pool to the lower one. It looks fun, it's not, it's very
bumpy. DOUBLE TAP: Campsites on north side of the bridge 0.1 mile up on the left.

1427.8 - Upper Jake Spring - BINK: Side trail on left of PCT goes to spring.
A few yards north from the sign on the PCT is a flat camping area.

1428.6 - Screwdriver Spring - BINK: Signed side trail drops 0.2 mile west off the PCT on what appears
to be an old skid road.

1430.0 - DOUBLE TAP: At trail to left down to spring, look to the right and you will see a flat open spot
(old abandoned jeep road) with many good campsites.

1432.7 - Peavine Creek - The PCT emerges at a logging road.
On the road, cross Peavine Creek, and come to an
intersection with road 37N30. Turn right and look for
a faint trail down to Peavine Creek. There is a large
pool here. SOCKS: There is a hunter's camp down
the road to the left about 0.25 mile. Nice open grassy
spaces for camping.

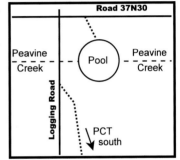

1436.2 - Red Mountain Pond-
BINK: Signed side trail
goes north 100 feet off the PCT.

1436.9 - Clark Spring - BINK: Go east down
road to spring. Good water all year.
DOUBLE TAP: Campsites at the road.

1438.8 - Junction of two roads to Deadman Creek - Creek
usually dry.
GIRL SCOUT: This road is marked "R3000" on a sign on a tree.

1440.4 - Kosk Spring - BINK: Sign indicates spring is 0.2 miles down west.

1442.9 - (approximately) - BINK: The trail will cross a wet muddy area. Look for a small trail going 25
feet up the hill (to the east) to where water issues from under a rocky ledge in a fast trickle.
There is a metal trough to channel the flow of water to fill bottles. This small "spring" (if you
can call it that) is mostly reliable, but the flow does diminish quite a bit in the fall. Hopefully the
metal trough will help.

1447.7 - Springs at Moosehead Creek's headwaters - BINK: There is side trail here signed
"Moosehead Springs" with a trail that drops north off the PCT down into the creek drainage
area. If water is not flowing across the trail, go 10 yards down past the campsite, where a
rough trail drops into the creek bed. Water can always be found here.

1455.1 - Alder Creek Trail - Water 0.5 off PCT. WOLF (2014): Follow Alder spur trail from PCT, spur
trail joins a dirt road which forks a couple of times; follow small cairns at forks. Half a mile
down from PCT a cairn on the left marks the place to leave the dirt road. There is a dry creek
bed right there, but follow it up to the right some 50 feet for ice cold running water.

1457.9 - Recross Grizzly Peak Road -
There are usually a few seasonal springs/streams in the next 2.6 miles.

1458.1 - Gold Creek Trail Junction - BINK: A signed side trail heads north 0.2 mile off the PCT here.

1461.6 - Deer Creek Spring - BINK: A signed side trail drops north off the PCT.

1462.6 - Deer Creek - Water here. BINK: Deer Creek always flows.

1463.7 - Side canyon with refreshing creek - Water here.

1467.1 - Butcherknife Creek - Water here.

1470.7 - McCloud-Big Bend Road - Water here.

1470.9 - Ash Camp - Water and privy here.

1473.1 - Fitzhugh Gulch Creek - Water and campsites here.

1473.4 - Jeep Road - DOUBLE TAP: Look to your right for a turnout with good campsites.

1476.5 - Abandoned unpaved jeep road - Camping here.

1480.4 to 1482.9 - DOUBLE TAP: A lot of poison oak here with some overhanging the trail.

1481.4 - Trough Creek - Water here. DOUBLE TAP: Lots of poison oak.

1484.6 - Squaw Valley Creek - Water here.
DOUBLE TAP: Cross the bridge and look left for the steep trails heading down to the creek.

1494.0 - Spring - Water here.

1494.8 - Fall Creek - Water here.

1496.4 - Campsite - DOUBLE TAP: When you hit the unpaved road, turn right and follow it up and around for ~200 ft. Once you see Mount Shasta to your left look to your right and climb small hill for a perfect campsite looking right at Mount Shasta.

1500.8 - Riverside Road - See Castella map:

Stay on the PCT: Two options:

(1) At PCT mile 1500.8, turn right, follow Riverside Road until it merges with Soda Creek Road. Continue on Soda Creek Road and immediately cross over Soda Creek. A few minutes later cross over the Sacramento River, then cross over the train tracks. Continue on Soda Creek Road up to the Interstate. Walk under interstate, then PCT tread continues uphill.

(2) At PCT mile 1500.8, cross over Riverside Road, and the trail tread continues on the other side of the road for just a couple minutes. The PCT re-emerges at a green gate at a V-intersection of Soda Creek Road and Riverside Road. Turn left onto Soda Creek Road, and immediately cross over Soda Creek. A few minutes later cross over the Sacramento River, then cross over the train tracks. Continue on Soda Creek Road up to the Interstate. Walk under interstate, then PCT tread continues uphill.

Go to Castella: Three options:

(A) At PCT mile 1500.8, turn right, follow Riverside Road until it merges with Soda Creek Road. Continue on Soda Creek Road and immediately cross over Soda Creek. A few minutes later cross over the Sacramento River, then cross over the train tracks. Continue on Soda Creek Road until you reach Frontage Road, turn left. Walk Frontage Road approximately 2 miles, turn right on Castle Creek Road. Go under the interstate, you will see the Post Office and Ammirati's on the left.

(B) At PCT mile 1500.8, turn left onto Riverside Road. Shortly after the Picnic Area, turn right, cross the train tracks, intersect Frontage Road. Turn left. Go to Castle Creek Road, turn right. Go under the interstate, you will see the Post Office and Ammirati's on the left.

(C) Follow (1) or (2) above.
Stay on PCT until mile 1503.7, then take Bobs Hat Trail down to Castella.

MT. SHASTA - DUNSMUIR - CASTELLA
Overview

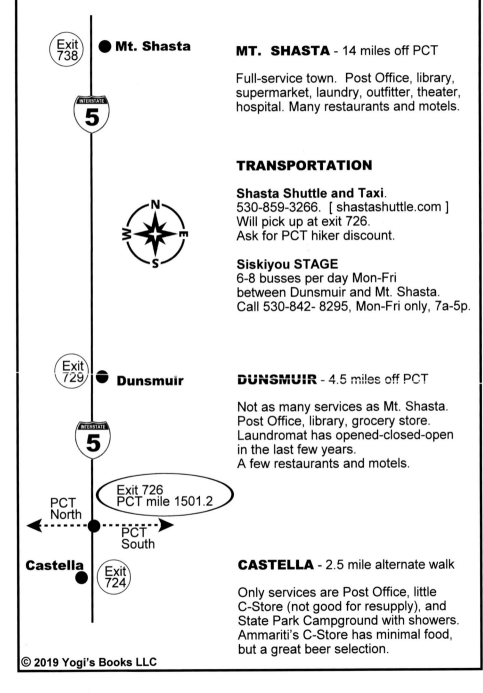

Exit 738 ● Mt. Shasta

MT. SHASTA - 14 miles off PCT

Full-service town. Post Office, library, supermarket, laundry, outfitter, theater, hospital. Many restaurants and motels.

TRANSPORTATION

Shasta Shuttle and Taxi.
530-859-3266. [shastashuttle.com]
Will pick up at exit 726.
Ask for PCT hiker discount.

Siskiyou STAGE
6-8 busses per day Mon-Fri
between Dunsmuir and Mt. Shasta.
Call 530-842- 8295, Mon-Fri only, 7a-5p.

Exit 729 ● Dunsmuir

DUNSMUIR - 4.5 miles off PCT

Not as many services as Mt. Shasta.
Post Office, library, grocery store.
Laundromat has opened-closed-open
in the last few years.
A few restaurants and motels.

Exit 726
PCT mile 1501.2

PCT North
PCT South

Castella ● Exit 724

CASTELLA - 2.5 mile alternate walk

Only services are Post Office, little
C-Store (not good for resupply), and
State Park Campground with showers.
Ammariti's C-Store has minimal food,
but a great beer selection.

1501.2 - Castella CA

OVERVIEW: Not much here. Just a store, PO, and campground.

GETTING HERE: See the Handbook map. Frontage road is best.

BUS SERVICE: Siskiyou County STAGE. Call 530-842-8220.
Service to/from Castella, travel to Dunsmuir, Mt. Shasta, Weed.
2018:   Mon, Wed, Fri only   Pick up at Castella PO at 10:40am
        Mon thru Fri   Pick up at Castella PO at 6:40pm

POST OFFICE: 530-235-4413, USPS only   Hiker's Legal Name
Mon-Fri 11a-3p   PCT Hiker, ETA: MM/DD/YY
Sat 8:40a-10a   General Delivery
General Delivery held for 30 days   20115 Castle Creek Road
                                              Castella, CA 96017

MAIL DROPS: Ammirati's (530-235-2676) accepts mail drops, no fee. USPS is best !!

USPS Address: UPS Address:
Hiker's Legal Name   Hiker's Legal Name
PCT Hiker, ETA: MM/DD/YY   PCT Hiker, ETA: MM/DD/YY
c/o Ammirati's Market   c/o Ammirati's Market
PO Box 90   20107 Castle Creek Road
Castella, CA 96017   Castella, CA 96017

RESUPPLY: Ammirati's Market. 530-235-2676.
Open approximately 7:30a-9p every day.
Store food shelves are sometimes bare.
Lots of beer and liquor on shelves. Excellent beer selection.

CAMPING: Castle Crags State Park Campground.
$ hiker site. Pay showers. No laundry.

RESTAURANTS: The diner is only open on the weekends – hours vary.

LAUNDRY: No.

SHOWERS: Pay showers at the State Park.

ATM: No.

FUEL: HEET, and sometimes canister fuel at Ammirati's.

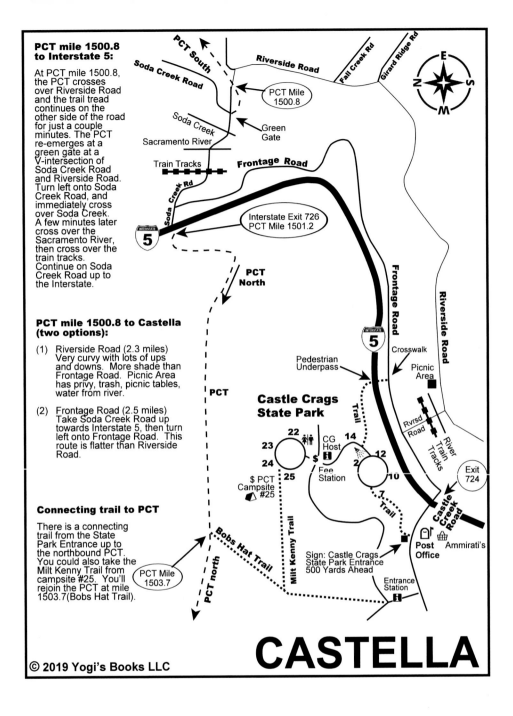

PCT mile 1500.8 to Interstate 5:

At PCT mile 1500.8, the PCT crosses over Riverside Road and the trail tread continues on the other side of the road for just a couple minutes. The PCT re-emerges at a green gate at a V-intersection of Soda Creek Road and Riverside Road. Turn left onto Soda Creek Road, and immediately cross over Soda Creek. A few minutes later cross over the Sacramento River, then cross over the train tracks. Continue on Soda Creek Road up to the Interstate.

PCT mile 1500.8 to Castella (two options):

(1) Riverside Road (2.3 miles) Very curvy with lots of ups and downs. More shade than Frontage Road. Picnic Area has privy, trash, picnic tables, water from river.

(2) Frontage Road (2.5 miles) Take Soda Creek Road up towards Interstate 5, then turn left onto Frontage Road. This route is flatter than Riverside Road.

Connecting trail to PCT

There is a connecting trail from the State Park Entrance up to the northbound PCT. You could also take the Milt Kenny Trail from campsite #25. You'll rejoin the PCT at mile 1503.7(Bobs Hat Trail).

Riverside Road

Fall Creek Rd

Girard Ridge Rd

PCT South

Soda Creek Road

PCT Mile 1500.8

Green Gate

Soda Creek

Sacramento River

Train Tracks

Soda Creek Rd

Frontage Road

INTERSTATE 5

Interstate Exit 726 PCT Mile 1501.2

PCT North

PCT

Frontage Road

INTERSTATE 5

Crosswalk

Pedestrian Underpass

Picnic Area

Castle Crags State Park

Riverside Road

Rvrsd Road

River Train Tracks

Trail

22

23

24

25

$ PCT Campsite #25

CG Host

$

Fee Station

14

2

12

10

7

Trail

Exit 724

Bobs Hat Trail

PCT north

PCT Mile 1503.7

Milt Kenny Trail

Sign: Castle Crags State Park Entrance 500 Yards Ahead

Entrance Station

Castle Creek Road

Post Office

Ammirati's

CASTELLA

OVERVIEW: Full service, yet smaller than Mt. Shasta.

GETTING HERE: Get to Interstate 5, Exit 726. Go north ~4.5 miles.

TAXI: Shasta Shuttle and Taxi. 530-859-3266.
Picks up at Exit 726. 2018: 10% PCT discount

BUS SERVICE: Siskiyou County STAGE. Call 530-842-8220.
Service to/from Castella, travel to Dunsmuir, Mt. Shasta, Weed.
2018: Mon, Wed, Fri only Pick up at Castella PO at 10:40am
Mon thru Fri Pick up at Castella PO at 6:40pm

POST OFFICE: 530-235-0338, USPS only
Mon-Fri 8:30a-5p. Sat closed,
but usually hikers can pick up
packages on Sat from 9a-11a.
Knock on back door inside lobby.

Hiker mail held for 30 days, unless
you call to ask to hold longer.

Hiker's Legal Name
PCT Hiker, ETA: MM/DD/YY
General Delivery
Dunsmuir, CA 96025

MAIL DROPS: Dunsmuir Lodge (530-235-2884)
Accepts mail drops for guests.
No fee. USPS, UPS, or FedEx.

Hiker's Legal Name
PCT Hiker, ETA: MM/DD/YY
c/o Dunsmuir Lodge
6604 Dunsmuir Ave
Dunsmuir, CA 96025

RESUPPLY: Dunsmuir Supermarket grocery store 530-235-4751
Mon-Sat 8a-9p. Sun 8a-8p.
Full resupply, but limited dinner choices.

RESTAURANTS: Yes.

LAUNDRY: Closed in 2018.
Laundromat in town has opened - closed - opened in the last several years.

ATM: In town. Also at Manfred's.

COMPUTER: Dunsmuir Library 530-235-2035

FUEL: Denatured alcohol at Dunsmuir Hardware 530-235-4539

DUNSMUIR LODGING ask for hiker rates		Rates	AC, TV, frig	micr	laundry	other
Cedar Lodge	530-235-4331	$$	Y	Y	no	
Cave Springs Motel	530-235-2721	$$$	Y	Y	Y	check website for specials
Dunsmuir Lodge	530-235-2884	$$ - $$$$	Y	no	no	
Dunsmuir Inn and Suites	530-235-4395	$$$ - $$$$	Y	Y	no	
Travelodge	530-235-4100	$$$	Y	Y	Y	
		B & B rate is approximately $8 more, which gets you two full breakfasts at Penny's Diner next door.				
		$ = usually less than $50 $$ = usually $50-$80 $$$ = usually $80-$110 $$$$ = usually greater than $110				

DUNSMUIR

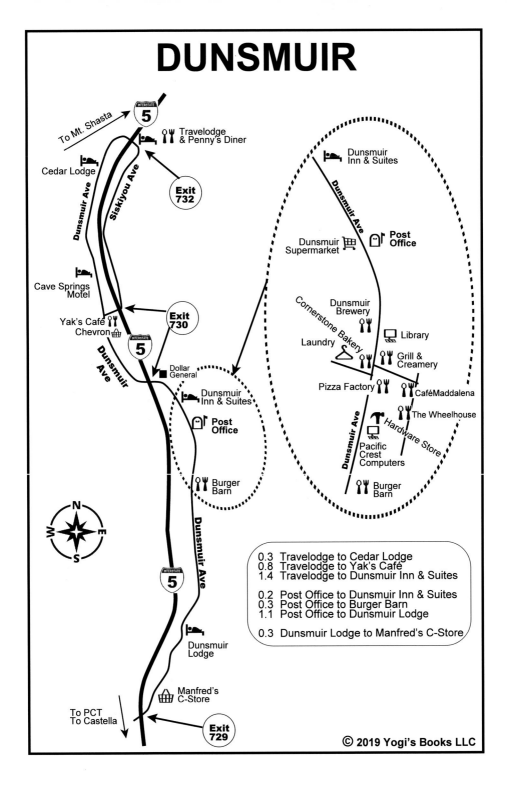

INTERSTATE 5

To Mt. Shasta

Travelodge & Penny's Diner

Cedar Lodge

Dunsmuir Ave

Siskiyou Ave

Exit 732

Dunsmuir Inn & Suites

Dunsmuir Ave

Dunsmuir Supermarket

Post Office

Cave Springs Motel

Yak's Café
Chevron

INTERSTATE 5

Exit 730

Dunsmuir Ave

Dollar General

Dunsmuir Inn & Suites

Post Office

Burger Barn

Dunsmuir Brewery

Cornerstone Bakery

Laundry

Library

Grill & Creamery

Pizza Factory

CaféMaddalena

The Wheelhouse

Dunsmuir Ave

Hardware Store

Pacific Crest Computers

Burger Barn

INTERSTATE 5

N
W   E
S

Dunsmuir Ave

INTERSTATE 5

0.3 Travelodge to Cedar Lodge
0.8 Travelodge to Yak's Café
1.4 Travelodge to Dunsmuir Inn & Suites

0.2 Post Office to Dunsmuir Inn & Suites
0.3 Post Office to Burger Barn
1.1 Post Office to Dunsmuir Lodge

0.3 Dunsmuir Lodge to Manfred's C-Store

Dunsmuir Lodge

Manfred's C-Store

To PCT
To Castella

Exit 729

© 2019 Yogi's Books LLC

OVERVIEW:	Good restaurants, fun tavern, cheap motel.

GETTING HERE:	Hitch north 12 miles on Interstate 5, or take the bus or a taxi.

TAXI:	Shasta Shuttle and Taxi. 530-859-3266.
	Will pick up at exit 726. Ask for PCT hiker discount.

BUS SERVICE:	Siskiyou County STAGE. Call 530-842-8220.
	Service to/from Castella, travel to Dunsmuir, Mt. Shasta, Weed.
	2018:	Mon, Wed, Fri only	Pick up at Castella PO at 10:40am
		Mon thru Fri	Pick up at Castella PO at 6:40pm

POST OFFICE:	If you want to bounce General Delivery mail from Mount Shasta to anyplace
	else, you cannot just call the Mount Shasta Post Office. Three options:

	(1)	File a forwarding address
	(2)	Go to the Mt. Shasta PO in person
	(3)	Go to any other PO, ask that PO to call the Mount Shasta PO to have your
		mail bounced ahead.

	530-926-1343, USPS only	Hiker's Legal Name
	Mon-Fri 8:30a-5p, Sat closed	PCT Hiker, ETA: MM/DD/YY
		General Delivery
	Hiker mail held until end of hiker season.	301 S. Mt. Shasta Blvd
		Mount Shasta, CA 96067

OUTGOING MAIL:	Pages	530-926-2520	UPS, FedEx, and USPS services.
		Mon-Fri 10a-5:30p. Sat 10a-3p. Sun closed.

RESUPPLY:	Ray's Food Place Supermarket	530-926-3390	7a-11p every day
	Mountain Song Natural Foods	530-926-3391
	Berryvale Natural Foods	530-926-1576	8a-8p every day
	Mt. Shasta Supermarket	530-926-2212	Mon-Sat 8a-7p, Sun 9a-7p

OUTFITTER:	Fifth Season	530-926-3606
	Sportsman's Den	530-926-2295

RESTAURANTS:	Everywhere. These are hiker favorites:
	Black Bear Diner	Great breakfast here.
	Round Table Pizza	AYCE lunch buffet.

LAUNDRY:	Yes.

ATM:	Yes.

COMPUTER:	Library	530-926-2031

FUEL:	Denatured alcohol at Ace Hardware	530-926-3482
	Canister fuel at Fifth Season	530-926-3606

MEDICAL:	Mercy Medical Center	530-926-6111

MOVIE:	Mount Shasta Cinema	530-926-1116

MT. SHASTA LODGING	ask for hiker rates!	Rates	TV AC	frig	micr	bkfst	laundry	other stuff
Alpine Lodge	530-926-3145	$$$	Y	Y	Y	cold	no	
Best Western	530-926-3101	$$$$	Y	Y	Y	hot	Y	pool, hot tub
Cold Creek Inn	530-926-9851	$$$	Y	Y	Y	cont	no	kitchenettes available
Evergreen Lodge	530-926-2143	$$	Y	Y	Y	no	no	pool, hot tub
A-1 Choice Inn	530-926-4811	$$	Y	Y	Y	no	no	pool, hot tub
Mt Shasta Inn & Suites	530-918-9292	$$$	Y	Y	Y	cont	no	hot tub
Strawberry Valley Inn	530-926-2052	$$$$	Y	in suites only		cont	no	
Travel Inn [www.visitmtshasta.com]	530-926-4617	$$	Y	some	some	no	no	
		Recommended. Rooms are small, location is good, and the price is right. Ask about a hiker/climber rate.						
KOA	530-926-4029	Laundry on-site. Shower included in stay. Tent sites and camping cabins.						
		$ = usually less than $50 $$ = usually $50-$80 $$$ = usually $80-$110 $$$$ = usually greater than $110						

Map Symbols

David "Awol" Miller has given us permission to use the map symbols he created for his excellent book "The AT Guide". These map symbols allow you to easily find town services with a quick glance at the town maps.

- Airport
- ATM or Bank
- Boat
- Bowling
- Bus
- Camping
- Car Rental
- Computer
- C-Store
- First Aid
- Grocery Store
- Hardware Store
- Hostel
- Hotel
- Information
- Internet/WiFi
- Laundry
- Light Rail
- Lounge/Bar
- Outfitter
- Outgoing Mail
- Pay Phone
- Pharmacy
- Picnic Table
- Pool
- Post Office
- Ranger Station
- Restaurant
- Restroom/Privy
- Shoe Store
- Shower
- Ski Lift
- Theater
- Train Station

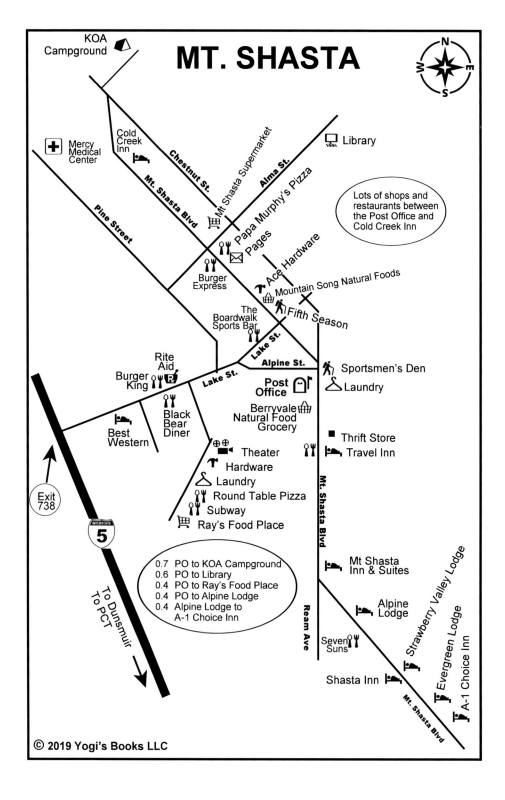

MT. SHASTA

KOA Campground

Mercy Medical Center

Cold Creek Inn

Chestnut St.

Mt. Shasta Supermarket

Alma St.

Pine Street

Mt. Shasta Blvd

Papa Murphy's Pizza

Pages

Library

Lots of shops and restaurants between the Post Office and Cold Creek Inn

Ace Hardware

Burger Express

Mountain Song Natural Foods

The Boardwalk Sports Bar

Fifth Season

Lake St.

Rite Aid

Alpine St.

Burger King

Lake St.

Post Office

Sportsmen's Den

Laundry

Black Bear Diner

Best Western

Berryvale Natural Food Grocery

Theater

Thrift Store

Travel Inn

Exit 738

INTERSTATE 5

Hardware

Laundry

Round Table Pizza

Subway

Ray's Food Place

Mt. Shasta Blvd

0.7 PO to KOA Campground
0.6 PO to Library
0.4 PO to Ray's Food Place
0.4 PO to Alpine Lodge
0.4 Alpine Lodge to A-1 Choice Inn

Mt Shasta Inn & Suites

Strawberry Valley Lodge

To Dunsmuir
To PCT

Ream Ave

Alpine Lodge

Evergreen Lodge

Seven Suns

A-1 Choice Inn

Shasta Inn

Mt. Shasta Blvd

© 2019 Yogi's Books LLC

1503.7 - Bob's Hat Trail - Take this down to Castle Crags Campground and Castella.

1504.5 to 1511.3 - Lots of water here. SOCKS: Water sources were good till 1504 or 1505, after that they were dry, pools, or trickling. Load up in the beginning of this stretch!

1515.3 - Cascading Creek - Water here.
If dry at trail, look upstream for pools of water or downstream for spring.

1516.2 - Densely vegetated creeklet - Water here. Trickling in 2012-2016.

1525.8 - Road 40N30 - BINK: Water at lake 0.25 to 0.5 mile off trail.

1529.0 - Spring - Piped spring on trail. Great water. Easy to miss. Watch for it! Watch for wildflowers.

1531.3 - Junction to Porcupine Lake - Nice clear lake, worth the side trip.

1536.7 - Spur trail to Deadfall Lake - Water here.

1538.2 - Gully with a permanent spring - Water here.

1542.7 - Cross an old trail by a small meadow's edge -
There is a creek about 0.1 mile after a trail sign. Unreliable in dry years.

1545.9 - Chilcoot Creek - Usually dry.

1550.5 - Two trail junctions - Go left at the second junction. Pay attention to trail signs.

1554.1 - Two Springs - Water here.

1556.0 - Masterson Meadow Trail - Water here.
DOUBLE TAP: Spring is ~100ft north of PCT at broken wooden sign.

1557.1 - Masterson Meadow Lake seasonal creek - Usually flowing, but slowly.

1560.2 - Scott Mountain Summit (Highway 3) -
Scott Campground is here. No fee. Tables, privy. No trash, no water.
Seasonal creek (barely flowing in mid-June) at back of campground.
Callahan CA is 8.3 miles north. Etna CA is 20 miles north.

1560.2 - Callahan CA

OVERVIEW: The only services in Callahan are the Post Office and the Callahan Emporium (C-Store and Bar). No lodging.

GETTING HERE: Hitch 8.3 miles north (right) on Hwy 3 from Scott Summit.

POST OFFICE:
530-467-5155, USPS only
Mon-Fri 11:30a-3:30p
Sat 10:30a-12:30p
Hiker mail held until end of hiker season

Hiker's Legal Name
PCT Hiker, ETA: MM/DD/YY
General Delivery
Callahan, CA 96014

STORE / BAR:
Callahan Emporium. 530-467-3395. Closed on Tuesdays.
Store is a small C-Store, not good for hiker resupply.
Deli open Wed-Mon 11a-3p.
Store / Bar open Thur-Fri-Sat 10a-6p. Sun-Mon-Wed 11a-5p.

1562.8 - Enter Trinity Alps Wilderness - Sign on a tree directs you to a spring 100 yards down the hill. Multiple springs/streams crossing the PCT beginning 1.5 - 2 miles north of here.

1564.7 - Spring - Many springs near here.

1565.9 - Road 40N63 - Water just past the road.

1566.1 - Mosquito Lake Creek - Water here.

1568.4 - Seasonal Creek - Usually flows.

1571.1 to 1575.4 - Lots of water.

1571.5 - Bloody Run Trail Junction - DOUBLE TAP: Follow Bloody Run trail to the left off of the PCT for ~0.1 mile to find a large campground with good campsites.

1579.0 - South Fork Scott River - Water here.

1579.1 - DOUBLE TAP:
Look for a great raspberry bush on the left side of the trail just after the Scott River.

1579.6 - Alder-lined creeklet - Water here.

1585.2 - Jeep trail to Siphon Lake - There is a seasonal spring here on the PCT.

1585.2 to 1590.8 - Lots of water.

1590.8 - Creek below Statue Lake - Water here. Starts to dry up in July.

1594.0 - Paynes Lake Creek - Water here. DOUBLE TAP: Many good campsites around the lake (which is ideal to swim in). Mice at campsites.

1594.7 - Glacial Bowl - Water here. Make sure you leave here with enough water. The next on-trail water is 15.6 miles north of here at Shelly Lake's outlet creek.

1599.7 - Sawyers Bar Road / Etna Summit

1599.7 - Yreka CA

If you want a larger town, consider taking the bus from Etna to Yreka. You'll find Motel6 ($$), Comfort Inn ($$$), and Baymont Inn ($$$) very close to a Raley's supermarket, Walmart, and restaurants. Bus is Siskiyou Stage (530-842-8220). You want the Montague/Scott Valley/Hornbrook bus. Etna to Yreka is 70 minutes.

OVERVIEW:	Etna is a really cool town. Perfect place for a zero day. The whole place is hiker-friendly.
GETTING HERE:	Not much traffic on the road at Etna Summit (hitch about 11 miles to the right), but everyone gets a ride. Trail supporters have worked hard to promote the trail in Etna, and the citizens are aware of hikers and our need for rides. But don't be surprised if you wait 45 minutes before the first car comes by.
SHUTTLE:	No cell service at Etna summit. Ride back to trail can be arranged (2018: $5). Ask at Alderbrook Manor.

POST OFFICE:

530-467-3981, USPS only.
Mon-Fri 9a-5p.
Sat package pick up only 8a-10a.
General Delivery mail MUST have a valid
domestic return address. If not picked up 15
days after mail arrives at PO, Postmaster will
scan as "delivered to agent", then she will
keep hiker mail until the end of hiker season.

Hiker's Legal Name
PCT Hiker, ETA: MM/DD/YY
General Delivery
119 Diggles Street
Etna, CA 96027

MAIL DROPS:

Alderbrook Manor (530-467-3917)
Accepts mail drops,
no fee for guests, $5 for non-guests.
USPS, UPS, FedEx.

Hiker's Legal Name
PCT Hiker, ETA: MM/DD/YY
c/o Alderbrook Manor
836 Sawyers Bar Road
Etna, CA 96027

RESUPPLY: Ray's Food Place (large grocery store) 530-467-5235   7a-10p every day

LODGING:

Hiker Hut at Alderbrook Manor   530-467-3917

2018: $25 PCT rate will get you a bed, shower, TV and VCR,
microwave, toaster, coffee pot, BBQ grill, and a computer.
Laundry, loaner clothes, and bikes available.
B&B rooms: $$$$

If Hiker Hut is full, you can camp at Alderbrook Manor for $20,
which includes all the amenities listed above.

Rough & Ready Bunkhouse. 716-930-9131. [www.randrbunkhouse.com]
Six hiker maximum. Laundry, shower, kitchen, Netflix. Website: "You can stay
1 or 2 nights and in return I'm asking for 1 hour per night in sweat equity/work."

Motel Etna. 530-467-5338. TV, frig, microwave, AC. Rates: $$

CAMPING:

2018: $5 Camping at City Park.
2018: $20 overflow camping at Hiker Hut, includes all Hiker Hut amenities.

CITY PARK:

2018: $5 camping, $5 hot showers, free WiFi, lockers, charging stations, rides
to/from Etna Summit. Locker and shower tokens available at Ray's Food Place.

RESTAURANTS:	Several restaurants. The pies at Bob's Ranch House are fantastic.
BREWERY:	Yes!
LAUNDRY:	At Hiker Hut, R & R Bunkhouse, also laundromat near Shell.
SHOWER:	RV Park, and at City Park.
ATM:	At Ray's Food Place and at Shell Station.
COMPUTER:	Library 530-467-3661
FUEL:	Denatured alcohol and HEET at the hardware store.
MEDICAL:	Scott Valley Rural Health Center 530-467-5393 Mon-Fri 9a-noon and 1p-4p
POISON OAK:	There is a lot of poison oak on the trail for the rest of California. Know what it looks like and avoid it. Carry Zanfel or Calamine.

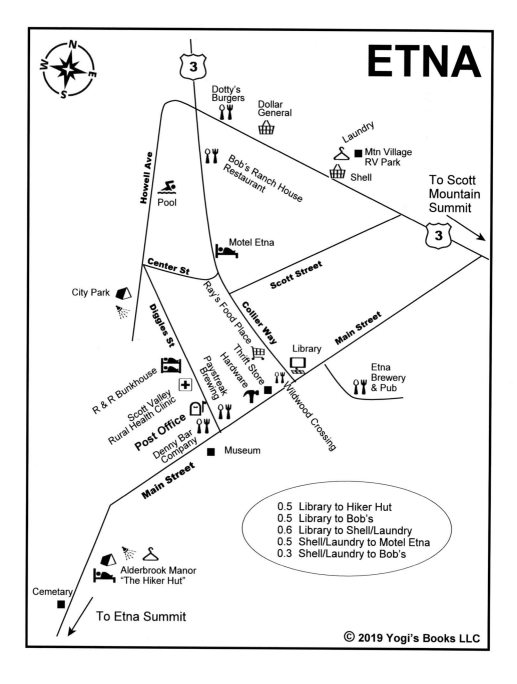

ETNA

To Scott Mountain Summit

0.5 Library to Hiker Hut
0.5 Library to Bob's
0.6 Library to Shell/Laundry
0.5 Shell/Laundry to Motel Etna
0.3 Shell/Laundry to Bob's

To Etna Summit

© 2019 Yogi's Books LLC

HINT - The next on-trail water is 10.7 miles north at Shelly Lake's outlet creek.

1607.2 - Cub Bear Spring - Water here 0.2 mile off PCT.

1610.4 - Shelly Lake's outlet creek - Water and 2 small campsites.

1613.5 - Creeklet with campsites - Water here.

1613.7 - Fisher Lake - Water here. Good tent sites, a nice fire pit, great swimming.

1614.0 - Marten Lake - Water here.

1620.4 - Trail to Cold Springs - Good water 0.3 mile off PCT. Take the second trail.

1621.3 - Soft Water Spring - Unreliable.

1621.5 - Second trail to Shadow Lake

1623.7 - Marble Valley Guard Station - Water here.

1624.1 - Marble Gap Trail, water nearby - A good-flowing spring can be heard from the trail. SCRUB (2013): You can hear it clearly but it does not cross the trail. It was the best water around for a long time.

1626.6 - Box Camp Trail Junction -
DOUBLE TAP: Be careful, the PCT takes a sharp turn to the left, almost 180 degrees.

1629.0 - Paradise Lake - Water here. DOUBLE TAP: Ice cold spring at the lake via a trail to the left of the lake. Spring is ~200 ft down this trail.

1634.5 - Buckhorn Spring -
Usually good water, 150 feet west of PCT in meadow NW of the big 3-forked tree.

1641.5 - Cold Spring Creek - Water here. Start watching for poison oak.

1642.5 - Grider Creek - Water here. Watch for poison oak.

1643.7 - Grider Creek - Water here. No camping opportunity here.

1645.4 - Bridge - Water here. Sleep on the bridge to avoid poison oak.

1645.7 - Bark Shanty Creek - Water here.

1647.7 - Junction with Old Grider Creek Trail - Water here.

1649.5 - Grider Creek Campground - Water and privy here.

1649.5 to 1655.9 - No camping between Grider Creek Campground and Seiad Valley. It's all road walk. Tons of blackberry bushes along the road.

1652.1 - Grider Road - Turn right.

1654.5 - Highway 96 - Turn left.

OVERVIEW: The PCT passes right through town, which is very small.
The PO, store, and diner are all on the trail (road)
in the same building. RV Park is next door.

GETTING HERE: The PCT goes right through town.

POST OFFICE: 530-496-3211, USPS only   Hiker's Legal Name
Mon-Fri noon-4p   PCT Hiker, ETA: MM/DD/YY
Sat noon-1:30p   General Delivery
Hiker mail held until end of hiker season   44717 State Highway 96
                                Seiad Valley, CA 96086

                 Put your name on every
side of your package.

MAIL DROPS: Store accepts mail drops, no fee,   Hiker's Legal Name
USPS, UPS, or FedEx. Must have real   PCT Hiker, ETA: MM/DD/YY
name on package, must show photo ID to   c/o Seiad Valley Store
pick up. See hours in "Resupply" section   44719 State Highway 96
below. 530-496-3399.   Seiad Valley, CA 96086

                 RV Park accepts mail drops. 530-496-3400.
$5 fee. If you camp here (2018: $15-$20), the $5 package fee is waived.
UPS or FedEx are recommended !!

                 USPS address: UPS or FedEx Address:
Hiker's Legal Name   Hiker's Legal Name
PCT Hiker, ETA: MM/DD/YY   PCT Hiker, ETA: MM/DD/YY
c/o Mid River RV Park   c/o Mid River RV Park
PO Box 707   44701 State Highway 96
Seiad Valley, CA 96086   Seiad Valley, CA 96086

RESUPPLY: Good resupply at the Seiad Valley Store. 530-496-3399.
This is a large C-Store, but it has good options for hiker resupply.
Hiker-friendly owner Rick knows what hikers want.
You could definitely pick up enough food to get to Ashland.
Beginning May 1, open 6a-8p every day. Stays open until 9 during high season.

CAMPING: The Mid-River RV Park is very hiker-friendly. 530-496-3400.
There is a hiker area with TV/VCR (free movies), frig, microwave.
It's a great place to hang out while in Seiad Valley.
2018: $15-$20 camping includes shower.

RESTAURANTS: Excellent shakes and BLT sandwich at the Seiad Valley Café!!
530-496-3360. Usually 7a-2p everyday. Hours vary.
If you try the pancake challenge, don't plan on hiking out of town
the same day. You've never seen pancakes this big.

LAUNDRY: At the RV Park. The dryer is very hot! Watch your clothes.

SHOWERS: At the RV Park.

ATM: No.

FUEL: Store has denatured alcohol, white gas, canister fuel.

## 19

LEAVING SEIAD VALLEY - You're going up 4500 feet in 8 miles. Hot, hot, hot.
Watch out for poison oak on the climb out of Seiad Valley. It's everywhere !!!!!

1657.6 - Fern Spring - Usually water here.

1661.8 - Lookout Spring - Watch for a spur trail on the left of the PCT.
BINK: My favorite PCT spring.
SCRUB (2013): Fill up here, because Kangaroo Springs was super gross.

1666.0 - Kangaroo Springs - Watch for these springs, which are sometimes just gross pools. After the PCT switchbacks down to bowl area, and after the PCT makes a right curve all the way around the bowl, there are a couple springs on the left of the PCT, and a couple springs on the right, down in a meadow.

1670.7 - Cook and Green Pass - Before crossing the road, look for a trail to your left. This is the trail to the water, 0.1 mile off PCT. RADAR: The second source along this trail flows better than the first. About another 3-4 minute walk mostly on a contour.

1676.2 - Bear Dog Spring - Good water. Dries up in late August.

1677.9 - Spring - Unreliable, often barely running. Difficult to get water.

1683.2 - Alex Hole Spring - DOUBLE TAP: Look for trail to the left of the PCT just after you pass the unpaved road on the right. About 0.1 mile and 100 ft down (after a sharp turn to the left) you will run into multiple small streams from the spring, which is ice cold. Plenty of camping spots back on the unpaved road and off the unpaved road.

1685.3 - Mud Spring - Good camping on north side of the trail.
There is a trickling spring 0.1 mile north on the gravel road.

1687.2 - Spring - After crossing Road 40S01, the trail goes down a hill then makes a left turn. Follow your ears to a spring down on the right. Get water here.

1687.6 - Bearground Springs -
Two sets of springs cross the PCT. Sometimes only trickling.

1690.5 - Donomore Creek - Water and lots of cows here. Water is nasty.

1691.7 - WELCOME TO OREGON !!!!!

1693.1 - Spring - BINK: A small spring flows from under a rock on the uphill side of the trail.

1696.1 - Sheep Camp Spring - This great spring is a few yards to the right where the PCT crosses a dirt road. DOUBLE TAP: Good campsites.

1708.2 - Grouse Gap Shelter - Water near the shelter, 0.2 mile off PCT. Privy.

1708.7 - Springs - A couple seasonal springs cross the PCT.

1710.0 - Mt. Ashland Campground - No water.

1711.6 - Mt. Ashland Road

1713.3 - Water faucet and picnic table

1717.1 - Spring-fed gully - Water here.

1717.7 - Callahan's Short Cut - Directions are in the "Callahan's" section (below).

1718.7 - Highway 99

OVERVIEW: 541-482-1299.
Hiker-friendly, excellent food, beautiful rooms, comfortable camping.

"Welcome Pacific Crest Trail hikers! Callahan's Lodge is delighted to be on your path whether you are a thru hiker or on a section jaunt! Enjoy dining hospitality: a tall cool lemonade sipped on the dining deck, a selection of one of a dozen beers on tap, a generous carb meal of Callahan's classic spaghetti or a T-bone steak cooked to your liking. Those who also long for a hot shower, laundry facility, and a soft spot to stay the night have found the right place."

GETTING HERE: (1) Side trail at PCT mile 1717.7 - Going North, approximately five miles after crossing the Mt. Ashland Ski Road, the PCT will cross 3 dirt roads spaced fairly close together. Above the 3rd road, there is a small rectangular, wooden, directional Callahan's sign posted high on a tree. Follow that road straight down the mountain approximately 400 feet. Cross a dirt road straight down to the railroad yard and across the RR tracks in a northeasterly direction.   You will see another steep short dirt road leading to the intersection of Interstate 5 and Exit 6. Cross under the freeway. Callahan's occupies the northeast quadrant of that intersection.

(2) Stay on PCT until you reach PCT mile 1718.7 (Highway 99).
Turn left, walk one mile. Cross under the interstate on a road.
You'll soon see Callahan's on the left.

MAIL DROPS: Accepts mail drops, $5 fee.   Hiker's Legal Name
USPS, UPS, FedEx.   PCT Hiker, ETA: MM/DD/YY
Mail must have ETA.   c/o Callahan's Lodge
No outgoing mail.   7100 Old Highway 99 South
                                Ashland, OR 97520

RESTAURANTS: Restaurant hours vary by season.

LODGING: Beautiful rooms. Rates: $$$$

HIKER SERVICES: **2019 rates:**

PCT hiker package $65: "We accept and hold your resupply box. When you arrive, check in at our front desk. You can do a load of laundry (no sleeping bags, please) take a hot shower, pitch your tent on any level spot you like, then have a seat on our dining deck or in the dining room. Order a salad, bottomless plate of spaghetti served with our artisan baked bread. Enjoy live music till 9pm, maybe later. You will sleep like a baby and later than usual. When you awaken, come to breakfast (after 8am, please) and dine on a dish of bacon, eggs, fresh fruit and all the pancakes you can eat."

A LA CARTE rates:

$5	Pick up your resupply package	
$12	Shower	Shampoo, conditioner, lotion, towel, washcloth, robe
$10	Load o' Laundry	Includes soap
$32	Clean and Camp	Shower, laundry, and camping
$14	Soft, Flat Place to Camp	With restroom privileges
$15	Breakfast	AYCE pancakes, 3 eggs, 3 bacon, fresh fruit
$1	First mug of beer	For thru hikers only, $1 goes to PCTA
$16	Callahan's Classic Spaghetti Dinner	AYCE spaghetti meal, salad, and house-made bread

OVERVIEW: Full-service, great restaurants, many lodging options.

GETTING HERE: (1)   PCT mile 1718.7 - Highway 99
                          Don't try to hitch to Ashland from the spot where the trail hits Highway 99.
                          Walk the mile along Highway 99 to Callahan's (with your thumb out!) then
                          try to hitch the interstate on-ramp from there. There is more traffic near
                          Callahan's. At this point, Highway 99 and I-5 are the same road. It's about
                          12 miles to Ashland.

                    (2)   PCT mile 1735.5 - Highway 66 - Hitch 17 miles left (east)

BUS SERVICE: RVTD (Rogue Valley Transportation District).
                    Busses DO NOT run on Sundays or holidays. One way $2. All day $5. Pick up
                    a bus schedule at the Chamber of Commerce (541-482-3486) or the Library (541-
                    774-6996). For an automated schedule, call RVTD at 541-608-2400. To talk to
                    an actual person, call 541-779-2877 Mon-Fri between 6a and 5:30p.

TAXI SERVICE: Cascade Shuttle   541-488-1998

POST OFFICE: Main Post Office: Hiker's Legal Name
                    541-552-1622. Mon-Fri 9a-5p, USPS only   PCT Hiker, ETA: MM/DD/YY
                    Sat closed, but usually hikers can pick   General Delivery
                    up packages on Saturdays from 8a-4p.   Ashland, OR 97520
                    Knock on double white door in lobby.

                    ● DO NOT include Post Office street address on General Delivery address.
                    ● Hiker mail held 30 days, or until ETA.
                    ● There is an Automated Postal Machine at the Main Post Office.
                      Ship packages 24 hours a day.

                    Postal substation in Rite Aid   Cash only. You can mail out from here.
                                                    541-482-7406, press 5, ask for Post Office.
                                                    Open Mon-Fri 9a-1p & 2p-6p. Sat & Sun closed.

MAIL DROPS: Rodeway Inn (541-482-5111)   Hiker's Legal Name
                    Accepts mail drops, free for guests,   PCT Hiker, ETA: MM/DD/YY
                    $5+ for non-guests. Clearly label your   c/o Rodeway Inn
                    mail drop as a hiker package, include   2359 Ashland Street
                    your ETA. USPS, UPS, FedEx: Ashland, OR 97520

OUTGOING MAIL: The UPS Store   541-482-6245   Mon-Fri 9a-6p. Sat 10a-3p. Sun closed.
                                                     Hours are likely to change.

RESUPPLY: Albertsons   541-482-6320   6a-11p every day
                    Shop 'n Kart   541-488-1579   7a-midnight every day
                    Food Co-Op   541-482-2237   7a-9p every day

OUTFITTER: Mountain Provisions   541-708-6350   10% PCT discount, DT exchange
                    Get 'n Gear   541-482-5181

RESTAURANTS: You'll find just about every type of restaurant in Ashland.

                    SCRUB: If you get the chance, go to Morning Glory for breakfast. There will be
                    a line out the door within 30 minutes of opening at 8a, and there's a reason for
                    that. We weren't just talking about it like, "Oh, best breakfast on the trail." It was
                    more like, "Top breakfasts for life."

LAUNDRY: Yes.
ATM: Many.
COMPUTER: Available at the hostel, in some bars/cafes, and at the Library (541-774-6996).

FUEL: <u>Mountain Provisions</u> 541-708-6350 Canisters

MEDICAL: <u>Ashland Community Hospital</u> 541-201-4000

WARM CLOTHES: When you finally reach Ashland Oregon, the last thing you think you'll need are your warm clothes. Northern California was hot, and you've decided to bounce your sleeping clothes, gloves, hat, and fleece up to Cascade Locks. DON'T DO IT. The Oregon nights are cold.

SHAKESPEARE FESTIVAL: 541-482-4331
Cheaper tickets go on sale a few hours before show time.

STEHEKIN MAILDROP: Make sure your resupply person mails your Canada and US entrance papers to Stehekin (General Delivery, 98852).

ASHLAND LODGING Ask for hiker rates Many lodging options Here are a few:	Rates	frig	micr	TV	laundry	pool	hot tub	bkfst	computer
Ashland Hostel 541-482-9217 ask for hiker rate	$ bunk $$ + private	Y	Y	no	Y	no	no	no	
Ashland Motel 541-482-2561	$$$	Y	Y	Y	Y	Y	no	no	no
Columbia Hotel 541-482-3726 ask for PCT rate	$$$ + some use shared bath	no	no	no	no	no	no	no	no
Best Western Bards Inn 541-482-0049	$$$$	Y	no	Y	no	outdoor	Y	hot	Y
Best Western Windsor Inn 541-488-2330	$$$$	Y	some	Y	Y	outdoor	no	hot	Y
Flagship Inn 800-547-6414	$$$	Y	Y	Y	no	outdoor	no	cont	Y
Holiday Inn Express 541-201-0202	$$$$	Y	Y	Y	Y	indoor	Y	hot	Y
Palm Motel 541-482-2636	$$$$	some	some	Y	no	outdoor	no	no	no
Relax Inn 541-482-4423 see Yelp reviews	$$	Y	Y	Y	no	Y	no	no	no
Rodeway Inn 541-482-5111	$$$ possible hiker rate	Y	Y	Y	no	outdoor	no	cont	no
Stratford Inn 541-488-2151	$$$$	Y	Y	Y	Y	indoor	Y	cont	Y
Super 8 541-482-8887	$$ +	Y	Y	Y	Y	indoor	Y	cont	no
Timbers Motel 541-482-4242	$$$	Y	Y	Y	no	outdoor	no	Y	no
	$ = usually less than $50 $$ = usually $50-$80 $$$ = usually $80-$110 $$$$ = usually greater than $110								

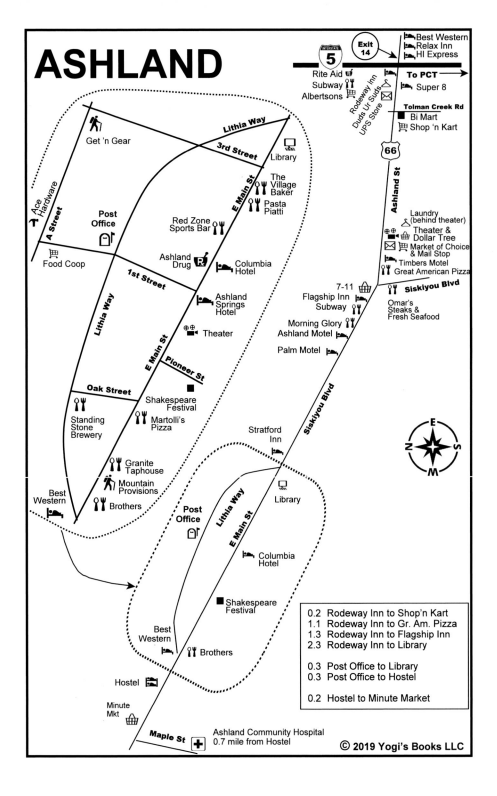

ASHLAND

Best Western
Relax Inn
HI Express

Interstate 5

Exit 14

To PCT

Rite Aid
Subway
Albertsons

Rodeway Inn
Duds Ur Suds
UPS Store

Super 8

Tolman Creek Rd
Bi Mart
Shop 'n Kart

66

Ashland St

Get 'n Gear

Lithia Way

3rd Street

Library

E Main St

The Village Baker

Pasta Piatti

Laundry (behind theater)

Theater & Dollar Tree

Market of Choice & Mail Stop

Ace Hardware

A Street

Post Office

Red Zone Sports Bar

Ashland Drug

Columbia Hotel

Timbers Motel
Great American Pizza

Food Coop

1st Street

7-11

Flagship Inn
Subway

Siskiyou Blvd

Lithia Way

Ashland Springs Hotel

Morning Glory
Ashland Motel

Omar's Steaks & Fresh Seafood

E Main St

Theater

Palm Motel

Pioneer St

Stratford Inn

Siskiyou Blvd

Oak Street

Shakespeare Festival

E
N S
W

Standing Stone Brewery

Martolli's Pizza

Granite Taphouse

Mountain Provisions

Lithia Way

Library

Best Western

Brothers

E Main St

Post Office

Columbia Hotel

Shakespeare Festival

Best Western

Brothers

0.2	Rodeway Inn to Shop'n Kart
1.1	Rodeway Inn to Gr. Am. Pizza
1.3	Rodeway Inn to Flagship Inn
2.3	Rodeway Inn to Library
0.3	Post Office to Library
0.3	Post Office to Hostel
0.2	Hostel to Minute Market

Hostel

Minute Mkt

Maple St

Ashland Community Hospital
0.7 mile from Hostel

© 2019 Yogi's Books LLC

Map Symbols

David "Awol" Miller has given us permission to use the map symbols he created for his excellent book "The AT Guide". These map symbols allow you to easily find town services with a quick glance at the town maps.

✈	Airport	✚	First Aid	⊻	Lounge/Bar
$	ATM or Bank	🛒	Grocery Store	🚶	Outfitter
🚢	Boat	🔨	Hardware Store	✉	Outgoing Mail
👥	Bowling	🛏	Hostel	📞	Pay Phone
🚌	Bus	🛌	Hotel	℞	Pharmacy
⛺	Camping	ℹ	Information	🪑	Picnic Table
🚗	Car Rental	📶	Internet/WiFi	🏊	Pool
💻	Computer	🧺	Laundry	📮	Post Office
🧺	C-Store	🚊	Light Rail		

🏠	Ranger Station
🍴	Restaurant
🚻	Restroom/Privy
👟	Shoe Store
🚿	Shower
🚡	Ski Lift
🎥	Theater
🚂	Train Station

Easy Food Resupply

Triple Crown Outfitters in Kennedy Meadows is known as "the best resupply on the PCT." This great selection is also available for online shipping.

www.triplecrownoutfitters.com

- Huge selection

- Fast shipping

- Relax in town instead of shopping

- Quickly pick up a box and get back on trail

- Perfect for international hikers

Questions? Call or email:
559-302-9943
jackie@triplecrownoutfitters.com

RESUPPLY SUMMARY

1735.3 Green Springs Inn - 1.8 mile walk or hitch

Mail Drops: Accepts mail drops, no fee.
USPS, UPS, or FedEx.
No outgoing mail.
541-890-6435
[info@greenspringsinn.com]

Hiker's Legal Name
PCT Hiker, ETA: MM/DD/YY
c/o Green Springs Inn
11470 Highway 66
Ashland, OR 97520

Resupply: No resupply.

1742.7 Hyatt Lake Resort - 1.4 mile walk or hitch

Mail Drops: 541-482-3331
Accepts mail drops, no fee, UPS or
FedEx only. Pick up packages at
Camper's Cove Store office, usually
open 8:30-5p every day. Call ahead if
you will arrive after office hours. No
outgoing mail. Put phone number on
mail drops.

Hiker's Legal Name
PCT Hiker, ETA: MM/DD/YY
c/o Hyatt Lake Resort
7900 Hyatt Prairie Road
Ashland, OR 97520

Resupply: No resupply. Only has a few snacks.

1773.4 Fish Lake Resort - 2 mile walk or hitch

Mail Drops: 541-949-8500
Accepts mail drops, $5 fee
UPS only!
No outgoing mail

Hiker's Legal Name
PCT Hiker, ETA: MM/DD/YY
c/o Fish Lake Resort
State Hwy 140, Mile Marker 30
Eagle Point, OR 97524

Resupply: Store has car camping snacks only. No hiker resupply.

1773.4 Lake of the Woods Resort - 3.7 mile hitch

Resupply: 541-949-8300. Store has car camping snacks only. No hiker resupply.

1820.9 Crater Lake Mazama Village - 0.8 mile walk using guardrail trail

Mail Drops: Mazama Store (541-594-2255, ext 3609) accepts mail drops
USPS, FedEx, or UPS. USPS is recommended.
Click-n-Ship does not work for any Crater Lake addresses.

Crater Lake recommends that
hikers send mail drops via USPS:

UPS or FedEx only:

Hiker's Legal Name
PCT Hiker, ETA: MM/DD/YY
c/o Mazama Village Camp Store
Mazama Village
Crater Lake, OR 97604

Hiker's Legal Name
PCT Hiker, ETA: MM/DD/YY
c/o Mazama Village Camp Store
569 Mazama Village Drive
Crater Lake, OR 97604

Resupply: Mazama Store (541-594-2255, ext 3609) has car-camping food.
Not good for hiker resupply.

1820.9 Crater Lake Post Office

Post Office: The Post Office is in the visitor information building on the road between
Mazama and the Rim (4 road miles from Mazama, 3 road miles from Rim).
541-594-3115, Summer hours: Mon-Sat: 9a-noon and 1p-3p
Does NOT accept General Delivery. Outgoing mail only.

Resupply: No resupply.

Crater Lake Rim Village - on Rim alternate, 4.4 trail miles north of Mazama Village

Resupply: No resupply.

RESUPPLY SUMMARY

1848.0 Diamond Lake Resort - 10 mile hitch or on trail alternate route

Post Office: 541-793-3116.
May 1-Oct 31: Mon-Fri 9a-noon, 1p-4:30p. Sat 8a-12:30p.
Beginning Nov 1, only open Tuesday and Friday 8a-12:30p.
Return address must have your phone number.
Mail must have an ETA.
Hiker mail held for approximately one month after ETA.
USPS, UPS, or FedEx to the Post Office at this address:

Hiker's Legal Name
PCT Hiker, ETA: MM/DD/YY
c/o Diamond Lake Resort
340 Resort Drive
Diamond Lake, OR 97731

Resupply: Small C-Store: South Shore Store (541-793-3333, press 8)
Limited snacks, cold drinks, beer

Large C-Store: Resort Store (541-793-3333, press 5)
Decent hiker resupply, and a better beer selection

1906.6 Shelter Cove Resort - 1.4 mile walk or hitch

Mail Drops: 541-433-2548
Accepts mail drops, $10 fee for
USPS, $5 fee for UPS or FedEx.
No outgoing mail at all, not even
letters. Allow an extra week if
shipping USPS.

Hiker's Legal Name
PCT Hiker, ETA: MM/DD/YY
c/o Shelter Cove Resort
27600 West Odell Lake Road
Highway 58
Crescent, OR 97733

Resupply: Extremely expensive, limited resupply.

1907.9 Crescent Lake OR - 7 mile hitch

Mail Drops: Willamette Pass Inn (541-433-2211)
Accepts USPS mail drops, no fee.

Hiker's Legal Name
PCT Hiker, ETA: MM/DD/YY
c/o Willamette Pass Inn
PO Box 1035
Crescent Lake OR 97733

Resupply: Small grocery, good resupply: Odell Sportsman Center   541-433-9355

1952.6 Elk Lake Resort - 1 mile walk

Mail Drops: 541-480-7378
Summer hours per website [www.elklakeresort.net]
Mon-Thur 10a-8p. Fri 10a-9p. Sat 9a-9p. Sun 9a-8p.

Accepts mail drops, $5 fee.
UPS or FedEx only. Make sure
your mail drop is mouse/chipmunk
proof. A hard plastic tote is ideal to
keep out the critters. Mail must
have ETA. No outgoing mail.

Hiker's Legal Name
PCT Hiker, ETA: MM/DD/YY
c/o Elk Lake Resort
60,000 Century Drive
Bend, OR 97701

Resupply: No resupply.

RESUPPLY SUMMARY

1952.6	Bend OR via Elk Lake Resort -	32 mile hitch or Trail Angel ride
1983.7	Bend OR via McKenzie Pass -	35 mile hitch or Trail Angel ride
2000.9	Bend OR via Santiam Pass -	35 mile hitch or Trail Angel ride

Post Office: General Delivery is at the Main
Post Office at 2300 NE 4th St.
Mon-Fri 8:30a-5:30p. Sat 10a-1p.
541-318-5068, USPS only.
Priority Mail held for 2 weeks.

Hiker's Legal Name
PCT Hiker, ETA: MM/DD/YY
General Delivery
Bend, OR 97701

Mail Drops: REI accepts mail drops, no fee.
USPS, FedEx, UPS. 541-385-0594.
Mon-Sat 10a-8p, Sun 11a-6p.
Clearly mark your mail drop
as a hiker package .

Hiker's Legal Name
PCT Hiker, ETA: MM/DD/YY
c/o REI #96
380 SW Powerhouse Drive
Bend, OR 97702

Mail Drops: Trail Angel Brian Douglass
Accepts mail drops, $5 fee.
USPS, UPS, or FedEx.
541-213-8510.
Bdouglass2014@centurylink.net

Hiker's Legal Name
PCT Hiker, ETA: MM/DD/YY
c/o Brian Douglass
1686 NE Tucson Way
Bend, OR 97701-6235

Resupply: Supermarkets: Albertsons 541-382-3661
Safeway 541-312-6480

| 1983.7 | Sisters OR via McKenzie Pass - | 20 mile hitch or Trail Angel ride |
| 2000.9 | Sisters OR via Santiam Pass - | 20 mile hitch or Trail Angel ride |

Post Office: 541-549-0412, USPS only.
Mon-Fri 8:30a-5p. Sat closed.
General Delivery held for 15 days.

Hiker's Legal Name
PCT Hiker, ETA: MM/DD/YY
General Delivery
Sisters, OR 97759

Mail Drops:

| Sisters Inn (541-549-7829) Accepts mail drops, no fee. Clearly label your box as a hiker package, including ETA. | USPS address: Hiker's Legal Name PCT Hiker, ETA: MM/DD/YY c/o Sisters Inn PO Box 938 Sisters, OR 97759 | UPS or FedEx address: Hiker's Legal Name PCT Hiker, ETA: MM/DD/YY c/o Sisters Inn 605 N. Arrowleaf Trail Sisters OR 97759 |

Resupply: Supermarket: Ray's Food Place 541-549-2222

1995.1 Big Lake Youth Camp - 0.7 mile walk

Mail Drops: Info: 503-850-3583. Direct line to camp: 503-805-2267 [www.biglake.org/pct-hikers/]
Open end of June thru Labor Day. After mid-August, the camp is not staffed full-time.

Accepts mail drops from the end of June
thru Labor Day, no fee, USPS or UPS only.
Hiker mail must state "PCT hiker" and ETA.
Hiker mail held for one month after ETA.
No outgoing mail.

Hiker's Legal Name
PCT Hiker, ETA: MM/DD/YY
c/o Big Lake Youth Camp
26435 Big Lake Road
Sisters, OR 97759

Resupply: No resupply.

2046.0 Olallie Lake Resort - on trail

Resupply: [www.olallielakeresort.com] Good hiker resupply. No mail drops accepted.

2092.2 Government Camp - 4.8 mile hitch from Barlow Pass
or bus from Timberline Lodge

Post Office: 503-272-3238, USPS only.
Mon-Fri noon-4p. Sat closed.
If mail has ETA, it is held until the
ETA date, otherwise it is held for 2 weeks.

Hiker's Legal Name
PCT Hiker, ETA: MM/DD/YY
General Delivery
88331 E Govt Camp Loop
Government Camp, OR 97028

Resupply: Small grocery with decent resupply: Govy General Store 503-272-3107

RESUPPLY SUMMARY

2092.2 Sandy OR - 34 mile hitch from Barlow Pass
or bus from Government Camp or Timberline Lodge

Post Office: 503-668-4055. Mon-Fri 8:30a-5p.
Sat closed, but package pickup possible
at the will-call window from 6a-11a.
General Delivery held for 15 days.
USPS only.

Hiker's Legal Name
PCT Hiker, ETA: MM/DD/YY
General Delivery
Sandy, OR 97055

Resupply: Supermarket: Safeway   503-668-3202.
Grocery Store: Grocery Outlet 503-668-6950.

2097.4 Timberline Lodge - on trail

Mail Drops: WY'East store in the ski building
takes mail drops, $5 fee. Write
"Hold for PCT Hiker" on your package.
No outgoing mail. WY'East Store
503-272-3311, ext3189.
USPS or UPS.

Hiker's Legal Name
PCT Hiker, ETA: MM/DD/YY
c/o Timberline Lodge Ski Area
27500 E Timberline Road
WY'East Store
Timberline Lodge, OR 97028

Resupply: WY'East Store: No resupply. Minimal snacks.

2147.1 Cascade Locks OR - on trail

Post Office: 541-374-5026. Mon-Fri 8:30a-1p and
2p-5p. Sat closed, but usually hikers
can pick up packages on Sat from
9a-10a. Knock on the wooden door
to the left in the lobby. USPS only.
Hiker mail held until end of October.

Hiker's Legal Name
PCT Hiker, ETA: MM/DD/YY
General Delivery
Cascade Locks, OR 97014

Mail Drops: Cascade Locks Ale House (541-374-9310) accepts mail drops.

USPS Address:
Hiker's Legal Name
PCT Hiker, ETA: MM/DD/YY
c/o Cascade Locks Ale House
PO Box 388
Cascade Locks OR 97014

UPS or FedEx Address:
Hiker's Legal Name
PCT Hiker, ETA: MM/DD/YY
c/o Cascade Locks Ale House
500 WaNaPa Street
Cascade Locks OR 97014

Mail Drops: Port Marine RV Park (541-374-8619)
Accepts mail drops,
UPS or FedEx only, no fee.
Pick up mail drops at Administration
Office Mon-Fri 8a-5p. Sat-Sun closed.

Hiker's Legal Name
PCT Hiker, ETA: MM/DD/YY
c/o Port Marine RV Park
355 WaNaPa Street
Cascade Locks, OR 97014

Resupply: Grocery Store, full resupply: Columbia Market 541-374-8425

2147.1 Stevenson WA - 3.2 mile hitch

Post Office: 509-427-5532, USPS only
Mon-Fri 8:30a-5p
Sat closed
General Delivery held for 15 days

Hiker's Legal Name
PCT Hiker, ETA: MM/DD/YY
General Delivery
Stevenson, WA 98648

Mail Drops: Rodeway Inn accepts mail drops. 509-427-5628

Resupply: Supermarket: A & J Market 509-427-5491

2147.1 Hood River OR - 20 mile Interstate hitch or bus

Post Office: 541-386-1584, USPS only
Mon-Fri 8:30a-5p, Sat closed
Do not put Post Office street address
on General Delivery address.
Hiker mail held for 30 days.

Hiker's Legal Name
PCT Hiker, ETA: MM/DD/YY
General Delivery
Hood River, OR 97031

Resupply: Supermarket: Safeway 541-386-1841

1719.2 - Cross under Interstate 5 - No interstate access here. To hitch, go down to Callahan's

1720.0 - Seasonal Spring - Spring is past the wooden bridge. Unreliable.

1728.1 - Piped spring - Good water.

1730.1 - Piped spring - BINK (2009): The black plastic pipe was sticking into the pond and it appeared no water was flowing, however upon pulling the end of the pipe out of the water, there was water flowing out of it. Better yet, on the way down to the pond you will pass an old metal water trough that is dry; however, on the backside of it is a pipe with very good flow. This is easily missed! You cannot see or hear this water until nearly upon it.

1735.3 - Shortcut trail to Green Springs Inn

1735.5 - Highway 66 / Green Springs Summit - Ashland is 17 miles to the left.
DOUBLE TAP: Flat campsites on the north side of the Highway in a turnout.

1735.4 - Green Springs Inn

CONTACT: [www.greenspringsinn.com]   [info@greenspringsinn.com]   541-890-6435

GETTING HERE: <u>Three options:</u>

(1) <u>PCT mile 1735.5</u> - <u>BEST OPTION</u> - <u>1.8-mile short cut trail.</u> Details: about 1/4 mile before reaching Hwy 66, drop off PCT on to old skid road (poorly marked, on right side of PCT). Cross Keene Creek Dam. Pick up service road alongside ditch which empties into reservoir above dam. Follow the ditch road for about 1.0 mile. Look for power lines crossing the ditch. Just under the power lines, turn left and cross a wooden game bridge. Follow the power line right-of-way uphill for about 50 feet. Look for a well-marked trail on your right. Follow that trail up to the cabin area. Turn left on the Cabin Loop Road and follow it past the shop until you see the restaurant building through the trees. Take a short trail from the Cabin Loop Road to the restaurant parking lot.

(2) <u>PCT mile 1735.5</u> - Stay on PCT until <u>Highway 66</u>.
Hitch or walk 1.7 miles to the right.

(3) <u>PCT mile 1735.5</u> - Stay on PCT until <u>Highway 66</u>.
Follow Hwy until you see a <u>faint two-track on the right</u>. Follow this to the dam, cross the dam, follow the service road to the right to Green Springs Inn. This saves you the 0.6-mile highway walk around the reservoir.

RIDES: GSI staff will help with rides for injured/sick hikers from the Hwy 66 trailhead if possible. Call 541-482-0614. Staff will also shuttle hikers back to the trailhead if the restaurant is not too busy.

RETURN TO PCT: Hyatt Lake Road is directly across Hwy 66 from Green Springs Inn. Take Hyatt Lake Road 3 miles directly north, intersect the PCT at PCT mile 1742.7.

MAIL DROPS: Accepts mail drops, no fee.   Hiker's Legal Name
USPS, UPS, or FedEx.   PCT Hiker, ETA: MM/DD/YY
No outgoing mail.   c/o Green Springs Inn
                                                    11470 Highway 66
                                                    Ashland, OR 97520

RESUPPLY: No resupply. A limited selection of soda, beer, candy for sale.

LODGING: Inn has 8 motel rooms. Rates: $$$ +
Rooms fill up quickly, especially on weekends.

BEER:	First beer is free!
RESTAURANT:	Restaurant usually open 8:30a-8:30p every day. A free beer for hikers!
	BUCKEYE (2010): The absolute BEST burger you will find on the trail is at Green Springs Inn. Homemade herb bread, hand-pressed fresh burger. Plus, at least five homemade pies to choose from.
CAMPING:	There is an area suitable for camping, free for PCT hikers.
OTHER:	No resupply, no laundry, no showers, no ATM.
RIDE:	Possible ride back to Green Springs Summit, if they have time.

1741.2- Hyatt Lake Recreation Road - Water on the PCT, just before the road.

1742.7 - Hyatt Lake

OVERVIEW:	Hyatt Lake Campground	$ camping, includes shower.
	Hyatt Lake Resort	541-482-3331. Open year-round. Hiker-friendly, great pizza.

GETTING HERE:	See Handbook map. Hyatt Lake Campground is 0.3 mile from PCT. Hyatt Lake Resort (aka Campers Cove) is 1.4 mile from PCT.
RIDES:	If they have time, Hyatt Lake Resort will pick you up. Call 541-482-3331.
MAIL DROPS:	No fee to pick up a box. Boxes are at the Camper's Cove store. Hyatt Lake says: "PLEASE include a phone number on your packages. We end up with unclaimed packages, and would like to get them back to the owner, but without a phone number we can't contact them."

UPS or FedEx only !!!! Pick up packages at office, usually open 8:30-5p every day. Call ahead if you will arrive after office hours. No outgoing mail.	Hiker's Legal Name PCT Hiker, ETA: MM/DD/YY c/o Hyatt Lake Resort 7900 Hyatt Prairie Road Ashland, OR 97520

RESUPPLY:	Campers Cove has the smallest store on the PCT. All it has is pop, small bags of chips, cookies, and a little candy. Credit cards accepted ($10 minimum).
RESTAURANT:	The old "Campers Cove" restaurant serves breakfast, lunch, dinner, and excellent pizza. Beer, wine, liquor. 2018 hours: Sun-Thur 9a-6p, Fri 9a-7p, Sat 9a-8p. Hours might be extended in the high season. Call for information.
LODGING:	Cabins: $$$ +
CAMPING:	Faucets were turned off in 2017, 2018. Camping is at the Hyatt Lake Campground. PCT camping rate $ includes shower. PCT campsite is behind restroom/shower. If Entrance Station is open, pay there. If not, pay at Fee Station. PCT campsite might move in future years.
SHOWER:	$ at Hyatt Lake Campground.
LAUNDRY:	No.
ATM:	No.

HYATT LAKE

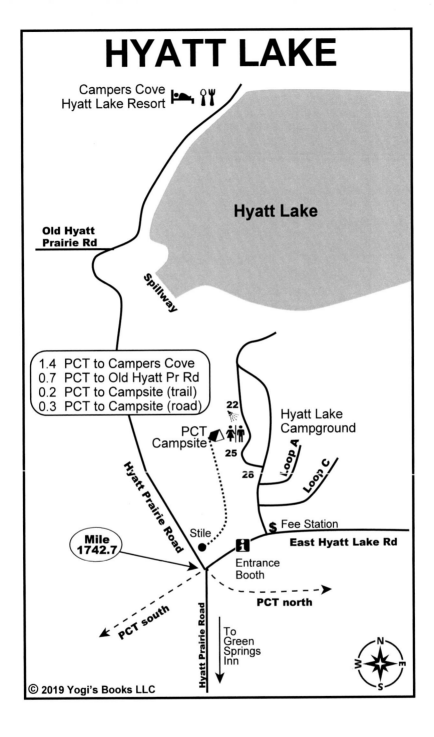

Campers Cove
Hyatt Lake Resort

Hyatt Lake

Old Hyatt
Prairie Rd

Spillway

1.4 PCT to Campers Cove
0.7 PCT to Old Hyatt Pr Rd
0.2 PCT to Campsite (trail)
0.3 PCT to Campsite (road)

22

PCT
Campsite

Hyatt Lake
Campground

25

Loop A

26

Loop C

Hyatt Prairie Road

Stile

$ Fee Station

Mile
1742.7

East Hyatt Lake Rd

Entrance
Booth

PCT north

Hyatt Prairie Road

PCT south

To
Green
Springs
Inn

N
W   E
S

© 2019 Yogi's Books LLC

1742.7 - If you don't go to Hyatt Lake Resort, continue on the PCT across the road. Very soon, you will see a sign indicating water is off trail to the left. Faucet was turned off in 2017, 2018.

1750.4 - Klum Campground - 0.3 mile off the PCT. Camping $20/site for up to 8 people. Water, showers. Contact Jackson County Parks 541-774-8183.

1751.1 - Grizzly Creek - First, the PCT crosses a canal which smells like sewage. About a minute later, you walk on a bridge over Grizzly Creek, which has disgusting water. BINK: 100% agree. I avoid this source at all costs.

1755.2 - Big Springs - Watch for a sign on the right side of the trail. The sign leads you about 3 minutes away to a good fenced-in spring.

DOUBLE TAP (2014): There are 2 junctions, sign to the spring at 2nd junction. If you accidentally take the 1st junction then turn left at the jeep road, walk ~0.15 miles to the trail on right. Good cold water coming out of a pipe at the end (good camping here too).

1761.6 - Dead Indian Memorial Road

1763.3 - South Brown Mountain Shelter - Nice shelter with well water from pump. Water often tastes like a pipe.

1773.2 - Fish Lake Trail - Fish Lake Resort is 2.0 mile to the left. Take the super easy side trail. Much better than hitching up on Hwy 140.

1773.4 - Fish Lake Resort

OVERVIEW:	541-949-8500 [info@fishlakeresort.net]

Owners Rob and Kaitlyn say: "Hikers are always welcome here at Fish Lake Resort. We have a PCT Register, laundry, warm showers, cold beer, hot food, and a game room with TV."

GETTING HERE: (1) <u>PCT mile 1773.2</u>: Take the Fish Lake Trail 2 miles to the west (left). This is a flat, super easy walk.

(2) <u>PCT mile 1773.4</u>: Hitch 2.1 miles to the left on Highway 140. Turn off Hwy 140, then it's 0.6 mile farther down to Fish Lake Resort.

MAIL DROPS: Accepts mail drops, $5 fee. No outgoing mail.

UPS only !!!!

Hiker's Legal Name
PCT Hiker, ETA: MM/DD/YY
c/o Fish Lake Resort
Highway 140, Mile Marker 30
Eagle Point, OR 97524

RESUPPLY: Store has car camping snacks only. No hiker resupply in past years. New owners took over in 2017; they are trying to stock hiker resupply items.

LODGING: <u>Cabins</u> Rates: $$$$. No TV. Include linens, bedding, dishes, cooking utensils, stove/oven, refrigerator, bathroom, shower.

<u>Rustic cabins</u> available. Ask for PCT hiker rate ($$).

CAMPING: Free hiker site.

RESTAURANT: Great burgers and cold beer!! Open 7 days a week. Close at 7p Mon, Tue, Wed.

LAUNDRY: Yes.

SHOWER: Yes.

FUEL: Usually fuel canisters and HEET at the store.

MOSQUITOES: Bugs are usually really bad north of here.

1773.4 - Lake of the Woods Resort

OVERVIEW:	541-949-8300. Open year-round. Cabins, restaurant, pizza parlor, C-Store (car camping snacks only). Restaurant food here is much better than at Fish Lake Resort.
GETTING HERE:	Hitch 3.7 miles east (right) on Highway 140, then turn off highway (right) and go 1.2 more miles to Lake of the Woods Resort.
RESUPPLY:	Store has car camping snacks only. No hiker resupply.
LODGING:	Cabins, 2-night minimum. Rates: $$$$
RESTAURANT:	Lake House Restaurant serves breakfast/lunch/dinner every day. Grill & Pizza Shop open every day at 11a.

1773.4 - Highway 140 - Mosquitoes are terrible north of here.

1773.5 - Bridge Over Large Creek -
Water just after the highway. Often dry by late August, usually dry in September.

1773.8 - Junction to Parking Lot - Water on the PCT here.

1781.5 - Twin Ponds Trail to Summit Lake - LIGHTFOOT (2007): The first pond is shallow and may dry up in late season, but about 0.25 miles further is the second which is deeper and would be expected to be a water source year round. There is limited, poor camping.

1784.9 - Junction to Christi's Spring - Great water!

SCRUB: There is nice camping for several people if you bushwhack about 25 yards down past the water at Christi's Spring. You can't see the sites from the spring itself.

1796.0 - Snow Lakes Trail 3739 -

1798.5 (Devils Peak/Lee Peak Saddle) to 1802.1 (Honeymoon Creek) - Many small creeks.

1799.3 - Seasonal Creek - Usually good water.

1799.3, 1799.7, 1800.7 - Get water from these spring-fed creeks.
You'll switchback across them a few times as you descend off Devils Peak.
These creeks have much better water than Honeymoon Creek (at 1802.1)

1802.1 - Honeymoon Creek - Not a good water source.

1804.3 - Ranger Springs - BINK: Good water, but quite a trek off trail.

1806.4 - Trail Junction to McKie Camp - PCT is the trail to the right.

1808.9 - Jack Spring - BINK: The water here is more than 0.5 mile off trail.
Small hole in a wet area, can be dry in late summer.

1820.9 - Highway 62 - Mazama Village is to the right.

1821.7 - Annie Creek Trail Junction

1823.0 - Dutton Creek - Water here. This is where the Stock PCT and the Hiker PCT split.

541-594-2255   press 3609   Mazama Village Store
                  press 2   Mazama Cabins & Campground
                  press 5   Mazama Village Annie Creek Restaurant & Gift Shop
                  press 0   Rim Village Lodge
                  press 1   Rim Village Lodge Dining Room
                  press 6   Rim Village Gift Shop
                  press 8   Resort Business Office

888-774-2728   Lodging Reservations

PERMIT - Permits are required to camp in Crater Lake National Park. Your PCTA permit covers you as long as you sign the trail register when entering Crater Lake National Park. Quoted from the Crater Lake "Plan Your Visit" page of the NPS website: "All campers not staying in the park's developed campgrounds must obtain a backcountry permit. The only exception is through-hikers on the Pacific Crest Trail, who may instead sign the trail register as they enter the park."

THREE PLACES IN HIKERS NEED/WANT TO GO

(1) Mazama Village - PCT mile 1820.9 - Off trail 1.4 mile by car (0.8 mile using guardrail shortcut). Mazama has a store (car-camping food), restaurant, showers, laundry, camping, and cabins. The Mazama Store accepts mail drops. Free trolley between Mazama Village and Rim Village.

(2) Post Office & Visitor Center - Off trail, approximately 4 road miles from Mazama, or approximately 3 road miles from the Rim Village. The Post Office is in the Visitor Information Building on the road (not on the PCT) in between Mazama and the Rim Village. PO does *NOT* accept General Delivery; it is outgoing mail only. There is nothing to eat here.

(3) Rim Village - On trail (Hiker Route). The Rim Village is 4.4 trail miles north of the PCT crossing of Highway 62; or 7 road miles north of Mazama Village. The Rim Village has a Café/souvenir shop (no resupply) and a Lodge. The Lodge has a restaurant which is open for breakfast, lunch, and dinner. Free trolley between Mazama Village and Rim Village.

HITCHHIKING IN CRATER LAKE NATIONAL PARK
Hitchhiking is illegal in CLNP. Free trolley between Mazama Village and Rim Village.

CRATER LAKE AREA MAP

Notice where Mazama Village, the PO, and the Rim Village are located in relation to each other. They're NOT near each other. Unless you want to do a lot of road walking, plan carefully for your Crater Lake resupply.

OFFICIAL PCT ROUTE

According to the PCTA, the Equestrian route is the "official" route. Are you really going to hike 1823.0 miles to Crater Lake, and then avoid the spectacular Rim Trail (Hiker PCT)? Really?

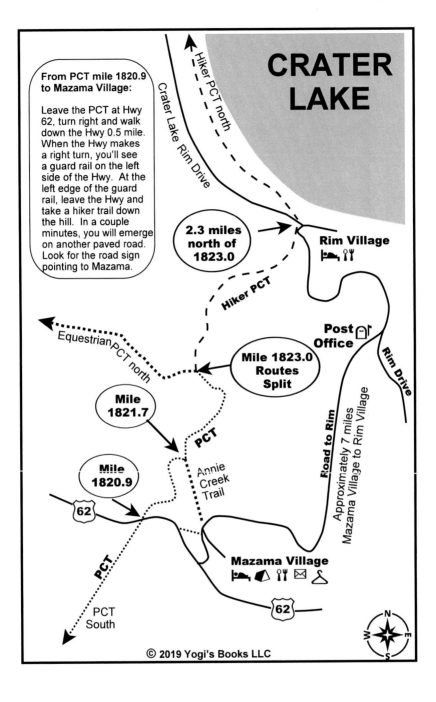

From PCT mile 1820.9 to Mazama Village:

Leave the PCT at Hwy 62, turn right and walk down the Hwy 0.5 mile. When the Hwy makes a right turn, you'll see a guard rail on the left side of the Hwy. At the left edge of the guard rail, leave the Hwy and take a hiker trail down the hill. In a couple minutes, you will emerge on another paved road. Look for the road sign pointing to Mazama.

CRATER LAKE

Hiker PCT north

Crater Lake Rim Drive

2.3 miles north of 1823.0

Rim Village

Hiker PCT

Post Office

Equestrian PCT north

Mile 1823.0 Routes Split

Mile 1821.7

Road to Rim

Approximately 7 miles
Mazama Village to Rim Village

Rim Drive

Mile 1820.9

62

PCT

Annie Creek Trail

PCT

Mazama Village

62

PCT South

N

© 2019 Yogi's Books LLC

OVERVIEW: C-Store with car camping food, restaurant, showers, laundry, cabins, campground. Pick up your maildrop at the Mazama Village Store.

GETTING HERE: Two options:

    (1) **PCT mile 1820.9** - Guardrail Trail: Walking the highway is faster and has less climbing than the Annie Creek Trail. Leave the PCT at Hwy 62, turn right and walk down the Hwy 0.5 mile. When the Hwy makes a right turn, you'll see a guardrail on the left side of the Hwy. At the left edge of the guard rail, leave the Hwy and take a hiker trail down the hill. In a couple minutes, you will emerge on another paved road. Look for the road sign pointing to Mazama. This is the quickest, cheapest way to get to the Mazama Store/campground. Hikers who walked the road all the way actually had to pay an entrance fee to walk through the car gate. If you stay on trails, there are no entrance gates where you would have to pay anything. Total distance: PCT at Hwy 62 to guardrail trail to Mazama is 0.8 miles.

    (2) **PCT mile 1821.7** - Annie Creek Trail: Cross the highway and stay on the PCT for 0.8 mile. Then take the Annie Creek Trail down to Mazama. It's about 1.1 mile from the PCT/Annie Creek junction to the Mazama Store. Total distance: PCT at Hwy 62 to Annie Creek Trail to Mazama is 1.9 miles.

TROLLEY: Free trolley between Mazama Village and Rim Village.

MAIL DROPS: Mazama store accepts mail drops, USPS, UPS, FedEx. 541-594-2255, ext 3609. **Crater Lake recommends that hikers send mail drops via USPS.** No fee to pick up mail drops. You cannot mail packages out from Mazama. Outgoing mail is letters only. Amazon PCT Hiker mail will arrive in Crater Lake via the USPS, no matter how it was originally shipped.

    USPS, UPS, and FedEx all deliver to the Mazama Store.

    Unclaimed mail: When Mazama closes in mid-October, all unclaimed USPS mail is taken to the Post Office. The Post Office returns them to the sender. So, be absolutely sure to include a valid domestic return address on all mail. UPS/FedEx packages are almost impossible to return.

    ★★ USPS Click-N-Ship will not work for Crater Lake addresses ★★

Crater Lake recommends that hikers send mail drops via USPS:	**UPS/FedEx only address:**
Hiker's Legal Name	Hiker's Legal Name
PCT Hiker, ETA: MM/DD/YY	PCT Hiker, ETA: MM/DD/YY
c/o Mazama Village Camp Store	c/o Mazama Village Camp Store
Mazama Village	569 Mazama Village Drive
Crater Lake, OR 97604	Crater Lake, OR 97604

RESUPPLY: Mazama Store 541-594-2255, ext 3609. Open approximately 7a-9p every day, June thru Labor Day. Hours reduced in off-season. Closes mid-October.

    Car-camping food. Not good for hiker resupply. Few dinners, expensive candy.

LODGING: Reservations 888-774-2728.

    There are cabins at Mazama Village and a Lodge at the Rim Village, but they're expensive and usually filled up. Don't count on staying indoors. No TV in the cabins or Lodge rooms.

    Mazama Village cabins $$$$. Rim Village Lodge rooms $$$$. Open late-May to mid-October.

CAMPING: Campground open mid-June to late-Sept/early-October. 541-594-2255, press 2. Ask about the hiker site $.

RESTAURANT:	Annie Creek Restaurant at Mazama.
	Excellent pizza, pasta, salads, soups, beer, wine.
	Restaurant open late-May to mid-September.
	Hours: 8a-8p late-May to late-June, and September.
	7a-9p late-June to late-August.
	541-594-2255, press 5.
LAUNDRY:	At the Mazama Store.
SHOWERS:	Coin-operated showers at the store and at the campground.
	Towel available at store.
ATM:	At the Mazama Store.
FUEL:	HEET and canister fuel at the Mazama store.
	Both often sell out in high hiker season.
WiFi:	Pay WiFi. Hourly and daily rates.

LEAVING MAZAMA: Two options:

(1) Go back to PCT mile 1820.9 (PCT crossing of Highway 62).

(2) Walk out of the main Campground entrance to the road to the Rim. Turn right. Walk maybe 200 yards to where the road turns right. Signed Annie Creek Trail is on the left. Hike this trail 0.6 miles and join the PCT at the PCT/Annie Creek Trail junction (PCT mile 1821.7).   DOUBLE TAP: Immediately after getting on the Annie Creek Trail the trail forks, take the left fork which goes up to the PCT.

1820.9 - Crater Lake Post Office & Visitor Center

OVERVIEW:	The Post Office is *not* along the PCT. The PO is in the visitor information building on the road between Mazama and the Rim (4 road miles from Mazama, 3 road miles from Rim). There is nothing to eat here.
GETTING HERE:	Leave the PCT at mile 1820.9, and go to Mazama Village. Then walk up the road from Mazama toward the Rim Village. The PO is about 4 road miles from Mazama. There is NOT a connecting trail from the Hiker PCT to the PO. The only way to get to the PO is on the road. Hitchhiking is illegal in Crater Lake National Park.
POST OFFICE:	Post Office is outgoing mail only. **NO GENERAL DELIVERY.**
	541-594-3115
	Summer hours: Mon-Sat: 9a-noon and 1p-3p

Crater Lake Rim Village

OVERVIEW:	The Rim Village is 4.4 trail miles or 7 road miles north of Mazama Campground. The Rim Village has a gift shop (no resupply) and a Café. The Lodge has a restaurant.
GETTING HERE:	Two options:

(1) PCT mile 1820.9 - Go to Mazama Village, then walk the road up to the Rim from Mazama or from the PO.

(2) PCT mile 1823.0 - Take the Hiker's PCT up to the Rim. When the trail emerges at a paved road, you'll see the Rim Village to your right.

TROLLEY:	Free trolley between Mazama Village and Rim Village.
MAIL DROPS:	No.
RESUPPLY:	No resupply at the Rim Village.
LODGING:	Reservations 888-774-2728.

There are cabins at Mazama Village and a Lodge at the Rim Village, but they're expensive and usually filled up. Don't count on staying indoors. No TV in the cabins or Lodge rooms.

Mazama Village cabins $$$$.

Rim Village Lodge rooms $$$$.

Rim Village Lodge is open late-May to mid-October.

RESTAURANTS:	Rim Village Café (541-594-2255, press 6) features "Grab and Go" items such as hot soups, sandwiches, salads, and snacks. Summer usually open 9a-6p. Shorter hours in off-season.

Lodge Dining Room (541-594-2255, press 1) serves breakfast, lunch, dinner. Reservations required for dinner. Reservations fill up fast.

ATM:	At the Gift Shop.
WATER:	Water fountain next to Visitor's Center. Also a bathroom with water.

Access these files as often as possible:

(1) **Pacific Crest Trail Water Report -** Current status of water sources.
Frequently updated during hiker season. [www.pctwater.com]

(2) **Yogi's PCT Handbook update file -** Changes to trail/town information which have occurred between the time your book was printed and now. Frequently updated during hiker season. [www.yogisbooks.com], then click UPDATES & LINKS

Do you have changes/updates to report?
If so, send them here: yogisbooks@gmail.com

1820.9 - Highway 62 - Mazama Village is to the right.

1821.7 - Annie Creek Trail Junction

1823.0 - Dutton Creek - Water here. This is where the Stock PCT and the Hiker PCT split.

WATER - The next on-trail water is at Thielsen Creek, 26.4 miles north of the Rim Village.

CAMPING ON THE RIM - SCRUB (2013): You might see signs and/or hear from a Ranger about the illegality of camping on the Crater Lake Rim. I did it anyway and got away with it. The next night, my friend tried and was woken up at 1am by a Ranger with a heat sensor (yes, really) and given $500 in citations for illegal camping and possession on federal lands. Yeah he was unlucky, but just know that you do it at your own risk and the Rangers don't necessarily look the other way about anything at Crater Lake.

Rim Trail / Hiker PCT (11.7 miles)	
0.0	**Leave Equestrian PCT at Dutton Creek Trail Junction (PCT mile 1823.0)**
2.3	**Rim Village**
4.6	**Junction to Lightning Spring -** Easy trail to Lightning Spring (0.8 mile off PCT). No Park permit required for PCT permit holders. Great water and camping.
5.9	**Trail to the Watchman.**
6.2	**Privy at parking lot.**
9.0	DOUBLE TAP: **Good campsites** to the right of the PCT ~100 ft off trail behind a grove of trees.
11.7	**Rim Trail / Hiker PCT joins Equestrian PCT (PCT mile 1839.2)**

1839.2 - Equestrian PCT joins Rim Trail / Hiker PCT

1847.8 - Highway 138

OVERVIEW: Diamond Lake Resort is along the east side of Diamond Lake. South Shore Pizza/C-Store is at the – you guessed it – south end of the lake. The Resort is 3 miles north. Resort has motel rooms, cabins, laundry, PO, two restaurants.

541-793-3333	press 1	Reservations
	press 4	Food Service
	press 5	North Store
	press 8	South Shore Pizza & Store

GETTING HERE: See Handbook map.
                Shuttles to/from PCT at Hwy 138 or Windigo Pass for a fee. 541-793-3333.

POST OFFICE: Post Office is inside the Lodge, next to the registration desk. 541-793-3116. Pick up mail drops only during PO hours. May 1-Oct 31: Mon-Fri 9a-noon, 1p-4:30p. Sat 8a-12:30p. Beginning Nov 1, only open Tuesday and Friday. Return address must have your phone number. Mail must have an ETA. Be sure your address is Diamond Lake, not Diamond ! ! Hiker mail held for approximately one month after ETA. USPS, UPS, or FedEx to the Post Office at this address:

                Hiker's Legal Name
                PCT Hiker, ETA: MM/DD/YY
                c/o Diamond Lake Resort
                340 Resort Drive
                Diamond Lake, OR 97731

RESUPPLY: South Shore Store   541-793-3333, press 8. Limited snacks, cold drinks, beer.

                Resort Store   541-793-3333, press 5. Large C-Store with decent hiker resupply, including Idahoans, and a better beer selection.

LODGING: Reservations   541-793-3333, press 1.
                Motel rooms   With TV, AC, and heat. Rates: $$$ +
                Cabins   With kitchens. Sleep 6 people. Rates: $$$$ +

CAMPING: Free Hiker/Biker Camping Area   Five non-motorized campsites, adjacent to the South Shore Picnic Area (see the bottom of the lake on Halfmile Oregon map D1a).

                Broken Arrow Campground   South of South Shore Store. See Halfmile Oregon map D1a, below "South Shore Picnic Area" at the bottom of the lake. Showers, flush toilets, trash. This is a pay campground.

                Diamond Lake Campground   Between South Shore Store and Diamond Lake Resort. Noted as "Diamond Lake Loop" on Halmfile map D1a. Showers, flush toilets, trash. This is a pay campground.

RESTAURANT: South Shore Pizza.   541-793-3333, press 8.
                                     Pizza, chicken, subs, scooped ice cream, cold drinks, beer. Open daily from Memorial Day weekend to Labor Day weekend.

                Resort: 541-793-3333, press 4.
                                     Diamond Lake Café and Mt. Bailey Sports Grill/Lounge.

LAUNDRY: At Diamond Lake Resort.
SHOWER: At campgrounds and at the Resort.
ATM: In main lodge.

RETURN TO PCT: Howlock Mountain Trail #1448. This is shown in the top right of Halfmile Oregon map D1a, and continues onto Halfmile Oregon map D2. From the Forest Service website: "The first 2 miles of trail is heavily used by horses. The trail passes through open stands of lodgepole pine for the first 3 miles. The timber type gradually changes to true fir-mountain hemlock as you gain elevation."

DIAMOND LAKE

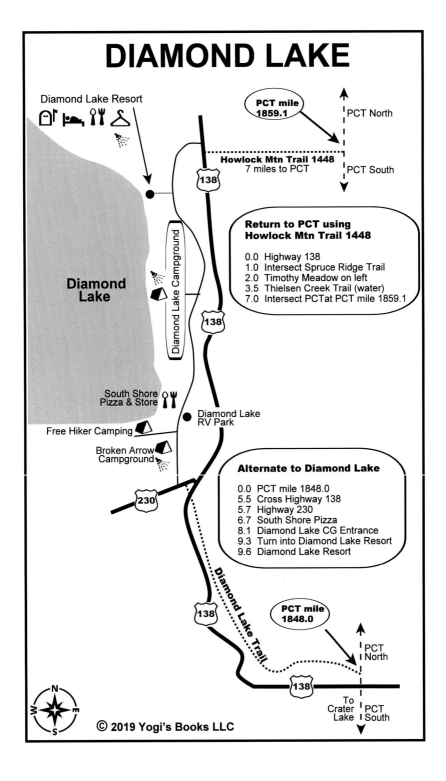

Diamond Lake Resort

PCT mile 1859.1

PCT North

138

Howlock Mtn Trail 1448
7 miles to PCT

PCT South

Diamond Lake Campground

Diamond Lake

138

**Return to PCT using
Howlock Mtn Trail 1448**

0.0 Highway 138
1.0 Intersect Spruce Ridge Trail
2.0 Timothy Meadow on left
3.5 Thielsen Creek Trail (water)
7.0 Intersect PCT at PCT mile 1859.1

South Shore
Pizza & Store

Diamond Lake
RV Park

Free Hiker Camping

Broken Arrow
Campground

230

Alternate to Diamond Lake

0.0 PCT mile 1848.0
5.5 Cross Highway 138
5.7 Highway 230
6.7 South Shore Pizza
8.1 Diamond Lake CG Entrance
9.3 Turn into Diamond Lake Resort
9.6 Diamond Lake Resort

138

Diamond Lake Trail

PCT mile 1848.0

PCT
North

138

To
Crater
Lake

PCT
South

© 2019 Yogi's Books LLC

1856.1 - Thielsen Creek - Cold water.

1859.1 - Howlock Mountain Trail - Goes down to Diamond Lake Resort.

1865.9 - Maidu Lake Trail 3725A - Maidu Lake is one mile off trail.
Get water here, and skip Six Horse Spring.

1872.1 - Tolo Camp, junction to Six Horse Spring -
Six Horse Spring is 0.4 mile down the ridge, usually has water. Lower pools are fresher.

1878.2 - Windigo Pass, Road 60 -
BINK: Walk east on the road about 0.5 mile to where a small creek crosses the under the road.
Dry 2012-2016.

1878.3 - Oregon Skyline Trail Alternate - Trail signs mark this as "Odell Lake Trail." On Halfmile
Oregon Skyline Alternate Map Page 2, the area near Crescent Lake Campground is very
confusing if you are going to Crescent Lake. The trail dumps you onto a road. Follow
northwest until you see NFCG sign "Spring Camp." On the same map, Whitefish Horse Camp
is for equestrians only, and reservations are required. Does have water.

DOUBLE TAP: OST not marked as OST anywhere on the trail from what I saw. Turn right at
Forest Rd 60 and hike for ~0.5 mile and you will see a sign on the left marked as the Oldenburg
Lake Trail, this is the OST. Right before you reach Crescent Lake look for trail signs that have
the letters MW inside of a horseshoe, follow that trail until you are ~0.5 mile away from
Crescent Lake.

1880.6 - Minor crest saddle to lakelet - You have to watch for this. Watch your maps and pay
attention to the trail. It's not really a saddle. Watch the left side of the PCT, the lake is downhill
through the trees. You can barely see it. It's just as the PCT gets steeper and the trees open
up. Before the PCT leaves the trees, look down to the left and you should see the lake, which
is sometimes dry. BINK: Usually has water as late as July.

1889.3 - Summit Lake - Water, and many yogi-ing opportunities.

1889.6 - Creek - Good water.

1889.6 to 1896.5 - Gross water in the ponds and lakes.

1896.5 - Spring - A fantastic on-trail spring. This is the beginning of Mountain Creek.

1899.4 - Pond - Water here.

1902.4 - Hidden Lake

1906.2 - Pengra Pass - Turn right to go to Shelter Cove Resort.

1906.6 - Shelter Cove Trail

1907.9 - Willamette Pass, Highway 58 - Privy across the highway.
It's pronounced "Willamette, Damn It!"

1906.6 - Shelter Cove Resort

OVERVIEW: 541-433-2548.
Open year-round. Small store, shower, laundry, camping.

GETTING HERE: (1)   Pengra Pass (PCT mile 1906.2) - Go down to the jeep road, turn right, stay on this jeep road. Cross the railroad tracks, then walk the jeep road to the right down to the highway. Turn right on the highway, walk 0.5 mile. You'll see a BLM campground on the left, then cross a bridge, then see a big green Shelter Cove sign on the left. Just past that on the left are 2 big logs. At the logs, you can leave the highway and take the cleared area about 0.3 mile to the resort.

(2)   Shelter Cove Trail (PCT mile 1906.6) - Turn right, follow trail 2.2 miles.

Or, stay on Shelter Cove Trail until you get to the Pengra Pass jeep road (see previous paragraph). Go left on the jeep road, cross the railroad tracks, then walk the jeep road to the right down to the highway. Turn right on the highway, walk 0.5 mile. You'll see a BLM campground on the left, then cross a bridge, then see a big green Shelter Cove sign on the left. Just past that on the left are 2 big logs. At the logs, you can leave the highway and take the cleared area about 0.3 mile to the resort.

PCT HIKER AREA: Walled tent, charging station, microwave.

MAIL DROPS: Accepts mail drops. UPS/FedEx are faster than USPS, because UPS/FedEx deliver to the Resort. USPS has to be picked up an hour round trip, and the Resort does not pick up mail every day. Allow an extra week if shipping USPS.

Hiker's Legal Name
PCT Hiker, ETA: MM/DD/YY
c/o Shelter Cove Resort
27600 West Odell Lake Road
Highway 58
Crescent, OR 97733

UPS or FedEx: $5 fee
USPS: $10 fee.

No outgoing mail at all,
not even letters.

RESUPPLY: Store usually open: Sun-Thur 8a-8p, Fri-Sat 7a-8p.
Hours vary!! Extremely expensive, limited resupply.

LODGING: Rooms and cabins: $$$ - $$$$

CAMPING: 2018: Backpacker's site $10.

RESTAURANT: 7a-7p every day. Grill serves pancakes, breakfast burritos, home made pizzas, burgers, fresh cut fries. There is a daily hiker special. Hiker lounge has a microwave.

LAUNDRY: One washer and one dryer.

SHOWER: Coin operated shower.

ATM: Yes.

FUEL: HEET and canister fuel.

OVERVIEW: Very small town with limited services, but it's got more than Shelter Cove!!

GETTING HERE: From Willamette Pass, hitch 7 miles to the right on Hwy 58.

SHUTTLES: Possible ride from Willamette Pass Inn owners. 541-433-2211.

MAIL DROPS: Willamette Pass Inn (541-433-2211)   Hiker's Legal Name
                 Accepts USPS mail drops, no fee.   PCT Hiker, ETA: MM/DD/YY
                                                             c/o Willamette Pass Inn
                                                             PO Box 1035
                                                             Crescent Lake OR 97733

RESUPPLY: Odell Sportsman Center   541-433-9355
                                           Small grocery, good resupply.

LODGING: Willamette Pass Inn   541-433-2211
                                           Rates: $$$ +
                                           Rooms have kitchenettes, refrigerator, utensils
                                           Cabins have full kitchens and utensils

RESTAURANT: Yes.

ATM: At Odell Sportsman Center.

FUEL: HEET at Odell Sportsman Center.

1910.7 (Lower Rosary Lake) to 1962.1 (North Fork Mesa Creek) - All good water.

1914.4 - Maiden Peak Ski Hut - Blue sign marks trail to shelter. Nobos can't miss it. BINK: This is a nice public ski hut has a wood stove, loft, and solar light system, but no nearby water supply.

1925.1 - Charlton Lake - Water here.

1927.7 - Harralson Trail - At an unsigned major trail junction, "Harralson" is carved into a downed log. The PCT goes to the right.

1941.5 - Snowshoe Lake Trail -

1944.0 - The PCT goes right where an unsigned lightly-used trail goes straight/left downhill. Minutes later is the signed Porky Lake Trail. PCT goes straight here. 10 yards later, there is an unsigned junction. The right-branching trail goes to Cliff Lake. The left-branching trail is the PCT.

1950.0 - Spring - Watch for a spring down 30 feet on the left.

1952.6 - Island Meadow Trail / Elk Lake Trail - Take this easy trail one mile to the right, and you'll reach Highway 46. Elk Lake Resort is across the highway. You could hitch Highway 46 to the north (left), and get to Bend in 32 miles.

1952.6 - Elk Lake Resort

OVERVIEW:	[www.elklakeresort.net] click [location] click [pacific crest trail] 541-480-7378 Open year-round. Hours change; see website for current info. Summer usually open Mon-Thur 11a-7p, Fri 11a-9p, Sat 9a-9p, Sun 9a-7p. Hiker-friendly. Good food and ice cream!!
GETTING HERE:	PCT mile 1952.6: Easy one-mile walk down the Island Meadow Trail. When you emerge at a trailhead parking lot, go to the left and follow the road down to the highway. Cross the highway, and continue walking straight toward the lake. The restaurant is on the left, just before you walk into the water.
RETURN TO PCT:	Take the Horse Creek Trail up the ridge to the PCT instead of backtracking up the Island Meadow Trail. The Horse Lake Trail will meet the PCT at mile 1953.9. Both trails are easy and well-maintained.
SHUTTLE:	Brian Douglass (UberDucky) provides rides from Elk Lake Resort, McKenzie Pass, and Santiam Pass to Sisters or Bend. Email is preferred contact method: [bdouglass2014@centurylink.net] 541-213-8510 Request 50¢ per mile reimbursement. Provide this information: Name of hiker(s) Cell phone number Trailhead pick up point Destination Date and Time transportation is being requested Don's Town & Country Shuttle cell 541-280-5076, business 541-647-2281
MAIL DROPS:	UPS or FedEx only!! $5 fee. Make sure your mail drop is mouse/chipmunk proof. A hard plastic tote is ideal to keep out the critters. Mail must have ETA. No outgoing mail.
	Hiker's Legal Name PCT Hiker, ETA: MM/DD/YY c/o Elk Lake Resort 60,000 Century Drive Bend, OR 97701
RESUPPLY:	No resupply. Small store only has very expensive drinks, candy, DEET.

RESTAURANT:	Summer usually open Mon-Thur 11a-7p, Fri 11a-9p, Sat 9a-9p, Sun 9a-7p. Hours may change. See website [www.elklakeresort.net] Great food here! Have an ice cream cone for dessert!
LODGING:	Rustic cabins 2018: $70. Furnished cabins $$$$.
CAMPING:	2018: $10 camping.
SHOWERS:	2018: Hot showers $5, includes towel and soap.
LAUNDRY:	No.
CANISTER FUEL:	Yes.

1953.9 - Horse Creek Trail - Take this easy trail one mile to the right, and you'll reach Highway 46. Elk Lake Resort is across the highway. You could hitch Highway 46 to the north (left), and get to Bend in 32 miles.

1962.1 - North Fork Mesa Creek - Usually dry.

1965.7 - Hinton Creek - Don't count on this.

1966.4 - Separation Creek - No water here.

1966.5 - Clear lakelet - This is off to the right. Good water.

1971.8 - Obsidian Trail 3528 - Keep walking past this junction until you're above Obsidian Falls, and the PCT will cross the creek. Continue upstream about one minute and get water directly from Sister Spring.

1971.5 to 1973.5 - Obsidian Limited Entry Area - Permit required for camping.
Your PCTA permit does not cover you for camping in this area.

1972.1 - Sister Spring - This is where you get water! Delicious!

1975.3 - Opie Dilldock Pass - Cell service here.

1976.2 - Minnie Scott Spring - GREAT spring.

1979.7 - South Matthieu Lake - Water.

1982.6 - Trail to Lava Lake Camp - BINK: Water 0.5 mile off trail at Lava Lake car campground. DOUBLE TAP: I recommend hiking to Hwy 242 via the Lava Lake Camp Trail and hitching from there as there is a big spot for cars to pull over at unlike right at McKenzie Pass. Plus, a lot of day hikers park their cars at Lava Camp Lake and they can be potential rides to Sisters or Bend.

1983.7 - McKenzie Pass / Highway 242 - Hitch 15 miles to the right to go to Sisters OR and farther to Bend OR. Some hikers have good luck getting rides at McKenzie Pass. Other hikers strongly state that Santiam Pass is better for catching a ride.

1986.6 - Belknap Crater - Off trail.

1993.7 - Coldwater Spring - BINK: Has never had water that I can ever remember. Consider it dry. Good camping, however.

1995.1 - Trail to Big Lake Youth Camp

1999.0 - Lily-pad pond - Water and camping here. DOUBLE TAP: Pond not visible from PCT.

2000.9 - Santiam Pass - US Highway 20 -
Hitch 15 miles to the right to go to Sisters OR and farther to Bend OR.

	BEND, OR	**SISTERS, OR**
OVERVIEW:	Large, spread out, all services.	Cool vibe. Good restaurants. Expensive lodging.
GETTING HERE:	(1) PCT 1952.6 (Island Meadow Trail) PCT mile 1953.9 (Horse Creek Trail) Take either trail one mile to the right, and you'll reach Highway 46. Elk Lake Resort is across the highway. Hitch Highway 46 to the north (left), and get to Bend in 32 miles. (2) PCT 1983.7 (McKenzie Pass) Hitch 15 miles to the right on Hwy 242 to Sisters. Then hitch 22 miles on Hwy 20 to Bend. (3) PCT 2000.9 (Santiam Pass) Hitch 15 miles to the right on Hwy 20 to Sisters. Then hitch 22 miles on Hwy 20 to Bend.	Hitch 15 miles to the right from: McKenzie Pass (PCT mile 1983.7) or Santiam Pass (PCT mile 2000.9)
RIDES:	REI (541-385-0594) has a list of people who give rides to trailheads. Any questions, call Cat Addison (Catdog, AT'04) 919-244-3338.	Blanche (541-241-0520) provides rides from McKenzie Pass or Santiam Pass to Sisters. She loves picking up hikers (when she's not doing her own hikes).
	Brian Douglass (UberDucky) provides rides from Elk Lake Resort, McKenzie Pass, and Santiam Pass to Sisters or Bend. Email is preferred contact method: [bdouglass2014@centurylink.net] 541-213-8510 Request 50¢ per mile reimbursement. Provide this information: Name of hiker(s), cell phone number, trailhead pick up point, destination, date and time transportation is being requested.	
BUS:	Cascade East. 541-385-8680. Local Bend transportation, and to nearby towns (including Sisters).	
CELL SERVICE:	Cell service above Obsidian Falls (mile 1972.0), at Opie Dilldock Pass (mile 1975.3), on top of Belknap Crater (off trail at 1986.6), and much of the trail between McKenzie Pass and Santiam Pass (mile 1983.7 - 2000.94)	
RESUPPLY:	Albertsons 541-382-3661 6a-11p every day Safeway 541-312-6480 6a-11p every day	Ray's Food Place Supermarket 541-549-2222. 7a-10p every day Melvin's Market 541-549-0711. 8a-7p every day. Natural foods grocery, deli, wine bar.
OUTFITTER:	Mountain Supply 541-388-0688 Mon-Sat 10a-6p, Sun 10a-5p REI 541-385-0594 Mon-Sat 10a-8p, Sun 11a-6 The Gear Fix 541-617-0022 Every day 10a-6p. Used gear and gear repair	OUTDOOR STORES: MacKenzie Creek 541-549-8424 Hike-N-Peaks 541-904-0778
SHOE STORE:	Foot Zone 541-317-3568 M-F 10a-7p, Sat 10a-6p, Sun 11a-5	
RESTAURANTS:	Yes. You gotta have Deschutes Brewery beer in Bend! The Mirror Pond Pale Ale is fantastic. Pilot Butte Drive-In has an 18-ounce burger. It's a Bend tradition since 1983.	Yes. Try the Hop N Bean: Pizzeria and Coffee Shop with 24 beers on tap.

	BEND, OR	**SISTERS, OR**
LAUNDRY & ATM:	Yes.	Yes.
SHOWER:		At City Park.
COMPUTER:	Library 541-617-7050	Library 541-549-2921
MEDICAL:	Several hospitals and clinics.	High Lakes Health Care 541-549-9609
POST OFFICE:	General Delivery is at the Main Post Office, 2300 NE 4th St 541-318-5068, USPS only Mon-Fri 8:30a-5:30p, Sat 10a-1p General Delivery Priority Mail held for 2 weeks. Hiker's Legal Name PCT Hiker, ETA: MM/DD/YY General Delivery Bend, OR 97701	541-549-0412, USPS only Mon-Fri 8:30a-5p, Sat closed General Delivery held for 15 days. Hiker's Legal Name PCT Hiker, ETA: MM/DD/YY General Delivery Sisters, OR 97759 If you want to bounce General Delivery mail from Sisters to anyplace else, you cannot just call the Sisters Post Office. Three options: (1) File a forwarding address (2) Go to the Sisters PO in person (3) Go to any other PO, ask that PO to call the Sisters PO to have your mail bounced ahead
MAIL DROPS:	REI (541-385-0594) Mon-Sat 10a-8p, Sun 11a-6p Accepts mail drops USPS, UPS, FedEx **Clearly mark your package as a hiker package.** Hiker's Legal Name PCT Hiker, ETA: MM/DD/YY c/o REI #96 380 SW Powerhouse Drive Bend, OR 97702 - Bunk & Brew Hostel (458-202-1090) Accepts mail drops, no fee for guests, $5 fee for non-guests. USPS, UPS, FedEx. Hiker's Legal Name PCT Hiker, ETA: MM/DD/YY c/o Bunk and Brew 42 NW Hawthorne Ave Bend, OR 97703 - Trail Angel Brian Douglass 541-213-8510 Accepts mail drops, no fee, USPS, UPS, and FedEx. Hiker's Legal Name PCT Hiker, ETA: MM/DD/YY c/o Brian Douglass 1686 NE Tucson Way Bend, OR 97701-6235	Sisters Inn (541-549-7829) Accepts mail drops, no fee. Clearly label your box as a hiker package, including ETA. USPS address: Hiker's Legal Name PCT Hiker, ETA: MM/DD/YY c/o Sisters Inn PO Box 938 Sisters, OR 97759 UPS or FedEx address: Hiker's Legal Name PCT Hiker, ETA: MM/DD/YY c/o Sisters Inn 605 N. Arrowleaf Trail Sisters OR 97759

	BEND, OR	SISTERS, OR
FUEL:	HEET: Gas stations and supermarkets Canisters: Mountain Supply and REI	HEET: Ray's Food Place Denatured: Ace Hardware Canisters: MacKenzie Creek

BEND LODGING		Rates	frig micr	TV	pool	laundry	computer	bkfst
Bunk and Brew Hostel	458-202-1090 info@bunkandbrew.com	$ bunk $$ private	first beer free, AC, laundry, storage lockers, full kitchen, light breakfast, outdoor BBQ grill, lighted outdoor gazebo, accepts mail drops					
Cascade Lodge	541-382-2612	$$$	Y	Y	Y	no	no	no
Chalet Motel	541-382-6124	$$	Y	Y	no	no	no	no
Days Inn	541-383-3776	$$	Y	Y	Y	Y	Y	hot
Dunes Motel	541-382-6811	$$	Y	Y	no	Y	no	no
EconoLodge	541-382-7711	$$	Y	Y	Y	no	Y	cont
Mill Inn B & B	541-389-9198	$$$	no	some	hot tub	Y	no	bkfst for 2
Motel 6	541-382-8282 possible hiker rate	$$	Y	Y	Y	no	no	no
Motel West	541-389-5577	$$	Y	Y	no	no	no	no
Rainbow Motel	541-382-1821	$$	Y	Y	no	no	no	no
Royal Gateway Motel	541-382-5631	$$	Y	Y	no	no	no	no
Sonoma Lodge	541-382-4891	$$	Y	Y	no	no	no	no

SISTERS LODGING		Rates	frig micr	TV	pool	laundry	computer	bkfst
Sisters Inn	541-549-7829	$$$	Y	Y	no	no	no	no
Sisters Motor Lodge	541-549-2551	$$$$	Y	Y	hot tub	no	no	no
Best Western	541-549-1234	$$$$	Y	Y	Y	Y	Y	cont waffles
Five Pine Lodge	541-549-5900	$$$$	Y	Y	Y	no	Y	no
Creekside Campground	541-323-5218	2018: Hiker/Biker site $5, includes shower Open May thru October [www.ci.sisters.or.us] click on: Visiting Sisters, then Creekside Campground						
Sisters RV Park	541-549-3861	Camping						
Three Sisters Horse Hiker and Guest Ranch	FB: Premila Tracey Pickett 541-852-1831 oregonrawlk@gmail.com	5 miles southeast of Sisters on Highway 20. Hitch to Sisters, then call for a ride. Lodging, camping, laundry, showers, WiFi, computer, home cooked meals. 2018: Room is $50, includes full house amenities and meals. Camping for donation. Hiker-friendly owner Premila Pickett says: "No smoking on property. I don't mind a beer or two, but our Ranch is not be a place to party and spend your time getting stoned; we have paying guests with families."						

	$	= usually less than $50
	$$	= usually $50-$80
	$$$	= usually $80-$110
	$$$$	= usually greater than $110

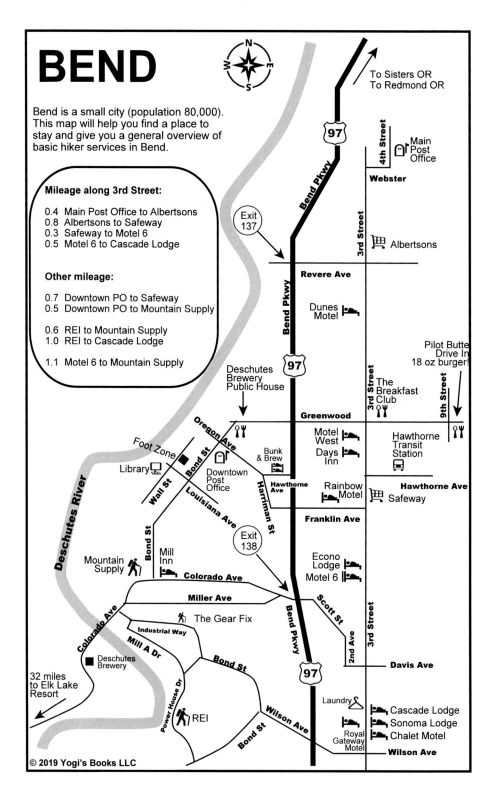

BEND

Bend is a small city (population 80,000). This map will help you find a place to stay and give you a general overview of basic hiker services in Bend.

Mileage along 3rd Street:

0.4 Main Post Office to Albertsons
0.8 Albertsons to Safeway
0.3 Safeway to Motel 6
0.5 Motel 6 to Cascade Lodge

Other mileage:

0.7 Downtown PO to Safeway
0.5 Downtown PO to Mountain Supply

0.6 REI to Mountain Supply
1.0 REI to Cascade Lodge

1.1 Motel 6 to Mountain Supply

To Sisters OR
To Redmond OR

97
Bend Pkwy

4th Street
Main Post Office
Webster

Exit 137

3rd Street
Albertsons

Revere Ave

Dunes Motel

Bend Pkwy

97

Deschutes Brewery Public House

3rd Street
The Breakfast Club

9th Street
Pilot Butte Drive In 18 oz burger!

Greenwood

Oregon Ave
Foot Zone
Bond St
Library
Downtown Post Office
Wall St
Louisiana Ave
Bunk & Brew
Hawthorne Ave
Harriman St

Motel West
Days Inn

Rainbow Motel

Hawthorne Transit Station

Hawthorne Ave
Safeway

Franklin Ave

Bond St
Mill Inn
Mountain Supply
Colorado Ave

Exit 138

Econo Lodge Motel 6

Miller Ave

The Gear Fix

Industrial Way

Colorado Ave
Mill A Dr

Deschutes Brewery

Bond St
Bend Pkwy

Scott St

2nd Ave
3rd Street

Davis Ave

97

32 miles to Elk Lake Resort

Power House Dr
REI

Wilson Ave

Bond St

Laundry

Royal Gateway Motel

Cascade Lodge
Sonoma Lodge
Chalet Motel

Wilson Ave

SISTERS

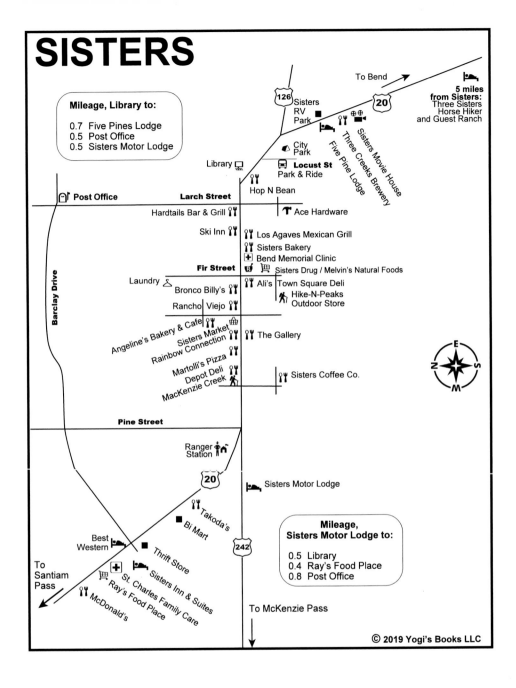

Mileage, Library to:

0.7 Five Pines Lodge
0.5 Post Office
0.5 Sisters Motor Lodge

To Bend

126 Sisters RV Park

20

5 miles from Sisters:
Three Sisters Horse Hiker and Guest Ranch

City Park

Library

Locust St
Park & Ride

Larch Street

Hop N Bean

Post Office

Hardtails Bar & Grill

Ace Hardware

Ski Inn

Los Agaves Mexican Grill

Sisters Bakery

Bend Memorial Clinic

Fir Street

Sisters Drug / Melvin's Natural Foods

Laundry

Ali's Town Square Deli

Bronco Billy's

Hike-N-Peaks Outdoor Store

Rancho Viejo

Barclay Drive

Angeline's Bakery & Cafe

Sisters Market

The Gallery

Rainbow Connection

Martolli's Pizza

Depot Deli

Sisters Coffee Co.

MacKenzie Creek

Sisters Movie House

Three Creeks Brewery

Five Pine Lodge

Pine Street

Ranger Station

20

Sisters Motor Lodge

Takoda's

Bi Mart

Best Western

**Mileage,
Sisters Motor Lodge to:**

0.5 Library
0.4 Ray's Food Place
0.8 Post Office

Thrift Store

242

To Santiam Pass

St. Charles Family Care

Sisters Inn & Suites

Ray's Food Place

McDonald's

To McKenzie Pass

© 2019 Yogi's Books LLC

1992.6 - Big Lake Youth Camp

OVERVIEW:

Info: 503-850-3583. Direct line to camp: 503-805-2267.
Very hiker-friendly. Open from the end of June thru Labor Day.
After mid-August, the camp is not staffed full-time.

2016: Accept packages, open for meals, showers, laundry 06-14-16 to 09-05-16
2017: Accept packages, open for meals, showers, laundry 05-29-17 to 09-14-17
2018: Accept packages, open for meals, showers, laundry 06-03-18 to 09-19-18
2019: Accept packages, open for meals, showers, laundry 06-02-19 to 09-18-19

GETTING HERE:

Take side trail off PCT, then walk 0.7 mile.
Go to the Headquarters building (look for flag poles).
That's where you register and pick up your maildrop.

PCT WELCOME CENTER:

Day use PCT cabin/lounge with kitchen, hot showers, lounge, charging, and WiFi.

MAIL DROPS:

Accepts mail drops (see dates above), no fee, USPS or UPS only.

Mail must state "PCT Hiker" and ETA.

Mail held for 30 days only. After 30 days, mail is returned to sender unless you request otherwise. If you arrive outside of dates listed above, pick up your mail at the Headquarters building.

No outgoing mail.

Hiker's Legal Name
PCT Hiker, ETA: MM/DD/YY
c/o Big Lake Youth Camp
26435 Big Lake Road
Sisters, OR 97759

LODGING:

No. Hikers may not stay overnight at the camp.
There are tent sites nearby in a cove by the lake.

MEALS:

Hikers are welcome for vegetarian meals, on a donation basis (not free).

2015 meal times: 8:15am, 12:30pm, 5:30pm
2016 meal times: 9:15am, 1:30pm, 6:30pm
2017 meal times: 9:15am, 1:15pm, 6:20pm
2018 meal times: 8:30am, 12:00pm, 5:30pm
2019 meal times: 9:15am, 1:15pm, 6:20pm

LAUNDRY:

Yes, for a donation.

SHOWERS:

Yes, for a donation.

PHONE:

Emergency use only.

STORE:

T-shirts, postcards, games. No food or fuel.

FUEL:

No.

HINT - For the rest of the trail, the PCT passes many old volcanoes covered with glaciers. The creeks from the glaciers have a lot of silt in them. Some of the glacial creeks are so silty that they look like milk. Pay attention to your maps. If a water source appears to come from a glacier, plan to get your water elsewhere.

2001.0 - Santiam Pass Northbound Trailhead -
After crossing Hwy 20, the trail curves to the right around a small rise, then a side trail goes to a parking lot with trash cans and privy.

2010.6 - Koko Lake

2015.1 - Rockpile Lake - Water and camping here.

2016.4 - Swallow Lake Trail 3488 - Four-way junction. PCT goes straight, then curves to the left and stays on the west side of the ridge. **DO NOT GO DOWNHILL.**

2022.3 to 2023.7 - Pamelia Limited Entry Area - Permit required to camp here.
Your PCTA permit does not cover you for camping in this area.

2023.0 - Shale Lake - Water and camping here.

2027.9 - Milk Creek - A glacial creek. Milky-white water.

2032.3 - Russell Creek - A glacial creek. Milky-white water. Cross this creek early in the morning if possible. The water is strong, and you can't see through it.

2032.7 - Whitewater Creek - A glacial creek. A little milky.

2033.6 to 2034.6 - Jefferson Park - Camping restrictions.
Camping within 250 feet of lakes requires an advance permit.

2034.5 (Creek) to 2046.0 (Olallie Lake) - All good water.

2039.9 - Skyline Road 42 near Breitenbush Lake - Breitenbush Lake is 0.3 mile off the PCT. It has two small 3-sided, dirt-floored, lakefront shelters.

SCRUB (2013): There is a great spring at Breitenbush Lake campground. Walk past the shelters, cross two footbridges and listen for it gushing.

2046.0 - Olallie Lake Resort	The store is about 0.1 mile off the PCT.

The store is about 0.1 mile off the PCT.
Does not accept mail drops. [www.olallielakeresort.com].
Good hiker resupply.
Canister fuel and denatured alcohol, batteries, beer.
Cash only.

2049.7 - Jude Lake - Water.

2050.4 - Stream - BINK: This stream always flows.

2055.1 - Lemiti Creek - Water and camping. Sometimes dry.

2055.5 - Trooper Springs - Usually has water. Look for a side trail on the right side of the PCT.

2063.0 - Seeping spring - BINK: Look for small side trail. Good water here always, located 200 feet off trail. TWODOG: Reach a marked junction to the seeping spring just a few minutes after you intersect the third of four dirt roads crossed on the way from North Pinhead Butte down to the Warm Springs River.

2065.1 - Warm Springs River - Water.

2065.4 - Spring - BINK: Good water here, short walk down side trail.

2073.1 - Clackamas Lake Campground - TWODOG (2006): Clackamas Lake Campground has piped water. You can visit the spring that is the source for Clackamas Lake by taking an obvious spur trail down to the head of the lake, about halfway along the Miller Trail between the PCT and the campground.

2074.6 - Oak Grove Fork Clackamas River - Water here.
TWODOG (2006): Joe Graham Horse Camp has piped water, dumpsters, and privys.

2074.9 - Spring along Oak Fork - Good water.

2078.5, 2078.7 - Springs next to the trail - Good water.

2078.9 - Crater Creek - Cross the creek on a long wooden boardwalk. Good water.

2079.3 - Little Crater Lake Trail -
BUCKEYE (2010): Crystal clear water in Little Crater Lake.

2083.2 - Campsite with a seeping spring - Watch the <u>left side</u> of the PCT for a "campsite" sign on a tree. The campsite and the spring are on the <u>right side</u> of the PCT. With your back to the "campsite" sign, cross the PCT, follow a large <u>downed</u> tree in front of you and a little to the right to the spring. This good spring is maybe 30 feet from the PCT.

2087.0 - US Highway 26 at Wapinitia Pass - Privy, picnic table, trash.

2088.4 - Switchback north to a near-crest junction to Twin Lakes Trail -
The upper lake is a better camping choice; the lower lake is heavily used by overnighters and can be very noisy. Also, the sign leading back to the PCT on the loop is old and misleading.

2092.0 - Barlow Pass Trailhead - Picnic table, trash, port-a-potty.

2092.2 - Barlow Pass, Highway 35 - Hitch to Government Camp or Sandy from here.

2095.0 - Gully with a campsite - Water here.
DOUBLE TAP: Account for slower going in the sand on the last part of this climb.

Approaching Timberline Lodge - SCRUB: There is a ton of camping on the climb up to Timberline; the closer you get, the more sites there are. There's excellent camping directly above the Lodge area on the PCT.

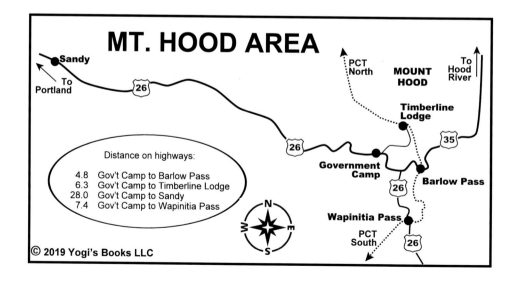

GETTING HERE: (1)   <u>Hitch from PCT mile 2092.2</u>: There is a trailhead at Barlow Pass. Out at the highway cars are going FAST. Hitch 2.1 miles left (west) on Highway 35, then 32 miles right (west) on Highway 26.

    (2)   <u>Bus from PCT mile 2092.2 or 2097.4</u>: Take the bus from Government Camp or Timberline Lodge.

BUS: <u>Mt. Hood Express</u>. 503-668-3466. Bus from Timberline Lodge to Government Camp to Sandy runs six times per day.

POST OFFICE: General Delivery held for 30 days only. 503-668-4055. USPS only. Mon-Fri 8:30a-5p Sat closed, but the will-call window is open from 6a-10a for pick up only. General Delivery held for 15 days.

    Hiker's Legal Name
    PCT Hiker, ETA: MM/DD/YY
    General Delivery
    Sandy, OR <u>97055</u>

RESUPPLY: Safeway Supermarket   503-668-3202
    Grocery Outlet   503-668-6950
    Dollar Tree   503-668-3041

LODGING: <u>Best Western</u>. 503-668-7100. Rates: $$$$, rooms have micr and frig Hot breakfast, indoor heated pool, hot tub, laundry, computer.

RESTAURANTS: Several.

LAUNDRY & ATM: Yes.

COMPUTER: Library. 503-668-5537.

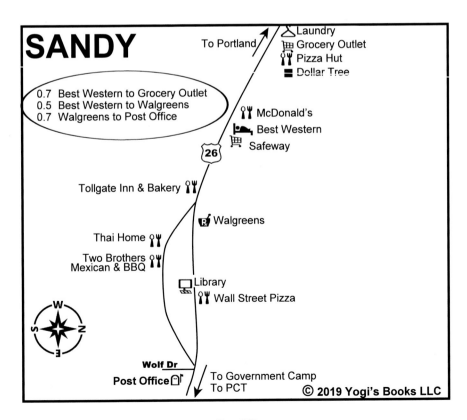

SANDY

To Portland

Laundry
Grocery Outlet
Pizza Hut
Dollar Tree

0.7 Best Western to Grocery Outlet
0.5 Best Western to Walgreens
0.7 Walgreens to Post Office

McDonald's
Best Western
Safeway

26

Tollgate Inn & Bakery

Walgreens

Thai Home

Two Brothers
Mexican & BBQ

Library
Wall Street Pizza

Wolf Dr
Post Office

To Government Camp
To PCT

© 2019 Yogi's Books LLC

OVERVIEW: Touristy / Ski village which supports Timberline Lodge.

GETTING HERE: There is a trailhead at Barlow Pass. Out at the highway cars are going FAST. Hitch 2.1 miles left (west) on Highway 35, then 2.7 miles right (west) on Hwy 26.

BUS: Mt. Hood Express. 503-668-3466.
Bus from Timberline Lodge to Government Camp runs six times per day.
Bus continues east from Government Camp to Sandy OR.

POST OFFICE: 503-272-3238, USPS only
Mon-Fri noon-4p. Sat closed.

If mail has ETA, it is held until the
ETA date, otherwise it is held for 2 weeks.

Hiker's Legal Name
PCT Hiker, ETA: MM/DD/YY
General Delivery
88331 E Govt Camp Loop
Government Camp, OR 97028

RESUPPLY: Govy General Store 503-272-3107
7a-8p every day. Small Grocery with decent hiker resupply.

LODGING: Cascade Ski Club Hostel 503-272-9204. Dorm-style bunks.

Huckleberry Inn 503-272-3325
Rooms sleep up to 6 people. $$$ +
Two bedrooms with living room and kitchen $$$$

Best Western 503-272-3205
Micr, frig, hot breakfast, laundry, indoor hot tub, $$$$

Collins Lake Resort 503-928-3498. 2-night minimum stay. $$$$$$$

RESTAURANTS:
Yes. Also a deli in the General Store.

LAUNDRY: Yes.
ATM: Yes.

FUEL: Sometimes HEET at Chevron.

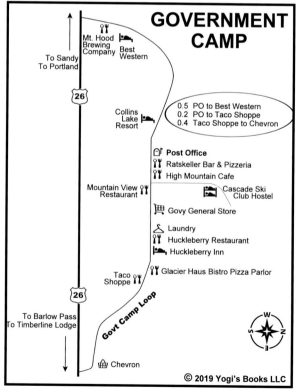

GOVERNMENT CAMP

Mt. Hood Brewing Company
Best Western
To Sandy
To Portland
26

Collins Lake Resort

0.5 PO to Best Western
0.2 PO to Taco Shoppe
0.4 Taco Shoppe to Chevron

Post Office
Ratskeller Bar & Pizzeria
High Mountain Cafe
Mountain View Restaurant
Cascade Ski Club Hostel
Govy General Store
Laundry
Huckleberry Restaurant
Huckleberry Inn
Glacier Haus Bistro Pizza Parlor
Taco Shoppe
26
To Barlow Pass
To Timberline Lodge
Govt Camp Loop
Chevron

© 2019 Yogi's Books LLC

OVERVIEW:	[info@timberlinelodge.com] 503-272-3311
	Timberline Lodge is a nice place to relax for a few hours. Eat in one of the restaurants in the Lodge or at the snack bar in the ski building, treat yourself to a beer, eat some ice cream. Good microbrews in the Lodge restaurants.
GETTING HERE:	On trail.
BUS:	Mt. Hood Express. 503-668-3466. Bus from Timberline Lodge to Government Camp runs six times per day. Bus continues east from Government Camp to Sandy OR.
MAIL DROPS:	The WY'East store in the ski building takes mail drops, $5 fee. USPS or UPS. WY'East Store 503-272-3311, ext 3189. Write "Hold for PCT Hiker" on your package. No outgoing mail.

High Season (June to late August):   7a-7p every day
Low Season: 9a-5p every day

Click-N-Ship USPS address:

Full Name:	Hiker's Legal Name, ETA/ PCT Hiker
Company Name:	c/o Timberline Lodge Ski Area
Address 1:	27500 E Timberline Road
Address 2:	WY'East Store
City:	Timberline Lodge
State/Zip:	OR 97028

RESUPPLY:	WY'East store 7:15a-7p thru Sep 5th, then hours reduced. Mountain House dinners and a very small selection of snacks (not enough for resupply), AquaMira, bug spray. Vending machines in Lodge have candy.
LODGING:	503-272-3311, ext. 4400.
RESTAURANTS:	Restaurants in the main Lodge. Snack bar in the ski building. I highly recommend both the Blue Ox and the Cascadia Dining room. Great microbrews here. The food at Timberline is terrific, the setting is unmatched, and the company of trail friends is . . . well . . . simply perfect.
LAUNDRY:	Free laundry for Lodge guests.
SHOWER:	Hiker shower in the parking lot.
ATM:	Yes.
COMPUTER:	Inquire at the front desk.
FUEL:	Denatured by the ounce at Wy'East Store.

2100.8 - Zigzag River - Silty water.

2101.8 - PCT splits to two routes - Purists will be very confused.

2102.5 - Lost Creek - DOUBLE TAP: Good flow. Great campsite to the right of the PCT with room for ~6 tents about 0.1 mile after you cross Lost Creek. You can't see it from the trail but look to the right after you round a bend to the right and it's pretty obvious there could be (and is) a good campsite up above a little hill. You also get a nice view of a waterfall in the distance towards the top of Mount Hood from the campsite overlooking Lost Creek.

2103.7 - The two routes are rejoined here.

2106.9 - Scout Camp after Sandy River - As you approach the Sandy River, you'll follow a creek for a while. This creek flows into the Sandy River at the same place you cross the Sandy River. Get your water from the creek, since the Sandy River is silty.

2107.3 - Ramona Falls Loop Trail - RECOMMENDED ROUTE: Go to Ramona Falls. It's beautiful.

2109.4 - Muddy Fork - DOUBLE TAP: There is a big log with a rope tied to it that you can hold as you walk across to go over Muddy Creek. With the rope it was easy.

2115.1 - Trickling Creek - Usually good water.

2118.9 - Junction with Huckleberry Mountain Trail 617 to Salvation Spring Camp -
BINK: Salvation Spring is located 100 feet below and off trail in a wet meadow.
Can be seen to the right from trail. Small sign on tree.

FIDGET(2010): This campsite and spring are 0.3 mile past the trail junction, not at the trail junction. You can follow the side trail down about 0.4 mile to the spring, or just stay on the PCT another 5 minutes.

2122.6 - Discover a small spring - NO WAY RAY: There are four talus slopes crossed by the trail. Just after the fourth one, a PVC pipe is sticking out just below the trail. Plenty of water.
BINK: On left side (downhill side) of trail for northbounders. Clearly visible, but easy to miss.

2128.1 - Indian Springs Campground - Shortly after the AMAZING panoramic view of Mt. St. Helens, Mt. Adams, and Mt. Rainier, you'll find Indian Springs Campground on the left side of the PCT. It looks more like a jeep turnaround than a campground. At the far left end of the turnaround/campground, look for a side trail leading to the spring, which has water. Continuing past the spring, take the Indian Springs Trail 435 down the ridge to the Eagle Creek Trail.

FIRE! There was a major fire in this area at the end of the 2017 season.
The Eagle Creek Trail was closed for 2018-2019 PCT'ers, and will probably be closed in 2020. Watch Halfmile's site [pctmap.net] and the PCTA site [pcta.org] for closure information. The PCT is open.

2128.1 or 2130.8 - Eagle Creek Trail Alternate Route

	S>N	Elevation
Leave PCT at Indian Springs CG	0.0	4242
Junction with Eagle Creek Trail	2.0	2567
Tunnel Falls	5.9	1092
4-mile Camp (Tenas Camp)	7.9	702
Bridge across gorge	8.6	551
Trailhead (see next paragraph)	12.2	121
Cascade Locks, OR	15.4	242

TRAILHEAD - When you finish the Eagle Creek Trail, you'll emerge at a large trailhead parking lot. Walk 0.5 mile down the road to the campground. You'll see Gorge Trail 400 on the right near some picnic tables. Take this trail. Stay on Gorge Trail 400 until you reach a paved bike path. Turn right, stay on the bike path all the way into Cascade Locks.

Along the bike path, you will reach a junction where a signed trail to the PCT leaves the bike path on the right. You could take this trail to Cascade Locks, but I recommend staying on the bike path. The bike path is easier, more scenic, and ends at the Bridgeside Restaurant!

2130.8 Junction with Eagle Creek Trail 440 to Wahtum Lake - Water.

2137.1 - Ruckel Creek Trail 405 - No water information.

2139.5 - Teakettle Spring - Pool on left side where trail widens - sign on tree.

2143.4 - Cross a creek - Water.

2145.3 - Cross a creek - Water.

2147.1 - Cascade Locks OR

2147.1 - Cascade Locks OR

OVERVIEW: Town is just a few blocks long. Great place for a zero day.
"PCT Days" is held here. 2020: Aug 14-16 [www.pctdays.com]

GETTING HERE: On trail.

SHUTTLES: Randi Nelson (360 669-3112) offers shuttles for a fee in these areas:
Cascade Locks, Snoqualmie Pass, White Pass, Packwood.

POST OFFICE: 541-374-5026. USPS only.   Hiker's Legal Name
Mon-Fri 8:30a-1p and 2p-5p.   PCT Hiker, ETA: MM/DD/YY
Sat closed, but usually hikers can pick up   General Delivery
packages on Sat from 9a-10a. Knock on   Cascade Locks, OR 97014
the wooden door to the left in the lobby.

Hiker Gen Del held until the end of October

MAIL DROPS: Cascade Locks Ale House   541-374-9310, accepts USPS, UPS, or FedEx.

USPS Address: UPS or FedEx Address:
Hiker's Legal Name   Hiker's Legal Name
PCT Hiker, ETA: MM/DD/YY   PCT Hiker, ETA: MM/DD/YY
c/o Cascade Locks Ale House   c/o Cascade Locks Ale House
PO Box 388   500 WaNaPa Street
Cascade Locks, OR 97014   Cascade Locks, OR 97014

Port Marine RV Park (541-374-8619)   UPS or FedEx Address:
Accepts mail drops, UPS or FedEx only, no fee. Hiker's Legal Name
Pick up mail at Administration Office   PCT Hiker, ETA: MM/DD/YY
Mon-Fri 8a-5p. Sat-Sun closed.   c/o Port Marine RV Park
                                      355 WaNaPa Street
                                      Cascade Locks, OR 97014

RESUPPLY: Columbia Market grocery store. 541-374-8425. 7a-9p every day.

RESTAURANTS: Yes. Don't miss Thunder Island Brewery!

LAUNDRY: Yes.

SHOWERS: Yes.

ATM: Yes.

COMPUTER: Library. 541-374-9317. Computer for guests at Best Western.

FUEL: HEET at the Shell station. Canister fuel at Columbia Market.

CASCADE LOCKS LODGING		Rates	TV	AC	micr	frig	cont bkfst	other stuff
Best Western	541-374-8777 ask for hiker discount	$$$$	Y	Y	Y	Y		free full breakfast at Bridgeside restaurant, indoor pool, hot tub, laundry, computer
Bridge of the Gods Motel & RV Park	541-374-8628	$$$$	Y	Y	some		no	laundry, some kitchenettes
Columbia Gorge Inn	541-374-0015	$$$ +	Y	Y	Y	Y	no	
Cascade Motel	541-374-8750	$$ +	Y	some	Y	Y	no	cabins
Port Marine RV Park	541-374-8619	2018: Camping $5, includes shower.						
		$$ = usually $50-$80 $$$ = usually $80-$110 $$$$ = usually greater than $110						

HUNTING SEASON: Looking ahead to Harts Pass (PCT mile 2619.5). The Pasayten Wilderness has early season rifle deer hunting in September. Be sure to wear bright orange.

REMINDER: Make sure your resupply person mails your passport and your Canada entrance papers to Stehekin (General Delivery, 98852)

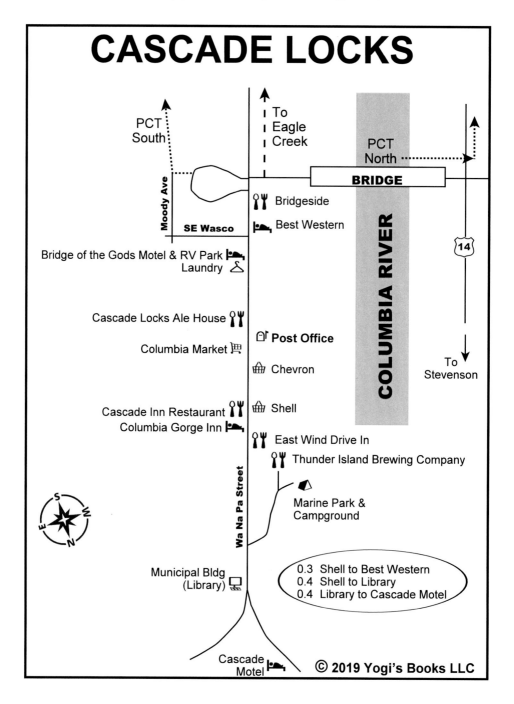

CASCADE LOCKS

Portland OR

Public transportation is available from Stevenson WA to Portland OR.

STEVENSON TO VANCOUVER WA:

Skamania County   509-427-3990   [www.skamaniacounty.org/public_transit.htm]
The WET Bus (Gorge West End Transit Bus) goes from Vancouver WA to Bridge of the Gods PCT Trailhead twice per day Mon-Thur, three times a day on Friday, and four times on Saturday and Sunday.

VANCOUVER WA TO PORTLAND: C-Tran   360-695-0123   [www.c-tran.com]

PORTLAND AND 'BURBS: Tri-Met   503-238-7433   [www.trimet.org]

HIKER-FRIENDLY OUTFITTER:

Next Adventure. 503-233-0706. 426 SE Grand Ave, Portland OR 97214.
"We offer thru-hiker discounts and carry all kinds of hiker gear like Tyvek by the foot, alcohol by the ounce, ULA packs, Gossamer Gear packs, Titanium gadgets, Aquamira, you name it!

2146.9 - Stevenson WA

OVERVIEW:	Grocery store is better than Cascade Locks. More restaurants, too.
GETTING HERE:	Cross the Bridge of the Gods, then take Highway 14 East 2.7 miles.
POST OFFICE:	509-427-5532, USPS only Mon-Fri 8:30a-5p Sat closed General Delivery held for 15 days	Hiker's Legal Name PCT Hiker, ETA: MM/DD/YY General Delivery Stevenson, WA 98648
RESUPPLY:	A & J Market (Supermarket). 509-427-5491. 7a-9p every day.
RESTAURANTS:	Many. Check out Walking Man Brewery 509-427-5520
LAUNDRY:	Yes.
ATM:	At supermarket and C-Store. Banks in Stevenson, too.
COMPUTER:	Library 509-427-5471
FUEL:	HEET at Napa Auto Parts 509-427-5601
MEDICAL:	North Shore Medical 509-493-2133 0.6 mile from Texaco

STEVENSON LODGING	Rates	TV, AC laundry	micr	frig	bkfst	
Rodeway Inn 509-427-5628	$$$ +	Y	some		cont	accepts mail drops
Columbia Gorge Riverside Lodge 509-427-5650	$$$ +	no	kitchenettes		no	
	$$ = usually $50-$80 $$$ = usually $80-$110 $$$$ = usually greater than $110					

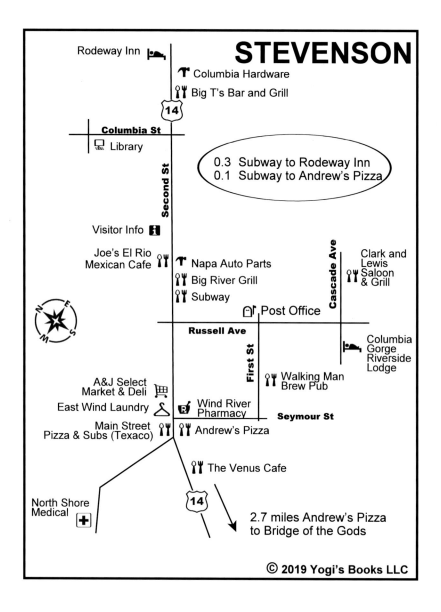

STEVENSON

Rodeway Inn

Columbia Hardware

Big T's Bar and Grill

14

Columbia St

Library

Second St

0.3 Subway to Rodeway Inn
0.1 Subway to Andrew's Pizza

Visitor Info

Joe's El Rio
Mexican Cafe

Napa Auto Parts

Big River Grill

Subway

Cascade Ave

Clark and
Lewis
Saloon
& Grill

Post Office

Russell Ave

First St

Columbia
Gorge
Riverside
Lodge

Walking Man
Brew Pub

A&J Select
Market & Deli

East Wind Laundry

Wind River
Pharmacy

Seymour St

Main Street
Pizza & Subs (Texaco)

Andrew's Pizza

The Venus Cafe

North Shore
Medical

14

2.7 miles Andrew's Pizza
to Bridge of the Gods

© 2019 Yogi's Books LLC

OVERVIEW: All hiker services in easy walking distance of Sunset Motel.

GETTING HERE: Hitch or take the bus. Go 20 miles east on Interstate 84.
Hood River services are near Interstate Exits 62 and 63.

BUS SERVICE: Columbia Area Transit (CAT) offers Dial-A-Ride, a door-to-door service in Cascade Locks and Hood River Mon-Fri. If you're going to Hood River, this is a sure way to get there. Trips must be scheduled at least one day in advance and may include other passengers going to different destinations. No walk-on passengers or additional unscheduled passengers will be accepted. This service is available Mon-Fri. To schedule a ride, call 541-386-4202, Mon-Fri 8a-4:30p.

CAT also has a fixed route schedule to Portland.

Columbia Gorge Express serves Portland, Cascade Locks, and Hood River. 888-246-6420.

POST OFFICE: 541-386-1584, USPS only
Mon-Fri 8:30a-5p, Sat closed
Hiker General Delivery held for 30 days

Hiker's Legal Name
PCT Hiker, ETA: MM/DD/YY
General Delivery
Hood River, OR 97031

DO NOT put Post Office street address
on General Delivery address.

OUTGOING MAIL: Postal Annex. 541-386-6122. Mon-Fri 8a-6p. Sat 9a-4p. Sun closed.
This is a private business, *not* a branch Post Office.
USPS, UPS, and FedEx.

RESUPPLY: Safeway   541-386-1841   Open 24 hours

SHOPPING: Wal-Mart   541-387-2300   6a-11p

SHOE STORE: Shortt Supply   541-386-5474

RESTAURANT: Yes.

LAUNDRY: Yes.

ATM: Yes.

COMPUTER: Library   541-386-2535

FUEL: HEET at Safeway   541-386-1841

MEDICAL: Hood River Memorial Hospital   541-386-3911

HOOD RIVER LODGING Many options. Here are a few:		Rates	micr	frig	bkfst	pool	laundry	computer
Comfort Suites	541-308-1000	$$$$	Y	Y	hot	indoor pool hot tub	Y	Y
Hood River Hostel	541-806-8525	$$$	Y	Y	gourmet	no	Y	Y
Lone Pine Motel	541-387-8882 see Yelp reviews	$$$	Y	Y	no	no	no	no
Oak Street Hotel	541-386-3566	$$$$	no	Y	cont	no	no	no
Riverview Lodge	541-386-8719	$$$ +	Y	Y	no	indoor pool hot tub	no	Y
Sunset Motel	541-386-6322	$$$ +	Y	Y	no	no	no	no
		$$$ = usually $80-$110 $$$$ = usually greater than $110						

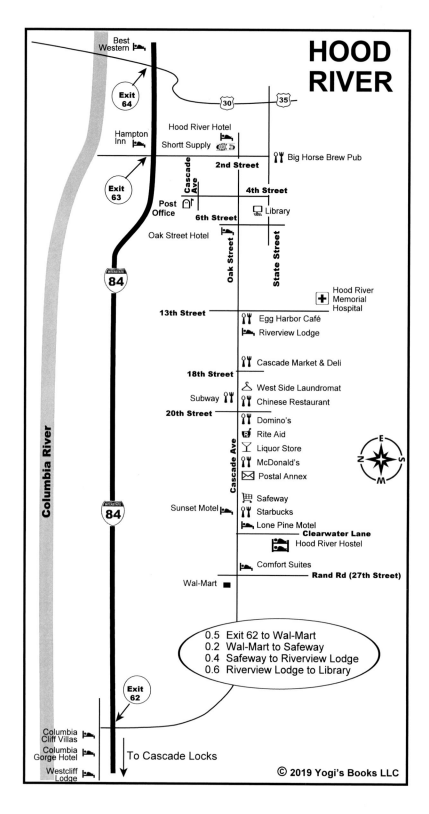

HOOD RIVER

Best Western

Exit 64

30   35

Hood River Hotel
Shortt Supply

2nd Street

Big Horse Brew Pub

Hampton Inn

Cascade Ave

Exit 63

4th Street

Post Office

Library

6th Street

Oak Street Hotel

Oak Street

State Street

Interstate 84

Hood River Memorial Hospital

13th Street

Egg Harbor Café

Riverview Lodge

Cascade Market & Deli

18th Street

West Side Laundromat

Subway   Chinese Restaurant

20th Street

Domino's

Cascade Ave

Rite Aid

Liquor Store

McDonald's

Postal Annex

Safeway

Sunset Motel   Starbucks

Lone Pine Motel

Clearwater Lane

Hood River Hostel

Comfort Suites

Rand Rd (27th Street)

Wal-Mart

Interstate 84

Exit 62

0.5 Exit 62 to Wal-Mart
0.2 Wal-Mart to Safeway
0.4 Safeway to Riverview Lodge
0.6 Riverview Lodge to Library

Columbia River

Columbia Cliff Villas

Columbia Gorge Hotel

Westcliff Lodge

To Cascade Locks

RESUPPLY SUMMARY

2229.4 Trout Lake WA - 13 mile hitch on backcountry road

Post Office: 509-395-2108, USPS only
Mon-Fri 9:30-12:30p and 1p-4p
Sat closed
If you won't arrive by your ETA date,
please call the Post Office.
Hiker General Delivery held
until end of hiker season.

Hiker's Legal Name
PCT Hiker, ETA: MM/DD/YY
General Delivery
2393 Highway 141
Trout Lake, WA 98650

Mail Drops: Trout Lake Grocery
(509-395-2777)
Accepts mail drops,
no fee.

USPS address:
Hiker's Legal Name
PCT Hiker, ETA: MM/DD/YY
c/o Trout Lake Grocery
PO Box 132
Trout Lake, WA 98650

UPS/FedEx address:
Hiker's Legal Name
PCT Hiker, ETA: MM/DD/YY
c/o Trout Lake Grocery
2383 Highway 141
Trout Lake, WA 98650

Resupply: Large C-Store: Trout Lake Grocery Store 509-395-2777

2295.4 White Pass WA - 0.5 mile walk

Mail Drops: Kracker Barrel Store (509-672-3105)
Accepts mail drops, $5 fee. Boxes
can be picked up any time the store
is open (usually 8a until 5p or 6p).
Outgoing mail is letters only, no boxes.
USPS, UPS, FedEx:

Hiker's Legal Name
PCT Hiker, ETA: MM/DD/YY
c/o White Pass Rural Branch PO
at the Kracker Barrel Store
48851 US Highway 12
Naches, WA 98937

Resupply: Large C-Store: 509-672-3105 Usually has good hiker resupply. Beer.

2295.4 Packwood WA - 20 mile hitch

Post Office: 360-494-6311, USPS only
Mon-Fri 8a-noon and 1p-4:45p
Sat closed
General Delivery held 30 days.

Hiker's Legal Name
PCT Hiker, ETA: MM/DD/YY
General Delivery
Packwood, WA 98361

Resupply: Large grocery store:
Blanton's Market 360-494-6101 Good hiker resupply

2393.6 Snoqualmie Pass WA - 0.3 mile walk

Mail Drops: Questions about Snoqualmie Pass USPS mail:
Call the North Bend WA Post Office 425-831-7020.

Mail Drops: Chevron (425-434-6688)
Accepts mail drops, no fee.
Hiker mail held for 3 weeks.
Note: Hikers often have trouble with
mail drops sent to Chevron. Better
option is to send UPS/FedEx to Summit
Inn.

Hiker's Legal Name
PCT Hiker, ETA: MM/DD/YY
c/o Chevron Station
521 State Route 906
Snoqualmie Pass, WA 98068

Mail Drops: Summit Inn (425-434-6300) accepts
mail drops. Be sure to label your box as
a hiker package. Box must clearly have
your name and ETA. No fee if you are a
guest, $15 fee (plus tax) for non-guests.
Per phone call in December 2017, this
address is good for USPS, UPS, FedEx:

USPS, UPS, FedEx address:
Hiker's Legal Name
PCT Hiker, ETA: MM/DD/YY
c/o Summit Inn Hotel
603 SR 906
PO Box 163
Snoqualmie Pass, WA 98068

Resupply: Two very expensive C-Stores, with good hiker resupply:

Chevron   425-434-6688
Lee's Summit Grocery   425-434-0024 Better selection than Chevron

RESUPPLY SUMMARY

2464.7   Stevens Pass Ski Area - on trail

Mail Drops: Contacts: Ticketing 206-812-4510, ext. 4350.
Summer/Fall only 206-812-7844.

Accepts mail drops, UPS or FedEx only. Pick up packages:

May 1-June 20	Mon-Thur 7:30a-4p
June 21-Sep 30	Every day 8a-5p
Oct 1-Oct 31	Mon-Thur 7:30a-4p

Hiker's Legal Name
PCT Hiker, ETA: MM/DD/YY
c/o Stevens Pass
93001 NE Stevens Pass Hwy, US2
Skykomish, WA 98288

Resupply: No resupply.

2464.7   Skykomish WA - 16 mile hitch

Post Office: 360-677-2241, USPS only.
Mon-Fri 11:30a-3:30p.
Sat closed, but there is package pick
up 8a-10a. Ring buzzer or knock on
door. Hiker mail must have valid
domestic return address. Hiker mail
held until end of season.

Hiker's Legal Name
PCT Hiker, ETA: MM/DD/YY
General Delivery
Skykomish, WA 98288

Resupply: C-Store: Sky Gas 360-677-2290 Limited resupply

2464.7   Baring WA / Trail Angel Jerry Dinsmore - 24 mile hitch

Post Office: 360-677-2230. Mon-Fri 11:45a-3:45p. Sat 8a-9:45a.
Does not accept General Delivery. Outgoing mail only.

Resupply: No resupply in Baring.
There is a big grocery store in Gold Bar, 13 miles west of Baring.

2464.7   Leavenworth WA - 35 mile hitch

Post Office: 509-548-7212, USPS only
Mon-Fri 9a-5p
Sat 9a-11a
General Delivery held for 30 days.

Hiker's Legal Name
PCT Hiker, ETA: MM/DD/YY
General Delivery
Leavenworth, WA 98826

Resupply: Supermarket: Safeway 509-548-5435

2572.4   Stehekin WA - 11 mile bus

Post Office: 509-699-2015, USPS only
May 1-Oct 15: M-F 10a-4p, Sat noon-2p.
After Oct 15: M-F 10a-4p, Sat closed.
Hiker mail held until end of season;
returned to sender in mid-November.

Hiker's Legal Name
PCT Hiker, ETA: MM/DD/YY
General Delivery
Stehekin, WA 98852

Resupply: No resupply in Stehekin.

Red Apple Market (509-682-4521) in Chelan will deliver groceries to
Stehekin. 3pm cut-off time for orders. Your items will arrive on the
ferry the next day.

RESUPPLY SUMMARY

2572.4   Chelan WA - 11 mile bus, then 2.5 hour or 4 hour ferry

Post Office: 509-682-2625, USPS only
Mon-Fri 8:30a-5p
Sat package pick up only 6a-2p
(close for lunch).
General Delivery held for 30 days.

Hiker's Legal Name
PCT Hiker, ETA: MM/DD/YY
General Delivery
Chelan, WA 98816

Resupply: Supermarkets: Red Apple Market   509-682-4521
  Safeway   509-682-2615
  Walmart   509-682-4291

2591.6   Mazama WA - 18 mile hitch

Mail Drops: Goat's Beard Mountain Supplies. 509-996-2515.
Accepts mail drops. Open 9a-6p every day. Hours vary.

Hiker's Legal Name
PCT Hiker ETA: MM/DD/YY
c/o Goats Beard Mountain Supplies
50 Lost River Road
Mazama WA 98833

Resupply: C-Store: Mazama Store   509-996-2855

2591.6   Winthrop WA - 35 mile hitch

Post Office: 509-996-2282, USPS only
Mon-Fri 9a-4:30p
Sat closed

Hiker's Legal Name
PCT Hiker, ETA: MM/DD/YY
General Delivery
Winthrop, WA 98862

Mail Drops: Hostel accepts mail drops, no fee. 206-940-4507.

USPS Address:
Hiker's Legal Name
PCT Hiker, ETA: MM/DD/YY
North Cascades Mountain Hostel
PO Box 1338
Winthrop, WA 98862

UPS / FedEx Address:
Hiker's Legal Name
PCT Hiker. ETA: MM/DD/YY
North Cascades Mountain Hostel
209 Castle Ave
Winthrop, WA 98862

Resupply: Supermarket: Evergreen IGA   509-996-2525

2661.9   Manning Park, BC, Canada

Mail Drops: The Lodge accepts mail drops for PCT Hikers. 800-330-3321. BE SURE
to write "Hold for PCT Hiker" along with your expected arrival date.

Be careful sending packages here.
You might be charged a customs fee ($45+).
Mail your package at least 4 weeks before you arrive.
Packages could take 3-4 weeks to clear customs.

Hiker's Legal Name
PCT Hiker, ETA: MM/DD/YY
c/o Manning Park Lodge
7500 Highway #3
Manning Provincial Park, BC V0X IR0
CANADA

Resupply: Large C-Store at the resort.

The end of the trail is near.
It's time to figure out how you'll get home.

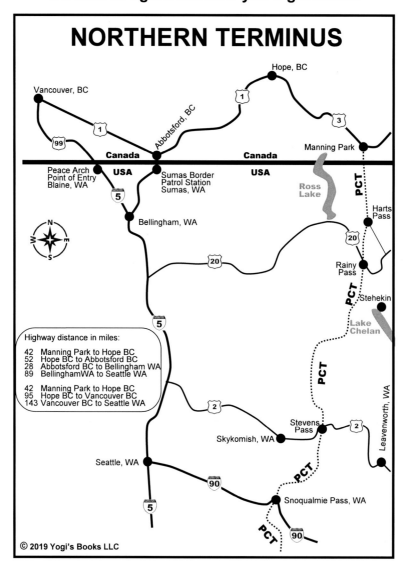

NORTHERN TERMINUS

Hope, BC

Vancouver, BC

Abbotsford, BC

Canada — USA

Manning Park

Peace Arch
Point of Entry
Blaine, WA

Sumas Border
Patrol Station
Sumas, WA

Ross
Lake

PCT

Harts
Pass

Bellingham, WA

20

Rainy
Pass

PCT

Stehekin

Lake
Chelan

Highway distance in miles:

42 Manning Park to Hope BC
52 Hope BC to Abbotsford BC
28 Abbotsford BC to Bellingham WA
89 BellinghamWA to Seattle WA

42 Manning Park to Hope BC
95 Hope BC to Vancouver BC
143 Vancouver BC to Seattle WA

PCT

Leavenworth, WA

2

Stevens
Pass

2

Skykomish, WA

Seattle, WA

90

5

PCT

Snoqualmie Pass, WA

PCT

90

© 2019 Yogi's Books LLC

HITCH FROM RAINY PASS TO BELLINGHAM OR SEATTLE

Hike to the PCT monument (PCT mile 2652.6). Do not go into Canada. Turn around and hike back to Rainy Pass (PCT mile 2591.1). Hitch west on Highway 20 to the Sedro-Woolley WA area near Interstate 5. From there, you can go north to Bellingham WA or south to Seattle WA. Both cities have airports and Amtrak.

Go to Skagit Transit [www.skagittransit.org] click on [Routes] click on [Trip Planner].
Enter Sedro Woolley as your starting location, and Seattle or Bellingham as your destination.
This will give you all bus numbers and connection information.

Classic Mountain Cabby   Serves trailheads, Bellingham, Wenatchee, Spokane, and the Seattle Airport.
509-996-2894.

USA to CANADA ON FOOT USING THE PCT

PCNST (**P**acific **C**rest **N**ational **S**cenic **T**rail) is border to border within the United States. Most hikers continue 8.8 more miles into Canada on the **PCT** (**P**acific **C**rest **T**rail), finishing at Manning Park. The PCT border crossing is unmanned. You can legally cross from the US into Canada on trail only if you have your "Application to enter Canada via the PCT" with you as you enter Canada.

CANADA to USA

It is illegal to cross from Canada into the US using the trail. You must enter the US at a manned border crossing. The PCT is not a manned border crossing. All travelers entering the US from Canada by air are required to have a passport book. US citizens entering the US by land or sea are required to have either a passport book, a passport card, or an enhanced Driver's License. Visit the US Department of State website [www.travel.state.gov] for current regulations.

MANNING PARK to USA - see "Northern Terminus" Yogi map

OPTION 1: Manning > Abbotsford BC / Sumas WA > Bellingham or Seattle

Manning Park to Hope BC:	**HITCH:**	Hitch 42 miles west on Highway 3.
Hope BC to Abbotsford BC:	**BUS:**	Ebus [https://myebus.ca] 877-769-3287
Abbotsford BC to US border:	**BUS:**	BC Transit Route 2 (Bluejay-Huntingdon GoLine). [www.bctransit.com] 604-854-3232
US border to Sumas WA:	**WALK:**	Walk across the border.
Sumas WA to Bellingham WA:	**BUS:**	Whatcom Transportation Authority Bus [www.ridewta.com] 360-676-7433
Bellingham WA to Seattle WA:	**BUS OR TRAIN:** Greyhound [www.greyhound.com] 800-231-2222 Amtrak [www.amtrak.com] 800-872-7245, press 0	

OPTION 2: Manning > Vancouver BC > Bellingham or Seattle

First, choose how you will get from Manning Park to Vancouver BC:	
PRIVATE SHUTTLE: Manning to Vancouver BC: Canadian Craft Charters. 778-320-3409 [https://www.vancouvershuttlehire.com/], then search "Manning Park". 2018: $499 for up to 14 hikers That's $35.71/person (14 people)	**HITCH:** Manning to Hope BC, 42 miles west **BUS or TRAIN:** Hope BC to Vancouver BC Ebus VIA Rail Canada 877-769-3287 888-842-7245 [https://myebus.ca] [www.viarail.ca]

Once you are in Vancouver BC, use the following information:	
Vancouver BC:	Public transportation (train and bus) Sky Train [www.translink.ca] 604-953-3333
Vancouver BC to Bellingham WA or Seattle WA:	Amtrak [www.amtrak.com] 800-872-7245, press 0 Greyhound [www.greyhound.ca] 800-661-8747 Greyhound [www.greyhound.com] 800-231-2222 Bolt Bus [www.boltbus.com] 877-265-8287 Quick Shuttle [www.quickcoach.com] 800-665-2122
Seattle, WA:	Public bus: King County Metro Transit 206-553-3000 [www.metro.kingcounty.gov] Light Rail: Sound Transit 888-889-6368 [www.soundtransit.org]

2147.5 - Oregon-Washington border

2151.3 - Gillette Lake - Water here, but it looked green.
RADAR: Plenty of water at the inlet creek *after* the obvious side trail going down to the shore. The PCT crosses the inlet creek soon after with a large campsite in this area.

2152.2 - Greenleaf Creek - Strong flow with a footbridge.

2513.1 - Seasonal Stream - DOUBLE TAP (2014): Good flow.

2153.5 - Campsite - DOUBLE TAP (2014): Stream running well with small footbridge.

2154.6 to 2162.6 - Between the two roads, listen for a creek down on the left. You'll have to bushwhack down to it.

2157.2 - Viewpoint, spring near Table Mtn. - BINK: Through here (I am unsure of its exact location) the trail climbs (northbound) very steeply up an old logging road for about 0.75 mile. Part way up this a spring is heard gushing to the left (northbounders) and downhill of the trail. A rough trail leads 25 feet down to it. This spring always flows. About 200 feet farther north up the PCT from here is a small flat large enough for one tent.

2162.6 - Spur trail to Three Corner Rock water trough - BINK: Great water flowing like a fire hose from 3" black PVC pipe. A bit off trail, not a trip many thru-hikers make, but worth it if in need. If you go this far, I recommend walking another 0.1 mile over to a dirt road and then a short walk up to Three Corner Rock, site of an old fire lookout. The best views of the Columbia River Gorge anywhere near the PCT that I have seen. Bring your camera!

2166.7 - Rock Creek - Always water here. SCRUB: Nice camping for several people on top of the rise to the left before you cross the creek. Not visible from the trail.

2167.1 - Snag Creek - Always water here.

2168.3 - Seasonal Creeklet - Usually water here.

2175.6- approximately - DOUBLE TAP: Look for a use trail to the left where the PCT makes a hard right. This trail will take you to a great scenic overlook in just 50 ft where you can dangle your feet over a cliff a few hundred feet above the forest floor below.

2177.1 - Trout Creek - Always water here. Good camping.

2180.2 - Wind River - Always water here.

2182.7 - Panther Creek - Always water and camping here.

2183.5 - Spring

2191.6 - Junction with the Big Huckleberry Mountain summit trail - Great views on summit.

2193.5 - Descend to a gully with a reliable spring - PCT curves left. About a minute after the curve, watch the left side of the PCT for a handmade "water" sign. Follow the spur trail to the left past a rugged picnic table and down to the spring.

2198.4 - Road 60 - Small FS campground with picnic tables and a privy. Road 60 is a gravel road. You could get to Trout Lake WA from here (hard hitch).

2200.1 - Duck Pond named as Sheep Lake - Gross, disgusting water.

2201.2 - Green Lake - Gross, disgusting water.

2205.5 - Outlet Creek of Lake Sebago - No water.

2205.8 - Blue Lake - Water and camping here.

2207.6 - Junction with East Crater Trail 48 - Camping at Junction Lake. Junction Lake has water, but it's very shallow.

2208.8 - Bear Lake, Elk Lake Trail - Bear Lake has water. Down off the PCT to the left.

2209.3 - Slope above east end of Deer Lake - Deer Lake (down off PCT) usually good water.

2215.2 - Road 24 - You could get to Trout Lake WA from here.

2219.1 - Outlet of Big Mosquito Lake - Has water. In the next mile, there are at least three good cold creeks.

2221.8 - Creek Below Steamboat Lake - Water here.

2224.3 - Trout Lake Creek - Water and campsite.

2229.4 - Road 23 - Water after the road.
DOUBLE TAP: Campsites for ~6 tents to the left of the PCT about 0.1 mile north of Road 23.

2229.4 - Mount Adams Zen Buddhist Temple

We are a small Spiritual retreat center, Buddhist Temple, and Druid sanctuary located 4.3 miles south of Trout Lake Washington.

We have a very small B&B where folks can rest up, get care for simple first aid, shower and do laundry, plus access to a kitchen to cook your own meals. We have WiFi.

B&B regular rate is $$$ +, includes breakfast. PCT hikers get 15% off weekdays.

Hostel $, includes breakfast.
You have access to a kitchen to cook your own meals, shower, and laundry facilities.

Camping $, meals not included.

Meals are available $.

We have daily meditation and we're a drug-free, party-free place to stay.

Check us out online
[www.TLAbbey.com], or
[www.Mtadamszen.org]

Contact:
Venerable Kozen
46 Stoller Rd
Trout Lake WA

cell 509-637-5995
home 509-395-2030

Mailing:

PO Box 487
Trout Lake, WA 98650

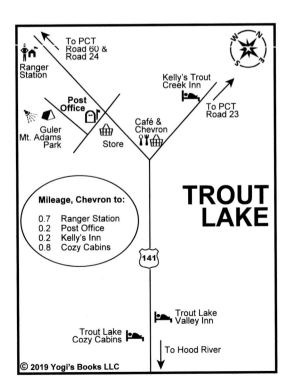

Mileage, Chevron to:

0.7 Ranger Station
0.2 Post Office
0.2 Kelly's Inn
0.8 Cozy Cabins

© 2019 Yogi's Books LLC

OVERVIEW: Small, hiker-friendly.
[www.troutlakewashington.com] then Activities, then PCT Information

GETTING HERE: Hitching easiest on weekends.

(1)   **PCT mile 2198.4 - Road 60** Hitch on Road 60 (right about 20 miles). Road 60 is a semi-traveled gravel road.

(2)   **PCT mile 2215.2 - Road 24** Hitch on Road 24 (right about 20-25 miles). Road 24 could be well-traveled during huckleberry season, but don't count on it.

(3)   **PCT mile 2229.4 - Road 23** Hitch on Road 23 (right about 13 miles). This paved road is the best option, especially if you want a ride from Trail Angels (call store). The Trail Angels prefer paved roads. Cell service for nobos on trail before reaching Road 23. If you can't get a ride, start walking toward town. After about 0.5 mile, you'll see an open space off the road; there is usually cell service there.

RIDES: Store (509-395-2777) has list of Trail Angels who give rides. There is usually a shuttle schedule. See Trout Lake website above. Doug Anderson can pre-arrange pickups from Road 23. Dougdjr@gorge.net   509-395-9307

POST OFFICE: 509-395-2108, USPS only
Mon-Fri 9:30-12:30p and 1p-4p. Sat closed.
If you won't arrive by your ETA date, please call the Post Office. Hiker Gen Del held until end of hiker season. Post Office prefers that hikers send boxes to the Trout Lake Grocery.

Hiker's Legal Name
PCT Hiker, ETA: MM/DD/YY
General Delivery
2393 Highway 141
Trout Lake, WA 98650

MAIL DROPS: Trout Lake Grocery Store (509-395-2777) accepts mail drops, no fee:

USPS address:
Hiker's Legal Name
PCT Hiker, ETA: MM/DD/YY
c/o Trout Lake Grocery
PO Box 132
Trout Lake, WA 98650

UPS or FedEx address:
Hiker's Legal Name
PCT Hiker, ETA: MM/DD/YY
c/o Trout Lake Grocery
2383 Highway 141
Trout Lake, WA 98650

RESUPPLY: Trout Lake Grocery Store. 509-395-2777. Summer hours: 7a-8p. Similar to a large C-Store. Not recommended for resupply.

RESTAURANTS: Café: Breakfast, burgers, baked goods, ice cream, beer.

LAUNDRY: Laundry machines at the Trout Lake Valley Inn.
Laundry for guests at Kelly's B&B and at the Grocery Rooms.

ATM: No ATM, but grocery gives cash back on debit card.
FUEL: HEET at Chevron.

TROUT LAKE LODGING ask for PCT rates		Rates	TV micr, frig	bkfst	laundry	other stuff
Cozy Cabins	509-395-2068	$$$ +	Y	no	Y	kitchenettes
Kelly's Trout Creek Inn	509-395-2769	$$ +	no	cont	Y	community room has TV
Trout Lake Valley Inn	509-395-2300	$$$	Y	cont waffles	Y	AC, hot tub
Rooms at the Grocery	509-395-2777	2018: $25	no	no	Y	bikes
Mount Adams Zen Buddhist Temple	509-395-2030	See previous page				
Guler Mt. Adams Park	509-773-4616	Camping and showers. 2018: camping $10				
Rates: $$ = usually $50-$80. $$$ = usually $80-$110. $$$$ = usually greater than $110.						

2233.0 - Spring, 100 yards past White Salmon River -
As the PCT curves to the left, you'll notice a PCT marker on a tree.
An obvious side trail on the right leads to the spring. Many hikers miss this.

2236.0 - Junction with Round the Mountain Trail 9 - RADAR: Take the Round the Mountain Trail about a quarter mile, you'll find nice camping just down the way with beautiful views of Adams.

2239.5 - Sheep Lake - Gross.

2239.6 - Riley Creek - Silty water.

2239.9 - Seasonal creek

2240.9 - Mutton Creek - No water.

2242.2 - Lewis River - Silty water.

2242.6 - Divide Camp Trail 112 - No water here.

2242.8 - Mt. Adams Creek - This ford is tricky.

2244.8 - Killen Creek - Water here.

2245.4 - Second Pond - Looked okay.

2249.1 - Muddy Fork - Clear in 2016, 2017, 2018.

2249.6 - Westward to a very good campsite - Water here.

2250.0 - Lava Spring - Great water. Good camping.

2254.2 - Midway Creek - Get water from the first small creek after the dirt road.

2257.0 - Last pond - They all have water, and they all look gross.

2259.3 - Climb to a saddle, pass two small ponds - RADAR: Look for an established campsite on the left. Not much camping along this part of the trail other than here. You could clear out a spot in the pines just south of here also. I wouldn't consider the ponds as water sources.

2260.1 - Prominent Ridgecrest -
Good camping spots off the trail to the right at the top of the ridge

2261.2 - Trickling Creek - Usually has water, but not in dry years.

2269.2 - Walupt Creek - Is dry.

2269.8 - Sheep Lake - Water here.

2273.4 - Tributary of Cispus River - Water here. SCRUB: Many unlisted campsites for at least the next mile after here. Good place to stage oneself for a morning sally up to Goat Rocks, or wait out bad weather.

2275.1 to 2277.1 - DOUBLE TAP: Many campsites off the PCT on the way up to the Packwood Glacier and the Knife's Edge.

2277.1 to 2280.0 - DOUBLE TAP: No good campsites in this stretch, which is basically the Knife's Edge. Try to hit this section before 3pm as to not get caught up on the Knife's Edge in the dark. If you take the Hiker PCT at junction ~mile 2276.6 to the right, you will have to traverse over some snow more than likely but it's only about 100 ft or so. If weather is good, take the Hiker PCT as it starts out much higher than the Equestrian PCT and the views are spectacular. I had clouds blowing in and out as I came down from the top of the Knife's Edge which was eerie but a lot of fun at the same time.

2277.1 - Old Snowy Alternate

2280.4 - Bleak Alpine Campsites - This is the first water after you come off the Knife's Edge. DOUBLE TAP: About 0.1 mile after coming down off the Knife's Edge look to the left and you will see a grove of trees ~200 ft off the PCT with some use trails. There are plenty of good campsites up in those trees and a tremendous view of Mount Rainier in the distance. Very windy here.

2282.8 - Lutz Lake - Water here. RADAR: Not enough water flowing into this lake. It was stagnant and too low to have any water at the outlet creek. There was water flowing in the creeks beyond Tieton Pass north of here.

2287.2 - Hidden Spring - TWODOG: Walk down the trail marked "Hidden Springs Tr 1117" for about 10 minutes until you reach a flat spot with an obvious campsite. Springs, and more camps, are just downhill to your left.

2292.0 - Chairlift Trail - Shortcut to White Pass. STRAIGHT JACKET: Once you get to the top of the ski lift, you can see exactly where you need to go, so no route-finding. Sure it's overgrown and steep in places (it *is* a ski slope), but it's quite doable, and was a fun adventure. Well worth it to get to food quicker.

2293.3 - Ginnette Lake - Water and camping here.

2295.4- Highway 12 / White Pass WA / Packwood WA
Walk to the left 0.5 mile to get to White Pass.
Hitch to the left 20 miles to get to Packwood.

2295.4 - White Pass WA

OVERVIEW: Not much here. A motel and a C-Store. That's it.

GETTING HERE: Two options:

(1) PCT mile 2292.0 - Chairlift trail. Steep and sometimes slippery.

(2) PCT mile 2295.4 - Highway 12, walk 0.5 mile to the left.

SHUTTLES: Randi Nelson (360 669-3112) offers shuttles for a fee in these areas:
Cascade Locks, Snoqualmie Pass, White Pass, Packwood.

MAIL DROPS: Kracker Barrel Store (509-672-3105) accepts mail drops.

2018: $5 fee for first package, $3 for additional packages. Mail can be picked up any time the store is open (usually 8a until 5p or 6p). Sometimes open until 7p on weekends. This is a Rural Post Office, which is not full-service. Outgoing mail is letters only, no boxes. USPS, UPS, FedEx:

Hiker's Legal Name
PCT Hiker, ETA: MM/DD/YY
c/o White Pass Rural Branch PO
at the Kracker Barrel Store
48851 US Highway 12
Naches, WA 98937

RESUPPLY: The Kracker Barrel in White Pass is NOT a Kracker Barrel Restaurant.
It is a large C-Store which serves a fresh pizza, sandwiches, ice cream.
Usually open 8a until 5p or 6p, sometimes open until 7p on weekends.
Usually has good hiker resupply. Good beer selection.

The motel rooms have microwaves, stoves, and ovens, so you could buy food at the store to cook: canned soups/stews, frozen pizzas, and hot pocket type microwave food. The store has fried food, like chicken strips and fries.

Backpacks not allowed inside the store.

LODGING: The Village Inn (509-672-3131) is next to the Store.
Different sized kitchenette rooms sleep 1-6 people.
Some rooms have stove, some have microwave.
Outdoor pool. Rates: $$$ +

FUEL: Sometimes the store has HEET, canisters, and white gas.

LAUNDRY, ATM: At the store.

FLEA MARKET: Packwood hosts a gigantic flea market over Labor Day weekend.
All motel rooms will be full beginning the Monday before Labor Day.

GETTING HERE: Hitch 20 miles to the left on Highway 12.
White Pass Cracker Barrel might be able to arrange a ride to Packwood.

SHUTTLES: Randi Nelson (360 669-3112) offers shuttles for a fee in these areas:
Cascade Locks, Snoqualmie Pass, White Pass, Packwood.

POST OFFICE: 360-494-6311, USPS only   Hiker's Legal Name
Mon-Fri 8a-noon and 1p-4:45p   PCT Hiker, ETA: MM/DD/YY
Sat closed   General Delivery
General Delivery held for 30 days   Packwood, WA 98361

RESUPPLY: Blanton's Market 360-494-6101
This is a large grocery store, good for resupply. 7a-8p every day.

OUTDOOR STORE: White Pass Sports Hut. 360-494-7321. Does not have camping
gear, but it does have some hats, gloves, socks, canister fuel.

RESTAURANTS: Yes.
LAUNDRY: At the RV Park.
SHOWERS: At the RV Park.
ATM: At Blanton's Market and Shell station.

COMPUTER: Packwood Timberland Library 360-494-5111

FUEL: HEET at Shell gas station
Denatured alcohol and canisters at Ace Hardware   360-494-2131
Canister fuel at White Pass Sports Hut   360-494-7321

PACKWOOD LODGING	Rates	TV	frig	micr	laundry	bkfst	other
The Bunkhouse 509-929-2468 UNCONFIRMED: All info for The Bunkhouse.	$	Y	full kitchen		Y	no	hostel-style dorm and private rooms
Packwood Inn 360-494-5500	$$ +	Y	some	some	Y	cont	private bath indoor pool
Hotel Packwood 360-494-5431	$$ +	Y	no	no	no	no	shared bath. 2 rooms have private bath.
Tatoosh Motel 360-494-7379		Y	Y	Y	no	cont	
Cowlitz River Lodge 360-494-4444	$$$	Y	some	some	Y	cont	sauna
Mtn View Lodge 360-494-5555	$$$	Y	some	some	no	cont	outdoor pool, hot tub
Crest Trail Lodge 360-494-4944	$$$$	Y	Y	some	no	hot	2 glasses of complimentary wine each evening
Packwood RV Park 360-494-5145	Due to disrespectful 2017 hikers, the RV park did not allow hikers to stay in 2018.						
	$ $$ $$$ $$$$	= usually less than $50 = usually $50-$80 = usually $80-$110 = usually greater than $110					

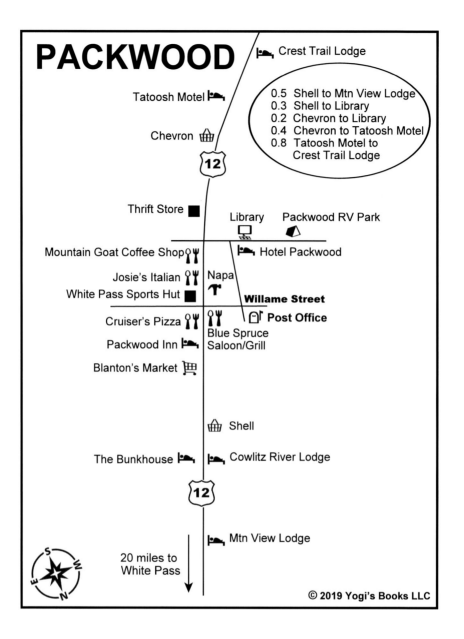

PACKWOOD

Crest Trail Lodge

Tatoosh Motel

Chevron

0.5 Shell to Mtn View Lodge
0.3 Shell to Library
0.2 Chevron to Library
0.4 Chevron to Tatoosh Motel
0.8 Tatoosh Motel to
     Crest Trail Lodge

12

Thrift Store

Library   Packwood RV Park

Mountain Goat Coffee Shop   Hotel Packwood

Josie's Italian   Napa
White Pass Sports Hut

Willame Street

Cruiser's Pizza   Post Office
                Blue Spruce
Packwood Inn   Saloon/Grill

Blanton's Market

Shell

The Bunkhouse   Cowlitz River Lodge

12

Mtn View Lodge

20 miles to
White Pass

© 2019 Yogi's Books LLC

2296.16- Dark Meadows Trail 1107 - No water here.

2297.6 (Deer Lake) to 2302.5 (Pipe Lake) -
Lots of lakes along here. Some are clear, some have floating green slime.

2305.3 - Snow Lake - Water here.

2309.1 (Bumping River) to 2340.4 (Morgan Springs) -
All the on-trail water sources had water. No water information for the off-trail sources.

2311.4 - Crag Lake - DOUBLE TAP: Follow use trail to the left of the PCT right after small stream that crosses the PCT. This trail leads down to a campground with room for ~4 tents on the east side of Crag Lake. The trail continues on the north side of Crag Lake to other smaller campsites.

2312.4 - Remy's Spring - REMY: Great spring right below the trail. For Sobos, this will be on the right, while descending after turning the corner at the last Rainier National Park regulations sign. Lots of water in this section, but this was the best.

2324.3 - Chinook Pass Parking Area - Privy and trash bins in parking lot.
There is a side trail to the parking area after you cross the road on the bridge.

2327.4 - Sourdough Gap - SCRUB: You finish a climb to a narrow saddle and look ahead to a nice gradual trail leading to another saddle. It looks very PCT, but halfway across to that next saddle the PCT actually splits off on a 180-degree turn down to the right that is marked by a knee-high, camouflaged rock-colored sign that faces away from northbounders.

2334.5 - Spring - DOUBLE TAP: Spring is visible ~100ft down the right side of the PCT.

2340.4 - Trail to Morgan Springs

2342.1 - Spur Trail to Arch Rock Shelter - This is a faint spur trail on the left side of the PCT.
There is water on the PCT about a minute past the shelter spur trail.

2347.5 - Urich Cabin - Get water as you cross the bridge just before the cabin.

DOUBLE TAP: Just after Camp Urich there is a horse camp.
Stay to the right of the horse camp (right before entering the camp) to stay on the PCT.

2352.2 - Just before a road, you'll see a campsite on the right side of the PCT.
Just past the campsite is a spring down on the right side of the PCT.
DOUBLE TAP: Another campsite on south side of spring ~50 ft down.

2357.6 - Granite Creek Trail 1326 on Blowout Mountain - RADAR: *After* this junction you climb up to the side of Blowout Mountain.

2358.0 - Blowout Mountain - RADAR: At the Blowout Mountain sign on the PCT, go off trail and follow a faint trail a short way to the top of Blowout Mountain (easy). Awesome 360 views from up here. Don't miss it.

2364.0 - Scott's Spring - Follow the signs to ice cold water.

2364.6 - Tacoma Pass Campsite - DOUBLE TAP: Good camping here for ~6 tents.

2366.3 - Seasonal Creek - BINK: Approaching this, northbounders will come to the remains of a wooden bridge over rust-colored nasty-looking water. This is not the source! The better water is found in a gully another 100 yards north on the trail. Also of note: approximately 2-2.5 miles north of this source is a small spring which lies to the right (for northbounders) of the trail in an open grassy area. This spring always has water and as far as I know is unmapped and in no guidebook.

2371.2 - Spring in spongy ground - TWODOG: Midway along the level, east-west stretch of trail north of Snowshoe Butte is a spring in spongy ground. It's in a tiny meadow immediately below the trail on the right. Northbound, it's after you leave the 200 yards of logging "track" and resume walking on trail. Southbound, it's after you've descended the edge of a large, sloping meadow with a probably-dry ravine at the far side. The spring should be obvious if you're watching for it. It was flowing at the end of September and is probably good all season. No camping here, but level spots on old logging spurs are nearby in both directions.

2373.1 - Scott's Spring - There is a sign for this spring. BINK: Hiking northbound, you will be doing a steep descent to this forested saddle. About halfway down at a switchback corner to the west, you will see a small grassy area only ten feet off the trail which has a normally reliable spring.

2374.4 - Weather Station Access Road - Weather Station closed; no water here.

2374.5 - Privy

2375.1 - Stampede Pass Road 54 - Lizard Lake has water, but it looks gross.

2377.3 - Trail follows to a hairpin on a road - Spring here. TWODOG: You could camp here, or better yet at a large flat spot 0.1 mile farther down the trail.

2379.5 (Creek) to 2391.8 (Beaver Lake) -
All the on-trail water sources had water.

2384.8 - Mirror Lake - DOUBLE TAP: In addition to campground bordering the left side of the PCT (room for ~4 tents), there are use trails to the left and right of here offering plenty of good camping. The one to the right goes up to a good size campground and the one to the left is ~50ft before the campground bordering the PCT. Follow the left use trail for ~200 ft for another large size campground.

2392.3 - Beaver Lake - After passing this lake, the PCT emerges on a ridge in a ski area. The buildings you see down to the right are the Snoqualmie Pass Ski Area. The Summit Inn is the large white building with a red roof. The PCT will cross a ski area access road, which you can take down to the Summit Inn, instead of walking the PCT all the way over to Interstate 90, just to turn around and walk the road back to the Summit Inn.

Access these files as often as possible:

(1) Pacific Crest Trail Water Report - Current status of water sources. Frequently updated during hiker season. [www.pctwater.com]

(2) Yogi's PCT Handbook update file - Changes to trail/town information which have occurred between the time your book was printed and now. Frequently updated during hiker season. [www.yogisbooks.com], then click UPDATES & LINKS

Do you have changes/updates to report?
If so, send them here: yogisbooks@gmail.com

OVERVIEW: Snoqualmie Pass is a ski resort and a great hiker stop.

GETTING HERE: (1) PCT mile 2392.9 - Leave the PCT on the ski slope and walk down the slope
                     directly to the Summit Inn (large white building with a red roof).

                (2) PCT mile 2393.6 - Stay on the PCT all the way to Interstate 90, then walk
                     0.3 mile on the road to the right until you see the Summit Inn on your left.

SHUTTLES: Randi Nelson (360 669-3112) offers shuttles for a fee in these areas:
              Cascade Locks, Snoqualmie Pass, White Pass, Packwood.

MAIL DROPS: Note: this is **SNOQUALMIE PASS**, not SNOQUALMIE.
              Get it right or you'll be sorry.

              Questions about Snoqualmie Pass USPS mail: North Bend PO 425-831-7020.

              Chevron (425-434-6688)   Hiker's Legal Name
              Accepts mail drops, no fee.   PCT Hiker, ETA: MM/DD/YY
              Mail held for 3 weeks only.   c/o Chevron Station
              Make your box easily identifiable.   521 State Route 906
              Note: Hikers often have trouble   Snoqualmie Pass, WA 98068
              with packages sent to Chevron.
              Better option is to send to Summit Inn.

              Summit Inn (425-434-6300)   Hiker's Legal Name
              Be sure to label your box as a hiker   PCT Hiker, ETA: MM/DD/YY
              package. Box must clearly have your   c/o Summit Inn Hotel
              name and ETA. No fee if you are a   603 State Route 906
              guest, $15 fee (plus tax) for non-guests. PO Box 163
              Per phone call in December 2017, this Snoqualmie Pass, WA 98068
              address is good for USPS, UPS, FedEx:

RESUPPLY: Two very expensive C-Stores, you could resupply at both.

              Chevron. 425-434-6688. 6a-11p every day. C-Store.
              No Knorr sides or Idahoans. Lots of Ramen and snacks. Beer.

              Lee's Summit Grocery. 425-434-0024. Large C-Store.
              Mon-Tue 8a-4p. Wed-Sun 7a-7p. Better selection than Chevron.
              Knorr sides and Idahoans, Ramen, lots of snacks. Beer.

LODGING: Summit Inn. 425-434-6300.
              It's a nice hotel. Hot tub, heated pool, sauna, laundry on site. Rooms have TV.
              Some rooms have refrigerator and microwave. Ask for hiker rate $$$.

              Washington Alpine Club Guye Cabin. [www.washingtonalpineclub.org/cabin]
              In August and September, we host PCT hikers as guests to rest and relax. Inside
              bunks, showers, library, full kitchen, hand laundry, outside area. Please check in
              with host. No wireless, absolutely no smoking, no alcohol/beer! 2019: $20/night.

RESTAURANTS: Summit Pancake House   Not just pancakes. Lunch & dinner, too.
              Webb's   Burgers, salad, full bar, PCT hiker specials.
              Red Mountain Coffee   Pizza by the slice, salads, breakfast burritos.

LAUNDRY: Laundry at the Summit Inn. Front desk sells laundry soap.
              Laundry at WAC Guye Cabin.

SHOWER: At WAC Guye Cabin.

ATM: Yes.

COMPUTER: In lounge of Summit Inn for guests only.

FUEL: HEET at the Chevron and Lee's Summit Grocery.

REMINDER: Make sure your resupply person mails your passport and your Canada entrance
              papers to Stehekin (General Delivery, 98852)

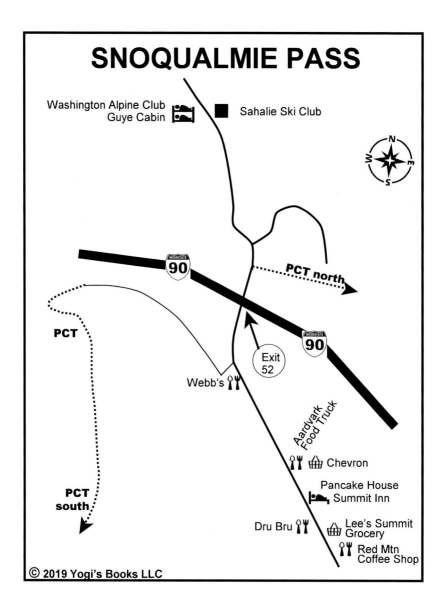

SNOQUALMIE PASS

Washington Alpine Club
Guye Cabin

Sahalie Ski Club

PCT north

90

90

PCT

Exit 52

Webb's

Aardvark Food Truck

Chevron

Pancake House
Summit Inn

PCT south

Dru Bru

Lee's Summit Grocery

Red Mtn Coffee Shop

© 2019 Yogi's Books LLC

2393.7 - Interstate 90

2300.8 - Ridge Lake - Water and camping here.

2403.3 - "Kenny Spring" near Forested saddle between Joe and Edds lakes -
BINK: Approximately 0.25 mile north of this saddle, the trail enters a small open meadow (lush green plant growth in this area) with a dry stream bed. If you go 20 yards down the steep gully to the right, there is a spring with a constant flow of water coming out of the rocks in the center of the gully. This always has water, but is tricky to locate. I named it "Kenny Spring" in honor of Kenny Gould.

2411.7 - Delate Creek - Water here.

2414.3 - Lemah Creek - Water here.

2414.9 - Lemah Meadow Trail 1323B - Water here.

2415.0 - A couple of campsites - No water here. RADAR: The first large camping area is hidden on a rise to the right of the PCT. Look for the short side trail. Beyond this on the PCT watch for a trail off to the left. This trail goes towards Lemah Creek to a large campsite. Water here instead of backtracking south on the PCT.

2421.7 to 2494.0 (Lake Sally Ann) -
All the on-trail water sources had water.

2428.3 - Waptus River Campsite - DOUBLE TAP: After crossing the bridge (north side) there is a use trail heading up the hill to the left of the PCT. Follow this trail to a nice campsite with room for ~4 tents and it also has a fire pit. You can also continue along the PCT for ~200ft and you will see other campsites to the right directly from the PCT.

2435.3 - Deep Lake's campsite access trail - Get water here before climb to Cathedral Pass.

2438.3 - Cathedral Pass Trail - TWODOG (2006): There is a large, reliable tarn down the Cathedral Pass Trail, about 100 yards from its junction with the PCT.

2446.7 - Cross outlet of Deception Lakes - Lots of mice here.

2450.3 - DOUBLE TAP: After hiking switchbacks down a big rock field you enter a forested area. You will start seeing campsites 0.2 miles after entering the forested area.

2464.3 - Trail to Granite Peaks Lodge at Stevens Pass Ski Area

2464.7 - Highway 2 / Stevens Pass - Hitch to Dinsmores, Skykomish, Leavenworth

---

Permit required to camp in North Cascades National Park (PCT mile 2571.6 to 2587.7). Your PCTA permit does not cover you for camping in this area. Northbound hikers can get the permit at the Golden West Visitor Center in Stehekin, or call the North Cascades National Park Wilderness Information Center (360-854-7245) from Stevens Pass.

STEVENS PASS

Lodging at The Mountaineers Stevens Lodge, a short walk from the resort's bike park, is open from mid-August through the end of September to host PCT thru-hikers. Bunk in a dorm, gear drying room, laundry tub and hot shower provided. More info: 206-521-6000 mountaineers.org/stevenslodge, info@mountaineers.org

Directions to the Mountaineers Lodge (hostel lodging), Northbound PCT hikers: Walk west through the parking lot to the base area. From Granite Peaks Lodge, follow the "Foot Traffic" signs, then pass to the right of the Hogsback Express chairlift. Walk uphill and west towards the maintenance building passing the Skyline Express and Brooks chairlifts on your right and crossing one bike trail. Walk the road on the uphill side of the maintenance building to the first sharp left bend and then up to our lodge. Stevens Lodge is the 4 story, dark red building at the first sharp, 90-degree bend in the road. Look for The Mountaineers sign on the balcony and come on in!

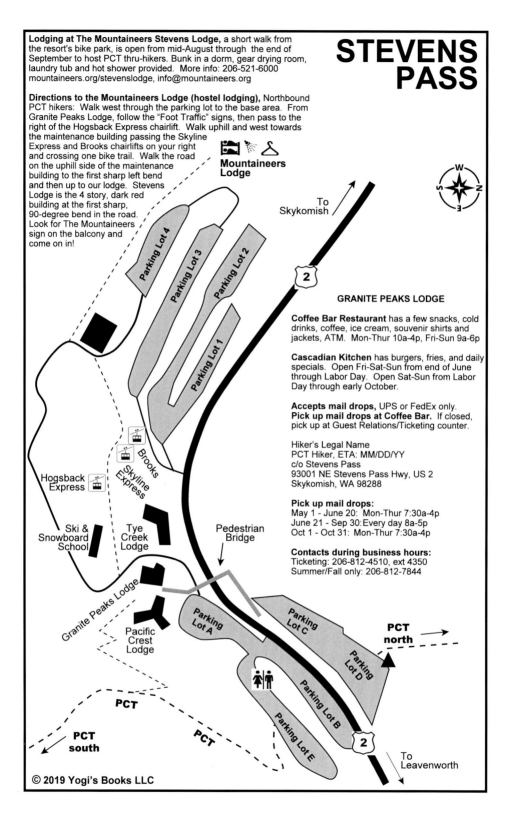

Mountaineers Lodge

To Skykomish

GRANITE PEAKS LODGE

Coffee Bar Restaurant has a few snacks, cold drinks, coffee, ice cream, souvenir shirts and jackets, ATM. Mon-Thur 10a-4p, Fri-Sun 9a-6p

Cascadian Kitchen has burgers, fries, and daily specials. Open Fri-Sat-Sun from end of June through Labor Day. Open Sat-Sun from Labor Day through early October.

Accepts mail drops, UPS or FedEx only.
Pick up mail drops at Coffee Bar. If closed, pick up at Guest Relations/Ticketing counter.

Hiker's Legal Name
PCT Hiker, ETA: MM/DD/YY
c/o Stevens Pass
93001 NE Stevens Pass Hwy, US 2
Skykomish, WA 98288

Pick up mail drops:
May 1 - June 20: Mon-Thur 7:30a-4p
June 21 - Sep 30: Every day 8a-5p
Oct 1 - Oct 31: Mon-Thur 7:30a-4p

Contacts during business hours:
Ticketing: 206-812-4510, ext 4350
Summer/Fall only: 206-812-7844

Parking Lot 4
Parking Lot 3
Parking Lot 2
Parking Lot 1

Brooks
Skyline Express
Hogsback Express
Ski & Snowboard School
Tye Creek Lodge
Pedestrian Bridge
Granite Peaks Lodge
Pacific Crest Lodge
Parking Lot A
Parking Lot C
Parking Lot D
Parking Lot B
Parking Lot E

PCT north
PCT
PCT
PCT south
To Leavenworth

© 2019 Yogi's Books LLC

GETTING HERE: Hitch 16 miles to the west from Stevens Pass (Highway 2).

BUS SERVICE: Northwestern Trailways (509-838-4029) has a route from Spokane to Seattle, with a scheduled stop in Leavenworth, a flag stop at Stevens Pass (you must flag the bus down), and an on call (reservations required) stop in Skykomish. Eastbound bus to Leavenworth crosses Stevens Pass at approximately 11:30am. Westbound bus to Skykomish crosses Stevens Pass at approximately 1:55pm.

POST OFFICE: Hiker mail must have valid domestic return address.
Hiker mail held until end of season.

Postmaster Ginnie is usually here Mon-Fri until 4p.
If you arrive after 3:30pm, ring buzzer or knock on door.

Ginnie posts her cell phone number on the board in the lobby. If the PO is closed, and if she is in town, she will come to the PO to give you your mail. Do not call after 8pm.

360-677-2241. USPS only.	Hiker's Legal Name
Mon-Fri 11:30a-3:30p	PCT Hiker, ETA: MM/DD/YY
Sat closed, but can pick up packages from	General Delivery
8a-10a. Ring buzzer or knock on door.	Skykomish, WA 98288

RESUPPLY: Sky Gas Chevron (large C-Store). 360-677-2290.
Sun-Thur 6a-11p, Fri-Sat 6a-midnight. Not recommended for resupply.

Sky Deli & Liquor. 360-677-2211. Good prices on candy bars.
Mon-Tue 9a-6p, Wed-Thur 6a-6p, Fri 6a-7p, Sat 9a-7p, Sun 9a-5p.

LODGING: Cascadia Inn. 360-677-2030. Weekday rates below.

Private rooms with shared bath: $$
Private rooms with private bath and TV: $$$

There is a community room downstairs with a big satellite TV. Internet available.

Train tracks are across the street from the Cascadia Inn.
Trains come through at night and they are LOUD.

LAUNDRY: Yes.

RESTAURANTS:

Sky Deli	360-677-2211	Sandwiches & ice cream
Cascadia Restaurant	360-677-2030	
Whistling Post Tavern	360-677-2111	Bar with pool tables

ATM: At Sky Gas Chevron.
There is *not* and ATM in Baring or in Stehekin.
The bus to Stehekin is *not* free. Bring $20 in small bills.

COMPUTER: Skykomish Library. 360-677-2660.

FUEL: HEET at Sky Gas Chevron.
Canister fuel at Sky Deli.

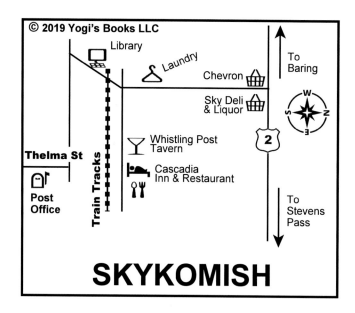

© 2019 Yogi's Books LLC

Library

Laundry

Chevron

Sky Deli & Liquor

To Baring

Whistling Post Tavern

Cascadia Inn & Restaurant

Thelma St

Train Tracks

Post Office

To Stevens Pass

2

SKYKOMISH

2461.6 - Dinsmore's Hiker Haven / Baring WA

GETTING HERE: Hiker Haven is in Baring (highway mile marker 41).
Baring is 8 miles west of Skykomish (Skykomish = highway mile marker 49).
We can pick you up from Skykomish, but NOT from Stevens Pass.

Hitch to Baring and get out at the Baring Store.
Go over the tracks and take the first left and down to the Dinsmore sign.

POST OFFICE: Baring PO (360-677-2230). Mon-Fri 11:45a-3:45p. Sat 8a-9:45a.
Does not accept General Delivery. Outgoing mail only.

MAIL DROPS: Dinsmores do not accept or pick up mail.
Do not address anything to the Dinsmores.
If you mail anything to the Dinsmores, it will be returned.

Send your mail General Delivery to Skykomish.

RESUPPLY: Small store, but not good for hiker resupply.
There is a big grocery store in Gold Bar, 13 miles west of Baring.

SERVICES: **One night stay only for dedicated PCT hikers who respect house rules and are willing to offset expenses with a donation.**

Dinsmores have an indoor bunkroom plus two acres of grass for pitching tents and hanging out. Shower, bathroom, laundry, a fire pit, and WiFi.

MEALS: There isn't any place to eat in Baring. You can have pizza delivered.
The Dinsmores try to give rides to the Cascadia in Skykomish for meals.

FUEL: Canister fuel ($) at Dinsmore's Hiker Haven.

OVERVIEW: If you want a real town, Leavenworth is the place.
It's crazy touristy, but that also means great places to eat.

GETTING HERE: From Stevens Pass, hitch 35 miles to the right (east).

BUS SERVICE: Northwestern Trailways (509-838-4029) has a route from Spokane to Seattle, with a scheduled stop in Leavenworth, a flag stop at Stevens Pass (you must flag the bus down), and an on call (reservations required) stop in Skykomish. Eastbound bus to Leavenworth crosses Stevens Pass at approximately 11:30am. Westbound bus to Skykomish crosses Stevens Pass at approximately 1:55pm.

POST OFFICE: 509-548-7212. USPS only.
Mon-Fri 9a-5p
Sat 9a-11a
General Delivery held for 30 days.

Hiker's Legal Name
PCT Hiker, ETA: MM/DD/YY
General Delivery
Leavenworth, WA 98826

RESUPPLY: Safeway 509-548-5435 6a-11p every day

OUTDOOR STORE: Leavenworth Mountain Sports 509-548-7864 M-F 10a-6p, Sat-Sun 9a-6p

RESTAURANTS: Many, including a Brewery.

LAUNDRY: No public laundromat. Laundry at KOA is for KOA guests only.

ATM: Yes.

COMPUTER: Library 509-548-7923

FUEL: HEET at gas stations and Safeway.
Canister fuel maybe at Leavenworth Mountain Sports.

MEDICAL: Cascade Medical Center. 509-548-5815.

LEAVENWORTH LODGING		Rates	frig	micr	TV	laundry	pool	hot tub	bkfst
Adventure Inn	509-548-5250	$$$ +	Y	Y	Y	no	no	no	no
Bavarian Lodge	888-717-7878	$$$$ +	Y	Y	Y	no	Y	Y	hot
Bavarian Ritz	509-548-5455	$$$ +	Y	Y	Y	no	no	no	
Der Ritterhof Inn	509-548-5845	$$$ +	Y	ask	Y	Y	Y	Y	cont
Enzian Inn	509-548-5269	$$$$ +	no	no	Y	no	Y	Y	full
Evergreen Inn	509-548-5515	$$$ +	some		Y	Y	no	Y	hot
Fairbridge Inn	509-548-7992	$$$ +	Y	Y	Y	Y	Y	Y	hot
Howard Johnson	509-548-4326	$$$ +	Y	Y	Y	no	Y	no	cont
Innsbrucker Motel	509-548-5401	$$$ +	Y	Y	Y	no	no	no	no
Linderhof Inn	509-548-5543	$$$ +	Y	Y	Y	no	Y	Y	cont
Obertal Inn	800-537-9382	$$$$ +	Y	Y	Y	$7	no	Y	cont
Village Inn	509-548-6620	$$$ +	Y	Y	Y	no	no	no	no
KOA	509-548-7709	$ Tenting $$$ Camping cabin (no bathroom) Pool, hot tub, laundry, showers							
		$ = usually less than $50 $$ = usually $50-$80 $$$ = usually $80-$110 $$$$ = usually greater than $110							

LEAVENWORTH

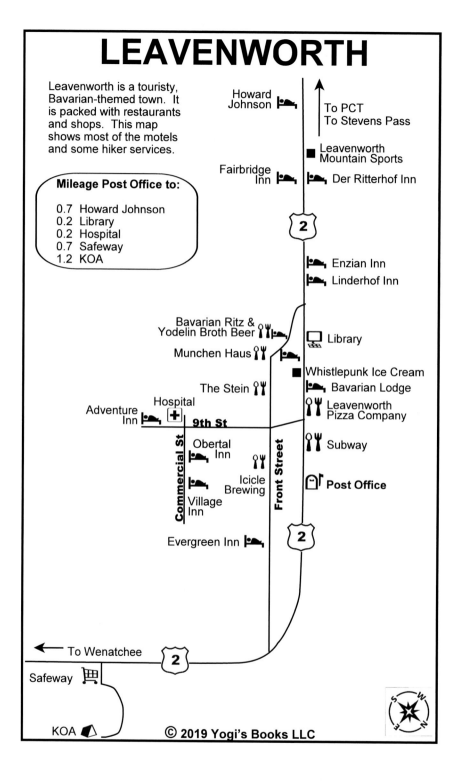

Leavenworth is a touristy, Bavarian-themed town. It is packed with restaurants and shops. This map shows most of the motels and some hiker services.

Mileage Post Office to:

0.7 Howard Johnson
0.2 Library
0.2 Hospital
0.7 Safeway
1.2 KOA

Howard Johnson

To PCT
To Stevens Pass

Leavenworth Mountain Sports

Fairbridge Inn

Der Ritterhof Inn

2

Enzian Inn

Linderhof Inn

Bavarian Ritz & Yodelin Broth Beer

Munchen Haus

Library

Whistlepunk Ice Cream

The Stein

Bavarian Lodge

Leavenworth Pizza Company

Adventure Inn

Hospital

9th St

Subway

Obertal Inn

Front Street

Commercial St

Post Office

Icicle Brewing

Village Inn

Evergreen Inn

2

To Wenatchee

2

Safeway

KOA

© 2019 Yogi's Books LLC

Permit required to camp in North Cascades National Park (PCT mile 2571.6 to 2587.7). Your PCTA permit does not cover you for camping in this area. Northbound hikers can get the permit at the Golden West Visitor Center in Stehekin, or call the North Cascades National Park Wilderness Information Center (360-854-7245) from Stevens Pass.

Alternates and bail-outs: "Anish" Heather Anderson, holder of the PCT female unsupported speed record (60 days, 17 hours, 12 minutes), is very familiar with the trails in Northern Washington (not just the PCT). Anish has graciously offered bail-out and alternate suggestions in case the weather gets bad, which often happens north of Skykomish. See the shaded boxes at mile points 2502.5, 2571.9, and 2661.4.

2468.2 (Tributary of Nason Creek) to 2494.0 (Lake Sally Ann) -
All the on-trail water sources have water.

2481.7 - Wenatchee Pass - DOUBLE TAP: At Pear Lake / PCT sign you will see campsites right off the PCT. Look left (if heading northbound) at this place to see a use trail heading back. Take that trail for ~300 ft to an even larger campground with great campsites. I could hear water in the distance, but I didn't look for it.

2486.1 - SCRUB (2013): You will be going gently downhill through a boulder field and should hear water flowing under the boulders to your left/downhill. Poke around and that water is reachable, and it is and clear and ICE COLD! I can only assume it's spring-fed. There had been no on-trail water before this for 10+ miles.

2487.2 - Campsite near a seasonal creek

2487.8 - Saddle Gap - TWODOG (2006): Sign pointing downhill to water is still there, but it looked steep and I didn't see any sign of a trail.

2494.0 - Lake Sally Ann - Campsites and privy.

2500.0 to 2535.0 - SCRUB: Count on a significantly slower pace in the area around Glacier Peak. In some areas, the trail is brand new like a sidewalk, but in other areas it is overgrown and rutted out. I was always behind where I thought I'd be at any given time from about mile 2499.5 to 2534.5.

2500.7 - Semi-clear reflection pond - Small, with gross water. Camping here.

2502.4 - White Pass

2503.0 - North Fork Sauk Trail - Bail out here if the weather is bad

ANISH: You've made it to White Pass (not the White Pass with the Kracker Barrel, but White Pass in the North Cascades at PCT mile 2502.4), and realize you need to get out. Or, perhaps you went on to Red Pass (PCT mile 2503.8) or even Fire Creek Pass (PCT mile 2520.5) before calling it. Either way, once you're this deep into the wilderness section, the North Fork Sauk Trail is a direct route out to civilization.

Just north of White Pass (PCT mile 2502.4), there is a junction with the North Fork Sauk Trail (PCT mile 2503.0). It drops steeply west before leveling out and following the river. There is plenty of water on this route. After about 8 miles, you will reach a gravel parking lot. Exit lot and walk right (north) on gravel FS Road 49. About 8 miles down this road you will reach the paved Mountain Loop Highway. This area is very busy all summer and into the fall. It's likely you'd find someone at the gravel parking lot and definitely on the highway. Hitch west to I-5.

2504.3 - Red Pass

2507.3 - Last crossing of a swelling creek - Water here. In the next mile you will cross a clear creek. It is the last clear on-trail water for the next 7.8 miles.

2508.2 (White Chuck River) to 2512.3 (Kennedy Creek) - All the on-trail water sources are silty-white glacial creeks.

2508.2 - White Chuck River - Bridge. Silty water.

2509.2 - Baekos Creek - Bridge. Silty water.

2511.3 - Sitkum Creek - Bridge. Silty water.

2512.4 - Spring - SCRUB (2013): There is a nice spring coming out of the ground just below the trail on the left for a nobo. There is a path to it.

2512.8 - Kennedy Creek - Silty water.

2513.0 to 2515.0 - DOUBLE TAP (2014): Many downed trees; expect a slower hiking rate.

2515.0 - Glacier Creek - Lots of mice. Good water.

2515.0 (Glacier Creek) to 2521.3 (outlet of Mica Lake) - All on-trail water sources have good water.

2520.5 - Fire Creek Pass

2521.3 - Mica Creek - Good water and camping.

2523.5 - Campsite - SCRUB: Good small campsite on the left of the trail at the corner of a rightward-turning downhill switchback.

2525.1 - Milk Creek - Bridge. Silty-white glacial creek.

2530.6 - Small knoll - Lots of creeks near the knoll.

2530.8 - East Fork Milk Creek - Water.

2532.0 - Dolly Vista Campsite

2532.7 (Saddle on Vista Ridge) to 2535.7 (Campsite beside Vista Creek) - Several small seasonal creeks, with good water.

2538.0 - Junction with old PCT to log crossing of Suiattle River

2540.1 - "The Big Grove" - BINK: "The Big Grove" is a grove of very large 10-15 foot diameter trees, the largest you will see on the entire PCT in a flat area. The new Suiattle River route is much longer than the former route, but overall is not a bad walk and the big trees grove is incredible. At one time prior to the creation of the Glacier Peak Wilderness, the Forest Service wanted to continue the Suiattle River Road all the way up to the vicinity of this grove so that they could be logged. Hopefully this stand of huge Douglas fir, Sitka Spruce, Western Hemlock, and some Western Red Cedar will now stand until they die natural deaths.

2541.1 - Bridge over Suiattle River - BINK: Camping on west side of river.

2542.8 - Clear Creek - Good water.

2544.2 - Clear Creek - Good water.

2544.5 - Clear Creek - Good water.

2544.9 - Miners Creek - Bridge, good water.

2544.9 (Miners Creek Bridge) to 2549.1 (Buck Creek Pass Trail) - Several (maybe 10) small creeks cross the trail. All have clear water.

2549.1 - Buck Creek Pass Trail

2549.7 - Miners Creek - SCRUB: Great camping a minute before the river (green glacial water). Fill up at the last creek you cross ~5 minutes before Miners.

25523 - Cloudy Pass - RADAR: If you are going to take the alternate route to save a couple of miles or avoid bad weather, take this turn. There is another junction in just 0.1 mile where you head down into the valley instead of towards Cloudy Pass.

YOGI: Don't take the alternate down Agnes Creek unless you absolutely have to. I've walked both the alternate and the PCT. The PCT here is beautiful!!

2552.5 - Suiattle Pass

2552.5 (Suiattle Pass) to 2572.4 (Stehekin) -
All the on-trail water sources have good water (except Trapper Creek).

2568.4 - Seasonal Trapper Creek - Dry during PCT hiker season.

2572.1 - Enter North Cascades National Park - Permit required for camping from 2571.6 to 2587.7.

2572.4 - Stehekin River Road / Agnes Creek Trailhead - The PCT emerges at a bend in the road. Walk down to the right, cross the Stehekin River on a bridge, and you will be at the High Bridge Ranger Station.

Permit required to camp in North Cascades National Park (PCT mile 2571.6 to 2587.7). Your PCTA permit does not cover you for camping in this area. Northbound hikers can get the permit at the Golden West Visitor Center in Stehekin, or call the North Cascades National Park Wilderness Information Center (360-854-7245) from Stevens Pass.

Map Symbols

David "Awol" Miller has given us permission to use the map symbols he created for his excellent book "The AT Guide". These map symbols allow you to easily find town services with a quick glance at the town maps.

Airport	First Aid	Lounge/Bar	Ranger Station
ATM or Bank	Grocery Store	Outfitter	Restaurant
Boat	Hardware Store	Outgoing Mail	Restroom/Privy
Bowling	Hostel	Pay Phone	Shoe Store
Bus	Hotel	Pharmacy	Shower
Camping	Information	Picnic Table	Ski Lift
Car Rental	Internet/WiFi	Pool	Theater
Computer	Laundry	Post Office	Train Station
C-Store	Light Rail		

OVERVIEW: General Stehekin info: [www.stehekin.com]. Services in Stehekin begin to shut down in late-September and early-October. No ATM.

Three areas of Stehekin:

(1)   The LANDING refers to the town of Stehekin: North Cascades Lodge at Stehekin, PO, satellite phone, small store, restaurant, Forest Service Office, campground. [www.lodgeatstehekin.com]   Lodge phone 509-682-4494, Mon-Fri 8a-6p.

(2)   The RANCH refers to the Stehekin Valley Ranch: Cabins for rent and quite possibly the best food on the entire trail. The 9-mile bus ride between the Ranch and the Landing takes 30 minutes. 509-682-4677, Mon-Fri 8a-5p. [www.stehekinvalleyranch.com]

(3)   The STEHEKIN BAKERY is along the bus route between the Ranch and the Landing. This is the best bakery on the trail. 509-682-7742 [www.stehekinpastry.com]

GETTING HERE: Stehekin is 11.1 miles from the PCT at High Bridge Ranger Station.

Current bus schedule: [www.stehekin.com] or call 509-682-4494
The last bus is usually on Columbus Day !!
Bus is not free. 2019: High Bridge to Stehekin $8, cash only.
The bus will stop at the bakery on the way into town.
Load up here; there's not much to eat when you get to Stehekin.

Bus runs mid-June to early-October. 2017 Schedule:		
Leave Stehekin Landing	**At High Bridge (PCT)**	Arrive Stehekin Landing
8:15 a	9:15 a	10:00 a
11:30 a	12:30 p	1:30 p
2:00 p	3:00 p	3:45 p
5:30 p	6:15 p	7:00 p

The week before Columbus Day, 2017 Schedule:		
Leave Stehekin Landing	**At High Bridge (PCT)**	Arrive Stehekin Landing
9:30 a	10:30 a	11:15 a
2:00 p	3:00 p	4:00 p

POST OFFICE: 509-699-2015   May 1-Oct 15:   Mon-Fri 10a-4p, Sat noon-2pm
                              After Oct 15:   Mon-Fri 10a-4p, Sat closed

USPS only.   Hiker's Legal Name
Hiker mail held until end of season;   PCT Hiker, ETA: MM/DD/YY
returned to sender in mid-November.   General Delivery
                                Stehekin, WA 98852

RESUPPLY: No resupply. Landing store has very minimal snacks.

Stehekin Bakery   Pack out pizza, sandwiches, calzones.
The Garden   Fresh fruit and vegetables.

Red Apple Market (509-682-4521) in Chelan will deliver groceries to Stehekin. 3pm cut-off time for orders. Your items will arrive on the ferry the next day.

OUTDOOR STORE: The outdoor store near the Landing is geared to tourists, but it does have some hiker food.

| LODGING: | **North Cascades Lodge at Stehekin**. [www.lodgeatstehekin.com] Reservations 509-682-4494. Direct line 509-699-2056. Huge rooms sleeping 2-6 people per room. Small motel rooms have either two twin beds or one double bed. No TVs in any of the rooms. Per room rates: $$$$ |

The Stehekin Valley Ranch. [www.stehekinvalleyranch.com]
509-682-4677. Rate is per person (not per cabin) and includes all transportation and three all-you-can-eat meals. Breakfast 7a-9a, Lunch noon-1p, Dinner 5:30p-7p. Since transportation and meals are included in the price to stay at the Ranch, the cost is really quite reasonable.

Tent cabins (log walls, canvas roof). No TV, no electricity, no running water. Kerosene lantern provided, use of shower/bath house. Per person rates: $$$

Ranch Cabins (fully enclosed) with electricity and private bathrooms with shower. Per person rates: $$$$

CAMPING: Free camping at Purple Point Campground.

LOUNGE: Above the store. When you're looking at the front of the store, go around to the left and up the stairs. Walk down the hall to the lounge (just a room; no food/beverages sold here) with big windows where you can look out on the lake. PCT hikers tend to congregate here.

MEALS: (1) EXCELLENT food at Stehekin Valley Ranch. If you are not staying at the Ranch, but you want to eat dinner (excellent food!!), make reservations at the Log Office in Stehekin. Dinner served from 5:30p-7p.

Stop by, email, or call: 509-682-4677 [ranch@stehekinvalleyranch.com]
Bus ride from Stehekin to the Ranch for dinner departs Landing at 5:30p.
Non-Ranch guests are welcome for dinner, but NOT for breakfast and lunch.

(2) There is also a restaurant at the Landing.

(3) The Stehekin Bakery has amazing baked goods plus a limited breakfast and lunch menu: croissants, pizza, and homemade hot pockets. This is a GREAT place for lunch. You can ride the bus from the Lodge to the Bakery. Credit cards accepted. Open through Columbus Day weekend.

LAUNDRY·   One washer and one dryer in the A-frame building.

SHOWER: Shower in the A-frame building.

ATM: No.

FUEL: Usually denatured by the ounce at the Ranch.
The Landing store carries canister fuel (509-699-2056).

PHONE: There is one pay phone in Stehekin, at the A-frame building.
You can purchase a phone card at the store.

Permit required to camp in North Cascades National Park (PCT mile 2571.6 to 2587.7). Your PCTA permit does not cover you for camping in this area. Northbound hikers can get the permit at the Golden West Visitor Center in Stehekin, or call the North Cascades National Park Wilderness Information Center (360-854-7245) from Stevens Pass.

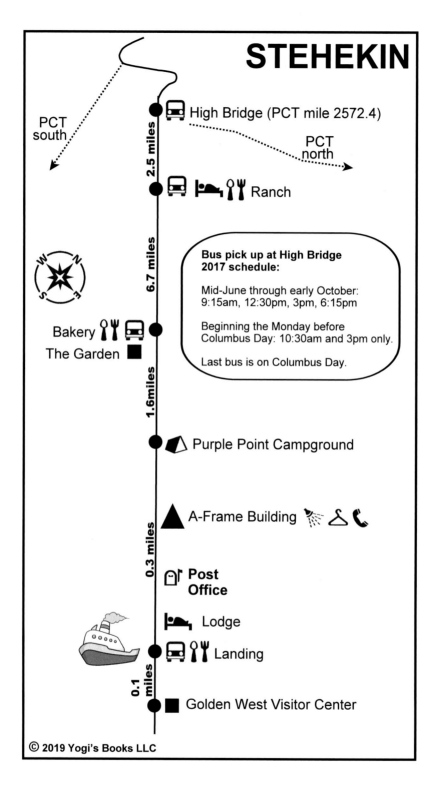

STEHEKIN

High Bridge (PCT mile 2572.4)

PCT south

PCT north

2.5 miles

Ranch

6.7 miles

Bus pick up at High Bridge 2017 schedule:

Mid-June through early October:
9:15am, 12:30pm, 3pm, 6:15pm

Beginning the Monday before
Columbus Day: 10:30am and 3pm only.

Last bus is on Columbus Day.

Bakery

The Garden

1.6miles

Purple Point Campground

A-Frame Building

0.3 miles

Post Office

Lodge

Landing

0.1 miles

Golden West Visitor Center

© 2019 Yogi's Books LLC

OVERVIEW: Typical touristy town. Good food.

GETTING HERE: Take the bus from High Bridge to Stehekin, then the ferry to Chelan.

BOAT TO CHELAN: Lady of the Lake. 509-682-4584. [www.ladyofthelake.com]

2019 Schedule Lady of the Lake		Leave Chelan	Arrive Stehekin	Leave Stehekin	Arrive Chelan	One Way	Round Trip
May 1 - Oct 15	every day	8:30a	12:30p	2:00p	6:00p	$24	$41
June 15 - Sep 30	every day	8:30a	11:00a	12:00p	2:45p	$37	$61
Oct 16 - Oct 31	Mon, Wed, Fri, Sat, Sun	10:00a	12:30p	1:30p	4:00p	$24	$41
November	Mon, Wed, Fri, Sun	10:00a	12:30p	1:30p	4:00p	$24	$41

POST OFFICE: 509-682-2625, USPS only   Hiker's Legal Name
                   Mon-Fri 8:30a-5p   PCT Hiker, ETA: MM/DD/YY
                   Sat package pick up only 6a-2p   General Delivery
                   (close for lunch). Knock on door. Chelan, WA 98816

                   General Delivery held for 30 days.

RESUPPLY: Safeway   509-682-2615   6a-10p every day
                   Super Walmart   509-682-4291   Open 24 hours
                   Red Apple Market 509-682-4521

RESTAURANTS: Many.

LAUNDRY: Yes.

SHOWERS: At Campground.

ATM: Yes.

COMPUTER: Library. 509-682-5131.

FUEL: HEET at gas stations and Safeway.

MEDICAL: Clinic and Hospital.

CHELAN LODGING		Rates	frig micr	TV	laundry	pool	hot tub
Apple Inn	509-682-4044	$$$	Y	Y	no	Y	Y
Campbell's Resort	509-682-2561	$$$$	Y	Y	Y	Y	Y
Deep Water Inn	509-888-5461	$$$	Y	Y	no	no	no
Midtowner Motel	509-682-4051	$$$ + Summer $$ + September	Y	Y	Y	Y	Y
Mom's Motel	509-682-5715	$$	Y	Y	no	no	no
Lakeshore Campground	509-682-8023	$ camping	showers				
		$ = usually less than $50 $$ = usually $50-$80 $$$ = usually $80-$110 $$$$ = usually greater than $110					

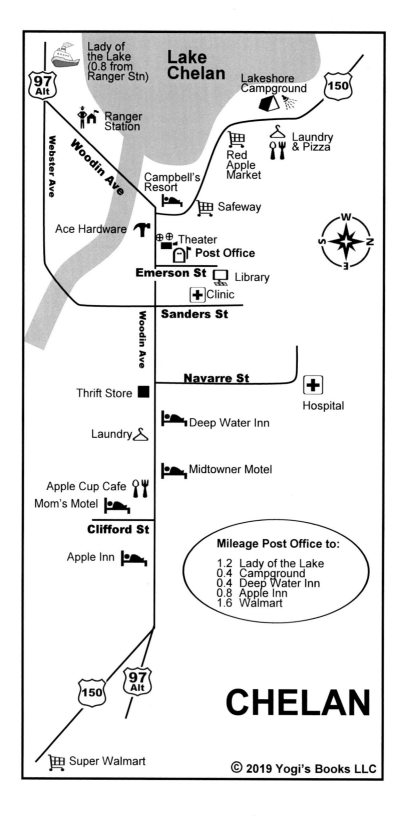

Lady of the Lake (0.8 from Ranger Stn)

Lake Chelan

Lakeshore Campground

97 Alt

150

Ranger Station

Webster Ave

Woodin Ave

Red Apple Market

Laundry & Pizza

Campbell's Resort

Safeway

Ace Hardware

Theater

Post Office

W N S E

Emerson St

Library

Clinic

Sanders St

Woodin Ave

Navarre St

Hospital

Thrift Store

Deep Water Inn

Laundry

Midtowner Motel

Apple Cup Cafe

Mom's Motel

Clifford St

Mileage Post Office to:

1.2 Lady of the Lake
0.4 Campground
0.4 Deep Water Inn
0.8 Apple Inn
1.6 Walmart

Apple Inn

150

97 Alt

CHELAN

Super Walmart

© 2019 Yogi's Books LLC

CELL SERVICE - There is no cell service from Stehekin to the border.

PERMIT - Permit is required to camp in North Cascades National Park (mile 2571.6 to 2587.7).
Northbound hikers: get permit at the Golden West Visitor Center in Stehekin.
Southbound hikers get permit at Ranger Station in Winthrop.

HIGHWAY 20 WEST OF RAINY PASS FROM STEHEKIN

ANISH: If for some reason you need to get to Highway 20 west of Rainy Pass from the Stehekin side (example: weather is forcing you to abandon your thru-hike, but landslides have closed Highway 20 as happened in 2013), you can take the Cascade Pass route out of the mountains, rather than the boat from Stehekin which is expensive and dumps you far from mass transit centers.

From High Bridge (PCT mile 2572.4), follow the PCT nobo to Bridge Creek Campground (PCT mile 2577.3 – you are on an old road here, and there is a trail crew camp with corral on the right).

Instead of continuing on the PCT as it makes a sharp right onto single track, continue straight toward Park Creek/Cascade Pass. The road will become more and more disused and trail-like as it follows the river. Ignore trails leading to Park Creek and Flat Creek. Pass Cottonwood Creek Campground and begin to climb. Follow signs for Cascade Pass.

From the pass, descend steeply to the Cascade Pass Road (gravel). It is a long (15 miles or so) road walk out to Highway 20, but Cascade Pass is quite possibly the most popular day hike in the North Cascades. You will most likely be able to hitch from the trailhead or the parking lot. The Cascade Pass Road will bring you out to Marblemount (about an hour's drive and easy hitch to 1-5).

2577.3 - Bridge Creek Campground - Creek, picnic tables, bear boxes.

2586.7 - Twisp Pass Trail - Per an email from the Wilderness Information Center Supervisor of the North Cascades National Park, "The actual PCT runs along the WEST side of Bridge Creek. The trail on the east of Bridge Creek is known as the Stiletto Spur Trail (provides access to Stiletto Peak) and it is not maintained to the same standards as the PCT: it generally has more brush, more stream crossings, and more downed trees. So please, stay on the main PCT (west side of Bridge Creek). It's a better trail for hikers!" Halfmile's Washington map K16 shows the PCT correctly on the west side of the creek.

2591.6 - Hwy 20 / Rainy Pass - Cross the highway to find a privy, trash, and some camping. If you don't want to go into Canada, you can get home from Rainy Pass. Hike to the PCT monument (PCT mile 2653.1). Turn around and hike back to Rainy Pass (PCT mile 2591.6). Hitch west on Highway 20 to the Sedro-Woolley WA area near Interstate 5. From there, you can go north to Bellingham WA or south to Seattle WA. Both cities have airports and Amtrak.

Go to [www.skagittransit.org] click [Routes] click [Trip Planner].
Enter Sedro Woolley as your starting location, and Seattle or Bellingham as your destination. This will give you all bus numbers and connection information.

Classic Mountain Cabby   509-996-2894. Serves trailheads, Bellingham,
Wenatchee, Spokane, and the Seattle Airport.

2591.6 - Mazama WA - at Rainy Pass, hitch 18 miles to the right on Highway 20.
The Inn, Store, and Outfitter are next to each other. There is nothing else here.

Country Inn   509-996-2681   Restaurant, quiet rooms, no TV. Rates: $$$ +
Ask for PCT discount.
Freestone Inn   509-996-3906   Jack's Hut Pizza and Brews nearby.
Mazama Store   509-996-2855   7a-6p every day.

Goat's Beard Mountain Supplies (outfitter)   Hiker's Legal Name
509-996-2515. 9a-6p every day.   PCT Hiker ETA: MM/DD/YY
Accepts mail drops USPS, UPS, FedEx: c/o Goats Beard Mountain Supplies
50 Lost River Road
Mazama WA 98833

WINTHROP

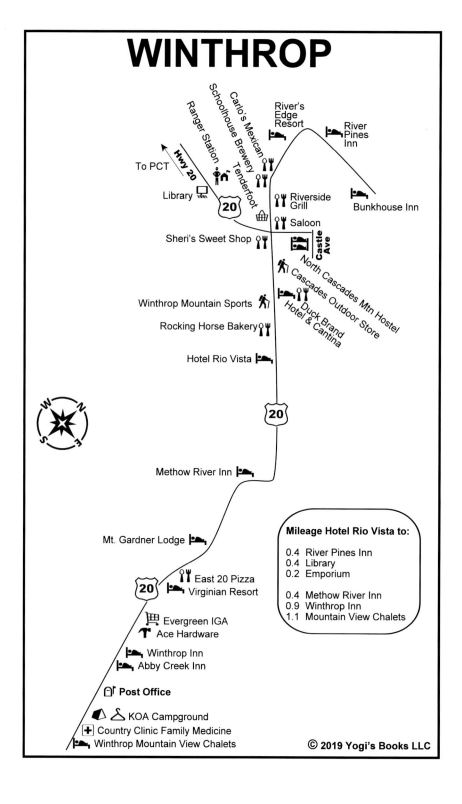

To PCT

Ranger Station

Schoolhouse Brewery

Carlo's Mexican

Tenderfoot

Hwy 20

Library

River's Edge Resort

River Pines Inn

Riverside Grill

Bunkhouse Inn

Saloon

Castle Ave

Sheri's Sweet Shop

North Cascades Mtn Hostel

Cascades Outdoor Store

Winthrop Mountain Sports

Duck Brand Hotel & Cantina

Rocking Horse Bakery

Hotel Rio Vista

Methow River Inn

Mt. Gardner Lodge

East 20 Pizza

Virginian Resort

Evergreen IGA

Ace Hardware

Winthrop Inn

Abby Creek Inn

Post Office

KOA Campground

Country Clinic Family Medicine

Winthrop Mountain View Chalets

Mileage Hotel Rio Vista to:

0.4 River Pines Inn
0.4 Library
0.2 Emporium

0.4 Methow River Inn
0.9 Winthrop Inn
1.1 Mountain View Chalets

© 2019 Yogi's Books LLC

OVERVIEW: Touristy, with many great restaurants. Excellent brewery!
GETTING HERE: Hitch 35 miles to the right on Hwy 20 at Rainy Pass.

TAXI: Classic Mountain Cabby serves trailheads, Bellingham, Wenatchee, Spokane, and the Seattle Airport. 509-996-2894.

BUS TO SEATTLE: [www.okanogantransit.com]

PERMIT: Southbound hikers, if you do not already have permit for the North Cascades National Park, you can get one at the Methow Valley Ranger Station in Winthrop.

POST OFFICE:
509-996-2282, USPS only
Mon-Fri 9a-4:30p
Sat closed
General Delivery held for 30 days

Hiker's Legal Name
PCT Hiker, ETA: MM/DD/YY
General Delivery
Winthrop, WA 98862

MAIL DROPS: Hostel accepts mail drops, no fee. 206-940-4507

USPS Address:
Hiker's Legal Name
PCT Hiker, ETA: MM/DD/YY
North Cascades Mountain Hostel
PO Box 1338
Winthrop, WA 98862

UPS / FedEx Address:
Hiker's Legal Name
PCT Hiker, ETA: MM/DD/YY
North Cascades Mountain Hostel
209 Castle Ave
Winthrop, WA 98862

RESUPPLY:
Evergreen IGA Supermarket   509-996-2525   Full resupply
Tenderfoot   509-996-2288   C-Store resupply

OUTFITTER:
Winthrop Mountain Sports   509-996-2886
Cascades Outdoor Store   509-996-3480

WINTHROP LODGING central reservations.net		Rates	frig	micr	TV	other
Abby Creek Inn	509-996-3100	$$$	Y	Y	Y	pool, cont bkfst
Bunkhouse Inn	509-996-2148	$$$	Y	Y		some rooms have TV (local reception only)
Duck Brand Hotel	509-996-2408	$$$	no	no	Y	
Hotel Rio Vista	509-996-3535	$$$$	Y	some	Y	hot tub
Methow River Lodge	509-996-4348	$$$$	Y	Y	Y	motel rooms and cabins (with kitchens)
Mt. Gardner Inn	509-996-2000	$$$	Y	Y	Y	
River Pines Inn	509-322-4062	$$$	Y	Y	Y	
River's Edge Resort	509-996-8000	$$$$	Y	Y	Y	cabins with kitchens, hot tub
Virginian Resort	509-996-2535	$$	some		Y	cont bkfst
Winthrop Inn	800-444-1972	$$$	Y	Y	Y	guest computer, pool, hot tub
Winthrop Mountain View Chalets	800-527-3113	$$$	Y	Y	Y	
North Cascades Mountain Hostel [info@ncascadesmtnhostel.com]	206-940-4507	Bunks $, Private Rooms $$ + All accommodations share common bathroom, shower, kitchen, living room. Laundry on site.				
KOA	800-562-2158	$ Tenting $$ + Camping cabin (no bathroom) Pool, laundry, showers on site.				
		Rates: $ = usually less than $50 $$ = usually $50-$80 $$$ = usually $80-$110 $$$$ = usually greater than $110				

RESTAURANTS:	Several. Don't miss the brewery! Huge scoops of ice cream at Tenderfoot.	
LAUNDRY:	At the KOA. Also at the Hostel. Call first 206-940-4507.	
SHOWER:	At the Hostel. Call first 509-699-0568.	
ATM:	Yes.	
COMPUTER:	Library. 509-996-2685.	
CANISTER FUEL:	Winthrop Mountain Sports	509-996-2886
	Cascades Outdoor Store	509-996-3480
MEDICAL:	Country Clinic	509-996-8180

2596.9 - Cutthroat Pass

2599.3 - Granite Pass

2601.4 - Campsite - DOUBLE TAP: Campsites are on the left ~300 ft off the PCT.
Creek is ~0.1 mile west of the campsite.

2602.3 - Methow Pass -
BINK: About a mile north of here is a small stream flowing across the trail, including campsites.

2603.9 - approximately - TWODOG: There is a trailside camp with water near the bottom of the switchbacks down from Methow Pass.

2609.9 - Brush Creek - DOUBLE TAP: Many small campsites scattered around this are before the creek. Follow a use trail to the left ~200 ft before crossing the creek which goes up to ~3 campsites all separated by ~50 ft.

2612.7 - Glacier Pass - BINK: Campsites here, but no apparent water. I have heard for years that there is a spring a short distance north of the campsite on a rough side trail but have never taken the time to investigate it.

TWODOG (2006): At Glacier Pass, there is a horse camp in a meadow with a seeping spring that had water during a dry spell in September. Take the spur trail down to your left just after passing the Glacier Pass sign.

2616.8 - Spring, Campsites - DOUBLE TAP: Spring is ~0.1 mile and ~100 ft down to the right of the PCT. Follow the use trail from the campground to the right of the PCT to many low flowing spring streams but it was good enough to get water.

2620.3 - 20 yards before Road 500 - TWODOG: The *reliable* water at Meadows Campground is located where Road 500 down from the Brown Bear Mines (and the PCT) reaches the Campground, a seeping spring in the center of the Campground loop. Leave the PCT at 2619.82619.8, walk down Road 500 to reach the spring. The unmarked and barely maintained trail back up to the PCT is across from the Campground entrance, where Road 500 continues towards Harts Pass. The trail heads toward the obvious low saddle, re-joining the PCT at mile 2620.7.

2621.2 - Low Saddle

2622.5 - Harts Pass - Campground with privy. No water at campground. Water about 0.5 mile up the road to Slate Peak. DOUBLE TAP: At the first road crossing, turn left and go down road for ~50 ft and you will see the PCT on the right side. The campground and bathroom are up and to the right at the first road crossing. Ranger Station is up and to the left.

Pasayten Wilderness has early season rifle deer hunting in September.
Be sure to wear bright orange.

2622.9 - Creek - BINK: Always has water.

2633.5 - DOUBLE TAP: Many good campsites (~6 tents) to the right just off the PCT.

2639.5 - Rock Pass - From Rock Pass, you can see Woody Pass. That trail in front of you on the ridge on the left side of the valley is not the PCT. It's not an alternate route. It is an old abandoned trail. Don't take it. Stay on the PCT, which switchbacks down into the valley, then switchbacks back up to Woody Pass.

SPECIAL AGENT: DO NOT take the old route to Woody Pass. Going North on the PCT there, right in front of you is the old route of the trail. You can see it cut into the side of the mountain going all the way to Woody Pass. It's a straight shot. But as you start along this old trail, you will pass a sign that says "abandoned trail." That alone there should tell you something. But Teatree and I hiked on and eventually had to turn around after 0.75 mile. The trail was so narrow and eroded that after you took a step, it would wash away down a steep-ass hill. So . . . . . don't ever take side trails that have signs that say "abandoned trail." And don't take this old alternate route, OK?

TEATREE: Special Agent is NOT kidding. Whatever you do, don't take this abandoned trail. I cannot stress this enough. Unless you want to DIE on your very last day of hiking, suck it up and hike your ass to the Pass on the official PCT. I honestly don't think you'll get there any other way. What were we thinking?

SCRUB: Washouts destroyed seven different 10-15 foot sections of trail between Rock Creek Pass and Woody Pass. They were fun to climb through and not especially dangerous by the time I got there, but they slowed everyone down and you would NOT want to go through them in snowy/icy weather.

2642.1 - Woody Pass

2647.0 - Hopkins Pass

2649.4 - Castle Pass

2653.1 - US-Canada Border

2661.2 - Gibson Pass Road

2661.9 - Highway 3 - Manning Park is 0.9 mile to the right.

2661.9 - Manning Park

OVERVIEW: 800-330-3321. Manning Park has a resort with a Lodge, pool, hot tub, store, 2 restaurants, and a bar. I've been told that if you pay for things with your credit card, you'll get a better exchange rate (therefore, things are cheaper) than if you exchange your American dollars for Canadian dollars and then pay with Canadian dollars.

GETTING HERE: When you get to the road, turn RIGHT. Walk 0.9 mile.

PCT HIKER INFO: [http://summer.manningpark.com/pct-hiker-info/]

MAIL DROPS: The Lodge accepts packages for PCT Hikers.
BE SURE to write "Hold for PCT Hiker" along with your expected arrival date.

Be careful sending packages here.
You might be charged a customs fee ($45+).
Mail your package at least 4 weeks before you arrive.
Packages could take 3-4 weeks to clear customs.

Hiker's Legal Name
PCT Hiker, ETA: MM/DD/YY
c/o Manning Park Lodge
7500 Highway #3
Manning Provincial Park, BC V0X IR0
CANADA

RESUPPLY: Country Store is a large C-Store. Open Sun-Thur 8a-7p. Fri-Sat 8a-8p.
Southbounders could resupply here, but not many choices.

LODGING:	Rooms have TV, microwave, refrigerator. Rates in Canadian dollars: $$$$ <u>Ask for the PCT hiker rate.</u>
	The Lodge also offers hostel accommodations. Rate: $ (Canadian dollars). Single and double private rooms with bunks and mattresses. Common kitchen, showers, TV, pay phone.
RESTAURANTS:	Two restaurants and a pub.
LAUNDRY: SHOWER: ATM:	Yes. Yes. Yes.
COMPUTER:	Computer for guests.
PHONES:	Warning: There is an access charge for EVERY call you make from your motel room phone. Every call. Even toll-free calls.
LOOKING AHEAD:	Go home and start planning your Continental Divide Trail hike! I happen to know of a great book which will help you with that hike: "Yogi's Continental Divide Trail Handbook," available at [www.yogisbooks.com].

LEGAL SOUTHBOUND ENTRY INTO THE US

ANISH: It may have changed, but in the past you were legally able to cross into the US from Canada via the manned trail/road crossing at Hozomeen near Ross Lake. You should verify this with the North Cascades National Park if you wish to attempt a southbound hike starting in this manner.

This is a dead end road in Canada. Once you cross into the US, you merge onto the East Bank Trail. Follow this about 11 miles to the Castle Pass Trail and go left (east). This trail is unmaintained, but follow-able. Just be prepared and carry detailed topo maps. At Castle Pass (15-20 miles), you intersect the PCT. There is mediocre camping here. Go left (north) and walk 3.7 miles to Monument 78.

NORTHBOUNDERS NOT CROSSING INTO CANADA

ANISH: If you are not entering Canada, you may return to Highway 20 via the Castle Pass and East Bank trails rather than taking the PCT. The Castle Pass / East Bank route is longer, but you will come out to the highway rather than attempting to hitch from Hart's Pass. Hart's Pass is a fairly easy hitch in the summer, especially on weekends, but the later in the season it gets (after Labor Day), the harder the hitch becomes, especially on weekdays and in inclement weather. You may have to walk 18 miles down a very narrow, eroded dirt road or walk the PCT all the way back to Rainy Pass.

To take the Castle Pass/East Bank Alternate: Once you've reached Monument 78, walk south 3.7 miles on the PCT to Castle Pass (PCT mile 2648.9). Go right (west) and follow the unmaintained Castle Pass Trail to the East Bank Trail. Carry detailed topo maps as this 15-20 miles is unmaintained.

At the East Bank junction, merge with the East Bank trail going left (west) 4 miles to Ross Lake. You will reach Ross Lake at the Lightning Creek camp area. If you are incredibly lucky or good at yogi'ing, you may discover boaters at the boat camp who will take you down lake. If not, hike south on the East Bank Trail 16 miles to Highway 20. Do not follow trails to Jack Mountain, Ruby Arm, or Hidden Hand Campground. To access Highway 20, go right at a major junction with the Happy Panther Trail. Cross the bridge and hitch right (west) from the large parking area.

PCNST (Pacific Crest National Scenic Trail) is border to border within the United States. Most hikers continue 8.8 more miles into Canada on the PCT (Pacific Crest Trail), finishing at Manning Park. The PCT border crossing is unmanned. You can legally cross from the US into Canada on trail only if you have your "Application to enter Canada via the PCT" with you as you enter Canada.

CANADA to USA

It is illegal to cross from Canada into the US using the trail. You must enter the US at a manned border crossing. The PCT is not a manned border crossing. All travelers entering the US from Canada by air are required to have a passport book. US citizens entering the US by land or sea are required to have either a passport book, a passport card, or an enhanced Driver's License. Visit the US Department of State website [www.travel.state.gov] for current regulations.

MANNING PARK to USA - see "Northern Terminus" Yogi map

OPTION 1: Manning > Abbotsford BC / Sumas WA > Bellingham or Seattle

Manning Park to Hope BC:	HITCH:	Hitch 42 miles west on Highway 3.
Hope BC to Abbotsford BC:	BUS:	Ebus [https://myebus.ca] 877-769-3287
Abbotsford BC to US border:	BUS:	BC Transit Route 2 (Bluejay-Huntingdon GoLine). [www.bctransit.com] 604-854-3232
US border to Sumas WA:	WALK:	Walk across the border.
Sumas WA to Bellingham WA:	BUS:	Whatcom Transportation Authority Bus [www.ridewta.com] 360-676-7433
Bellingham WA to Seattle WA:	BUS OR TRAIN: Greyhound [www.greyhound.com] 800-231-2222 Amtrak [www.amtrak.com] 800-872-7245, press 0	

OPTION 2: Manning > Vancouver BC > Bellingham or Seattle

First, choose how you will get from Manning Park to Vancouver BC:

PRIVATE SHUTTLE: Manning to Vancouver BC: Canadian Craft Charters. 778-320-3409 [https://www.vancouvershuttlehire.com/], then search "Manning Park". 2018: $499 for up to 14 hikers That's $35.71/person (14 people)	HITCH: Manning to Hope BC, 42 miles west BUS or TRAIN: Hope BC to Vancouver BC Ebus VIA Rail Canada 877-769-3287 888-842-7245 [https://myebus.ca] [www.viarail.ca]

Once you are in Vancouver BC, use the following information:

Vancouver BC:	Public transportation (train and bus) Sky Train [www.translink.ca] 604-953-3333
Vancouver BC to Bellingham WA or Seattle WA:	Amtrak [www.amtrak.com] 800-872-7245, press 0 Greyhound [www.greyhound.ca] 800-661-8747 Greyhound [www.greyhound.com] 800-231-2222 Bolt Bus [www.boltbus.com] 877-265-8287 Quick Shuttle [www.quickcoach.com] 800-665-2122
Seattle, WA:	Public bus: King County Metro Transit Light Rail: Sound Transit 206-553-3000 888-889-6368 [www.metro.kingcounty.gov] [www.soundtransit.org]

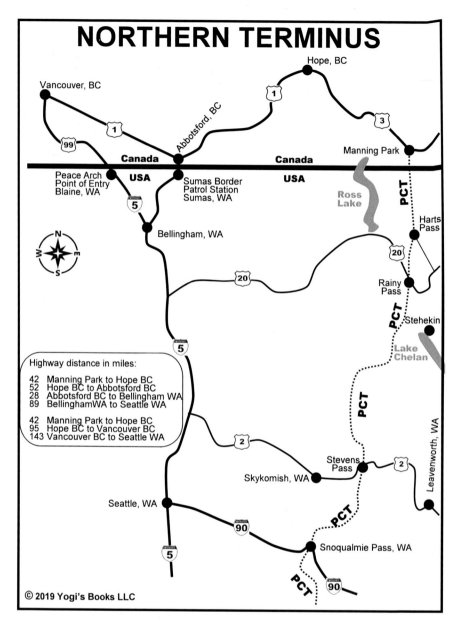

NORTHERN TERMINUS

Hope, BC

Vancouver, BC

Abbotsford, BC

1

99

Canada

USA

Peace Arch
Point of Entry
Blaine, WA

Sumas Border
Patrol Station
Sumas, WA

Manning Park

Canada

USA

Ross
Lake

PCT

Harts
Pass

5

Bellingham, WA

20

N
W E
S

20

Rainy
Pass

PCT

Stehekin

Lake
Chelan

5

Highway distance in miles:

42 Manning Park to Hope BC
52 Hope BC to Abbotsford BC
28 Abbotsford BC to Bellingham WA
89 BellinghamWA to Seattle WA

42 Manning Park to Hope BC
95 Hope BC to Vancouver BC
143 Vancouver BC to Seattle WA

PCT

Leavenworth, WA

2

Stevens
Pass

Skykomish, WA

2

Seattle, WA

90

PCT

Snoqualmie Pass, WA

5

PCT

90

© 2019 Yogi's Books LLC

	Motel	Restaurant	Bus	Train	Car Rental	Airport
Manning Park	✔	✔				
Hope, BC	✔	✔	✔	✔		
Abbotsford, BC	✔	✔	✔	✔	✔	✔
Vancouver, BC	✔	✔	✔	✔	✔	✔
Sumas, WA		✔	✔			
Blaine, WA	✔	✔	✔			
Bellingham, WA	✔	✔	✔	✔	✔	✔
Seattle, WA	✔	✔	✔	✔	✔	✔